SCOTLAND *the* BEST!
THE ONE TRUE GUIDE

Peter Irvine

With additional research and opinions by
Keith Davidson

HarperCollins*Publishers*

HarperCollins Publishers
Westerhill Rd, Bishopbriggs Glasgow G64 2QT

First published in Great Britain in 1993
by Mainstream Publishing Company (Edinburgh) Ltd

First published by HarperCollins Publishers in 1997

This edition published in 1999

ISBN 0 00 472399 6

www.**fire**and**water**.com

Printed in Scotland by The Bath Press

CONTENTS

A DECLARATION OF FALLIBILITY

This guide is 'true', but it may not always be absolutely accurate. Since this may seem like a contradiction in terms, I should explain. *Scotland the Best!* is a handbook of information about all the 'best' places in Scotland. 'Best' you will understand is a subjective term; it means 'best' according to what I think. Needless to say, there seem to be a lot of readers who agree with my judgement and even if you don't, you may see that I and my associates have gone to some efforts to reach our assertions. It's intended to be obvious that I am conveying opinions and impressions. They're true because the motives are true; we believe in what we are saying. We take no bribes and and have no vested interest in any of the places recommended, other than that we do talk things up and shamelessly proclaim the places we like or admire.

Along with observations, every 'item' conveys factual information; I hope it's plain where the facts end and the opinions begin. In guide books this is not always the case. However, it's with 'the facts' that inconsistencies may appear. We try to give accurate and clear directions explaining how to find a place and basic details that might be useful. This information is gleaned from a variety of sources and may be supplied by the establishment concerned. We do try to verify everything usually by visiting, but the process of acquiring and transcribing information is tricky when there's so much of it. Things change and because nowhere we mention has solicited their inclusion (or if they have, it has made little difference), nor been invited to check what we say … well, mistakes can be made. With this density of information it's impossible to run it past proprietors, and they might not like what we say because it's our opinion, not theirs. So I'm sorry if we get a number wrong. We hope there aren't any mistakes, but we may not find out until you let us know. Please do so we can fix it.

This admission is therefore made in advance. I hope you haven't gone up the glen with no cash to find that after all they don't accept credit cards, or arrive at the golf club to find that you've booked into a sauna parlour. My cringing excuse is that we are merely human. This guide is made by fallible humans like me for fallible humans, of which I hope you are one. However, be clear of one thing, this book is about searching for something better, it is actually about striving for perfection.

INTRODUCTION

This is the Millennium edition of *Scotland the Best!* it doesn't say so on the cover and by the time you read this you may well be weary or have forgotten about the whole damned thing anyway. Most likely, the year 2000 will be a year like any other with its good times and its bad times.

But I do think this edition is millennial in one respect. I always see my book as a barometer, a gauge of how we are doing, so this is a report or perhaps a snapshot of all the best things about Scotland at the turn of the century. Though many things have not changed since I prepared the last edition in 1997 and lochs and hills and castles have changed little over centuries, we check out everything again nevertheless. The emerging restaurant culture, not only in Edinburgh and Glasgow but even in places like Perth and Skye, and the fluctuating patterns of hotels and pubs are hard to keep up with but even outdoor places are subject to changes in, for example, their accessibility or what's available for visitors. If regular users of this guide find that many entries are unaltered, they can assume it's because the information and the received perception remains the same. Taken in the context of the whole, what we have tried to do as always, is to produce an accurate and coherent report on the state of the nation … at the time of going to press. Unlike many other guides, *Scotland the Best!* is published very quickly after the final compilation of material. This edition was researched in the summer and autumn of 1999.

New readers should be aware that *Scotland the Best!* is not an everything-goes-in kind of guidebook. It is highly selective and subjective and we do not list places just because they're there – only if they are above the ordinary and beyond the mediocre. We don't provide any orientation information and we assume you can follow a map. In short, we assume you are an intelligent and curious human being who perhaps doesn't have a lot of time to spend in Scotland or to sift through guides and the the piles of promotional print that's available. This book is supposed to be the only one you need, a discerning distillation of all the other pub and hotel guides, restaurant guides, walking books and local attraction brochures. Remember, we've eliminated all the not very good stuff no matter how it presents itself or how indignant they may be that we've ignored them. We include major attractions only if they're worth visiting in the same way that we include a little home-made ice-cream shop. In the year 2000, anywhere that's decent in Scotland should be in this book. We hope we've saved you time and helped you to have a more engaging experience. We know Scotland and we're proud of it; we want you to see the good bits – with time to stop and smell the roses en route.

In the collection and evaluation of the huge amounts of info (and disinfo) and in the writing and editing of this edition, I am grateful for the efforts and commitment of my one true researcher, the endlessly intrepid and cheerful Keith Davidson. Intrepid because no glen is too long to bring back the latest word on the last bothy, cheerful because sixteen attractions in a day is not necessarily an attractive proposition. And thanks again go to my long-suffering PA Georgia.

Though I say one and only researcher, this is not to diminish the vast amount of feedback I now get from readers, not by mail but by e-mail via the internet site provided by The Famous Grouse (www.famousgrouse.com/scotlandthebest). Though I cannot reply to them, every one is noted and anywhere recommended or rubbished, is checked. Of course, I am sorry if I recommend somewhere highly and you then have a bad experience. Though I can't enter into correspondence with the place or the writer, we will be very wary of it in future. As is obvious with *Scotland the Best!*, nobody here pays for inclusion and cannot affect what we write about them. We purposefully carry no ads or sponsorship and there is no editor breathing down my neck to conform or capitulate. This book survives on its sales alone and because we, and you, believe in it. I hope you will keep using it and keep writing in. I'd like to think that everyone recognised and listed between these covers, every chef, baker and candlestick maker has the same aspiration as I do: to think always of their readers/customers first. And to help make Scotland the best!

OTHER GUIDES

As mentioned in the Introduction, *Scotland the Best!* is supposed to encompass and replace all the other selective guides to restaurants, pubs, walks, etc. However, you'll notice that I often refer to the *AA Restaurant Guide* or *Michelin*. These are the only two that I think are reliable. They have loads of inspectors and back-up, so they are better placed than I am to be specific about food. Having said that, a restaurant has to have three rosettes before you can be fairly sure that it won't let you down. Only one restaurant in Scotland has five rosettes (Altnaharrie, see p.136) and for 1999, there are no fours.

I also refer to the *Taste of Scotland* guide which is readily available in bookshops and participating hotels and restaurants. I say participating because TOS is an association of members who have some say over their entries. It is currently introducing more quality control and as an organisation it is committed to improving standards.

A whole bunch of generic guides to Scotland and to Edinburgh have appeared recently. We've been discovered – we should be flattered, even if they don't know what they're talking about half the time. What can I say? They compete with *Scotland the Best!* even if we are the only one that is actually made here. Anyway, it looks like you just bought this book, so thanks. You made the right choice.

HOW TO USE THIS BOOK

There are three ways to find things in this book:

1. There's an index at the back. Towns are in bold type and may have a number of entries. A number in bold type means there is a whole page or section devoted to the town (the numbers listed are page numbers).

2. The book can be used by category, e.g. you can look up the best restaurants in the Borders or the best scenic routes in the whole of Scotland. Each entry has an item number in the outside margin. These are in numerical order and allow easy cross-referencing.

3. You can start with the maps and see how individual items are located, how they are grouped together and how much there is that's worth seeing or doing in any particular area. Then just look up the item numbers. If you are travelling round Scotland I would urge you to use the maps and this method of finding the best of what an area or town has to offer.

The maps correspond to the recognisable regions of Scotland. There's also an overall map to show how the regions fit together. The list of maps is on p.321 and the map section is at the back of the book.

All items have a code which gives (1) the specific item number; (2) the map on which it can be found; and (3) the co-ordinate. For space reasons, items in Glasgow and Edinburgh are not marked on Maps A and B, although they do have co-ordinates in the margin to give you a rough idea of the location. City maps are readily available from any tourist office or newsagent.

TICKS FOR THE BEST THERE IS

Although everything listed in the book is notable and remarkable in some way, there are places that are outstanding even in this superlative company. Instead of marking them with a rosette or a star, they have been 'awarded' a tick.

 Amongst the very best in Scotland

 Amongst the best (of its type) in the UK

 Amongst the best (of its type) in the world, or simply unique

Listings generally are not in an order of merit although if there is one outstanding item it will always be at the top of the page and this obviously includes anything which has been given a tick.

Hotels and restaurants are also grouped according to price and this is why a cross-marked place may appear further down the page (ticks also indicate exceptional value for money).

A NOTE ON CATEGORIES

Edinburgh and Glasgow, the destinations of most visitors and the nearest cities to more than half of the population, are covered in the substantial Sections 1 and 2. Both have been extended from the last edition mainly to cover the proliferation and diversification of restaurants. You will probably need a city map to get around, although Maps A and B should give you the rough layout.

For the purposes of maps, and particularly in Section 3 (Regional Hotels and Restaurants), I have used a combination of the subdivision of Scotland based on the current standard political regions along with the historical ones, e.g. Argyll, Clyde Valley. From Sections 4 to 11, categories are based on activities, interests and geography and refer to the whole of Scotland. Section 12 covers the islands, with a page-by-page guide to the larger ones.

Section 13 is intended to give a comprehensive and concise guide to the best of the major Scottish towns in each area. Some of the recommended hotels and restaurants will be amongst the best in the region and will have been referred to in Section 3, or even amongst the best in Scotland and referred to in Sections 4 to 12, but otherwise they have been selected because they are the best there is in the town or the immediate area.

There are some categories like Bed and Breakfasts, Fishing Beats, Antique Shops that haven't been included because they are impracticable to assess (there are too many of them, they are too small, or they change hands too often). Fishing places would be spoiled if too many people knew about them, and for similar reasons I've declined to draw attention to (for example) Places to see Birds of Prey. In this edition there are several new categories that might be useful like diving sites and annual events.

If there are other categories that you would like to see in future editions, please let us know (*see p. 12*).

The codes

1.   The Item Code

At the outside margin of every item is a code which will enable you to find it on a map. Thus **917** MAP 2 *B3* should be read as follows: **917** is the item number, listed in simple consecutive order; MAP 2 refers to the Highlands – the map section is at the back of the book; *B3* is the map co-ordinate, to help pinpoint the item's location on the map grid. A co-ordinate such as *xC1* indicates that the item can be reached by leaving the map at grid reference *C1*.

2.   The Hotel Code

Below each hotel recommended is a band of codes as follows:

20RMS   JAN-DEC   T/T   PETS   CC   KIDS   TOS   LOTS

20RMS means the hotel has 20 bedrooms in total. No differentiation is made as to the type of room. Most hotels will offer twin rooms as singles or put extra beds in doubles if required. This code merely gives an impression of size.

JAN-DEC means the hotel is open all year round. APR-OCT means approximately from the beginning of April to the end of October.

T/T refers to the facilities: T/ means there are direct-dial phones in the bedrooms while /T means there are TVs in the bedrooms.

PETS means the hotel accepts dogs and other pets, probably under certain conditions (e.g. pets should be kept in the bedroom). It's usually best to check first.

XPETS indicates that the hotel does not generally accept pets.

CC means the hotel accepts major credit cards (e.g. Access and Visa).

XCC means the hotel does not accept credit cards.

KIDS indicates children are welcome and special provisions/rates may be available.

XKIDS does not necessarily mean that children are not able to accompany their parents, only that special provisions/rates are not usually made. Check by phone.

TOS means the hotel is part of the Taste of Scotland scheme and has been selected for having a menu which features imaginative cooking using Scottish ingredients. The Taste of Scotland produces an annual guide of members.

LOTS Rooms which cost more than £65 per night per person. The theory is that if you can afford over £130 a room, it doesn't matter too much if it's £135 or £150. Other price bands are:

EXP Expensive: £50-65 per person.

MED.EX Medium (expensive): £38-55.

M NX Medium (inexpensive): £30-38.

INX Inexpensive: £25-30.

CHP Cheap: less than £25.

Rates are per person per night. They are worked out by halving the published average rate for a twin room in high season and should be used only to give an impression of cost. They are based on 1999 prices. Add between £2 to £5 per year, though the band should stay the same unless the hotel undergoes improvements.

3.   The Restaurant Code

Found at the bottom right of all restaurant entries. It refers to the price of an average dinner per person with a starter, a main course and dessert. It doesn't include wine, coffee or extras.

EXP Expensive: more than £30

MED Medium: £20-30.

INX Inexpensive: £12-20.

CHP Cheap: under £12.

These are based on 1999 rates. With inflation, the relative price bands should stay about the same. Where a hotel is notable also for its restaurant, there is a restaurant line below the hotel entry and a separate code in the corner.

4.   The Walk Code

A great number of walks are described in the book, especially in section 8.

2-10km   CIRC   BIKE   1-A-1

2-10km means the walk(s) described may vary in length from 2km to 10km.

CIRC means the walk can be circular, while xCIRC shows the walk is not circular and you must return more or less the way you came.

BIKE indicates the walk has a path which is suitable for ordinary bikes.
xBIKE means the walk is not suitable for, or does not permit, cycling.
mtBIKE means the track is suitable for mountain or all-terrain bikes.

The 1-A-1 Code

First number (1, 2 or 3) indicates how easy the walk is.
1 the walk is easy.
2 medium difficulty, e.g. standard hillwalking, not dangerous nor requiring special knowledge or equipment.
3 difficult: care and preparation and a map are needed.

The letters (A, B or C) indicate how easy it is to find the path.
A the route is easy to find. The way is either marked or otherwise obvious.
B the route is not very obvious, but you'll get there.
C you will need a map and preparation or a guide.

The last number (1, 2 or 3) indicates what to wear on your feet.
1 ordinary outdoor shoes, including trainers, are probably okay unless the ground is very wet.
2 you will need walking boots.
3 you will need serious walking or hiking boots.

Apart from designated walks, the 1-A-1 code is employed wherever there is more than a short stroll required to get to somewhere, e.g. a waterfall or a monument. Found at bottom-right corner of item.

LIST OF ABBREVIATIONS

As well as codes and because of obvious space limitations, a personal shorthand and ad hoc abbreviation system has had to be created. I'm the first to admit some may be annoying, especially 'restau' for restaurant, but it's a long word and it comes up often. The others which are used are …

Aber	Aberdeen	accom	accomodation
adj	adjacent	admn	admission
app	approach	approx	approximately
atmos	atmosphere	av	average
AYR	all year round	bedrms	bedrooms
betw	between	br	bridge
BYOB	bring your own bottle	cl	closes/closed
		dining-rm	dining room
E	east	Edin	Edinburgh
esp	especially	excl	excluding
exhib(s)	exhibition(s)	exp	expensive
facs	facilities	ft	fort
Glas	Glasgow	gr	great
grd(s)	garden(s)	HS	Historic Scotland
hr(s)	hour(s)	incl	including
inexp	inexpensive	info	information
j/tie	jacket and tie	jnct	junction
L	loch	LO	last orders
min(s)	minute(s)	mt(s)	mountain(s)
N	north	NTS	National Trust for Scotland
no smk	no smoking		
nr	near	o/look	overlook(s)/ing
opp	opposite	o/side	outside
pl	place	poss	possible
pt	point/port	R	river
r/bout	roundabout	rd	road
refurb	refurbished/ment	restau	restaurant
rm(s)	room(s)	RSPB	Royal Society for the Protection of Birds
rt	right		
S	south	sq	square
stn	station	st	street
SYHA	ScottishYouth Hostel Association	TDH	Table d'hôte
		TO	tourist office
t/off	turn off	trad	traditional
tratt	trattoria	univ	university
v	very	vegn	vegetarian
W	west	w/end(s)	weekend(s)
yr(s)	years		

YOUR HELP NEEDED
(AND WIN GOOD WHISKY)

Scotland the Best! wouldn't be the best if I didn't receive feedback and helpful suggestions from so many people. It really has become an interactive book because so many of you seem to know what sort of places are likely to fit. With each new edition I believe I get closer to the definitive best guide including everywhere in Scotland that's any good. It bothers me if I miss something – a new restaurant might be forgiveable, but there may be an established one that I've omitted from this edition. There are pubs for example that have been doing great food for years and as each edition passes I get closer to knowing all of them. This completeness is because people write to tell me. And I hope very much that they will continue to do so. *Scotland the Best!* is supposed to follow the inside track to Scotland and you who live here, or are experiencing it as a visitor, are on it. Send me the word!

Write and let me know whether you have found the information helpful and accurate and whether you agree or disagree with my selections. Have places lived up to your expectations and, in particular, are there any superlative places that ought to have been mentioned? Even if it's your own place and you think it deserves wider attention, let me know. Everywhere you recommend will be checked out for the next edition in 2001/2002. Please send your comments or suggestions to:

Peter Irvine/*Scotland the Best!*
Reference Department
HarperCollins Publishers
Westerhill Rd
Bishopbriggs
Glasgow
G64 2QT

For sharing this information, HarperCollins will be happy to share out some good whisky and cheese. A bottle of malt (any from the list of my suggestions on p.170) together with a drum of Tobermory cheddar will be presented at the launch of the next edition, to the best three suggestions received by 30 September 2001. Recommendations can be for any category or for any number of categories, and anywhere that you recommend will be included next time, if it checks out. Please give reasons for your recommendation and specific directions if it is difficult to find.

You can also contact me on the internet through the *Scotland the Best!* website which is sponsored by Famous Grouse whisky. The address is

www.famousgrouse.com.

SECTION 1

Edinburgh

The telephone code for Edinburgh is 0131
Refer to MAP A, *unless otherwise stated*

THE BEST HOTELS

1
D2 ✓ ✓ **THE BALMORAL:** 556 2414. Princes St at E end above Waverley Stn. Capital landmark with its clock always 2 min fast (except at Hogmanay) so you don't miss your train. The old pile especially dear to Sir Rocco Forte's heart. Exp for a mere tourist but if you can't afford to stay there's always afternoon tea in the Palm Court. Few hotels anywhere are so much in the heart of things. Good business centre, fine sports facs; luxurious and distinctive rms with some ethereal views of the city. Main restau, Number One Princes Street (74/BEST RESTAUS), excellent and less formal brasserie, Hadrian's, adequate. 186RMS JAN-DEC T/T PETS CC KIDS LOTS

2
C3 ✓ ✓ **THE CALEDONIAN:** 459 9988. Princes St, W End. Edin institution – former stn hotel built in 1903. Owners have spent a fortune recently upgrading it from merely grand to Grand and Businesslike. Sparkling spa (with pool). Endearing lack of uniformity about the rms. Executive rms on fifth floor (and deluxe rms elsewhere) have gr views as well as facs. Capital kind of place in every respect. Main restau, The Pompadour, part of the big refurb for fine dining, Chisholm's brasserie is a … brasserie. Cally Bar a famous rendezvous. 249RMS JAN-DEC T/T XPETS CC KIDS TOS LOTS

3
xE4 ✓ ✓ **PRESTONFIELD HOUSE:** 668 3346. Off Priestfield Rd, 3km S of city centre. The Heilan' coos in the 14-acre grounds tell you this isn't your average urban bed for the night. 17th-century building with period features still intact. Architect Sir William Adam, responsible for the ceiling in the Tapestry Rm, also 'did' the ornamental ceilings in Holyrood Palace. Bulk of rms – 26 – added in a sympathetic 1997 refurb, though older ones possibly have more character. Sleep thro' history. 31RMS JAN-DEC T/T PETS CC XKIDS LOTS

4
B2 ✓ **CHANNINGS:** 315 2226. S Learmonth Grds, parallel to Queensferry Rd after Dean Br. tasteful alternative to hotel chain hospitality. 5 period town houses joined to form a v tasteful and discreet hotel. Impeccable décor with efficient and individual service. Gr views from top-floor rms, incl the Prime Minister's alma mater – Fettes College. A chic retreat from downtown throngs. Brasserie has 2 AA rosettes. 48RMS JAN-DEC T/T XPETS CC KIDS LOTS

5
C1 ✓ **THE HOWARD:** 557 3500. 36 Gr King St. Elegant establishment in the heart of the New Town – gr individual rms with cupboards big enough for a horse and some baths ditto. Basement restau, Number 36, is one of the city's finest (71/BEST RESTAUS) and a marked design contrast to what's upstairs. Same owners as Channings (*see above*). 15RMS JAN-DEC T/T XPETS CC XKIDS TOS LOTS

6
E2 **ROYAL TERRACE:** 557 3222. 18 Royal Terr. Romanesque plunge pool, other sports facs, multi-level terraced grd out back, deceptively large number of rms and town house décor a tad on the Baroque side. In other words, fabulous darling! Bar/restau not so notable among the natives, so good place for discreet meets. 110RMS JAN-DEC T/T XPETS CC KIDS LOTS

7
D3 **HOLIDAY INN CROWN PLAZA:** 557 9797. 80 High St. Modern but sympathetic building on the Royal Mile, handy for everything. Good facs but some say service lacking. Thin walls, not gr views. Piano bar can be fun if taken in the right spirit (lots of). Gym and small pool. Unlike other hotels nr here, does have parking. 238RMS JAN-DEC T/T PETS CC KIDS TOS LOTS

8
C3 **THE SHERATON:** 229 9131. Festival Sq on Lothian Rd and nr Conference Centre, this city-centre business hotel won no prizes for architecture when it opened late 1980s, but it's settling in now and the 'square' is looking better. A reliable stopover with excellent service. Larger rms and castle views carry premiums, but make big difference. Terr restau adequate, but The Grill menu prepared under the supervision of Nicolas Laurent is elegant, Scottish and innovative (3 Michelin Forks). 261RMS JAN-DEC T/T PETS CC KIDS TOS LOTS

9
C2 **THE GEORGE:** 225 1251. George St (betw Hanover St and St Andrew Sq). An Inter-Continental Hotel but Robert Adam-designed and dating back to late 18th century. Good views to Fife from the top 2 floors. Pricey, but you pay for the location and the Georgian niceties. Busy and grandiose carvery plus good Gallic restau, the Chambertin (102/FRENCH RESTAUS). Good Hogmanay hotel if you like a touch of carnival – the Latin stage is outside. Taken over by luvvies during TV Festival. 195RMS JAN-DEC T/T PETS CC KIDS LOTS

THE MORE INDIVIDUAL HOTELS (AND GUEST HOUSES)

10
xE1 ✓ ✓ **THE MALMAISON:** 468 5000. Tower Pl, Leith, at the dock gates. Award-winning, praise-laden designer hotel with individual and rather natty rms. Appeals to smart, young thrusting types like me and Robbie Williams. CD players in each chambre (borrow CDs from reception). Brasserie and café-bar have stylish ambience too (90/BEST BISTROS) and there are many others nearby in this waterfront quarter. Also in Glas, Newcastle, Manchester and spreading.
60RMS JAN-DEC T/T PETS CC KIDS EXP

11
C3 ✓ ✓ **THE POINT:** 221 5555. 34 Bread St. You'd never guess this used to be a Co-operative department store. Space and colour combinations manage to look simultaneously rich and minimal, some castle views. Suites (LOTS) come with side-lit Jacuzzis. Considered one of the gr designery hotels in world terms and features on the cover of *Hotel Design*. Café-bar Monboddo and restau have modern and spacious, mid-Euro feel. Good places to meet Edinburgers.
140RMS JAN-DEC T/T PETS CC KIDS EXP

12
B3 ✓ ✓ **THE BONHAM:** 226 6050. 35 Drumsheugh Grds. Discreet townhouse in elegant W End cres. Cosmo service and ambience. *Conde Naste Travel* called it 'one of the coolest' (in the world). Owned by same people as the Howard and Channings (4/5/BEST HOTELS). Rms stylish but not minimalist. Dining in calm, spacious restau where chef Pelham Hill excels. No bar.
48RMS JAN-DEC T/T XPETS CC XKIDS LOTS

13
C3 ✓ **INNER SANCTUM** and the **OLD RECTORY** at the **WITCHERY:** 225 5613. Castlehill. 2 highly individual rms and an apartment above the Witchery restau (70/BEST RESTAUS) at the top of the Royal Mile. Prob the most exceptional and atmospheric in town – designed by owner James Thomson and Mark Rowley – fairly camp/theatrical, OTT and v sexy. Go with somebody good (see Aonach Eagach Ridge 2215/BEFORE YOU DIE).
2+1 APT JAN-DEC T/T XPETS CC XKIDS LOTS

14
B3 ✓ **EDINBURGH RESIDENCE:** 226 3380. 7 Rothesay Terr. Another town house affair, this where several Georgian town houses have been joined into an elegant residencia (or time-share). Usually rms (or suites available), but pricey. No restau but 24 hr room service. Drawing rm if you're feeling lonely. Quiet W End but nr nightlife and shops.
21RMS (8 SUITES) JAN-DEC T/T XPETS CC KIDS LOTS

15
C2 **SIBBET HOUSE, 26 NORTHUMBERLAND ST:** 556 1078. The definitive New Town B & B. Some rms adj and apartment over the way. Georgian town house hospitality that has been wowing guests for yrs. Timeless.
8RMS(+APT) JAN-DEC T/T XPETS CC KIDS MED.EXP

16
C2 **24 NORTHUMBERLAND ST:** 556 8140. Next door to 26 above so similar apartments – these full of antiques (owner is notable dealer). Several people wrote to suggest this place for inclusion. It's been a secret so far – now you'll have to book.
3RMS JAN-DEC X/X XPETS CC XKIDS MED.EXP

17
C2 **17 ABERCROMBY PLACE:** 557 8036. Another plush and private Georgian town house; discreet lack of signage. Once abode of the New Town's architect, Playfair, now belongs to advocate Eirlys Lloyd. No smk, 2 rms in a self-contained mews; main house for breakfast.
8RMS JAN-DEC T/T XPETS CC KIDS MED.EXP

18
D2 **THE ALBANY:** 556 0397. 39 Albany St. Refurb townhouse hotel handy for trend-spotting Broughton St, but too exp for its denizens. New Town splendour and *politesse* – only a few mins walk uphill to Princes St. Basement restau, Haldane's (74/SCOTTISH RESTAUS), is pretty good.
21RMS JAN-DEC T/T PETS CC KIDS LOTS

19
xD4 **THE GRANGE:** 667 5681. 8 Whitehouse Terr. In southern sedate suburb and set in beautiful grds, this is a quiet country-house kind of retreat from which to venture into the city (centre 3km). Restau but we haven't tried.
15RMS JAN-DEC T/T PETS CC KIDS EXP

20   **SIX ST MARY'S PLACE:** 332 8965. Vegn GH. On main st of Stockbridge (St
B1   Mary's Pl part of Raeburn Pl) and busy main rd out of town for Forth Rd Br and
N, this is a tastefully converted Georgian town house. Informal, friendly, well-
cared-for accom popular with academics and people we like. No smk. Vegn
breakfast in conservatory. Jolly; nice people.

8RMS JAN-DEC X/X XPETS CC KIDS MED.INX

21   **STUART HOUSE:** 557 9030. 12 E Claremont St. Nr the corner of main rd and
D1   pleasant walk up to Princes St (1.5km). Residential New Town st and family
house decorated with taste and attention to detail – bonny flower grd out
front. Book well in advance. No smk.

5RMS JAN-DEC T/T XPETS CC KIDS MED.EXP

22   **TEVIOTDALE HOUSE:** 667 4376. 53 Grange Loan, towards E end. Fabulous
xD4   fecund flower grd out front and bargain accom within. Ground-floor rm (popular with honeymooners) has a 4-poster with adj chaise longue and the
whole effect is undeniably, unexpectedly sexy – although v respectable you
understand. Healthy breakfasts.   7RMS JAN-DEC T/T XPETS CC KIDS MED.INX

23   **HOTEL JAVA:** 467 7527. Constitution St, Leith, next to the estimable Port O'
xE1   Leith (258/GR EDIN PUBS). Friendly, contemporary bar with basic but inexp rms
in Leith nr docks and with many of the city's best bars and restaus nearby.
Phillipa and Sue run a laid-back and happy house. Rms at back and round
courtyard.   10RMS JAN-DEC X/X PETS CC KIDS CHP

24   **TAYLORS HALL:** 622 6800. Cowgate. If you don't mind the racket (or want to
D3   be part of it), this is a clubby/young thing kind of hotel in the heart of the
throbbing Cowgate area and above the hugely popular 3 Sisters pub. 3 bars
to choose from(Irish/American/Goth) 24 hr license for residents. Can do 4 in a
rm.   42RMS JAN-DEC T/T PETS CC XKIDS MED.EX

25   **FREDERICK HOUSE:** 226 1999. 42 Frederick St nr George St. Central refurb
C2   making the most of its location and booming Edinburgh to charge a tad over
the odds for basic tho' contemp facs. B/fast over the rd at Cafe Rouge for
example.   42RMS JAN-DEC T/T XPETS CC XKIDS MED.EX

26   **WEST END HOTEL:** 225 3656. 35 Palmerston Pl. Capital haunt for Highlanders
B3   and Islanders who feel like a blether in Gaelic or a good folk music session in
the bar (decent measures). Popular with folkie non-guests too. Spacious rms
with oddly familiar furniture.   8RMS JAN-DEC T/T XPETS CC KIDS INX

27   **PARLIAMENT HOUSE:** 478 4000. 15 Calton Hill. Good central location, only
E2   200m from E end of Princes St and adj to Calton Hill (380/BEST VIEWS), although
tucked away. Small bar in residents lounge and recent ('99) restau for b/fast,
even meals – but OK town house-style décor.

53RMS JAN-DEC T/T XPETS CC KIDS EXP

28   **STATION HOTEL:** 226 1446. 9-13 Market St, behind Waverley Stn. Some good
D3   views from upper floors to Princes St. Couldn't be handier for the stn or city
centre. Rms feel a bit 'holiday package deal', basic but acceptable. No smk. Its
restau is Italian-ish and curiously, always empty.

30RMS JAN-DEC T/T XPETS CC KIDS MED.EXP

THE BEST 'ECONOMY' HOTELS AND TRAVEL-LODGES

Hotels/B&Bs below are included on grounds of price, convenience or just because we like them for some idiosyncratic reason.

29 **APEX INTERNATIONAL:** 300 3456. 31-35 Grassmarket. Once part of Heriot-
C3 Watt Univ, a determined conversion resulted in a central hotel with contemporary Euro-bland façade. Civilized although a tad characterless and no longer inx. Rms with castle view, are more exp, but worth the extra. Fifth-floor restau (INX) also has nice outlook. Another Apex (474 3456) nr Haymarket with 68 rms and a restau called Tabu (mixed reviews).

168RMS JAN-DEC T/T XPETS CC KIDS EXP

30 **STAKIS EDINBURGH AIRPORT:** 519 4400. At the airport, 10km W of city cen-
xA3 tre. No way 'economy', but a reliable travellers' tryst. An L-shaped box with the buzz of a high-class transit camp; charming staff. You can virtually roll out of bed and check in. That smell over the airport by the way is due to some unconscionable thing they do to chickens in their concentration camp nearby. Stay indoors and don't have the fricassee!

134RMS JAN-DEC T/T XPETS CC KIDS LOTS

31 **TRAVEL INN:** 228 9819. 1 Morrison Link, nr Haymarket Stn. Likeable for the
B3 fact it makes no pretence to be anything other than a bed factory. Big, orthogonal and dull but v cheap – flat charge of under £40 applies per rm which can take 2 adults or a family of 4. 7 rms specially adapted for wheelchair users.

280RMS JAN-DEC X/T XPETS CC KIDS CHP

32 **FORTE POSTHOUSE:** 334 0390. Corstorphine Rd next to Zoo. Entrance feels
xA3 like an underground car park, but there's a gr view across to the Pentlands. Bit of a featureless bed box, although recently refurbed, but has all the facs expected of a big chain hotel and you hear real wolves howling in the night.

303RMS JAN-DEC T/T PETS CC KIDS MED.EXP

33 **THISTLE INN:** 220 2299. 94-96 Grassmarket. Basic and boisterously located
C3 accom joined to Biddy Mulligan's next door which is open to 1am, 7 days. So don't bring grandma, do come on a night out with the lads (or lassies).

29RMS JAN-DEC X/T PETS CC KIDS MED.INX

34 **IBIS:** 240 7000. Hunter Sq. First in Scotland of the Euro budget chain and first
D3 in Edin of a huge rash of Parliament boom hotels. Dead central behind the Tron so good for Hogmanay stays (or not). Serviceable and efficient. For tourists, poss the best of the ones above for location.

99RMS JAN-DEC T/T PETS CC KIDS MED.INX

THE BEST HOSTELS

Edin has some YHA hostels (nae drinking) and independents (young and Hoochy, open 24 hrs), also some handy univ halls of residence to let o/side term time. With all the independent hostels, it's best to turn up around 11/11.30am if you haven't booked. The SYHA is the Scottish Youth Hostels Association. 01786 891400.

35 ✓ ✓ **THE HIGH STREET HOSTEL:** 557 3984. 105 High St. On the Royal
D3 Mile, nr the Cowgate with its late-night bars. Ideal central cheap 24 hr crash-out dormitory accom with all the facs for itinerant youth seeking a capital experience. At the time of writing, the original hostel also called **THE HIGH ST HOSTEL**, but at 8 Blackfriars St and under threat from the neighbouring Holiday Inn, was still open. Original here means best. Sister hostel: **CASTLE ROCK**, 15 Johnston Terr (225 9666) in the old Council Environmental Health HQ, is huge (190 beds in various dorms, but no singles/doubles) and has some gr views across the Grassmarket or to the castle which is just over there. Same folk (Mr Backpacker himself, Peter Macmillan) also have places in Ft William, Inverness, Oban and Skye. CH

36 ✓ ✓ **S.Y. HOSTEL, EGLINTON:** 337 1120. 18 Eglinton Cres. From the
A3 stained glass over the main door to the tartan and wood entrance foyer, you know you're not in a typical hostel. Grand late-Victorian pile in a quiet W End st with 156 beds – majority in dorms but some rms for 4 (single sex dorms). Members only but you can join at reception. Booking recommended. Doors locked at 2am. CHP

37 ✓ **BELFORD HOSTEL:** 225 6209. Douglas Grds, nr Gallery of Modern Art
A2 (excellent café, 199/BEST TEAROOMS) and quaint Dean Village, but still fairly central. Bizarre concept – 98 beds in partitioned-off 'rms' of 6-10 in a converted church. Top-bunk berth gets you a view of the vaulted wooden ceiling way above. Games rm, bar, MTV. Sister establishment **EDINBURGH BACKPACKERS HOSTEL**, 65 Cockburn St (220 1717), is closer to action. CHP

38 **PRINCES ST HOSTEL:** 556 6894. 5 W Register St. Behind Burger King at E end
D2 of Princes St. Incredibly central for cheap accom. Basic and attracts the usual international crowd. Same people now have **PRINCES ST WEST**, 3 Queensferry St (226 2939) with bar. CHP

39 **S.Y. HOSTEL, BRUNTSFIELD:** 447 2994. 7 Bruntsfield Cres. S of Tollcross about
xC4 10 min walk from W End. Buses from Princes St (grd side), nos 11, 15, 16. Reliable and secure hostel accom in a verdant corner of Bruntsfield. 130 beds but booking 2-3 months in advance is essential at peak times. Again, members only, join at reception and doors locked at 2am. CHP

40 From July-Sep, SYHA also opens a temporary hostel in **ROBERTSON'S CLOSE**
D3 off Cowgate. Phone Edin district office for info 229 8660.

41 **POLLOCK HALLS:** 667 0662. Off Dalkeith Rd. The main accom for Edin Univ –
xE4 a village of modern low-rise blocks, situated 3km S of centre next to the Royal Commonwealth Swimming Pool (349/MAIN ATTRACTIONS) and in the shadow of Arthur's Seat, on which to gaze or jog. Refectory, bar, shared kitchens and showers. Huge number of rms – 800 basic singles and more than 400 others, some doubles. Vacs only. MED.INX

42 **NAPIER UNIVERSITY:** 455 4621. Craiglockhart campus off Colinton Rd.
xC4 College halls in high-rise blocks about 10km SW of centre. In grounds of imposing Craiglockhart Hospital where Siegfried Sassoon met Wilfred Owen. Far out for some, but good sports facs, incl pool. Vacs only. CHP

43 **QUEEN MARGARET COLLEGE:** 317 3310. Clerwood Terr. Way out, midway
xA2 betw main rds W to Glas and N to Forth Br; about 10km, so transport probably essential (or bus). Campus facs, e.g. refectory, laundry, bank, good sports. Shared bathrms, etc. and a bit dreary, so not exceptional value, but a private and well-equipped refuge from uptown hassles. Phone first. Also self-catering flats. Vacs only. CHP

44 **ARGYLE PLACE:** 667 9991. 14 Argyle Pl, in Marchmont area of up-market stu-
xD4 dent flats. Quiet area though Argyle Pl the most happening st. 2 km to centre across 'The Meadows' (not advised for women at night). Nice garden. CHP

THE BEST CAMPING AND CARAVAN PARKS

Refer to Lothians map on pages 340–341.

45
MAP 7
D1

✓ **THE MONKS' MUIR:** 01620 860340. 4 km S of Haddington and signpost-ed off A1 40 km from centre. Convenient location (good rd to town) and attractive site. Good shop and bike hire point. Floodlit *terrain de pétanque* (here they do try harder). 67 pitches. Open AYR.

46
MAP A
xE4

MORTONHALL PARK: 664 1533. Off Frogston Rd E, a kind of inner-city ring rd. About 12km S of centre. From S and city bypass: take Lothianburn jnct into town and rt at first lights for 4km. From centre: take A702 via Morningside to last left turn before bypass. Mortonhall marked, but enter via (and pass) Klondyke Grd Centre. No. 7 or 11 bus from town. Well-equipped park with 4 toilet/shower blocks, shop, laundry, lounge, play area and fully serviced pitch-es. Also bar/restau in converted stables/courtyard serving food till 9pm. Coffee shop with decent home-baking at grd centre. Mar-Oct. 268 places.

47
MAP A
xA1

THE EDINBURGH CARAVAN CLUB SITE: 312 6874. Marine Dr, Silverknowes. 8km NW of centre via Ferry Rd then rt on Pennywell Rd, continue over r/bout to Marine Dr. Former local authority site, taken over and substantially refurbed by the Caravan Club of GB – reopened 1997. Accepts non-members. 150 pitch-es for caravans, tents and motor homes – all with electricity. Two heated toilet blocks, laundry, disabled facs. Open AYR.

48
MAP 7
B1

FORDEL, DALKEITH: 660 3921. Lauder Rd. On A68, 4km S of Dalkeith; 18km SE of centre. V well equipped and serviced site secluded from the busy rd. Behind a 24 hr garage and pub/café (Fordel Inn). Some work done recently so improved pitches and more landscaping. Best to have a car; reasonable bus service to Dalkeith, but fewer go past gate. 35 caravan sites, 100 pitches.

49
MAP 7
B1

DRUM MOHR, MUSSELBURGH: 665 6867. Levenhall. 4km out of Musselburgh on the coast rd to Prestonpans. 22km E of centre. Go through Musselburgh, signed off bypass and take rd rt at Mining Museum. Award-win-ning site is 400m up a country lane, within sight of the sea, quiet (apart from some traffic noise) and well maintained. You will be rather removed from Edin, but within easy reach of the golf/beaches/walks and ice cream of E Lothian. Disabled facs. Mar-Oct. 120 pitches.

See Lothians map on pages 340–341.

50
MAP 7
B1
✓ ✓ **GREYWALLS, GULLANE:** 01620 842144. On the coast, 36km E of Edin off A198 just beyond golfers' paradise of Gullane. O/looks Muirfield, the championship course (no right of access) and nr Gullane's 3 courses and N Berwick's 2 (395/396/SPORTS FACS). No grey walls here but warm sandstone and light, summery public rms in this Lutyens-designed manor with grds attributed to Gertrude Jekyll. It's the look that makes it special and the roses are legendary. Sculpture grd in July and literary w/ends. Library like a London club, and service. Golf ain't everything.

23RMS APR-OCT T/T PETS CC XKIDS TOS LOTS

51
MAP 7
A1
✓ ✓ **CHAMPANY INN:** 01506 834532. On A904 , 3km off Linlithgow on way to Forth Rd Bridge and S Queensferry. Exemplary restau with rms format with 16 comfortable rms annexed to the restau which is legendary for steaks and seafood (184/RESTAUS FOR BURGERS AND STEAKS). Lovely rm for b/fast. Extraordinary wine-list with dinner. Veggies should not venture here.

16RMS JAN-DEC T/T XPETS CC KIDS LOTS

52
MAP 7
B2
✓ **BORTHWICK CASTLE, NORTH MIDDLETON:** 01875 820514. On B6367, 3km off the A7, 18km bypass, 26km SE of centre. So this is a real Border castle, a big red one. Walls 30m high, this magnificent tower house knocks you off your horse with its authenticity – Mary Queen of Scots was blockaded here once and at night you expect to see her swishing up the spiral stairs. 8 rms in castle, 2 in gatehouse, the (v) grand banqueting hall is impressive, dinner (EXP) is not.

10RMS MAR-DEC T/X PETS CC KIDS LOTS

53
MAP 7
A1
✓ **NORTON HOUSE, INGLISTON:** 333 1275. Off A8 nr airport, 10km W of city centre. Virgin hotel in extensive grounds (hence quiet) with those Bransonesque touches you'll love or loathe – teddy bear on the bed, ducks in the bath. But high standard of service and accom with country house feel and handy for airport, points N or SW, even Edinburgh. Conservatory Restau is easily worth its two AA rosettes.

47RMS JAN-DEC T/T XPETS CC KIDS TOS LOTS

54
MAP 7
B2
JOHNSTOUNBURN HOUSE, HUMBIE: 01875 833696. On B6457 2km from A68 and 25km SE of centre. Bypass 22km. Country class in this 17th-century manor with relaxed and friendly service. Some rms in its coach house, all have that upbeat frilliness. Public areas v cool, esp the panelled 18th-century dining-rm. Feels like a true escape. Mavis Hall park adj offers clay pigeon shooting, fishing, off-road, etc., so it's an excellent all-round centre v close to the city. Dinner so-so, good wine-list.

20RMS JAN-DEC T/T PETS CC KIDS LOTS

55
MAP 7
B2
DALHOUSIE CASTLE, BONNYRIGG: 01875 820153. Just off B704 2km from the A7, 15km from bypass and 23km S of centre. The castle that tries too hard? It looks fantastic in its setting and dates way back to the 13th century but the facs are everything you would expect from a contemporary city hotel, which is perversely disappointing. (Previous guests incl Edward I, Cromwell, Queen Victoria, some rock stars.) Our Braveheart researcher was quite fond of the William Wallace rm; dinner is taken in the dungeon. Another 5 rms in adj Victorian lodge.

34RMS JAN-DEC T/T PETS CC KIDS TOS LOTS

56
MAP 7
A1
HOUSTON HOUSE, UPHALL: 01506 853831. On A899 at end of Broxburn/Uphall Main St, 8km from r/bout at the start of the M8 Edin–Glas motorway. Airport 10km, 18km W of centre. Bits of this tower house date to the 16th century, others far more recent (extension with 46 rms completed summer 1997). Yet more 4-posters, nice open fire in the bar, restau is rated and the place is stuffed with farmers during Royal Highland Show week. Set on 20 acres of greenery, atypical Uphall. Sports facs, incl a pool.

71RMS JAN-DEC T/T XPETS CC KIDS TOS LOTS

57
MAP 7
A1
DALMAHOY, KIRKNEWTON: 333 1845. On A71 (Kilmarnock rd) on edge of town – bypass 5km, 15km W of centre, airport 6km. In the beginning was the word, and the word was golf. 2 good courses, European Tour venue and that's what the groups of chaps (and occasionally ladies) come for. Hotel itself is Georgian with 7 distinctive rms, rest in new annex where the extensive sports facs reside. Part of the Marriott chain. 60 new rms '99.

215RMS JAN-DEC T/T XPETS CC KIDS TOS LOTS

58 **MARINE HOTEL, NORTH BERWICK:** 01620 892406. The grand old seaside

MAP 7 hotel of N Berwick reeks of holidays gone by – you almost expect to see

B1 Margaret Rutherford on the putting green. Snooker, open-air swimming pool.
O/looks links and Fidra. Good for kids and golf.

83RMS JAN-DEC T/T PETS CC KIDS EXP

59 **OPEN ARMS, DIRLETON:** 01620 850241. Dirleton is 4km from Gullane

MAP 7 towards N Berwick. Comfortable if pricey hotel in centre of village, opp ruins

B1 of 13th cent castle. Location means it's a golfers' paradise and special packages are available. Restau has 2 AA whatsits.

10RMS JAN-DEC T/T PETS CC KIDS TOS LOTS

60 **HAWES INN, SOUTH QUEENSFERRY:** 331 1990. From city take rd N via

MAP 7 Queensferry Rd heading for Forth Rd Br. On front at Hawes Pier and literally

A1 under the famous rail br (351/MAIN ATTRACTIONS). Pick the rt rm and lie back in
the 4-poster to soak up an atmos that made RLS escape into *Kidnapped*. Facs
far from fab, but genuine 16th century with unique situation. Some nights,
many bikers.

8 RMS (NONE EN SUITE) JAN-DEC T/T PETS CC KIDS MED.INX

61 **QUEENSFERRY LODGE HOTEL, nr NORTH QUEENSFERRY:** 01383 410000. At

MAP 7 Fife end of rd br (so Edin is a toll away), but a good stopping-off place for all

A1 points N. Dramatic setting with estuarine views. Restaus/bars/shop – a modern purpose-built roadhouse. N Queensferry less crowded than S (except for
Deep Sea World – 1541/KIDS); nice bistro – the Channel (01383 412567).

77RMS JAN-DEC T/T PETS CC KIDS MED.INX

62 **THE OLD ABERLADY INN:** 01875 870503. Main St. Straightforward drop inn

MAP 7 with simple, well-kept rms, a good farmhouse-style bistro with interesting

B1 menu and a trad howf for drinks and bar food. Popular with golfers – OK for
anyone.

8RMS JAN-DEC T/T PETS CC KIDS MED.INX

63 **TWEEDDALE ARMS, GIFFORD:** 01620 810240. One of 2 inns in this heart of E

MAP 7 Lothian village 9km from the A1 at Haddington, within easy reach of Edin. Set

B2 among rich farming country, Gifford is conservative and couthy. Some
bedrms small, but public rms pleasant if chintzy. Smells like a country inn
should.

16RMS JAN-DEC T/T PETS CC KIDS MED.INX

64
C3 ✓ ✓ **THE ATRIUM:** 228 8882. Foyer of the Traverse Theatre (421/GOOD NIGHTLIFE), Cambridge St off Lothian Rd. Every year the taxing question – which are the very best restaus in town? More difficult to assess now because there are so many contenders. Michelin and AA differ widely. I'll still settle for Andrew Radford's stylish restau behind the Usher Hall in the atrium of an office block. AA Gill can get back on that London train, leave us to our excellent dinner and our non-metropolitan ways. Remarkable food that's both modish and subtle, still the capital's best all-rounder. The newer **BLUE** (77/BEST BISTROS) is upstairs. Lunch and dinner Mon-Sat. LO 10pm. Cl Sun.
EXP

65
xE2 ✓ ✓ **LA POTINIÈRE:** Main St, Gullane. 01620 843214. 36km W of city on A198 coast rd off A1. David and Hilary Brown's intimate, much-celebrated caff, the first truly gr restau in SE Scotland, enduring elegance although facing that stiff competition in town. I came back here summer of '99 after a long absence – it *is* still *the* best and worth the 45 min drive for the elegant simplicity of their set menu of French classic and contemporary cooking. Outstanding wine list. Dinner: Fri/Sat only (or groups by arrangement). Lunch: Tue-Sun. Famously booked in advance, but lunch and Fri easier and often cancellations. No smk.
MED

66
D3 ✓ ✓ **THE TOWER:** 225 3003. Corner of Chambers St and George IV Br above the new Museum of Scotland. Top end and top floor restau in the distinctive 'tower' on the corner of the new museum building. Benefits from the much-admired grand design and detail of Gordon Benson's architectural vision. Décor has been described as retro-futurist; it feels that it could be anywhere except for Edin rooftops and castle skyline outside the windows (and in summer, the terr). Gr private dining-rm in the tower itself. Kitchens far below in prehistoric Scotland, but food everything one would expect – Scottish slant on modern British. The steaks are good. 7 days. Lunch and dinner. LO 11pm. W/end booking essential. Smokers to the balcony!
EXP

67
xE1 ✓ ✓ **(FITZ)HENRY:** 555 6625. 19 Shore Pl. Dave Ramsden's warehouse brasserie in an off-the-waterfront st in Leith – one of Edin's top spots and the only one (1997/98/99) apart from The Atrium (*see above*) to get a Michelin red M. Great chefs have come and gone – currently Brett Morman, a Sydney man. Fastidious, but non-intrusive service in a stylish setting. 6 days. Lunch and dinner. Cl Sun.
MED

68
C2 ✓ **RHODES & CO:** 220 9190. 3 Rose St opp M & S and Jenners of which it is a part. Totally professional dining out experience from Gary, the Rhodes boy. High expectation so not always entirely realized. Stark, modern rm upstairs and bar by big windows on the street. Perhaps a bit soulless, but the Edin bourgeoisie have taken to heart the fairly plain fare generally impeccably prepared and presented without fuss (but not by Gary who has moved on). Mashed potatoes, for example, and sticky toffee pud rarely come better than this. Lunch 7 days. Dinner Mon – Sat. LO 10.30pm.
MED

69
xD4 ✓ **THE MARQUE:** 466 6660. 19 Causewayside. Discreet Southside bistro/restau owned by chefs Glyn Stevens and John Rutter. At first ('98) the 'menu you must', now settled into a more measured response. Food v sound but smallish rm somewhat bereft of atmos. You feel you'd bring your mum 'n' dad here on Graduation Day. They would be impressed. Tue-Sun, lunch and dinner. LO 11pm.
EXP

70
C3 ✓ **THE WITCHERY:** 225 5613. Castlehill. At the top of the Royal Mile where the tourists come, many will be unaware that this is one of the city's best restaus and certainly its most stylishly atmospheric. 2 salons, the upper more witchery; in the 'secret grd' downstairs, a converted school playground, James Thompson has created a more spacious ambience for the (same) elegant Scottish menu. 7 days. Lunch and dinner. (232/LATE-NIGHT RESTAUS)
EXP

71
C1 ✓ **NUMBER 36:** 556 3636. 36 Gr King St. Basement restau of the Howard Hotel (5/BEST HOTELS) in the New Town and in design contrast to the Georgian opulence upstairs. Number 36 is bold and clean-cut verging on minimalist. The food also is contemporary in every respect and this is one of the

city's great discreet eats. Innovative cuisine, service is snappy. 7 days. Lunch and dinner (cl Sat lunch). No smk. MED

72 ✓ **MARTIN WISHART:** 553 3557. 54 The Shore. Small, chic restau on the
xE1 shore in Leith formerly Silvios. Chef/prop the eponymous Martin has trained with some big names to drop (but I won't). Some people rave about this place (some don't). I'm on the fence, but can sometimes be found in the window when I'm with the kind of friend who thinks that food is the new rock 'n' roll. Contemp, stylish, no fuss – the food I mean! Lunch Tues – Fri, Dinner Tues – Sat. EXP

73 ✓ **THE VINTNER'S ROOM:** 554 6767. 87 Giles St, Leith. Cobbled courtyard
xE1 to wine bar, with woody ambience and open fire. Vaults, formerly used to store claret (Leith was an important wine pt), also incl a restaurant lit by candlelight. Bar and restau have same evening menu (French tone using fresh Scottish produce), but cheaper options at lunch in the bar and less formal. Excellent cheeseboard and wine list. Mon-Sat lunch and 6.30-10pm. MED

74 ✓ **NUMBER ONE PRINCES STREET, BALMORAL HOTEL:** 556 2414. Address
xE1 with a certain ring for the principal restau of the Balmoral (1/BEST HOTELS) entered through lobby or off st. Based apparently on the Mandarin Grill, Hong Kong, these opulent subterranean salons have ample space around the tables, but the lighting and lacquering do little to cosify the ritziness. Chef Jeff Bland ensures that **HADRIAN'S BRASSERIE,** a peppermint lounge at st level, complements well. Cl Sat/Sun lunch. LO 10.30pm. EXP

75 ✓ **MARTIN'S:** 225 3106. 70 Rose St N Lane. Quiet lane behind busy shop-
C2 ping precinct nr Princes St – odd place to find a decent restau but this is one of Edin's most consistently top eateries. Good service, v high standard of contemporary cooking, delicate desserts and an unsurpassed, unpasteurized Celtic cheeseboard. Good on game and Martin knows his wines. 3 AA rosettes. Lunch Tue-Fri, dinner Tue-Sat. LO 10pm. EXP

76 **THE ROCK:** 555 2225. Commercial St/Quay, Leith. In a row of 'waterfront'
xE1 restaus in converted warehouses opp the new Scottish Office, this is the one that stands out for excellent food (though others are notable). Modern setup with good sightlines to other diners and open kitchen. Grill menu of burgers and steaks (and salmon) is simple and à la carte menu widens choice for non red-meaters. Mick Jagger and some women ate here '99. We hear changes may be afoot in 2000. 7 days. Lunch and dinner. Cl Sun lunch. MED

THE BEST BISTROS AND CAFÉ-BARS

77
C3 ✓ ✓ **BLUE:** 221 1222. Cambridge St. Upstairs in the Traverse Theatre building. From the makers of The Atrium (64/BEST RESTAUS), a lighter, informal lunch, indeed the same menu continues all day till late. Still one of most fashionable place in town to graze, you can eat for under a tenner; the menu, which changes seasonally, tempts you to more. Sound levels high, but partly because it's full of people with something to say. 12noon-3pm and 6pm-12midnight daily. Set snacks only in the afternoon, bar open to 1am daily. It's where we go. Same people now have **THE HUB** (*see below*).   CHP.INX

78
xE1 ✓ ✓ **SKIPPERS:** 554 1018. 1a Dock Pl. In a corner of Leith off Commercial Rd by the docks. Look for Waterfront (see below) and bear left into adj cul-de-sac. The pioneer restau in the pre-yuppie Leith, it's still after all these yrs quite the best real bistro in town. V fishy, v quayside intimate and friendly. Look no further out to sea. Dinner: Tue-Sat, LO 10pm.   MED

79
C3 ✓ **TUSCAN SQUARE:** 221 9728. 30 Grindlay St, part of the Lyceum Theatre. At last a formula in this site that has worked. Iain McMaster's light Mediterranean menu is of the moment, inx and v well done. Tables o/stairs and on the street for cafe-bar stuff. Upstairs for the evening (or 'suits' having lunch). Some big tables. Lunch and dinner Cl Sun/Mon.   INX

80
E4 ✓ **HOWIE'S:** 668 2917. 75 St Leonard's St. Up on the S side, this extended set of rms is always busy. Unfussy, extensive and eclectic menu the epitome of good Edin bistro food that's affordable. Totally reliable and inexp eating out. Though this is the original Howie's, 2 others hit the same spot S and W of the city. 63 Dalry Rd, 313 3334. The best place to eat in the neighbourhood 100m up from Haymarket Stn. 208 Bruntsfield Pl, 221 1777. In a converted church. All 7 days, lunch and dinner. LO 10/10.30pm. Cl Mon lunch. BYOB (with corkage) or unpretentious wine list. Also …   INX

81
B1 ✓ **HOWIE'S CANTEEN:** 225 5553. Glanville Pl by the br in Stockbridge. David Howie Scott's latest venture, turning a white elephant site into an instant success (maybe because they Feng Shui'd the room). Similar approach and menu to other Howies and not exactly a canteen, more a buzzy bistro with good value contemporary food. 7 days, lunch till 4pm, LO 10pm.   INX

82
C4 ✓ **THE APARTMENT:** 228 6456. 7 Barclay Pl, up from the Kings Theatre. Contemporary eating-out experience with almost surprisingly good food, courtesy of chef Mark Lawrence in the kitchen and Malcolm Innes. You may meet Malcolm! Grazing menu and big helpings at comfortably inx prices. Some art, some thought. An instant hit, autumn '99. This must be how to do it. 7 days, dinner only, LO 11pm.   INX

83
C3 ✓ **CAFE HUB** 473 2067. Castlehill, top of Royal Mile. The cafe of the Hub (the International Festival Centre). Light ground floor cafe in expensively converted church and o/side terrace (smokers brave all weathers). Run by Andrew Radford (of Blue, *above*) and a strong team. Newish at time of writing, it may move up this page. At moment more functional than fab, but we go loads. Phone for hrs.   INX

84
B2 ✓ **INDIGO YARD:** 220 5603. 7 Charlotte Lane. Food in bar area and in restau upstairs in converted and glazed-over yard behind the W End. Enormously popular and always buzzing so you may not hear your wine pop or your coin drop in the condom machine. Earlier therefore better for conversational meals, but snackier supper menu from 10pm-1am is worth remembering. Food modern Med/Mex-Scottish and better than café-bar standard. 7 days, lunch and evening menu LO 10pm, then supper. (316/THESE ARE HIP) INX

85
C4 ✓ **MONTPELIERS:** 229 3115. 159 Bruntsfield Pl. Same ownership as above and similar buzz and noise levels, but more accent on food. From b/fast menu to late supper, they've thought of everything. All the contemp faves. Gets v busy. 7 days, 9am – 1am, lighter menu after 10pm.   INX

86
C2 ✓ **BROWNS:** 225 4442. 131 George St nr Charlotte Sq. First Scottish venture of this carefully-run small seventies chain, taken over for expansion by Bass. One of the most successful packaging of the late 90s Menu-U-Like, this is a reliable meal out. Huge rm can be noisy but excellent service. Quite the

best of the big restaus at this end of George St. Don't even think about the others. 7 days, 10am-11.30pm (Sun open at 12noon). No booking. INX

87
xE1 ✓ **THE WATERFRONT:** 554 7427. 1c Dock Pl. In this foody corner of the waterfront, The Waterfront conservatory o/looks the backwater dock. It's *the* place to head in summer, but the warren of rms is cosy in winter. Food has wavered a bit over the yrs and still does, but site, setting and gr friendly service are mostly what you come for. 7 days, LO 10pm. MED

88
xE1 ✓ **THE SHORE:** 553 5080. 3 The Shore, Leith. Bar (often with live light jazz) where you can eat from the same menu as the dining-rm/restau. Real fire and large windows looking out to the quayside – strewn with bods on warm summer nights. Food, listed on a blackboard, changes daily but is consistently good. Lots of fish, some meat, some vegn. No smk in restau/OK in bar. 7 days, LO 10pm. (291/PUB FOOD) MED

89
B2 ✓ **BOUZY ROUGE:** 225 9594. 1 Alva St, nr corner with Queensferry St. Edin branch of the hugely successful bistros opened first in Airdrie, but most notably in Glas. This is well thought out accessible dining with some flair for the money (well you know what I mean). This basement can seem cramped (esp the seats), but reliable, contemporary and inx. 7 days, lunch and dinner, LO 9.30pm (Fri/Sat 10.30pm). INX

90
xE1 ✓ **MALMAISON BRASSERIE:** 555 6969. Tower Pl at Leith dock gates. Restau and café-bar of Malmaison (10/INDIVIDUAL HOTELS). Authentic brasserie atmos and menu, as in all Malmaisons in the expanding chain, with linen cloths, big windows, steak frites. **CAFÉ MAL** with snackier food, is less successful. 7 days. Lunch and dinner. MED.INX

91
D4 ✓ **NICOLSON'S:** 557 4567. 6a Nicolson St, opp Festival Theatre. '99 makeover but same proprietors (they also have The Grain Store (154/SCOTTISH RESTAUS) and the coffee shop nearby (208/BEST TEAROOMS) and vastly improved layout. Still with good window seats o/looking the theatre. Revamped menu huge improvement, esp since it's available later than most. 7 days. Lunch and dinner, LO 11pm (Fri/Sat 12midnight). MED

92
xE1 **DANIEL'S:** 553 5933. 88 Commercial Quay, off Dock Pl. Versatile with small deli, takeaway and bistro. Main eaterie is housed in conservatory at back of old bonded warehouse. Clean lines, modern look and v popular. Offers contemporary French menu with Alsace and external influences that has been packing us in. Also tables by the water 7 days, 9am-10pm. INX

93
D3 **THE DORIC:** 225 1084. 15 Market St. Opp the Fruitmarket Gallery and the back entrance to Waverley Stn. Upstairs bistro with chequered cloths, awful paintings, eclectic menu. Famous for their unaccommodating attitude to latecomers and the rude expulsion you get when they want to close the bar; it ain't cheap like the old days. All this aside it's still a gr bistro; we always go back. 7 days, LO 10.30pm. MED

94
D3 **LE SEPT:** 225 5428. 7 Old Fishmarket Close. The cobbled close winds steeply off the High St below St Giles. Wee o/side terr in summer and narrow woody rm inside for nonsmokers (but smokey rm too). Crêpes, omelettes, plats du jour and Franco-bistro food. Cheerful, busy rendezvous with well-regarded staff. Mon-Thu lunch and LO 10.30pm; Fri 12noon-11.30pm; Sat 12noon-11pm; Sun 12.30-10.30pm. INX

95
D3 **THE DIAL:** 225 7179. 44-46 George IV Br. Modern Scottish with an international spin in this subterranean designer eaterie. Some swear by this place, but some drawbacks, e.g. v basementy, variable service. But then it looks cool, does a bargain pre-theatre menu and much effort has gone into the aesthetics, edible or otherwise. On balance: dial their number. MED

96
C2 **A ROOM IN TOWN:** 225 8204. 18 Howe St, corner of Jamaica St. No one can work out why they didn't call it 'A Room in the New Town' which is better and describes where it is. We're not sure about the mural either. However, good bistro menu and friendly service. 7 days, lunch and dinner. BYOB. LO 10pm. INX

97 ✓ **DUCK'S AT LE MARCHE NOIR:** 558 1608. 2-4 Eyre Pl. Malcolm Duck pre-
C2 sides with meticulous attention to detail in his bistro/restau at the lower
end of the New Town. In a residential neighbourhood, an easy-going but still
business-like atmos. Various *menus complets*, with some imaginative regional
variations and regular gourmet evenings. Good-value wine list. Dinner 7 days,
lunch Mon-Fri. LO 10.30pm (earlier Sun). MED

98 ✓ **CAFÉ SAINT-HONORÉ:** 226 2211. 34 Thistle St Lane, betw Frederick St
C2 and Hanover St. Suits a-plenty, New Town regulars and occasional lunch-
ing ladies all to be found in this busy, shiny bistro-cum-restau where menu
smacks of *fin de siècle* Paris. No starving artists, or bohemia just a *fin de 20th
siècle* restau with a distinct French flavour. Veggies should phone ahead. EXP

99 ✓ **BISTRO PROVENCALE:** 229 4404. 21 Argyle Pl. Authentic corner de
xD4 France in Marchmont's main st. Could be Montparnasse. Straight talking
menu has some French flair. Even frogs legs. Cheap cheap lunch. BYOB. Cl
Mon/Tues. INX

100 ✓ **JACQUES:** 229 6080. 8 Gillespie Pl, Bruntsfield. Endearing French staff and
xC4 atmos. Hard-working wee rustic eaterie close to the King's Theatre. Has all
those French dishes – mussels, roulade – and throws in left-fielders like
ostrich, yes, ostrich! Loyal following, you may need to book. Also Sun brunch.
Lunch and LO 11pm Mon-Sat, 10am-10pm Sun. INX

101 ✓ **BONARS:** 556 5888. 58 St Mary's St. The Bonars moved from their highly-
E2 regarded country restau in Gifford to take over this once formal eaterie.
Still a sense that *beurre* wouldn't melt in the mouth, but some dishes are quite
inspired. When the new Parliament opens round the corner, intrigue may add
more piquancy to the sauce. 7 days (though may be closed Sun, so check)
lunch and dinner. LO 9.30pm. EXP

102 ✓ **CHAMBERTIN:** 225 1251. 21 George St. Discreet, v professionally run
C2 main restau of George Hotel (9/BEST HOTELS) in opulent salon where suits
dine at lunch time and other members of the Edin establishment compare
chips (on the shoulder). More relaxed in the evenings. Food more *au courant*
than previously. Lunch Mon-Fri, LO 10pm Mon-Sat. Cl Sun. EXP

103 **LA BONNE VIE:** 667 1110. 49 Causewayside. Popular bistro in Edin's S side. V
D4 agreeable. Sitting among the garlands, stone walls, shining glassware and
candles for a few mins, there's a growing sense of personality, then it hits you.
This is the Felicity Kendall of capital restaus – and that's a compliment.
Scottish produce, French outlook. Lunch and LO 10.30pm daily. MED

104 **PIERRE VICTOIRE:** 225 1721. 10 Victoria St. For those who followed the rise
D3 and fall of Pierre Levicky who created the Pierre Victoire 'cheap, cheerful ...
and authentic' bistro chain, took over the world and then, suddenly went
under, this place is of some interest. It was his first venture. There are others in
town, all privately managed – this is still the one to try. 7 days. Lunch and dinner. LO 10.30pm. INX

105 **BLEU:** 557 8451. 4 Union St. The branch we prefer (less claustrophobic) of this
D1 'new concept' former Pierre Victoire 'Bouchées' are mouthfuls, like tapas but
helpings are huge so food is a gr deal. Other branches in Stockbridge (8
Gloucester St 225 1037) and Victoria St (226 1900). 7 days, lunch and dinner. INX

106 **LA P'TITE FOLIE** 225 7983. 61 Frederick St. Formerly Chez Jules. The word is
C2 unpretentious. – mismatched furniture, inx French *plat du jour*. Cheap lunch. 7
days. Cl sun lunch. INX

107 **CAFÉ D'ODILE:** 225 5366. 13 Randolph Cres. A secret grd and small cafeteria
B2 downstairs at the French Institute. Lunch only but can be booked for parties
at night. Gr views over the New Town, simple French home-cooking, patron-
ized by ladies who lunch and students. BYOB. Tue-Sat. CHP

LA POTINIÈRE: 01620 843214. Main St, Gullane. Report: 65/BEST RESTAUS.

THE VINTNER'S ROOM: 554 6767. 87 Giles St, Leith. Report: 73/BEST RESTAUS.

108 ✓ **SCALINI:** 220 2999. 10 Melville Pl. Downstairs (*the scalini*) bistro restau in
xE1 a low-ceilinged sliver of a basement with a straightforward and personal
approach to Italian cooking – Silvio will tell you what's good tonight and he'll
be right. They have an amazing collection of vintage Barberas, probably one
for your birthday. Smoking upstairs. Cl Suns. MED

109 ✓ **VALVONA & CROLLA:** 556 6066. 19 Elm Row. Cafe at the back of the leg-
E1 endary deli, and with all the flair and attention to detail that you would
expect. First-class ingredients, produce shipped in from Italy (fresh veg from
Milan markets) and gr Italian domestic cooking. This place is a treat without
the trappings. Everything from vegn breakfast to fab lemon polenta cake and
coffee for afternoon nibblers via a damned fine lunch. May be queues. No
smk. Mon-Sat 8am-5pm. Not cheap, but who's counting the lira. INX

110 ✓ **COSMO:** 226 6743. 58 N Castle St (a no through rd). V much in the old, dis-
C2 creet style for those with some time and cash on their hands. In Edin
terms, has been the up-market Italian restau for yrs and it is often fully
booked. Famous people like Sean do get brought here. The lighting and the
music are soft, the service impeccable and the (Italian) wine list exemplary.
Menu pragmatically brief; allow time to enjoy it. 6 days. Cl Sun and Sat lunch.
EXP

111 ✓ **LIBRIZZI'S:** 668 1997. 22a Nicolson St. Small basement ristorante opp
D3 Festival Theatre. Intimate and personal place ignored by other guides.
Underrated, but reliable, esp for fish. Good service, well-selected wines. Cl Sun,
LO 11pm. MED

112 ✓ **TINELLI:** 652 1932. 139 Easter Rd. Small and neat restau with unassuming
xE2 frontage on unfashionable st that was serving air-dried beef long before
anyone else. Many fans swear by it! Not a pizza/pasta joint – grilled liver with
balsamic vinegar more their style. One of the city's best Italians. Lunch and LO
10.30pm Mon-Sat. MED

113 ✓ **BAR ROMA:** 226 2977. 39 Queensferry St. One of Edin's long-standing
B3 fave Italians, now revamped and hurtled into the 90s. Almost looks like a
Pizza Express from the outside. Inside always bustling (this includes the
menu) with real Italian rude waiters as the floor show. 7 days, all day. LO
11.30pm. INX

114 **EST EST EST:** 225 2555. 135 George St at W End. Though my own feeling
C2 about this place (the food) is ugh, ugh, ugh, there's no question that it works
in a super-restaurant way. Busy, noisy, sleek and modern – it's a New Labour
kinda thing. Food and service – who cares? The people say yes. 7 days. LO
11.00pm. INX

115 **TONY'S:** 226 5877. 42 St Stephen St. Identifiable by the floral window box,
C1 this small tratt features a high standard of Italian cooking, comparable with
the standard of patter from Tony himself. V popular so book. Daily, evenings
only, LO 11pm. Slightly larger **TONY'S** at 19 Colinton Rd, 447 8781. Same
menu, excellent service. INX

116 **PEPE'S TAVERNA:** 337 9774. 96 Dalry Rd. Taverna's just the word – checked
A4 tablecloths, dark wooden fixtures and hanging pots and pans. Food is stan-
dard Italian but when virtually everywhere else has packed up for the night,
Pepe's keeps on keeping on. A Dalry haven 6pm-2.30am. Cl Tue. (240/LATE-
NIGHT RESTAUS) INX

117 **GIULIANO'S:** 556 6590. 18 Union Pl, top of Leith Walk nr the main r/bout, opp
D2 Playhouse Theatre. No change at Giuli's but something sets it apart as it's usually heaving with happy punters, many birthdays! It's just pasta and pizza but
in a no-nonsense menu that appeals. The food is great, the din is loud. Lunch
and LO 2am daily. Also another 'on the shore' in Leith (554 5272) which is esp
good for kids (192/KID-FRIENDLY). INX

UMBERTO'S: 554 1314. Off Bonnington Rd. (190/KID-FRIENDLY PLACES).

GORDON'S TRATTORIA: 225 7992. 231 High St. (238/LATE-NIGHT RESTAUS).

THE BEST PIZZA

118 ✓ **PIZZA EXPRESS:** 332 7229. 1 Deanhaugh St, Stockbridge. Burgeoning
B1 national chain, same formula everywhere, but what-the-hell, it's great pizza (and ambience). Stockbridge branch best, in refurbed bank with Water of Leith gurgling below. Simple, no-nonsense, affordable pizza with good service. Award for architecture. Edin W End branch, 225 8863, 32 Queensferry St. Both open till 12midnight daily. Also North Br, adj Calton Highland Hotel, but these 2 branches best vibes. No booking   INX

119 **JOLLY:** 556 1588. 9 Elm Row. The original, unaltered '70s pizza point with
E1 wood-burning oven. Frilly, democratic and no irony – but gt pizzas and gt service. Mon-Sat and LO 11.30pm Sun 4-10.30pm.   INX

120 **MAMMA'S:** 225 6464. 30 Grassmarket. Brash, American-style with informal
C3 booking system (chalk your name on the board then nip off to the pub to wait). Some alternatives to pizza, but you come to mix 'n' match – haggis, calamari and BBQ sauce and 40 other toppings. 12noon-10.30pm Sun-Thu, till 1am Fri-Sat (later if you're still eating). Also 1 Howard St, Canonmills.   INX

121 **CAPRICE:** 554 1279. 325-331 Leith Walk. Old-style – hip in the '70s but bought
xE1 over a few years back and not quite what it was. But – wood-burning oven, packed with Leithers at peak times; the pizza's fine. Lunch Mon-Sat, LO 11pm Mon-Thu, 11.30pm Fri-Sat, 10pm Sun.   INX

122 **MARIO'S:** 337 6711. 105 Dalry Rd. Well-kept secret in this not so up-market
A4 part of town (1 km Haymarket Stn) with loyal clientele – Mario knows 90% of his customers by name. Good for kids, gr for pizza. Lunch and LO 10pm (Fri-Sat 11.30pm).   INX

THE BEST MEDITERRANEAN FOOD

123 ✓ **IGG'S:** 557 8184. 15 Jeffrey St, nr Royal Mile. Maybe misleading to include
D3 Igg's here because although it serves the best tapas in town, they're only available at lunch. Overall, it's a v smart eaterie serving some of the best victuals in Edin – Spanish/Scots crossover. Excellent sauces and riojas. People in the know eat here. Lunch LO 10.30pm. Cl Sun.   MED

124 ✓ **BARIOJA:** 557 3622. 19 Jeffrey St. And after Iggs, a tapas bar opened sum-
D3 mer '99 – they are joined together in the basement. Small tables and not much room to move upstairs; more space, less ambience down. Sound, authentic tapas menu. 11am – 11pm. Cl Suns.   INX

125 ✓ **MEDITERRANEO:** 557 6900. 73 Broughton St. Fairly discreet frontage on
D2 busy little Broughton St. Family feel (the Crollas, scions of the V and C – 1336/DELIS) to this cafe/bistro/restau serving not unsurprisingly Mediterranean snacks and meals, but not pasta. Deli counter, various coffee. 7 days lunch and Thur-Sat, dinner LO 9.30pm.   INX/MED

126 ✓ **TAPAS TREE:** 556 7118. 1 Forth St. Bustling wee restau with upbeat
D2 Spanish staff and gypsy/Cajun soundtrack. Starter/main/pud is the heavier option but 3 well-chosen tapas (veg, fish and something else) with some robust bread and a bottle of house red makes for a v decent meal. Snappy service. This place unusual in that it gets better and better. Tapas in the £2 to £5 range, so not a pocket buster. 11am-10.30pm daily.   INX

127 **PHENECIA:** 662 4493. 55-57 W Nicolson St, on corner nr Edin Univ. Unfussy
D4 yellow N African/Spanish eaterie with couscous, lots of grilled meats and wide vegn choice. Poss to eat v cheaply at lunch-time – some people just pop in from that univ for hummus and salad. Lunch Mon-Sat, LO 11pm daily (10pmSun). They have the Château Musar.   INX

128 **TAPAS OLÉ:** 556 2754. 8-10 Eyre Pl and 225 7069, 4 Forrest Rd, nr the Univ.
C2 Tapas restau/bar. Meat/vegn/seafood menus and the usual vinos. Spacious rather than cosy with Spanish proprietor and waiters. Live music on Sun. 7 days, lunch and LO 10.30 pm.   INX

THE BEST SEAFOOD RESTAURANTS

129
xE1
✓✓ **SKIPPERS:** 554 1018. 1a Dock Pl, Leith. Bistro with truly maritime atmos; mainly seafood. Best to book. Many would argue Skippers *is* the best place to eat seafood in town. Full report: 78/BEST BISTROS.

130
xE1
✓✓ **FISHERS:** 554 5666. Corner of The Shore and Tower St, Leith. At the foot of an 18th-century tower opp Malmaison Hotel and rt on the quay (though no boats come by). Seafood cooking with flair and commitment in boat-like surroundings where trad Scots dishes get an imaginative twist. Hugely popular, some stools around bar and tables o/side in summer (can be a windy corner). Often all are packed. Cheeseboard has some gr Brits if you have rm for a third course. 7 days. 12noon-10.30pm. MED

131
D3
CREELERS: 220 4447. 3 Hunter Sq. Tim and Fran James still holding on to their excellent seafood restau and smokehouse in Arran, also called Creelers. But they're mainly to be found in this corner of the revamped Hunter Sq behind the Tron Church, just a short cast from the Royal Mile (tables alfresco in summer). One of the best seafood spots in town. Nice paintings, good atmos, not exp. Bar meals at front, restau at back. Lunch and LO 10.30/11pm (Cl Sun in winter). MED

132
C2
THE MUSSEL INN: 225 5979. 61 Rose St. In the heart of the city centre where parking ain't easy, a gr little seafood bistro specializing in mussels and scallops (kings and queens) which the proprietors rear/find themselves. Also 'catch of the day' and a non-fish pasta option. Good chips. Lunch and dinner. Cl Sun, Mon. LO 10pm. INX

133
D2
CAFÉ ROYAL OYSTER BAR: 556 4124. W Register St. 'under new management', still a place for a flourish of insanity or sheer exhibitionism. Beluga caviar followed by Homard Newburg with a bottle of Bolly will cost you an arm and a leg. But you can also snack. Higher celeb quotient there for the classy surroundings with spillover atmos from adj bar. Tiles, linen, dark wood, v Victorian. Visitors usually find it all v groovy; locals lament that it ain't what it was. Lunch and LO 10.15pm daily. EXP

134
D4
LA BONNE MER: 662 9111. 113 Buccleuch St, nr the Univ. Discreet, some would say, tidy little seafood bistro. On a site which has seen many different cuisines in the past, this time it seems to work. Food simple, prices esp inx; 'student' 2-course lunch £5. BYOB. Tue-Sat, lunch and LO 10pm. Related to **LA BONNE VIE** (94/FRENCH RESTAUS). INX

THE BEST FISH 'N' CHIPS

135
C1
✓ **L'ALBA D'ORO:** Henderson Row, nr corner with Dundas St. Large selection of deep-fried goodies, incl many vegn savouries. Inexp proper pasta, real pizzas and even the wine's OK. A lot more than your usual fry-up – as several plaques on the wall attest (incl *Scotland the Best!*). Open till 12midnight. CHP

136
D2
✓ **THE RAPIDO:** 77 Broughton St. Fine chips. Popular with late-nighters stumbling back down the hill to the New Town, and the flotsam of the 'Pink Triangle'. Open till 1.30am (3.30am Fri-Sat). CHP

137
D2
✓ **THE DEEP SEA:** Leith Walk, opp Playhouse. Open late and often has queues but these are quickly dispatched. The haddock has to be 'of a certain size'. Trad menu. Still one of the best fish suppers you'll ever feed a hangover with. Open till 2am (-ish) (3am Fri-Sat). CHP

138
D4
✓ **SUSIE'S DINER:** 667 8729. 51-53 W Nicolson St. Cosy, neighbourhood (univ) self-service diner. Nice people behind and in front of the counter. Mexican and Middle-Eastern dishes, occasional live music and belly dancing nights. Licensed, also BYOB. Mon 9am-8pm, Tue-Sat 9am-10pm. Cl Sun.　CHP

139
D3
✓ **BANNS:** 226 1112. 5 Hunter Sq, just off Royal Mile at the Tron Church. Veggie burgers, Mexicana and many less predictable things in this informal eaterie on a redeveloped corner of the Old Town; tables outside in summer. Snacks and full meals all day, some vegan. Organic wines and beers, decent coffee from Gaggia machine. Daily 10am-11pm.　INX

140
C2
✓ **HENDERSON'S:** 225 2131. 94 Hanover St. Edin's original and trail-blazing basement vegn self-serve café-cum-wine bar. Canteen seating to the left (avoid), candles and live piano or guitar downstairs to the rt (better). Happy wee wine list and bottles of some excellent organic real ales. Good cheese. Cl Sun. LO 10pm. Also has the Farm Shop upstairs with a deli and takeaway and the more bar-like **HENDERSON'S THISTLE BISTRO** round the corner in Thistle St and a **TAKEAWAY IN CANONMILLS**, nr the clock with tables (some hot dishes), NOTE: Henderson's organic oatcakes are *the* best.　CHP

141
D3
✓ **BLACK BO'S:** 557 6136. 57 Blackfriars St. Unlike other eateries below, this is a restau, not a way of life. You could just about bring your meaty boyfriend here. Not precious, not perfect, but good vegn ideas and combos. Woody, laid-back set-up. Adj bar has been cool for yrs. Food less fruity than formerly and not so stodgy. 7 days, not Sun lunch. LO 10.30pm.　INX

142
D4
✓ **KALPNA:** 667 9890. 2-3 St Patrick Sq. Ingredients taken seriously in this long-established vegn restau which is also something else – a good Indian one – so more interesting than many. Thali gives a good overview while bargain Wed buffet features regional cuisine. No smk. Lunch Mon-Fri, dinner Mon-Sat, LO 10.30pm. (164/INDIAN RESTAUS)　INX

143
D4
✓ **ANN PURNA:** 662 1807. 45 St Patrick Sq. Excellent vegn restau nr Edin Univ with genuine Gujerati/S Indian cuisine. Good atmos – old customers are greeted like friends. Indian beer, some suitable wines. Lunch Mon-Fri, dinner 7 days, LO 11pm. (165/INDIAN RESTAUS)　INX

144
E4
ENGINE SHED CAFÉ: 662 0040. 19 St Leonard's Lane. Hidden away off St Leonard's St, this is a lunch-oriented vegn café where much of the work is done by adults with learning difficulties on training placements, so worth supporting. Simple, decent food and gr bread – baked on premises, for sale separately. Nice stopping-off point after a tramp over Arthur's Seat. (Also has a shop at 123 Bruntsfield Pl.) Mon-Thu 10.30am-3.30pm, Fri 10.30am-2.30pm, Sat 10.30am-4pm, Sun 11.30am-4pm.　CHP

145
C3
HELIOS FOUNTAIN: 229 7884. 7 Grassmarket. Old hippies eat sugar-free cake, their kids play with building blocks and browsers check out the tenets of Steinerism (Rudolf, not George). Reliable self-service vegn caff, anthroposophical bookshop and gewgaw emporium. No smk. Mon-Sat 10am-6pm, Sun 12noon-5pm.　CHP

146
C3
CORNERSTONE CAFÉ: 229 0212. Underneath St John's Church at the corner of Princes St and Lothian Rd. V central and PC self-service coffee shop in church vaults. Home-baking and hot dishes at lunchtime. Some seats outside in summer (in graveyard!) and market stalls during the Festival. One World Shop adj is full of Third World-type crafts and v good for presents. A respite from the fast-food frenzy and money round of Princes St. Open 9.30am-5pm (later in Festival). Cl Sun.　CHP

147
E4
ISABEL'S: 662 4014. 83 Clerk St (in basement of Nature's Gate wholefood shop). V small café selling vegn standards. Pop in some time. Mon-Sat 11.30am-6.30pm. (Cl earlier Tues/Sat)　CHP

148
C2 ✓ **WINTER GLEN:** 477 7060. 3a1 Dundas St, which is on the rt going down-hill opp the Scottish Gallery. Comfortable, intimate basement restau. Pleasing name comes not from sentiment, but from the surnames of the owners. Nevertheless this mainly Scottish menu originates from glen and loch and bay; Scotland's first-class ingredients featured and presented to exemplary effect. Smart service, urbane atmos. In most of the other guides too (tho' only 1 AA rosette). 6 days. Cl Sun.   MED

149
D3 ✓ **DUBH PRAIS:** 557 5732. 123b High St. Slap bang (but downstairs) on the Royal Mile opp the Holiday Inn. Only 9 tables and a miniature galley kitchen from which proprietor/chef James McWilliams and his team produce a remarkably reliable à la carte menu from sound and sometimes surprising Scottish ingredients. Remarkable and surprising because you might not expect the largely suburban clientele to feast so enthusiastically on ostrich or rabbit, but they do. Testimony to the chef; there are many more conventional options. An outpost of culinary integrity on the Royal Mile. Cl Sun-Mon. LO 10.30pm.   MED

150
D2 **HALDANE'S:** 556 8407. 39 Albany St. In basement of The Albany (18/INDIVID-UAL HOTELS). Fine dining nr Brougton St and prob the best meal in the area. Scottish by nature rather than hype. Everything done in a country house style, down to the bar snacks. Lunch Mon-Fri, LO 9.30pm daily.   MED

151
D3 **OFF THE WALL:** 667 1597. 11 S College St, nr Univ and round corner from Festival Theatre (hence inx pre and aprés 'theatre menu'). Not so much off the wall as in the wall, a discreet bistro often missed by the ravening foodies (but not Gillian Glover of *Scotland on Sunday* who loved it … and if it's good enough for her …). Short, simple menu with all the Scottish stalwarts (salmon, venison, beef) all nicely concocted with contemporary ingredients and twist. Mon-Sat, lunch and LO 10pm or later by arrangement.   MED

152
D3 **JACKSONS:** 225 1793. 209 High St. In the midst of the Mile, Jacksons plays the Scottish card big time. Here for over 15 yrs, this is a v TOS experience. In the cellar so to speak, but tables o/side in summer. Not sure about the haggis timbale thing, but Lyn MacKinnon I like and she's so … well, very Scottish. 7 days, lunch and dinner.   MED

153
C3, D2 **STAC POLLY:** 229 5405. 8a Grindlay St. Opp Lyceum Theatre and not far from Usher Hall, Traverse and cinemas. Those haggis filo parcels that divide opinion are still on the menu which is largely local produce cooked up a storm (Scottish beef, salmon, game). The restau – dark wood and tartan curtains – is quietly smart. Cheeses come from Iain Mellis. There's another basement **STAC POLLY** at 29-33 Dublin St in the New Town (556 2231). Similar menu but it feels clubbier. V fine. Both: lunch Mon-Fri (Sat lunch at Dublin St). Dinner 7 days LO 10/11pm (Grindlay St later).   MED

154
D3 **THE GRAIN STORE:** 225 7635. 30 Victoria St. Regulars climb the stairs for the pigeon, salmon or guinea fowl – perhaps the vegn alternative – then hang around this laid-back first-floor eaterie drinking wine or coffee. Informal and welcoming, there are few better places for a relaxed Sun lunch extending far into the afternoon. Perhaps more 'mod Brit' than simply 'Scottish'. Lunch and dinner daily, LO 11pm. Tho' much earlier Mon-Thur, so check.   MED

155
xE4 **FENWICK'S:** 667 4265. 15 Salisbury Pl. Tucked away in the depths of Newington tho with plenty students and tourists from the drab hotel belt to attract, this 90s kind of restau is an honest-to-goodness treat. Excl value. The cooking, with assorted international manoeuvres, offers local produce turned out with a goodly degree of style and honesty. Affordable wine list chalked up on the wall, but can BYOB. Lunch and LO 10.30pm.   INX

THE BEST MEXICAN (AND CENTRAL AMERICAN) RESTAURANTS

156 ✓ **VIVA MEXICO:** 226 5145. Anchor Close, Cockburn St. Has it really been
D3 here more than a dozen yrs? That says something about its position among the come-and-go Mexicans. Still throws in something innovative now and again, although all the expected dishes are here. Reliable venue for those times when nothing else fits the mood but sour cream, tacos and limey lager; nice atmos downstairs. Another branch nr Tollcross at 50 E Fountainbridge. Lunch (not Sun) and LO 10.30pm. INX

157 ✓ **MOTHER'S:** 662 0772. 107-109 St Leonard's St. Gr wee neighbourhood
E4 restau that manages to do the basics well (unlike many other Tex/Mexicans in town). Burgers, beef, burritos and one or two departures like Cajun veggie kebabs. Simple décor, good staff, proper coffee, home-made desserts. A hit, a palpable hit. Dinner 6-10pm Tue-Thu and Sun, 6-10.30pm Fri-Sat. Cl Mon. INX

158 **TEX MEX:** 225 1796. 47 Hanover St. Young, dumb and full of, er, tequila. A
C2 Primal Scream of a place in the city centre with all the usual Mexican faves, José Cuervo experiments and jolly soundtrack. Probably the best appointed of its ilk in Edin; infinitely preferable to others nearby. Slammersville. 12noon-1am Mon-Sat, till 12midnight Sun. INX

159 **PANCHO VILLAS:** 557 4416. 240 Canongate. This spartan cantina remains a
E3 reliable exponent of what we've come to regard as Mexican cooking with nosh of the 'chilada, 'ajita, 'ichanga school. Plain décor, decent edibles, happy place for parties. Lunch 12noon-2.30pm Mon-Sat, dinner 6-10.30pm daily. INX

160 **CUBA NORTE:** 221 1430. Morrison St (W End nr Haymarket Stn). Yes, we know
B3 it's not Mexican and perhaps not Cuban either, but this bar/restau with Latin vibes has been a success since it opened late '98 (despite the pundits poo-pooing that a cool place could be this far W). Bar at front, tables upstairs through back serving Cuba-style cuisine (though we know they don't have any food, never mind a cuisine, over there). Success in stretching the imagination and the ingredients all down to Oz chef. Some tango, flamenco and DJ salsa (various w/end nights) may drown out the flava later on, but a better attempt at Havana than others. 7 days lunch and LO 10.30pm. INX

THE BEST INDIAN RESTAURANTS

161
D3
✓ **SURUCHI:** 556 6583. 14a Nicolson St. Upstairs opp Festival Theatre. Owner from Jaipur called Mr Rodriguez plus chefs from Bengal, Delhi and S India equals eclectic Indian menu. Unfussy décor and food with light touch (good coconut rice) attracts students/academics from nearby univ as well as theatregoers. This place is routinely praised to the skies; mostly we agree. Live music some nights. Lunch and LO 11.30pm daily. INX

162
D3
✓ **KEBAB MAHAL:** 667 5214. 7 Nicolson Sq. Nr Edin Univ and Festival Theatre. Gr vegetable biryani and delicious lassi for under a fiver? Hence high cult status. Late-night Indo-Pakistani halal caff that attracts Asian families as well as students and others who know. Kebabs, curries and excellent sweets. One of Edin's most cosmopolitan restaus. Sun-Thu 12noon-12midnight, Fri-Sat 12noon-2am. No alcohol baby! CHP

163
xE1
✓ **THE RAJ:** 553 3980. 89 Henderson St on S corner of The Shore, Leith. Take a certain amount of care with the food, add Tommy Miah's marketing nous and wadda-you-get? The most successful Indian/Bangladeshi restau in town. Regular events (Bangladeshi New Year and Food/Culture Fest) add to the jollity; jars of things available to buy and take home, also recipe books. Sun-Thu still does food 'at 1983 prices'. Try to sit up on the raised front area – better than the back. Totally Raj, in the non-Irvine Welsh sense (in-joke for Edin readers). Lunch and LO 11.30pm, 7 days. INX

164
D4
KALPNA: 667 9890. 2-3 St Patrick Sq. The original Edin Indian veggie restau and still ragingly popular. Lighter, fluffier and not as attritional as so many tandooris. Wed buffet a bargain. Report: 142/VEGN RESTAUS. INX

165
D4
ANN PURNA: 662 1807. 45 St Patrick Sq. Friendly and family-run Gujerati/S Indian veggie restau with seriously value-for-money business lunch. Report: 143/VEGN RESTAUS. INX

166
C1
LANCERS: 332 3444. 5 Hamilton Pl. Bengali/N Indian, off busy Hamilton Pl in Stockbridge/New Town area. A 'Brits in India, those were the days' type restau which can mean service on the precious side, but the food speaks for itself. Dining area not so comfortable, but New Townies with lovely kitchens do phone for a kerry-oot. 7 days. LO 11pm. INX

167
B3
INDIAN CAVALRY CLUB: 228 3282. Athol Pl, W End, just off the main Glas rd, about 250m from Princes St the upmarket one tho'. Bargain business lunch attracts the suits. Another restau you'll like if you go for the retro colonial style. We don't esp – but no quibbles about the nibbles or the mainly excl main dishes. This seems an unlikely carry-out place, but they do, and it's one of the best in town. Lunch and LO 11.30pm daily. INX

168
C4
SHAMIANA: 228 2265. 14 Brougham St, Tollcross. Recommended by everyone from Egon Ronay (not a recommendation we'd rely on) to Gordon Brown our dear Treasurer, a prominent sign outside proclaims, 'Voted Best Restau in Scotland'. Well, up to a point Lord Copper. Small eaterie with quiet décor and v popular after rough patch. The food's good again, the kulcha is fine; the staff could lighten up a bit. MED

169
D3
KUSHI'S: 556 8996. 16 Drummond St. Long regarded as the only real Indian, this basic Punjabi café (no restau twiddly bits) has been drawing in students and others for cheap eats since Nehru was in his collar, or at least in the news. It's just round the corner from Edin Univ's Old College. Short no-nonsense menu, cheap no-nonsense prices. Unique, this is the stripped-down curry. Lunch Mon-Sat, dinner Mon-Thu 5-8.30pm, Fri-Sat 5-9.30pm. Cl Sun. CHP

THE BEST FAR-EASTERN RESTAURANTS

170 ✓ **ERAWAN ORIENTAL:** 556 4242. 14 S St Andrews St. The latest and most
D2 upmarket part of the dynasty (see below), betw Princes St and the soon-to-come Harvey Nix. Location the thing, but large brasserie-type rm with competent Thai cuisine mainly business at lunch and pleasure at night. Prob the best Thai in town. 7 days. LO 11pm.

171 **SIAM ERAWAN:** 226 3675. 48 Howe St. On corner of Stockbridge area, the first
C2 proper Thai in town and still rated – manages that quiet Eastern elegance v well. Same people also have **ERAWAN EXPRESS**, 220 0059, 176 Rose St, a kind of Thai canteen but not quite as inspired as its big sis. Both establishments lunch Mon-Sat, dinner daily, LO 11pm. INX

172 **AYUTTHAYA:** 556 9351. 14b Nicolson St, opp Festival Theatre. Decent
D3, C4 prospect pre- or post-show. Long, thin, not atmos restau, but attentive service, good vegn selection and a steady hand in the kitchen. Under the same ownership is **SUKHOTHAI:** 229 1537. 23 Brougham Pl, Tollcross. Funkier eaterie where the waitresses do their best to look delicate but would perhaps feel better in baseball caps. Sip your Singha – think not of Phuket. LO 10pm. INX

173 **YUMI:** 337 2173. 2 W Coates (continues from Haymarket Terr, W End). The
B3 classier and more polite of the capital's Japanese restaus. Our researcher thought it the cleanest rip in town. Still Michelin awards 2 forks. One day when we are loaded, we'll be back. Go if you must have sushi. Dinner only. LO 11pm. Cl Sun. EXP

174 **DARUMA-YA:** 554 7660. 82 Commercial St (entry via Dock Pl). Japanese din-
xE1 ing in the capital has a history of high prices and high snob value but at last one that is affordable. Bargain set meals. Not the most stylish, mouth-watering sushi you've ever had in your life, but it's a long way from Tokyo or Soho. Lunch Tue-Sat, LO 10.30pm Mon-Sat. Cl Sun. MED

175 **TAMPOPO:** 220 5254. 25a Thistle St. Not a restau at all but a gr wee Japanese
C2 noodle bar where you can pick up a ramen to go or one of those meal-on-a-tray things. Open lunch Mon-Sat, also 6-9pm Tue-Sat. Cl Sun. CHP

176
C2 ✓ **KWEILIN:** 557 1875. 19 Dundas St. Large New Town place with imaginative Cantonese cooking (real chefs); v good seafood and genuine dim sum in pleasant but somewhat uninspired setting. No kids allowed in the evening – somewhere for grown-ups to eat their quail in peace. Book. LO 10.45pm. Cl Sun/Mon   MED

177
xE4 ✓ **DRAGON WAY:** 668 1328. 74 S Clerk St. First thing that hits you as you go in – a big lacquer dragon wrapped around a pillar. Décor gloriously OTT and often described as 'Hollywood film set'. Good food mind you, and service, so one of the more interesting Chinese nights out. Lunch Mon-Fri and LO mid-night.   INX

178
C3 ✓ **ORIENTAL DINING CENTRE:** 221 1288. 8 Morrison St, opp cinema complex. It's a restau (**RAINBOW ARCH**), a dim sum basement bar and a late-night noodle shack (**HOHOMEI** – cash only, eat in or takeaway). Noodles 5.30pm-2.30am Mon-Sat. The restau is best by far in this neck of the W End. 12noon-midnight daily.   INX

179
xE1 ✓ **YEE KIANG:** 554 5833. 42 Dalmeny St. Authentic Chinese home cooking courtesy of Michael Wong deep in the heart of Hibbie land – recent refurb but feels like someone's living rm. Small, democratic. Does the real Chinese tea ceremony. An inside track choice. 7 days, 5.30pm-10.30pm (11.30pm w/ends).   INX

180
B3 ✓ **LUNE TOWN:** 220 1688. 38 William St. The wee one hidden away behind the W/End. A classy Chinese, often busy. Predominantly Cantonese cuisine. Lunch and LO 11.30pm Mon-Fri. Open 3pm-12midnight Sat-Sun.   MED

181
C1 ✓ **LOON FUNG:** 556 1781. 2 Warriston Pl, Canonmills. Upstairs (and down when it's crowded) the famous lemon chicken and crispy duck go round for ever. And damned fine seaweed. Lunch and LO 11.30pm (Sun-Thu), 12.30am (Fri-Sat).   INX

182
B3 **NEW EDINBURGH RENDEZVOUS:** 225 2023. 10a Queensferry St. Hardly new and easy to miss (upstairs, next door to travel agents). Functional décor, short wine list to be taken seriously and dishes you won't find in any other Scottish Chinese restaus, e.g. shredded sea blubber. Sound nice? Well this restau is for diehards. They'd say nobody does better Peking food in this town. 7 days. Lunch and LO 11pm Mon-Sat, 1-11pm Sun.   INX

183
C4 **LEE ON:** 229 7732. 3-5 Bruntsfield Pl. Through purple porthole-effect windows, a restau popular with the Chinese community. Feels a bit *Man From UNCLE*, but food fine. 7 days. Lunch and dinner. LO 12midnight.   INX

THE BEST RESTAURANTS FOR BURGERS AND STEAKS

184
xA2
✓ ✓ **CHAMPANY'S:** 01506 834532. On A904, Linlithgow to S Queensferry rd (3km Linlithgow), but nr M9 at jnct 3. Accolade-laden restau (and 'Chop and Ale House') different from others below because it's out of town (and out of some pockets). Both surf 'n' turf with live lobsters on premises. Good service, huge helpings (Americans may feel at home). Chop House 7 days, lunch and LO 10pm; restau lunch (not Sat) and LO 10pm. Cl Sun. Hotel rms adj (51/HOTELS O/SIDE TOWN)   INX.EXP

185
C1
✓ **BELL'S DINER:** 225 8116. 7 St Stephen St, Stockbridge. Bill Allan will understand why I can't say anything more about this legendary American diner. Nothing has changed in 20 yrs except the annual paint job. Burgers, steaks, shakes and coincidentally, the best veggie (nut) burger in town. Mon-Fri 6-10.30pm, Sat-Sun 12noon-10.30pm.   INX

186
xE1
✓ **THE ROCK:** 555 2225. Commercial St, Leith. Where to go for lunch with clients or dinner out when all you want is a decent steak/burger (there are other options). Best in Leith, with Bell's the best in town, and the most up-market on this page. Poss changes in 2000. Report: 76/BEST RESTAUS.   MED

187
D4, B1
✓ **BUFFALO GRILL:** 667 7427. 12-14 Chapel St. and 1 Raeburn Pl, Stockbridge (332 3864). Burn that beef! Although this diner trades on its reputation for steaks and such-like, there are some Mexican concessions to veggies. Book and BYOB Lunch Mon-Fri, LO 10.15pm (Sun 10pm).   INX

188
D4
SMOKE STACK: 556 6032. 53-55 Broughton St. From the makers of The Basement (262/GR EDIN PUBS) came something across the rd – a burgundy and blue diner rather than an orange and blue bar. Modish décor has a soothing effect. Loads of burgers (Scottish beef or vegn), seared salmon, etc. jollied along by a gr staff. (Santana at lunch time, old times/new times.) Proper menu available lunch and dinner, but food of some sort all day. Also does a good Sun brunch (248/SUN BREAKFAST). Open 12noon-10.30pm daily.   INX

189
C2
WIGWAM: 225 6127. 64 Thistle St. Bright colours in this central, but backstreet Native Americana diner. Mainly meat – a buffalo wings kinda joint – but vegn burgers too, with a good guacamole. Tex-Mex obviously, handy business lunch venue. Lunch and LO 11pm daily.   INX

190 ✓ **UMBERTO'S:** 554 1314. Bonnington Rd Lane off Bonnington Rd to E of
xE1 ✓ Newhaven Rd jnct. Whitewashed coach house hidden away in a v unlikely part of Leith. In contrast to some other 'kiddie' places, grown-ups would
actually want to eat here too. Downstairs is a civilized restau, upstairs a theme
area for kids where some booths form part of a big toy train and mobile
youngsters can run in and out of the Wendy house. Excl Italian cooking with
a Scottish twist. Upstairs open Mon-Fri 12noon-2pm then 5-7.30pm, Sat
12noon-7.30pm, Sun 12noon-5.30pm. Downstairs lunch and LO 10pm Mon-
Sat. INX

191 ✓ **LUCAS:** 446 0233. 16 Morningside Rd. '99 leap into town for the ice cream
xC4 ✓ kings (1321/ICE CREAM) to this modern ice-creamerie and caff where kids
with dads will enjoy their spag and their sundae. Crowded if not claustrophobic upstairs – they'll love it! 7 days. INX

192 ✓ **GIULIANO'S ON THE SHORE:** 554 5272. 1 Commercial St, by the br. With
xE1 ✓ its checked tablecloths, accented waiters and cheerful pizza/pasta menu,
this is almost a cartoon version of an Italian restau – no slight intended – and
kids love it. Always a birthday party happening at w/ends. Lunch and LO
10.30/11pm. INX

193 **YE OLDE PEACOCK INN:** 552 8707. Newhaven Rd nr Newhaven Harbour and
xC1 opp Harry Ramsden's (a more obvious place to take kids perhaps, *see below*),
but this has been one of Edin's unsung all-round family eateries for yrs, and
deserves wider recognition. The fish here really is fresh, the menu is more
adventurous than you'd think with lots that wee kids and we kids like. High
tea is a treat. Lunch and LO 9.30pm Mon-Thu, 12noon-9.30pm Fri-Sun (till
6pm). CHP

194 **FAT SAM'S:** 228 3111. 56 Fountainbridge. Cavernous gr Italian-style barn with
C4 a couple of enormous television screens, fish tank and animatronic cartoon-
like Fat Sam to scare the unwary. The scale and sheer chutzpah appeal to children of all ages (i.e. students' night out). Kids' menu has usual burgers, pizzas
and all that jazz. Main menu has all that's jazzier (swordfish, mezzelune) but
really a place for the young at heart and brain. 7 days, LO 10.30pm. INX

195 **BRIDGE INN, RATHO:** 333 1320. Canal Centre, Ratho, W Lothian. 14km W of
xA3 centre via A71, turning rt opp Dalmahoy Golf Club. Well worth the drive for an
afternoon on, or by, the Union Canal. The Pop Inn Restau has special menus for
kids, play areas and numerous distractions. Sailings and walks. LO food 9pm,
bar open 12noon-11pm (12midnight Fri-Sat). (302/PUB FOOD) INX

196 **CRAMOND BRIG HOTEL:** 339 4350. At the R Almond as you hit Edin on the
xA2 dual carriageway from the Forth Rd Br. This inn has put a lot of effort into
attracting families with its indoor/outdoor play areas (Funky Forest). If you've
driven for hrs with a whingeing child and want steak and chips while wee
Daniel or Amy play themselves into a stupor then it's v convenient. Otherwise
a bit characterless. Lunch and LO 9.30pm, 7 days. Open from lunch straight
through to close on Sat-Sun. INX

197 **HUNTER'S TRYST:** 445 3132. 97 Oxgangs Rd. Adj to Safeway, corner of
xC4 Oxgangs Rd N. Big steaks in the 'burbs. If this place was another half mile S it
would be up the Pentlands so a long schlep from town – but nr Fairmilehead
exit from bypass, so convenient for travellers. Alloa's bid for kid-friendliness
sees a bright Wacky Warehouse play area (it is a warehouse and it's v wacky)
connected to pub/inn selling pub/inn food. WW closes 8pm 7 days. Inn till
11pm daily, LO food 10pm (snacks till close). INX

198 **HARRY RAMSDEN'S:** 551 5566. Newhaven Rd. Edin branch of national chain.
xD1 Bright, tacky, predictable menu, but nice location by harbour nr *Britannia* and
the other new big developments. With seats o/side. All day, 7 days. CHP

THE BEST TEAROOMS AND COFFEE SHOPS

199
A2
✓✓ **GALLERY OF MODERN ART CAFÉ:** Belford Rd. Utterly unbeatable on a fine day when you can sit out on the patio by the grass, with sculptures around, have some wine and a plate of Scottish cheese and oat-cakes. Hot dishes are excellent. Coffee and cake whenever. Then it's back to the art. Oh well! Mon-Sat 10am-4.30pm, Sun 2-4.30pm. (354/OTHER ATTRACTIONS)

200
D3
✓ **FRUITMARKET CAFÉ:** 226 1843. 29 Market St. Attached to the Fruitmarket Gallery, a cool spacious place for coffee, cake or a light lunch. Big windows to look out; good mix of tourists, Edin faithfuls and art seekers – the latter go upstairs. Mon-Sat 10.30am-5.30pm, Sun 12noon-5pm.

201
xC4
✓ **MANGO AND STONE:** 229 2987. 165 Bruntsfield Pl. Juice bar in Bruntsfield, the first we suspect of many (in airports etc.). 'They squeeze to please' and they do eg 'Growing bones' (blueberry, orange, banana, pineapple), the 'Detox' – carrot, orange, beetroot. Filled rolls, good coffee, few chairs. Juice not cheap – health at a premium. 7 days 8am-6pm (Sun 9am-6pm).

202
C2
✓ **QUEEN STREET CAFÉ:** National Portrait Gallery (353/OTHER ATTRACTIONS), Queen St, betw Hanover and St Andrew's Sq. And through the arched window … a civil slice of old Edin gentility. Serving seriously good light meals, tasteful sandwiches, coffee and cake – best scones in town, among other things. Mon-Sat 10am-4.30pm, Sun 2-4.30pm.

203
D3,C4
✓ **FAVORIT:** 220 6880. 20 Teviot Pl, nr Univ. and 30 Leven St nr Kings Theatre (221 1800). First of several branches planned by people who brought us Indigo Yard (316/THESE ARE HIP) and Iguana nearby (321/THESE ARE HIP). All- day, all-round drop-in café in contemporary style reminiscent of City Café (325/THESE ARE HIP). They've thought of everything. Great late (333/LATE BARS). Both: 7 days, 8am-3am.

204
C2
✓ **THE LAIGH:** 225 1552. 117 Hanover St. Long before the coffee revolution, this basement coffee/bake house was the place to go for cafe culture. Trad furniture and atmos. Old faves - hazelnut meringue cake, tuna salad - remain despite new owners and are still the best you'll taste anywhere. Ingredients organic where poss. This place is essential Edin. Mon-Sat 8.30am-5pm Cl Sun.

205
C3
✓ **WHERE TO?:** 229 6886. 103 Highriggs, Tollcross. Excl caff/coffee shop for food, information, inspiration. Report 727/INTERNET CAFÉS.

206
D3
CAFÉ FLORENTIN: 225 6267. 8 St Giles St. Have turned an entire generation of Edimbourgeois on to almond croissants and wicked tartelettes. Uptown café with downtown décor, this establishment is the capital in a nutshell (or short-crust pastry case). Advocates rub shoulders with student grunge queens over a blast of caffeine. Aficionados feel that Florentin is not what it was. Discuss (over croissants)! Open 7am-11pm daily later during the Festival. Also at 5 NW Circus Pl, Stockbridge – with shop, 7am-7pm daily. (241/SUN BREAKFAST)

207
xD4
KAFFE POLITIK: 446 9873. 146-148 Marchmont Rd. All black and white and wood and middle-Euro chic at another converted bank in the heart of student flat land. Rear wall speckled with quotes from assorted celebs. Damn fine cup of coffee, sodas, juice, soup 'n' sandwiches and unfussy hot dishes. Small choice of v good breakfasts (246/SUN BREAKFAST). 10am-10pm daily.

208
D3
BLACK MEDICINE COFFEE SHOP: 622 7209. 2 Nicolson St, corner of Drummond St. Newish coffee shop by the same people as Nicolsons (91/BEST BISTROS) on busy Southside corner opp Festival Theatre and Univ Old Quad. Good place to take your book from Thins; get a window seat! Good smell. Big bagels. 7 days. 8am-8pm.

209
D2
STARBUCKS: 226 3610. 128 Princes St, 2nd floor of Waterstone's bookshop. Dare we say better than the cramped original (Seattle Coffee Co) at London's Covent Garden? Easily. In among the books, a young and friendly staff dispense everything from caffè latte to iced Americano. Savouries and pâtisserie courtesy of The Auld Alliance Bakery. View of the Castle. Open 8am-8pm Mon-Sat, (till 7pm on Sat) and 10.30am-6pm Sun. Another more business-like branch in the basement of the Edin Solicitors Property Centre at 85 George St

and a more stand-alone branch in Lothian Rd, on the corner of Bread St opp the ABC cinema.

210 **CLARINDA'S:** 557 1888. 69 Canongate. Nr the bottom of the Royal Mile nr the
E2 Palace (and the new Parliament building). A small tearoom with hot dishes and snacks that may seem more of a sit-down stop on the tourist trail but actually has probably the best home-baking in town (esp the apple pie). V reasonable prices; run by good Edin folk. 10am-4.45pm (from 12noon Sun).

211 **THE ELEPHANT HOUSE:** 220 5355. 21 George IV Br. Nr libraries and Edin Univ,
D3 a rather self-conscious but big-time and well-run coffee shop with light snacks and multifarious choice of caffeines and tannins to speed your research. Cakes/pastries are bought in but can be taken out. Mon-Fri 8am-11pm, Sat-Sun 10am-11pm. Same people have **ELEPHANT'S & BAGELS** at Nicolson Sq. Soup 'n' a bagel t/away and sit-in. 7 days 8am-6pm (w/ends 10am-5pm).

212 **COMMON GROUNDS:** 226 1416. 2-3 N Bank St, top of The Mound. The kind of
D3 coffee emporium where tourists wander in by accident and women can breast feed with impunity. Cake, light meals, insane range of espressos, incl the 'Keith Richards' (a quadruple). Live music some nights. 9am-10pm, Sat-Sun 10am-8pm.

213 **G&T (GLASS & THOMPSON):** 557 0909. 2 Dundas St. Patrician New Town cof-
C2 fee shop and deli with contemporary food and attitude. A Clarissa Dickson-Wright kind of place: they love food. Gr *antipasti*, salads and sandwiches to go. 8.30am-6.30pm, Sat till 5.30pm, Sun 11am-4.30pm. (251/TAKEAWAYS)

214 **BOTANIC GARDENS CAFETERIA:** By 'the House' (where there are regular
xB1 exhibs), within the grds (352/OTHER ATTRACTIONS). For café only, enter by Arboretum Pl. Recent major revamp but still catering-style food with light meals at lunchtime. O/side tables; the view of the city is why we come. And the squirrels. 10am-5pm.

215 **METROPOLE:** 668 4999. 33 Newington Rd. Once a bank, now a civilized coffee
xE4 house – the premises lend an air of Art Deco something. On a quiet afternoon it's where a Newington mum might mull over her life, the children at the nursery. Accompanied by their excl cappuccino with cinnamon … and a 'friend'. 9am-10pm daily.

216 **THE LOWER AISLE:** Underneath St Giles' Cathedral (357/OTHER ATTRACTIONS),
D3 enter round back via Parliament Sq, or through the body o' the kirk. Proximity of courts sees many legal eagles swooping in, tourists who have this book and regulars for coffee, tea, light meals. Mon-Fri 9am-4.30pm, Sun 10am-2pm. Cl Sat.

217 **CAFFE SARDI:** 220 5553. 18-20 Forrest Rd. More a restau perhaps with all the
D3 expected dishes but also serves a mean Danish pastry and espresso. Coffee machine is a Big Gold Dream and with waitresses from the old country and Italian television on cable, a hint, just a hint, of Soho's Bar Italia. Mon-Sat 9.30am-11pm. Cl Sun.

218 **ROUND THE WORLD:** 15 NW Circus Pl, Stockbridge. Exceptional gift shop and
C2 kitchenware vendor with startling coffee bar in converted bank (once mine). Tea, cake and one of the v best espressos. Open 10am-6pm Mon-Sat.

219 **LA GRANDE CAFETIÈRE (CAFÉ GRAND):** 228 1188. 182-184 Bruntsfield Pl.
xC4 Coffee shop during the day, popular bistro at night (INX). In among assorted coffees and herbal teas, Bovril can be had. Nice restful alternative to brash Montpeliers opp. 9am-11pm, till 12midnight Thu-Sat. Sun 10am-9pm.

220 **CALIFORNIA COFFEE CO:** 228 5001. By the Odeon cinema (Clerk St), top of
E4, D4 Middle Meadow Walk (opp Forrest Rd). 7.45am-9pm Mon-Fri, 10am-9pm Sat-Sun. Hope Park Cres, 8.30am-7pm Mon-Fri, 10am-7pm Sat-Sun. Caffeine kiosks in former police boxes. Similar fare to Starbucks (*see above*), but this is on the hoof and home-grown. Others imminent at time of going to press.

GREAT CAFÉS AND GREASY SPOONS

221 ✓ **BLUE MOON CAFÉ:** 557 0911. 36 Broughton St. Longest-established gay
D2 café in the capital and still evolving (2055/GAY EDIN). Now houses an espresso bar as well as the main bit with breakfast, snacks, meals or a drink. Female staff efficient, boys more spacey. Free condoms in the gents for the impecunious or impatient. 11am-12midnight Mon-Fri 9am-12.30 am Fri-Sat. LO 40 min before close.

222 ✓ **NDEBELE:** 221 1141. 59 Home St, Tollcross. The Ndebele are a southern
C4 African people, but this café has dishes from all over the continent so get your ostrich, mielie bread and moi moi here – or just have a coffee. Does loads of sandwiches, light meals and has a good groovalong soundtrack. Africa distant and usually hot, this delightfully chilled. Daily 10am-11pm. T/away and sit-in.

223 ✓ **LUCA'S:** 446 0233. 16 Morningside Rd. In town version of legendary ice
xC4 cream parlour in Musselburgh (1321/ICE CREAM). Ice cream and snacks d/stairs, more pasta parlour up. Cheap and cheerful food. Gr for kids. 7 days.

224 **LOST SOCK DINER:** 557 6097. Corner of E London St/Broughton St, adj
D1 Sundial laundrette. An innovation and caused a whirl when it opened – a café/restau attached to a laundrette where you could eat well while your washing spun. Several changes of chef and food policy since, still a cool place to snack with or without your powder. 7 days. LO 4pm Mon, 10pm Tue-Sat. Sun 10am-5pm. Some people do the caff at Stills Gallery, Cockburn St.

225 **CENTRAL CAFÉ:** 228 8550. 42 Home St, next to the Cameo Cinema. Graham
C4 Main's downtown deli/takeaway with urban cool and gr snacks and coffee (no cooking). Best music and crack in the area, 9am-6pm. Cl Sun.

226 **CANASTA:** 554 5190. 10 Bonnington Rd, nr corner with Gr Jnct St, Leith. Café
xD1 for locals, not one of your downtown cappuccino numbers. Best omelettes in the burg, and usual café grub (haddock and chips, grills) and cakes homemade before you (I) get up. Tea in a mug. Takeaway. We should honour these people. Cl Sun.

KEBAB MAHAL: 667 5214. Nicolson Sq. Cult I. Report: 162/INDIAN.

KUSHI'S: 556 8996. 16 Drummond St. Cult II. Report: 169/INDIAN.

INTERNET CAFÉS

227 ✓ **WHERE TO?:** 229 6886. 103 Highriggs where Laurieston Pl becomes
C3 Tollcross. Odd name, odd combo of what are perhaps the preoccupations of proprietor Crawfurd Hill: going out, eating out and IT. Great outdoors lifestyle informs food and decor. Euro food: from rosti to sachertorte and gr fluffy omelettes. Screens incl 2 iMacs (£5 an hr session), but newspapers as well as Internet, so an all-round information destination with good food. A bold and imaginative venture. Then log off – there's hills to climb! 7 days, 7.30am-10pm (10.30 w/ends).

228 **CYBERIA:** 220 4403. 88 Hanover St. If we can split hairs and say there's a dis-
C2 tinction between cool and hip, then Cyberia takes the silicon wafer for coolest capital Internet café. Good coffee, fine sandwiches and cakes – you'd come for an espresso even if you had no interest in cyberspace. 12 terminals, E-mail drop box facility, surfing sessions by the half hr, etc. V chic, understated décor with sculpturey bits. E-mail: edinburgh@cybersurf.co.uk. Mon-Sat 10am-10pm, Sun 12noon-7pm.

229 **WEB 13:** 229 8883. 13 Bread St. The city's most homely Internet boutique, 19
C3 terminals. At quieter times, bloke who looks much more attuned to messing around with motherboards will muck in to make you a sandwich. Again, all the usual facs for web, e-mail, etc. Quarter- and half-hr rates, dozen PCs, colour scanning, printing and all that jazz. E-mail: queries@web13.co.uk. The breakfast sc(ram)bled egg and mushroom baguette is recommended. Mon-Fri 9am-8pm, Sat 9am-6pm, Sun 11am-5pm.

230
C3
✓ ✓ **BLUE:** 221 1222. Cambridge St. Upstairs in the Traverse Theatre building. The café-bar associated with The Atrium (34/BEST RESTAUS), so the food's pretty good and you can graze and snack till 12midnight (same menu all day) in the place to be seen. (77/BEST BISTROS)

231
D3
✓ **FAVORIT:** 220 6880. 20 Teviot Pl and 30 Leven St (221 1800). New, happening café/restau – salads, pasta, wraps, Ben and Jerry's from dawn till almost dawn. More to come. **7 days, 8am-3am.** (203/BEST TEAROOMS)   MED

232
C3
✓ **THE WITCHERY:** 225 5613. Castlehill, top of Royal Mile nr the Castle. Not open v late, but does take bookings up till 11.30pm, that crucial half hr beyond 11 that allows you to eat after the movies. Special after-theatre menu from 10.30pm has 2 courses for under £10, a v good deal from one of the best restaus in town. 7 days, lunch and **LO 11.30pm.** (70/BEST RESTAUS)

233
B2
✓ **PIZZA EXPRESS:** Best branch in Stockbridge 332 7229. 1 Deanhaugh St and W. End at 32 Queensferry St (225 8863). **Open till midnight** and no booking policy, so a good bet. Report 118/BEST PIZZA.

234
B3,xC4
✓ **INDIGO YARD:** 220 5603. 7 Charlotte Lane and **MONTPELLIERS:** 229 3115. 159 Bruntsfield Pl. **Late supper menu till 1am** in fashionable, throbbing and related bistro bars (with similar clientele). Seductive menu, but loud. Report: 84/BEST BISTROS.

235
D2
GIULIANO'S: 556 6590. 18 Union Pl, Leith walk opp Playhouse. Buzzing Italian tratt day and night. **Handily open till 1am.** Report 117/ITALIAN. ·

236
D3
NICOLSON'S: 557 4567. 6a Nicolson St, upstairs opp Festival Theatre. Convenient and v Edin kind of bistro till **11pm (12midnight Fri/Sat).** Diverse menu; late-night people. (91/BEST BISTROS)

237
D2
BLUE MOON CAFÉ: 556 2788. 36 Broughton St. Gay café-bar in the quarter. Burgers to bagels. Go on, they won't bite you (or maybe they will). **LO 11.30pm (12.30am Fri-Sat).** (221/CAFÉS)

238
D3
GORDON'S TRATTORIA: 225 7992. 231 High St. Although some late-night visitors mistake this for a kebab house, it's v definitely Italian. Pasta 'n' pizza until tomorrow. **Sun-Thu 12noon-12midnight, Fri-Sat 12noon-3am.**   INX

239
D3
BAR ROMA: 226 2977. 39a Queensferry St, nr W End of Princes St. Buzzing day and night. An Edin institution but with recent revamp. Better than your av pasta, smarter than your av wine list. **12noon-12midnight Sun-Thu; 12.45am Fri-Sat.**   INX

240
A4
PEPE'S TAVERNA: 337 9774. 96 Dalry Rd. Finally, here's one to remember; good and friendly and **open till 2.30am** (though Cl Tue). (116/ITALIAN RESTAUS)

GOOD PLACES FOR SUNDAY BREAKFAST

241
D3
✓ **CAFÉ FLORENTIN:** St Giles St, off Royal Mile opp Cathedral. The first to open for a civilized start (or finish). The authentically French coffee shop with croissants/pain au chocolat and the best whirly pastries in town. May be too early to eat cake. **From 7am.** (206/BEST TEAROOMS)

242
C3
✓ **WHERE TO?:** 229 6886. 103 Highriggs where Laurieston Pl becomes Tollcross. Excl all-round caff with outdoorsy slant, Internet access (727/INTERNET CAFÉS) and good grub. Healthy b/fasts incl Swiss muesli, porridge, kedgeree, bagels, squeezed juice and coffee. Newspapers as well as cyberstuff. **From 7.30am.**

243
D3
FAVORIT: 220 6880. 20 Teviot Pl. The hip all-rounder. **Open 7 days from 8am.** Report: 203/BEST TEAROOMS and 231/LATE-NIGHT RESTAUS.

244
D3
NEGOCIANTS: 45-47 Lothian St. Nr univ. Gr all-round pub (322/THESE ARE HIP), open v late and v early on Sun for breakfast. **From 9am (brunch till 6pm).** May be tables o/side.

245 **MANGO AND STONE:** 229 2987. 165a Bruntsfield Pl. **Open at 9am** for the
xC4   healthiest start on this page – the Detox, the pure orange juice – whatever.
Good juice, good coffee. Report: 201/COFFEE SHOPS

246 **KAFFE POLITIK:** 446 9873. 146-148 Marchmont Rd. Quite possibly the best
xD4   scrambled eggs with emmental and chives on toast in town. And good coffee
in serenely cerebral surroundings. **From 10am.** (207/BEST TEAROOMS)

247 **CITY CAFE:** Blair St. It's been here so long, it's easy to take for granted … but
D3   for that 'BIG' breakfast (carnivore or veggie), few places in the city beat the
content or American diner atmos. **From 11am**.

248 **SMOKE STACK:** 556 6032. 53-55 Broughton St. Proper brunch in bar-strewn
D2   Broughton St (*see below*) – Arbroath smokies, Eggs Florentine or Benedict, all-
out brekkers, vegn or carnivore style in burgundy and blue diner. **12noon-
4pm.** (188/BURGERS)

249 **THE BROUGHTON ST BREAKFAST:** Meanwhile, elsewhere in Edin's hippest
D2, D1   st, the upsurge of café-bar culture offers many good bets for brekkers. From
the top down: **THE CATWALK** opens at **10am** for both veggies and carnivores, while **BAROQUE** kicks in from **12.30pm** with similar nosh (slightly
more exp). Round the corner in Broughton St Lane, **THE OUTHOUSE** opens at
12.30pm and serves a more elaborate brunch menu through to 4pm (see
THESE ARE HIP for details). For a pubbier experience, try the **BARONY** further
down the st (261/GR EDIN PUBS). Cheap, cheerful, papers to peruse. **LOST SOCK
DINER** is at the bottom and round the corner. Neighbourhood caff **from
10am** (they also do laundry – see 224/CAFÉS).

THE BEST TAKEAWAY PLACES

250 ✓ **ROWLAND'S:** 225 3711. 42 Howe St. Still the Top-notch New Town take-
C2   away with creative hot dishes that change daily. Despite the t/away
explosion, still leaves the others standing for real food. Interesting sandwich
rolls, excellent cheeses, bread, cakes and other carefully selected fare. Also
does o/side catering (mmm … those Thai prawns) and you can phone your
order. Mon-Fri 8am-5pm. Cl Sat-Sun.

251 ✓ **G&T (GLASS & THOMPSON):** 557 0909. 2 Dundas St. Deli and coffee
C2   shop on main st in New Town, but also takeaway sandwiches/rolls in infinite formats using their drool-making selection of quality ingredients (breads,
cheeses, salamis, etc.). Take away to office, grds or dinner party. Excellent sit-in
area and small terr for whiling away Edin days. Mon-Fri 8.30am-6.30pm, Sat
8.30am-5.30pm, Sun 11am-4.30pm. (213/BEST TEAROOMS)

252 **THE GLOBE:** 558 3837. 42 Broughton St. A bright spot on the corner in the
D2   middle of Edin's coolest st; this place is one of the reasons why. Open all day
till 3/4pm for sandwiches/rolls and toasted focaccia. Big window for people
watching. Branches at 23 Henderson Row and Castle St. Cl Sun.

253 **FOOD PLANTATION:** High St. Friendly takeaway with homemade feel (all the
D2   baking is fresh and they make the best muffins in town). Sandwiches to go
and to order, wraps, crêpes and interesting soups. Odd spot, but definitely
worth the detour into the tourist strip. Cl Sun.

254 **MANGO AND STONE:** 229 2987. 165a Bruntsfield Pl. Mentioned elsewhere
xC4   and report 201/COFFEE SHOPS, but takeaway food (or juice) that is good for
you. Open early and late.

255 **THE DELTA:** 346 8973. 27 Roseburn Terr. Seriously good Indian t/away in the
xA3   west of the city. Good fish and vegn choice. Huge selection, so t/away the
menu. Some delivery. 7 days, 5pm-11pm.

256 **EASTERN SPICES:** 558 3609. 2 Canonmills Br, by the clock. On the grapevine,
C1   this place is better than most – phone in your order or turn up and wait. Also
home delivery. Full Indian menu from pakora to pasanda and vegn meals for
one – if you're down at the end of lonely st.

257 **HENDERSONS:** 556 7737. Canonmills opp the Clock. T/away and bakery
C1   branch of venerable vegn restau (140/VEGAN RESTAUS). Excl wholemeal meals
and s/wiches. Salads, puds etc. Tables to eat. Other t/away selection in main
shop above restau at 94 Hanover St. Bakery, lunch with 5pm. Cl Sun.

SOME GREAT 'EDINBURGH' PUBS (THOSE PUBS YOU WON'T FIND ANYWHERE ELSE)

258
xE1
✓ ✓ **PORT O' LEITH:** 58 Constitution St. You could walk into this bar once every 5 yrs and be hard pushed to see any changes. Occasionally wild, always interesting; a gr leveller and no place for snobs. The distilled spirit of auld Leith untouched by the new Leith around it. Good soundtrack both verbal and musical. Mary Moriarty is queen of all she surveys. Till 12.45am.

259
D2
✓ **CAFÉ ROYAL:** Behind Burger King at the E end of Princes St, one of Edin's longest celebrated pubs. Unrelated to the London version, though there is a similar Victorian/Baroque elegance. Through the partition is the Oyster Bar (133/SEAFOOD RESTAUS). Central counter and often standing rm only. If you're going out on the tiles, the tiles here are a good place to start. New management, may smarten it up. Mon-Wed 11am-11pm, Thu to 12midnight, Fri-Sat to 1am, Sun 12.30pm-11pm.

260
C4
✓ **BENNET'S:** Leven St, by King's Theatre. Just stand at the back and watch light stream through the stained glass on a sunny day. Same era as Café Royal and similar ambience, mirrors and tiles. Decent food at lunch (296/PUB FOOD). Till 11.30pm Mon-Wed, 12.30am Thu-Sat, 11pm Sun.

261
D2
BARONY BAR: 81 Broughton St. Real-ale venue with a young profile and occasional live music; also some Belgian and wheat beers. Newspapers on hand to browse over a Sun afternoon breakfast or a (big) lunchtime pie. Till 12midnight Mon-Thu, 12.30am Fri-Sat, 11pm Sun.

262
D2
THE BASEMENT: 109 Broughton St. Much-imitated, still crucial, this is a chunky, happening sort of, er, basement where you can have Mex-style food during the day served by laaarvely staff in Hawaiian shirts. At night, the punters are well up for it – late, loud and lively. Till 1am daily.

263
xE4
SHEEP'S HEID: 656 6952. The Causeway, Duddingston Village. Not central, but a pleasant and dramatic drive away behind Arthur's Seat in the Queen's Park. Old coaching inn with good crack, some locals, patio grd and decent grub (294/PUB FOOD). Food till 9pm, pub 11pm (12midnight Fri-Sat).

264
C2
KAY'S BAR: 39 Jamaica St. The New Town – incl Jamaica St – sometimes gives the impression that it's populated by people who were around in the late 18th century. It's an Edinburgh thing (mainly male). And they care for their beer (285/REAL-ALE PUBS). Until 11.45pm (11pm Sun).

265
B3
MATHER'S: 1 Queensferry St. Edin's W End has a complement of 'smart' bars that cater for people with tight haircuts and powerbooks. The alternative is here – a stand-up space for old-fashioned pubbery, slack coiffure and idle talk (276/'UNSPOILT' PUBS). Till 12midnight Mon-Thu, 1am Fri-Sat, 11pm Sun.

266
E1
ROBBIE'S: Leith Walk, on corner with Iona St. Some bars on Leith Walk are downright scary – but not this one. Tolerant, good range of beer, TV will have the football on often as not. Wild mix of Trainspotters, locals and the odd dodgy character or 3, even a stray social worker (HQ is nearby). Oddly clean after early '99 refurb (274/'UNSPOILT' PUBS). Till 12midnight Mon-Sat, 11pm Sun.

267
D3
CITY CAFÉ: 220 0127. 19 Blair St. Seems ancient, but 11 yrs on, the retro Americana chic has aged gracefully. Pool tables, all-day food, decent coffee. A hip Edin bar that has stood the test of time. Music downstairs later courtesy of guest DJs (247/SUNDAY BREAKFAST). 11am-1am daily.

268
D3
CAFÉ AQUARIUS: 557 6337. 10 Drummond St. Token hip bar in this section for this edition. Swirly lilac pop-tart deco from the makers of Bar Sirius in Leith (323/THESE ARE HIP). Gr soundtrack (guest DJs Fri-Sun evenings), effort goes into the food, eager staff. We are the children of … . 11am-1am daily.

269
D3
THREE SISTERS: Cowgate. Of the many booming bars in the Cowgate, we may as well select this one, the latest superbar at the time of going to press and already 'Edinburgh's busiest bar'. Nothing v special but good conversion of old warehouse and better than your av super bar (3 to choose from). Also has rms. 7 days, 11am-1am.

THE BEST OLD 'UNSPOILT' PUBS

Of course it's not necessarily the case that when a pub's done up, it's spoiled, or that all old pubs are worth preserving, but some have resisted change and that's part of their appeal. Money and effort are often spent to 'oldify' bars and contrive an atmos. The following places don't have to try.

270
xA4
✓ **THE DIGGERS:** 1 Angle Park Terr. (Officially the Athletic Arms.) Jambo pub *par excellence*, stowed with the Tynecastle faithful before and after games. Still keeps a gr pint of McEwan's 80/-, allegedly the best in Edin. The food is basic pies and stovies. Till 12midnight Mon-Sat, 6pm Sun.

271
xA3
✓ **ROSEBURN BAR:** 1 Roseburn Terr, on main Glas rd out W from Haymarket and one of the nearest pubs to Murrayfield Stadium. Wood and grandeur and red leather, bonny wee snug, fine pint of McEwan's and wall-to-wall rugby of course. Heaving before internationals. Till 11pm Sun-Wed, 12midnight Thu-Sat.

272
C1
✓ **CLARK'S:** 142 Dundas St. A couple of snug snugs, red leather, brewery mirrors and decidedly no frills. Good McEwan's – just the place to pop in if you're tooling downhill from town to Canonmills. A local you would learn to love. Till 11pm (11.30pm Thu-Sat).

273
C3
BLUE BLAZER: 2 Spittal St. No frills, no pretensions, just wooden fixtures and fittings, pies and toasties in this fine S&N-owned howf that usually carries half a dozen real ales. More soul than any of its competitors nearby. Mon-Thu 11am-12midnight, Fri-Sat 11am-12.30am, Sun 12.30pm-11pm.

274
xE1
ROBBIE'S: Leith Walk, on corner with Iona St. Real ales a-go-go in a smoky old neighbourhood howf that tolerates everyone from the wifie in her raincoat to multi-pierced yoof of indeterminate gender. More rough than smooth of course, but with the footy on the box, pint of Bass, packet of Hula Hoops – this bar can save your life (and it's cleaner than it used to be). Till 12midnight Mon-Sat, 11pm Sun. (266/GR EDIN PUBS)

275
C2
OXFORD BAR: 8 Young St, one of the lanes behind W end of George St. No time machine needed – just step in the door to see an Edin that hasn't changed since yon times. Careful what you say; this is an off-duty cop shop. Some real ales but they're beside the point. Till 1am (12midnight Sun).

276
B3, D2
MATHER'S: 1 Queensferry St. Not only a reasonable real-ale pub but almost worth visiting just to look at the ornate fixtures and fittings – frieze and bar esp. The latter looks as if it was carefully hewn from a single lump of wood by a Stakhanovite Victorian – they don't make 'em like that these days. Unreconstructed in every sense. Till 12midnight Mon-Thu, 1am Fri-Sat, 11pm Sun. (265GR EDIN PUBS) There's another, unrelated, MATHER'S in Broughton St which is managing to keep its head above water in the city's grooviest thoroughfare by remaining pub-like and unpretentious.

277
D3
STEWART'S: 14 Drummond St on the S Side and just off S Br. Lino, beer, pensioners and folk who sing when in their cups. Few concessions to anything that has happened to the licensed trade since the 1960s. Till 12midnight Mon-Sat, 11pm Sun.

278
D3
THE ROYAL OAK: Infirmary St. Tiny upstairs and not much bigger down. During the day, pensioners sip their pints (couple of real ales) while the cellar opens till 2am.

279
C1 ✓ **THE CUMBERLAND BAR:** Cumberland St, corner of Dundonald St. After work this New Town bar attracts its share of suits, but later the locals reclaim it and Camra (Campaign for Real Ale) supporters seek it out too. Av of 12 real ales on tap. Nicely appointed, decent pub lunches, unexpected beer grd. Mon-Wed till 11.30pm, Thu-Sat to 12midnight. Sun 12.30-10pm.

280
xC1 ✓ **STARBANK INN:** 64 Laverockbank Rd, Newhaven. On the seafront rd W of Newhaven harbour. Usually 9 different ales on offer. Gr place to sit with pint in hand and watch the sun sink over the Forth. The food is good (299/PUB FOOD). Bar till 11pm Sun-Wed, 12midnight Thu-Sat.

281
D3 ✓ **THE BOW BAR:** 80 W Bow, halfway down Victoria St. They know how to treat drink in this excellent wee bar. Ask for a whisky – a fair few available – and there's no insane rigmarole about ice in the glass. Laphraoig, for example, comes straight as nature intended. Bliss. Till 11.30pm Mon-Sat, 11pm Sun.

282
D2 ✓ **THE GUILDFORD ARMS:** 1 W Register St. Behind Burger King at E end of Princes St (opp Balmoral Hotel) on same block as the Café Royal (259/GR EDIN PUBS). Lofty, ornate Victorian hostelry with loadsa good ales. There are real ales you won't find anywhere else in the city. Pub grub available on 'gallery' floor as well as bar. Sun-Wed till 11pm, Thu-Sat till 12midnight.

283
B3, B1 **BERT'S:** 29 William St. Rare ales, a suit and twinset crowd after work but a fair mix at other times in this *faux* Edwardian bar. Decent pies for carnivores or veggies alike and a good place to escape from uptown neurosis. Till 11pm Sun-Thu, 12midnight Fri-Sat. More local **BERT'S** at 2 Raeburn Pl, Stockbridge.

284
xC4 **THE CANNY MAN:** 237 Morningside Rd. Officially known as the Volunteer Arms, but everybody calls it the Canny Man. Good smorrebrod at lunch time (293/PUB FOOD), and wide range of real ales. Casual visitors may feel that management have an attitude (problem).

285
C2 **KAY'S BAR:** 39 Jamaica St, off India St in the New Town. Go on an afternoon when gentlemen of a certain age talk politics, history and football over pints of real ale. The bow-tied barman patiently serves. All red and black and vaguely distinguished with a tiny snug – The Library. Till 11.45pm (11pm Sun). (264/GR EDIN PUBS)

286
D2 **CASK & BARREL:** 115 Broughton St. Wall-to-wall distressed wood, gr selection of real ales and the only bar in Edin where they've realized that samosas make ideal snacks. Also does pub grub, sometimes Thai-flavoured. Till 12.30am Sun-Wed, 1am Thu-Sat.

287
C4 **CLOISTERS:** 26 Brougham St, Tollcross. Nine real ales on tap in this simple and unfussy bar with its wooden panelling and laid-back app. Same owners as Bow Bar (*see above*). Basic pub grub at lunchtimes, bar closes 12midnight (12.30am Fri-Sat).

288
A4 **CALEY SAMPLE ROOM:** 5-8 Angle Park Terr. Half-owned by the nearby (independent) Caledonian Brewery, the CSR sells all the expected Caledonian real ales and a couple of guests besides. A neighbourhood bar most of the time, a haven for home and away fans before and after games at Tynecastle. Basic pub lunches Mon-Fri, drink served till 12midnight Sun-Thu, 1am Fri-Sat.

289
E4, **FIRKINS:** Physician & Firkin, 58 Dalkeith Rd; Footlights & Firkin, 7 Spittal St;
C3 Fling & Firkin, 49 Rose St, etc. Coming to us courtesy of Alloa – they brew their
C2 own at Dalkeith Rd and supply all the local Firkins. Formula pubs – wood, food and real ales from light Summer Swallow to mental Dogbolter. F*rk*n jokes wearing thin. Generally till 1am daily.

290
A4 **CALEDONIAN BEER FESTIVAL:** An annual event held around the first w/end in June at Edin's own – and independent – Caledonian Brewery, a red-brick Victorian pile at 42 Slateford Rd (on rt-hand side going out of town). It's a gr site, 50 real ales from Adnams to Whitbread on tap, food and music (esp jazz) on Thu-Sat evenings and Sun afternoon in the brewery's own 'Festival Hall', a refurbed bottling plant. See local press for details or call 337 1286. The 'Festival Hall' also hosts ceilidhs every Sat. (438/CEILIDHS)

PUBS WITH GOOD FOOD

291
xE1
✓ **THE SHORE:** 553 5080. 3 The Shore. A bistro/restau but the same (black-board) menu faster and friendlier in the bar (where you can smoke). Light meat dishes, lots of fish and always something vegn. Lunch and LO 10pm. (88/BEST BISTROS)

292
xE1
✓ **KING'S WARK:** 554 9260. 36 The Shore, on the corner of Bernard St. Woody, candlelit, absolutely fine. A business haunt at lunchtimes and a good informal restau-cum-bar in the evenings. Scottish slant on the menu, incl excellent fish in beer batter and chips; also food at the bar and real ales. Lunch and LO10pm. Bar open to 11pm, 12midnight Fri-Sat.

293
xC4
✓ **THE CANNY MAN:** 447 1484. 237 Morningside Rd (aka The Volunteer Arms) on the A702 via Tollcross, 7km from centre. Idiosyncratic renowned eaterie with a certain hauteur. Carries a complement of malts as long as your arm, serious wine list and excellent smorrebrod lunches (12noon-3pm daily). B-listed building with monkey-jacketed bar staff, cigars for sale – a shrine to the good life. No loonies or undesirables are welcome (you may be tested). Till 12midnight Mon-Sat, 11pm Sun. (284/REAL-ALE PUBS)

294
xE4
SHEEP'S HEID: 656 6952. Causeway, Duddingston Village. An 18th-century coaching inn 10km from centre behind Arthur's Seat and reached most easi-ly through the Queen's Park. Restau upstairs (not summer) and decent pub food down, incl alfresco dining when poss. The village and the nearby wild-fowl loch should be strolled around if you have time. Food till 9pm, incl Sun.

295
C4
THE GOLF TAVERN: 229 3235. 31 Wright's Houses. Off Bruntsfield Pl facing onto the links. V English country pub style with hearty food (beef 'n' ale pie, sausage and mash), couple of Chesterfields for slumping purposes; clientele can be v MOR. LO food 7.30pm. Bar closes 12midnight daily.

296
C4
BENNET'S: 229 5143. 8 Leven St, next to the King's Theatre. An Edin standby, listed for several reasons (260/GR EDIN PUBS), not least for its honest-to-good-ness (and cheap) pub lunch. À la carte (sausage, fish, steak pie, etc.) and daily specials under the enormous mirrors. Lunch only, 12noon-2pm.

297
D2
THE ABBOTSFORD: 225 5276. 3 Rose St. A doughty remnant of Rose St drink-ing days of yore, and still the best pub lunch nr Princes St. Nothing fancy in the à la carte of grills and mainly meaty entrées. Huge portions. LO in bar 3pm. Restau upstairs serves food in evening too – LO 9.45pm. Bar till 11pm. Cl Sun.

298
C2
THE DOME: 624 8624. 14 George St. Edin's first megabar and not a chain. Former bank and grandiose in the way that only a converted temple to Mammon could be. Main part sits 15m under elegant domed roof with island bar and raised platform at back for determined diners. Staff almost impecca-ble, pricey menu; you come for the surroundings more than the victuals (MED). Lunch 12noon-6pm, LO dinner 10pm daily. Also snack menu for casual diners away from roped-off posh nosh area. Adj real-ale Art Deco bar Frazers is sep-arate, more intimate, better for a blether. Final bit, downstairs: Why Not?, a nightclub for over-25s still lookin' for lurvv. Main bar Sun-Thu till 11.30pm, Fri-Sat till 1am.

299
xC1
STARBANK INN: 552 4141. 64 Laverockbank Rd, the seafront rd in New Haven. Long - est family pub with real ales (280/ALES) and excl value food, with big help-ings. Gr seafood platter. 7 days lunch and dinner LO 9pm (Sun all day menu).

300
xD1
OLD CHAIN PIER: 552 1233. 1 Trinity Cres, on the Forth just W of Newhaven Harbour. Rt on the waterfront, off the beaten track. V approachable with friendly staff. Well-kept real ale, gr bar snacks (stilton with oatcakes, interest-ing toasties) and excellent-value bar meals. LO food 8pm (but ask nicely after 8 and you never know). Bar 12noon-11pm Sun-Wed, till 12midnight Thu-Sat.

OUTSIDE TOWN

Refer to Lothians map on pages 340–341.

301
xE4
THE SUN INN, LOTHIANBURN: 663 2456. On a bend of the A7 nr t/off for Newtongrange, under mega viaduct, 18km S of city centre. Happy, homely

pub in the unfashionable netherlands of Midlothian. Bistro-style food, lunch and LO 9.30pm. Always a couple of real ales – one from the Broughton Brewery.

302 **THE BRIDGE INN/THE POP INN, RATHO, W LOTHIAN:** 333 1320. 16km W of
MAP 7 centre via A71, turning rt opp Dalmahoy Golf Club. Large choice of comfort-
B1 ing food in canalside setting. Has won various awards, incl accolades for its kids' menu. Restau, bar food and canal cruises with nosh. Pop Inn 12noon-9pm daily. Restau lunch daily and LO 9pm Mon-Sat. Bar till 11pm, 12midnight Fri-Sat. (195/KID-FRIENDLY)

303 **DROVER'S INN, EAST LINTON:** 01620 860298. 5 Bridge St. Off the A1, 35km S
MAP 7 of city. Fair way to go for eats, but don't think about the A1, think about this
B1 welcoming pub with notable food. A classic village pub with warmth and deli-cious meals in bistro beside bar or restau up top. Beer grd out back is o/looked and trains whoosh by, but on a sunny day, partake their excellent lunch here. Lunch and dinner (6-9.30pm) daily.

304 **GOBLIN HA', GIFFORD:** 01620 810244. 35kms town in neat E Lothian vill.
MAP 7 Report 304/PUB FOOD
B1

305 **THE WATERSIDE, HADDINGTON:** 01620 825674. 28kms town off A1. Long-
MAP 7 est, landmark pub food watering hole. Report 865/LOTHIANS.
B1

THE BEST PLACES TO DRINK OUTDOORS

306 **THE HUB:** 473 2067. Castlehill. The café-bar of the International Festival
C3 Centre run by Andrew Radford of the Atrium. Enclosed terrace, big brollies, people-watching and gr food. Report: 83/BISTROS.

307 **THE SHORE:** 553 5080. 3 The Shore, Leith. Excellent place to eat (78/BEST
xE1 BISTROS), some tables just o/side the door, but it's fine to wander over to the dock on the other side of the st and sit with your legs over the edge. Do try not to fall in. From 11am daily.

308 **THE WATERFRONT:** 554 7427. 1c Dock Pl. Another v good Leith eaterie
xE1 (87/BEST BISTROS) but with waterside tables and adj barge for those who fancy a float. Gr wine list. From 12noon Mon-Sat, 12.30pm Sun.

309 **PEAR TREE:** 667 7533. 38 W Nicholson St. Adj to parts of Edin Univ so real stu-
D4 dent style with biggest beer grd in the capital and refectory-style food. From 11am Mon-Sat, 12.30pm Sun. Round the corner on the main drag, **BAR CE LONA** spills out onto the wide pavement. (317/THESE ARE HIP).

310 **THE OUTHOUSE:** 557 6668. 12a Broughton St Lane. Large patio out back,
D2 home to summer Sun afternoon barbecues. (Not a gr view unfortunately.) (315/THESE ARE HIP)

311 **THE PLEASANCE:** In The Pleasance. Open during the Festival only, this is one
E3 of the major Fringe venues, and has a large open courtyard. If you're here, you're certainly plugged into the centre of things.

312 **THE CATWALK CAFÉ:** 478 7770. 2 Picardy Pl. Catwalk café becomes sidewalk
D2 café in warm weather. Busy corner on major r/bout, but also the apex of the pink triangle and a traffic light system where traffic stops so maximum peo-ple-watching potential. (326/THESE ARE HIP)

General locations: try **GREENSIDE PL** (THEATRE ROYAL), bars in **THE GRASS-MARKET**, and **IGUANA** and **NEGOCIANTS** (321/322/THESE ARE HIP) on **LOTH-IAN ST**. All make a stab at pavement café culture when the sun's out.

THESE ARE HIP

313 **THE POND:** Corner of Bath Rd and Salamander St, Leith. Turn rt at the foot of
xE1 Constitution St past the warehouses. This bar is so cool it's on the edge of nowhere. Run by the people who had Edinburgh's most groovy club, Going Places, the Edinburgh Beige Cricket Team and the fanzine, *Shavers Weekly*. This bar is where you'll find the people who know how this town ticks. It's a find and I hope to hell you do – I have a certain interest. Open when you are.

314 **PO-NA-NA:** 226 2224. 43b Frederick St. A case of souk it and see in this popu-
C2 lar N African theme bar – part of a chain but not obtrusively. Functions as a bar till 11pm, then it's more of a club with entry charge and DJs, and maybe a queue to get in. 7 days till 3am. The fag machine is covered in zebra skin. Fun, so crowded.

315 **THE OUTHOUSE:** 557 6668. 12a Broughton St Lane. Not an avowedly gay
D2 establishment, but happily mixed of an evening when there's a nice atmos in this v contemporary café-bar. Modish food available 12noon-4pm for self-conscious business diners and a regular Sun barbecue on the patio (not the greatest of views though). One of the few bars in the UK doing the absinthe thing – drink more than 2 at your peril. Till 1am.

316 **INDIGO YARD:** 220 5603. 7 Charlotte Lane, off Queensferry St. Tucked away in
B3 the WEnd, this spacious designer café-bar offers exposed brickwork, balcony tables, booths and babes in blue of both genders serving good food and drink. More MED than Mex cuisine with flexible menu, but poss too loud later on for serious dining (84/BEST BISTROS). Till 1am daily. Same people have **IGUANA** (*see below*) and **FAVORIT** (203/BEST TEAROOMS).

317 **BAR CE LONA:** 662 8860. 2 W Cross causeway. Big plate glass frontage makes
D3 fashion statement in student-land. On busy rd for traffic, but often tables o/side. Menu does make serious attempt at Mediterranea, but mainly a cooler hang out than most on this corner of the University. 7 days, all day till 1am.

318 **BARACOA:** 225 5846. 7 Victoria St. Cuban-style, Cuba Norte (160/RESTAU) may
D3 be preferable and more laid back, but 90s UK-Style this Cuban café-bar prob sets the pace. There is a proper menu till 9pm and wrap snacks after, but it's for the Havana Club and rhythm, this younger crowd come. Ché would think this was only about money – and he'd be right! 7 days all day till 3am.

319 **CAFÉ AQUARIUS:** 557 6337. 10 Drummond St. Pre-club bar spitting distance
D3 from Cowgate venues if you know how to dodge down a close. Guest DJs from Tribal Funktion, Manga, and elsewhere spin tunes. Good chips as well. 11am-11pm daily.

320 **TRAVERSE THEATRE BAR:** Downstairs at the Traverse Theatre, Cambridge St
C3 (421/NIGHTLIFE). One of the first Edin bars to go in for designer furniture, rolling art exhibs and all that jazz. Still trendy if a bit arch. Food 10am-8pm if no show, till 10pm when there's something on. Gr buzz pre- and post-performance. Bar till 12midnight Sun, Tue, Wed; 11pm Mon; 1am Fri-Sat. Much later during Festival when it's one of the nerve centres and around Hogmanay. Good place to meet nice people.

321 **IGUANA:** 220 4288. 41 Lothian St. From the makers of Indigo Yard (*see above*)
D3 comes this self-consciously clubby café-bar over the road from Edin Univ's Bristo Sq buildings – so v studeny in term time. DJs (Thu-Sat) play ambi-ent/dub/dance later on. During the day people eat, drink or sip coffee in calm, cool surroundings (by Glasgow's Graven Images). LO food 8.30pm. 9am-1am daily. (332/LIVE MUSIC)

322 **NEGOCIANTS:** 225 6313. 45-47 Lothian St. (Pron 'Nigoshunts' by locals.)
D3 Mirrors, food, space and shooters (non-lethal variety) upstairs; dancefloor, DJs (every night), drink and more drink down. Range of clients from civilized bagel-nibblers mid-morning to Chimayed-out dance fiends in the wee small hrs. Zanier and less pretentious than Iguana next door,– but just as studeny. Table service lacks pace – but hey! LO food 2.30am. Open 9am-3am daily.

323 **SIRIUS:** 555 3344. 7-10 Dock Pl, Leith. 'Designed' without being dreadful –
xE1 quite harmonious really and almost democratic in the clientele mix it attracts. Gr energy about the place on the night-out nights, cocktail pitchers abound

– wet Wed afternoon muzak would be Massive Attack. Does coffee and food in that eclectic, flexible style (i.e. Med-Mex). Till 12midnight Sun-Wed, 1am Thu-Sat.

324 **THE WATER SHED:** 220 3774. 44 St Stephen St. Neighbourhood café-bar with
C1 *de rigueur* light wood, blue and orange décor. Coffee/food served 10am-7pm (yes, Med-Mex inevitably), really kicks in as a bar later on – open till 1am daily. Share a cocktail or some cheap Chardonnay with Stockbridge's shiny happy people.

325 **CITY CAFÉ:** 220 0127. 19 Blair St. A true original that went from *the* hippest, to
D3 nowhere, and now back again with the cool night people. Buzzing at the w/end, downstairs the DJs play all kinds depending on the night. Watch the flyers. 11am-11pm daily.

326 **THE CATWALK CAFÉ:** 478 7770. 2 Picardy Pl. Opened as the bright new thing
D2 (concrete grey) in autumn '97 then seemed to go through an identity crisis in '98. Still a cool space for the be-seen crowd though, with DJs in the basement open decks etc. And food. Till 1am daily. Tables o/side on a corner of the pink triangle. (312/DRINK OUTDOORS)

GOOD LIVE MUSIC

327 **THE VENUE:** 557 3073. Calton Rd, behind Waverley Stn. Edin's major live
D2 venue at club level with well-established dance clubs at w/ends like Pure and Tribal Funktion. For live music, it's on the UK club circuit, so often notable bands and the best of the Scottish wannabes. Watch for posters and flyers. (434/ROCK AND POP)

328 **LA BELLE ANGELE:** 225 2774. 11 Hasties Close. Combines its role as a DJ club
D3 and live music venue well. Rm has attitude and atmos. (434/ROCK AND POP) Some showcases, parties and special nights.

329 **THE CAS ROCK:** 229 4341. 104 W Port. Nr art college. Musical oasis in Edin's
C3 pubic triangle, the area full of bars with 'dancers'. No-nonsense, Indie/alternative thrashing in small space. Hot, sweaty, beery rock 'n' roll. Till 1am daily.

330 **THE LIQUID ROOM:** 225 2564. At the top of Victoria St. Probably the city's
D3 best turned-out venue for live music. Enter at st level and descend to watch bands before they go on to greater things (or not). For details consult *The List*. Times vary. Also a major club venue.

331 **SUBWAY:** 225 6766. Cowgate, under George IV Br. Cavernous grungey rock 'n'
D3, C3 roll. Fairly studenty, live music some nights, DJs on others playing 1960s to cheesy dance. 5pm-3am daily. Also **SUBWAY WEST END**, 23 Lothian Rd. Glitzier than its Cowgate cousin. Nothing live; DJs playing Indie, 1970s, 1980s.

332 **NEGOCIANTS:** 225 6313. 45 Lothian St. Basement DJs in bar for young dudes.
D3 Upstairs café-bar serving interesting food; bustling with studentish crowd, LO food 2.30am. 9am-3am daily. **IGUANA** next door also does cool tunes. Reports: 322/321/THESE ARE HIP.

333 **HENRY'S CELLAR BAR:** 538 7385. Morrison St. Has established itself as an
B3 alternative jazz venue over the last couple of years with sounds of every stripe taking the tiny floor of this crowded basement. Everything from drum 'n' bass experiments to Latin, nightly. Older, mellow crowd. Till 3am.

334 **NEGOCIANTS:** 45 Lothian St, by Univ Union buildings. Civilized
D3 café/restau/bar upstairs and basement with DJs. Open till 3am every night.
Full reports: 322/THESE ARE HIP, 332/LIVE MUSIC.

335 **PO-NA-NA:** 43b Frederick St. More of a club than a bar later on perhaps but
C2 open to 3am daily. Think Morocco. Young crowd; queue at w/ends. (314/THESE
ARE HIP)

336 **THE THREE SISTERS:** Cowgate. 3 themed bars, o/side courtyard and a 'hotel'
D3 ensure that this converted warehouse complex goes like a fair – full 3am, 7
nights.

337 **BARACOA:** 7 Victoria St. Cuban nitespot, some food, some salsa. Mainly rum-
D3 fuelled furore and jamming till 3am, 7 nights.

338 **THE ROYAL OAK:** Infirmary St, nr the top and S Br. Run by ex-White Heather
D3 Club dancer Sandra Adams, this place is a folk institution. Locals drink in the
tiny bar upstairs during the day, live sessions kick-off downstairs every night
around 10pm with well-kent faces dropping in occasionally for the tunes and
the singaround. Till 2am daily. (278/'UNSPOILT' PUBS)

339 **FAVORIT:** 19 Teviot Pl, nr Univ. Not so much a bar, but a café/restau (203/BEST
D3 TEAROOMS), but has intentional informal bar atmos, so more 'civilized' than
those above if you want more than a pint or a pull. 7 days till 3am.

340 **CC BLOOMS:** Greenside Pl. Late-night gay venue with bar upstairs (catch the
D2 floor show and eye contact generally) and downstairs dance floor. Till 3am.
(2052/GAY EDIN)

Not-so-very late bars (till 1am) include **IGUANA**, **INDIGO YARD**, **THE WATER-
SHED** (all THESE ARE HIP), **BAROQUE**.

General area for late-bars and ebb and flow of party and night-time animals
is **THE COWGATE – VICTORIA ST – FORREST RD** triangle. Pub hrs vary, but
many places open later than 1am.

341
C3 ✓ ✓ ✓ **EDINBURGH CASTLE:** Go to Princes St and look up. The main attraction, extremely busy AYR. Tartan tea cosies on sale in the shop rake in the bawbees. And yet. St Margaret's 12th-century chapel is simple and beautiful, the rolling history lesson that leads up to the display of Scotland's crown jewels is fascinating; the Stone of Destiny is a big deal to the Scots (though others may not see why). And, ultimately, the Scottish National War Memorial is one of the most genuinely affecting places in the country – a simple, dignified testament to shared pain and loss. Last ticket 45 min before closing. Apr-Sep 9.30am-6pm, Oct-Mar 9.30am-5pm. HS

342
E2 ✓ ✓ **HOLYROOD PALACE:** Foot of the Royal Mile. Queenie's N Brit timeshare – she's here for a wee while at end June/beginning July every yr. Large parts of the palace are dull (Duke of Hamilton's loo, Queen's wardrobes) so only a dozen or so rms are open, most dating from 17th century but a couple from the earlier 16th-century bit. Lovely cornices abound. Anomalous Stuart features, adj 12th-century abbey ruins quite interesting. Upper-class shop, so get your souvenirs here. Apr-Oct: Mon-Sat 9.30am-5.15pm (last ticket), Sun 9.30am-4.30pm (last ticket). Nov-Mar: 9.30am-3.45pm (last ticket) daily. HS

343
C3
D3 ✓ ✓ **THE ROYAL MILE:** The High St, the medieval main thoroughfare of
E3 Edin following the trail from the volcanic crag of Castle Rock and
E4 connecting the 2 landmarks above. Heaving during the Festival but if on a winter's night you chance by with a frost settling on the cobbles and there's no one around, it's magical. Always interesting with its wynds and closes (Dunbar's Close, Whitehorse Close, the secret grd opp Huntly House), but lots of tacky tartan shops too. See it on a walking tour – there are several esp at night (ghost/ghouls/witches, etc.). Some of the best actually take you under the st. Mercat Tours (661 4541) are pretty good. Also Robin's (661 0125) and Witchery (225 6745).

344
D3 ✓ ✓ **ROYAL SCOTTISH MUSEUM:** Chambers St. From the big whale skeleton to archaeological artefacts, design exhibs to stuffed elephants, it's all here. Building designed by Captain Francis Fowkes, Royal Engineers, and completed in 1888. Ab fab atrium soars way up high. Mon-Sat 10am-5pm, Sun 12noon-5pm. ADMN

345
D3 ✓ ✓ **MUSEUM OF SCOTLAND:** Chambers St. The story of Scotland from geological beginnings to Kirsty Wark's Saab Convertible, all housed in a marvellous new building by Gordon Benson and Alan Forsyth. Opened in Dec '98, it's even worth paying to get in. World-class space with resonant treasures like St Fillian's Crozier and the Monymusk Reliquary, said to contain bits of St Columba. Mon-Sat 10am-5pm, Sun 12noon-5pm. Open late on Tue and from 4.30-8pm it's free. ADMN

346
E3 ✓ ✓ **DYNAMIC EARTH, THE WILLIAM YOUNGER CENTRE:** 550 7800. Foot of Holyrood Rd. Edin's Millennium Dome, a brand new interactive museum/visitor attraction, made with Millennium money and a huge success since it opened summer '99. Salisbury Craigs rise above, the universe and everything below. Vast restau, outside an amphitheatre. 7 days 10am-6pm.

347
C3 ✓ ✓ **NATIONAL GALLERY** and **ROYAL SCOTTISH ACADEMY:** The Mound. The National is the rear of the 2 Neoclassical buildings on Princes St and houses a superb collection of Old Masters in a series of hushed salons. Many are world famous, but you don't emerge goggle-eyed as you do from the National in London – more quietly elevated (FREE). The Playfair 'temple' on Princes St itself is the RSA; changing exhibs which in early summer and midwinter show work from contemporary Scottish artists (ADMN). Both galleries Mon-Sat 10am-5pm, Sun 2-5pm. Major refurb underway 2000.

348
xA3 ✓ ✓ **EDINBURGH ZOO:** 334 9171. Corstorphine Rd. 4km W of Princes St, buses from Princes St Grds side. Whatever you think of zoos, this one is highly respected and its serious zoology is still fun for kids (organized activities in Jul/Aug). The penguins waddle out at 2pm daily and the melancholy, accusing eyes of the wolves connect with onlookers in a profoundly disconcerting manner. Open AYR. Mon-Sat 9am-6pm, Sun 9.30am-6pm. (1534/KIDS) ADMN

349 ✓ **ROYAL COMMONWEALTH POOL:** 667 7211. Dalkeith Rd. Hugely suc-
xE4 cessful pool complex which includes a 50m main pool, a gym, sauna/steam rm/suntan suites and a jungle of flumes. Goes like a fair, morning to night. Some people find the water overtreated and over noisy, but Edin has many good pools to choose from; this is the one that young folk prefer. Some lane swimming. Mon-Fri 9am-9pm, Sat-Sun 10am-4pm (7pm in summer).

350 ✓ **BRITANNIA:** Ocean Dr, Leith, in the docks, enter by Commercial St at end
xE1 of Gr Junction St. Done with ruling the waves, the royal yacht has found a permanent home as a tourist attraction (and prestigious corporate night out). Close up, the Art Deco lines are surprisingly attractive, while the interior was one of the sets for our best-ever soap opera. Daily 10am-5pm. Bookings 0131 555 5566. ADMN

351 ✓ ✓ ✓ **THE FORTH BRIDGE:** S Queensferry, 20km W of Edin via A90.
xA1 First turning for S Queensferry from dual carriageway; don't confuse with signs for road br. Or train from Waverley to Dalmeny, and walk 1km. Knocking on now and showing its age, the br was 100 in 1990. But still … Can't see too many private finance initiative wallahs rushing in to do anything of similar scope these days – who would have the vision? An international symbol of Scotland, it should be seen, but go to the N side, S Queensferry's getting v crowded – and I live there, goddamit!

THE OTHER ATTRACTIONS

352 ✓ ✓ ✓ **ROYAL BOTANIC GARDEN:** 552 7171. Inverleith Row, 3km from
C1 Princes St. Bus nos 23, 27. Enter from Inverleith Row or Arboretum Pl. 70 acres of ornamental grds, trees and walkways; a joy in every season. Tropical plant houses, the newly landscaped rock and heath grd and enough space just to wander. Chinese Grd coming on nicely, precocious squirrels everywhere. The 'Botanics' have talks, events (info 552 5339) and other impt outstanding gardens throughout Scotland. Gallery with occasional exhibs and café with outdoor terr for serene afternoon teas (214/BEST TEA-ROOMS). Total integrity and (the natural high). Open 7 days 10am-4pm (Nov-Feb), 6pm (Mar-Apr/Sep-Oct) and 8pm (May-Aug).

353 ✓ ✓ **NATIONAL PORTRAIT GALLERY:** 556 8921. 1 Queen St. Sir Robert
D2 Rowand Anderson's fabulous and custom-built neo-Gothic pile houses paintings and photos of the good, gr and merely famous. Danny McGrain hangs out next to the Queen Mum and Nasmyth's familiar pic of Burns is here. Good venue for photo exhibs, beautiful atrium with star-flecked ceiling and frieze of (mainly) men in Scottish history from a Stone-Age chiel to Carlyle. Splendid. Gr café (202/BEST TEAROOMS). Mon-Sat 10am-5pm, Sun 2-5pm.

354 ✓ **GALLERY OF MODERN ART:** 556 8921. Belford Rd. Betw Queensferry Rd
xA2 and Dean Village (nice to walk through). Best to start from Palmerston Pl and keep left or see below. Former school with permanent collection from Impressionism to Hockney and the Scottish painters alongside. An intimate space where you can fall in love (with paintings). Important temporary exhibs. The café is excellent (199/BEST TEAROOMS).

355 **THE DEAN GALLERY:** 624 6200. Belford Rd. Across the (busy) rd from GOMA.
xA2 New (1999) addition to Edin art and love life – sexy, intimate spaces, communal coffee shop, grds to wander. Superb 20th-century collection. Gr way to app both galleries is by Water of Leith Walkway (360/WALKS IN THE CITY). Same hrs as GOMA. Mon-Sat 10am-5pm, Sun 2-5pm.

356 **MUSEUM OF CHILDHOOD:** 200 2000. 42 High St. Local authority-run shrine
D3 to the dreamstuff of tender days where you'll find everything from tin soldiers to Lady Penelope on video. Full of adults saying, 'I had one of them!' Child-size mannequins in upper gallery can foment an *Avengers*-era spookiness if you're up there alone. Mon-Sat 10am-5pm. Cl Sun. (1537/KIDS)

357 **ST GILES' CATHEDRAL:** Royal Mile. Not a cathedral really, although it was
D3 once – the High Kirk of Edin, Church of Scotland central and heart of the city since the 9th century. The building is mainly medieval with Norman frag-

ments and all encased in a Georgian exterior. Lorimer's oddly ornate Thistle chapel and the 'big new organ' are impressive. Simple, austere design and bronze of John Knox set the tone historically. Holy Communion daily and other regular services. Good coffee shop in the crypt (216/BEST TEAROOMS). Summer: Mon-Fri 9am-7pm, Sat 9am-5pm, Sun 1-5pm. Winter: Mon-Sat 9am-5pm, Sun 1-5pm.

358 **THE GEORGIAN HOUSE:** 225 2160. 7 Charlotte Sq. Built in the 1790s, this *B2* town house is full of period furniture and fittings. Not many rms, but the dining-rm and kitchen are drop-dead gorgeous – you want to eat and cook there. Delightful ladies from the National Trust for Scotland answer your queries. Moderator of the General Assembly of the Church of Scotland bides up the stair. Apr-Oct 10am-5pm, Sun 2-5pm. Last admn 4.30pm. NT

359 **LAURISTON CASTLE:** 336 2060. 2 Cramond Rd S. 9km W of centre by A90, *xA1* turning rt for Cramond. Elegant architecture and gracious living from Edwardian times. A largely Jacobean tower house set in tranquil grounds o/looking the Forth. The liveability of the house and the preoccupations of the Reid family make you wish you could poke around for yourself, but there are valuable and exquisite decorative pieces and furniture and it's guided tours only. You could always continue to Cramond for the air (362/WALKS IN THE CITY). Apr-Oct 11am-5pm (cl lunch, cl Fri); Nov-Mar 2-4pm, w/ends only. ADMN

BUTTERFLY FARM, NR DALKEITH: Report: 1538/KIDS.

DEEP SEA WORLD, NORTH QUEENSFERRY: Report: 1541/KIDS.

ARTHUR'S SEAT: Report: 361/WALKS IN THE CITY.

THE PENTLANDS: Report: 364/WALKS O/SIDE THE CITY.

THE SCOTT MONUMENT/CALTON HILL: Report: 382/380/BEST VIEWS.

THE BEST WALKS IN THE CITY

See page 10 for walk codes.

360
A2
B2
B1
C1
D1

WATER OF LEITH: The indefatigable wee river that runs from the Pentlands through the city and into the docks at Leith can be walked for most of its length, though obviously not by any circular route. (A) The longest section from Balerno 12km o/side the city, through Colinton Dell to the Tickled Trout pub car park on Lanark Rd (4km from city centre). The 'Dell' itself is a popular glen walk (1-2km). All in all a superb urban walk.

START: A70 to Currie, Juniper Green, Balerno; park by High School. (B) Dean Village to Stockbridge: enter through a marked gate opp Hilton Hotel on Belford Rd (combine with a visit to the art galleries)(354/355/ATTRACTIONS). (C) Warriston, through the spooky old graveyard, to The Shore in Leith (plenty of pubs to repair to). Enter by going to the end of the cul-de-sac at Warriston Cres in Canonmills; climb up the bank and turn left. Most of the Water of Leith Walkway (A, B and C) is cinder track. 12KM (OR LESS) XCIRC BIKE BUS 43,44 1-A-1

361
xE3

ARTHUR'S SEAT: Of many walks, a good circular one taking in the wilder bits, the lochs and gr views (381/BEST VIEWS) starts from St Margaret's Loch at the far end of the park from Holyrood Palace. Leaving the car park, skirt the loch and head for the ruined chapel. Pass it on your rt and, after 250m in a dry valley, the buttress of the main summit rears above you on the rt. Keeping it to the rt, ascend over a saddle joining the main route from Dunsapie Loch which appears below on the left. Crow Hill is the other peak crowned by a triangular cairn – both can be slippery when wet. From Arthur's Seat head for and traverse the long steep incline of Salisbury Crags. Paths parallel to the edge lead back to the chapel. (Incidentally, nae mt bikes off tarmac or the polis will have words.)

START: Enter park at palace at foot of the High St and turn left on main road for 1km; the loch is on the rt.

PARK: There are car parks beside the loch and in front of the palace (paths start here too, across the rd). 5-8KM CIRC MT BIKE (RESTRICTED ACCESS) 2-B-2

362
xA1

CRAMOND: This is the charming village (not the suburb) on the Forth at the mouth of the Almond with a variety of gr walks. (A) To the rt along the 'prom'; the trad seaside stroll. (B) Across the causeway at low tide to Cramond Island (1km). Best to follow the tide out; this allows 4 hrs (tides are posted). People have been known to stay the night in summer, but this is discouraged. (C) Cross the mouth of the Almond in the tiny passenger boat which comes on demand (summer 9am-7pm, winter 10am-4pm) then follow coastal path to Dalmeny House which is open to the public in the afternoons (May-Sep, Sun-Thu); or walk all the way to S Queensferry (8km). (D) Past the boathouse and up the R Almond Heritage Trail which goes eventually to the Cramond Brig Hotel on the A90 and thence to the old airport (3-8km). Though it goes through suburbs and seems to be on the flight path of the London shuttle, the Almond is a real river with a charm and ecosystem of its own. The Cramond Bistro (312 6555) on the riverside is not a bad wee bistro and awaits your return. BYOB. Cl Mon.

START: Leave centre by Queensferry Rd (A90), then rt following signs for Cramond. Cramond Rd N leads to Cramond Glebe Rd; go to end.

PARK: Large car park off Cramond Glebe Rd to rt. Walk 100m to sea. 1/3/8KM XCIRC BIKE BUS 41 1-A-1

363
xA2

CORSTORPHINE HILL: W of centre, a knobbly hilly area of birch, beech and oak, criss-crossed by trails. A perfect place for the contemplation of life's little mysteries and mistakes. Or walking the dog. It has a radio mast, a ruined tower, a boundary with the wild plains of Africa (at the zoo) and a vast redundant nuclear shelter that nobody's supposed to know about. See how many you can spot. If it had a tearoom in an old pavilion, it would be perfect.

START: Leave centre by Queensferry Rd and 8km out turn left at lights, signed Clermiston. The hill is on your left for the next 2km.

PARK: Park where safe, on or nr this rd (Clermiston Rd). 1-7KM CIRC XBIKE BUS 26, 85 1-A-1

Refer to Lothians map on pages 340–341.

364
MAP 7
A2

✔ **THE PENTLANDS:** A serious range of hills rising to almost 600m, remote in parts and offering some fine walking. There are many paths up the various tops and round the lochs and reservoirs. (A) A good start in town is made by going off the bypass at Colinton, follow signs for Colinton Village, then the left fork up Woodhall Rd. Second left up Bonaly Rd (signed Bonaly Scout Camp). Drive/walk as far as you can (2km) and park by the gate leading to the hill proper where there is a map showing routes. The path to Glencorse is one of the classic Pentland walks. (B) Most walks start from signposted gateways on the A702 Biggar Rd. There are starts at Boghall (5km after Hillend ski slope); on the long straight stretch before Silverburn (a 10km path to Balerno); from Habbie's Howe about 18km from town; and from the village of Carlops, 22km from town. (C) The most popular start is probably from the visitor centre behind the Flotterstone Inn, also on the A702, 14km from town (decent pub lunch and 6-10pm, all day w/ends); trailboard and ranger service. The remoter tops around Loganlea reservoir are worth the extra mile.

1-20KM CAN BE CIRC MTBIKE BUS 4 OR ST ANDR SQ 2-B-2

365
MAP 7
A2

HERMITAGE OF BRAID: Strictly speaking, still in town, but a real sense of being in a country glen and from the windy tops of the Braid Hills there are some marvellous views back over the city. Main track along the burn is easy to follow and you eventually come to Hermitage House info centre; any paths ascending to the rt take you to the ridge of Blackford Hill. In winter, there's a gr sledging place over the first br up to the left and across the main rd.

START: Blackford Glen Rd. Go S on Mayfield to main T-jnct with Liberton Rd, turn rt (signed Penicuik) then hard rt. 1-4KM CAN BE CIRC XBIKE BUS 7 1-A-1

366
MAP 7
A2

ROSLIN GLEN: Special: spiritual, historical and enchanting, with a chapel (1681/CHURCHES), a ruined castle and woodland walks along the R Esk.

START: A701 from Mayfield or Newington (or bypass, t/off Penicuik, A702 then fork left on A703 to Roslin). Some parking at chapel (1681/CHURCHES), 500m from corner of Main St/Manse Rd, or follow B7003 to Rosewell (also marked Rosslynlee Hospital) and 1km from village the main car park is to the left.

1-8km XCIRC BIKE BUS ST ANDR SQ 1-A-1

367
MAP 7
A1

ALMONDELL: A country park to W of city (18km) nr (and one of the best things about) Livingston. A deep, peaceful woody cleft with easy paths and riverine meadows. Fine for kids, lovers and dog walkers. Visitor centre with teashop. Trails marked.

START: Best app from Edin by A71 via Sighthill. After Wilkieston, turn rt for Camp (B7015) then follow signs. Or A89 to Broxburn past start of M8. Follow signs from Broxburn. 2-8KM XCIRC BIKE BUS ST ANDR SQ 1-A-1

368
MAP 7
A1

BEECRAIGS AND COCKLEROY HILL: Another country park SW of Linlithgow with trails and clearings in mixed woods, a deer farm and a fishing loch. Gr adventure playground for kids. Best is the climb and extraordinary view from Cockleroy Hill, far better than you'd expect for the effort. From Ben Lomond to the Bass Rock; and the gunge of Grangemouth in the sky to the E.

START: M90 to Linlithgow (26km), through town and left on Preston Rd. Go on 4km, park is signed, but for hill you don't need to take the left turn. The hill, and nearest car park to it, are on the rt.

2-8KM CIRC MTBIKE BUS ST ANDR SQ 1-A-1

369
MAP 7
B2

BORTHWICK AND CRICHTON CASTLES: Takes in 2 impressive castles, the first a posh hotel (52/HOTELS O/SIDE TOWN) and the other an imposing ruin on a ridge o/looking the Tyne. A walk through dramatic Border Country steeped in lore. Path obvious at first in either direction, then peters out, but the castle you're going to is always in view. Nice picnic spots nr Crichton.

START: From Borthwick: A7 S for 16km, past Gorebridge, left at N Middleton; signed. From Crichton: A68 almost to Pathhead, signed then 3km.

7KM XCIRC XBIKE BUS ST ANDR SQ 1-B-2

WOODLAND WALKS NR EDINBURGH

Refer to Borders map on pages 342–343 and Lothians map on pages 340–341.

370 **DAWYCK GARDENS, nr STOBO:** 10km W of Peebles on B712 Moffat rd.
MAP 8 Outstn of the Edin Botanics; a 'recent' acquisition, though tree planting here
A2 goes back 300 yrs. Sloping grounds around the Scrape Burn which trickles into the Tweed. Landscaped woody pathways for meditative walks. Famous for shrubs and blue Himalayan poppies. Mar-Oct 10am-6pm. ADMN

371 **HUMBIE WOODS:** 25km SE by A68 t/off at Fala. Follow signs for church. Most
MAP 7 open woods (beech) beyond car park, through paddock. The churchyard is as
B2 reassuring a place to be buried as you could wish for; if you're set on cremation, come here and think of earth. Deep in the woods with the burn besides; after-hrs the sprites and the spirits must have a hell of a time.

372 **SMEATON GARDENS, EAST LINTON:** 2km from village on N Berwick rd
MAP 7 (signed Smeaton). Up a drive in an old estate is this walled grd going back to
B1 the early 19th century. An additional pleasure is the Lake Walk halfway down the drive through a small gate in the woods. A 1km stroll round a secret finger lake in magnificent woodland. Grd hrs 10am-4.30pm, Sun from 11.30am; cl w/ends Jan and Feb.

373 **WOODHALL DENE, NR DUNBAR:** A1 Dunbar bypass, E to Spott then rd to
MAP 7 left, 5km. Small car park in river hollow. Follow river to important ancient
B1 woodland site (2km). Can be damp. Few folk.

374 **DALKEITH COUNTRY PARK:** 15km SE by A68. The wooded policies of
MAP 7 Dalkeith House; enter at end of Main St. Surprisingly extensive area so close to
B1 town and conurbation. Under these stately deciduous trees, carpets of bluebells, daffs and snowdrops, primroses and wild garlic according to season. Adventure playground for kids, natural playground for the rest of us.

375 **VOGRIE COUNTRY PARK, NR GOREBRIDGE:** 25km S by A7 then B6372 6km
MAP 7 from Gorebridge. Small country park well organized for 'recreational pursuits'.
B2 9-hole golf course, tearoom and country ranger staff. May be busy on Sun, but otherwise a corral of countryside on the v edge of town.

376 **CARDRONA FOREST/GLENTRESS, NR PEEBLES:** 40km S to Peebles, 8km E
MAP 8 on B7062 and similar distance on A72. Cardrona on same rd as Kailzie Grd
B2 Tearoom (Apr-Oct) is excl. Forestry Commission woodlands so mostly regimented firs, but Scots pine and deciduous trees up the burn. Set trails incl mt bikes. Nice in late autumn and winter. Some dark mysterious bits.

THE BEST BEACHES

Refer to Lothians map on pages 340–341.

377 ✓ **SEACLIFF:** The best beach, least crowded/littered; perfect for picnics,
MAP 7 beachcombing, and gazing into rock pools. There is a harbour, still in use,
B1 which is also good for swimming. 50km from Edin, Seacliff is off the A198 out of N Berwick, 3km after Tantallon Castle (1625/RUINS). At a bend in the rd and a farm (Auldhame) there is an unsigned rd off to the left. 2km on there's a barrier, costing 2 x 50p to get car through. Car park 1km then walk. From A1, take E Linton t/off, go through Whitekirk towards N Berwick, then same.

378 **PORTOBELLO:** Edin's town beach, 8km from centre by London Rd. When
MAP 7 sunny – chips, lager, bad ice cream. When miserable – soulful dog walkers.
B1 Arcades, mini-funfair, long prom. A 'used to be' place. (386/SPORTS FACS) – maybe the *Evening News* will shame the council enough and it will be reinstated to its former glory.

379 **YELLOWCRAIGS:** Nearest decent beach (35km). A1 or bypass, then A198
MAP 7 coast rd. Left o/side Dirleton for 2km, park and walk 100m across links to fair-
B1 ly clean strand and sea. Gets busy, but big enough to share. Hardly anyone swims, but you can. Scenic. **GULLANE BENTS**, a sweep of beach, is nearby and reached from village main st. Connects westwards with Aberlady Nature Reserve. One of the cleanest.

THE BEST VIEWS OF THE CITY

380 ✓ ✓ **CALTON HILL:** Gr view of the city easily gained by walking up from
E2 E end of Princes St by Waterloo Pl, to the end of the buildings and
then up stairs on the left. The City Observatory and the Greek-style folly lend
an elegant backdrop to a panorama (unfolding as you walk round) where the
view up Princes St and the sweep of the Forth estuary are particularly fine. At
night, the city twinkles. Popular cruising area for gays – but can be dangerous.
Destination of the Torchlight Procession (part of Edin Hogmanay celebra-
tions) with gr firework finale.

381 ✓ ✓ **ARTHUR'S SEAT:** W of city centre. Best app through Queen's Park
xE3 from foot of Canongate by Holyrood Palace. The igneous core of an
extinct volcano with the precipitous sill of Salisbury Crags presiding over the
city and offering fine views for the fit. Top is 251m; on a clear day you can see
100km. Surprisingly wild considering proximity to city. (361/WALKS IN THE CITY)

382 **SCOTT MONUMENT:** Princes St. Design inspiration for Thunderbird 3. This
D2 1844 Gothic memorial to one of Scotland's best-kent literary sons rises 61.5m
above the main drag and provides scope for the vertiginous to come to terms
with their affliction. 287 steps mean it's no cakewalk; narrow stairwells weed
out claustrophobics too. Those who make it to the top are rewarded with fine
views. Underneath, a statue of the mournful Sir Walter gazes across at Jenners.
Apr-Sep 9am-6pm; Oct-Mar 9am-3pm. Cl Sun. ADMN

383 **CAMERA OBSCURA:** Castlehill, Royal Mile. At v top of st nr castle entrance, a
C3 tourist attraction that, surprisingly, has been there for over a century. You
ascend through a shop, photography exhibs and holograms to the viewing
area where a continuous stream of small groups are shown the effect of the
giant revolving periscope thingie. All Edin life is visible – amazing how much
fun can be had from a pin-hole camera with a focal length of 8.6m. Apr-Oct
9.30am-6pm, sometimes later. Nov-Mar 10am-5pm. ADMN

384 **NORTH BERWICK LAW:** The conical volcanic hill, a beacon in the E Lothian
MAP7 landscape. **TRAPRAIN LAW** nearby is higher, tends to be frequented by rock-
A1 climbers, but has major prehistoric hillfort citadel of the Goddodin and a def-
inite aura. BOTH 1-A-1

THE PENTLANDS/HERMITAGE: Reports: 364/365/WALKS O/SIDE CITY.

CASTLE RAMPARTS: Report: 341/MAIN ATTRACTIONS.

THE BEST SPORTS FACILITIES

SWIMMING AND INDOOR SPORTS CENTRES

385 **ROYAL COMMONWEALTH POOL:** 667 7211. Dalkeith Rd (349/MAIN ATTRAC-
xE4 TIONS). The biggest, but Edin has many others. Recommended are
xD4 **WARRENDER** (447 0052), Thirlestane Rd 500m beyond the Meadows S of cen-
xE1 tre; **LEITH VICTORIA** (555 4728), in Jnct Pl off the main st in Leith, now
C1 refurbed with Pulse centre; **GLENOGLE** (343 6376) in Stockbridge, the New
Town choice, v friendly. All these pools are old and tiled, 25yd long, seldom
crowded and excellent for lane swimming – at certain times. All tend to have
different sessions, so phone to check.

386 **PORTOBELLO:** Portobello Esplanade (378/BEACHES). Similar to others.
xE1 Recently refurbed, excellent Turkish baths still there, ladies-only, gents-only
and mixed days. Phone for details 0131 669 6888.

387 **AINSLIE PARK:** 551 2400. Pilton Dr, off Ferry Rd, N of centre, 5km from Princes
xC1 St; and **LEITH WATERWORLD:** 555 6000. Foot of Leith Walk. Leisure centres
xE1 with water thrills for kids. Ainslie has serious keep-fit side, Leith has financial
troubles and opens 10am-5pm Fri-Sun, restricted otherwise.

388 **THE NEXT GENERATION:** 554 5000. Newhaven Harbour. V much part of the
xD1 regeneration of the waterfront, this sportsarama complex in the David Lloyd
stable, in fact son of hence naff name. Terms, gym, 2 pools incl one outdoor
o/looking Forth (only in non-wet weather). Not cheap, but not as exp as some
in town. 7 days till 11.30pm.

389 **MEADOWBANK:** 661 5351. London Rd. City athletics stadium with courts for
xE2 squash and badminton (often booked), Pulse centre, weights room, 13m indoor climbing wall, outdoor football/hockey pitches and velodrome. No pool.

390 **MARCO'S:** 228 2141. 51 Grove St. Labyrinthine commercial centre with aero-
B3 bic classes, gym, squash and snooker. No pool. Little Marco's will look after your kids while you sweat.

391 **UNIVERSITY GYM:** 650 2585. The Pleasance. No-nonsense complex, v cheap.
E3 The best in town for weights (all the right machinery) and circuit training. Squash, badminton, indoor tennis, etc. Quiet in vacs, membership not required. For a reasonable fee, the Fitness and Sports Injury Centre (FASIC) is an excellent alternative to the 'take 2 aspirin and go away' school of GP. Few fake suntans.

392 **EDINBURGH CLUB:** 556 8845. 2 Hillside Cres. Probably the most civilized of
E1 non-hotel-type clubs. Usually members only, longer-stay visitors may be able to negotiate a rate. Good weights (mainly Universal), sauna/steam/sun/bistro. Good aerobics classes. And spinning, apparently. No pool.

393 **DRUMSHEUGH BATHS CLUB:** 225 2200. 5 Belford Rd, W End. Private swim-
A2 ming club in elegant building above Dean Village that costs a fortune to join and has an 18-month waiting list (so nae chance readers). But gorgeous Victorian pool with rings and trapeze over the water, sauna, multigym and bar. Frequented by the quality. If you're chums with New Town lawyer, get him to sign you in as a guest.

GOLF COURSES

There are several municipal courses (see phone directory under City of Edin Council) and nearby, esp down the coast, some famous names that aren't open to non-members. Refer to Lothians map on pages 340–341.

394 **BRAID HILLS:** 447 6666. Braid Hills app. 2 18-hole courses (no. 2 summer
MAP 7 only). Thought to be the best in town. Never boring; exhilarating views.
A1 Booking usually not essential, except w/ends. Women welcome (and that ain't true everywhere round here).

395 **GULLANE NO. 1:** 01620 842255. The best of 3 courses around this pretty, twee
MAP 7 village (35km down the coast) that was built for golf. Now you are really
B1 golfing! (though not on Sat).

960 **GLEN GOLF CLUB (AKA NORTH BERWICK EAST):** 01620 895288. Some say
MAP 7 W is best (01620 892135) but most say E and few would argue that N Berwick
B1 on a fair day was worth the drive (36km, A1 then A198) from Edin. That's the Bass Rock out there, and Fidra. Open to women.

397 **MUSSELBURGH:** The original home of golf (really: golf recorded here in
MAP 7 1672), but this local authority-run 9-hole links is not exactly top turf and is
B1 enclosed by Musselburgh Racecourse. Nostalgia still appeals though. **ROYAL MUSSELBURGH** nearby compensates. It dates to 1774, the fifth-oldest in Scotland. Busy early mornings and Fri afternoons, 01875 801139.

398 **GIFFORD:** 01620 810267. Dinky inland course on the edge of a dinky village,
MAP 7 bypassed by the queue for the big E Lothian courses and a guarded secret
B1 among the regulars. (Can't play after 4pm Tue/Wed/Sat or Sun afternoons.) 9 and 11 holes.

OTHER ACTIVITIES

399 **TENNIS:** There are lots of private clubs though only the **GRANGE** (332 2148)
xD4 has lawn tennis and you won't get on there easily. There are places you can slip on (best not to talk about that), but the municipal centres (Edin residents/longer-stay visitors should get a Leisure Access card [661 5351] allowing advance reservation) are:

400 **SAUGHTON:** 444 0422. Stevenson Dr. 8km W of city centre. 2 astroturf courts
xA4 and one other. Also used for football, so phone to book.

401 **CRAIGLOCKHART:** 444 1969. Colinton Rd. 8km SW of centre via Morningside
xC4 and Colinton Rd. 6 indoor courts, 7 outdoor and a 'centre court' – best to
check/book by phone. Other separate sports facs incl squash, badminton and
gym, 443 0101. Centre open Mon-Fri 9am-11pm, Sat-Sun 9am-10.30pm.

402 **SKIING:** Artificial slopes at **HILLEND** on A702, 10km S of centre. 445 4433.
xC4 Excellent fac with various runs. The matting can be bloody rough when you
fall and the chairlift is a bit of a dread for beginners, but once you can ski here,
St Anton is all yours. Tuition every evening (not Thu) and w/ends. Open till
10pm in winter, 9pm in summer. Snowboarders welcome but it ain't Whistler.

403 **PONY-TREKKING: LASSWADE RIDING SCHOOL:** 663 7676. Lasswade exit
xE4 from city bypass then A768, rt to Loanhead 1km and left to end of Kevock Rd.
Full hacking and trekking facs and courses for all standards and ages.

404 **PENTLAND HILLS TREKKING CENTRE:** 01968 661095. At Carlops on A702
xA4 (25km from town) has sturdy, steady Icelandic horses who will bear you good-
naturedly into the hills. Exhilarating stuff. Bus from St Andrew's Sq.

405 **ICE-SKATING: MURRAYFIELD ICERINK:** 337 6933. Riversdale Cres, just off
xA3 main Glas Rd nr zoo. Cheap, cheerful and chilly. It has been here forever and
feels like a gr 1950s B movie … go round! Sessions daily from 2.30pm. Also …
WINTER WONDERLAND: E Princes St Gardens. Big open-air ice rink in the gardens below the Scott Monument. Open late Nov-early Jan. 7 days. Mass fun!

406 **ALIEN ROCK:** 552 7211. Old St Andrew's Church, Pier Pl, Newhaven. Indoor
xD1 rock climbing in a converted kirk. Laid back atmos, bouldering rm and interesting 12m walls of various gnarliness to scoot up. Daily; phone for sessions.
Have a pint after in **THE STARBANK** or **THE OLD CHAIN PIER** nearby
(299/300/PUB FOOD).

THE BEST GALLERIES

407 **CITY ART CENTRE:** 529 3993. Market St. Quite big. This is the place the pop-
D3 ulist blockbuster exhibs come to as well as excellent social/educational displays. Sensibly curated city asset. Convenient and carefully run café.

408 **THE FRUITMARKET GALLERY:** Across the rd in Market St, a smaller, more
D3 warehousey space for more contemporary collections, retrospectives, installations. Café (200/BEST TEAROOMS) highly recommended for meeting and eating, watching the world go by.

409 **THE COLLECTIVE GALLERY:** 220 1260. 22 Cockburn St. Installations of
D3 Scottish and other young contemporary trailblazers. Members' work won't
break the bank.

410 **INGLEBY GALLERY:** 556 4441. 6 Calton Terr. Important, chic gallery in a pri-
E2 vate house backing onto Calton Hill. Often shows work by significant contemporary artists. 10am-6pm Wed-Sat.

411 **THE SCOTTISH GALLERY:** 558 1200. 16 Dundas St. Guy Peploe's influential
C2 New Town gallery on 2 floors. Where to go to buy something painted, sculpt-
ed, thrown or crafted by up-and-comers or established names – everything
from affordable jewellery to original Joan Eardleys at £10k plus. Or just look.

412 **OPEN EYE GALLERY:** 557 1020. 75-79 Cumberland St and **EYE-2** opp.
C1 Excellent small galleries in residential part of New Town. Always worth checking out for accessible contemporary painting and ceramics. Almost too accessible (take cheque book).

413 **THE PRINTMAKERS' WORKSHOP AND GALLERY:** 557 2479. 23 Union St, off
D1 Leith Walk nr London Rd r/bout. Workshops that you can look over. Exhibs of
work by contemporary printmakers and shop where prints from many of the
notable names in Scotland are on sale at reasonable prices. Bit of a treasure.

414 **BELLVUE GALLERY:** 557 1663. 4 Bellvue Cres. Edin's newest small gallery at
D1 the bottom of fashionable Broughton St. Selected contemporary work in light
salons (gallery is part of a house). The one to watch, the openings to go to.
Afternoons.

415 **PHOTOGRAPHY:** Edin is blessed with 2 contemporary photo-art venues.
D3 **STILLS:** 622 6200, 23 Cockburn St, with a café. **PORTFOLIO:** 220 1911, 43 Candlemaker Row, is a small 2-floor space in what used to be the city's left-wing bookshop.

GOOD NIGHTLIFE

For the current programmes of the places recommended below and all other venues, consult The List *magazine, on sale at most newsagents.*

MOVIES

Multiplex chains apart, these ones take movies seriously:

416 **THE CAMEO:** 228 4141. Home St in Tollcross. 3 screens showing important
C4 new films and cult classics. Some late movies at w/ends. Good bar.

417 **FILMHOUSE:** 228 2688. Lothian Rd, opp Usher Hall. 3 screens with everything
C3 from first-run art-house movies to subtitled obscurities and retrospectives. Home of the annual Film Festival; café-bar (till 11.30pm Sun-Thu, 12.30am Fri-Sat) is a haven from the excesses of Lothian Rd. Open to non-cinephiles.

418 **THE DOMINION:** 447 2660. Newbattle Terr, off Morningside Rd. Friendly, fam-
xC4 ily-run cinema with 3 screens (one of them's like sitting in a plane). Nice wee place to see big films with the kids. Luca's ice cream.

THEATRE

419 The main city theatres are **THE FESTIVAL THEATRE:** 529 6000. Nicolson St.
D3 Edin's showcase theatre re-created from the old Empire with a huge glass frontage of bars and a stage and screen dock large enough to accommodate the world's major companies. Eclectic programme AYR.

420 **THE KING'S:** 229 1201. Leven St, Tollcross. **THE LYCEUM:** 229 9697. Grindlay St.
C4, C3 Ornate and lately refurbed theatres with wide-ranging popular programmes.

421 **THE TRAVERSE:** 228 1404. Small but influential, dedicated to new work
C3 (though mainly touring companies) in modern Euro, v architectural 2-theatre premises in Cambridge St (behind Lyceum). Good rendezvous bar in theatre (320/THESE ARE HIP) plus excellent adj restau (64/BEST RESTAUS) and café-bar (77/BEST BISTROS).

422 **THEATRE WORKSHOP:** 226 5425. 34 Hamilton Pl. A small neighbourhood
C1 theatre in Stockbridge with a wide reputation for vital, innovative work. Café-bar run by the Helios Fountain people (145/VEGN RESTAUS).

CLASSICAL MUSIC

423 Usually from one of Scotland's national orchestras at regular concerts in the
C3, E4 **USHER HALL** 228 1155. Lothian Rd. Smaller ensembles more occasionally at **THE REID, ST CECILIA'S** or **THE QUEEN'S HALL.** See *The List* or the Sat edition of the *Scotsman* newspaper.

JAZZ

424 **THE QUEEN'S HALL:** 668 2019. Clerk St. Occasional 'concerts'; see press.
E4

425 **HENRY'S CELLAR BAR:** 538 7385. Morrison St opp cinema nr corner with
C3 Lothian Rd. small, integral jazz cellar (with other funky music). Report: 333/LIVE MUSIC.

426 **NOBLES:** 554 2024. 44a Constitution St. Dependable bar food and real ales in
xE1 a fine-sized rm. Folk on Thu, R&B Fri and jazz Sat, but phone to confirm.

427 **LEITH JAZZ FESTIVAL/EDINBURGH JAZZ FESTIVAL:** Late May/early Aug.
xE1 Selected venues. Check *The List* for details or TO.

FOLK

See LIVE MUSIC. *Best bets on a regular basis are:*

428 **SANDY BELL'S** aka **THE FORREST HILL BAR:** Forrest Hill. Famous and forev-
D3 er. Sometimes you could look in and wonder why; other times you know
you're in exactly the rt place. Music every night except Tue and Sun.

429 **THE FIDDLER'S ARMS:** Grassmarket. And fiddle they do on Mon nights. Good
C3 crack and blether at all times.

430 **WEST END HOTEL:** 225 3656. Palmerston Pl. A good place to stay or just to
B3 hang out with the Highlanders. Some trad folk live at w/ends and whenever.
(26/INDIVIDUAL HOTELS)

431 **THE ROYAL OAK HALL:** Infirmary St. Late-night singalong. (338/LATE BARS)
D3

THE BEST ROCK AND POP MUSIC

432 **PLAYHOUSE THEATRE:** 557 2590. Greenside Pl. Major theatre in Scotland,
D2 most regular programme, holds 3,000. More infrequent as concert venue
while they get through the musicals (not many to go).

433 **USHER HALL:** 228 1155. Lothian Rd. Gr auditorium. Classier acts. Undergoing
C3 refurb, so may be absent from current listings.

434 **THE VENUE:** 557 3073 and **LA BELLE ANGELE:** 225 2774. Main small club
D3 venues for emerging and local bands. Check *The List* (fortnightly) for programmes. (327/328/LIVE MUSIC, 2099/ROCK AND POP)

435 **QUEEN'S HALL:** 668 2019. Clerk St. Most diverse (choral, jazz, art pop). Good
E4 atmos. Used every night; your best bet if you just want to go somewhere for
decent music.

THE BEST CEILIDHS

436 **THE ASSEMBLY ROOMS:** 220 4349. George St. Municipal halls but grand, the
C2 venue for all kinds of culture (esp during the Festival), and though a long way
from the draughty village hall kind of jig, they've been positively reeling to
the sounds of the Robert Fish Band. Ceilidhs generally last Fri of the month.
Watch local press, e.g. *The List* (fortnightly), for details and pay at the door.

437 **WEST END HOTEL:** 225 3656. 35 Palmerston Pl. Edin's Heilan' hame hotel has
B3 occasional sessions of music/singing and storytelling (more like a trad ceilidh)
but no dancing. This is where to come (or phone) to find out where the others are (occasional ceilidhs held in the church hall nearby). (26/INDIVIDUAL
HOTELS)

438 **CALEDONIAN BREWERY:** 01698 385251. Slateford Rd. At time of going to
xA4 press, ceilidhs every Sat in the Festival Hall in the brewery 8-11.45pm. Bands
vary but the couple of hundred heuchin' teuchin' punters have a good time
regardless. (290/REAL-ALE PUBS)

SECTION 2

Glasgow

The telephone code for Glasgow is 0141
Refer to MAP B, *unless otherwise stated*

439 ✓ ✓ **ONE DEVONSHIRE GARDENS:** 339 2001. 1 Devonshire Grds. Off Gr
xB1 Western Rd (the A82 W to Dumbarton). After yrs at the front – it's still
at the front. 3 separate houses in leafy Victorian terr, and after accolades and
write-ups galore, remains the most notable urban hotel in Scotland. It's all
down to detail and service, fab fixtures and fabrics: it's all down to DESIGN.
Every rm is different but all have the things that we modern travellers look out
for: CD players, big beds, deep baths, thick carpets/towels/curtains. Some
Ralph Lauren rms; the supersuites all in house 3 (rms 21, 27, 28) if you're
Pavarotti or just celebrating. Restau a foodie experience in itself (490/BEST
RESTAUS). Stars aplenty – well it's the obvious choice.
27RMS JAN-DEC T/T PETS CC KIDS LOTS

440 ✓ **THE ARTHOUSE HOTEL:** 221 6789. 500 129 Bath St, nr Sauchiehall Centre
D3 and above Sarti (523/ITALIAN RESTAUS), so gr coffee downstairs. New (summer '99) and v smart town-house hotel with wide, tiled stairwell and funky lift
to 3 floors of individual rms (so size, views, etc. vary). Fab gold embossed wallpaper in the hallways, notable stained glass in 'fine' drawing-rm (The Arc) and
nice pictures and prints. Grill downstairs has tepenyaki dishes and adj oyster
bar. Chef John Quickley home at last. Bar, a fashionable rendezvous for this,
the sexiest stopover in town. 68RMS JAN-DEC T/T XPETS CC KIDS MED.EXP

441 ✓ **THE MALMAISON:** 572 1000. 278 W George St. Sister hotel of the one in
C3 Edin and same team as One Devonshire (*see above*) so no surprise that
this is an outstanding hotel. The 'chain' of good design hotel spread through
England as we speak (dulcet tones of course). Café Mal downstairs contrasts
with the woody clubbiness of the brasserie next door (504/BEST BISTROS). Well-
proportioned rms (some suites), with CDs, cable, etc. Stylish excellence. This is
indeed the Blair New World. 72RMS JAN-DEC T/T XPETS CC KIDS MED.EXP

442 ✓ **THE DEVONSHIRE HOTEL:** 339 7878. 5 Devonshire Grds. Confusingly
xB1 perhaps for first-time visitors, this similarly sumptuous town house hotel
is at the other end of the short block containing One Devonshire (*see above*).
I say 'similarly' (pictures, plants, atmos, etc.), but it is less deluxe, less designey,
some may find more easy on the pocket – and you don't have to be so cool.
Dining for residents only. All bedrms different.
16RMS JAN-DEC T/T PETS CC KIDS LOTS

443 ✓ **CARLTON GEORGE:** 353 6373. 44 W George St. Adj Queen St Stn and
D3 George Sq, this is a smart new addition to Glasgow and apart from parking (a hike to carpark behind the stn) prob the best hotel in the city centre for
the business traveller. Its more fun than that though with a huge Irish bar
downstairs and airy restau up top. Residents lounge and drinks in rm all on
the house. Excl service and the usual comforts.
65RMS JAN-DEC T/T XPETS CC KIDS EXP

444 ✓ **NAIRN'S:** 353 0707. 13 Woodside Cres, nr Charing Cross. 4 rms above Nick
B2 Nairn's eponymous restau and clearly one of the best places in town to
have breakfast (and dinner) (487/BEST RESTAUS). Each rm v individual with different themes (one definitely more S&M than M&S), but all with good light
and good bathrms. 4RMS JAN-DEC T/T XPETS CC KIDS EXP

445 **GLASGOW HILTON:** 204 5555. 1 William St. App from the M8 slip rd or from
C4 city centre via Waterloo St. It has a forbidding Fritz Lang/*Metropolis* appearance which isn't really dispelled once inside. But hotel is one of the best in
town with good service and appointments. Japanese people made esp welcome. Huge atrium. Cameron's, the hotel's main restau, is present and correct,
and the most highly Michelin-rated restau in town ('99). Minsky's bistro and
Raffles bar are not so special. 319RMS JAN-DEC T/T PETS CC KIDS LOTS

446 **THE MARRIOTT:** 226 5577. 500 Argyle St, nr motorway. Modern and function-
C4 al business hotel where parking is a test for the nerves. Nevertheless, there's a
calm, helpful attitude from the staff inside; for further de-stressing you can
hypnotize yourself by watching the soundless traffic on the Kingston Br o/side;
or there's a pool to lap. No-smk floors. 298RMS JAN-DEC T/T PETS CC KIDS LOTS

447 **THE COPTHORNE:** 332 6711. 50 George Sq. Situated on the sq which is the
D3 municipal heart of the city and next to Queen St Stn (trains to Edin and pts N),
Glas will be going on all about you and there's a conservatory terr, serving
breakfast and afternoon tea, from which to watch. Bedrms vary greatly; some
perhaps overdone and over dear. Busy brasserie.

141RMS JAN-DEC T/T PETS CC KIDS LOTS

448 **THE MOAT HOUSE:** 306 9988. Congress Rd. Beside the SECC, on the Clyde, this
B4 towering, glass monument to the 1980s feels like it's in a constant state of
'siege readiness'. The Marine Restau, in the lobby, has a good reputation and
ring-side seating for river-gazing. Somewhat removed from city centre (about
3km, you wouldn't want to walk), it's esp handy for SECC and Armadillo
goings-on.

282RMS JAN-DEC T/T PETS CC KIDS LOTS

449 **THE CENTRAL HOTEL:** 221 9680. Gordon St. Once the last word in gracious
D3 living, the elegance is now distinctly faded, although a certain atmos still
remains in the sweep of the staircase and in the grandiose public rms. Rms are
individual, though may be small (and too hot). Corridors stretch forever but
you're at the hub of a gr city.

221RMS JAN-DEC T/T PETS CC KIDS EXP

THE BEST OF THE LESS EXPENSIVE HOTELS

450 ✓ ✓ **GROUCHO ST JUDES:** 352 8800. 190 Bath St. New (summer of '99) col-
D3 laboration betw Paul Wingate and Bobby Patterson of Glasgow and
the Groucho Club of Soho. D'stairs bar, u'stairs rms and restau on ground floor.
New at time of going to press, but an instant hit. Membership not reqd, just a bit
of credential and credit card.

6RMS JAN-DEC T/T XPETS CC XKIDS MED.EXP

451 ✓ **CATHEDRAL HOUSE:** 552 3519. 28-32 Cathedral Sq/John Knox St. Next
E3 to the Cathedral (some rms o/look) and close to the Merchant City, this
detached old building has been tastefully refurbed (though a redec may be
due) and converted into a café-bar (with occasional live music), a separate
restau (check opening though) and comfortable bedrms above. Discreet and
informal hospitality for the traveller; much as it always has been here, in the
ancient heart of the city.

7RMS JAN-DEC T/T PETS CC KIDS MED.EXP

452 ✓ **THE TOWN HOUSE:** 357 0862. 4 Hughenden Terr. Quiet st off Gr Western
xB1 Rd via Hyndland Rd, o/looking the cricket grounds. Spacious rms faith-
fully restored – even if you don't happen to live in a well-appointed town
house on a gracious terr yourself, you'll feel at home. Close to the W End. Don't
confuse with the Townhouse Hotel, Royal Cres.

10RMS JAN-DEC T/T XPETS CC KIDS MED.INX

453 ✓ **THE LODGE INN:** 221 1000. 10 Elmbank Grds, above Charing Cross Stn.
C3 Once an office block, then the Charing Cross Tower Hotel, this under new
ownership (S&N) is still a vast city-centre budget hotel, with no frills and no
pretence, but a v adequate rm for the night. Not a pile of charm and you
wouldn't want to spend your holidays here, but its functionalism, anonymity
and urban melancholy may suit the very modern traveller. M8 rms less quiet.

276RMS JAN-DEC T/T XPETS CC KIDS MED.EX

454 ✓ **THE BRUNSWICK:** 552 0001. 104-108 Brunswick St. V contemporary, min-
E4 imalist hotel in Merchant City. Bright and cheerful rms economically
designed to make use of tight space; low Japanese-style beds. Good base for
nocturnal forays into pub and club land. Restau has had mixed response, but
breakfast v pleasant. Check out the penthouse.

21RMS JAN-DEC T/T XPETS CC KIDS MED.EXP

455 ✓ **RAB HA'S:** 572 0400. 83 Hutcheson St. Rms above a pub in the urban
E4 heart of the Merchant City that have had a recent overhaul. Good food
and friendly folk make this a place to go if you're in the know. But noisy late
night and if you lie in.

4RMS JAN-DEC T/T PETS CC XKIDS MED.INX

456 ✓ **THE MERCHANT LODGE HOTEL:** 552 2424. 52 Virginia St. Conversion of
D4 the old Tobacco Merchants house (in Merchant City) that has managed
to retain the original staircase (ask the porter to take your bags, there's no lift).
Surprisingly quiet area nr shops; in the gay zone (in case you didn't notice).

34RMS JAN-DEC T/T PETS CC KIDS CHP

457 **HOLIDAY INN EXPRESS:** 0800 897121. Corner of Stockwell and Clyde St (but
D4 you don't get a room on the river). Functional bed-box that's still a good deal.
All you do is sleep here. Nr Merchant City, so plenty of restaus, nightlife and
other distractions and curiously midway betw 2 of Glasgow's oldest, funkiest
bars The Scotia and Victoria (638/637/PUBS).

120RMS JAN-DEC T/T XPETS CC KIDS MED.INX

458 **BABBITY BOWSTER:** 552 5055. 16-18 Blackfriars St. This carefully renovated,
E4 late 18th-century town house was pivotal in the redevelopment of the
Merchant City. Renowned for its hospitality; bar (659/REAL-ALE PUBS, 672/PUB
FOOD) and beer grd, Schottische restau upstairs and simple accom above. A
welcoming howf, some Culture thrown in, a basic rm.

6RMS JAN-DEC X/X XPETS CC XKIDS MED.INX

159 **WICKETS HOTEL:** 334 9334. 52 Fortrose St. Probably best app via Dumbarton
xA2 Rd, turning up Peel St before railway br. O/looking W of Scotland Cricket
Ground, family-run hotel with decent rms, conservatory restau and a beer grd
made for long summer afternoons (684/DRINKING OUTDOORS).

10RMS JAN-DEC T/T PETS CC KIDS MED.INX

460 **KIRKLEE:** 334 5555. 11 Kensington Gate. The Stevens keep a tidy house and
xA1 most notably a tidy grd in this leafy suburb nr Botanics and Byres Rd.

9RMS JAN-DEC T/T XPETS CC KIDS MED.INX

461 **THE WHITE HOUSE:** 339 9375. 12 Cleveden Cres. Not really a hotel, more self-
xA1 catering apartments nr Botanics. V civilized alternative, esp if there are a few
of you or you are staying a week. Nightly lets, cool place.

6UNITS JAN-DEC T/T PETS CC KIDS MED.INX

462 **NUMBER 52 CHARLOTTE STREET:** 553 1941. Serviced apartments in superb
E4 conversion of the one remaining Georgian town house in historic (now decimated) st betw the Barrows Market and Glas Green. V good rates for
bedrm/lounge/kitchen; everything but breakfast.

6RMS JAN-DEC X/T XPETS CC KIDS MED.INX

463 **THEATRE HOTEL:** 227 2772. 27 Elmbank St. The theatre is the Kings in the W
C3 End, this reasonably appointed budget hotel is just down the (rather bleak)
road. But it is ok inside, better than most and inx. No dining rm ('continental
b/fast' served in your rm). But there's 'a wide variety of eating places nearby',
as they say.

59RMS JAN-DEC T/T PETS CC KIDS MED.INX

464 **THE VICTORIAN HOUSE:** 332 0129. 214 Renfrew St. Expansive guesthouse
C3 which has swallowed up adj houses in hill-top terr behind Sauchiehall St nr
Art School (746/MACKINTOSH). Basic accom. Rms without facs cheaper but
bathrms can be a floor away. Location is the appeal.

55RMS JAN-DEC X/T PETS CC KIDS INX

465 **RENNIE MACKINTOSH HOTEL:** 333 9992. 218-220 Renfrew St and the **GREEK**
C2, B3 **THOMSON:** 332 6556, 140 Elderslie St, have both cheekily borrowed the
names of 2 of Glasgow's most famous sons. The Mockintosh isn't too over-
bearing, the service is friendly and helpful, and there's alfresco breakfasting in
the summer.

24/17RMS JAN-DEC T/T X/PETS CC KIDS INX

THE BEST HOSTELS

*The SYHA is the Scottish Youth Hostel Association, of which you have to be a
member (or a member of an affiliated organization from another country) to stay
in their many hostels round Scotland. Phone 01786 451181 for details, or contact
any YHA hostel.*

466 ✓ **SY HOSTEL:** 332 3004. 7 Park Terr. Close to where the old Glas hostel used
B2 to be in Woodlands Terr, in the same area of the W End nr the univ and
Kelvingrove Park. This building was converted in 1992 from the Beacons
Hotel, which was where rock 'n' roll bands used to stay in the 1980s. Now the
bedrms are converted into dorms for 4-6 (some larger) and the public rms are
common rms with TV, games, café, etc. Still feels more like a hotel than a hos-
tel and is a gr place to stay. Late opening. You must be a member of the YHA.
See above.

160BEDS

467
B2 ✓ **GLASGOW BACKPACKERS:** 332 9099. 17 Park Terr. Along from the SYH (*see opposite*), the funkier alternative. Mostly dorms but some twins available. Only open summer months. Close to W End thrills and spills. 92BEDS

468
C3 ✓ **BAIRD HALL, STRATHCLYDE UNIV:** 553 4148. 460 Sauchiehall St. The landmark Grade A-listed Art Deco building near the Art School and the W End. Originally the Beresford Hotel, built 1937 and once Glasgow's finest (v Miami Beach). 194 rms in vacs and 11 available AYR. Spartan, almost drab, though the rms are fine, like an American Y. Reeks of nostalgia as well as disinfectant. Dining-rm, TV and reading rm. Lots of groovy places nearby such as Bar Ce Lona, Variety Bar, Baby Grand and the Griffin. All are listed further on. 185BEDS

469
D4 **CLYDE HALL, STRATHCLYDE UNIV:** 553 4148 318 Clyde St. A v central block, off-campus at the bottom of Union/Renfield St and almost o/looking the river. 165 single and twin rms, mainly in summer vac. Refectory and TV rm. Some smaller rms on lower floor are available cheaply as self-catering specifically for backpackers, and are a v good deal. 128BEDS

470
E3 **MURRAY HALL, STRATHCLYDE UNIV:** 553 4148 (ext 3560). Collins St. Modern, but not sterile block of single rms on edge of main campus and facing towards Cathedral. Part of large complex (also some student flats to rent by the week) with bar/shop/laundrette. Quite central, close to Merchant City bars. Vacs only. 70BEDS

Note: Both Strathclyde and Glasgow univs have other halls of residence available for short-term accom in the summer months. For those above (the best of them) and others, you may also phone: Glasgow 330 5385 or Strathclyde 553 4148 (central booking).

THE BEST HOTELS OUTSIDE TOWN

471
MAP 1
C2 ✓ **GLEDDOCH HOUSE, LANGBANK, NR GREENOCK:** 01475 540711. Take M8/A8 to Greenock, then B789 signposted Langbank/Houston, then 2km – hotel is signed. 30km W of centre by fast rd. A château-like country-house hotel, formerly the home of the Lithgow shipping family. High above the Clyde estuary, there are spectacular views across to Dumbarton Rock and the Kilpatrick Hills. Rms not lavish but comfortable – only a few have the view. Reputable dining-rm strong on Scottish ingredients and cuisine. Pleasant conservatory. Excellent 18-hole golf course (738/SPORTS FACS); health club, tiny pool. 38RMS JAN-DEC T/T PETS CC KIDS TOS LOTS

472
MAP 1
C2 ✓ **CAMERON HOUSE, NR BALLOCH, LOCH LOMOND:** 01389 755565. A82 dual carriageway through W End or via Erskine Br and M8. 45km NW of centre. Highly regarded mansion-house hotel complex with excellent leisure facs in open grounds on the bonny banks of the loch. Sports incl 9-hole golf, good pool, tennis and a busy marina for sailing/windsurfing, etc. Notable restau (The Georgian Rm) and all-day brasserie. Many famous names from Gazza to Pavarotti have holed up here (but they wouldn't have Oasis). 96RMS JAN-DEC T/T XPETS CC KIDS TOS LOTS

473
MAP 6
B3 ✓ **THE BLACK BULL HOTEL, KILLEARN:** 01360 550215. 2 The Sq. A81 towards Aberfoyle, take the rt fork after Glengoyne Distillery, and the hotel is at the top end of the village next to the church. Open-plan bar/restau with excellent reputation for food (2 AA rosettes), spacious conservatory with enclosed grd, and tastefully decorated, comfortable rms. (473/O/SIDE GLAS) 11RMS JAN-DEC T/T PETS CC KIDS MED.EXP

474
MAP 1
D3 ✓ **NEW LANARK MILL HOTEL, LANARK:** 01555 667200. From Glasgow, take M74, then follow signs for Lanark and esp New Lanark, the conservation vill of Robert Owen (45 mins). Excl retreat from Glasgow, where you wake up on the banks of the Clyde and sleep to the sound of its running water. Serene spot tho' many visitors. Good walks up river (1464/WATERFALLS) and an excl restau in Lanark (10 mins), La Vigna (810/RESTAUS CLYDE VALLEY). 38RMS JAN-DEC T/T PETS CC KIDS MED.INX

475
MAP 1
D3
✓ **SCORETULLOCH HOUSE HOTEL, DARVEL:** 01560 32331. M74, jnct 8 for A71 Kilmarnock. Signed and 2km from rd E of Priestland nr Darvel. Restau (incl brasserie) with rms in the country. Report 802/AYRSHIRE.

476
MAP 6
A3
✓ **THE LODGE ON LOCH LOMOND:** 01436 860201. Edge of Luss on A82 N from Balloch. About 40 mins W End. Linear not lovely, but gr lochside setting. Wood-lined rms o/look the bonny banks, tho' Luss is not everybody's cup of tea (and sausage roll). Restau also has the view and terrace and is surprisingly good – AA rosette; booking may be necessary w/ends.
29RMS JAN-DEC T/T PETS CC KIDS MED.INX

477
MAP 6
B3
COUNTRY CLUB HOTEL, STRATHBLANE: 01360 770491. 20km N and only 20mins from Maryhill Rd on a good day (follow A81, the Milngavie rd, to Strathblane). Not new (refurbed '97), but fresh outlook. A civilized lodging to N of city with good restau (1 AA rosette) and more informal brasserie. Rms individual, reasonably well appointed; carefully chosen pictures.
10RMS JAN-DEC T/T PETS CC KIDS EXP

478
MAP 1
D3
BOTHWELL BRIDGE HOTEL, BOTHWELL: 01698 852246. Uddingston t/off from M74, 15km SE of centre. Main St. Nr castle (478/O/SIDE GLAS) and pub (648/'UNSPOILT' PUBS). Comfortable, family-run hotel with an Italian ambience. V kid-friendly.
90RMS JAN-DEC T/T XPETS CC KIDS EXP

479
MAP 6
B3
CULCREUCH CASTLE HOTEL, FINTRY: 01360 860555. Off B818 in Campsie Fells, 32km N of centre via A81 Milngavie rd from Glas. Fintry is well kept and in a valley betw the Fells and the Fintry Hills. Some fine walking (714/WALKS O/SIDE THE CITY). Ancestral home of the Galbraiths with many old features, incl a half-tester bed. Dungeons converted into bar/bistro. Many weddings, so check w/ends.
8RMS JAN-DEC T/T PETS CC KIDS TOS MED.INX

480
MAP 1
C2
THE INVERKIP HOTEL, INVERKIP: 01475 521478. M8 from Glas then A8 and A78 from Pt Glas heading S for Largs. 50km W of centre. Inverkip is a wee bypassed village now dominated from the other side of the main rd by the Kip Marina (1910/WATERSPORTS). Hotel is in Main St; a family-run coaching inn with busy pub downstairs. The most reasonable place to stay on this part of the Clyde coast.
6RMS JAN-DEC X/T PETS CC KIDS INX

481
MAP 1
A4
KIRKTON HOUSE, CARDROSS: 01389 841951. Darleith Rd. A814, past Helensburgh to Cardross village then N up Darleith Rd. Kirkton House is 1km on rt. 18th-century Scottish farmhouse that combines rustic charm with *every* mod con (check your web site). Informal and unpretentious ('no hang-ups'), quality home-cooking and a stone's throw from L Lomond. International clientele.
6 RMS FEB-NOV T/T PETS CC KIDS MED.INX

THE BEST CAMPING AND CARAVAN PARKS

482
MAP 1
D3
STRATHCLYDE PARK: 01698 266155. 20km SE of Glas. M74 at jnct 6 or M8/A725. On the edge of a large popular country park and easily reached by the motorway system. Go left just after park entrance. Check in until 9.30pm. Stay up to 2 weeks. Usual but good standard facs on site and many others nearby, e.g. café, windsurfing, gym till 8.30pm, 500m away. Motorway close, so traffic noise, but no visual intrusion on this well-managed parkland site. Caravans and tents separate. Glasgow's most accessible caravan park by car. 250 pitches. Apr-Oct. (1398/COUNTRY PARKS)

483
MAP 1
C3
BARNBROCK, LOCHWINNOCH: 01505 614791. 40km SW of Glas via M8/A8 Pt Glas then Kilmacolm rd A761, then B786; or via Johnstone on A737, A760 to Lochwinnoch. Let's face it, it's not exactly convenient, but this beautiful, remote site (camping only) is on the edge of the wild and wonderful Muirshiel Country Park and Lochwinnoch Nature Reserve, and it's not far to go to leave the city behind completely. 15 tents. (1584/WILDLIFE)

484
MAP 1
C2
CLOCH CARAVAN PARK, GOUROCK: 01475 632675. 45km W of Glas along the coast. Take M8 then A8 through Greenock and Gourock; continue for 6km. Residential caravan park (no tents) with only a few touring pitches. Best feature is that it o/looks the historical Cloch Pt Lighthouse and the R Clyde. 10 places only.

485 **TULLICHEWAN, BALLOCH:** 01389 759475. 40km NW of Glas. A fair distance
MAP 6 from the city, but fast rds in this direction via A82 (dual carriageway all the
B3 way), or via Erskine Br and then M8. Best to leave the car here and take frequent train service from Balloch Stn nearby; 30mins to Glas Central Stn. This
park is nicely situated nr L Lomond and tourist centres, and is well managed
and good fun for kids. Shop, laundrette, games rm, TV, sauna, sunbeds, etc.
Probably the best park for holiday-making hereabouts. 140 places.

486 **ARDLUI, LOCH LOMOND:** 01301 704243. Continue on A82 (*from above*). At
MAP 6 the other end of the loch in an ideal spot for exploring by boat (they have hir-
A2 ing facs and a 100 berth marina) or on foot. For self-catering, 6-8 berth caravans are available and there's an on-site hotel (11 rms, 2 bars and 2 restaus) if
your tent blows away in the night. Laundry, children's play area, shop. 97
places.

487
B2 ✓ ✓ **NAIRN'S:** 353 0707. 13 Woodside Cres, nr Charing Cross. Ubiquitous telly chef Nick Nairn's notable and first Glas venture (another restau imminent at time of going to press) on 2 floors in this W End town house (accom in 4 rms upstairs – 444/BEST HOTELS). Hits all the right spots in urban contemporary dining – smart, confident cuisine and service. You'd be hard put to find anywhere else of this quality at these prices. *Michelin Bib Gourmand* '99.

MED

488
C3 ✓ ✓ **GAMBA:** 572 0899. 225a W George St. Mellow minimalist seafood restau in basement at corner of W Campbell St. Brave opposition in the seafood stakes to Two Fat Ladies (*see below*) in a city more inclined to the other steaks, but owner Alan Tomkins of Papingo (505/BEST BISTROS) knows exactly what he's doing and, as expected, the wine list is well chosen. Fashionable foodie choice for '99 and winner of the Highland Spring Restaurant of the Year. Lunch and dinner. LO 10.30pm. Cl Sun. (577/SEAFOOD RESTAUS)

MED

489
B2 ✓ ✓ **STRAVAIGIN:** 334 2665. 28-30 Gibson St. Constantly changing, innovative and consciously eclectic menu from award-winning chef Colin Clydesdale. Mixes cuisines, esp Asian and Pacific Rim. Pleasant café-bar upstairs is more continental. Excellent, affordable food without the foodie formalities and open later than most. One of 2 Glas restaus with 3 AA rosettes '99 (other is One Devonshire Gardens). Mon-Thu 12noon-12midnight, Fri-Sat 12noon-1am, Sun 5pm-12midnight.

INX

490
xB1 ✓ ✓ **ONE DEVONSHIRE GARDENS:** 339 2001. Glasgow's most stylish hotel (1/BEST HOTELS) has a restau which has won accolades in its own rt. Like the sumptuous surroundings, dishes on the fixed-price menu are contemporary, voguish and seductive. Staff are young and friendly. All in all, a smart food experience that doesn't feel like you're in a hotel.

EXP

491
C3 ✓ **ROCOCO:** 221 5004. 202 W George St. corner of Wellington St and just along from Bouzy Rouge to which it is related (522/BISTROS). But this is the upmarket, fine dining and impeccable service version. Excl contemp menu has the lot in the mix. Nice private dining area and smokers courtyard o/side for post-prandial chat and coffee. Lunch and LO 10.30pm, cl Sun.

492
A3 ✓ **AIRORGANIC:** 564 5201. 36 Kelvingrove St. Much-applauded, media-friendly bar/café and upstairs restau in the former Bar Miro. Proprietor Colin McDougal and designer Dene Happell have created an airy and stylish ambience for the purposefully organic bar and cuisine. This includes beer and wine list, bar snacks and a full menu upstairs. All as organic as poss. Menu not vegn – does include meat and fish. Bar: food LO 9pm. Restau LO 11pm, 12midnight w/ends. (668/PUB FOOD)

INX

493
D3 ✓ **YES:** 221 8044. 22 W Nile St. Downtown and downstairs (though street-level café-bar is a good place to meet and the 'Express Menu' one of the best-value light meals in town) is the airy and uncluttered creation of Ferrier Richardson. Some Asian/Pacific influence to superbly balanced dishes presented with flair and no fuss. Lunch and LO 11pm (upstairs 9pm). Both cl Sun.

MED

494
B3 ✓ **THE BUTTERY:** 221 8188. 652 Argyle St. Central but curious location for Glas's most consistently superb restau owned, as is the Rogano (*see below*), by Alloa Breweries. Occupying the only remaining tenement block in an area carved up by urban developers, the Buttery and its little brother downstairs, the Belfry (515/BEST BISTROS), are best reached via the westerly extension of St Vincent St then Elderslie St. Comfortable old-fashioned elegance will probably outlive most of the makeovers in these pages. Don't miss the winning sample-all-desserts option. 6 days, lunch and 7-10pm. Cl Sun and Sat lunch.

EXP

495
A1 ✓ **THE UBIQUITOUS CHIP:** 334 5007. 12 Ashton Lane. A cornerstone of culinary Glasgow. 2-storey, covered courtyard draped with vines, off a bar strewn cobbled lane in the heart of the W End, heaped with accolades over 27 yrs in residence. The main bit is still one of the most atmospheric of rms. The menu is exemplary Scottish seafood, the best of seafood, game and beef and

fine, original cooking. An outstanding wine list. Chip upstairs is cheaper. (519/BISTROS). Daily lunch and 6.30-11pm. EXP

496 ✓ **TWO FAT LADIES:** 339 1944. 88 Dumbarton Rd, along from Kelvingrove
A2 Museum nr the end of Byres Rd. Calum Mathieson's long-established seafood bistro still takes the best line on fish in the city. Easy on the eye and palate (nothing too fancy) and for this degree of integrity and reliability, easy on the pocket. Simply sound. Tue-Sat LO 10pm, lunch Fri-Sat only. Cl Sun. (576/SEAFOOD RESTAUS) MED

497 ✓ **THAI FOUNTAIN:** 332 2599. 2 Woodside Cres, Charing Cross. Same own-
B2 ership as Amber Regent (*see below*), this is probably Glasgow's best Asian restau. Genuinely Thai and not at all Chinese. Innovative dishes with gr diversity of flavours and textures, so sharing several is best. Of course you will eat too much. Cl Sun. (555/FAR-EASTERN RESTAUS) MED

498 ✓ **LA PARMIGIANA:** 334 0686. 447 Gr Western Rd. Simply the best Italian
B1 for many discriminating Glaswegians (convenient location nr Kelvin Br – usually parking nearby), the favourite posh place to eat without the ceremony and dulcet tones. Contemporary, perhaps predictable, cuisine. For when you can't face anything that isn't lightly done in olive oil. LO 11pm. Cl Sun. (524/ITALIAN RESTAUS) MED

499 ✓ **ROGANO:** 248 4055. 11 Exchange Pl. Betw Buchanan St and Queen St. An
D3 institution in Glas since the 1930s. Décor replicating a Cunard ship, the *Queen Mary*, is the major attraction. *The* place to take visiting friends or clients, even if just for cocktails. Restau spacious, perennially fashionable, with fish and seafood the specialities. Downstairs has a lighter/cheaper menu, and though a bit sub-Rogano its informality is easier on the pocket. Restaurant: lunch and 6-10.30pm. Café Rogano: lunch and 6-11pm (Fri-Sat until 12midnight, Sun until 10pm). EXP.MED

500 **THE CABIN:** 569 1036. 996 Dumbarton Rd. Beautifully cooked fresh seafood
xA2 and Scottish game, home-made Irish soda bread and delicious puds. You'll probably have to linger after dinner, when Wilma, legendary waitress and *chanteuse*, does her diva thing. A Glas original. BYOB if you like. Tue-Fri lunch, Tue-Sat dinner. LO 9pm. MED

501 **PUPPET THEATRE:** 339 8444. 11 Ruthven Lane. In a converted mews behind
A1 Byres Rd, one of Scotland's most stylish restaus. Intimate dining areas; the crescent-shaped conservatory is the most popular and may be tightly packed. Fixed-price menus. Contemporary British with Scottish slant. Chefs do come and go a bit. Lunch (not Sat); LO 10.30pm. Cl Mon. EXP

502 **BUDDA:** 243 2212. 142 St Vincent St. Downstairs bar with N African slant and
D3 this atmospheric restau behind the drapes at the back. Good fusion cooking with all the right contemporary references. Mon-Sat lunch and LO 10.30pm. Sun dinner only. INX

AMBER REGENT: 50 W Regent St. Report: 559/FAR-EASTERN.

KILLERMONT POLO CLUB: 2002 Maryhill Rd. Report: 545/INDIAN.

THE BEST BISTROS AND CAFÉ-BARS

503 **MITCHELLS:** 204 4312. 2 branches, both W. 157 N St on the left bank of
C3 M8 at the Mitchell Library, next to the Bon Accord (656/REAL-ALE PUBS).
Ales here too, but notably *the* place for informal and v good food with a gen-
uine bistro atmos. Intimate, more colourful version in busy Ashton Lane off
Byres Rd (339 2220) has helpful BYOB, inx pre-theatre menu and more laid-
back atmos. Both have food until 11pm, bar till 12midnight. Cl Sun.   INX

504 **MALMAISON:** 221 6401. 278 W George St. The brasserie in the basement
C3 of the hotel (441/BEST HOTELS) with the same setup in Edin and a v similar
menu. Excellent brasserie ambience in meticulously designed woody salon.
Seating layout and busy waiters mean lots of buzz; also private dining-rms and
the adjacent **CAFÉ MAL** in bright contrast. Fixed-menu lunch or dinner
Mediterranean style with daily specials. 7 days, lunch and LO 10.30pm.   MED

505 **PAPINGO:** 332 6678. 104 Bath St. Bright bistro in a cool basement an
C3 enduring success story and still feels ... well good enough to eat. The food
is Scottish/French and perfectly portioned, esp for pre-theatre dinner. Wines
and waiters are esp well chosen. A smooth operation! Daily till 10.30/11pm.
INX

506 **BABY GRAND:** 248 4942. 3-7 Elmbank Grds. Inviting haven among high-
C3 rise office blocks opp hotel (453/LESS EXP HOTELS); a downtown-USA location. (Go behind the King's Theatre down Elmbank St, rt at gas stn and look for
the hotel.) Narrow rm with bar stools and banquettes, often with background
music from resident mad pianist. Light, eclectic menu from tapas to full meals
materialize in the tiny gantry. Daily 8am-12midnight/1am.   CHP

507 **GROUCHO ST JUDES:** 352 8800. 190 Bath St. Ground floor restau/bistro
D3 of the hotel (450/LESS EXP HOTELS)outpost of the Soho hostelry we've all
read about. Not so bohemian rhapsody and no sign of Robbie Coltrane or
Williams, but a fairly stylish station on the far northern line. Almost excludes
anyone who isn't self-important somehow. Fortunately there's a lot of us. Can't
remember what the food's like.   MED

508 **TUN TON:** 572 1230. 157 Hope St nr corner of St Vincent St. Cool, current,
D3 has been described as 'retro-futurist': from chairs to mirrored ceiling tiles
very Graven Images. Bar/restau downstairs and mezzanine at the back.
Accessible smart food and friendly New World wine list. Pre-theatre menu inx
and otherwise good value maintaining early promise will depend on the chef.
Lunch and dinner, Sun dinner only. LO 10.30pm but bar till 12midnight.   MED

509 **BLUE BAR CAFÉ:** The Lighthouse, Mitchell Lane. Opened after going to press,
D3 the first Glas venture of Andrew Radford and intended to be a replica of his
highly-regarded Edin café/bar of the same name. 7 days, 10am-12midnight
(11pm Sun/Mon). **THE DOOCOT**, an organic café and bar by the people who
brought us Antipasti (528/ITALIANS) is on the top floor of The Lighthouse. More
fashion than food. Same hrs as Blue.   INX

510 **COTTIER'S:** 357 5827. 93 Hyndland Rd. Off the top of Hyndland St nr
xA1 Highburgh Rd. Converted church that encompasses a bar; regular live music
(693/LIVE MUSIC) and benches o/side, a restau with an interesting menu made
up of light, spicy dishes and a theatre that stages a broad range of music
throughout the yr. A v broad church. (622/SUN BREAKFAST and other references.) 7 days.   INX

511 **JANSSENS:** 334 9682. 1355 Argyle St opp Kelvingrove Art Gallery. I missed it
A2 out last time and hundreds of people complained. Ok, you go there, you like
it – it's unpretentious, gr atmos (esp at night). You feel safe. It's because I'm not
Glaswegian, it's because oops ... I've never been there. Now I have. OK I agree.
It's in the book. 7 days noon-late.   INX

512 **16 BYRES RD:** 339 2544. 16 Byres Rd. Tiny restau at the tackier end of Byres Rd
A2 in a site that has seen many menus. Now at last a winning combo – good bistro
food, no fuss and inx. Sublime puds. Lunch and LO 10pm. Cl Sun. Best book! INX

513 **MADELEINE'S:** 564 1233. 1138 Argyle St. Far W in Argyle St, this friendly bistro
A3 is a bit of a secret. Homemade rather than trying to be trendy. All v

Glaswegian; some jazz and as they say, 'it rocks'. Open all day from 12noon. LO 10.30pm. INX

514 **STAZIONE:** 576 7576. 1057 Gr Western Rd. Nr Gartnavel Hospital, which for
xB1 non-Glaswegians means a long way down Gr Western Rd from the Botanic corner. Informal bar/bistro bit of the rather more formal **LUX** (upstairs). Mediterranean/Italian, relaxed ambience. O/side tables in summer. 7days, lunch and 5-11pm. INX

515 **THE BELFRY:** 221 0630. 652 Argyle St. App via W extension of St Vincent St,
B3 Elderslie St and left at the conical church. The basement of the Buttery, one of Glas's finest restaus (494/BEST RESTAUS), in the one remaining tenement of an area savaged by the M8. Bistro version of the Scots/French cuisine served up top, in study-like cellar rms with dark wood and books. Mon-Sat lunch, 6-11pm. Cl Sun.

516 **LOOP:** 572 1472. 64 Ingram St, Merchant City. Main Rd for traffic nr
E4 Fruitmarket venue. Contemp cafe-restau, light and stylish design. Seems like there's a lot like this in Glas, but Loop may last. From risotto to bangers and mash, so hits most of the now buttons. We shall see (you there). 7 days, 11am – LO 10.30pm. MED

517 **CUL DE SAC:** 334 8899. 44 Ashton Lane, the main lane off Byres Rd with the
A1 Grosvenor Cinema (775/NIGHTLIFE) and The Ubiquitous Chip (495/BEST RESTAUS). Perennially fashionable crêperie/diner dedicated to serving good, simple food with flair, even wit. The atmos is relaxed and conversational, the burgers are exceptional and the fresh exotic flowers add a final *touché* (623/SUN BREAKFAST). Daily 12noon-11pm (Fri-Sat 12midnight). CHP

518 **BAR BREL:** 342 4966. 39 Ashton Lane. Another Billy McAnnanie (Baby Grand,
A1 Cottiers) translation of an idea from elsewhere. This is a Gallic bar/bistro across the lane from the Cul de Sac (*see above*). Flagstone floor, metal tables and enormous folding doors. No mistaking the Belgian influence in the cooking; fat, crispy chips served with large bowls of steaming mussels, or with steak. No Belgian jokes, but Belgian beers and a good wine list. Daily 11am-11pm (Fri-Sat till 12midnight). INX

519 **UPSTAIRS AT THE CHIP:** 334 5007. 12 Ashton Lane. At other end of lane from
A1 Cul de Sac (*see above*) and upstairs from The Ubiquitous Chip (495/BEST RESTAUS), this is the wine bar and cheap seats version of the celebrated restau. Some tables are around the gallery of the courtyard below. There's a different menu with some similar seafood and puds, as well as bar-type salads and soups, etc. The bill will be less and you still get the celebrated wine list. Lively atmos from the adj bar. LO 10.45pm. (624/SUN BREAKFAST) INX

520 **TRON CAFÉ-BAR:** 552 8587. 63 Trongate. Attached to the important Tron
E4 Theatre (781/NIGHTLIFE), has undergone a major face-lift. The buzzing bar/bistro at the back has New Glas clientele, decent house wines and an eclectic menu. Not always the best grub in the city, but definitely up there for atmos and generally good vibes. Food until 10.30/11pm. Cl Sun evening. CHP

521 **BARGO:** 553 4771. 80 Albion St. Huge bar and bistro in lofty stylish design. Big
E4 windows through which to watch the further transformation of the Merchant City. The menu is a bit of a contemporary mix and match, but ain't bad considering this is more of a bar to be seen in (dreaming of Manhattan). Popular pre-club venue (676/PRE-CLUB BARS) but often quiet midweek. 7 days, 10am-12midnight. LO for food 7pm. INX

522 **BOUZY ROUGE:** 221 8804. 111 W Regent St. Sister restau of the Bouzy Rouge
C3 in Airdrie (01236 763853) and now in Edin, this is an excellent unpretentious downtown bistro. Owned by the Brown family, it repeats the Airdrie formula of eclectic, affordable contemporary food and wine. Gr for breakfast and Sun lunch. 7 days, 9.30am-12midnight. Sun 12noon-12midnight. LO 10pm. Popular; booking may be necessary. INX

FIREBIRD: 1321 Argyle St. Report: 534/BEST PIZZA.

ARTHOUSE GRILL: Basement, 129 Bath St. Report: 440/HOTELS.

523
D3 ✓✓ **SARTI:** 248 2228, 133 Wellington St, and 204 0440 (best number for bookings), 121 Bath St. Glasgow's famed *emporio d'Italia* combining a deli in Wellington St, wine shop in Bath St and restaus in each. Gr bustling atmos. Cultivated and celebrated by anyone who has ever managed to get a table at lunchtime. Good pizza, specials change every day, *dolci* and *gelati* in super-calorific abundance. You may wait! LO 10.30pm. Cl Sun. (536/PIZZA, 584/COFFEE)   CHP

524
B1 ✓ **LA PARMIGIANA:** 334 0686. 447 Gr Western Rd. Sophisticated ristorante that blends trad service and contemporary Italian cuisine into a seamless performance. Carefully chosen dishes and wine list; solicitous service. Milano rather than Napoli. Expect to find Italians (who consider this to be one of the city's gr restaus – 498/BEST RESTAUS). Mon-Sat lunch and 6-11pm. Cl Sun.   MED

525
B4 ✓ **LA FIORENTINA:** 420 1585. 2 Paisley Rd W. Not far from river and motor-way over Kingston Br, but app from Eglinton St (A77 Kilmarnock Rd). It's at the Y-jnct with Govan Rd. Trad tratt Little Tuscany (and pizzeria next door) in an imposing listed building with an angel on top. Always busy, usually seafood specials and off-hand waiters who break into the occasional aria. As Italian as you want it to be, gr atmos with enormous menu and wine list. Mon-Sat lunch and 5.30-11pm (though LO 9.30pm). Cl Sun.   MED

526
D3 **RISTORANTE CAPRESE:** 332 3070. 217 Buchanan St. Basement café nr the Concert Hall. Glaswegians (and footballers) love this place judging by the rogues' gallery of happy smiling punters. Checked tablecloths and crooning in the background create the authentic 'mamma mia' atmos. Friendly service, constantly mobbed (well, not *mobbed*). LO 10/11pm. Book at w/ends.   INX

527
C3 **PAPERINO'S:** 332 3800. 283 Sauchiehall St. When you look into it, you find good restaus of a certain type are often owned by the same people. That explains why this ordinary-looking though smart restau is better than the rest – it's the Giovanazzi brothers who also own La Parmigiana (*see above*) and The Big Blue (670/PUB FOOD). Pasta and pizza here are always just fine. 7 days. LO 11pm/12midnight.   INX

528
A1 **ANTIPASTI:** 337 2737. 337 Byres Rd. Popular restau on 2 levels that spills onto the st in warm weather, bringing a touch of *la dolce vita* to the corner of Observatory Rd. Good pasta. Breakfast time until late (12midnight w/ends). Also at 305 Sauchiehall St (332 9002). Same hours, food, and same vibe. 7 days. LO 10.30pm.   INX

529
B1 **TREVI:** 334 3262. 526 Gr Western Rd. Tiny family-run tratt with celebrity pho-tos next to cool football memorabilia on the walls. The staff can get a bit dis-tracted on international fixture nights. Loyal clientele; specials change every day. Tasty home-made focaccia. Mon-Fri lunch and 6-10.30pm, Sat-Sun 6-10.30pm.   INX

530
xC5 **ARIGO:** 636 6616. 67 Kilmarnock Rd, Shawlands. Smart little Italian joint on busiest stretch of this main drag. Waiters in the long aprons-u-like. Spare, colour-tint décor. Some surprises on the menu, e.g. *pollo e crozzo risotto* (with mussels). Proper wines. 7 days, lunch and dinner. 7 days LO 10.30pm.   INX

531
D3 **FAZZI'S:** 332 0941. 67 Cambridge St. Across the rd from the Glas Thistle Hotel. This once gr deli/café (and some say it's gone rt down the pasta tube) includ-ed here more for nostalgia than now. Decent cappuccino. Mon-Sat 8am-10pm, Sun 11am-9pm.   INX

532
xB1 **LA SCARPETTA, BALLOCH:** 01389 758247 Balloch Rd nr the bridge. Not per-haps many reasons to linger in Balloch – the loch (Lomond) here is not one of them, but this family – run restau is. Fave of writer A. L. Kennedy and she ain't easy to please. 7 days LO 10.30pm   INX

THE BIG BLUE: 445 Gr Western Rd. Report: 670/PUB FOOD.

LA VIGNA: Lanark. Report: 810/CLYDE VALLEY.

THE BEST PIZZA

533   ✓   **PIZZA EXPRESS:** 221 3333. 151 Queen St and 402 Sauchiehall St (332
D4, D3   ✓   6965). The national chain who set the pizza standard here in 2 well-situ-
ated and classy restaus. Always a reliable standby when pizza's the only thing
you can agree on and it's sometimes handy that you can't book.

534   ✓   **FIREBIRD:** 334 0594. 1321 Argyle St. Big-windowed, spacious bistro at
A3   ✓   the far W end of Argyle St. Mixed modern menu but notable for wood-
smoked dishes, of which their light, imaginative pizzas are excellent. 11am-
12midnight (till 1am w/ends).   INX

535   **LITTLE ITALY:** 339 6287. 205 Byres Rd. Ready-made slices and 3 sizes of
A1   superb made-to-order takeaway pies. You'll have to wait, but it's worth it. Have
a coffee. Mon-Thu 8am-10pm, Fri-Sat 8am-1am, Sun 5-10pm. (631/TAKEAWAY)

536   **SARTI:** 248 2228. 133 Wellington St and 121 Bath St. Excellent, thin-crust pie,
D3   buffalo mozzarella and freshly-made *pomodoro*. 6 days, 8am-10pm. Cl Sun.
Full report: 523/ITALIAN RESTAUS.

537   **SAL E PEPE:** 341 0999. 18 Gibson St. Nr Glas Univ, this is the newest of the new
B2   crop of Tuscan-influenced Italian bistros and part of the Di Maggio family
chain (610/KID-FRIENDLY). Good thin-crust base and a chilli *pomodoro* option
that makes a change for veggies. 7 days, 9.30am-11pm.

538   **CINE CITTÀ:** 332 6789. 327 Sauchiehall St. Trad oven-baked, thin-based pizza
C3   with all the usual freshly-prepared goodies that go on top; in the nite-zone. 7
days until 11pm.

539   **SANNINO:** 332 8025, 61 Bath St, and 332 3565, 61 Elmbank St. Famous for its
D3, C3   enormous 16 inch pizzas, made for sharing. You can half and half the toppings. 7 days, 12noon-12midnight.

THE BEST FRENCH RESTAURANTS

540   **78 ST VINCENT:** 221 7710. 78 St Vincent St. Impressive split-level rm with an
D3   enormously high ceiling and a big mural by Glas artist Donald McLeod. Stylish
cuisine balancing the tried and tested with some touches of originality.
Slightly formal with an atmos of discreet efficiency. Not bad wines. Lunch (not
Sun) and LO 10.30pm (10.45pm Sat-Sun).   MED

541   **THE BRASSERIE:** 248 3801. 176 W Regent St. Related to Rogano (499/BEST
C3   RESTAUS), so seafood is their forte and menu has seasonal v Scottish note. Busy
in evenings, but you can usually find a nook for that tête-à-tête. Here you will
find a genuine steak tartare. Good wine list, especially bin-ends and halves.
Mon-Fri 12noon-11pm, Sat lunch and 6-11pm. Sun, parties only.   MED

542   **FROGGIE'S:** 572 0007. 53 W Regent St. Café/bistro with French owners and
C3   French home-cooking app. Gone a bit cajun/creole of late, but there are still a
few reminders left, viz the classic Marseillaise *soupe de poisson*. Bustling
brasserie atmos. Some reasonable wines and you can BYOB. Open every day,
best to book at w/ends. Mon-Sat 9am-12midnight; Sun 5pm-12midnight. INX

543   **PIERRE VICTOIRE:** 221 7565, 91 Miller St, and 221 9130, 165 Hope St. Two sur-
D4, D3   viving Pierres from the shakedown which followed Pierre Levicky's 'bankrupt-
cy' and general demise. Hope St was always a separate concern and showed
more flair than most in its high-ceilinged two-chambered room. It's still a res-
onable lunch and French bistro supper at v affordable prices. Lunch and 5-
10.30pm.   INX

544   **CAFÉ DU SUD:** 332 2054. 8 Clarendon St. Popular intimate restau tucked away
C2   behind St George's Cross. Mediterranean/French-style cooking from hus-
band-and-wife team who run it with an emphasis on the personal touch.
Everything seems fresh and home-made. Better book. Tue-Sat 12noon-3pm
and 6-10.30pm. Cl Sun and Mon. Lunch Fri/Sat only, Dinner Tues-Sat LO
9.45pm   INX

THE BEST INDIAN RESTAURANTS

545
xC1
✓ **KILLERMONT POLO CLUB:** 946 5412. 2022 Maryhill Rd. The more genuine traditions of the days of the Raj are still in evidence at Killermont. Within a hill-top restau, at the Milngavie end of Maryhill Rd, you will find courteous manners, attentive service and a clubby atmos in the front rm, which is kept as a shrine to all things polo (and they *do* run their own team). The food is fresh, light and the spices are sprinkled with care. Here Indian cuisine is taken seriously and they experiment – the introduction of their Dum Pukht menu (slow cooked) has been a huge success. Lunch seriously inx. Lunch (not Sun) and 5pm-12midnight (LO 10.30pm).
MED

546
B3
✓ **MOTHER INDIA:** 221 1663. 28 Westminster Terr. A kitchen-style restau where 'on-the-bone', a touchstone of authentic Indian home-cooking, is used to gr effect. Tired of the old trad buffet round, they've devised a new app where you can make up your own buffet – as many dishes as you like all freshly prepared. Lots of vegn choice. V relaxed neighbourhood atmos. BYOB. 7 days, lunch and LO 11pm, 11.30pm Fri/Sat.
INX

547
B3
✓ **CRÈME DE LA CRÈME:** 221 3222. 1071 Argyle St. The biggest, the most flash (and god knows they love flash) restau in town – or anywhere for that matter – so *they* say. Still at the hot edge of all things curried and they even show movies (*sic*), incl cartoons (612/KID-FRIENDLY). Frequently busy with office parties and leaving-dos, which keeps the place buzzing. Behind the flambé and the razzmatazz this is a restau that is run with care and, dare we say, precision. 7 days, lunch (not Sun) and LO 11pm.
MED

548
A1, B3
✓ **ASHOKA ASHTON LANE:** 357 5904. 19 Ashton Lane. Front-line curry shop for students from Glasgow Univ, just up the lane. V popular, v customer-led, so the food is strong on flavour and generously portioned. Can do no wrong, some say. **ASHOKA WEST END:** 339 0936. 1284 Argyle St. Has always been a good, simple and dependable place to go for curry, but now seeming pricey to the faithful. Still, the healthy option menu is a good idea and on Sun family night, kids eat free. Both 7 days, lunch and open till 12midnight (W End even later).
INX

549
B3
MR SINGH'S INDIA: 204 0186. 149 Elderslie St. In an area stuffed with curry houses, this one shows panache and some design. Menu is a triumph of trying to please. And they do. 7 days, lunch and LO 11.30pm.
INX

550
B3
CAFÉ INDIA: 248 4074. 171 N St. Enormous brasserie, big on a glamour that seems a bit time-warped now, but the food is pretty good. The extensive menu is busy with herbs and spices and is not merely hot. A night on the town kind of joint. Buffet and à la carte, Sun-Mon. 7 days, lunch and LO 11.30pm/12midnight.
INX

551
B1
SHISH MAHAL: 339 8256. 68 Park Rd. First-generation Indian restau that still, after 30 yrs, remains one of Glasgow's faves. At last in '99 a major refurb has brought it back into the light. Menu also completely recharged and the toilets seriously posh. Many different influences in the cooking. 7 days. Till 11pm/12midnight.
INX

552
C3
KAMA SUTRA: 332 0055. 331 Sauchiehall St. Part of the Ashoka group, this restau has built a reputation for good food. An extensive and adventurous menu where each dish comes with a breakdown of contents and region of origin. Extracts from the original Indian sex-guide dotted here and there are peered at, surreptitiously, but this all seems a bit ragged now. 7 days, lunch and till 12midnight (Fri-Sat till 1am).
INX

553
B3
THE ASHOKA: 221 1761. 108 Elderslie St. Confusingly, no relation to those above. Designery interior but that old pink pakora sauce still runs through the veins. Once voted No. 1 in the 'Best curry houses in Scotland' – that's a matter of taste but it is hot (and hot). Mon-Sat lunch, 7 days dinner. LO 11.30pm. INX

554
xC5
SHIMLA PINKS: 423 4488. 777 Pollokshaws Rd. V serviceable Indian restau in Shawlands on the S side of town. Another branch in Johnstone (01505 322588 at 4 William St) and part of a national chain hailing from Brum. Only Indian restau in Glas recommended by Michelin. 7 days. Cl lunch Sat/Sun. LO 11.30pm.
INX

THE BEST FAR-EASTERN RESTAURANTS

555
B2
✓ **THAI FOUNTAIN:** 332 2599. 2 Woodside Cres. Charing Cross, nr M8, Mitchell Library, etc. The best Thai in town (and probably in Scotland). Owned by Chinese Mr Chung (*see* Amber Regent, *below*), but the Thai chefs know a green curry from a red. Tom yam excellent and weeping tiger beef v popular with those who really just want a steak. Lots of prawn and fish dishes and real vegn choice. Lunch and LO 11pm. Cl Sun.   MED

556
A3
✓ **THAI SIAM:** 229 1191. 1191 Argyle St (W End side). Trad homely (if crepuscular) atmos but fashionable clientele who swear it has the prawniest crackers and greenest curry in town. Prop/chef Pawina Kennedy ensures authenticity and a packed house at w/ends. Lunch Mon-Fri LO 11pm. Cl Sun.   MED

557
A2
✓ **FUSION:** 339 3666. 41 Byres Rd. Small, stylish and reasonably authentic Japanese bistro at bottom end of Byres Rd. Beef, chicken, salmon and vegn sushi/sashimi combos. Generally minimalist approach, incl wines and puds. Excellent value (how do they do it?). Lunch Tue-Sat, dinner Tue-Sun, 6pm-12midnight (but they may close earlier and the chefs do dictate).   CHP

558
E4
✓ **MAO:** 564 5161. Corner of Brunswick and Wilson St in Merchant City. Bright, hip east-Asian restau transplanted not of course, from Bejing but from Dublin. Good service, right-on wine-list. Open all day. 7 days. LO 10/11pm.   INX

559
D3
✓ **AMBER REGENT:** 331 1655. 50 W Regent St. Elegant Cantonese restau that prides itself on courteous service and the quality of its food. The menu is trad with dishes designed to be eaten using chopsticks, although cutlery, of course, is provided. Candle-lit booths, sumptuous décor and a creditable wine list. Quite romantic, and just about always in *Michelin*. Lunch, LO 11pm (Fri 11.30pm, Sat 12midnight). Cl Sun.   MED

560
D4
HO WONG: 221 3550. 82 York St, in city centre nr river, betw Clyde St and Argyle St. Discreet, urbane Pekingese/Cantonese restau which relies on its reputation and makes few compromises. Décor dated now, but still up-market clientele; roomful of suits at lunch and champagne list. Notable for seafood and duck. Good Szechuan. Lunch (not Sun) and LO 11.30pm.   MED

561
D3
PEKING INN: 332 8971. 191 Hope St. The revolving hot-plate/server at the centre of the table was an innovation when introduced here. Since then there has been many a slip 'twixt cup and lip in the course of lengthy, exploratory meals fuelled by endless hot saki. Famous for its spicy, Szechuan specials; and good times. Lunch and LO 11.15pm (w/ends 12.15am).   MED

562
C3
LOON FUNG: 332 1240. 417 Sauchiehall St. Poss Glasgow's most 'respected' Cantonese restaurants. Traditionally the place where the local Chinese community meet for lunch with their families and on a Sun/Mon/Tue, the pace is fast and friendly while the food, as you would expect, is fresh and authentic. Everybody on chopsticks. 7 days, 12noon-10/11pm.   MED

563
C3
THE NOODLE BAR: 333 1883. 482 Sauchiehall St. Authentic, Chinese-style noodle bar, 100m from Charing Cross. Along with **CANTON EXPRESS** opp at 407 Sauchiehall St (332 0145), two gr fast food joints with genuine, made on the spot – in the wok – food late into the AM. Quite groovy. 7days, 12noon-5am. (616/615/LATE-NIGHT RESTAUS)   CHP

564
A1
AMBER RESTAURANT: 339 6121. 130 Byres Rd. Trad Chinese restau with an informal attitude and helpful staff. Recently extended selection of vegn dishes. V popular takeaway/home-delivery service; their chow mein is the best in the W End. Lunch except Sat-Sun and 5-11.30pm.   INX

565
C2
CHINA TOWN: 353 0037. 42 New City Rd. Out of centre and out of Glasgow; in fact you're in Hong Kong (almost). Endless food for lunch (esp Sun) or dinner. Divine dim sum. If you love Chinese food, you must come here. 7 days, noon – 11.30pm.   INX

566
D4
ICHIBAN: 204 4200. 50 Queen St. Upstairs noodle bar based loosely on the Wagamama formula. Ramen, udon, soba noodle dishes; also chow meins, tempuras and other Japanese snacks. Long tables, eat-as-it-comes 'methodology'. Light, calm, hip. Lunch and LO 11pm (10pm Sun).   INX

THE BEST MEXICAN RESTAURANTS

Glas has innumerable restaus and café-bars with Mexican choices on a menu that mixes food from all over (best to stick to the potato skins). The places below are close to genuine Mex (UK style):

567 **PANCHO VILLAS:** 552 7737. 26 Bell St. Bright, colourful restau free of the clut-
E4 tered cantina stereotype, run by real, live Mexican, Maira Nunez. Menu in Spanish/ingredients in English. No burritos ('an American invention'). Plenty of veggie choices but you really have to try the *albondigas en salsa* (that's spicy meatballs). Mon-Sat lunch and 6-11pm, Sun until 10pm.   INX

568 **CANTINA DEL REY:** 552 4044. 6 King's Court in E End nr St Enoch's glasshouse.
D4 Frozen margaritas a must in this spacious bar/restau which actually does feel like a cantina. Fajitas (with floury tortillas and spicy dips) a favourite among the *comidas* (which also includes blackened fish) and brought sizzling across the rm to your table. Free nachos; you keep on drinking. 7 days, 12noon till LO 10pm (Fri-Sat till 11pm).   INX

569 **SALSA:** 337 1416. 184 Dumbarton Rd. Western off-shoot of the Cantina (*see*
xA2 *above*), smaller, more neighbourhood-friendly. Spicy salsas of the title and all the things they accompany. As with all Mexican places, food can vary with the chef, most of whom have never been N, never mind S, of the Rio Grande, but here it's more conscientious than most. Good vegn choice. 7 days, 12noon-10pm (Fri 11pm).   INX

570 **TEX MEX:** 332 8338. 198 Bath St. Western extension of original in Edin and
D3 every bit as slammin'. More Tex than Mex, though chicken-fried steak notable by its absence, and howzabout some corn bread while we're at it. Adj Sublime Bar goes a bit Alamo at the w/end. 7 days, lunch and dinner. LO 10-11pm. INX

THE BEST RESTAURANTS FROM AROUND THE WORLD

571 ✓ **OBLOMOV:** 339 9177. 372 Gr Western Rd, nr Kelvinbridge. Bar/restau
B1 with E European 'bohemian' twist. Small (12 tables) raised dining area with light and bar meals during day and heartier à la carte. Most dishes have Euro influence with some classics, e.g. blinis, goulash, strudel. Drink vodka. Often must book! Lunch and LO 8.30pm. Bar till 12midnight/1am. (667/PUB FOOD)   INX

572 **CAFÉ SERGHEI:** 429 1547. 67 Br St, just over the Jamaica St (or Glas) Br. Greek
D4 island evenings on a bleak rd heading S, a restau in an interesting conversion of a former bank with upstairs balcony beneath impressive cupola. In a tough world, this place has survived. Talkative waiters advise and dispense excellent Greek grub, incl vegn dishes. Fri is Greek dancing night. Lunch (not Sun) and 6-11pm, 7 days.   INX

573 **PONTE VECCHIO:** 572 1881. 333 Gt Western Rd opp Oblomov (above) as it
B1 happens. Not a merely Italian restau as you might think from the title and most of the menu, but a Spanish – Italian joint with a genuine paella, risotto and a way with the gambas. Nice place too. 7 days, lunch and LO 10.15pm INX

574 **STRAVAIGIN:** 334 2665. 28-30 Gibson St. The best fusion restau in town with
B2 influences from all over, though mainly E of Suez. Report: 47/BEST RESTAUS.

575 **BAR BREL:** 342 4966. 39 Ashton Lane. Belgian would you believe? Report:
A1 518/BEST BISTROS.

576
A2 ✔ ✔ **TWO FAT LADIES:** 339 1944. 88 Dumbarton Rd. Informal and bright restau that serves some of Glasgow's most underrated food. Quality and freshness of seafood and imaginative cooking, in the hands of chef/proprietor Calum Mathieson. A reliably fine prospect whether you're a fishhead or not, and a bloody good place – no pun, no hype intended. Pre-theatre menu. Sensible short wine list. Mon/Tue-Sat 6-10pm, lunch Fri-Sat. (496/BEST RESTAUS) MED

577
C3 ✔ ✔ **GAMBA:** 572 0899. 225a W George St, in basement at corner of W Campbell St. 1998 addition to the hitherto limited selection of seafood restaus in Glas and an instant catch. Mostly down to stylish setting and snappy service, as well as excellent fresh fish unfussily presented à la mode. Exemplary wine list. Unlike many, open on Mon (cl Sun). Lunch and dinner. LO 10.30pm but may stay open later so check. (488/BEST RESTAUS) MED

578
xB1 ✔ **GINGERHILL:** 956 6515. Hillhead St, Milngavie. Upstairs at the end of the main st in this northern suburb of Glas (you are at the start of the W Highland Way), is a restau run entirely by women mostly from the island of Gigha (like much of the seafood they serve). Fixed menu and daily specials depending on what's landed. Vegn options and some chargrilled meat. One dinner sitting only, Thu-Sat (other nights if there are more than 6 of you); light lunches Mon-Sat. BYOB, no corkage. MED

ROGANO: 11 Exchange Pl. Report: 499/BEST RESTAUS.

579
E4 ✔ **THE 13TH NOTE:** 553 1638. 50-60 King St. Good attitude/good vibes café-bar with sometimes live music downstairs (Tue/Thu). Extended and big range menu from excellent vegeburgers (100% less meat than MacDonald's) to Indian and Greek dishes. All suitable for vegans. Organic booze on offer, but also normal Glas bevvy. 7 days, 12noon-12midnight. Food LO 10.30pm. Also 13th Note Club at Clyde St. (694/LIVE MUSIC).

580
B2, C2 ✔ **GRASSROOTS:** 353 3278. 48 Woodlands Rd. The foremost emporium for all things organic in Glas. Now has a restau round the corner at 97 St Georges Rd (333 0534). This is proper food, prepared before your eyes. Round the world dishes as vegn food should be and some simply splendid salads. Calming as well as healthy. 7 days 10am-10pm. CHP

581
B1 **BAY TREE:** 334 5898. 403 Gr Western Rd. Long-established vegan restau nr Kelvinbridge. Wide range of dishes, esp Greek, Turkish and Arabic (owners are Iraqis). All strictly vegan, the sole concession being a jug of milk marked 'cows'. 7 days till 9pm (Sun till 8pm). (621/SUN BREAKFAST) CHP

582
B1 **CAFÉ ALBA:** 337 2282. 61 Otago St. Popular neighbourhood café with excellent, trad vegn food. Hot dishes of the day, good salads/dressings and homemade cakes, scones and slices. Hungry univ crowd, so there's not much left beyond 2.30pm. Mon-Sat 10am-5pm. (588/BEST TEAROOMS) CHP

583
B3 **THE ASHA:** 221 7144. Elderslie St. Intimate, vegn restau among many other Indians. All dishes can be be made to order; your choice of sauce and chilliness. 3 fixed-price Thalis and a selection of starters that are moreish than most. Some wines, but a jug of lager is probably the answer here. Lunch (except Sun), and 5-11.30pm. INX

THE GRANARY: 82 Howard St, nr St Enoch Centre. Report: 587/BEST TEAROOMS.

Restaurants serving good vegn food but which are not exclusively vegn:

YES, PUPPET THEATRE, THE UBIQUITOUS CHIP and **THAI FOUNTAIN.** Reports: 493/501/495/497/BEST RESTAUS.

TUN TON, BABY GRAND and **TRON CAFÉ-BAR.** Reports: 508/506/520/BEST BISTROS.

MOTHER INDIA. 28 Westminster Terr. Report: 546/INDIAN RESTAUS.

CAFÉ GANDOLFI. 64 Albion St. Report: 585/BEST TEAROOMS.

584 ✓ ✓ **SARTI:** 248 2228. 133 Wellington St and 121 Bath St. Full report:
D3 523/ITALIAN RESTAUS, but mentioned here just in case you want a light
snack or an excellent cappuccino – definitive. 8am-10pm. Cl Sun.

585 ✓ ✓ **CAFÉ GANDOLFI:** 552 6813. 64 Albion St, Merchant City nr City
E4 Halls. The vaguely bohemian, Europe-somewhere atmos, the stained
glass and the heavy, over-sized wooden furniture create a unique ambience
that has stood the fashionability test of recent times. The food is light and
imaginative and served all day. You may have to queue (because it's good). 7
days, 9am-11.30pm, Sun from 12noon. (619/SUN BREAKFAST)

586 ✓ ✓ **TINDERBOX:** 339 3108. 189 Byres Rd, on busy corner with
A1 Highburgh Rd. Stylish, designery but unlikely to date, a kind of state
of the art neighbourhood coffee shop. Stuff for kids, stuff to buy. Snacks and
Elektra, the good-looking coffee machine. 7 days, 8am-10pm.

587 ✓ **THE GRANARY:** 226 3770. 82 Howard St, beside/behind the glass pyra-
D4 mid of the St Enoch Centre towards river. A calm style-free oasis away
from the bustling shoppers on Argyle St that serves mainly vegn dishes but
the emphasis is on home-baking. The apple pie is still the best in town. Hard
to believe that this place exists in an area decimated by the mall-mongers.
Vive la resistance! Mon-Sat 8.30am-6pm, Sun 11-5pm.

588 ✓ **CAFÉ ALBA:** 61 Otago St. Just after the dog-leg on this busy st that's
B1 always in danger of falling into the river you'll find this supremely unruf-
fled little café. Fresh mainly vegn fare, none of which exists much beyond
lunchtime, and home-baked cakes that also have a tendency to disappear
quickly. Draws a slightly arty (but not starving in garrets obviously) crowd.
Mon-Sat 10am-5pm. (582/VEGN RESTAUS)

589 ✓ **MANGO AND STONE:** 221 3449. Princes Sq. The juice bar from
D4 Edinburgh upstairs in Princes Sq at the top of the elevator. Mainly t/away,
but some seats on concourse. Excl and healthy juice combos incl 'the Detox'.
Also bagels, muffins, smoothies – the usual, but here done with some
panache. Excl coffee. 7 days till 6pm. (Sun 5pm).

590 **THE WILLOW TEAROOMS:** 217 Sauchiehall St. Another level (The Gallery),
C3, D4 has been added upstairs, and a new sister tearoom has now opened at 97
Buchanan St. Both, under the discerning eye of proprietor Anne Mulhern,
recreate the interiors of the original Miss Cranston's Tearooms, designed by
C.R. Mackintosh. 30 blends of loose-leaf tea, all manner of cakes, scones and
sandwiches and now, hold on … a wee glass of wine. Mon-Sat 9.30am-
4.30pm. (750/MACKINTOSH)

591 **CAFÉ ROBERTA:** 204 0860. 84 Gordon St, opp main canopied entrance to
D3 Central Stn. Popular downtown foodstop and famous cappuccino on your
way to the train (or the work). 7 days. Mon-Sat 7.30am-7pm, Sun 10.30am-
5pm. (591/COFFEE)

592 **EXHIBITION CAFÉ:** 353 4779. 10 Dumbreck Rd, Bellahouston Park. On the
xA5 ground floor of House for an Art Lover (753/MACKINTOSH). This bright rm has a
modern Spanish feel; tan leather couches, tubular steel chairs and gallery
space. Nicely prepared, light, lunch menu without fuss, like the surroundings.
Excellent latte/espresso/cappuccino. Daily 10am-10pm. (till 4pm Fri and Sun).

593 **BRADFORDS:** 245 Sauchiehall St. Coffee shop/restau upstairs from the
C3 flagship shop of this local and estimable bakery chain. Familiar wifie waitresses, the macaroni cheese is close to mum's and the cakes and pies from downstairs represent Scottish bakery at its best. Mon-Sat 9am-5.30pm.

594 **PICKERING AND INGLIS, THE CHAPTERHOUSE:** 26 Bothwell St. A self-serve
D3 coffee shop at the back of a bookshop. Wholesome and home-baked; busy
Christian rendezvous, behind the tracts and concordances. Mon-Sat 8.30am-
4.30pm.

595 **THE JENNY TRADITIONAL TEAROOMS:** 20 Royal Exchange Sq, opp new
D4 Gallery of Modern Art. Trad they are; inside, a chintzy parlour just as you might
like to imagine it (though not perhaps off a main st in Glas). Sombrely lit and

low-voiced for the serious business of taking tea (several varieties) with scones, cakes (not all home-made – tut-tut) and their famous fudge. Hot dishes and interesting sandwiches. Busy pavement tables in summer. 7 days, 8am-6.30pm (Sun till 6pm)

596
xC5
TASHA BLANKITT: 423 5172. 378 Cathcart Rd. An out-of-the-way and unusual gift/coffee shop/bistro S of the river with a loyal following. 'Hampstead in Govanhill' home-cooking that's truthful, often imaginative and selective; micro's only there to heat things up. Mon, lunch only Tues-Sat, lunch and LO 8pm (Fri/Sat Midnight) Sun 10.30am-6pm. Dinner w/ends only, 7-11pm. (606/KID-FRIENDLY)

597
A1
LA FOCACCIA: 337 1642. 291 Byres Rd. Italian coffee shop on busy Byres Rd with freshly-made sandwiches on a variety of continental breads, strong java and cakes and pastries. Those tiny wrought-iron and polished wood island thingies to perch at and babelicious counter staff – all gals … this is, after all, an Italian gaff. Soaves ice cream. Mon-Sat 7am-11pm, Sun 9am-10pm.

598
D3
STARBUCKS: 353 3149. 27 Sauchiehall St opp concert Hall and branches (33 Bothwell St and 13 Renfield St). Formerly Seattle Coffee Houses from NW USA at the forefront of the caffeine revolution. Excl coffee, ambience and service. They practically invented the flavoured variants. 7 days till 7pm (8pm Thur).

599
D3
COSTA COFFEE: 221 9305. Royal Exchange Sq and innumerable branches incl Waterstones, Sauchiehall St. On a sunny day, you can't miss it – many tables o/side. The expanded version of the regular coffee house. All the steamy noises and aromas, double filled sarnies, etc. plus flapjacks and some hot dishes, but coffee is their business. A swift espresso should see you round the Gallery of Modern Art (703/OTHER ATTRACTIONS).

GREAT CAFÉS AND GREASY SPOONS

600
A2
✔ ✔ **UNIVERSITY CAFÉ:** 87 Byres Rd. When your granny, in the lines of the well-known song, was 'shoved aff a bus', this is where she was taken afterwards and given a wee cup of tea to steady her nerves. People have been coming here for generations to sit at the 'kneesy' tables and share the salt and vinegar. Run by the Verecchia family who administer advice, sympathy and pie, beans and chips with equal aplomb. A gem. Daily till 10pm (w/ends till 10.30pm). Cl Tue. Takeaway open later.

601
xC5
✔ ✔ **THE UNIQUE:** 223 Allison St. Not exactly central, but if you're on the S-side you'll find the best fish 'n' chips in town here. Through the curtain in the café they serve lunches, fish teas and spam fritters. Veg oil used. Old-fashioned hrs, viz 8.15am-1.15pm, 3-8pm. That's right, 8pm – closed!

602
A1
✔ **GROSVENOR CAFÉ:** 35 Ashton Lane, behind Byres Rd nr Hillhead Stn. For over 30 yrs they've been serving hot, filled rolls and bowls of steaming broth to students, and all the rest of us who have happily crammed into the wee booths. New patio at rear and licence. More extensive suppery menu after 7pm. 7 days, 9am-11pm (Mon till 7pm, Sun till 5.30pm).

603
xE4
✔ **COIA'S CAFÉ:** 473 Duke St. Since 1928, supplying this E End high st with ice cream, gr deal breakfasts and the kind of comforting lunch (you would call it dinner) café-bar places just cannot do. There's a telly in the corner but it's really only there to spark off open debate. Sit-in or takeaway. Sweeties of all sorts; and Havana cigars. 7 days, 7.30am-9pm (LO 7.30pm); Sun from 11am.

604
xC1
CAFE D'JACONELLI: 570 Maryhill Rd nr the Queens Cross Church (747/MACKINTOSH). Neighbourhood caff with toasties, macaroni cheese and ice-cream to go that's been here for ever. Disappearing Glasgow! Take to the baguettes. 7 days, 9am-10pm.

605
xA5
ALLAN'S SNACK BAR: 6 Storie St, Paisley. Off the High St, a chip shop with classic greasy spoon adj and a chips-with-everything menu in a Paisley days-gone-by atmos. Happy waitresses. Mon-Thu 11am-7pm, Fri-Sat 11am-8pm. Cl Sun.

JACK MCPHEES: 285 Byres Rd. Report: 611/KID-FRIENDLY.

KID-FRIENDLY PLACES

606
xC5
✓ **TASHA BLANKITT:** 423 5172. 378 Cathcart Rd. Bit out of the way, but not far from Pollokshaws Rd on the S-side. A friendly spot to take the kids, commandeer a comfy corner and have some macaroni cheese. High chairs and half portions. 7 days, 8.30am-5.30pm (Sun 10.30am-4.30pm). (596/BEST TEAROOMS)

607
xC1
✓ **THE BLACK BULL HOTEL, KILLEARN:** 01360 550215. Take them for a run! Main sq in village on A81 towards Aberfoyle. Gr pub food (473/BEST HOTELS O/SIDE GLAS), but esp if you've got kids and a fine day. Enclosed grd and adventure playground in parkland out the back. Ancient oaks, a Tarzan slide and views of distant hills. Sound nice? You'd better believe it. They'll all be happy here. 7 days.

608
D3
TGI FRIDAYS: 221 6996. 113 Buchanan St. The Glas branch of the national chain adored by kids because of the way they get fussed over and are given, pretty much, a free run of the place. The food is from everywhere via America and when added, free-hand, to the crayon drawings on the tablecloth, can look quite spectacular. Huge range of cocktails available for parents who may need them. 7 days, 11am-11.30pm, Sun till 11pm.

609
B4
HARRY RAMSDEN'S: Paisley Rd W, beside M8 flyover – not far from centre, but difficult without a car. Not a bad branch of the national chain that caters well for kids. Greasy, cooked in lard and in cheerfully tacky surroundings, the chips and peas, sausage and fishcakes come in kids' portions and there's a playground to throw up into before you get back in the car.

610
A1
xC5
D4
DI MAGGIO'S: 334 8560. 61 Ruthven Lane, off Byres Rd, W End; 632 4194, 1038 Pollokshaws Rd, on a busy corner S of the river; and 248 2111, 21 Royal Exchange Sq. Bustling, friendly pizza joints with good Italian attitude to bairns. There's a choice to defy the most finicky kid. High chairs, special menu. 7 days.

611
A1
JACK MCPHEES: 285 Byres Rd. Squeaky booths, gingham table covers … Cuthbert, Dibble and grub. Kids' meal and drink £1.95. Beat that you MacBurger Wimpy King Huts! 6 days, 8am-10pm, Sun till 7pm.

612
B3
CRÈME DE LA CRÈME: 221 3222. 1071 Argyle St. Big (huge), bustling Indian emporium which makes special allowances for kids (there are 40 high chairs available!), incl cartoons on giant screens. Tempt them with a korma, then the ice cream. 7 days, lunch and LO 11.30pm. (547/INDIAN RESTAUS)

613
xE2
FAMILY FUN PUB: 0345 023028 (linkage to the other areas). Belziehill 'Farm' off the Jnct 5 M74 on A725 to Coatbridge. It just sounds awful, but they have 'funday roasts', an ice-cream factory where you make your own and a Charlie Chalk menu for 'them'. But then kids are easy to please, no? And you will keep having them! 7 days.

THE BEST LATE-NIGHT RESTAURANTS

614
B2
✓ **INSOMNIA/CRISPINS DELI:** 564 1700. 38 Woodlands Rd. 24hr café/deli that dispenses food, infusions, strong coffee and drinks to those who just *will not go to their beds*. In a rm full of higgledy-piggledy bits of furniture, baths full of goldfish and a clock noticeable by its absence, Glasgow's demi-monde plot and sip tea into the wee hrs of the afternoon. **7 days, 24hr.**

615
C3
✓ **CANTON EXPRESS:** 332 0145. 407 Sauchiehall St. The first fast-food Chinese joint on this block and still the genuine fast Chinese article. Not as wok-tastic as once was, but still feels like Hong Kong to us. 7 days, **12noon-4am.**

616
C3
THE NOODLE BAR: 333 1883. 482 Sauchiehall St. Major competition to the above (even gets the edge in opening hrs). Authentic, Chinese fast food, no frills (ticket service and eezee-kleen tables). The noodle is 'king' here; cooking is taken seriously. 7 days, **12noon-4.30am.** (563/FAR-EASTERN RESTAUS)

617 **KING'S CAFÉ:** 332 0898. 71 Elmbank St. Here for yrs, for that special, deep-
C3 fried pizza need that sometimes, inexplicably, gets you at 3am. Not er …
plush. Restau **till 11pm**; takeaway **till 5am Thu/Fri/Sat**.

618 **GUIDO'S CORONATION RESTAURANT:** 552 3994. 55 Gallowgate. Nr the
E4 Barrowland for as long as people have been going there. Fish and chips and
home-made pizza/ice cream. Sit-in or takeaway. **Sun-Thu till 1am, Fri-Sat till
2am.**

The following are also open till late 7 days:

CRÈME DE LA CRÈME: 1071 Argyle St. Report: 547/INDIAN RESTAUS. **11pm**.

BABY GRAND: Elmbank Gdns, Charing X. (506/BISTROS) **12pm**.

PIZZA EXPRESS: Sauchiehall St/Queen St. (533/PIZZAS) **11.30pm**.

ASHOKA ASHTON LANE: Ashton Lane. (548/INDIAN RESTAUS) **12.30pm**.

MR SINGH'S INDIA: Elderslie St. (549/INDIAN RESTAUS) **11.30pm**.

LOON FUNG: Sauchiehall St. (562/FAR EASTERN RESTAUS) **11.30pm**.

GOOD PLACES FOR SUNDAY BREAKFAST

619 ✓ **CAFÉ GANDOLFI:** 552 6813. 64 Albion St. Atmospheric rm, with soft day-
E4 light filtering through the stained glass and the comforting, oversized
wooden furniture. This is a pleasant start to another Sun, that day of rest and
more shopping made even better with some baked eggs, a pot of tea and the
Sun papers. **From 12noon.** (585/BEST TEAROOMS)

620 **GRASSROOTS:** 97 St Georges Rd at Charing X is another healthy Sun thing
C2 and it **opens at 10am.** (580/VEGN RESTAUS)

621 **BAY TREE:** 403 Gr Western Rd. This excellent caff (581/VEGN RESTAUS) provides
B1 another antidote to the toxins of Sat night. A hearty vegan breakfast is served
all day. **From 11am.**

622 **COTTIER'S:** 93 Hyndland St, off Hyndland Rd. Off the top of Hyndland St nr
xA1 Highburgh Rd. Deep in the hefty-mortgage belt of Hyndland, this converted
church probably gets more of a congregation now than it ever did. Eclectic
menu from fruit plate to the full monty and eggs benedict to cajun kedgeree.
12noon-4pm. Papers provided. (510/BEST BISTROS)

623 **CUL DE SAC:** 44 Ashton Lane, off Byres Rd. A smart relaxed place to phase into
A1 Sun. Clubby staff, so revival may take until late afternoon. The fry-up includes
potato scones and comes in a vegn version, and there are the better-than-
average burgers and exotic crêpes. Brunch **12.30pm-4pm.** (517/BEST BISTROS)

624 **UPSTAIRS AT THE CHIP:** 334 5007. 12 Ashton Lane. 'Sair heid' or not, their
A1 Bloody Marys are the best in town and combined with a veggie breakfast (gr
potato crowdie), famously restorative. Selection of papers. Unhurried. **From
12.30pm.** (519/BEST BISTROS)

625 **BABBITY BOWSTER:** 552 5055. 16 Blackfriars St. The seminal Merchant City
E4 bar/hotel recommended for many things (672/PUB FOOD, 686/DRINKING OUT-
DOORS), but worth remembering as one of the best and earliest spots for Sun
breakfast. **From 9am.**

THE BEST TAKEAWAY PLACES

626 **MISE EN PLACE:** 424 4600. 122 Nithsdale Rd. S-side specialist caterer and deli
xC5 run by Suzanne Ritchie, who knows that rocket leaves are not enough.
Everything from dinner *à deux* to full-on alfresco bash with cool waiters and
other trimmings. Delivered to your door or drop in for delish lunch. New caff
next door from late '99. Mon-Fri 9.15am-5.45pm, Sat 9.15am-2pm.

627 **HUNGRYS:** 353 1889. 98 Bath St. 'American-style' deli/sandwich shop in down-
D3 town Glas. It's a long way from 34th St, NYC, but it's much better than most on
these blocks, as long lunch queues attest. Several kinds of bread, good soup.
Try a pepper and tuna mayo on herb focaccia. Mon-Fri 8am-4pm.

628 **FIRST CHOICE:** 331 2272. 138 Renfield St. At the top of the town, across the st
D3 from Scottish Television. Good selection of cheeses and sandwich meats –
their pastrami and Swiss toastie is v popular and v Glas. Freshly-made coffee
and a selection of cakes – but the empire biscuits don't last much beyond
11am. What is it about STV and empires? Mon-Fri 6.30am-5pm, Sat 6.30am-
3pm.

629 **NUMBER ONE SANDWICH ST:** 248 2050, 104 St Vincent St and 221 2002, 9
D3, C3 Waterloo St. 2 other downtown locations where office-workers and shop
assistants descend in droves for assembly-line and some bespoke sandwiches and baked potatoes. Betw them they produce over 1,000 lunches a day.
Mon-Fri 8am-4pm.

630 **SANSIRO:** 248 9553. 539 Sauchiehall St. Smart, little Italian lunch-box W of
B3 Charing Cross. Pizza, pasta, over-stuffed ciabatta, crostino and good coffee to
take away in this constantly changing part of Sauchiehall St. Mon-Fri 8am-
4pm.

631 **LITTLE ITALY:** 339 6287. 205 Byres Rd. Gr pizza focaccia and pasta (535/PIZZA),
A1 freshly-baked breads, ice cream, loadsa Italian wines and a no-bad (meaning
'not at all bad') cup of coffee. Mon-Thu 8am-10pm, Fri-Sat 8am-1am, Sun 5-
10pm.

632 **LE PETIT PAIN:** 337 1118. 239 Byres Rd. Bright, little continental baguette/cia-
A1 batta shop, baking on premises. Most fillings a combination of 2 or 3 ingredients and the whole effect is … fresh. Good coffee. Mon-Fri 8.30am-6pm, Sat
10am-6pm, Sun 11am-6pm.

633 **TOSCANA:** 956 4020. 46 Station Rd, Milngavie. It's a long way from town, but
xB1 this family-run Italian café does gr takeaway pasta and pizza and home-made
puds. Till 10pm.

Those pubs you won't find anywhere else.

634 ✓ **THE HALT BAR:** 160 Woodlands Rd. On the old tram route W, this
B2 Edwardian pub remains largely unspoiled. Original counter and snug
intact, but v much moves with the times. Always gr atmos – model of how a
pub should look and feel. Live music and DJs some nights. (646/'UNSPOILT'
PUBS, 692/LIVE MUSIC) Open till 11pm (12midnight w/ends).

635 ✓ **CORINTHIAN:** 191 Ingram St. Mega makeover of former Lanarkshire
D4 house to form cavernous bar/restau, 2 comfy lounge/cocktail bars and a
restau nr George Sq and Gallery of Modern Art. Awesome ceiling in main rm
much much better than megabars elsewhere. Food in main rm excl and good
coffee. Older, richer, well-heeled clientele, some Armani. Totally Glas. 7 days, till
12midnight. (Piano bar Thur-Sun).

636 ✓ **THE HORSESHOE:** 17 Drury St. A mighty pub since 1884 (and before) in
D3 the small st betw Mitchell and Renfrew Sts nr Central stn. Early example
of this style of pub, dubbed 'gin palaces'. Island rather than horseshoe bar and
an upstairs lounge where they serve high-tea. The food is amazing value
(636/PUB FOOD). Caledonian and Maclays. Daily till 12midnight.

637 ✓ **VICTORIA BAR:** 157 Bridgegate. 'The Vicky' is in the 'Briggait', one of Glas's
D4 oldest streets, nr the Victoria Br over the Clyde. Once a pub for the
fishmarket and open odd hrs, now it's a howf for all those who like an atmos
that's old, friendly and uncontrived. Real ales. Mon-Sat till 12midnight, Sun till
11pm. (767/FOLK MUSIC)

638 ✓ **SCOTIA BAR:** 112 Stockwell St. Nr the Victoria (*see above*), late-1920s
D4 Tudor-style pub with a low-beamed ceiling and intimate, woody 'snug'.
Long the haunt of folk musicians, writers and raconteurs. Music and poetry
sessions, folk and blues. Daily till 12midnight. (766/FOLK MUSIC)

639 ✓ **CLUTHA VAULTS:** 167 Stockwell St. This and the pubs above are part of
D4 the same family of trad Glas pubs. The Clutha (ancient name for the
Clyde) has a Victorian-style interior and an even longer history. Known for live
music. Mon-Sat till 12midnight, Sun till 11pm. (764/FOLK MUSIC)

640 ✓ **BLACKFRIARS:** 36 Bell St. Contemporary, but pub-like in middle of
E4 Merchant City – predates most of those around it. Hugh selection of
European and E European beers. Eclectic menu (673/PUB FOOD) till 6pm.
Regular programme of live music. 7 days noon-12midnight.

641 ✓ **UISGE BEATHA:** 246 Woodlands Rd. 'Oo-i-skay Bay' (or something like
B2 that) means 'the water of life' and is a unique Highland outpost in the city.
Shooting-lodge chic wearing a bit thin now, but cosy. More than a mere
draught of the Gael. Good grub at lunchtime. Related to one of the gr Highland
bars, The Drover's Inn, Inverarnan. Sun-Thu till 11pm, Fri-Sat till 12midnight.

642 **BAR 10:** 10 Mitchell Lane, off Buchanan St. Opp new Lighthouse and nr the
D3 Tunnel, this is a well-placed 'cool' bar. Mongrel furniture and sliced-brawn tiles,
high ceiling and design by Ben Kelly of Manchester's Hacienda fame, this
place looks like it's been transported from Canal St, NYC. Good food, gossip
and strong coffee served with a shot of iced water during the day; the place
to go pre-club at night. Regular DJs at w/ends. (675/PRE-CLUB BARS)

643 **MCPHABBS:** 23 Sandyford Pl. 2 blocks W of Charing Cross. Non-aligned booz-
B3 er, more of a 'shebeen' than anything else. *Laissez-faire* attitude. Postage-
stamp patio at rear, tasty bar food, endorsed by local MP George Galloway
(669/PUB FOOD). Good malts. 7 days, till 12midnight Fri-Sat.

644 **LISMORE:** 206 Dumbarton Rd, main rd w after Byres rd. Lismore/Liosmor
xA2 named after the long island off Oban. Gr neighbourhood (Partick) bar that
welcomes all sorts. Gives good atmos, succour and malts. Daily till midnight.

645 **THE MITRE:** 12 Brunswick St, but more in the lane behind Trongate opp the
E4 backwards EMPIRE sign by Douglas Gordon who may be inside. Despite many
fashionable bars nearby in the Merchant City, this more trad pub is where the
not dressed up people drink. Cheap food, karaoke upstairs on a Sat night. V
old labour. Till 11pm, 12midnight w/ends.

One type of bar/café/restau that Glas does v well is THE STYLE-BAR, with complete makeover à la mode. For a limited lifespan they are the place to be seen. At time of going to press the best of these are:

AIRORGANIC (492/BEST RESTAUS), **GROUCHO** (450/HOTELS), **BAR CE LONA** 427 Sauchiehall St, **SPY BAR** (679/PRE-CLUB BARS) and **ARTHOUSE** (440/HOTELS)

THE BEST OLD 'UNSPOILT' PUBS

Of course it's not necessarily the case that when a pub's done up it's spoiled, or that all old pubs are worth preserving, but some have resisted change and that's part of their appeal. The following places don't have to recreate 'atmos'. Most of them close no later than 12midnight.

646
B2
✓ **HALT BAR:** 160 Woodlands Rd. In the classic trad of the stand-up bar with a 'snug' (for the ladies), behind a wooden partition, with 'pulpit' serving-hatch. Varied (free) live music through the back (692/LIVE MUSIC). Sun-Thu till 11pm, Fri-Sat till 12midnight. Music usually from 9pm. (634/GR GLAS PUBS)

647
C3
✓ **THE GRIFFIN (AND THE GRIFFINY AND THE GRIFFINETTE):** 266 Bath St. Corner of Elmbank St nr King's Theatre. Built 1903 to anticipate the completion of the theatre and offer the patrons a pre-show pie and a pint. Stand at the Edwardian Bar like generations of Glaswegians. Main bar still retains 'snug' with a posh, etched-glass partition; booths have been added but the atmos is still 'Old Glasgow'. Sun-Thu till 11pm, Fri-Sat till 12midnight. (665/PUB FOOD)

648
xE2
THE ROWAN TREE, UDDINGSTON: 12km SE of centre via M74. In Old Mill Rd off Main St where sign points (in opp direction) for Bothwell Castle (1618/RUINS). A cottagey pub in the shadow of the world-famous Tunnock's Caramel Wafers factory and long frequented by the wafermakers. Food at lunchtime, coal fire in winter, folk music on Fri. Maclays. Mon-Sat till 11.45pm, Sun till 11pm.

649
xE4
THE SARACEN'S HEAD: Gallowgate, nr Barrowlands. An establishment of this name has existed in the neighbourhood since 1755, playing host to a multitude of colourful characters; not least Boswell and Johnson, on the return leg of their grand Highland tour. This, the most recent incarnation, opened in 1905 and is famous for its lethal 'White Tornado' cider. The atmos is more 'wild west' than E End, although the 'one singer, one song' rule still prevails. 7 days, Cl 10.30pm during week.

650
E4
THE MITRE: The lane of Brunswick St, off Argyle St opp C&A. Untouched by the 'gentryfiers' and full of character. Gem of a bar, just quietly getting on with its business. Bit of music at w/ends, food at lunch, Belhaven; nothing fancy. 7 days till 11pm or 12midnight. (645/GR GLAS PUBS)

651
xC5
M J HERAGHTY: 708 Pollokshaws Rd. More than a touch of the Irish about this pub and easily more authentic than recent imports. A local with loyal regulars who'll make you welcome; old pub practices still hold in this howf in the sowff. Sun-Thu till 11pm, Fri-Sat till 12midnight.

652
A5
BRECHIN'S: 803 Govan Rd. Nr jnct with Paisley Rd W and motorway overpass. Established in 1798 and, as they say, always in the same family. A former shipyard pub which, despite the proximity to Rangers FC, is not partisan. It's behind the statue of shipbuilder Sir William Pearce (which, covered in sooty grime, was known as the 'Black Man') and there's a feline 'rat-catcher' on the roof (making it a listed building). Unaffected neighbourhood atmos. Mon-Sat till 11pm, Sun till 6.30pm.

653
B4
THE OLD TOLL BAR: 1 Paisley Rd W. Opp the site of the original Parkhouse Toll, where monies were collected for use of the 'turnpikes' betw Glas and Greenock. Opened in 1874, the original interior is still intact; the *fin de siècle* painted glass and magnificent old gantry preserved under order. A 'palace pub' classic. Real ale and some single malts. 7 days till 11pm.

654
D3
THE HORSESHOE: 17 Drury St. The celebrated city-centre bar with the famous 'longest bar in the world' and an assortment of Old and New Glaswegians ranged along it. (636/GR GLAS PUBS, 666/PUB FOOD)

655 **BAIRDS BAR** and **THE DISTRICT:** 2 bars from opp sides of the gr divide.
E4 **BAIRDS** in the Gallowgate adj Barrowlands is a Catholic stronghold green to
xA5 the gills where, on days when Celtic play at home up the rd at Parkhead, you'd
have to be in by 11am to get a drink. **THE DISTRICT,** 252 Paisley Rd W, Govan,
nr Ibrox Park, is where Rangers supporters gather and rule in their own blue
heaven. Both pubs give an extraordinary insight into what makes the Glas
time bomb tick. Provided you aren't wearing the wrong colours (or say something daft), you'll be very welcome in either.

THE BEST REAL-ALE PUBS

*Pubs on other pages may purvey real ale, but the following are the ones where
they take it seriously and/or have a good choice.*

656 ✓ **BON ACCORD:** 153 N St. On a slip rd of the motorway swathe nr the
B3 Mitchell Library. One of the first real-ale pubs in Glas. Over 100 malts as
well as up to 12 beers; always McEwan's 80/-, Theakston and Old Peculier, plus
many guest ales on hand pump. Food at lunchtime and light bites till 9pm.
Light, easy-going atmos here, but they do take their ale seriously; there's even
a 'tour' of the cellars if you want it. Mon-Sat till 12midnight, Sun till 11.00pm.

657 ✓ **THREE JUDGES:** 141 Dumbarton Rd, opp the bottom of Byres Rd. Named
A2 after the triumvirate of boxing judges that used to own it. These days
you're more likely to find professors than practitioners of the 'gentlemanly art'.
Maclays and 9 guest ales that change regularly from a cast of hundreds. 7
days.

658 **TENNENTS:** 191 Byres Rd. Nr the always-red traffic lights at Univ Ave, a big,
A1 booming watering-hole of a place where you're never far away from the
horseshoe bar and its several excellent hand-pumped ales, incl Maclays,
Caledonian and Theakston. Revamped to take it into the next century, but the
'old century' crowd will still be there.

659 **BABBITY BOWSTER:** 16 Blackfriars St. In a pedestrianized part of the
E4 Merchant City and just off the High St, a highly successful pub/restau/hotel
(458/LESS EXP HOTELS); but the pub comes first. Maclays is heavily featured and
make their own Babbity Thistle Ale, but there's always an English guest and
lots of malts. Food all day (672/PUB FOOD), occasional folk music (esp Sun),
o/side patio (686/DRINK OUTDOORS) and exhibs. Proprietor Fraser Laurie has
thought of everything.

660 **THE CASK AND STILL:** 154 Hope St. 8 ales (always Youngers No. 3, McEwan's
D3 80/- and Old Peculier), but also noted for a mind-boggling range of malts.
They've got over 200. Mon-Sat till 11pm/12midnight. Cl Sun.

661 **THE BREWERY TAP:** 1055 Sauchiehall St, up w by the park on UNIV. All-round
A2 studenty kind of bar with food all day till 9pm, music on Sats (jazz-blues) and
at least 5 ales on tap. 7 days.

662 **THE TAVERNA:** 778 Pollokshaws Rd. Intimate wine bar/lounge On the S-side
xC5 with 2 Czech beers on draft and a large selection of German wheat-beers.

663 **THE HORSESHOE:** 17 Drury St. Gr for lots of reasons (636/GR GLAS PUBS), not
D3 the least of which is its range of beers: Caledonian, Greenmantle, Maclays and
Bass on hand pump.

664 **VICTORIA BAR:** 157 Bridgegate. Another pub mentioned before (196/GR GLAS
D4 PUBS) where IPA, Maclays and others can be drunk in a dark woody atmos
enlivened by occasional trad music (767/FOLK MUSIC).

PUBS WITH GOOD FOOD

665 ✓✓ **THE GRIFFIN:** 266 Bath St. On corner of Elmbank St across from
C3 King's Theatre. The Griffin, the Griffiny and the Griffinette: they're
always there on that corner and your basic pie/chips/beans *and a pint* will not
be bettered at this price (£2.80 lunchtime, Griffin only at time of going to press,
the equivalent 80 yrs ago of 8 old pence). Other staples available and a more
elaborate menu in the lounge or the Griffinette next door. Food: 12noon-3pm
and evenings till 7.30pm. Pub till 12midnight. (647/'UNSPOILT' PUBS)

666 ✓✓ **THE HORSESHOE:** 17 Drury St. The classic pub to be recommended
D3 for all kinds of reasons. But lunch is a particularly good deal with 3
courses for £2.60 (pie and beans still 80p), and old favourites on the menu like
mushy peas, macaroni cheese, jelly and fruit. Lunch 12noon-2.30pm and all
afternoon upstairs, incl hightea till 7.30pm (not quite the same atmos, but
pure Glas). Pub open daily till 12midnight. (636/GR GLAS PUBS)

667 ✓ **OBLOMOV:** 339 9177. 372 Gr Western Rd, Kelvinbridge. The latest bar by
B1 Ron McCulloch (designer and entrepreneur of this parish). This time the
timeless appeal of sepia, softly-lit pre-war kinda thing. Booths and chaises, big
drapes. Crepuscular dining-rm. Contemporary menu. Their food is good and
not too foreign. (571/ROUND THE WORLD). 7 days. Served 11.30am-8.30pm.

668 ✓ **AIRORGANIC:** 564 5200. 36 Kelvingrove St nr the park. Restau upstairs
A3 was definitely flavour of the month (or season 98/99), but snackier food
in bar, e.g. Thai curry sandwiches, sushi boxes, so the hip place to graze. Open
fire among cool minimalism and cool music. 7 days, 11am–11pm. (492/BEST
RESTAUS)

669 ✓ **MCPHABBS:** 221 0770. 23 Sandyford Pl. 2 blocks W of Charing Cross. Gr
B3 Scottish/Irish bar food; smoked haddies, salmon and steaks, beef and
Guinness stew, etc. Given the 'parliamentary seal of approval' by local MP
George Galloway who particularly rates the stew. 7 days, open till 12midnight
at w/ends. (643/GR GLAS PUBS)

670 **THE BIG BLUE:** 445 Gr Western Rd. A modern bar/bistro in a gr uptown loca-
B1 tion literally on the (river) Kelvinside. Drinking may drown the eating later on,
but till mid/late-evening there's excellent Italian pasta/pizza pub grub. LO
10/10.30pm. Bar 12midnight.

671 **THE DRUM AND MONKEY:** 93 St Vincent St, on corner of Renfield St.
D3 Cavernous but comfortable, and once fashionable bar/bistro with a sombre
gentlemen's club atmos – 'the odd libation for the overworked'. Comfort and
more contemporary food with a bistro through the back which has an à la
carte menu in the evening. 7 days till 11pm.

672 **BABBITY BOWSTER:** 16 Blackfriars St. Already listed as a pub for real ale and
E4 as a hotel (there are rms upstairs), the food is mentioned mainly for its
Scottishness (haggis and stovies) and all-day availability. It's also pleasant to
eat o/side on the patio/grd in summer. There is a restau upstairs (lunch
Mon–Fri, dinner Mon–Sat) but we prefer down. Also breakfast served from
8am (Sun 9am). (659/REAL-ALE PUBS, 458/LESS EXPENSIVE HOTELS)

673 **BLACKFRIARS:** 36 Bell St. Candleriggs is one of the focal points in the
E4 Merchant City. Gr Glas pub for all-round ambience, provision of real ale and
music, and food available all day till 12midnight (but drinkers loud after 9pm).
(640/GR GLAS PUBS, 690/LIVE MUSIC)

674 **FOX AND HOUNDS, HOUSTON:** On B790 village main st in Renfrewshire,
xA5 30km W of centre by M8 jnct 29 (A726), then cross back under motorway on
B790. Village pub with real fire and dining-rm upstairs for family meals and
suppers. Folk come from miles around. Sun roasts. Lunch and 6-10pm (all day
w/ends).

STRAVAIGIN: 28-30 Gibson St. Excellent pub food upstairs from one of the
best restaus in town. Report: 489/BEST RESTAUS.

PRE-CLUB BARS

675 **BAR 10:** 221 8353. 10 Mitchell Lane, halfway up Buchanan St pedestrian
D4 precinct on the left. There's an NYC look about this joint that is so loved by its
habitués, they make an exhib out of themselves. Designed by Ben Kelly of
Hacienda fame, after 6 yrs it has stood the fashion test and is as happening as
ever. Someday you should play it again Sam! (642/GR GLAS PUBS)

676 **BARGO:** 553 4771. 80 Albion St. In the Merchant City, this spacious, designer-
E4 theque is much in demand for fashion shoots and, posing on a Sat night. Can
be attractively, if not spookily, quiet during the week when surprisingly OK
food is served. (521/BEST BISTROS)

677 **CUL DE SAC:** 649 4717. 44 Ashton Lane. This upstairs bar is a perennial W End
A1 fave. Close to the underground for that last-minute dash into town to beat
club curfews. The Attic up top has diff vibe, more grown up and clubby as in
drinking clubby. (517/BEST BISTROS)

678 **MOJO:** 331 2257. 158a Bath St. City centre, underground bar with comfy
D3 couches and a smart, urban atmos. Good food through the back. DJs obliter-
ate the food thing, but raise the temperature later on.

679 **SPY BAR:** 221 7711. 151–155 Bath St. Central bar-restau kind of place though
D3 *The Herald* trashed the food bigtime not long after it opened (bit-of-every-
thing menu from Cajun to pasta). Otherwise a funky basement bar where
styly people gather. 7 days, 11am-12midnight (Sun from 6pm).

680 **POLO LOUNGE:** 553 1221. 84 Wilson St. Urbane and stylish bar/disco by the
E4 irrepressible Stefan King. Unmistakably gay in the heart of the quarter.
Clubbable rather than clubby crowd until late on arranged around the comfortable furniture; at w/ends you go downstairs to disco. Mellow Sun afternoons; papers and jazz. (2063/GAY GLAS)

681 **YANG:** 248 8484. 31 Queen St. Neon-lit style bar for v young young things.
D4 Next door to Archaos (755/BEST CLUBS). May seem clinical/spartan for some
tastes; it's the antithesis of the old Glas pub. (456/BEST CLUBS)

AIRORGANIC: 36 Kelvingrove St. Report: 668/PUB FOOD. '99 Flava.

PLACES TO DRINK OUTDOORS

682 **LOCK 27:** 1100 Crow Rd. At the very N end of Crow Rd beyond Anniesland, an
xA1 unusual boozer for Glas: a canalside pub on a lock of the Forth and Clyde
Canal (711/WALKS IN THE CITY), a touch English (a v wee touch), where of a summer's day you can sit o/side. Excellent bar food, always busy. 7 days.

683 **COTTIER'S:** 357 5825. 93 Hyndland St. First on the left after the swing park on
xA1 Highburgh Rd (going W) and the converted church is on your rt, around the
corner. Gr place for many reasons (510/BEST BISTROS, 622/SUN BREAKFAST), but a
cold beer on a hot day sitting in leafy shade is one of the best; or into the
evening – life can be good! 7 days.

684 **WICKETS HOTEL:** 334 9334. 52 Fortrose St. Probably best app via Dumbarton
xA2 Rd, turning up Peel St before railway br. O/looking W of Scotland Cricket
Ground (hence name). Large terr beer grd, made for long summer afternoons.
You can at least imagine the thwack of balls in the distance. Good place to
bring kids, even if you don't see them very often (Dad!). 7 days. (459/LESS EXP
HOTELS)

685 **ASHTON LANE:** As soon as the sun comes out, so do the punters. With the
A1 **CUL DE SAC** and **BAR BREL** at one end and **JINTY MCGINTY'S** at the other,
benches suddenly appear and the whole lane becomes a cobbled, alfresco
pub. It's the nearest Glas gets to Euro, even Dublin, drinking. 7 days.

686 **BABBITY BOWSTER:** 552 5055. 16 Blackfriars St. Unique in the Merchant City
E4 for several reasons (659/REAL-ALE PUBS, 672/PUB FOOD), but in summer certainly for its napkin of grd in an area bereft of greenery. Though enclosed by surrounding sts, it's an oasis many head for. Feels like Soho, Soho NYC? Naw, feels
like Glas. Always good crack. 7 days.

PUBS AND CLUBS WITH GOOD LIVE MUSIC

Many other places have live music but programmes and policies can vary quickly. Best to look out for posters or consult The List *magazine, on sale fortnightly in the city centre.*

687 ✓ **KING TUT'S WAH WAH HUT:** 221 5279. 272 St Vincent St. Every bit as
C3 good as its namesake in Alphabet City used to be; the room for interesting new bands, make-or-break atmos and cramped. Bands on the club circuit play to a damp and appreciative crowd. See flyers. Doors open 8.30pm. Tickets at bar or Tower Records, Argyle St.

688 **NICE 'N' SLEAZY:** 333 9637. 421 Sauchiehall St at the W End. Not esp sleazy
C3 and fairly rock 'n' roll. Popular art school hang-out. Every flavour of alco-pop and voddie to drink. Good indie jukebox and play station for hire. Bands downstairs (esp Thu-Sun) with a nominal entrance charge. Usually from 9pm. All over before midnight.

689 **THE CATHOUSE:** 248 6606. 15 Union St, and **THE GARAGE** , Sauchiehall St, W
D4, C3 End (same owners). Live rock clubs with mixed programme on various nights depending on availability of touring bands (other 'clubs' on other nights). Recent broadening of musical taste so no longer necessary to turn up with leather strides and pointy boots. Tickets in advance, as for King Tut's (*see above*).

690 **BLACKFRIARS:** 552 5924. 36 Bell St. Merchant City pub with everything
E4 (640/GR GLAS PUBS) which includes all kinds of live music and, if you are a player, 'Glasgow songwriters' on Tue nights features an open mic guest policy. Turn up early to book your spot. Free. (673/PUB FOOD)

691 **SCOTIA BAR** and **THE CLUTHA VAULTS:** 552 8681/552 7520. Nr each other in
D4 the E End nr the river and under same management (112 and 167 Stockwell St). Integral part of the Glas folk scene for yrs (766/764/FOLK MUSIC), but also readings and other sessions (e.g. Clutha has bluegrass and country). Glas Folk Club on Wed at Scotia and always at w/ends. Free. (638/639/GR GLAS PUBS)

692 **HALT BAR:** 564 1527. 160 Woodlands Rd. Gr pub rock atmos with booked live
B2 acts on Thu and 'open mic' spots on Wed and Sat. Music starts around 9pm and admn is free. (634/GR GLAS PUBS, 646/'UNSPOILT' PUBS)

693 **COTTIER'S:** 357 5825. 93 Hyndland St. In the densely populated quadrant
xA1 betw Dumbarton Rd and Byres Rd. A neighbourhood atmos to this converted church (not in, but off the top of Hyndland St nr Highburgh Rd); it has the same management as the Baby Grand (506/BEST BISTROS) and Cathedral House (451/INX HOTELS). Restau upstairs (510/BEST BISTROS). Bar and theatre, on the ground level, serve as a platform for local talent and cult-ish acts from abroad. Regularly features special gigs with 3 or more bands on the bill and, occasionally, entire, musically-themed, w/ends. Expect good programming.

694 **THE 13TH NOTE:** 221 0414. CAFE 60 King St and CLUB, Clyde St. The vegn
D4 restau in King St (579/VEGN RESTAUS) and the gig thing down nr the river. Various combos of the indie or merely hip in both. These are the ones to watch. Tue-Sun 8pm-3.30am.

THE MAIN ATTRACTIONS

695
A2
✓ ✓ **KELVINGROVE ART GALLERY AND MUSEUM:** 287 2700. At westerly extension of Argyle St and Sauchiehall St by Kelvingrove Park. Huge Victorian sandstone edifice with awesome atrium. On the ground floor is a natural history/Scottish history museum. The upper salons contain the city's superb British and European art collection. There are strong contemporary exhibs as well as the permanent collection. Pipe-organ recitals every alternate Sun. Tearoom. The Museum of Transport (701/OTHER ATTRACTIONS) is across the rd. Mon-Sat 10am-5pm, Sun from 11am.   FREE

696
xC5
✓ ✓ **THE BURRELL COLLECTION AND POLLOK PARK:** 649 7151. S of river via A77 Kilmarnock Rd (over Jamaica St Br) about 5km, following signs from Pollokshaws Rd. Set in rural parkland, this hugely successful attraction is an award-winning modern gallery built to house the eclectic acquisitions of Sir William Burrell. Showing a preference for medieval works, among the 8,500 items the magpie magnate donated to the city in 1944 are artefacts from the Roman empire to Rodin. The building itself integrates old doorways and whole rms reconstructed from Hutton Castle. Self-serve café and restau on the ground floor. Pollok House and Grds further into the park (with works by Goya, El Greco and William Blake) is worth a detour and has, below stairs, the better tearoom. Both open Mon-Sat 10am-5pm, Sun from 11am. (712/WALKS IN THE CITY)   FREE

697
xE3
✓ **GLASGOW CATHEDRAL/PROVAND'S LORDSHIP:** 552 8198/552 8819. High St. Across the rd from one another they represent what remains of the oldest part of the city, which (as can be seen in the People's Palace, *see below*) was, in the early 18th century, merely a ribbon of streets from here to the river. The present Cathedral, though established by St Mungo in AD 543, dates from the 12th century and is a fine example of the v real, if gloomy, Gothic. The house, built in 1471, is a museum which strives to convey a sense of medieval life. Watch you don't get run over when you re-emerge into the 20th century and try to cross the st. In the background, the Necropolis piled on the hill invites inspection and offers a viewpoint and the full Gothic perspective.

698
xE5
✓ **THE PEOPLE'S PALACE:** 554 0223. Reopened after renovations in spring 1998. App via the Tron and London Rd, then turn rt into Glas Green. This has long been a folk museum *par excellence* wherein, since 1898, the history, folklore and artefacts of a proud city have been gathered, cherished and displayed. But this is much more than a mere museum; it is the heart and soul of the city and together with the Winter Grds adj, shouldn't be missed if you want to know what Glasgow's about. Tearoom in the Tropics, among the palms and ferns of the Winter Grds, will still be part of the attraction for any visitor in the future. Opening times as other museums (*see above*).   FREE

699
xE3
ST MUNGO MUSEUM OF RELIGIOUS LIFE AND ART: 553 2557. In the Cathedral precinct or sq dubbed 'Ft Weetabix' by Glas cabbies. Opened with some gnashing of teeth and wringing of hands in 1993, it houses art and artefacts representing the world's 6 major religions arranged tactfully in an attractive stone building with a Zen grd in the courtyard. The dramatic Dalì *Crucifixion* seems somehow lost, and the assemblage seems like a good and worthwhile vision not quite realized. But if you like your spirituality shuffled but not stirred, this is for you. The punters' comments board is always … enlightening. Mon-Sat 10-5pm, Sun from 11am.   FREE

700
A1
HUNTERIAN MUSEUM AND GALLERY: 330 5431. Univ Ave. On one side of the st, Glasgow's oldest museum with geological, archaeological and social history displayed in a venerable building. The cloisters outside and the **UNIVERSITY CHAPEL** should not be missed. Across the st, a modern block contains part of Glasgow's exceptional civic collection – Rembrandt to the Colourists and the Glas Boys, as well as one of the most complete collections of any artist's work and personal effects to be found anywhere, viz that of Whistler. It's fascinating stuff, even if you're not a fan. There's also a print gallery and the superb **MACKINTOSH HOUSE** (748/MACKINTOSH). Mon-Sat 9.30am-5pm.   FREE

701 ✓✓ **MUSEUM OF TRANSPORT:** 287 2700. Off Argyle St behind the Kelvin
A2 Hall and opp Art Gallery. May not seem your ticket to ride, but this is
one of Scotland's most fascinating museums. Has something for everybody, esp
kids. The reconstruction of a cobbled Glas st c1938 is an inspired evocation.
There are trains, trams and unique collections of cars, motorbikes and bicycles.
And model ships in the Clyde rm, in remembrance of a mighty river. Make a
donation and the Mini splits in two. Mon-Sat 10am-5pm, Sun 11am-5pm. FREE

702 ✓✓ **BOTANIC GARDENS AND KIBBLE PALACE:** 334 2422. Gr Western
xB1 Rd. Smallish park close to R Kelvin with riverside walks (710/WALKS IN
THE CITY), and pretty much the 'dear green place'. Kibble Palace (built 1873) is
the distinctive domed glasshouse with statues set among lush ferns and
shrubbery from around the (mostly temperate) world. A wonderful place to
muse and wander. Grds open till dusk; palace 10am-4.45pm.

703 ✓✓ **GALLERY OF MODERN ART:** 331 1854. Queen St. Central, contro-
D4 versial and housed in former Stirling Library, Glasgow's big visual
arts attraction opened in a hail of art world bickering in 1996. Director Julian
Spalding's choice of inclusion raised to record levels both the ire of critics and
the interest of the public. This 'Modern Art' incl contemporary and populist
from elsewhere, but little from the influential movements and bugger all from
the Saatchi side in which many Glas artists have made notable contributions.
Smart café up top. Same hrs as Museum of Transport (*see above*). FREE

704 ✓✓ **THE BARROWS:** (pronounced 'Barras') The sprawling st and indoor
xE4 market area in the E End of the city around the Gallowgate. An experience, an institution, a slice of pure Glas. If you're only in town for one w/end,
it's a must, and like no other market anywhere. Sat and Sun only.

705 **THE TENEMENT HOUSE:** 333 0183. 145 Buccleuch St. Nr Charing Cross but
C2 can app from nr the end of Sauchiehall St and over the hill. The typical
'respectable' Glas tenement kept under a bell-jar since Our Agnes moved out
in 1965. She had lived there with her mother since 1911 and wasn't one for
new-fangled things. It's a touch claustrophobic, with hordes of visitors, and is
distinctly voyeuristic, but, well … your house would be interesting, too, in 50
yrs time if the clock were stopped. Daily, Mar-Oct 2-5pm. ADMN

706 **SHARMANKA KINETIC GALLERY:** 552 7080. 2nd floor, 14 King St, Trongate. A
E4 small and intimate experience cf most others on this page, but an extraordinary one. The gallery/theatre of Russian emigre Eduard Bersindsky shows his
meticulous and amazing mechanical sculptures. He and his partner prob
around to get them in motion. Sat/Sun 12-4pm. NTS

707 **GREENBANK GARDENS:** 10km SW of centre via Kilmarnock Rd, Eastwood
xC5 Toll, Clarkston Toll and Mearns Rd, then signposted (3km). A spacious oasis in
the suburbs; formal grds and 'working' walled grd, parterre and woodland
walks around elegant Georgian house. V Scottish. Grds open AYR dawn-dusk,
shop/tearoom Apr-Oct 11am-5pm. NTS

708 **CITY CHAMBERS:** 287 2000. George Sq. The hugely impressive building along
D3 the whole E end of Glasgow's municipal central sq. Let's face it, it's not often
that one could seriously recommend a visit to the City Council offices, but this
is a wonderfully over-the-top monument to the days when Glas was the second city of the empire, a cross between an Italian Renaissance palace and an
Escher marble maze. Guided tours Mon-Fri, 10.30am and 2.30pm.

709 **FINLAYSTONE ESTATE:** 01475 540505. 30km W of city centre via fast M8/A8,
xA5 signed off dual carriageway just before Pt Glas. Delightful grds and woods
around mansion house with many pottering places and longer trails (and
ranger service). Various 'attractions', e.g. that rare thing: a walled grd and
Victorian laundry and kitchen, etc. Visitor centre and conservatory tearoom.
Much better family outing than McDonalds or the grd centre. 7 days,
10.30am-5pm.

PAISLEY ABBEY: 15km from Glas. Report: 1713/ABBEYS.

BOTHWELL CASTLE, UDDINGSTON: 15km E, via M74. Report: 1618/RUINS.

See page 10 for walk codes.

710 **KELVIN WALKWAY:** A path along the banks of Glasgow's other river, the
B1 Kelvin, which enters the Clyde unobtrusively at Yorkhill but first meanders
through some of the most interesting parts and parks of the NW city. Walk
starts at Kelvingrove Park through the Univ and Hillhead district under Kelvin
Br and on to the celebrated Botanic Grds (702/OTHER ATTRACTIONS). The trail
then goes N, under the Forth and Clyde Canal (*see below*) to the Arcadian
fields of Dawsholm Park (5km), Killermont (posh golf course) and Kirkintilloch
(13km from start). Since the river and the canal shadow each other for much
of their routes, it's possible, with a map, to go out by one waterway and return
by the other (e.g. start at Gr Western Rd, return Maryhill Rd).

START: Usual start at the Eildon St (off Woodlands Rd) gate of Kelvingrove
Park or Kelvin Br. St parking only. 2-13+KM XCIRC BIKE 1-A-1

711 **FORTH AND CLYDE CANAL TOWPATH:** The canal, opened in 1790 and once
D2 a major short cut for fishing boats and trade betw Europe and America, pro-
xC1 vides a fascinating look round the back of the city from a pathway that
stretches on a spur from Pt Dundas just N of the M8 to the main canal at the
end of Lochburn Rd off Maryhill Rd and then E all the way to Kirkintilloch and
Falkirk, and W through Maryhill and Drumchapel to Bowling and the Clyde
(60km). Much of the route is through the forsaken or redeveloped industrial
heart of the city, past waste ground, warehouses and high flats, but there are
open stretches and curious corners and, by Bishopbriggs, it's a rural waterway.
More info from British Waterways (332 6936). Revitalizing the whole Edin–Glas
link is a major Millennium project.

START: (1) Top of Firhill Rd (gr view of city from Ruchill Park, 100m further on
– 722/BEST VIEWS). (2) Lochburn Rd (*see above*) at the confluence from which to
go E or W to the Clyde. (3) Top of Crow Rd, Anniesland where there is a canalside pub, Lock 27 (682/DRINK OUTDOORS), with tables o/side, real ale and food
(12noon-7/8pm). (4) Bishopbriggs Sports Centre, Balmuildy Rd. From here it is
6km to Maryhill and 1km in other direction to the 'country churchyard' of
Cadder or 3km to Kirkintilloch. All starts have some parking.

ANY KM XCIRC BIKE 1-A-1

712 **POLLOK COUNTRY PARK:** The park that (apart from the area around the
xC5 gallery and the house – 696/MAIN ATTRACTIONS) most feels like a real country
park. Numerous trails through woods and meadows. The leisurely Sun guided
walks with the park rangers can be educational and more fun than you would
think (632 9299). Burrell Collection and Pollok House and Grds are obvious
highlights. There's an 'old-fashioned' tearoom in the basement of the latter.
Enter by Haggs Rd or by Haggs Castle Golf Course. By car you are directed to
the entry rd off Pollokshaws Rd and then to the car park in front of the Burrell.
Train to Shawlands or Pollokshaws W from Glas Central Stn.

713 **MUGDOCK COUNTRY PARK:** 956 6100. Not perhaps within the city, but one
xB1 of the nearest and easiest escapes. Park which incl Mugdock Moor, Mugdock
Woods (SSSI) and 2 castles is NW of Milngavie. Regular train from Central Stn
takes 20 min, then follow route of W Highland Way for 4km across Drumclog
Moor to S edge of park. Or take Mugdock Bank bus from stn (not Sat) to end.
By car to Milngavie by A81 from Maryhill Rd and left after Black Bull Hotel (on
left) and before railway stn (over to rt) up Ellengowan Rd. Continue past reservoir then pick up signs for park. 3 car parks, visitor centre is at second one.
Many trails marked out and further afield rambles. This is a godsend betw Glas
and the Highland hills. 5-20KM CAN BE CIRC BIKE 1-A-2

CATHKIN BRAES: On S edge of city with impressive views. Report: 720/BEST
VIEWS.

See page 10 for walk codes.

714 **CAMPSIE FELLS:** Range of hills 25km N of city best reached via Kirkintilloch
xC1 or Cumbernauld/Kilsyth. Encompasses area that includes the Kilsyth Hills,
Fintry Hills and Carron Valley betw. (1) Good app from A803, Kilsyth main st up
the Tak-me-Doon *(sic)* rd. Park by the golf club and follow path by the burn. It's
poss to take in the two hills to left as well as Tomtain (453m), the most east-
erly of the tops, in a good afternoon; views to the E. (2) Drive on to the jnct
(9km) of the B818 rd to Fintry and go left, following Carron Valley reservoir to
the far corner where there is a forestry rd to the left. Park here and follow track
to ascend Meikle Bin (570m) to the rt, the highest peak in the central
Campsies. (3) The bonny village of Fintry (479/HOTELS O/SIDE TOWN) is a good
start/base for the Fintry Hills and Earl's Seat (578m). (4) Campsie Glen – a sliver of glen in the hills. App via Clachen of Campsie on A81 (decent tearoom) or
from veiwpoint high on the hill on B822 from Lennoxtown-Fintry. This is the
easy Campsie intro.　　　　　　　　　　10KM+ CAN BE CIRC XBIKE 2-B-2

715 **GLENIFFER BRAES, PAISLEY:** Ridge to the S of Paisley (15km from Glas) has
xA5 been a favourite walking-place for centuries. M8 or Paisley Rd W to town centre then: (1) S via B775/A736 towards Irvine or (2) B774 (Causewayside then
Neilston Rd) and sharp rt after 3km to Glenfield Rd (Bus: Clydeside 24). For (1)
go 2km after last houses, winding up ridge and park/start at Robertson Park
(signed). Here there are superb views and walks marked to E and W. (2) 500m
along Glenfield Rd is a car park/ranger centre. Walk up through grds and formal parkland and then W along marked paths and trails. Eventually, after 5km,
this route joins (1).　　　　　　　　　　2-10KM CAN BE CIRC MTBIKE 1-A-2

716 **GREENOCK CUT:** 45km W of Glas. Can app via Pt Glas but simplest route is
xA5 from A78 rd to Largs. Travelling S from Pt Glas take first left after IBM, signed
L Thom. Lochside 5km up winding rd. Park at Cornalees Br Centre. Walk left
along lochside rd to Overton (5km) then path is signed. The Cut, an aqueduct
built in 1827 to supply water to Greenock and its 31 mills, is now an ancient
monument. Gr views from the mast over the Clyde. Another route to the rt
from Cornalees leads through a glen of birch, rowan and oak to the Kelly Cut.
Both trails described on board at the car park.　　15/16KM CIRC MTBIKE 1-B-2

717 **MUIRSHIEL:** General name for vast area of 'Inverclyde' W of city, incl Greenock
xA5 Cut *(see above)*, Castle Semple Country Park and Lunderston Bay, a stretch of
coastline nr the Cloch Lighthouse on the A770 S of Gourock for littoral
amblings. But best wildish bit is Muirshiel Country Park itself, with trails, a
waterfall and Windy Hill (350m). Nothing arduous, but a breath of air. From Pt
Glas head S on A761 for Kilmalcolm then S for Lochwinnoch on B786.

718 **THE WHANGIE:** On A809 N from Bearsden about 8km after last r/bout and
xB1 2km after the Carbeth Inn, is the car park for the Queen's View (721/BEST
VIEWS). Climb uphill towards the stand of conifers and over the stile. Of 2 paths,
one leads along the top of the scarp, while the other lower down runs parallel to it and offers more protection from the elements. Both lead to the westerly end of the escarpment. Once you get to the summit of Auchineden Hill,
take the path that drops down to the W (a half-rt-angle) and look for crags on
your rt. This is the 'back door' of The Whangie. The path then seems to disappear into the side of the hill but carry on and you'll suddenly find yourself in
a deep cleft in the rock face with sheer walls rising over 10m on either side.
The Whangie is more than 100m long and at one pt the walls narrow to less
than 1m. As you emerge, take the lowest path, back along the face of the hill
to the stile and then down to the car park. Local mythology has it that The
Whangie was made by the Devil, who lashed his tail in anticipation of a witchy
rendezvous somewhere in the N, and carved a slice through the rock, where
the path now goes.　　　　　　　　5KM CIRC XBIKE XDOGS 1-A-1

719 **CHATELHÉRAULT, nr HAMILTON:** Jnct 6 off M74, well signposted into
xE2 Hamilton, follow rd into centre, then bear left away from main rd where it's
signed for A723. The gates to the 'château' are about 3km o/side town. A drive
leads to the William Adam-designed hunting lodge of the Dukes of Hamilton,
set amid ornamental grds with a notable parterre and extensive grounds.
Tracks along the deep, wooded glen of the Avon (ruins of Cadzow Castle) lead

to distant glades. Ranger service and good guided walks (01698 426213). 20km SE of city centre. House open 10.30am-4.30pm, walks at all times.

2-7KM CIRC BIKE 1-A-2

THE BEST VIEWS OF THE CITY AND BEYOND

Refer to Around Glasgow map on pages 328–329.

720
xC5
CATHKIN BRAES, QUEEN MARY'S SEAT: The southern ridge of the city on the B759 from Carmunnock to Cambuslang, about 12km from centre. Go S of river by Albert Br to Aikenhead Rd which continues S as Carmunnock Rd. Follow to Carmunnock, a delightfully rural village, and pick up the Cathkin Rd. 2km along on the rt is the Cathkin Braes Golf Club and 100m further on the left is the park. Marvellous views to N of the Campsies, Kilpatrick Hills, Ben Lomond and as far as Ben Ledi. Walks on the Braes on both sides of the rd.

721
xB1
QUEEN'S VIEW, AUCHINEDEN: Not so much a view of the city, more a perspective on Glasgow's Highland hinterland, this short walk and sweeping vista to the N has been a Glaswegian pilgrimage for generations. On A809 N from Bearsden about 8km after last r/bout and 2km after the Carbeth Inn which is a v decent pub to repair to. Busy car park attests to its popularity. The walk, along path cut into ridgeside, takes 40-50 min to cairn, from which you can see The Cobbler (1759/HILLS), that other Glas favourite, Ben Ledi and sometimes as far as Ben Chonzie 50km away. The fine views of L Lomond are what Queen Victoria came for. Further on is The Whangie (*see opp*).   1-A-1

722
xC1
RUCHILL PARK: An unlikely but splendid panorama from this overlooked, but well-kept park to the N of the city nr the infamous Possilpark housing estate. Go to top of Firhill Rd (past Partick Thistle football ground) over Forth and Clyde Canal (711/WALKS IN THE CITY) off Garscube Rd where it becomes Maryhill Rd. Best view is from around the flagpole; the whole city among its surrounding hills, from the Campsies to Gleniffer and Cathkin Braes (*see above*), becomes clear.

723
xE2
BAR HILL AT TWECHAR, nr KIRKINTILLOCH: 22km N of city, taking A803 Kirkintilloch t/off from M8, then the 'low' rd to Kilsyth, the B8023, bearing left at the 'black-and-white br'. Next to Twechar Quarry Inn, a path is signed for Bar Hill and the Antonine Wall. Steepish climb for 2km, ignore strange dome of grass. Over to left in copse of trees are the remains of one of the forts on the wall which was built across Scotland in the 2nd century AD. Ground plan explained on a board. This is a special place with strong history vibes and airy views over the plain to the city which came a long time after.   1-A-2

724
xE2
BLACKHILL, nr LESMAHAGOW: 28km S of city. Another marvellous outlook, but in the opp direction from above. Take jnct 10/11 on M74, then off the B7078 signed Lanark, take the B7018. 4km along past Clarkston Farm, head uphill for 1km and park by Water Board mound. Walk uphill through fields to rt for about 1km. Unprepossessing hill which unexpectedly reveals a vast vista of most of E central Scotland.   1-A-2

725
xA5
PAISLEY ABBEY: About one Sat a month betw May and Oct (1-5pm) on Abbey 'open days', the tower of this amazing edifice can be climbed. The tower (restored 1926) is 50m high and from the top there's a grand view of the Clyde. Obviously this is a rare experience, but phone TO (889 0711) for details; next Sat could be your lucky day. M8 to Paisley; frequent trains from Central Stn.

726
xA5
LYLE HILL, GOUROCK: Via M8 W to Greenock, then round the coast to relatively genteel old resort of Gourock where the 'Free French' worked in the yards during the war. A monument has been erected to their memory on the top of Lyle Hill above the town, from where you get one of the most dramatic views of the gr crossroads of the Clyde (Holy L, Gare L and L Long). Best vantage-point is further along the rd on other side by trig pt. Follow British Rail stn signs, then Lyle Hill. There's another gr view of the Clyde further down the water at **HAYLIE, LARGS**, the hill 3km from town reached via the A760 rd to Kilbirnie and Paisley. The island of Cumbrae lies in the sound and the sunset.

CAMPSIE FELLS and **GLENIFFER BRAES** : 714/715/WALKS O/SIDE THE CITY.

THE BEST OF THE SPORTS FACILITIES

SWIMMING AND INDOOR SPORTS CENTRES

The best 2 pools, Arlington Baths (332 6021) and the Western Baths (339 1127), are private. Temporary memberships may be negotiable. Others are:

727 **WHITEHILL POOL:** 551 9969. Onslow Dr parallel to Duke St at Meadowpark St
xE4 in the E End nr Alexandra Park (phone for times but usually Mon-Fri till 8.30pm and Sat-Sun till 1.45pm). 25m pool with sauna/multigym (Universal).

728 **NORTH WOODSIDE LEISURE CENTRE:** 332 8102. Braid Sq. Not far from St
B2 George's Cross nr Charing Cross at the bottom of Gr Western Rd. In a rebuilt area; follow AA signs. Modern pool (25m) and sauna/steam/sun centre. Mon-Fri 8/9am-7/8pm (Sat-Sun 10am-4pm).

729 **POLLOK LEISURE CENTRE:** 881 3313. Cowglen Rd. Not a do-your-lengths
xC5 kind of a pool – more a family water outing. Mon-Fri 9.30am-9pm, Sat/Sun 10am-4pm.

730 **GOUROCK BATHING POOL:** 01475 631561. On rd S, an open-air heated pool
xA5 on the Clyde. Gr prospect for summers like they used to be. (1893/SWIMMING POOLS)

731 **KELVIN HALL:** 357 2525. Argyle St by Kelvingrove Museum and Art Gallery
A2 (695/MAIN ATTRACTIONS). Major venue for international indoor sports competitions, but open otherwise for weights/badminton/tennis/athletics. Book hr-long sessions. No squash.

732 **SCOTSTOUN LEISURE CENTRE:** 959 4000. Danes Dr. Huge state-of-the-art
xA2 sports multiplex. 10 lane pool, indoor halls and outdoor pitches. 9am-10pm, w/ends till 6pm.

733 **MARCO'S:** 554 7184. Templeton Business Centre (beside the fabulous
xE4 Templeton Carpet Factory, by Glas Green in the E End. Like the Edin one, a labyrinthine and massively successful complex with squash/snooker/gym (Universal and First Class)/indoor jogging track (even though it is next to the Green). Nonmembers OK. 10am-10pm (Sat till 8pm). No pool.

734 **ALLANDER SPORTS CENTRE:** 942 2233. Milngavie Rd, Bearsden, 16km N of
xC1 centre via Maryhill Rd. Best by car. Squash (2 courts) badminton/snooker and swimming pool (open late, but times vary; usually till 10.30pm Tue/Thu/Fri and 9pm Sat-Sun). Waiting list for gym.

GOLF COURSES

Glas has a vast number of parks and golf courses. The following clubs are the best open to nonmembers. Refer to Around Glasgow map on pages 328–329.

735 **CATHKIN BRAES:** 634 0650. Cathkin Rd, SE via Aikenhead Rd/Carmunnock Rd
xC5 to Carmunnock village, then 3km. Best by car. Civilized hilltop course on the v southern edge of the city. Non-members Mon-Fri (though probably not Fri am).

736 **HAGGS CASTLE:** 427 1157. Dumbreck Rd nr jnct 22 of the M8; go straight on
xC5 to clubhouse at first r/bout. Part of the grounds of Pollok Park; a convenient course, perhaps overplayed, but not difficult to get on.

737 **POLLOK GOLF CLUB:** 632 1080. On the other side of the White Cart Water and
xC5 Pollok House and rather more up-market. Well-wooded parkland course, flat and well kept, but not cheap. Women not permitted to play.

738 **GLEDDOCH, LANGBANK:** 01475 540711. Excellent 18-hole course adj and
xA5 part of Gleddoch House Hotel (471/HOTELS O/SIDE TOWN). Restricted play.

THE BEST GALLERIES

*Apart from those listed previously (*MAIN ATTRACTIONS, OTHER ATTRACTIONS*) the following galleries are always worth looking into. The* Glasgow Gallery Guide, *free from any of them, lists all the current exhibs.*

739 ✓✓ **GLASGOW PRINT STUDIOS:** 552 0704. 22 King St. Influential and
E4 accessible upstairs gallery with print work on view and for sale from many of Scotland's leading and rising artists. Cl Sun. Print Shop over rd.

740 ✓✓ **TRANSMISSION GALLERY:** 552 4813. 28 King St. Cutting edge and
E4 often off-the-wall work from contemporary Scottish and international artists. Reflects Glasgow's increasing importance as a hot spot of conceptual art. Stuff you might disagree with. Cl Sun-Mon.

741 ✓✓ **THE GLASGOW ART FAIR:** George Sq in tented pavilions. Held
D3 every yr in mid-Apr. Most of the galleries on this page and many more are represented; highly selective and good fun.

742 ✓ **COMPASS GALLERY:** 221 6370. 178 W Regent St. Glasgow's oldest estab-
C3 lished commercial contemporary art gallery. Their 'New Generation' exhib in Jul-Aug shows work from new graduates of the art colleges and has heralded many a career. Combine with the other Gerber gallery (*see below*). Cl Sun.

743 ✓ **CYRIL GERBER FINE ART:** 221 3095. 148 W Regent St. British paintings
C3 and esp the Scottish Colourists and 'name' contemporaries. Gerber, the Compass (*see above*), and Art Exposure (*see below*) have Christmas exhibs where small, accessible paintings can be bought for reasonable prices. Cyril will know what's good for you. Cl Sun.

744 **ART EXPOSURE GALLERY:** 552 7779. 19 Parnie St. Behind the Tron Theatre.
E4 Showcase gallery with a friendly, down-to-earth attitude exhibiting the work of contemporary/graduate Scottish artists. Sort of 'affordable'. 11am-6pm. Cl Sun.

745 **SHARMANKA KINETIC GALLERY:** 552 7080. 14 King St, nr Trongate. Upstairs.
E4 Extraordinary gallery (theatre?) full of the fully-working mechanical sculptures of Russian emigre Eduard Berudsky. Unique and fascinating. W/ends 2-4pm. (706/OTHER ATTRACTIONS).

THE MACKINTOSH TRAIL

The gr Scottish architect and designer Charles Rennie Mackintosh (1868–1928) had an extraordinary influence on contemporary design. Glas is the best place to see his work.

746 ✓✓✓ **GLASGOW SCHOOL OF ART:** 353 4500. 167 Renfrew St.
C3 Mackintosh's supreme architectural triumph. It's enough almost to admire it from the st (and maybe best, since this is v much a working college) but there are guided tours at 11am and 2pm (Sat 10.30am) of the sombre yet light interior, the halls and library. You might wonder if the building itself could be partly responsible for its remarkable output of acclaimed painters. The Tenement House (705/OTHER ATTRACTIONS) is nearby.

747 ✓✓ **QUEEN'S CROSS CHURCH:** 870 Garscube Rd, where it becomes
xC1 Maryhill Rd (corner of Springbank St). Built 1896-99. Calm and simple, the antithesis of Victorian Gothic. If all churches had been built like this, we'd go more often. The HQ of the Charles Rennie Mackintosh Society, which was founded in 1973 (phone 946 6600). Mon-Fri 10am-5pm, Sat 10am-2pm, Sun 2-5pm. DONATION

748 ✓✓ **MACKINTOSH HOUSE:** 330 5431. Univ Ave. Opp and part of the
A1 Hunterian Museum (700/MAIN ATTRACTIONS) within the univ campus. The Master's house has been transplanted and methodically reconstructed from the next st (they say even the light is the same). If you've ever wondered what the fuss is about, go and see how innovative and complete an artist, designer and architect he was, in this inspiring yet habitable set of rms. Mon-Sat 9.30am-5pm (cl 12.30-1.30pm). Cl Sun. FREE

749   ✔   ✔ **SCOTLAND STREET SCHOOL:** 429 1202. 225 Scotland St. Opp
B5   Shields Rd underground and best app by car from Eglinton St (A77 Kilmarnock Rd over Jamaica St Br). Entire school (from 1906) preserved as museum of education through Victorian/Edwardian and wartimes. Original, exquisite Mackintosh features, esp tiling, and powerfully redolent of happy school days. This is a uniquely evocative time capsule. Café and temporary exhibs. Mon-Sat 10am-5pm, Sun 2-5pm.   FREE

750   **THE WILLOW TEAROOMS:** Sauchiehall St. The café he designed (or what's left
D3   of it); certainly where to go for a tea break on the trail (590/BEST TEAROOMS).

751   **THE HILL HOUSE, HELENSBURGH:** 01436 673900. Upper Colquhoun St. Take
xA3   Sinclair St off Princes St (at Romanesque tower and TO) and go 2km uphill, taking left into Kennedy Dr and follow signs. A complete house incorporating Mackintosh's typical total unity of design, built for Walter Blackie in 1902-4. Much to marvel over and wish that everybody else would go away and you could stay there for the night. There's even a library full of books to keep you occupied. Tearoom; grds. Apr-Oct 1.30-5.30pm. Helensburgh is 45km NW of city centre via Dumbarton (A82) and A814 up N Clyde coast.   ADMN

752   **MARTYR'S PUBLIC SCHOOL:** 946 6600. Parson St. Latest renovation and pub-
xE3   lic access to another spectacular Mackintosh building. Check those roof truss-es. Phone for times.   FREE

753   **HOUSE FOR AN ART LOVER:** 353 4770. Bellahouston Park. 10 Dumbreck Rd.
xA5   Take the M8 W, then the M77, turn rt onto Dumbreck Rd and it's on your left. These rms were designed, nearly a century ago, specifically, it would seem, for willowy women to come and go, talking of Michelangelo. Detail is the essence of Mackintosh, and there's plenty here, but the overall effect is of space and light and a complete absence of clutter. Design shop and Exhibition Café (592/BEST TEAROOMS) on the ground floor. Daily 10am-5pm.   ADMN

THE BEST CLUBS

Many of the best clubs come and go and there's little point in mentioning them here. Some are only on once a week with no permanent venue. Consult The List *(fortnightly) for up-to-date info, and look for flyers. Glas is a club city, but the dreaded curfew remains – check the following for current 'rules'.*

754   **CLUBS AT THE ARCHES:** 221 9736. At the Arches Theatre, Midland St
D4   (779/NIGHTLIFE), w/ends only. Glasgow's finest. 2/3 vaulted archways, serious sound system and v up-for-it crowd. Major millennium makeover to building but club nights set to continue. Best clubs: Inside Out, Slam one-offs.

755   **ARCHAOS:** 204 3189. 25 Queen St. Huge dance emporium on 3 floors, incl
D4   Betty's Mayonnaise. Central dance floor has state-of-the-art lighting. Balconies upstairs for action-checking and chilling. Atmos more rarified the higher you go.

756   **YANG:** 248 8484. 31 Queen St. Same crowd as Archaos *above*, but newer and
D4   fresher. Different clubs/DJs each night but open all week from 6pm.

757   **ALASKA:** 248 1777. 142 Bath Lane. Lane behind Bath St (behind the Spy Bar –
C3   679/PRE-CLUB BARS – same management). Laid-back bar area, hard-hitting dance floor. Cool as in … 1999.

758   **THE TUNNEL:** 221 7500. 84 Mitchell St. Once defined club culture in Glas. Still
D4   high-glam quotient and designer ambience with vogue-ish crowd. W/ends (Ark and Triumph) and student nights. On same circuit as Liverpool's Cream so big-name DJs every month.

759   **THE APARTMENT:** 221 7080. 23 Royal Exchange Sq. Colin and Kelly Barr's
D4   drinking club kind of disco for older, more discerning types. Exclusivity is part of the deal, but they have been known to let in any old footballer and hair-dresser. Similar crowd to be found downstairs in **BABAZA** (owned by King City Leisure). Apartment open Thu–Mon from 11pm.

760   **TRASH:** 572 3372. 197 Pitt St. Mega disco thing in W End. Student-ish crowd
C3   so not teensy. Clubs vary, till 3am.

761 **THE SUB CLUB:** 248 4600. 22 Jamaica St. Long-running, but revamped and
D4 still v much a scene. Eclectic music policy. Fri-Sat (some Thu and Sun).

762 **THE GARAGE:** 332 1120. 490 Sauchiehall St. The big night out for cheap
C3 drinks, chart sounds and copping off. Totally unpretentious. Live bands as
advertised.

THE BEST FOLK MUSIC AND CEILIDHS

763 ✓ ✓ **CELTIC CONNECTIONS:** 332 6633. Major jamboree every Jan. 3
D3 weeks of concerts, ceilidhs and gatherings. Broad appeal. Mainly at
the Glasgow Royal Concert Hall, but also at other venues city-wide, incl the
Old Fruitmarket in Albion St.

764 ✓ **CLUTHA VAULTS:** 167 Stockwell St. E end nr Clyde. Gr atmos for the drink
D4 and the music. Mixed programme: readings Tue, bluegrass Sat afternoons. (639/GR GLAS PUBS)

765 ✓ **THE HALT BAR:** Woodlands Rd. Among a mixed music programme, always
B2 some folk for the kind of folk who inhabit the bar. (634/GR GLAS PUBS)

766 ✓ **SCOTIA BAR:** 112 Stockwell St. The folk club and writers' retreat and all
D4 things non-high cultural. Club meets Wed night and Sat afternoons.
Always the 'right folk' here. (638/GR GLAS PUBS)

767 ✓ **VICTORIA BAR:** Bridgegate. Nr the Scotia (*see above*) and a similar set-up.
D4 Fri and Sat night sessions of Irish/Scottish trad music. (196/GR GLAS PUBS)

768 ✓ **THE RENFREW FERRY:** Enter by Clyde Pl via Jamaica St Br from N of river
C4 or Br St. A real ferry moored on the Clyde – brilliant ambience for ceilidhs
and gigs of all kinds. Fri 9pm-2am. Tickets at quay or in advance from Ticket
Centre, Candleriggs (227 5511), usually sold out by 10pm. Visitors and locals.
Gr bands.

769 **THE RIVERSIDE:** 248 3144. Fox St, off Clyde St. The place that started the
D4 ceilidh revival in Glas. Upstairs in quiet st, the joint is jumping. Fri-Sat from
8pm, fills up quickly. Good bands. Good, mixed crowd.

THE BEST ROCK AND POP MUSIC

For live music in smaller venues, see PUBS AND CLUBS WITH GOOD LIVE MUSIC.

770 ✓ ✓ ✓ **BARROWLAND BALLROOM:** Gallowgate. When its lights are
xE4 on, you can't miss it. The Barrowland is world-famous and for
many bands one of their favourite gigs. It's tacky and a bit run-down, but distinctly venerable; and with its high stage and sprung dance floor, perfect for
rock 'n' roll. The Glas audience is one of 'the best in the world'. True!

771 **SECC:** 248 3000. Finnieston Quay beyond the city centre and, for many,
A3 beyond the pale as far as concerts are concerned (big shed, not big on atmos),
but there are 3 different-sized halls for mainly arena-sized acts and everyone
from Eric to Pav and Oasis have played here. Glasgow's own, Wet Wet Wet, currently hold the record for numbers of nights sold – bet we won't see that
again!

772 **CLYDE AUDITORIUM, aka THE ARMADILLO:** Adj to the SECC. A smaller the-
A3 atre space, a belter for concerts, but not big enough for the megas.

*Neither of the above venues has its own box office. For tickets and information
check with Tower Records, Argyle St, 204 2500 and Virgin Records, Argyle St, 204
5151, and for credit card bookings 227 5511.*

773 **PAVILION THEATRE:** 332 1846. Renfield St. Regular concerts and a cosier
D3 place to watch a band.

GOOD NIGHTLIFE

For the current programmes of the places below and all other venues, consult The List *magazine, on sale fortnightly at most newsagents.*

CINEMA

There are all the usual multiplexes, but the best picture houses are:

774 **GLASGOW FILM THEATRE:** 332 6535. Rose St at downtown end of
C3 Sauchiehall St. Known affectionately as GFT, has bar and 2 screens for essential art house flicks.

775 **GROSVENOR:** 339 4928. Ashton Lane, off Byres Rd behind Hillhead Stn. Busy
A1 lane for eats and nightlife as well as this old cinema with 2 screens and a selected programme of mainly current hits.

THEATRE

776 ✓ ✓ **THE CITIZENS':** 429 0022. Gorbals St, just over the river. Fabulous
D5 main auditorium and 2 small studios. Drama at its v best. One of Britain's most influential theatres, esp for design. Reopened after lottery-funded renovations, now ready to take on the world – this is the one we love!

777 ✓ ✓ **THE TRAMWAY:** 422 2023. 25 Albert Dr on S-side. A theatre and vast
xC5 performance space. Dynamic and widely influential with an innovative and varied programme from all over the world. Seasonal programme. Reopening at time of going to press.

778 ✓ **CCA:** 332 7521. Centre for Contemporary Arts, 350 Sauchiehall St. Central
C3 arts-lab complex, notable as a theatre for modern dance (esp in spring with its New Moves programme), but also has gallery and other performance space and a good café. Cl 1999 for renovation.

779 ✓ **THE ARCHES:** 221 9736. Midland St, betw Jamaica St and Oswald St.
D4 Experimental and vital theatre on a tight budget in the railway arches under the tracks of Central Stn. Andy Arnold will not lie down. Opening times vary. W/end clubs among the best (754/BEST CLUBS). Major millennium renovations underway.

780 **RSAMD:** 332 4101. 100 Renfrew St. The Royal Scottish Academy of Music and
D3 Drama. Part and wholly student productions often with guest directors. Eclectic, often powerful mix.

781 **THE TRON THEATRE:** 552 4267. 63 Trongate. Contemporary Scottish theatre
E4 and other interesting performance, esp music. Recent face-lift. Gr café-bar with food before and *après* (520/BEST BISTROS).

782 **KING'S THEATRE:** 227 5511. Bath St. Trad theatre with shows like pantos,
C3 Gilbert and Sullivan and major touring musicals.

CLASSICAL MUSIC

783 **THEATRE ROYAL:** 332 3321. Hope St. Home of Scottish Opera, with a mainly
D3 high-brow diet of opera, ballet (from Scottish Ballet) and some drama.

784 **GLASGOW ROYAL CONCERT HALL:** 332 6633. Top of Buchanan St. Sep-Apr
D3 subscription series and Jun Proms from the Royal Scottish National Orchestra, plus visits from national and international orchestras.

785 **CITY HALLS:** 227 5511. Candleriggs. Winter subscription series provided by
E4 the Scottish Chamber Orchestra and BBC Scottish Symphony Orchestra.

786 **RSAMD:** 332 4101. 110 Renfrew St. Student productions often excel.
D3

787 **HUTCHESON'S HALL:** 552 8391. 158 Ingram St. Chamber concerts and
E4 recitals, many at lunchtime, in this NTS property.

JAZZ

788 See *The List* or *Live Scene*, a monthly freesheet. Best venues: **INTERNATIONAL JAZZ FESTIVAL** in early Jul (227 5511). Rest of the year: **BOURBON STREET** (552 0141), **THE BABY GRAND, THE BREWERY TAP** and **BLACKFRIARS.** Sun afternoon jazz at the **PAISLEY ARTS CENTRE,** New St (887 1010). Occasional gigs at **PIZZA EXPRESS**, 151 Queen St (221 3333), and concerts at the **MITCHELL THEATRE** (287 4855).

SECTION 3

Regional Hotels and Restaurants, including Aberdeen and Dundee

THE BEST HOTELS AND RESTAURANTS IN ARGYLL

See also 2169/CENTRES: OBAN. *Refer to Map 1.*

789
B1 ✔✔ **AIRDS HOTEL, PORT APPIN:** 01631 730236. 40km N of Oban 4km off A828. A gourmet experience and all round welcome from the Allens awaits you here in this refined hotel in a charming corner of Scotland. Member of cosmopolitan *Relais et Châteaux* group (and in all the other guide-books that count). Many ingredients come from v nearby incl a lovingly tended kitchen garden; Graeme Allen is a consummate chef. Nice short walk behind the house and they also arrange field trips and picnics. The family guesthouse up the rd is a cheaper stopover. Lismore passenger ferry 2km away (2117/MAGIC ISLANDS). 14RMS MAR-DEC T/T XPETS CC KIDS LOTS/MED.INX

EAT One of the best meals you will find in the N (and S, E and W). EXP

790
B2 ✔ **KILFINAN HOTEL, KILFINAN:** 01700 821201. 13km from Tighnabruaich. On B8000 which, 7km further N, joins L Fyne at Otter Ferry and continues to Strachur. Coaching inn, nestling in terraced grds, comfortably furnished throughout. Quality is paramount to Lynne and Rolf Mueller and it comes over in everything, not least the food. An elegant and cosy retreat. 11RMS JAN-DEC T/T PETS CC KIDS TOS MED.EXP

EAT Rolf's expertise with local produce: 3 AA rosettes; also barmeals. EXP

791
C1 ✔ **TAYCHREGGAN, KILCHRENAN:** 01866 833211. Signed off A85 just before Taynuilt, 30km from Oban and nestling on a bluff by L Awe in imposing countryside. Quay for the old ferry to Portsonachan is nearby with boats available. The Pauls have turned this long-established loch side inn into a fine and not too exp hotel with a restau where even locals come the long and winding (and enchanting) rd to eat. Pleasant rms and bar. That awesome loch is always there outside. 19RMS JAN-DEC T/X PETS CC KIDS TOS LOTS

EAT Nicely judged menu, always interesting. Euan's good wine list.

EXP

792
C2 **STONEFIELD CASTLE HOTEL, TARBERT (ARGYLL):** 01880 820836. Just o/side town on the A83, a castle which evokes the 1970s more than preceding centuries. Splendid grds leading down to L Fyne. Swimming pool no longer (shame). The surrounding luxuriant grds are fabulous. Dining-rm with crazy carpet and staggering views. Friendly, flexible staff; overall, it seems quintessentially Scottish and ok, esp for families (1098/KIDS) though style people may moan. They prefer that you have dinner too. (MED). 33RMS JAN-DEC T/T PETS CC KIDS MED.EX

793
C2 **ARDENTINNY HOTEL, DUNOON:** 01369 810209. 20km N via A880/A885. Trad, Clydeside inn by Glen Finart forest adj L Long. Beer garden on cove with moorings. Back on course after a management hiccup – same owner and chef. Good value. Alternative access on L Goil Cruiser 'water taxi', 01301 703349. 11RMS DEC-OCT T/T PETS CC KIDS TOS MED.INX

794
C2 **WEST LOCH HOTEL, TARBERT (ARGYLL):** 01880 820283. Picturesque 1710 former coaching inn on the cusp of Kintyre, just o/side of Tarbert on A83. Within easy reach of ferries to Islay, Gigha and Arran. Lovely views of loch over rd, freshly furnished whilst retaining authentic features. New owners since last edition, but aside from the odd extra here and there, they're keeping the character. Good food, relaxing though roadside rms may be noisy. Feel at home here (1124/INNS). 9RMS JAN-DEC X/T PETS CC KIDS MED.INX

795
C2 **COLUMBA HOTEL, TARBERT:** 01880 820808. Ideal budget hotel on water front in this perfect Argyll town. 'Net Store' bar v popular with yachties and locals. Bedrms seem constantly to be refurb; 4 huge superior rms ideal for families. Unusual gym and sauna. 10RMS JAN-DEC T/T PETS CC KIDS TOS MED.INX

796
B1 **BARRIEMORE, OBAN:** 01631 566356. Corran Esplanade. This hotel, the v last one in a st full of them along the coast to Ganavan, is a good bet if you're in Oban. Front rms have excellent views of Kerrera and Lorne. B&B only. 13RMS MAR-JAN X/X PETS CC KIDS INX

ARDANAISEIG, LOCH AWE: 01866 833333 (1086/COUNTRY-HOUSE HOTELS).
ISLE OF ERISKA: 01631 720371. 20km N of Oban (1078/COUNTRY-HOUSE HOTELS).
LOCH MELFORT: 01852 200233. 22km S of Oban (1085/COUNTRY-HOUSE HOTELS).

RESTAURANTS

797 ✓ **CREGGANS INN, STRACHUR:** 01369 860279. 2km N Strachur on A815 to
C2 Cairndow, a busy rd in summer along L Fyne. Road house bar/restau and
more formal dining-rm a successful combination of the popular and the more
particular. From burgers in the bar to Arran queenies eaten off crisp linen, to
cream teas in a coffee shop where you can sit o/side. The fiefdom of the late
Sir Fitzroy and Lady Maclean, the coffee shop sells their considerable canon of
books. Something for everybody, as they say. Excl wine-list.   CHP/MED/EXP

798 ✓ **CHATTERS, DUNOON:** 01369 706402. 58 John St next to Safeway. Rosie
C2 Macinnes' excellent restau in town rather than on esplanade is, by itself,
a good reason for getting the ferry. The Cowal peninsula awaits your explorations (and Benmore Grds 1376/GARDENS). Bar menu and à la carte, and a
small grd for drinks or lunch on a good day. All delightful. Mon-Sat 10am-3pm;
6-10pm. Cl Feb.   MED

799 ✓ **THE KILBERRY INN:** 01880 770223. Superlative home-cooking in road-
B3 side pub betw Tarbert and Lochgilphead by the coastal route (B8024).
Better than many more highfalutin' restaus. Fuller report: 1205/BEST FOOD. INX

THE BEST HOTELS AND RESTAURANTS IN AYRSHIRE & CLYDE VALLEY

See also 2163/AYR. Refer to Map 1.

800 ✓✓ **TURNBERRY HOTEL, TURNBERRY:** 01655 331000. Not just a hotel
C4 on the Ayrshire coast, more a way of life centred on golf. Looks over
the 2 courses which are difficult to get on unless you're a guest (1839/GREAT
GOLF). All that should be expected of a world-class hotel except, perhaps, the
buzz; but plenty of golf chat and time moving slowly. The spa complex adj has
state-of-the-art 'treatments', even exercise. Special £105 deal incl lunch and
all-day use of facs – you could pop down from Glasgow! Brasserie here has
excl 'light' all day menus; main dining-rm looks over the courses to Ailsa Craig
beyond – dinner only, and epic Sun lunch.

132RMS JAN-DEC T/T PETS CC KIDS TOS LOTS

EAT The Bay is the light place to eat; pastas, risottos, etc. Also main restau.
MED/EXP

801 ✓ **GLEDDOCH HOUSE, LANGBANK, nr GREENOCK:** 01475 540711. 35km
C2 from Glas by fast rd – M8/A8 t/off marked Langbank/Houston after jnct
31, follow signs. Set in extensive grounds (including 18-hole golf course), with
commanding view of Clyde by Dumbarton Rock (but only from a few rms).
Small leisure club adj. Excellent conservatory and dining-rms. Most civilised
place to stay close to Glas.   38RMS JAN-DEC T/T PETS CC KIDS

EAT Excellent restau with 2 AA rosettes. Scottish accents.   EXP

802 ✓ **SCORETULLOCH HOUSE HOTEL, DARVEL:** 01560 32331. Signed 2km off
D3 A71 at E end of Priestland E of Kilmarnock. On a hillside o/looking the R
Irvine. An unimposing country house with notable restaus – the Loudoun rm
for imaginative fine dining (2 AA rosette) and Oscar's Brasserie. Go for it attitude here (they even have a newsletter) and gr attention to comfort and
detail. Good hideaway from Glasgow (they say, $1/2$ hr up the rd).

8RMS JAN-DEC T/T PETS CC KIDS TOS MED.EX

803 **CHAPELTOUN HOUSE HOTEL, STEWARTON:** 01560 482696. 12km from
C3 Irvine. On A735 S of Stewarton, B769 to Irvine, then signposts. The Dobson
family always refurbing, retaining the oakiness and charming grounds (but
they must improve the pictures). Keen to raise from 2 to 3 AA rosettes, this is
a dining-rm to watch around here. 8RMS JAN-DEC T/T XPETS CC XKIDS TOS LOTS

804 **MONTGREENAN, nr KILWINNING:** 01294 557733. Take A736 (5km) from the
C3 A78 around Irvine and several r/bouts later you arrive in a surprisingly woody
enclave and a civilised country-house hotel (phone for directions). Woody
and friendly inside too, and recently taken over by the estimable Leckies
who own Crieff Hydro, so we can expect improv. Restau open non res. A Best
Western hotel.   21RMS JAN-DEC T/T PETS CC KIDS TOS LOTS

805 **PIERSLAND HOTEL, TROON:** 01292 314747. Craig End Rd opp Portland Golf
C3 Course which is next to Royal Troon (1837/GREAT GOLF). Mansion house of
some character and ambience much favoured for weddings. Wood-panelling,
open fires, lovely grds only a 'drive' away from the courses (no preferential
booking on Royal, but Portland usually poss) and lots of gr golf nearby.
Notable locally for bar meals.   28RMS JAN-DEC T/T PETS CC KIDS TOS EXP

806 **LOCHGREEN HOUSE, TROON:** 01292 313343. Elegant country-house hotel in
C3 golfing green Ayrshire (2163/AYR). Astute owners, the Costleys, also have the
BRIG O'DOON HOTEL, ALLOWAY, nr AYR: 01292 442466. On bank and by br
over the Doon, and grds. Good setting visited by hordes of tourists, since in
this corner are also found the old Brig (at end of the grd), the Alloway Kirk and
the Monument in question (1740/LITERARY PLACES). Mostly weddings, only
5rms.

RESTAURANTS

807 ✓ **FOUTERS, AYR:** 01292 261391. 2a Academy St. Off Sandgate. The best
C3   meal in town. Laurie and Fran Black, amazingly here 25 yrs on and still
caring about food and wine and Scotland's efforts to do better. Creative cooking and here the phrase 'best local ingredients' means what it says. Tue-Sat:
lunch and LO 10.30pm.   MED

808 ✓ **BRAIDWOODS, nr DALRY:** 01294 833544. Off main A78 coast rd, take
C3   Dalry Rd at Saltcoats, 6km along country rd: the Braidwood's white-
washed cottages and Keith's legendary cooking. This is better than most of
Glas and much better value (incl wines). Wed/Sat lunch and Tues-Sat dinner.
MED

809 ✓ **WILDINGS, GIRVAN:** 01465 713481. 56 Montgomerie St opp Ailsa Craig
C4   Hotel, off rd into Girvan from Ayr. Colourful, cosy restau effortlessly pre-
eminent in the area. Big menu exceedingly well done. Tues-Sat: lunch and LO
9 pm.   MED

810 ✓ **RISTORANTE LA VIGNA, LANARK:** 01555 664320. 40 Wellgate. Famously
D3   good Italian restau in a back st in Lanark. 7 days, lunch and dinner. Must
book.   MED

811 **VICTORIA HOUSE, GOUROCK:** 01475 630033. Main st above the trad Victoria
C2 pub, an excl new restau; still not in the foodie guides but big local reputation
(book a month ahead for w/ends). 7 days, dinner only LO 9.30pm.   INX

C3 **FINS, FAIRLIE, nr LARGS:** 01475 568989. 8 km S of Largs on A78. Excellent
seafood bistro. Report: 1250/SEAFOOD RESTAUS.   MED

MACCALLUMS, THE HARBOUR, TROON: 01292 319339. Harbourside
seafood bistro. Report: 1244/SEAFOOD.   MED

THE BEST HOTELS AND RESTAURANTS IN THE SOUTH-WEST

See also 2164/CENTRES: DUMFRIES. *Refer to Map 9.*

812
A3 ✓ ✓ **KNOCKINAAM LODGE, PORTPATRICK:** 01776 810471. Tucked away on dream cove, historic country house full of fresh flowers, gr food, sea air and informal, but v good service. Run by Canadians who know and love what they're doing. Their enjoyment is yours (1080/COUNTRY-HOUSE HOTELS).

10RMS JAN-DEC T/T PETS CC KIDS TOS LOTS

EAT Best meal in the S. from outstanding chef, Tony Pierce. Fixed menu – lots of unexpected treats. *Michelin* Star. EXP

813
A3 ✓ **CORSEWALL LIGHTHOUSE HOTEL, STRANRAER:** 01776 853220. A718 to Kirkcolm 3km, B738 to Corsewall 6km (follow signs). Wild location on cliff top. Cosily furnished clever but cramped (or snug) conversion. Best with a suite and a close personal friend. The adj fully functioning lighthouse (since 1817) makes for surreal evenings. No one night stays at w/ends.

6RMS (+ COTTS) JAN-DEC T/T PETS CC KIDS LOTS

814
B3 **KIRROUGHTREE HOTEL, NEWTON STEWART:** 01671 402141. On A712. Built 1719, Rabbie Burns' was once here. Extensive country house newly refurb with heavy drapes and plush atmos. Original panelled hall and stairs, spacious rms. Food here gets 3 AA rosettes and is probably the main reason for coming. Golf at the Cally Palace nearby, the other big hotel around here.

17RMS FEB-DEC T/T PETS CC KIDS TOS LOTS

815
C3 **BALCARY BAY, AUCHENCAIRN, nr CASTLE DOUGLAS:** 01556 640311. 20km S of Castle Douglas and Dalbeattie. Off A711 at end of shore rd. Watch fishermen casting their nets in the hazy bay. Ideal base for walking and birdwatching: hotel may be deserted by day. Gr hideaway spot but perhaps time for a makeover.

17RMS MAR-NOV T/T PETS CC KIDS TOS EXP

816
C3 **CLONYARD HOUSE, COLVEND, nr ROCKCLIFFE, nr DALBEATTIE:** 01556 630372. On Solway Coast rd nr Rockcliffe and Kippford (1418/COASTAL VILLAGES; 1640/ COASTAL WALKS) but not on sea. Later extension to house provides bedrms adj to patio grd with own private access and … aviary! A bit dated furniture-wise, but friendly family atmos presided over by Hudson, the parrot. Decent pub grub.

15RMS JAN-DEC T/T PETS CC KIDS MED.INX

817
B3 **CORSEMALZIE HOUSE, PORT WILLIAM, nr NEWTON STEWART:** 01988 860254. A714 from main A75 S of Newton Stewart then B7005 through Bladnoch; follow signs after br (8km). Trad granite house with comfortable rms, hidden in beautiful bluebell woods. Fishing on R Bladnoch and their own loch. Kitchen garden cooking.

14RMS MAR-JAN T/T XPETS CC KIDS TOS EXP

818
D3 **COMLONGON CASTLE, CLARENCEFIELD, nr DUMFRIES:** 013878 70283. 14km S of Dumfries. Early 20th-century house beside 15th-century castle, set in lush acreage extending down to the Solway. Atmos, panelled rms, armour and weaponry. Popular wedding venue (200 a year!), 4-poster beds. The smell of apples when the ghost's around.

11RMS FEB-DEC T/T XPETS CC KIDS MED.EX

819
C3 **GOOD SPOTS IN KIRKCUDBRIGHT:** pronounced 'cur-coo-bree'; a gem of a town. 3 fine hotels. **GLADSTONE HOUSE:** 01557 331734, a 'Gleneagles' guesthouse with grds, is superb and v inexp but only has 3rms; **GORDON HOUSE HOTEL:** 01557 330670 (12 rms, cheap and cheerful); and **THE SELKIRK ARMS:** 01557 330402 (17 rms, all mod cons, but not cheap). Selkirk Arms has probably the best food in town (*see over*).

820
C3 **ANCHOR, KIPPFORD:** 01556 620205. Seaside hotel in cute vill 3km off main A710. Good pub food and atmos (*see below*).

7RMS (+ COTT) JAN-DEC X/T PETS CC KIDS INX

821
C3 **ABBEY ARMS & CRIFFEL INN, NEW ABBEY, nr DUMFRIES:** 01387 850489/850244. Opp each other on village sq, comfy rms above village inns with loads of atmos nr Sweetheart Abbey and Criffel (1765/HILLS) 12km S of Dumfries.

CHP

RESTAURANTS

822
C3
✓ **WISHARTS, DUMFRIES:** 01387 259679. Best restau in the S in unusual location ie. Dumfries. Inconspicuous atop the Robert Burns Centre o/look R.Nith. Find it opp the TIC and cross one of the 2 pedestrian bridges. Excl contemp British food by star chef Mark Wishart. Hrs may change but currently Tues-Sat dinner LO 9.30pm and Sun lunch in summer.   MED

823
A3
THE CROWN, PORTPATRICK: 01776 810216. Harbourside hotel/pub restau with better than your av pub-grub. Goes a like a fair in summer. Lounge and conservatory. Most excl chips. 7 days. LO 10pm.   INX

824
A3
CAMPBELLS, PORTPATRICK: 01776 810314. Further round harbour from Crown, above – this is where the chef came. More upmarket but medium range seafood bistro. Unpretentious fishy fare (some pork/lamb/beef/duck/chicken dishes ie something for every one). 7 days lunch and LO 10pm. Cl Mon and Jan – Mar.   INX

825
C3
ANCHOR, KIPPFORD: 01556 620205. Waterfront hotel/bar on the 'Scottish Riviera'. Gr atmos in snug lounges and gr for family meals. 7rms above (so also rec as an inx hotel, above). 7 days, lunch and dinner.   CHP

826
C3
THE SELKIRK ARMS, KIRKCUDBRIGHT: 01557 330402. At east end of High st. Small country hotel with surprisingly good cuisine. Conservatory dining rm and less formal bistro. Lunch and dinner 7-9.30pm (bistro from 6pm). 7 days.
                                                                                        INX/MED

827
C3
THE AULD ALLIANCE, KIRKCUDBRIGHT: 01557 330569. Solway scallops and salmon, etc. 7 nights. (Easter-Oct) – no credit cards though. Also **LA DOLCE VITA**, 01557 331391. OK Italiano in gr town. Cl Sun, Mon. Both restaus are central and easy to find.

828
C3
CARLO'S, CASTLE DOUGLAS: 211 King Street, 01556 503977. Bustling atmos in small rm with odd green phone box. Best Italian food in S. Cl Mon.   INX

THE BEST HOTELS AND RESTAURANTS IN CENTRAL SCOTLAND

See also 2171/CENTRES: STIRLING. *Refer to Map 6.*

829
C2 ✓ ✓ **CROMLIX HOUSE, DUNBLANE:** 01786 822125. 3km from A9 and 4km from town on B8033; first follow signs for Perth, and then Kinbuck. A long drive through an old estate with splendid mature trees to this spacious, not gloomy Victorian house, meticulously redecorated by Ailsa and David Assenti. Unquestionably one of the gr country-house hotels in Scotland with excellent service and attention to detail. Staff ratio 2:1 and a happy crew. Who wouldn't be in these glorious Perthshire acres with fishing lochs (the House Loch nearby complete with swans and solitude) and Paul Devonshire's 2 AA rosette menu.   14RMS (8 SUITES) FEB-DEC T/T PETS CC KIDS LOTS

EAT Non-residents: drive that drive for dinner (or Sun lunch)! Gr conservatory.
EXP

830
C2 ✓ ✓ **THE ROMAN CAMP, CALLANDER:** 01877 330003. Behind the main st (at E or Stirling end), away from the tourist throng and with extensive grds on the R Teith; another, more elegant world. Roman ruins nearby, but the house was built for the Dukes of Perth and has been a hotel since the war. Rms low-ceilinged and snug; period furnishings; some rms small, many magnificent. O/side, the corridors do creak. Delightful drawing rm and conservatory. Round dining-rm v sympatico. Private chapel should a prayer (or wedding) come on. Rods for fishing – and the river swishes the lawn.
14RMS JAN-DEC T/T PETS CC KIDS TOS LOTS

EAT Dining-rm effortlessly the best food in town (with chef Ian McNaught).
EXP

831
D3 ✓ **GEAN HOUSE, ALLOA:** 01259 219275. On edge of town on B9096 to Tullibody (turn up by Town Hall). Untypical Scottish manor house, Edwardian and reminiscent of Lutyens' Greywalls at Gullane, and turned into a hotel which is the epitome of stylish comfort. Warm, wood-panelled and furnished in simple good taste; cosy inglenook fireplace. Comfy bedrms, terraced grds. New owners at time of going to press, so changes anticipated. Old Ochils not far away.   7RMS JAN-DEC T/T PETS CC KIDS LOTS

832
C3 **STIRLING HIGHLAND, STIRLING:** 01786 475444. Reasonably sympathetic conversion of former school (with modern accom block) in the historic section of town on rd up to castle. Serviceable modern hotel in prime location; light 17m pool. 'Sophisticated' Scholars restau up top (2 AA rosettes); the Italian bistro, Rizzios at st level, is not so *al dente*, but pleasant enough.
78RMS JAN-DEC T/T PETS CC KIDS MED.EX/EXP

833
C3 **BLAIRLOGIE HOUSE, STIRLING:** 01259 761441. 7km E of town centre on A91. A Victorian house truly nestling at the foot of the hills, in this case the splendid Ochils (1777/HILL WALKS). Well-kept grds (with azaleas and bluebells in spring) tumble to the rd. Cosy and accommodating (nice) family home; bright dining-rm. Much better value than many self-conscious country-house hotels. Views over Forth flood plain. Wallace Monument is nearby (1665/MONUMENTS). Michelin listed.   7RMS JAN-DEC T/T PETS CC KIDS MED.INX

834
B2 **LAKE HOTEL, PORT OF MENTEITH:** 01877 385258. A v lake side hotel on the Lake of Menteith in the purple heart of the Trossachs. Good centre for touring and walking. The Inchmahome ferry leaves from nearby (1727/MARY, CHARLIE AND BOB). Only a few rms o/look lake (3 newer ones carry supplement, but are worth the extra). Splendid conservatory for sunset supper. Romantic or what?
16RMS JAN-DEC T/T PETS CC KIDS TOS MED.EX

835
C2 **DUNBLANE HYDRO, DUNBLANE:** 01786 822551. One of the huge hydro hotels left over from the last health boom, this one is part of the Stakis chain. Nice views for some and a long walk down corridors for most. Exercise also in the gym and the pool. It's a dinner-dance world.
215RMS JAN-DEC T/T PETS KIDS CC TOS EXP

836
A2 **INVERARNAN HOTEL/THE DROVER'S INN, INVERARNAN:** 01301 704234. N of Ardlui on L Lomond and 12km S of Crianlarich on the A82. Much the same

as it was when it began in 1705; bare floors, open fires, shared facs and heavy drinking (1178/BLOODY GOOD PUBS). Highland hoolies here much recommended Bar staff wearing kilts look like they mean it. Rms are not Gleneagles. A wild place in the wilderness. 20RMS JAN-DEC X/X PETS CC KIDS CHP

837 **HOTELS IN KILLIN:** Killin is on the corner of the old 'Central' region, but is a v
B2 Highland sort of a place. Famous for the Falls of Dochart, the rocky course of the river that runs through the town, and with mighty Ben Lawers nearby, it is a good gateway for pts N and W. There are 2 good inexp hotels. **THE KILLIN HOTEL:** 01567 820296. V Scottish, tartan everywhere, pleasant old-fashioned feel; conservatory on front. **DALL LODGE:** 01567 820217. Smaller, more personal, many *objets*. Both hotels on main st.

32/10RMS JAN-DEC T/T PETS CC KIDS MED.INX

RESTAURANTS

838 ✓ **THE UNICORN INN, KINCARDINE:** 01259 730704; 15 Excise St. Nr
D3 Kincardine Br in village (Stirling 20km, M9 5km jnct 7). I get lost and ask at the petrol stn. Unique spot in this part of the world; bistro atmos, most excellent food. Light, Mediterranean app (and Spanish music). Seafood medley is a signature dish (there are live lobsters in a tank downstairs). Tapas at lunchtime. Gr cheeseboard. Nice people, chef Brian Ainslie taught by a maestro. MED

839 ✓ **BLACK BULL, KILLEARN:** 01360 550215. Good-looking village, 30mins N
B3 of Glasgow betw L Lomond (Drymen) and the Campsies. Excellent pub food and conservatory restau. 2 AA rosettes & Michelin only open w/ends. Other nights food in bar area. Good service, cuisine way beyond usual pub standard. Excellent puds. Live jazz. MED

840 ✓ **CREAGAN HOUSE, STRATHYRE:** 01877 384638. End of the village on
B2 main A84 for Crianlarich. Creagan House is the place to eat in Rob Roy country and there are some wonderful walks pre and *après* (1761/HILLS). They have 5 inexp rms and the Gunns (incl the v large hound) are an extremely congenial bunch. Gordon Gunn is also an innovative and individualist chef and ingredients come local, incl the grd. Going from 1 to 2 AA rosettes reflects their continuing commitment to good grub. Cl Feb. MED

841 ✓ **CROSS KEYS HOTEL AND BAR, KIPPEN:** 01786 870293. Main st of
C3 couthie town 15km W of Stirling by A811. Excellent pub-food winning accolades for yonks. Gr for families and generally for informal unpretentious approach and atmos. A wee treasure. (1210/PUB FOOD). LO 9.30pm. INX

842 ✓ **THE ALLAN WATER CAFÉ, BRIDGE OF ALLAN:** Caff that's been here for
C3 ever at the end of the main st in Bridge of Allan. Original features, gr feel, gr fish 'n' chips and, of course, the ice cream (1276/CAFÉS). 7 days, 9am-9pm.
CHP

843 **KIPLINGS, BRIDGE OF ALLAN:** 01786 833617. Well Rd off the main st and up
C3 the hill towards Sherriffmuir in dreaming and amazingly well-heeled suburb of Stirling/Bridge of Allan. Even the birds twitter politely. Like much of this, the restau probably looks better from the o/side. But Stirling comes over. EXP

THE BEST HOTELS AND RESTAURANTS IN THE BORDERS

See also 2167/CENTRES: HAWICK AND GALASHIELS, p. 297. *Refer to Map 8.*

844
C2 ✓ ✓ **ROXBURGH HOTEL, nr KELSO:** 01573 450331. *The* best country-house hotel in the Borders. Owned by the Duke and Duchess of Roxburghe, who have a personal input. Refurb ongoing, incl 4-poster beds, etc. Reliable wine list (by the Duke) and menu (safe and satisfying). The newish 18-hole golf course has broadened appeal – it's challenging (championship standard) and in a beautiful riverside setting (1865/GOLF). Compared with other hotels hereabouts, the Roxburgh can be good value. A taste of the high life without being stuffy. 22RMS JAN-DEC T/T PETS CC KIDS TOS EXP

EAT Where to go for fine dining and wining in the E Borders. Chef Keith Short. Also the Brasserie o/looking golf course open w/ends. EXP

845
C2 ✓ ✓ **CRINGLETIE HOUSE, PEEBLES:** 01721 730233. Country house 5km from town just off A703 Edin rd (35km). Late 19th-century Scottish baronial house in 28 acres. Recently refurb and more comfortable & civilized than ever. Conservatory does light lunches and nice aft tea. Walled garden provides all fruit and veg. 13RMS JAN-DEC T/T PETS CC KIDS TOS LOTS

EAT Gracious dining (o/looking) conservatory & garden. Friendly, relaxing city escape MED

846
C3 ✓ **BURTS, MELROSE:** 01896 822285. In Market Sq/main st, some (double-glazed) rms o/look. Busy bars, esp for food, The dining-rm is *where to eat* in this part of the Borders. Trad, but comfortably modernised small town hotel, though some rms also feel small. Convenient location. Good service (1718/ABBEYS; 1776/HILL WALKS; 1386/GARDENS).
21RMS JAN-DEC T/T PETS CC KIDS TOS MED.EX

EAT Jolly and busy bar, more refined dining-rm. Has 2 AA rosettes. EXP

847
C2 **DRYBURGH ABBEY HOTEL, nr ST BOSWELLS:** 01835 822261. Secluded, elegant 19th-century house in Abbey grounds banking R Tweed. Peaceful atmos; good swimming pool, and riverside walks.
26RMS JAN-DEC T/T PETS CC KIDS TOS EXP

848
B3 **PHILIPBURN, SELKIRK:** 01750 720747. 1km from town centre on A707 Peebles Rd. Recent complete refurb for long est family-run hotel (new owners). Used to be my favourite Borders hotel, not tried since makeover but looks good. Dining rm bar-bistro and rare outdoor pool. (with garden rms o/looking)
17RMS JAN-DEC T/T PETS CC KIDS EXP

849
C3 **JEDFOREST COUNTRY HOTEL, nr JEDBURGH:** 01835 840222. On A68 about 12km from the border at Carter Bar (the first hotel in Scotland!) and 5km from Jedburgh, my home town. A hotel that always had potential, now finally under competent ownership. Refurb rms and notable restau (French chef, 2 AA rosettes). You must walk down to that magic river.
8RMS JAN-DEC T/T XPETS CC KIDS MED.INX

850
C2 **EDNAM HOUSE, KELSO:** 01573 224168. Just off town sq, o/look R Tweed; a majestic Georgian mansion with original features incl some of the guests! Dated in a comfy way, fishing regalia dotted around; the restau's river view is poss its main attraction. 32RMS JAN-DEC T/T PETS CC KIDS TOS MED.INX

851
C2 **CLINT LODGE, ST BOSWELLS:** 01835 822027. Phone for directions, but on B6356 (1489/SCENIC ROUTES). Small country-house GH in gr border country with some tranquil views from rms and good home cooking. A wee bit special.
5RMS JAN-DEC X/T PETS XCC KIDS INX

RESTAURANTS

EATING IN MELROSE (the Borders best bet):

852
C2 ✓ **MARMIONS:** 01896 822245. Buccleuch St nr the abbey. Local fave bistro, now going a long time, but on our last visit it was better food-wise than ever. Lunch and dinner. Cl Sun. INX

853 ✓ **KINGS ARMS:** 01896 822143. High St. Excl barfood in 17th cent coaching
C2 inn. The locals choice. LO 9pm (9.30pm Sat).

854 **MELROSE STATION RESTAURANT:** 01896 822546.TOS. Another French-
C2 inspired eaterie, in stn conversion. Jostles for bistro slot with Marmions. (Wed-
Sun lunch, Wed-Sat dinner) INX

BURTS and **CRINGLETIE** (*see above*): Burts for fine dining in town, Cringletie
for country treat.

HORSESHOE INN, EDDLESTON: 01721 730225. Edin Rd o/side Peebles
(1228/PUB FOOD). CHP

855 **CASTLEGATE TEAROOMS and RESTAURANT, JEDBURGH:** 01835 862592.
C3 26 Castlegate nr Abbey. Home-made food incl puds in homely parlour. Not
licensed BYOB. Lunch and dinner 7 days. INX

856 **CULTER MILL, nr ABINGTON:** 01899 220950. A respite from the frustration of
MAP 9 crawling along in a convoy on the A702 (the main Edin – S route). Neatly con-
C1 verted mill – delicious fuel for the rd (fresh fish in batter is perfection). Cl Mon-
Tue. Lunch, LO 9pm (10pm Sat). Book at w/ends. INX

857 **KAILZIE GARDENS and RESTAURANT TEAROOM nr PEEBLES:** 01721
B2 722807. Report: 1284/TEAROOMS, but also a gr spot for dinner. CHP

THE BEST HOTELS AND RESTAURANTS IN THE LOTHIANS

See section 1 for Edin. Refer to Map 7.

858 ✓✓ **GREYWALLS, GULLANE:** 01620 842144. On the coast, 36km E of
B1 Edin off A198 just beyond golfers' paradise of Gullane. O/looks
Muirfield, the championship course (no right of access) and nr Gullane's 3
courses and N Berwick's 2 (1841/1842/GREAT GOLF). No grey walls here but
warm sandstone and light, summery public rms in this Lutyens-designed
manor with grds attributed to Gertrude Jekyll. It's the look that makes it special and the roses are legendary. Sculpture grd in July and literary lunches.
Library like a London club, and service. Golf ain't everything.
22RMS APR-OCT T/T PETS CC XKIDS TOS LOTS

EAT Fine and subtle dining in elegant rm adj course; experienced chef Simon
Burn is a confident player. Wine list has depth and character. EXP

859 ✓✓ **CHAMPANY INN nr LINLITHGOW:** 01506 834532. Excl restau with
A1 rms nr M9 jnct 3 (Edinburgh-Stirling), 30rms Edin city centre, 15 mins
airport. Convenient high standard hotel adj nationally famous restau
(184/EDIN RESTAUS) esp if you love your meat. Separate b/fast rm. Superlative
wine-list, esp S. African vintages. 16RMS JAN-DEC T/T XPETS CC XKIDS LOTS

860 **GREEN CRAIGS, ABERLADY:** 01875 870301. Individual hotel in superb set-
B1 ting on Edin side of Aberlady (A198, 8km A1). Décor may be iffy for some, but
overall it's comfortable and cared about. If you're staying elsewhere, they can
fetch you for dinner in a limo! Sun lunch recommended.
6RMS JAN-DEC T/T PETS CC KIDS EXP

861 **MARINE HOTEL, NORTH BERWICK:** 01620 892406. The grand old seaside
B1 hotel of N Berwick reeks of holidays gone by – you almost expect to see
Margaret Rutherford on the putting green. Snooker, open-air swimming pool.
O/looks Links and Fidra. Good for kids and golf.
83RMS JAN-DEC T/T PETS CC KIDS EXP

862 **OPEN ARMS, DIRLETON:** 01620 850241. Dirleton is 4km from Gullane
B1 towards N Berwick. Comfortable if pricey hotel in centre of village, opp ruins
of castle. Location means it's a golfers' haven and special packages are available. Restau has two AA whatsits. 10RMS JAN-DEC T/T PETS CC KIDS TOS LOTS

863 **THE OLD ABERLADY INN:** 01875 870503. Main St. Straightforward drop inn
B1 with simple, well-kept rms, a good farmhouse-style bistro with interesting
menu and a trad howf for drinks and bar food. Popular with golfers – OK for
anyone. 8RMS JAN-DEC T/T PETS CC KIDS MED.INX

864 **TWEEDDALE ARMS, GIFFORD:** 01620 810240. One of two inns in this heart
B1 of E Lothian village 9km from the A1 at Haddington, within easy reach of Edin.
Set among rich farming country, Gifford is conservative and couthy. Some
bedrms small, but public rms pleasant if chintzy. Smells like a country inn
should. 16RMS JAN-DEC T/T PETS CC KIDS MED.INX

JOHNSTOUNBURN HOUSE: 01875 833696. An excellent and relaxing country-house hotel within easy reach of town. Report: 54/HOTELS OUTSIDE TOWN.

RESTAURANTS

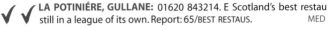

✓ ✓ **LA POTINIÉRE, GULLANE:** 01620 843214. E Scotland's best restau
still in a league of its own. Report: 65/BEST RESTAUS. MED

865 ✓ **THE WATERSIDE, HADDINGTON:** 01620 825674. 115 Waterside. On the
B1 river, opp side of the pedestrianised old br from St Mary's (1696/CHURCH-
ES). Upstairs restau is more of a pink napkin affair, bistro/bar down has various
rms. Separate vegn menu. Famously generous helpings. This is the reliable nay
definitive Lothian bistro. Daily lunch/supper, LO 10pm. INX

866 ✓ **DROVER'S INN, EAST LINTON:** 01620 860298. Bridge St, middle of neat
B1 vill just off A1. Pub with good atmos; bistro downstairs and more elebo-
rate dining up. Beer gdn out back. Lunch and dinner all areas, LO 9.30pm Pub
till 11pm. Don't drink and drove now! INX/MED

867 **LENNOXLOVE GARDEN CAFE nr HADDINGTON:** 01620 823720. 3km town
B1 on B6369 to Gifford. The tearoom of beautiful Lennoxlove House (1731/MARY,
CHARLIE, BOB) run by the bountiful Clarissa Dickson-Wright (of Fat Ladies fame).
As one might expect, excl home-baking, lunches and coffee. Open AYR 11am-
5pm. CHP

868 **POLDRATE'S, HADDINGTON:** 01620 826882. On B6369 out of Haddington to
B1 Lennoxlove and Gifford. Converted mill; bistro atmos, blackboard menu and
small, selected wine list changes frequently some say the management and
service can vary. Tue-Sun lunch and dinner (not Sun/Mon) LO 9.00pm. INX

869 **STARFISH, DUNBAR:** 01368 865384. On quayside of working harbour 500m
B1 from Main St. A seafood bistro with Eyemouth-landed fish and local seabass
and lobster washed down with Belhaven best. Lunch and dinner, LO 9pm. Cl
Mon/Tues. Hrs may vary in winter. INX

870 **THE OLD CLUBHOUSE, GULLANE:** 01620 842008. E Links Rd behind main st
B1 on corner of Green. Large woody clubhouse; a bar/bistro serving food all day
till 9.45pm. Gr busy atmos. Surprising wine selection; but puds are bought in. INX

871 **LIVINGSTON'S, LINLITHGOW:** 01506 846565. Thro arch at E end of High St
A1 opp PO. Cottage conversion with conservatory and garden – a quiet bistro
with imaginative modern Scottish cuisine 2AA rosettes. Tues-Sat, lunch and
dinner. Cl Jan. INX

CHAMPANY'S INN, nr LINLITHGOW: 01506 834532 (184/EDIN RESTAUS) and
see above.

THE BEST HOTELS AND RESTAURANTS IN FIFE

See also 2165/CENTRES: DUNFERMLINE AND KIRKCALDY, *p. 294*; 2176/HOLIDAY CENTRES: ST ANDREWS, *p.308*. Refer to Map 5.

872
C2 ✔ ✔ **OLD COURSE, ST ANDREWS:** 01334 474371. This world-famous hotel is the one you come to first on the A91 from N or W. Unlike many de luxe hotels in the UK, this has lightness to it and accessibility – it is after all surrounded by greens and full of golfers coming and going. Most rms o/look the famous course and sea (immaculate and tastefully done with no fac or expense spared), as do the Conservatory and less informal Road Hole Grill up top. Bar here also for lingering views and whisky in the glass. Truly gr for golf, but anyone could unwind here, towelled in luxury.

125RMS JAN-DEC T/T PETS CC KIDS LOTS

EAT Rd Hole Grill for spectacular dinner esp in late light summer. Mark Barker's menu has 2 AA rosettes. Young, keen v exp wine list.   EXP

873
B3 ✔ **BALBIRNIE HOUSE, MARKINCH:** 01592 610066. Signed from the rd system around Glenrothes (3km) in surprisingly sylvan setting of Balbirnie Country Park. One of the most sociable and comfortable country-house hotels in the land (and Taste of Scotland Hotel of the Yr 1996), with high standards in service and décor that's easy to be at home with. Elegant restau and more informal downstairs bistro (lunch only). New Orangery extension 1999. Their 'pamper breaks' – aft tea on arrival, Bucks Fizz with b/fast are a gr deal *à deux*. No leisure facs, but good golf in the park. Wake to the thwack of balls!

30RMS JAN-DEC T/T PETS CC KIDS TOS LOTS

EAT Elegant hotel dining and bistro for lunch. 2 AA rosettes.   EXP

874
C2 **RUFFLETS, ST ANDREWS:** 01334 472594. 4km from centre via Argyle St opp W Pt along Strathkinness Low Rd past univ playing fields. Serene feel to this country-house hotel on edge of town. The celebrated grds are a joy to walk in after dinner …or after getting married.

25RMS JAN-DEC T/T PETS CC KIDS TOS EXP

875
C3 **KILCONQUHAR CASTLE ESTATE, nr ELIE:** 01333 340501. On B942 nr Colinburgh, 3km from Elie (that famously nice town). Mainly time-share villas, but 'club rms' available in castle itself with access to all facs incl pool, tennis, golf and esp riding. Daily rates poss.

11RMS JAN-DEC T/T PETS CC KIDS MED.INX

876
D2 **CAMBO ESTATE, nr CRAIL:** 0800 980 5445. 2km E of Crail on A917. Huge country pile in glorious grds on the coastal rd betw St Andrews and Crail. Only 2/3 rms, but this is B&B in the grand manner. Rattle around, pretend you're house guests and be grateful you don't have to pay the bills.

2RMS JAN-DEC X/X PETS CC KIDS MED.INX

877
C3 **THE GOLF HOTEL, ELIE:** 01333 330209. Earlsferry end of favourite village (1419/COASTAL VILLAGES) o/look not bad golf. Recent improvements make this a good value and friendly billet.   22RMS MAR-OCT T/T PETS KIDS MED.INX

878
C3 **THE SHIP INN, ELIE:** 01333 330246. 6 basic rms adj pub notable for food and good life (1215/PUB FOOD) close to beach in an excellent neuk of Fife.

6RMS JAN-DEC X/X PETS CC KIDS CHP

879
D3 **THE HERMITAGE, ANSTRUTHER:** 01333 310909. Small B&B-type family house in the essential East Neuk town. Tasteful (unlike most round here) and friendly. The Cellar (*see below*) for the treat of your stay.

4RMS JAN-DEC X/X XPETS CC KIDS INX

880
B4 **WOODSIDE HOTEL, ABERDOUR:** 01383 860328. Refurb inn in main st of pleasant village with prize-winning rail stn, castle and church (1689/CHURCHES), coastal walk and nearby beach. This is where to come from Edin (by train, of course) with your bit on the side. 20RMS JAN-DEC T/T PETS CC KIDS MED.INX

881
B4 **FORTH VIEW, ABERDOUR:** 01383 860402. Brilliant setting by a jagged jetty on the Forth beneath a cliff for airy walks (and famed for rock-climbing). On foot by path from harbour; or car from corner of Silver Sands beach car park,

by extreme track. Accom is basic in family house, but you wake up with Edin over the sea. Novel still waiting to be written here.

5RMS APR-OCT X/X PETS CC KIDS CHP

SANDFORD HILL: 01382 541802. 7km S of Tay Br. Underrated country-house hotel in N Fife nr Dundee. Report: 1088/COUNTRY-HOUSE HOTELS.

PEAT INN nr CUPAR: 01334 840206. The definitive 'restaurant with rooms' (*see below*).

RESTAURANTS

882 ✓ ✓ **THE PEAT INN, nr CUPAR and ST ANDREWS:** 01334 840206. At a
C2 crossroads of the county, the hamlet of Peat Inn (signed from all over), this was one of the first gr Scottish restaus and David Wilson our first outstanding chef. Standards have improved immeasurably and now you don't need to go 50 miles to be sure of superb food. But on occasion come here – it is still an epicurean experience and should you not need to navigate the backrds of Fife, there are 8 rms for staying the night and looking forward to breakfast. 3 AA rosettes. Tue-Sat 1-3pm and 7-9.30pm.   EXP

883 ✓ ✓ **THE CELLAR, ANSTRUTHER:** 01333 310378. Off courtyard behind
D3 Fisheries Museum in this busy E Neuk town (1419/COASTAL VILLAGES) – you'd call this entrance unassuming. As is the whole app, though seafood here is among the v best you'll find in Scotland. Peter Jukes sources the best produce and then lets it do its own thing. One meat dish, but no bull on this menu. Tue-Sat lunch and 7-9pm (7 days high season, not Mon lunch, no lunch in wint). (1071/SEAFOOD RESTAUS)   MED

884 ✓ **OSTLER'S CLOSE, CUPAR:** 01334 655574. Down a close of the main st,
C2 Amanda and Jimmy Graham run a bistro/restau that has Cupar on the gastronomic map (for almost 20 yrs). But no pretence here about 'fine cuisine'; this is honest with thought and flair. Often organic, big on wild mushrooms. Tue-Sat 1-3pm; 7-9.30pm.   MED

885 ✓ **BOUQUET GARNI, ELIE:** 01333 330374. High St of genteel town
C3 (1419/COASTAL VILLAGES). Here for nearly 10yrs with consistently good dining and accolades (3 AA rosettes). However, may change hands, so check if Andrew Keracher still here (his family are famous for fish). Lunch and 7-9pm. Cl Sun. No smk.   MED

886 **OLD RECTORY, DYSART:** 01592 651211. 2km E of Kirkcaldy (5km centre); still
B3 'the best restuarant in W Fife' tho' foodie critic Gillian Glover disagreed. Loyal regulars know better. Tue-Sat lunch; Tue-Sun dinner.   MED

887 **CHANNEL RESTAURANT, NORTH QUEENSFERRY:** 01383 412567. Main st on
B4 way to harbour or lure of Deep Sea World (1541/KIDS). The rail br, however, is the real attraction (351/MAIN ATTRACTIONS) and provides stunning backdrop to this informal bistro with young, innovative owners. Their mum grows organic ingredients. Writer Ian Banks lives nearby and is a fan; so am I. Tues-Sat lunch/dinner. No frills, fine food – LO 9.30pm   INX

888a **VALENTE'S, KIRKCALDY & THE ANSTRUTHER FISH BAR:** 2 gr fish 'n' chip
B3, D3 shops with queues every day, but hang about for the real Saturday night (1258/1269/FISH AND CHIPS).   CHP

THE SHIP INN, ELIE: 01333 330246. Report:1215/PUB FOOD.

888b **THE SEAFOOD RESTAURANT, ST MONANS:** 01333 730327.
C3 Report:1253/SEAFOOD RESTAUS.

THE BEST HOTELS AND RESTAURANTS IN PERTHSHIRE AND TAYSIDE

See also DUNDEE HOTELS AND RESTAURANTS, *p. 132–133*; 2170/CENTRES: PERTH, *p. 302; and 2174/HOLIDAY* CENTRES: PITLOCHRY. *Refer to Map 4.*

889 ✓✓ **FARLEYER HOUSE, nr ABERFELDY:** 01887 820332. 4km town on
B3 B846 to Tummel Br. Cool country house in grounds with fine trees
and 6-hole golf course, nr Castle Menzies. Excellent dining-rm and informal
bistro. Library for whiling away afternoons. Homely with light, yet sophisticated touch. Serve yourself bar after hrs. Lovely b/fast.

19RMS+COTT JAN-DEC T/T PETS CC KIDS LOTS

EAT Almost like a city bistro, except woody acres o/side. Open to non-residents. Blackboard menu. Most exquisite food in the area. INX

890 ✓✓ **BALLATHIE HOUSE, nr PERTH:** 01250 883268. 20km N of Perth and
C3 more fully reported in the town section (2170/PERTH), but a true
country-house hotel on the Tay that you fall in love with. Good dining, good
fishing; good for the w/end away. 27RMS JAN-DEC T/T PETS CC KIDS TOS LOTS

EAT Award-winning chef Kevin MacGillivray. Gr local produce esp beef/lamb.
EXP

891 ✓ **KINFAUNS CASTLE, PERTH:** 01738 620777. A90 Dundee rd (Perth 7km).
C3 Once a walkers' hostel, a lavish restoration has turned this Scottish baronial pile into a sumptuous country-house hotel preserving glorious staircase,
ceilings and wood panelling and creating 16 lavish suites incl, 'Famous
Grouse' (and may my Internet site be with you). Restau open to non res with
chef Jeremy Ware's well-judged *table d'hôte* and long wine-list (tho' reviews
have varied, haven't they Marc?). 16RMS FEB-DEC T/T PETS CC KIDS LOTS

892 ✓ **DUNKELD HOUSE, DUNKELD:** 01350 727771. Former home of Duke of
B3 Atholl, a v large impressive country house on the banks of the R Tay just
outside Dunkeld. Leisure complex with good pool etc and many other activities laid on. V decent menu. Fine for kids. Pleasant walks. Not cheap but often
good deals available. Managed by Stakis chain. Huge but does fill up, so book
early! 97RMS JAN-DEC T/T PETS CC KIDS LOTS

893 ✓ **ROYAL HOTEL, COMRIE:** 01764 679200. Central sq of cosy town, a sym-
B3 pathetic and stylish upgrading of trad small-town hotel. Excellent restau
with good light and superb pub out back with real ale and atmos (1194/REAL
ALES). Exquisite rugs and pictures. A pleasing bit of style in the county bit of
the country. Delightful restau and bar meals.

11RMS JAN-DEC T/T XPETS CC KIDS MED.EX

894 **KINLOCH HOUSE, nr BLAIRGOWRIE:** 01250 884237. 5km W on A923 to
C3 Dunkeld. A country house with open views to the Sidlaw Hills. Panelled and
galleried, and rather formally attired and run – definitely one for snobs rather
than slobs. But the food is both spectacular and PC (some organic). Gr malt
whisky selection. 3 AA rosettes 21RMS JAN-DEC T/T PETS CC KIDS EXP

895 **HUNTINGTOWER HOTEL, nr PERTH:** 01738 583771. 3km from town, 1km
C3 ring rd (direction Crieff). Serviceable, good looking hotel in gardens close to
Perth and the rds north and west. Report: (2170/PERTH).

21RMS JAN-DEC T/T PETS CC KIDS EXP

896 **CASTLETON HOUSE, EASSIE, nr GLAMIS:** 01307 840340. 13km W of Forfar,
C3 25km N of Dundee. App from Glamis, 5km SW on A94. Family-run country-
house hotel with good restau. Not over-pricey or stuffy; bar meals as well as
dining-rms/conservatory. Popular Sun lunch.

6RMS JAN-DEC T/T PETS CC KIDS TOS EXP

897 **PINE TREES HOTEL, PITLOCHRY:** 01796 472121. A safe haven in visitor-ville –
B2 it's above the town and above all that (there are many mansions here). Take
Larchwood Rd off W end of main st (signed for golf course). Woody grds,
woody interior. There's a piano-player at dinner (Fri/Sat). Scots owners – now
there's a change. 19RMS JAN-DEC T/T XPETS CC KIDS MED.EX

898 **KILLIECRANKIE HOTEL, KILLIECRANKIE:** 01796 473220. 5km N of Pitlochry.
B2 Village inn ambience; cosy rms of individual character. Carefully run. Gr food.
Plenty walks round about.   10RMS MAR-DEC T/T PETS CC KIDS TOS EXP

EAT V fine home-cooking in restau and bar (LO 9.30pm). In every guide book
that counts. Pop over from Pitlochry.   INX

899 **KENMORE HOTEL, KENMORE:** 01887 830205. Ancient coaching inn in quaint
B3 conservation village. Excellent prospect for golfing (at Taymouth Castle adj,
1866/GOLF IN GREAT PLACES) and fishing. On river (Tay) itself with terrace. Comfy
rms.   35RMS JAN-DEC T/T PETS CC KIDS MEDINX

900 **CLOVA HOTEL, GLEN CLOVA:** 01575 550222. Nr end of Glen Clova, one of the
C2 gr Angus Glens (1449/GLENS), on B955 25km N of Kirriemuir. A walk/climb/
country retreat hotel with multifarious activities thought up by Graham
Davie. Hot soup, warm stove, warm welcome. Superb walking nearby. Often
full, tho v basic.   7RMS JAN-DEC T/T PETS CC KIDS INX

901 **HOTEL COLL EARN, AUCHTERARDER:** 01764 663553. Off main st.
B4 Extravagant Victorian mansion with exceptional stained glass. Comfy rms,
huge beds. Pleasant garden.   9RMS JAN-DEC T/T XPETS CC KIDS EXP

902 **GUINACH HOUSE, ABERFELDY:** 01887 820251. On A826 Crieff rd and among
B3 the famous 'Birks' (1816/WOODLAND WALKS). Small mansion in pleasant grd.
Chef prop Bert MacKay has 2 AA rosettes.
7RMS JAN-DEC X/T PETS CC KIDS MED.EX

903 **ATHOLL ARMS, BLAIR ATHOLL:** 01796 481205. Main st opp castle, the major
B2 attraction hereabouts (1596/CASTLES) and part of the estate. Refurb has
improved rms and tartanised downstairs. Magnificent lofty dining-rm, the old
ballrm for the castle. A v Highland experience.
31RMS JAN-DEC T/T PETS CC KIDS INX

904 **LINKS HOTEL, MONTROSE:** 01674 671000. French chef, Dutch coffee house
D2 and corporate approach. Oil industry types during the week, weddings at the
w/end. Smartest in town, if you're stopping.
25RMS JAN-DEC T/T PETS CC XKIDS MED.EX

GLENEAGLES: 01764 662231 (1079/COUNTRY-HOUSE HOTELS).

KINNAIRD HOUSE: 01796 482440 (1077/COUNTRY-HOUSE HOTELS).

AUCHTERARDER HOUSE: 01764 663646 (1082/COUNTRY-HOUSE HOTELS).

OLD MANSION HOUSE, AUCHTERHOUSE: 01382 320366 (1051/DUNDEE
HOTELS).

CRIEFF HYDRO, CRIEFF: 01764 655555. Superb for many reasons, esp kids.
Quintessentially Scottish (1091/KIDS).

RESTAURANTS

905 ✓ ✓ **LET'S EAT, PERTH:** 01738 643377. Corner of Kinnoull St. Tony Heath
C3 and Shona Drysdale's perfect county town eaterie. Cuisine without
the trappings, but all the rt trimmings. Extremely good value and valued
(Macallan TOS award '97 and '98). Also the niftily-named **LET'S EAT AGAIN** at
33 George St (633771), lighter, more Mediterraneao.   MED

906 ✓ **LOCHSIDE LODGE, BRIDGEND OF LINTRATHEN:** 01575 560340. 9km
C3 from Alyth towards Glenisla on B954 past Reekie Linn (1465/WATERFALLS),
or via Kirriemuir. Deep in watery countryside. Converted stone steading nr
loch; gr setting, gr food. Accom (3rms). Lunch/dinner LO 9pm. Cl Mon.   MED

907 ✓ **THE BUT 'N' BEN, AUCHMITHIE, nr ARBROATH:** 01241 877223. 2km off
D3 A92 N from Arbroath, 8km to town or 4km by cliff-top walk. Village
perched on cliff top where ravine leads to small cove and quay. Adj cottages
converted into cosy restau open noon-3pm for lunch, 4-5.30pm for high-tea
(2 sittings Sun, no dinner), 7.30-9.30pm for dinner. Cl Tue. Menus vary but all v
Scottish and informal with emphasis on fresh fish/seafood. Brilliant value –
Margaret Horn continues to provide a Scottish experience for her ain folk and
all others.   INX

908 **GORDONS, INVERKEILOR, nr ARBROATH:** 01241 830364. Halfway betw
D3 Arbroath and Montrose on the A92. Contemporary cuisine comes to Angus,
so 'polenta' and jus crop up on the menu alongside trad Scottish ingreds. Two
AA rosettes. Tues-Sun, and LO 9pm (Cl Sat) MED

909 **CARGILLS, BLAIRGOWRIE:** 01250 876735. Cosy wine bar ambience, busy à la
C3 carte menu and blackboard. Serviceable, reliable and a bit of a hidden gem.
Unprepossessing frontage, but on river side. Adj coffee shop/gallery. The
place to eat in this corner of the country. LO 10pm. Cl Mon. INX

910 **THE LOFT, BLAIR ATHOLL:** 01796 481377. Off the A9, in vill turn left at Tilt
B2 Hotel. Odd kind of location (corner of a caravan park) for this reputable restau
which gets 2 AA rosettes for chef Douglas Wright. Hearty food with a good
combo of new and traditional touches. 7 days, lunch and LO 9.30pm. INX

911 **CROFTBANK HOUSE, KINROSS:** 01577 863819. Stn Rd; on the M9: 1km on
C4 main rd from motorway jnct. Discreet hotel with notable dining-rm (2 AA
rosettes). Also bar meals (5rms). Cl Sun dinner and Mon (MED). **GROUSE AND
CLARET:** 01557 864212. Heatheryford on other (W) side of jnct, about 1km.
On fishing lochans, converted farm buildings with popular pleasant restau
and 3 rms. INX

KERRACHERS, PERTH: 01738 449777 (2170/PERTH) MED

THE BEST HOTELS AND RESTAURANTS IN THE NORTH-EAST

Excludes city of Aberdeen (p 127-8); see also 2176/CENTRES: BALLATER. *Refer to Map 3.*

912
C2
✓✓ **PITTODRIE HOUSE, PITCAPLE:** 01467 681444. Large 'family' mansion house on estate in one of the best bits of Aberdeenshire with Bennachie above. 40km Aber but 'only 30mins from airport' via A96. Follow signs off B9002. Lots of activities available on the estate, croquet lawn, billiards and lots of comfortable rms. Exquisite walled grd 500m from house. Fine menu, veg from grd; good esp French wine list.

27RMS JAN-DEC T/T PETS CC KIDS TOS LOTS

913
B3
✓✓ **DARROCH LEARG, BALLATER:** 01339 755443. On main A93 at edge of town. The Franks have carefully brought this hotel (long in the family) forward. With superior standards, but a relaxed ambience and an excellent dining-rm, it is the best in this hotel-studded town. Three AA rosettes; other Deeside hoteliers aspire to its good standards. Comfortable, informal with attentive and considerate staff. No bar, but civilised drinks before and *après*. Good base for touring.

18RMS JAN-DEC T/T PETS CC KIDS TOS LOTS

EAT Conservatory dining-rm and one of best restaus in NE; Chef David Mutter continues to hit the heights. Nice grd view, fab food. EXP

914
C2
✓ **OLD MANSE OF MARNOCH:** 01466 780873. On B9117, 1km from A97, the Huntly to Banff rd. Exactly as you'd imagine it, a charming old manse nr the banks of R Deveron. Bucolic surroundings; bright and healthy breakfast. They're planning some refurbs which would mean more rms but it's proving difficult, so we'll see. 5RMS JAN-DEC X/X PETS CC XKIDS TOS MED.EX

EAT Keren Carter's imaginative 4-course menu changes daily. May seat round the one table, like a dinner party. Must book. 2 AA rosettes. MED

915
B2
✓ **CRAIGELLACHIE HOTEL, CRAIGELLACHIE:** 01340 881204. The quintessential Speyside hotel, off A941 Elgin to Perth and Aber rd by the br over Spey. Esp good for fishing, but well placed for walking (Speyside Way runs along bottom of grd, see 1791/LONG WALKS) and distillery visits (1371/WHISKY). Informal; some fab rms. Nice snug and, of course, this is where to drink the drink. 25RMS JAN-DEC T/X XPETS CC KIDS TOS MED.EX

916
D2
✓ **UDNY ARMS, NEWBURGH:** 01358 789444. A975 off A92. Village pub with gr food and character run by the Craig family for many yrs. Rms tasteful and individually furnished. Folk come from Aber (22km) to eat here. Golf course Cruden Bay (1846/GREAT GOLF) 16km N and walks beside Ythan estuary (1582/WILDLIFE). 26RMS JAN-DEC T/T XPETS CC KIDS TOS MED.INX

EAT Excellent grub in bar or dining-rm. Good ambience and the dessert assiette is a gobsmacker. Lunch; LO 9.30pm. MED

917
B3
✓ **CRAIGENDARROCH, BALLATER:** 013397 55858. On the Braemar rd (A93). Part of a country-club/time-share operation with elegant dining, good leisure facs and discreet resort-in-the-woods feel. In the process of being sold from one major hotel chain to another as we went to press. Good service, 2 restaus, one by pool and the conscientiously up-market Oaks. Lodges can be available on short lets, a good idea for a group holiday or w/end. Refurb since last edition means big improvements around the pool/bar area; still a fab view from outside the Bar Bacoq restau.

45RMS JAN-DEC T/T XPETS CC KIDS TOS LOTS

918
D2
MELDRUM HOUSE, OLDMELDRUM: 01651 872294. 1km from village, 30km N of Aber via A947 Banff rd. Immediately impressive and solid establishment – Scottish baronial style. Fishing in the grounds; lots of corporate/wedding business. Altogether, v swish, and look out for the stuffed half tiger. Shame to say still haven't eaten but always looks tempting.

9RMS JAN-DEC T/T PETS CC KIDS LOTS

919 **THE MANSION HOUSE, ELGIN:** 01343 548811. In town centre (beneath the
B2 left hand of the statue on the hill). Comfortable and elegant town house in a
comfortable and gentle town with 'leisure facs', incl pool/gym and drop-in
bistro. Good dining-rm. 23RMS JAN-DEC T/T XPETS CC KIDS TOS LOTS

920 **MANSEFIELD HOUSE, ELGIN:** 01343 540883. Refurb hotel on edge of town
B2 centre considered locally to be the place to eat. Haven't stayed (or eaten), but
do what the Elginites do. 21RMS JAN-DEC T/T XPETS CC KIDS TOS MED.INX

921 **BANCHORY LODGE HOTEL, BANCHORY:** 01330 822625. A sporting-lodge
C3 hotel nr town centre, but superbly situated on the banks of the Dee. No longer
hold fishing rts, but can arrange. Public rms and many bedrms o/look the river.
Sporty rather than staid atmos but some sunglasses in evidence during the
summer. Actually served as a role model for Auchendean Lodge (962/LESS
EXPENSIVE HIGHLAND HOTELS). People come back, like the fish.
22RMS FEB-DEC T/T PETS CC KIDS EXP

922 **RAEMOIR HOUSE, BANCHORY:** 01330 824884. 5km N from town via A980 off
C3 main st. Mansion in the country with old-fashioned (1970s going on Victorian)
feel, so fairly relaxed. 9-hole golf and tennis. Stable annex and self-cat apts. The
Bishop-Milnes have taken over since last time, v sussed about the food; 2 AA
rosettes and aiming to improve under the direction of Stewart Dourst in the
kitchen. 20RMS JAN-DEC T/T PETS CC KIDS LOTS

923 **DELNASHAUGH INN, BALLINDALLOCH, nr GRANTOWN ON SPEY:** 01807
A2 500255. Road-side and Speyside (actually the Avon, pron 'Arn') inn, comfy,
unpretentious. On bend of A95 betw Craigellachie and Grantown nr confluence of main rds and rivers. Laura Ashley/Sarah Churchill décor, not minimalist, but simple. Food also. Much ado about fishing.
9RMS MAR-NOV T/T PETS CC KIDS MED.EX

924 **CASTLE HOTEL, HUNTLY:** 01466 792696. Behind Huntly Castle ruin; app from
C2 town through castle entrance and then over R Deveron up impressive drive.
Large but family-scale lodge-house; former seat of the Dukes of Gordon. Rms
have character and views. Fishing fixed.
20RMS JAN-DEC T/T PETS CC KIDS MED.INX

925 **SEAFIELD HOTEL, CULLEN:** 01542 840791. On the main Brae; an activity-ori-
C1 ented hotel with lots to do on nearby Seafield estate (hunt, shoot, fish). Single
rms can be a bit pokey but there's a comfortable lounge with a fair range of
malts. Restau good for fresh fish. Mr and Mrs Cox work at this.
22RMS JAN-DEC T/T PETS KIDS CC MED.INX

926 **ARCHIESTOWN HOTEL, ARCHIESTOWN:** 01340 810218. Main st of small vil-
B2 lage in heart of Speyside nr Cardhu Distillery (1374/WHISKY). A village inn with
comfortable rms and celebrated food in bistro setting (LO 8.30pm). Fishers
and locals. 8RMS FEB-SEPT T/T PETS CC KIDS MED.EX

927 **WATERSIDE INN, PETERHEAD:** 01779 471121. Edge of town on A952 to
D2 Fraserburgh on tidal R Ugie. Standard, well-run modern hotel, recommended
for its service and convenience and because it's the best option around. Good
for kids (1101/KIDS). 109RMS JAN-DEC T/T PETS CC KIDS MED.EX

928 **GRANT ARMS, MONYMUSK:** 01467 651226. The village inn on a remarkable
C3 small square, a good centre for walking (1772/HILLS), close to the 'Castle Trail'
(1606/CASTLES; 1662/COUNTRY HOUSES) and with fishing rts on the Don.
10RMS JAN-DEC X/T PETS CC KIDS MED.INX

EAT Best pub food for miles, and dining. Daily lunch, 6.30-9pm. INX

929 **BRAEMAR LODGE, BRAEMAR:** 013397 41627. Down-home granite country
A3 house where the owners won't look down their nose at muddy walkers. Few
frills but a haven after a long day in the Cairngorms. Have a whisky. Log cabins for hire out back. 7RMS JAN-DEC X/T PETS CC KIDS MED.INX

RESTAURANTS

930 ✓ ✓ **LAIRHILLOCK, nr STONEHAVEN:** 01569 730001. 15km S of Aber off
C3 A92. Excellent country pub and restau, good for kids. Full report
1009/ABER RESTAUS; 1206/PUB FOOD.

931 ✓ **THE GREEN INN, BALLATER:** 01339 755701. On the green in touring cen-
B3 tre of Royal Deeside, a restau with rms (3, above the shop). Rms often
booked, but phone for availability, then you get an excellent start to the day
as well. Jeff Purves' generally healthy and PC app to food means it's good all
the way through. The salmon will be wild, the scallops dived; no-fry policy and
heather honey instead of sugar, etc., but no preciousness here, just efficiency
and quality. MED

932 **THAINSTONE HOUSE, by INVERURIE:** 01467 621643. Smart corporate coun-
C3 try house hotel owned by the Macdonald group, but the restau has a
throughly deserved two AA rosettes. Catch it on a quiet night with a gathering haar in the grounds and it's sepulchral. But please, no more pop-classics
muzak, particularly not the theme from Twin Peaks. Too spooky. Lunch and LO
9.30pm daily. LOTS

933 **WHITE COTTAGE, ABOYNE:** 01339 886265. Just before Aboyne going W on
C3 A93 the Royal Deeside rd. Cottage it is, but not quite white. Laurie Mill's
straightforward app – ambitious food, simply pleasant surroundings.
Undeniably worthwhile stop on the rd; nice with kids. Lunch and dinner LO
9pm. Cl Sun/Mon. INX.MED

934 **MILTON RESTAURANT:** 01330 844566. On main A93 Royal Deeside rd 4km E
C3 of Banchory opp the entrance to Crathes (1379/GARDENS; 1663/COUNTRY HOUS-
ES). Roadside and surprisingly contemporary café/restau in old steading.
Pottery adj also craft shop with some v good jewellery. Light and exceeding-
ly pleasant space. Snack/hot food menu by day and dinner at night. 7 days,
not Sun eve. INX

935 **THE OLD MONASTERY, nr BUCKIE:** 01542 832660. Best first: a lovely space,
B1 gt views W along the coast, idyllic on a fine summer eve. But changed hands
since last time and new props still finding their feet; trying too hard perhaps?
Nice folk – so await developments. Tues-Sat Lunch and LO 8.30/9pm EXP

936 **FAGINS, WHITEHILLS nr BANFF:** 01261 861321. Loch St on rt as you app this
C1 coastal village 3km W of Banff off B9139. Long-standing local reputation for
surf 'n' turf suppers cooked in galley kitchen in corner of dining-rm above an
unpromising pub. Honest to goodness food with some flair. Wed-Sat dinner,
LO 9pm. Lunch Sun only. INX

937 **BALGONIE HOUSE HOTEL, BALLATER:** 01339 755482. Another contender in
B3 Royal Deeside's culinary centre. V neat hotel where John Finnie's cooking has
earned two AA rosettes. Friendly folk, no surprises, but lots of care. L and LO
9pm. If you want to stay, rms are exp. MED.EXP

TOLBOOTH, STONEHAVEN: 01569 762287 (1249/SEAFOOD RESTAUS).

THE BEST HOTELS AND RESTAURANTS IN THE HIGHLANDS

See also Ft William, p.296; Ullapool, p.305; Skye, p. 282; Western Isles, p. 284. Refer to Map 2.

938
C3 ✓✓ **INVERLOCHY CASTLE, FORT WILLIAM:** 01397 702177. 5km from town on A82 Inverness rd, Scotland's flagship Highland (*Relais et Châteaux*) hotel. Now less stuffy than it used to be, but still stuffed with sumptuous furnishings, objects and occasional film stars, luminaries and royalty. Everything you expect of a 'castle'; the epitome of grandeur and service. Huge colourful, comfortable rms, set in acres of rhododendrons with rainbow trout in the lake and the big Ben over there. Dine in (3 AA rosettes).

16RMS JAN-DEC T/T PETS CC KIDS LOTS

939
D2 ✓✓ **CLIFTON HOUSE, NAIRN:** 01667 453119. Seafield St off A96 to Inverness. A suburban mansion o/look park and seafront of genteel town nr Inverness. For over 50yrs (can it really be 50yrs?) one of the most distinctly individual hotels in the Highlands run by the inimitable J Gordon MacIntyre and full of his good taste. Last time I was there he was working in the grd from which herbs and glorious flowers come. Sometimes he chefs though his son does most. Excellent wine list. Sept-June there are musical and theatrical evenings; (send for prog). Every rm is a different experience; dinner is not merely a meal. It's a house party and demonstrates that all the management training, spas and gyms, trouser-presses and unctuous waiters in the world will never make up for style.

12RMS JAN-DEC X/X PETS CC KIDS EXP

EAT Dining never dull, often dramatic. Hand-picked excellent value wine list.

EXP

940
C2 ✓✓ **CULLODEN HOUSE, INVERNESS:** 01463 790461. 5km E of town nr A9, follow signs for Culloden village, not the battlefield. Hugely impressive, Georgian mansion and lawn a big green duvet on edge of suburbia and, of course, history. The most conscientiously de luxe hotel hereabouts. Some fab grd suites. Excellent chef. Part of Virgin marketing group.

28RMS JAN-DEC T/T PETS CC KIDS TOS LOTS

941
D2 ✓ **THE BOATH HOUSE, AULDEARN, nr NAIRN:** 01667 454896. Slam-dunking into BEST HIGHLAND HOTELS, this fab establishment (signed from the main A96 3km E of Nairn) only opened in '98 after Don and Wendy Matheson spent several years on a refurb of their 19th C mansion. Classic contemporary look, grounds to wander, health and beauty spa in the basement, and 2 AA rosettes for food already. Third on the way? Our kind of people.

7RMS JAN-DEC T/T PETS CC KIDS LOTS

942
C2 ✓ **DOWER HOUSE, nr MUIR OF ORD:** 01463 870090. On A862 between Beauly and Dingwall, 18km NW of Inverness and 2km N of village. Charming, personal place; you feel like a house guest. Cottagey-style small country house, with comfy public rms. Also lodge house accom.

5RMS JAN-DEC T/T PETS CC XKIDS EXP

EAT Michelin chef Robyn Aitchison, simple, sophisticated. Fixed menu.   MED

943
B2 ✓ **LOCH TORRIDON HOTEL, L TORRIDON, nr KINLOCHEWE:** 01445 791242. At the end of Glen Torridon in immense scenery. Highland Lodge atmos, big hills to climb. Report: 1139/GET-AWAY-FROM-IT-ALL

20RMS JAN-DEC T/T XPETS CC XKIDS LOTS

944
C2 ✓ **DUNAIN PARK, INVERNESS:** 01463 230512. 6km SW town on A82 Ft William rd. Mansion-house just off the rd, a quiet and more civilised alternative to hotels in town, esp for those on business. Some good deals out of season. Nice grds, small pool in outhouse; real countryside beyond. Notable restau/dining-rm with sound Scottish menu; lots of creamy puds. Excellent wine and malt list. Fresh donuts for breakfast now and again.

13RMS JAN-DEC T/T PETS CC KIDS TOS EXP

EAT Ann Nicholl's no-nonsense menu and sideboard of delicious puds.   MED

945
C2
✓ **THE SUMMER ISLES HOTEL, ACHILTIBUIE:** 01854 622282. 40km from Ullapool with views over the isles and an Antipodean welcome from Bob; Stac Polly and Suilven are close by to climb. V popular restau, comfortable rms above; with *Swiss Family Robinson* log cabins in grds. Adj pub offers similar quality food at half the price.   13RMS APR-OCT T/X PETS CC XKIDS TOS EXP

EAT Fairly formal dining, but awfully good. All would-be restaurateurs should be shown this cheeseboard. Seafood lunches and bar meals a must if nearby.
MED.EX

946
MAP 1
B2
✓ **CRINAN HOTEL:** 01546 830261. At the w end of the Crinan Canal, Nick Ryan and Frances Macdonald's place has splendid situation o/looking the canal lock, art (by Frances) and two excellent restaus (1241/SEAFOOD RESTAUS)   22RMS JAN-DEC T/T PETS CC KIDS LOTS

947
C2
BUNCHREW HOUSE, nr INVERNESS: 01463 234917. On A862 Beauly rd only 5km from Inverness yet completely removed from town; on the wooded shore of the Beauly Firth. Dining-rm and some bedrms o/look water; you might see Ben Wyvis. Gr club bar, esp for late dram. New owners, Oct'98, and they're working away at refurbishing the rms, and on raising food standards.
11RMS JAN-DEC T/T PETS CC KIDS TOS LOTS

948
C2
COUL HOUSE, CONTIN, nr STRATHPEFFER: 01997 421487. Comfortable country-house hotel on the edge of the wilds with some elegant public rms, partic the octagonal lounge. Family-run (Martyn and Ann Hill) with nice dogs. Well-kept lawns where a piper plays in summer (Fri evenings). V Taste of Scotland menu, Martyn keeps an excellent wine list and they have a small bistro now too.   20RMS JAN-DEC T/T PETS CC KIDS TOS MED.EX

949
C3
POLMAILY HOUSE, DRUMNADROCHIT, LOCH NESS: 01456 450343. 5km from Drumnadrochit on A831 to Cannich in Glen Urquhart and nr awesome Glen Affric (1444/GLENS). Unpretentious country-house retreat in lived-in unmanicured grounds. Many walks; tennis, riding and covered-in pool. Small, comfy public rms, individual bedrms. Sensible dinner and wine list. Everything on hand for kids (1094/KIDS), but ok for those without. The house and the glen are yours.   10RMS JAN-DEC T/T PETS CC KIDS EXP

950
C4
LODGE ON THE LOCH, ONICH: 01855 821237. In my view the best hotel in this strip S of Ft William (16km). Notable relaxed ambiance, colour scheme, furnishings etc. Not chp but 2 rms not en suite, are better value.
20RMS MAR-OCT T/T PETS CC KIDS TOS EXP

951
C4
ONICH HOTEL, ONICH, by FORT WILLIAM: 01855 821214. As above 16km S on main A82, one of many roadside and in this case, loch side hotels which are more attractive than many in Ft William. Onich is the best value and about half its rms o/look L Linnhe. Busy bars and grassy terrace.
25RMS JAN-DEC T/T PETS CC KIDS MED.EX

952
C4
HOLLY TREE, KENTALLEN, ARGYLL: 01631 740292. On A828 Ft William (Ballachulish) – Oban rd, 8km S of Ballachulish Bridge. On road and sea and once the railway; formerly a station. Now a slightly idiosyncratic hotel with decor of mixed taste (incl Mockintosh), but fab views from bdrms and dining rm. Nice for kids.   10RMS JAN-DEC T/T PETS CC TOS EXP

953
C1
KINLOCHBERVIE HOTEL, KINLOCHBERVIE: 01971 521275. Serviceable hotel on hill o/looking important fishing pt (go see evening fish market). 1970s kind of rms and restau, bar and bistro.   14RMS JAN-DEC T/T PETS CC KIDS EXP

954
D3
MUCKRACH LODGE, DULNAIN BRIDGE nr GRANTOWN and AVIEMORE: 01479 851257. 1km from Dulnain Bridge on A938 Cambridge Rd, so about 17km from A9. Small co house hotel, known locally for food and wine-list (open non-res).   13RMS JAN-DEC T/T PETS CC KIDS TOS MED.EX

955
C2
SUTHERLAND ARMS HOTEL, LAIRG: 01549 402291. Town hotel o/look L Shin. Not such gr value, but in a wide swathe of big country, this is the best option. Go fish.   27RMS APR-OCT T/T PETS CC KIDS MED.INX

KNOCKIE LODGE, LOCH NESS: 01456 486276 (1083/COUNTRY-HOUSE HOTELS).

ARISAIG HOUSE, ARISAIG: 01687 450622 (1161/SCOTTISH HOTELS).

ACKERGILL TOWER, nr WICK: 01955 603556 (1138/GET-AWAY-FROM-IT-ALL).

RESTAURANTS

956
D3
✔ ✔ **THE CROSS, KINGUSSIE:** 01540 661166. Off main st at traffic lights, head 200m uphill then left into glen. Perfect setting for the best restau in the ski zone, part of 'restau with rms' hotel in converted tweed mill (963/INEXP HIGHLANDS HOTELS). Airy rm, doesn't feel like Kingussie. Ruth Hadley, master chef, works wonders in the kitchen and Tony talks you through amazing wine list and the cheese, both fastidiously selected with gr flair and enthusiasm. Open to non-res but many people stay and eat. Mar-Nov. Cl Tue.   EXP

957
C3
✔ ✔ **OLD PINES, nr SPEAN BRIDGE:** 01397 712324. Medium-priced dining in inexp hotel, still one of the best meals in the Highlands (with new big table and crocks). How Sukie Barbour does it with all those kids, God knows, but the food can be brilliant. Essentially an award-winning restau with rms. Kids may eat with theirs. BYOB as well as carefully selected wine list. Phone to book. No smk. See also 767/LESS EXEP HIGHLAND HOTELS.   MED

958
C2
✔ **LA RIVIERA at the GLEN MORISTON HOTEL & RIVA/PAZZOS, INVERNESS:** 01463 223777 & 237377. Italian restaus in Inverness owned by the same people and probably best food in town. La Riviera is dining-rm, Riva is riverside downtown café/tratt and not exp, Pazzos is the new pasta-pizza parlour adj. Fuller reports: 2168/INVERNESS.   EXP/INX

959
D2
MANSFIELD HOUSE HOTEL, TAIN: 01862 892052. Smart baronial-style hotel on Scotsburn Rd (rms are LOTS). Owners, the Lauritsen family, know their business – a serious kitchen with a Scottish slant. L and LO 9pm   MED

GOOD LESS EXPENSIVE HOTELS IN THE HIGHLANDS

Refer to Map 2.

960
C2
✔ ✔ **THE CEILIDH PLACE, ULLAPOOL:** 01854 612103. Jean Urquhart's unconventional app and individual hotel still out in front; an oasis up-N. What started out in the 1970s as a coffee/exhibition shop in a boat shed, has spread along this row of cottages now comprising a restau, bookshop, self-serve wholefood/coffee area, and bedrms upstairs. In winter food is served in front of the roaring fire in the Parlour Bar. Bunkhouse across the rd offers cheaper accom but is not a substitute for the hotel. Live music and events throughout the yr, or you can simply sit on the lounge/terrace upstairs and wonder about Ullapool.   23RMS JAN-DEC T/X PETS CC KIDS EXP

EAT Coffee shop/bistro 8am-11pm. Restau informal, but urbane.   MED

961
C1
✔ ✔ **THE ALBANNACH, LOCHINVER:** 01571 844407. 2km up rd to Baddidarach as you come into Lochinver on the A837, at the br. Lesley and Colin have created a unique and comfortable haven in their 18th-century house. The suite in the grounds used to be a byre; the croft walk behind has gr views over the water to Suilven. After one of their winning dinners you get the sun on the terrace o/looking the grd (you have to go there to smoke) and drink the tranquility; and their whisky.
5RMS MAR-DEC T/X XPETS CC XKIDS MED.INX

EAT When in Assynt, eat at The Albannach. Simply good.   MED

962
D3
✔ **AUCHENDEAN LODGE, DULNAIN BRIDGE, nr GRANTOWN ON SPEY:** 01479 851347. An urbane enclave in an area of stunning scenery nr Aviemore skiing and Whisky Trail. Tastefully and cosily furnished Edwardian lodge with log fires, good malts and cellar, and books. Food with flair and imagination – they know their oysters and their mushrooms. Intimate. Dinner can turn into a house party as Ian patiently serves: Eric takes care of the kitchen.   7RMS JAN-DEC X/T PETS CC KIDS TOS MED.EX

EAT Most imaginative menu in wide area of S Speyside, incl Aviemore.   MED

963
D3
✔ **THE CROSS, KINGUSSIE:** 01540 661166. Tasteful hotel in converted tweed mill by river which gurgles o/side most windows. Lots of bespoke wooden fixtures. Restau superb.   9RMS MAR-NOV T/X XPETS CC XKIDS EXP

EAT To stay, you're expected to eat; you'd be mad not to (956/HIGHLANDS HOTELS).

964 ✓ **GLENGARRY CASTLE, INVERGARRY:** 01809 501254. A family-run hotel
C3 in the Highlands for over 40 yrs. The MacCallums still show how a friendly welcome and relaxed ambience need not be forced, and that value for
money can still be found. A real castle; large bedrms beams incl. Extensive
grounds, down to the loch. Tennis, fishing and a good base for touring the
'Ness' area. And check out the notoriously debauched 15th Earl.

26RMS MAR-NOV T/T PETS CC KIDS MED.EX

965 ✓ **GLENFINNAN HOUSE HOTEL, GLENFINNAN:** 01397 722235. Victorian
B3 mansion with lawns down to L Shiel and the Glenfinnan Monument over
the water. No shortbread-tin twee or tartan carpet here; instead a warm welcome from the MacFarlanes. You are piped into dinner and the bar has gr
atmos. A cruise on this stunning loch in the ex-admiralty launch prob a must!
(1163/SCOTTISH HOTELS). 20RMS APR-OCT X/X PETS CC KIDS MED.INX

966 ✓ **BALLACHULISH HOUSE, BALLACHULISH:** 01855 811266. Surprisingly
C4 spookyless considering it's reputed to be one of the most haunted houses in Scotland. Historic but comfortable GH ambiance. Many antiques. Hill
views. Billiard rm and games, 'trust' bar, and Liz Grey's expertise at the Aga.

8RMS JAN-DEC T/X PETS CC KIDS MED.EX

967 ✓ **OLD PINES, nr SPEAN BRIDGE:** 01397 712324. 3km Spean Br via B8004
C3 for Garlochy at Commando Monument. This award-winning 'restau with
rms' is a home from home. Open-plan pine cabin with log fires, games,
enough books for a public library and bedrms each named after a flower and
furnished accordingly. Enjoy Sukie Barber's exceptional cooking and the
ducks on the stream (1092/KIDS; 957/HIGHLAND HOTELS).

8RMS JAN-DEC X/X XPETS CC KIDS TOS MED.INX

968 **THE PLOCKTON INN, PLOCKTON:** 01599 544222. Neat village inn and
B3 seafood restau in neat little seaside vill (1412/COASTAL VILLAGES). Stone's throw
from the front. Simple, quiet tasteful rms. Bar and bistro, mainly seafood.
Tables on terrace in summer back garden for kids.

9RMS JAN-DEC T/T PETS CC KIDS MED.INX

969 **LOCH MAREE HOTEL, TALLADALE:** 01445 760288. On A832 15km from
B2 Kinlochewe and rt by the loch side (1470/LOCHS). A Highland fishing hotel
catering for discriminating tourists (incl Queen Victoria) since 1872. All fishing
arrangements made including ghillies. A good base for walking in Torridon. Nr
Inverewe (1378/GARDENS) and Gairloch. Unpretentious comfort, good value.

20RMS JAN-DEC T/T PETS CC KIDS MED.INX

970 **BEN LOYAL HOTEL, TONGUE:** 01847 611216. Taken over in autumn '98 by
C1 Elaine & Paul Lewis who have injected a little more verve. They're serious
about the food and this is now one of the best places to eat along the whole
north coast. Ask Elaine where the views are!

11RMS MAR-NOV X/T PETS CC KIDS TOS MED.EX

971 **TIGH-AN-EILEAN, SHIELDAIG:** 01520 755251. Lovely freshly-furnished hotel
B2 on waterfront o/look Scots Pine island on loch. The Fields, City of London
lawyers, bought the hotel in '99 and were only weeks into their first season
when we visited. Chris is a folk-buff so look out for music in the adj pub.
Dinner (MED) is well worth having. The view remains fab, just like the Colin
Baxter postcard. 11RMS APR-OCT X/X PETS CC KIDS EXP

972 **EDDRACHILLES HOTEL, nr SCOURIE:** 01971 502080. Not the friendliest of
C1 places but the rms are ok and the setting is exceptional; if you're a nice couple and you keep your traps shut, you'll be all rt. Handy for Handa Island
(1562/BIRDS). S of Scourie on A894. 12RMS MAR-OCT T/T XPETS CC XKIDS MED.EX

973 **SUTHERLAND ARMS HOTEL, GOLSPIE:** 01408 633234. Roadside inn at N end
D2 of town nr Dunrobin Castle and Big Burn Walk (1803/GLEN WALKS). First coaching inn in Scotland changed hands again in '98: a stopover on the way north.

14RMS JAN-DEC T/T PETS CC KIDS INX

974 **DORNOCH CASTLE HOTEL, DORNOCH:** 01862 810216. Atmos 16th-century
D2 castle in main st. Dinner in the dungeons (huge stone fireplace) and drinks
upstairs in the turreted bar o/look cathedral. Bedrms in old part and new
wing. Beach and golf nearby (1848/GREAT GOLF).

17RMS MAR-OCT T/T PETS CC KIDS MED.EX

975 **ROYAL HOTEL, CROMARTY:** 01381 600217. Marine Terr on seafront nr har-
D2 bour. Unfussy hostelry o/look Cromarty Firth with its oil stuff and dolphins in
this gr wee town at the end of the rd in the Black Isle (1414/COASTAL VILLAGES).
Conservatory, busy bar, afternoon teas. Some locals find it 'pricey'.

10RMS JAN-DEC X/T PETS CC KIDS MED.INX

976 **LOVAT ARMS, BEAULY:** 01463 782313. Best hotel of many in main st of mar-
C2 ket town 20km from Inverness. Relaxed, welcoming family-run hotel with gr
bar meals and comfy public rms. Much tartan upstairs.

23RMS JAN-DEC T/T PETS CC KIDS MED.EX

977 **TOMICH HOTEL, TOMICH, nr DRUMNADROCHIT:** 01456 415399. The inn of
C3 a quiet conservation village, part of an old estate on the edge of Guisachan
Forest. Nr fantastic Plodda Falls (1456/WATERFALLS) and Glen Affric
(1444/GLENS). Basic facs, but use of pool nearby in farm steading (9am-9pm);
esp good for fishing holidays. 25km drive from Drum by A831.

8RMS JAN-DEC T/T PETS CC KIDS MED.INX

978 **PORT-NA-CON, nr DURNESS:** 01971 511367. Ken and Lesley Black's guest-
C1 house on this idyllic shore is gr value. Comfortable rms (1 en suite), 600 books
in the library and mts all around waiting to be climbed, ensure guests return
regularly. Seafood from the loch often on the dinner menu (INX). Non-residents should book. If they're full, Lesley might be able to find you a rm at her
mum's house.

3RMS JAN-DEC X/X PETS CC KIDS CHP

979 **BALCRAGGAN HOUSE, nr FESHIEBRIDGE, nr KINCRAIG:** 01540 651488. On
D3 the B970 rd betw Kingussie and Inverdruie nr Aviemore, Helen Gillies' family
house and B&B rather than hotel, though dinner is available. Modern house
on bend of rd 1km Feshiebridge, only 2 rms, but of a standard too good not
to mention. Helen knows all the good walks near here.

2RMS JAN-DEC X/T PETS XCC KIDS INX

980 **LYNWILG HOUSE, nr AVIEMORE:** 01479 811685. 1.5km S of Aviemore, sign-
D3 posted. As per Balcraggan (above) a v superior B&B and with excellent food
on offer in the evenings. A reader recommendation, run by the Clearys, TOS
award winner. A civilised choice. 4RMS JAN-OCT X/T PETS CC KIDS TOS MED.INX

981 **HEATHBANK HOUSE, BOAT OF GARTEN:** 01479 831234. Quirky taste in wall
D3 decorations, lots of fans but fewer pics than before. Hotel taken over in Aug
'99 (just in time for the book) by Janet and David Lawton – we await developments. Colonial-type house in neat village nr skiing and osprey reserve
(1569/BIRDS). The Mackintosh conservatory continues the idiosyncracy. No
smk.

7RMS JAN-DEC X/X XPETS CC KIDS TOS MED.INX

982 **THE OLD SMIDDY, LAIDE:** 01445 731425. This book doesn't feature many
B2 B&Bs, but after those readers' letters … Kate MacDonald's place in jolie Laide
(Gruinard Bay, Wester Ross on the A832) is one of the superior examples. She's
a fine cook and does serious dinners (book then BYOB) but if you want to stay
these are only 3rms (and self-cat cottages out the back).

3RMS APR-OCT X/T PETS CC KIDS MED.INX

GLENELG INN, GLENELG: 01599 522273 (1121/INNS).

TOMDOUN HOTEL, nr INVERGARRY: 01809 511218 (1127/INNS).

OLD LIBRARY LODGE, ARISAIG: 01687 450651 – report RESTAURANTS, *opposite*.

GOOD INEXPENSIVE RESTAURANTS IN THE HIGHLANDS

Refer to Map 2.

C2 ✓ **CAFÉ NUMBER ONE, INVERNESS:** 01463 226200. Castle St. New favourite spot to eat in the Highland capital. See 2168/INVERNESS for full report. INX

983
C3 ✓ **OLD STATION, SPEAN BRIDGE:** 01397 712535. Richard and Helen Bunney's excl railway stn-restau conversion. Gr Scottish contemp cooking. We still say their single AA rosette (1999) should be 2. W coast seafood, and good vegn selection. Apr-Oct Tues-Sun, dinner only: 6.30-9pm. MED

984
B3 ✓ **SEAGREEN, KYLE OF LOCHALSH:** 01599 534388. Café by day and dinner at night. Eclectic eco-atmos with wholefood products to buy, art exhibitions and books. Dinner menu of interesting wholefood, organic ale, and excl organic wines. Local cheeses and handmade chocolates with your decaff. Restau May-Sept; LO 9pm; café AYR 10am-6pm (1230/VEGN RESTAUS). MED

985
B3 ✓ **THE SEAFOOD RESTAURANT, KYLE OF LOCHALSH:** 01599 534813. Gt atmos bistro nr (and still an actual station platform) the busy port, off the rd to Skye and with that bridge in the distance. Seafood (with unusual dressings; 'raspberry and poppy seed') and vegn selection. Apr-Oct: lunch Mon-Sat 10am-3pm; dinner 7 days 6.30-9pm. V popular, so maybe book. MED

986
B3 ✓ **OFF THE RAILS, PLOCKTON:** 01599 544423. On the platform of this working railway stn; but no droopy sandwiches here, just good home-baking and snacks in the day; 10.30am-5pm. Blackboard specials and evening menu 6.30-9.30pm. Good spot on edge of perfect little Plockton (1412/COASTAL VILLAGES). You may have to book. INX

987
D1 ✓ **LA MIRAGE, HELMSDALE:** 01431 821615. Dunrobin St nr the Br Hotel. A little piece of Las Vegas in Caithness; this glitterati parlour is a novelty in this wee village by the sea. Snacks of every kind all day; with life-size photos of the inimitable proprietor Nancy Sinclair and various celebs gracing the walls – you never know who might pop over! Great fish and chips and salmon fresh from the river in season. Daily noon-8.45pm (Dec-Apr, noon-7pm). Good family fare. INX

988 **THE BOATHOUSE, KINCRAIG:** 01540 651394. 2km from village towards
D3 Feshiebridge along L Insh. Part of L Insh Water sports (1912/WATER SPORTS), a balcony restau o/look beach and loch. Fine setting and ambience, friendly young staff, but they come and go. Some vegn. Salmon from the loch. You're in competition with the ospreys. Bar menu and home-baking till 6pm; supper till 9pm. Apr-Oct. CHP

989 **OLD LIBRARY LODGE, ARISAIG:** 01687 450651. Nr the end of the infamous
B3 'Road to the Isles' just as they start to hove into view. Converted stables with 6 bedrms (MED.INX) above and behind. Hot and cold lunch snacks (INX) 11.30am-2.30pm. Good selection of not only seafood but also meat and veg for the evening table d'hôte (MED) 6.30-9.30pm, booking advisable. Quay and beach nearby (with boats to Rum, Eigg and Muck), bask in the sunset behind them. INX

990 **OLD SCHOOL, INSHEGRA, nr KINLOCHBERVIE:** 01971 521383. B801 Betw
C1 Rhiconich and Kinlochbervie. Not exactly converted but *adapted*, which is what makes it atmos (the huge ruler on the wall helps). Snacks and kids menu during day; 3 courses at night with nursery puds. The world map from 1945 is not the only nostalgia. Gourmet it is not, but you're usually glad you stopped. Daily 12-2pm and 6-8pm. Also accom. Open AYR. INX

991 **RIVERSIDE BISTRO, LOCHINVER:** 01571 844356. On way into town on A837.
C1 Self-serve during day; vast array of Ian Stewart's home-made pies and calorific cakes. You can eat in, sit out at the picnic tables, or take away. Conservatory restau beside river serves v popular meals at night; using local seafood, venison, vegn – something for everyone incl, apparently, Michael Winner (though don't let that put you off). Daily lunch and 6-9pm. MED

992 **THE OYSTERCATCHER, PORTMAHOMACK, nr TAIN:** 01862 871560. On
D2 promontory of the Dornoch Firth (Tain 15km) this hidden seaside village
could bring back childhood memories (even somebody else's). Brightly
coloured murals adorn the caff, fish swim in lit tanks. Locals come for
Charlotte's snacks in the day and bistro at night. We come further, because it's
quite wonderful here. Open AYR (not Feb) 11am-6pm and 7-8.30pm. Cl Mon.

CHP

993 **MORANGIE HOUSE, TAIN:** 01862 892281. On way into/out of Tain from A9.
D2 Popular locally for its food; there's a huge menu with pages of food (grills,
roasts, etc.) catering for everyone. You scoff in the conservatory, quaff in the
pine and tartan lounge; a good choice for Sun lunch. Lunch and 6-9.30pm.

MED/INX

994 **FALLS OF SHIN COFFEE SHOP, nr LAIRG:** Self-serve café/restau in the visitor
C2 centre and shop across the rd from the Falls of Shin on the Achany Glen rd
8km S of Lairg (1469/WATERFALLS). Excellent basic food, among best I've seen
in similar situations. Somebody there cooks and cares. Mar-Oct 7days, LO
5.30pm.

CHP

995 **THE DUNNET HEAD TEA-ROOM, DUNNET HEAD, nr THURSO:** 01847
D1 851774. 15km N of Thurso on the coast rd via Castletown. A cliff-top café serving snacks, meals, puddings and a good selection of kids' faves. John has now
retired to his radio and email shack out the back, but can sometimes be seen
looking for puffins or distributing his newsletter about the the weather and
the wildlife. Only 3km from the famous Head; it's a good stop. 7 days; 3-8pm
(Apr-Oct).

INX

996 **KYLESKU HOTEL, nr KYLESTROME:** 01971 502231. On A894; tucked down
C1 beside L Glencoul where the boat leaves to see Britain's 'highest waterfall'
(1461/WATERFALLS). Gr pub seafood, delicious desserts; with similar formal
menu in adj restau. Both o/look loch; windswept/sunstroked atmos. Good
value.

INX

THE BEST PLACES TO STAY IN AND AROUND ABERDEEN

It's been said before, but in oil city, hotels are expensive. But remember, though full during the week, many places offer surprisingly good w/end deals. Refer to Map 3.

997 ✓✓ **MARCLIFFE OF PITFODELS:** 01224 861000. N Deeside Rd (en route to Royal Deeside 5km from Union St). Aberdeen's premiere hotel. A member of the Small Luxury Hotels of the World group, it is a successful mix of the intimate and the spacious, the old (mansion house) and the new (1993 refurb). Personally run by the Spence family, the sort of hoteliers whom no detail or face escapes. 2 excellent restaus, breakfast in light conservatory. Often dinners and dos attended by the gr and the good Aberdonians; always efficient and friendly service. *42RMS JAN-DEC T/T PETS CC KIDS TOS LOTS*

998 ✓ **MARYCULTER HOUSE HOTEL, MARYCULTER:** 01224 732124. Another out-of-town hotel, in the same direction as Ardoe below (and same owners) but 7km further on. Excellent situation on banks of Dee with river side walks and an old graveyard and ruined chapel. Newer annex; 8/9 rms o/look river. Poacher's Bar and dining-rm. We've heard murmurs of dissent about service, but still like the Knights Templar atmos lurking under the polite surface; hotel on site of 13th C preceptory. *23RMS JAN-DEC T/T XPETS CC KIDS TOS LOTS*

999 **ARDOE HOUSE, BLAIRS:** 01224 867355. 12km SW of centre on the S Deeside (it's poss to turn off the A92 from Stonehaven and the S at the first br and get to the hotel avoiding the city). The Dee is on other side of rd from hotel, but nearby. A goodly chunk of Scottish Baronial with few, but more individual rms and an annex where most rms have pleasant countryside views. Huge redevelopment over 1999/2000 will see 40 more rms and a leisure complex, but not open as we went to press. *71RMS JAN-DEC T/T PETS CC KIDS TOS LOTS*

1000 **THE PATIO HOTEL:** 01224 633339. Beach Boulevard. Accom in the developing Beach pleasure zone, not such a bad place to be. Leisure Centre, Virgin Multiplex and Really Big Disco nearby; and the long beach and seafront. This place, part of an emerging UK chain, wins no architectural plaudits from the o/side, but is comfortable and contemporary in its inner courtyard. Lightsome though bedrms have curiously wee windows. Own pool etc. Not far to Silver Darling for dinner (1010/ABER RESTAUS). *124RMS JAN-DEC T/T PETS CC KIDS EXP./ LOTS*

1001 **CALEDONIAN THISTLE HOTEL:** 01224 640233. Victorian edifice on Union Terr. Of several city centre hotels just off Union St, this always seems the most easy to deal with, the most calm and efficient. All the facs you'd expect; 2 restaus; rms on first and second floors refurbished recently. *80RMS JAN-DEC T/T PETS CC KIDS TOS LOTS*

1002 **ATHOLL HOTEL:** 01224 323505. 54 King's Gate. W towards Hazelhead, an Aber stalwart, the sort of place you put your rellies and join them for dinner or a bar meal. I've never stayed, but people say this is the best among many mansions. Hotel says it's 'in a class of its own'. *35RMS JAN-DEC T/T XPETS CC KIDS MED.EX*

1003 **THE BRENTWOOD HOTEL:** 01224 595440. 101 Crown St. In an area of many hotels and guesthouses to the S of Union St, this one is surprisingly commodious and a better prospect than most. An adequate business hotel on a budget. Close to Union St and bars/restaus. Bar meals recommended and the ale is real. *65RMS JAN-DEC T/T PETS CC KIDS MED.INX*

1004 **THE CULTS HOTEL, CULTS:** 01224 867632. 9km from centre on A93 Deeside rd so well-placed for touring/Castle Trail and nr Faradays to eat (1011/ABER RESTAUS). Fine roadside pub/hotel with local following and quite comfortable with recent refurb; but it's still good value and decent value is hard to find. Owners can organise all kinds of outdoors stuff, espec golf. *6RMS JAN-DEC T/T PETS CC KIDS MED.INX*

1005 **WATERWHEEL INN, BIELDSIDE:** 01224 861659. 12km centre also via A93 N Deeside Rd. Busy (Toby) roadhouse with various bars/restaus though rms at back are reasonably quiet. *21RMS JAN-DEC T/T PETS CC KIDS MED.EX*

1006 **CRAIGLYNN HOTEL:** 01224 584050. 36 Fonthill Rd. With the number of over-priced hotels in the city, glad to include this family-run establishment (Chris & Hazel Mann). Former townhouse with nice touches like central wooden staircase and stained glass. Rowies for breakfast! Handy for centre, small car/pk.

9RMS JAN-DEC T/T XPETS CC XKIDS MED.INX

1007 **HOSTELS: SYHA:** 8 Queen's Rd, an arterial rd to W. Grade 1 hostel 2km from centre (plenty buses). No café. Rms mainly for 4 to 6 people. You can stay out till 2am. Other hostels and self-catering flats c/o Univ, of which the best is probably the **ROBERT GORDONS**, 01224 2621344. Northern College have self-catering flats all over (check Aberdeen TO). Campus in Old Aberdeen which is good place to be though 6km city centre has univ halls accom 01224 272664. All vacs only.

1008 **CAMPING AND CARAVAN PARK:** Only one I recommend is at **HAZELHEAD**, 8km W of centre. Follow signs from ring rd. Swimming pool nearby. Grassy.

THE BEST RESTAURANTS IN ABERDEEN

THE TOPS

1009 ✓ ✓ **THE LAIRHILLOCK INN:** 01569 730001. Not in the city at all, but a roadside inn at a country crossroads to the S, reached off either the rd to Stonehaven or the S Deeside Rd W. Easiest is: head S on main A92, turn off at 'Durris' then 5km. Long-famous for its pub food and informal atmos (1206/PUB FOOD), now the restau has established itself as one of the best in the NE. Captain Budd runs a tight ship and shows what can be done even when location is not up your st. The quarterly newsletter is a model of friendly marketing. Restau: daily dinner and Sun lunch. LO 9.30pm. Inn: 7days lunch and LO 9.30-10.30pm.

MED/INX

1010 ✓ ✓ **SILVER DARLINGS:** 01224 576229. Didier Dejean's breakthrough bistro still going strong in this perfect spot. Not so easy to find – head for Beach Esplanade, the lighthouse and harbour mouth (Pocra Quay). The light winks and boats glide past. New dining rm upstairs since last visit, nice design and better views; the seafood superb. Mostly chargrilled; the smell pleasantly pervades. Different menu for lunch and dinner, changes seasonally and depends on the catch. Apposite wines, wicked desserts. Mon-Fri lunch and Mon-Sat dinner 7-9.30pm.

EXP

1011 ✓ **FARADAYS:** 01224 869666. Kirkbrae, Cults. 8km W on A93, turning uphill opp Kelly's. John Inches' assured contemporary dinner menu and superior versions of Scottish comfort food for lunch, e.g. mince with skirlie and peas, stew with doughboys. Intimate bistro ambience in former hydro-electricity station. Aber's reliably good repast. Tue-Sat lunch and LO 9.30pm.

EXP

1012 ✓ **SOHO BAR/RESTAU:** 01224 211111. Dee St. Bar in front. Brasserie downstairs, restau upstairs. Does look v 'SoHo' so a surprise to find it here. Design and food both light and chic (oysters, pigeon). What's happening to Abdn? Mon-Sat L and dinner LO 'late'.

MED

1013 ✓ **OLIVE TREE:** 01224 208877. 32 Queen's Rd. A late 90's addition to smart dining in the Granite City and Mike Reilly certainly made sure it had the look. Bargain lunches and suppers (5.30-7pm) preferred (INX). Service and presentation tip top but à la carte (MED) has some catching up to do before it's considered among the best in the land. Mon-Sat L and LO 10pm.

EXP

1014 ✓ **Q BRASSERIE:** 01224 595001. 9 Alford Pl. Shut for a major refurb in summer '99 – was one of the city's best, is it still? Chef Paul Whitecross has gone, so reports please.

MED

SEAFOOD

✓ ✓ **SILVER DARLING:** 01224 576229. The Tops (*see above*).

1015 ✓ **THE ASHVALE:** 01224 596981. 46 Gt Western Rd nr Union St and branches (incl Elgin, Br of Don, Inverurie and Brechin). The famous Ashvale fish 'n' chip shop, the NE equivalent, I suppose, of Harry Ramsden's, but we'd say better, esp here at original branch. Sit in (room for 300) or take away. Long, varied menu; you'd be daft not to have fresh fried fish (1260/FISH AND CHIPS). INX

1016 **ATLANTIS at the MARINER HOTEL:** 01224 591403. 349 Gr Western Rd. Those that know where to go in Aber for excellent fish and seafood may not necessarily go to Silver Darling or the Ashvale, but come here. Hotel dining-rm atmos is not too evident (tables in conservatory) and the fish v good. Moderately priced wines. Lunch (not Sat) and dinner LO 9.30pm . MED

ITALIAN

1017 ✓ **LITTLE ITALY:** 01224 572240. 79 Holburn St nr W end of Union St. The authentic good-fun and esp late-night Italian eaterie. Usual pasta/pizza mix. Can be raucous. Food till midnight Mon-Wed, till 2am Thur-Sat. MED

1018 **BORSALINO:** 01224 732902. Peterculter on main A93 (after Rob Roy Br), 15km W of city centre but famously worth the drive. For over 20yrs Franco's unlikely cantina in a roadside cottage. Here is a remote corner of Tuscany: pasta, the (awful) veal, tiramisu. Morning coffee, lunch and LO 10.30pm. MED

1019 **POLDINO'S:** 01224 647777. 7 Little Belmont St. Enduring haunt of Aberdonians in search of pasta etc. Good Italian home-cooking, incl puddings. City centre, always buzzy. Mon-Sat lunch and 6-10.45pm. INX

1020 **VIA MILANO:** 01224 593222. Bon Accord St. Designer Italian opened '98 as part of swish new shop mall, The Galeria. Big and familiar menu, but TVs? Daily L and LO 9pm. (later on Fri/Sat) INX

1021 **CARMINE'S PIZZA:** 01224 624145. 32 Union Terr. This tiny slice of a rm for *the* best pizza in town and on the wall, a few famous faces who've eaten them (well… Adam Faith). Noon-5.30pm. Cl Sun. CHP

EASTERN

1022 ✓ **THE ROYAL THAI:** 01224 212922. Crown Terr (off Crown St which is off Union St). The first and best of the welcome Asian invasion rated above all others by locals. 'Banquets' with sample dishes are a good idea. Good service, moody lighting. Daily lunch and 7-11pm. The Royal Thai is now bracketed by a Vietnamese restau and a Chinese/Thai called **PACIFIC WINDS** – not eaten, but heard good things. 01224 572362. Daily L and LO 11pm. MED

1023 **DIM SUM INN:** 01224 636750. 303 George St. Way down this long st off Union (about 1km), but the Chinese of choice for calm interior and good Cantonese cookery. 7 days, lunch and LO 10.30pm. INX

1024 **YU:** 01224 580318. 347 Union St. Central, stylish, airy and relaxed Peking Chinese. Good fish; light, imaginative sauces. Daily lunch and 7-11pm. MED

1025 **NARGILE:** 01224 636093. 77 Szene St. Turkish survivor that made its regulars happy for 18yrs. Turkish owner, Doric staff, reliable meze, kebabs, swordfish etc. Daily dinner, LO INX. Cl lunch. 11pm Sun 10pm. MED

1026 **DOWNSTAIRS AT BORSALINO'S, PETERCULTER** (1018/*above*): Tiny takeaway doing Chinese, unrelated to adj Italian; they drive from Cults! (see Borsalino's for directions). MED

FRENCH

1027 **GERARDS:** 01224 639500. 50 Chapel St. The longest-established major restau in city. Trad French and très exp (set meal a good idea). Good ambience and the discreet charm of the bourgeoisie. Open 7 days. EXP

1028 **CAFE ROUGE:** 01224 624324. 8 Golden Sq. Part of a chain, but reliable cafe/bistro with regular jazz downstairs. Fin-de-siècle metro-french as imagined by marketeers. Daily until 11pm. INX

1029 **LA BONNE BAGUETTE:** 01224 644445. Off Union St down steps at side of graveyard. Très popular and quite French café. Pâtisserie, snacks (baguettes, etc.) and specials. Daytime only 8.30am-5pm. Cl Sun. CHP

BISTROS

1030 **OWLIES:** 01224 649267. Littlejohn St. All-day brasserie in warehouse setting, a long-time Aber fave. Plain French fare (with provincial and more cosmo variations e.g. gado gado, couscous and good vegn menu). Tues-Sat LO 10pm (11 w/ends). Good atmos, good attitude.   INX

1031 **THE WILD BOAR:** 01224 625357. 19 Belmont St. Narrow, intimate and usually buzzing bar-bistro. From big cake selection to steaks/noodles to Thai additions. Funkier than it used to be: occ DJs 7 days, food LO 8pm (9pm w/ends).   INX

1032 **THE LEMON TREE:** 01224 642230. 5 W North St. From E end of Union St heading for beach, W North St is off King St. Excellent arts centre with café-bar/restau. Food ok rather than fantastic, but gr ambience. Another Aberdeen refurb in summer '99. so perhaps even better now?   INX

1033 **LA BAMBA:** 01224 590088. Crown Terr. Tex-Mex with attitude hits town. Good buzz in city centre. Dinner daily 7pm and 9pm 'seatings', L Fri-Sat   INX

1034 Also: another local fave worth checking is **THE COURTYARD ON THE LANE** in Alford Lane: 01224 213795. Meanwhile a Med-style piazza has appeared up Belmont St – The Academy Mall. **RSVP** was doing bargain breakfasts when we visited (a spacious chain café-bar); but the Scot/Med collision cuisine in **ZINC BAR/GRILL** looked the pick of the bunch (01224 640900) MED, and there's even **JAZZ CAFE** upstairs.

THE BEST PUBS AND CLUBS IN ABERDEEN

PUBS WITH ATMOSPHERE AND ATTITUDE

1035 ✓ **THE PRINCE OF WALES:** 7 St Nicholas Lane, just off Union St at George St. An all-round gr pub always mentioned in guides and one of the best places in the city for real ale: Old Peculier, Caledonian 80/-, Younger's No 3 and guest beers. V cheap self-service food at lunchtime. Lots of wood, flagstones, booths. Large area but gets v crowded. 7 days, 11am-11pm.

1036 **THE BLUE LAMP:** Gallowgate. Snug pub with nice ambience and long-established clientele and up the st large stone-floored lounge (The Blue Lampie) with gr atmos and live music w/ends (so open 1am). Pub has pics of that '83 team and a jukebox unchanged forever (Atomic Rooster, Julie Driscoll, Hendrix).

1037 **MA CAMERON'S INN:** Little Belmont St. The 'oldest pub in the city' (though the old bit is actually a small portion of the sprawling whole – but there's a good snug). No nonsense oasis in buzzy street. Food: lunch and early evening. Cl Sun.

1038 **THE GLOBE:** 13 N Silver St. Urban and urbane bar in single rm – a place to drink coffee as well as lager, but without self-conscious, pretentious 'café-bar' atmos. Known for its food at lunch and 5-7.45pm (not w/ends).

1039 **UNDER THE HAMMER:** 11 N Silver St. Basement bar along the st from above, v intimately Aberdonian and a good place to meet them. Slightly older and mixed crowd. Only open evenings (till midnight) and best late on. My kind of place.

1040 **THE LEMON TREE:** 5 W North St. A theatre (upstairs) and a spacious bar/restau on st level where there's lunchtime food (1032/ABER RESTAUS) and a mixed programme of entertainment. Phone (01224 642230) or watch for fliers, but prog will include comedy, jazz, folk, pop and cabaret. No membership required. Haven't seen it since the '99 refurb though, so perhaps looking rather fresher now.

CONTEMPORARY PUBS

1041 **COLLEGE:** Alfred Pl at W end of Union St. Hugely popular 'sports' and MTV kind of bar by Q Brasserie with stylish interior. Screens hanging everywhere for the footie, boxing, and other bodies disporting and competing as they do around the bar.

1042　**THE OLD TOWN SCHOOL:** Little Belmont St as Ma Cameron's above, but the v up-to-date equivalent with everything from themed interior, balcony and patio to many ales, gr wine selection (by glass), malts and grub. All works, gets busy.

1043　**CAFÉ SOCIETY:** 9 Queens Rd. An enduring nitespot on the oil slick circuit where an older crowd can dispose of their income and some of their sexual angst. Sub-Steven Conroy pictures and fake chandeliers 'create' a lounge-lizard atmos; the o/side patio is nice of a summer evening. Food served till 10pm, bar midnight. Refurb due and underway.

1044　**PARAMOUNT:** Bon Accord St. Designer café-bar looking a little worn now, but v popular and gr place to check out the club scene (flyers etc). Food to 5pm, open to midnight.

1045　**ESKOBAR:** Bridge st. Basic dance/grungy bar with food during the day, DJs at night and aspirins available from the toilet vending machine. This used to be the Wimpy.

1046　**ILLICIT STILL:** Betw Broad St and Netherkirkgate. Studenty, wooden real ale labyrinth with brews from Tomintoul among others. Also bar food. Also, **PO-NA-NA**, the dance-soul chain has landed at 5 Union St.

1047　**JUSTICE MILL LANE and WINDMILL BRAE:** Many pubs to choose from. JM Lane has bigger selection and slightly older age gp – **FLARES** 70's bar packs em in. Windmill Brae for under – 25 pre-clubbers. All loud and lively.

CLUBS

With more ready cash than most, the Aberdonian has many clubs to choose from. Once again we tried loads, those below are the ones we recommend. Open Fri-Sun mostly, but check flyers for details.

1048　✓ **MINISTRY OF SIN:** 01224 211661. 16 Dee St off Union St. Converted church and, after all these yrs still a good bet mainly because proprietor Mike Wilson put it together properly in the first place. Studenty but a pleasant mix – in Aber they generally don't mind oldies on the dancefloor. You have to be smart on Sats; students, glowsticks and guest DJs on Suns.

1049　**GLOW 303:** 9 Belmont St. Underneath a vodka bar, a zinc-lined, corrugated kind of a clubland disco with gr lay out and a young jumpy crowd (you could say enthusiastic). Underground dance, sometimes open to 3am.

1050　**THE PELICAN at the METRO HOTEL:** Market St. Funky subterranean beatbox in the basement of this plastic hotel. No bad attitude, moustaches, or white slingbacks thank you! Yet more underground dance.

THE BEST HOTELS IN AND AROUND DUNDEE

Refer to Map 4.

1051 ✓ **THE OLD MANSION HOUSE, AUCHTERHOUSE:** 01382 320366. 15km NW of centre on B954 to Alyth (take Coupar Angus rd from ring route). Every important Scot in history is reputed to have stayed in this 16th-century castellated hse. It hasn't changed a lot; but what would William Wallace make of the surprising outdoor pool? We loved it.
6 RMS JAN-DEC T/T PETS CC KIDS TOS EXP

EAT Elegant dining in the green world beyond Dundee. EXP

1052 **THE QUEENS HOTEL:** 01382 322515. Nethergate/Perth Rd. Convenient location with parking round the back. Old-style Victorian city hotel bang in the middle nr Arts Centre. Old-fashioned feel but better than the new-furnished feel of much of opposition. 47RMS JAN-DEC T/T PETS CC KIDS MED.EX

1053 **THE SHAFTESBURY:** 01382 669216. 1 Hyndford St just off Perth Rd (about 3km from city centre). A suburban (jute baron's) mansion converted into a comfortable hotel with neat back grd. All rms different; loungeable lounge. Decent value. 12RMS JAN-DEC T/T PETS CC KIDS INX

1054 **DRUMNACREE HOUSE HOTEL, ALYTH:** 01828 632194. St. Ninians Rd. Take A923 off ring rd in Dundee; follow signs for Alyth B954: 12km. Quiet house in residential rd of a sleepy farming town. Frilly décor, friendly hosts.
6RMS APR-DEC X/T PETS CC KIDS MED.INX

EAT All home-grown veg, local produce cooked traditionally or exotically – you choose (Cajun twist when we were there). 7pm onwards. Must book first. 2 AA rosettes. MED

1055 **FISHERMAN'S TAVERN:** 01382 775941. Broughty Ferry, Fort St nr the river/sea. Rms above and beside but noise not bad esp new rms adj which are en-suite – others more basic but chp. Excl pub (*see below*) and grub.
13RMS (5 EN-SUITE) JAN-DEC T/T PETS CC KIDS CHP.INX

1056 **HOTEL BROUGHTY FERRY, BROUGHTY FERRY:** 01382 480027. 16 W Queen St. On main rd into the 'Ferry' (*see below*). Cleanly refurb inside, with conservatory. Pool and sauna rm lurking surprisingly in the basement. On busy corner, but calm inside. Bar/restau. 16RMS JAN-DEC T/T PETS CC KIDS MED.INX

1057 **WOODLANDS, BROUGHTY FERRY:** 01382 480033. From Broughty Ferry main st, take left after 1.5km into Abercromby St, second left into Panmure Terr. High falutin' house in substantial acreage. One of the 'Bett Inn' chain, popular out-of-town wedding venue quite complete with small swimming pool and gym. 38RMS JAN-DEC T/T PETS CC KIDS MED.INX

1058 **FORT HOTEL, BROUGHTY FERRY:** 01382 737999. 58 Fort St. The 'Ferry' is easily reached by bus/train or Arbroath A92, then A930. About 8km along Tayside and a pleasant, less urban place with good pubs and restaus. This recently modernised rooming house is in main area, above the Fort Bar. Basic but adequate. 10RMS JAN-DEC T/T PETS CC KIDS MED.INX

SANDFORD HILL: 01382 541802. Excellent rural retreat over the water 7km S of Tay Br via A92/914 (1088/COUNTRY-HOUSE HOTELS).

SWALLOW HOTEL: 01382 641122. Modern, all-purpose chain hotel on town ring rd, but good for families (1102/KIDS).

HOSTELS: There is no S.Y.H. in the area, although in summer months univ hall accom is available – info from TO. 01382 434664. **THE WHITE HOUSE** 208 Broughty Ferry Rd. Caters for backpackers.

1059 **RIVERVIEW CARAVAN PARK:** 01382 535471. Take A92 Arbroath rd, 3 miles along take 3rd sign for Monifieth and follow caravan signs. **TAYVIEW EAST HOLIDAY PARK :** 01382 532837. Union St. Monifieth has gr sea views. Good site also at **TAYPORT:** across Tay Br, 8km SE of centre. 100 pitches on sandy/grassy site nr Tentsmuir (1586/WILDLIFE).

1060 ✓ **THE SHIP INN:** 01382 779176. On front at Broughty Ferry. Weathered by the R Tay since the 1800s, this cosy pub has sustained smugglers, fishermen and foody folk alike. Upstairs restau's Scottish menu has earned them their solid reputation. Lunch and 5-10.30pm, w/ends noon-10.30pm.   CHP

1061 ✓ **JUTE at DUNDEE ART CENTRE:** 01382 432000. Perth Rd. The bar/cafe/restau of the fab new arts centre which in a oner provided a national gallery space, cinema, classy craft shop and this much needed rendezvous for Dundee. Snacks, during day, main dishes in even. Good coffee. Gr space to eat in. 7 days 10.30 - midnight. Food LO 8.45pm.   CHP

1062 ✓ **SOUTH KINGENNIE HOUSE:** 01382 350562 Out of town. From A92 nr Arbroath rd take B978 to Kellas (2km). At app to village, restau signed to rt (1km along). Major Sun lunch destination for Dundonians needing a lungful of air, an eyeful of green fields and a stomach full of roast beef with all the trimmings. Modern Scottish menu at other times. Cl Sun evening and Mon.   INX

1063 ✓ **THE AGACAN:** 01382 644227. 113 Perth Rd. Fabled bistro for Turkish eats and wine. Art on the walls. Even non-meaties might dig the bohemian ambience. Cl Mon.   INX

1064 ✓ **PIZZA EXPRESS:** 01382 226677. 31A Albert Sq behind McGanns Galleries. Dundee branch of the dependable pizza chain. Easily the classiest looking restau in town. Less crowded than PEs elsewhere – Dundonians unimpressed by the slightly more exp pizza, may actually prefer Pizza Hut. Oh, well! 7 days LO 11.30pm   INX

1065 **CAFE MONTMATRE:** 01382 739313. Gray St nr station, Broughty Ferry. Charming and genuine French bistro with extensive menu. Dinner only Mon-Sat, LO 9.45pm   CHP

1066 **CUL DE SAC:** Tay Square, off S Tay St next to Repertory Theatre Café/bar/restau similar (same owners) as perenially hip Cul de Sac in Glasgow (517/BISTROS). Noon – 10.30pm.   INX

1067 **CAFÉ BUONGIORNO:** 01382 221179. 11 Bank St. Fairly authentic Italian job. Café by day and restau from 7-10pm.   MED

1068 **VISOCCHI'S:** 01382 779297. 40 Gray St, Broughty Ferry. More of a café than the original Kirriemuir branch caff. After almost 70yrs they're still making mouthwatering Italian flavoured ice creams (*amaretto*, *cassata* etc.) alongside home-made pasta and snacks.   CHP

1069 **ROYAL OAK:** 01382 229440. 167 Brook St nr W Pt. Excellent pub food with an Indian emphasis that's quietly quirky. Dundee's funky find. Bar and dining-rm. Lunch and LO 9pm.   INX

1070 **MANDARIN GARDEN:** 01382 227733. 40 S Tay St. V acceptable Chinese. Low key décor, peaceful atmos; food is the thing. Excellent seafood and different meats covered sauce-u-like. Lunch and 5-11pm. Cl Sun.   INX

1071 **BEIDERBECKES:** 304 Perth Rd. Jazz influenced pizzas (there's a Satchmo and a Hoagy Carmichael) with topping and base proportioned evenly for a change. Dundee-wise they've hit the rt note. Laid-back sounds. 10.30am-5pm; Sun 12-5pm.   CHP

PUBS

1072 **THE FISHERMAN'S TAVERN:** 12 Fort St, Broughty Ferry. Good pub lunches here, but notable for real ales. Listed 17th-century fisherman's cottage, snug portside atmos. 1am-midnight (1am Thur-Sat).

1073 **LAINGS:** Roseangle, off Perth Rd. V popular with 20s-30s crowd. Beer gdn gets crowded in summer, typical pub food to fill you up and the *de rigeur* Banoffee pie. 11am-11.30pm.

1074 **MERCANTILE BAR:** Commercial St. Huge newly fashioned trad style pub with circular gallery brimming with regulars. Food till 7pm. V mixed crowd.

1075 **TAYBRIDGE BAR:** 129 Perth Rd. Legendary drinking place. Est 1867: smell of spit and sawdust still lingers; women are present, but usually accompanied by their 'man'.

1076 **PUBS IN THE WEST PORT: THE GLOBE, TALLYS, THE PARAMOUNT etc:** Popular student hang-outs in W Port (end of S Tay St & off Marketgait; behind univ). The Irish one more authentic than usual. CHP

SECTION 4

Particular Places to Eat and Stay throughout Scotland

SUPERLATIVE COUNTRY-HOUSE HOTELS

Houses (both large and small, grand and intimate) in the country that have been turned into hotels. Usually family-run/owner-occupied, expensive but stress-free.

1077a
MAP 4
B3

✓ ✓ **KINNAIRD HOUSE, DUNKELD:** 01796 482440. 12km N of Dunkeld (Perth 35km) via A9 and B898 for Dalguise. In bucolic setting beneath woody ridge of Tay Valley, a country house which envelops you with good taste and comfort. Good, unobtrusive service; impeccable detail. The CDs are Domingo/Cole/Beethoven, the books are ones you'd want to read, the postcards are Scottish Wildlife Trust. You get a teddy on your bed and there's a stylish 'K' on everything. Gr snooker rm. Elegant dining; chef Trevor Brooks on the stove. Silently beyond the grounds and river, endless traffic ploughs N and S on the A9. One day you'll have to join it again. Until then, live Kinnaird. Also 9 superb individual cottages (esp 'Castle Peroch' and new one, 'keepers') on the estate. 9RMS (9 COTT) JAN-DEC T/T PETS CC KIDS LOTS

1077b
MAP 6
C2

✓ ✓ **CROMLIX HOUSE, DUNBLANE:** 01786 822125. Improved and perfected over the last few years – full report (829/CENTRAL HOTELS), but now unquestionably one of the best country-house hotels in the UK. Fabulous grounds, fastidious service, excellent food.

1078
MAP 1
B1

✓ ✓ **ISLE OF ERISKA, LEDAIG:** 01631 720371. 20km N of Oban (signed from A85 nr Benderloch Castle). As you drive over the Victorian iron br onto the isle (a real island), you enter a more tranquil and gracious world. Its 300 acres are a sanctuary for wildlife; you are not the only guests. The famous badgers, for example, come almost every night to the door of the bar for their milk. Comfortable baronial house with fastidious service and facs. Highly picturesque 9 hole golf, gr 17m pool (and gym) (excl in summer when it opens on to the garden). Also putting, tennis and clay shooting; it's all there if you feel like action, but it's v pleasant just to stay still (and aromatherapy is avail). Dining, with a Scottish flavour and impeccable local ingredients from a rich backyard and bay, has 2 AA rosettes.
17RMS FEB-DEC T/T PETS CC KIDS TOS LOTS

1079
MAP 4
B4

✓ ✓ **GLENEAGLES, AUCHTERARDER:** 01764 662231. On A824 and rather difficult to miss. Scotland's truly luxurious resort hotel. For facs on the grand scale others pale into insignificance; and it equates on an international level. Only the sun may be missing, but the famous golf (3 courses), the Equestrian Centre, Shooting School, Falconry Centre and Country Club make up for the climate. The Club now has 2 pools and an outdoor tub. Strathearn Restau is a foodie heaven but fabulously expensive. Club bistro lighter and brighter. When you are in love and rich go here; there are no cheap w/ends. 236RMS JAN-DEC T/T PETS CC KIDS TOS LOTS

1080
MAP 2
C2

✓ ✓ **ALTNAHARRIE INN, ULLAPOOL:** 01854 633230. 2km from town, but other side of L Broom access by boat. Comfortable haven in a wild setting; some rms in the grounds. But it's Gunn Eriksen's dinners that you come for – two Michelin stars (only one in Scotland) puts it on a par with Le Gavroche or La Tante Claire in London. But then, Gordon and Marco and Nico don't have the setting, do they? 8RMS APR-OCT X/X PETS CC KIDS LOTS

1081
MAP 9
A3

✓ ✓ **KNOCKINAAM LODGE, PORTPATRICK:** 01776 810471. An ideal place to lie low; an historic Victorian house nestled between two hills, on its own cove. The Irish coastline is the only thing on the horizon, apart from your considerate N American hosts proferring discreet service, excellent food (chef Tony Pierce excels with a fixed menu which is full of surprises), drink (over 400 wines and eclectic malts) and calm congeniality. 15km S of Stranraer off A77, nr Lochans. 10RMS MAR-DEC T/T PETS CC KIDS LOTS

1082
MAP 4
B4

✓ **AUCHTERARDER HOUSE, AUCHTERARDER:** 01764 663646. Off B8062 Crieff rd 3km from this village more commonly associated with Gleneagles. In contrast, it is intimate, sumptuous and there are few activities to impinge on your slobbing out. Much loved by not very right-on politicians, the Reagans came and the Majors (remember them) probably not PC enough for the Blairs. I've always had the average rms, but there are big suites in there somewhere. Public rms formal verging on gloomy; conservatory bar exquisite.
15RMS JAN-DEC T/T PETS CC KIDS TOS LOTS

1083
MAP 2
C3

✓ **KNOCKIE LODGE, nr FORT AUGUSTUS, LOCH NESS:** 01456 486276. 3km down rd/ track from B862, the quiet E bank rd round L Ness (1492/SCENIC ROUTES); 15km Ft Augustus. Rambling mansion on bluff o/looking a loch, set among farmlands with wide open views. Delightful laid-back atmos almost like an exclusive English pub. Gr chef should have 3 not 2 AA rosettes. Fishing and shooting on tap. Gr snooker rm. A fine retreat. Fixed dinner not J/T.   10RMS MAY-OCT T/X PETS CC XKIDS LOTS

1084
MAP 4
C3

✓ **BALLATHIE HOUSE, KINCLAVEN, nr BLAIRGOWRIE and PERTH:** 01250 883268. Superb situation on R Tay; culinary delights, comfortable, relaxing: a chance to enjoy the finer things in (Perthshire) life. Merits longer mention than this, but because it is handy for Perth and probably the best place to stay nr the town; full report and codes: 2170/PERTH.

1085
MAP 1
B2

✓ **LOCH MELFORT, ARDUAINE, nr OBAN:** 01852 200233. 22km S of Oban on the A816 and on one of the most commanding sites on this picturesque coast. The fabulous view is not everything, but the rms and the restau make the most of it. 20 rms in an annex have either patios or (better) balconies. Large light dining-rm with notable seafood (EXP); Skerry Bistro (MED) more informal fare. The wonderful Arduaine Gardens (1384/GARDENS) run by the NTS are on your doorstep.   26RMS MAR-DEC T/T PETS CC KIDS EXP

1086
MAP 1
C1

✓ **ARDANAISEIG, LOCH AWE:** 01866 833333. 16km from Taynuilt signed from main A85 to Oban down beautiful winding rd and 7km from Kilchrenan. In sheltered landscaped gardens dotted with funny faux Roman statuary and sculptures that burst from the rhododendrons. Nice to wander in even if you're not a guest – go for afternoon tea or lunch. On a promontory of the loch. Under the management of Robert Francis, this venerable hotel is thriving. Rooms have some partic antiques, and decor. O/side by the loch, deer wander and bats flap at dusk. Pure romance. Chef Gary Goldie deserves some plaudits too.   16RMS MAR-DEC T/T PETS CC KIDS TOS LOTS

1087
MAP 2
B3

✓ **ARISAIG HOUSE, ARISAIG:** 01687 450622. On A830, rd to the Isles from Ft William to Mallaig. 2km before Arisaig and 18km from Mallaig in stunning countryside on one of Scotland's most romantic coasts. The Smithers smother you with their good taste. 3AA. The grds are a joy. Civilised and relaxed. Fuller report: 1161/SCOTTISH HOTELS.

14RMS JAN-DEC T/T XPETS CC XKIDS TOS EXP

1088
MAP 5
C2

✓ **SANDFORD HILL, nr WORMIT (nr DUNDEE & ST ANDREWS):** 01382 541802. 7km S of Tay Bridge via A92 and A914, 100m along B946 to Wormit. In an unpromising landscape of quarries and pigfarms, a civilised withdrawal from the jams of Dundee and bunkers of St Andrews. An austere mansion with unusual layout and mullioned windows looking out to gorgeous grds. Wild but romantic tennis court, pub lunches. 750 acres adj farmland of 'activities' – clay-pigeon shooting, fishing in Farm Loch, off-road driving.   16RMS JAN-DEC T/T PETS CC KIDS TOS EXP

1089
MAP 2
B2

✓ **FLODIGARRY COUNTRY HOUSE, SKYE:** 01470 552203. Nr Staffin, 32km N of Portree. Set on a the face of a hill with amazing views across Staffin bay and the mighty Quirang behind. Gr crack in the bar (sessions at the drop of a fiddle) and lounge; the piano is often played. Flora MacDonald's cottage in the grounds with its tastefully refurbished bedrooms offers a rare opportunity actually to stay in a romantic place redolent of this island's history. Relaxed atmos; breakfast at your leisure with gr sky and Skye all around you.

16RMS JAN-DEC X/T PETS CC KIDS TOS EXP

1090
MAP 2
D3

✓ **CORROUR HOUSE, AVIEMORE:** 01479 810220. Small country house 3km from the concrete moor of Aviemore, handy for the ski slopes. Without airs but not without graces, this family-run hotel is extremely good value. Young deer in the garden at daybreak, fine-size rms, the best deal for miles.

8RMS JAN-DEC T/T PETS CC KIDS MED.INX

2 COUNTRY HOUSE HOTELS IN THE BORDERS

THE ROXBURGH HOTEL nr KELSO: 01573 450331 Report: 844/BORDERS

CRINGLETIE HOUSE nr PEEBLES: 01721 730233. Report: 845/BORDERS

HOTELS THAT WELCOME KIDS

1091
MAP 4
B3

✔ ✔ **CRIEFF HYDRO, CRIEFF:** 01764 655555. A national institution and still a family business; your family is part of theirs. App via High St, turning off at Drummond Arms Hotel uphill then follow signs. Vast Victorian pile with activities for everybody from bowlers to babies. Still run by the Leckies from hydropathic beginnings but with recent refurbs, incl the fabulous winter gardens moving graciously with the times. The Brasserie (best for food) is open all day. Gr tennis courts, riding school, Lagoon Pool. Tiny cinema shows family movies; nature talks, donkey rides. Kids endlessly entertained (even while you eat). Beyond are the Trossachs.

225RMS JAN-DEC T/T PETS CC KIDS MED.INX

1092
MAP 2
C3

✔ ✔ **OLD PINES, nr SPEAN BRIDGE:** 01397 712324. 3km Spean Br via B8004 for Garlochy at Commando Monument. Bill and Sukie Barber have 7 kids so will be unfazed by the demands of yours. One level pine log cabin – all bedrms individually furnished; bunk beds with wee teddies to cuddle and take home. Playrm with books, videos and games for kids of all ages, and the Barber brood are also on hand to play with. Menagerie of animals around the stream (many ducks) and Sukie's legendary cooking. Kids can eat separately (not pizza and chips). (657/HIGHLANDS HOTELS).

8RMS JAN-DEC X/X XPETS CC KID TOS MED.INX

1093
MAP 2
B3

✔ **GLENFINNAN HOUSE, GLENFINNAN:** 01397 722235. Just off the 'Road to the Isles' (the A830 from Ft William to Mallaig). V large Highland 'hoose' with so many rms and such large grds you can be as noisy as you like. Great intro to the Highland heartland; music, scenery and local characters. Cruise of the loch leaves from the foot of the lawn. (965/INEXP HIGHLAND HOTELS).

17RMS APR-OCT X/X PETS CC KIDS MED.INX

1094
MAP 2
C3

POLMAILY HOUSE, nr DRUMNADROCHIT: 01456 450343. 5km from main L Ness rd at Drumnadrochit via A831 to Cannich (and glorious Glen Affric), a good country-house hotel for adults that is excellent for kids. The Whittington-Davis's have 4 themselves. Their lucky kids and yours have lots to do in the grds – trout pond where older kids can fish, pet rabbit run, bikes, indoor swimming pool, friendly pet goat. Tree house and swing up the back esp popular. Separate kids' meal time; special rates.

12RMS + 2SUITES APR-OCT T/T PETS CC KIDS MED.EX

1095
MAP 2
A1

BAILE-NA-CILLE, TIMSGARRY, UIG, HARRIS: 01851 672242. 58km W of Stornoway, a long way to go, perhaps, and although this isolation might be more usually sought by adults, the beach here is one that kids will remember all their lives – wide, safe, untouched. Kids eat earlier and they will be tired. General air of anything goes (except smoking). Pollution-free zone.

9+3RMS MAR-OCT X/X PETS CC KIDS MED.INX

1096
MAP 1
C1

DRIMSYNIE: 01301 703247. Lochgoilhead, Argyll. Hotel(s) – they have 3 in the area/chalet/caravan/leisure complex – a holiday village, in fact, on the loch and on the rd to Carrick Castle. Every activity you could poss want (pool, ponies, golf and boating) to divert attention from the scenery. Chalets best for larger families – then you don't have to eat in the restau. The delights of the Sheep and Wool Centre may not detain you long.

17RMS+CHALETS JAN-DEC X/T PETS CC KIDS MED.INX

1097
MAP 8
B2

PEEBLES HYDRO, PEEBLES: 01721 720602. Innerleithen Rd. One of the first Victorian hydros, now more Butlins than Bath. Huge grounds, corridors (you get lost) and floors of rms where kids can run around. Water fun downstairs in small pool. Entertainment and baby-sitting services. V traditional and refreshingly untrendy. Rms vary.

137RMS JAN-DEC T/T PETS CC KIDS TOS MED.INX/EXP

1098
MAP 1
B2

STONEFIELD CASTLE HOTEL, TARBERT: 01880 820836. O/side Tarbert on A83 on slopes of L Fyne with wonderful views. A real castle with 60 acres of woody grounds to explore and a gr open-air pool. Full report and codes: 792/ARGYLL HOTELS.

1099 **ISLES OF GLENCOE HOTEL, BALLACHULISH:** 01855 811602. Beside the A82
MAP 2 Crianlarich to Ft William: a modern hotel and leisure centre jutting out onto
C4 L.Leven. New adventure playground o/side and nature trails. Conservatory
restau o/looking the water, adj. to refurb lounge. 'Mysteryworld' centre in grds
with its spooky actors retelling the local Celt history and 'astromyths' is fairly
awful. Snacks in the restau all day, new age gift shop (sic). Glencoe and 2 ski
areas nearby. 39RMS JAN-DEC T/T PETS CC KIDS MED.INX/EXP

1100 **COYLUMBRIDGE HOTEL, nr AVIEMORE:** 01479 810661. 8km from Aviemore
MAP 2 Centre on B970 rd to ski slopes and nearest hotel to them. 2 pools of decent
D3 size, sauna, etc. Plenty to do in summer and winter (1100/KIDS) and certainly
where to take Daniel and Amy when it rains. Best of the often-criticised
Aviemore corporate hotels, the most facs, huge new shed with kids play area
and staff wandering around in animal costumes (Cyril the Squirrel, Tadger the
Badger etc) 175 (INCL FAMILY)RMS JAN-DEC T/T PETS CC KIDS LOTS

1101 **WATERSIDE INN, PETERHEAD:** 01779 471121. Edge of town on A952 to
MAP 3 Fraserburgh. Modern hotel with pool etc and some activities for kids. Aden
D2 Country Park nearby (1101/KIDS). Kids' menu and meal times and family rms.
Ugie and Deedee (the bears) are a gr success, but you wouldn't want to take
them to bed. Adventure playground. Go-karts. Sometimes special family
w/ends. 109(16 FAMILY)RMS JAN-DEC T/T PETS CC KIDS TOS MED.EX

1102 **SWALLOW HOTEL, DUNDEE:** 01382 641122. Conveniently placed on the
MAP 4 edge of town, just off ring rd system and the rd in from Perth. A link in the
C3 commercial chain; but pleasantly sprawling with surprisingly lush grds, nature
trails and leisure facs. Deals available. 110RMS JAN -DEC T/T PETS CC KIDS EXP

1103 **INGLEDENE HOTEL, ARDROSSAN:** 01294 464998. 14 South Cres nr ferry to
MAP 1 Arran. I haven't been to this hotel with any travel and world weary brats, but I
C3 know a family who have and they said the welcome and the whole kids bit
was dealt with remarkably here. Large play area. On seafront.
8RMS JAN -DEC T/T PETS CC KIDS INX

THE BEST HOSTELS

For hostels in EDINBURGH, *see p.18; for* GLASGOW, *see p.66-7. SYHA Info: 01786
891400. Central reservations (SYHA) 01541 553255.*

1104 ✓ ✓ ✓ **CARBISDALE CASTLE, CULRAIN, nr BONAR BRIDGE:** 01549
MAP 2 421232. The flagship hostel of the SYHA, an Edwardian castle in
C2 terraced grds o/looking the flood plain of a river on the edge of the
Highlands. Once the home of the exiled King of Norway, it still contains original works of art (nothing of gr value though the sculptures are elegant). The
library, ballrm, lounges are all in use and it's only a few quid a night. Shared
dorms as usual but no chores. Kitchens and café. Bike hire in summer; lots
scenic walks. Stn (from Inverness) 1km up steep hill. Buses:
Inverness/Thurso/Lairg. 80km Inverness, 330km Edin. 226 beds.

1105 ✓ **STIRLING:** 01786 473442 Fax 445715. Modern, superb conversion. Gr part of
MAP 6 town, close to castle, adj ancient graveyard and with fine views from some
C3 rms. One of the new hotel-like hostels with student-hall standard and facs. Café
(open 8-8.30am and 6-6.30pm) or self-catering. Access till 2am. 130 beds.

1106 ✓ **LOCH LOMOND S.Y.H.:** 01389 850226 Fax 850623. Alexandria,
MAP 1 Dumbarton. Built in 1866 by George Martin, the tobacco baron (as
C2 opposed to the other one who produced the Beatles), this is hosteling on the
grand scale. Towers and turrets, galleried upper-hall, space for banqueting
and a splendid view across the loch, of where you're going tomorrow. 30km
Glas. Stn (Balloch) 4km. Buses 200m. Access till 2am. 184 beds.

1107 **THE BORDERS** *There are some ideal wee hostels in this hill-walking tract of*
MAP 8 *Scotland (where it all began) and one major one:*
C2, B3

MELROSE: 01896 822521. Grade 1, 90 beds, v popular. Well-appointed mansion looking across to the Abbey; student-hall standard.

BROADMEADOWS: 8km from Selkirk off A7, the first hostel in Scotland (1931)
is a cosy howf with a stove and a view.

SNOOT: 10km S of Hawick, Snoot is cute; a country church by the Borthwick Water converted into bunkrooms. Pastoral.

The 3 hostels above are all within an easy day's walk of one another.

1108
MAP 2
C2
INVERNESS STUDENT HOSTEL: 01463 236556. Independent hostel opp the SYH at 8 Culduthel Rd, uphill from town centre (some dorms have views). Run by same folk who have the great Edin one (35/HOSTELS), with similar laid-back atmos and camaraderie. Another independent hostel has opened down st when this one's full.

1109
MAP 6
B3
ROWARDENNAN, LOCH LOMOND: 01360 870259. The hostel at the end of the rd up the E (less touristy) side of L Lomond from Balmaha and Drymen. Large, well managed and modernised and on a water-side site. On W Highland Way and obvious base for climbing Ben Lomond (1780/MUNROS). Good all-round activity centre and lawns to the loch of your dreams. Rowardennan Hotel boozer nearby.

1110
HOSTELLING IN THE HEBRIDES: Simple hostelling in the crofting communities of Lewis, Harris and the Uists. Run by a trust to maintain standards in the spirit of Highland hospitality with local crofters acting as wardens, all hostels are about Grade 3 SYH. 2 in Lewis, 2 in Harris and one each in N and S Uist. No advance bookings necessary or accepted (suggests they will always fit you in). No smk and no Sun arrival or departure. Check local TOs for details (2159/WESTERN ISLES).

1111
MAP 1
B1
TOBERMORY, MULL: 01688 302481. Looks out to Tobermory Bay. Central but simple island hostel (grade 3), reception closed, tho' hostel open during the day. Members' kitchen. Nr ferry to Ardnamurchan, but main Oban ferry is 35km away (1416/COASTAL VILLAGES).

1112
MAP 2
C4
GLENCOE: 01855 811219. Deep in the glen itself, 3km off A82/4km by back rd from Glencoe village and 33km from Ft William. Modern timber house o/looking river; especially handy for climbers and walkers. Clachaig pub, 2km for good food and crack. (Also 1482/SCENIC ROUTES; 1747/SPOOKY PLACES; 1722/BATTLEGROUNDS; 1183/PUBS; 1877/SKIING; 1794/SERIOUS WALKS.).

1113
MAP 2
B3
RATAGAN: 01599 511243. 29km from Kyle of Lochalsh, 3km Shiel Br (on A87). A much-loved Highland hostel on the shore of L Duich and well situated for walking and exploring some of Scotland's most celebrated scenery e.g. 5 Sisters of Kintail/Cluanie Ridge (1796/SERIOUS WALKS), Glenelg (1483/SCENIC ROUTES; 1649/PREHISTORIC SITES), Falls of Glomach (1455/WATERFALLS). From Glenelg there's the short and dramatic crossing to Skye through the Kylerhea narrows (continuous, summer only), quite the best way to go.

1114
MAP 2
B2
INDEPENDENT HOSTELS IN SKYE: DUN FLODIGARRY, nr STAFFIN: 01470 552212. In far N 32km from Portree beside Flodigarry Country-House Hotel, whose pub is one of the best on the island and has great ceilidhs (2158/SKYE), and amidst big scenery. O/looks sea. Bunkrms for 2-6 (holds up to 66) and great refectory. Open AYR.

1115
MAP 2
B3
SKYE BACKPACKERS GUEST HOUSE, KYLEAKIN: 01599 534510. Convenient guest house with mainly 4-bunk rms and smallish gantry/lounge nr br for last/first stop on what used to be the island. Open AYR. There are many other independent hostels on Skye incl 2 in Portree.

1116
MAP 2
D3
GLEN FESHIE, nr AVIEMORE: 01540 651323. Privately-run hostel in farmhouse by the rd-side in Glen Feshie, signed Achlean from Feshiebridge on the B970. A walkers' refuge which has a genuine, friendly atmos. Store sells basics; free porridge, but also meals provided. Good base for Cairngorm walking (1797/SERIOUS WALKS). Open AYR.

THE BEST ROADSIDE, SEASIDE AND COUNTRYSIDE INNS

1117
MAP 2
A2

✓✓ **THE THREE CHIMNEYS, COLBOST, SKYE:** 01470 511258. 7km W of Dunvegan on B884 to Glendale. Rms in a new build across the yard from the excl and long-established Three Chimneys restau (2138/ISLAND RESTAU) called 'The House Over-by'. Roadside tho few cars and within sight and smell of the sea. Exceptionally high standard split level rms with own doors to the sward. Breakfast lounge, s/serv v healthy buffet. A model of its kind in the Highlands.

8RMS JAN-DEC T/T PETS CC KIDS LOTS

1118
MAP 1
C1

✓ **BRIDGE OF ORCHY HOTEL, BRIDGE OF ORCHY:** 01838 400208. Unmissable on the A82 (the rd to Glencoe, Ft William and Skye) 11km N of Tyndrum. Old inn extensively refurbished and run as an excl stopover hotel. Simple, quite stylish rms. Hearty pub grub and dining. Good spot for the malt on the W Highland way (1789/LONG WALKS). Also bunkhouse (v chp).

10RMS JAN-DEC T/T PETS CC KIDS MED.INX

1119
MAP 1
B1

✓ **PIER HOUSE, PORT APPIN:** 01631 730302. An inn at the end of the rd (the minor rd that leads off the A825 Oban to Ft William) and at the end of the 'pier', where the tiny passenger ferry leaves for Lismore (2117/MAGIC ISLANDS). Bistro restau with decent seafood (1257/SEAFOOD RESTAUS) in gr setting. Comfy motel-type rms o/look the sea and island and jazzy lounge.

11RMS JAN-DEC T/T XPETS CC KIDS MED.EX

1120
MAP 2
C3

✓ **CLUANIE INN, GLENMORISTON:** 01320 340238. On main rd to Skye 15km before Shiel Br, a trad inn surrounded by the mt summits that attract the walkers and travellers who frequent the place. Refurb to unusually good standard. Gym, sauna – even a sunbed. Good bar food LO 8.30pm. The Cluanie Ridge and the 5 Sisters await you in the morning (1796/SERIOUS WALKS).

13RMS JAN-DEC T/X PETS CC KIDS MED.EX

1121
MAP 2
B3

✓ **GLENELG INN, GLENELG:** 01599 522273. At the end of that gr rd over the hill from Shiel Br on the A87 (1483/SCENIC ROUTES)…well, not quite the end because you can drive further round to ethereal L Hourn, but this halt is a v civilised hostelry of fame and infamy. Decent food, good drinking, snug lounge. Grd with tables and views. Charming rms. From Glenelg, take the best route to Skye (2184/FAVOURITE JOURNEYS).

6RMS APR-OCT X/X PETS XCC KIDS MED.EXP

1122
MAP 4
B3

WEEM HOTEL, WEEM, nr ABERFELDY: 01887 820381. 2km from Aberfeldy on the rd to Glen Lyon which is a rd worth taking (1445/GLENS) and points N to L Rannoch. Old coaching inn, good base for some gr scenery and L Tay fishing. Basic accom; see the rm first.

14RMS JAN-DEC T/T PETS CC KIDS INX

1123
MAP 4
A3

FORTINGALL HOTEL, FORTINGALL, nr ABERFELDY: 01887 830367. Same area as above, 15km from Aberfeldy but close to the Glen. Trad inn, incl. flock wallpaper and other such furnishings. Often booked. The 'oldest tree' in Europe is next door in the churchyard. Good for fishing and walking and kids are welcomed.

9RMS MAR-OCT T/T PETS CC KIDS INX

1124
MAP 1
C2

WEST LOCH HOTEL, TARBERT: 01880 820283. Beside A83 just W of Tarbert; ideal stopover en route to the islands. Comfortably furnished; with original features sympathetically retained. Board games and books dotted around, children welcome in relaxed, friendly atmos. 9-hole golf course across the rd. Good value, but roadside rms may be noisy.

7RMS FEB-DEC X/T PETS CC KIDS MED.INX

1125
MAP 5
B3

KILDRUMMY INN, KILDRUMMY, nr BALLATER: 01975 571227. 30km N of Ballater via A97 off main A93 Deeside Rd. Nr Kildrummy Castle and Kildrummy Castle Hotel and grds. Roadside inn with nice walks around. Basic but basically fine; and v Scottish.

4RMS JAN-DEC X/T PETS CC KIDS INX

1126
MAP 4
C2

GLENISLA HOTEL, KIRKTON OF GLENISLA: 01575 582223. 20km NW of Kirriemuir via B951 at head of this secluded story-book glen. A home from home: hearty food, real ale and local colour. Fishers, stalkers, trekkers and walkers all come by. Miles from the town literally and laterally. Newish owners making many improvements. Still decidedly a non-TV kind of a place.

6RMS JAN-DEC X/X PETS CC KIDS INX

1127   **TOMDOUN HOTEL, nr INVERGARRY:** 01809 511218. 20km from Invergarry,
MAP 2   12km off the A87 to Kyle of Lochalsh. A 19th-century coaching inn that
C3   replaced a much older one; off the beaten track but perfect (we do mean perfect) for fishing, walking (L Quoich and Knoydart have been waiting a long time for you) and naturalising. Superb views over Glengarry and Bonnie Prince Charlie's country. Excellent value; old-fashioned style.

10RMS MAR-OCT X/X PETS CC KIDS CHP

1128   **ST MICHAEL'S INN, nr ST ANDREWS:** 01334 839220. On A919 towards
MAP 5   Dundee, 10km from St Andrews. At crossrds, a 200-year-old inn, seems
C2   Englishy, often busy, with pub food and restau. Plenty of golf and other attractions within reach. Good bet given cost of board in St Andrews.

8RMS JAN-DEC X/T PETS CC KIDS INX

1129   **TRAQUAIR ARMS, INNERLEITHEN:** 01896 830229. 100m from the A72
MAP 8   Gala–Peebles rd towards Traquair, a popular village and country inn that
B2   caters for all kinds of folk (and, at w/ends, large numbers of them). Notable for bar meals, real ale and family facs. Rms recently refurb.

10RMS JAN-DEC T/T PETS CC KIDS MED.INX

1130   **THE KAMES HOTEL, TIGHNABRUAICH:** 01700 811489. Frequented by passing yachtsmen who moor alongside and pop in for lunch. Good base for all
MAP 1   ing yachtsmen who moor alongside and pop in for lunch. Good base for all
C2   things offshore; marine cruises or a nostalgic journey on a 'puffer', with a gr selection of malts to warm you up before or after.

10RMS JAN-DEC X/T PETS CC KIDS MED.INX

1131   **BRIDGE OF CALLY HOTEL, BRIDGE OF CALLY:** 01250 886231. Exemplary
MAP 4   roadside pub on a bend of the road betw Blairgowrie and Glenshee/Braemar
C3   (the ski zone and Royal Deeside). Cosy and inexpensive betw gentle Perthshire and the wilder Grampians.

9RMS JAN-DEC T/T PETS CC KIDS INX

1132   **CLACHAIG INN, GLENCOE:** 01855 811252. Basic accom but you will sleep
MAP 2   well, esp after walking/climbing/drinking, which is what most people are
C4   doing here. Gr atmos both inside and out. Food avail bar/lounge and dining rm.

19RMS JAN-DEC X/T XPETS CC KIDS INX

1133   **MOULIN HOTEL, PITLOCHRY:** 01796 472196. Kirkmichael Rd; at the landmark
MAP 4   crossrds on the A924. Rms above and beside notable pub for food and esp
B2   ales – they brew their own out the back. (1193/REAL ALES).

17RMS JAN-DEC T/T MED.INX

1134   **CULFAIL HOTEL by KILMELFORD:** 01852 200274. On A816 20 km S of Oban
MAP 1   and nr a gr bit of W Highland coast that includes Seil Island, Luing etc. The bar
B2   of this hotel is the watering hole for the neighbourhood and people travel serious distances for the privilege. A gantry full of choice single malt whiskies and bar food provided as and when. A friendly hotel with a lounge that speaks of time gone by.   12RMS JAN-DEC X/T PETS CC KIDS MED.INX

1135   **GALLEY OF LORNE, ARDFERN:** 01852 500284. Roadside/seaside inn in
MAP 1   yachty haven of Ardfern. Salts, locals and other worthies mingle at the bar and
C3   the restau/bistro is good for families early in the evening and for drinking much wine later on. Rms basic, but Ardfern is a good berth.

JAN-DEC X/T PETS CC KIDS INX

1136   **GLENMORISTON ARMS HOTEL, INVERMORISTON, LOCH NESS:** 01320
MAP 2   351206. On main A82 betw Inverness (45km) and Ft Augustus (10km) at the
C3   Glen Moriston corner, and quite the best corner of this famous loch side to explore. Busy local bar, fishermen's tales. Bistro over-by (LO 8.30pm) table o/side in summer. Bar meals look ok and extensive malt list – certainly a good place to drink them.   8RMS JAN-DEC T/T PETS CC KIDS MED.INX

ANCHOR HOTEL, KIPPFORD: 01556 620205. Report: 820/SW HOTELS/RESTAUS

THE OLD ABERLADY INN: 01875 870503 Report: 863/LOTHIANS HOTELS

THE GREAT GET-AWAY-FROM-IT-ALL HOTELS

1137
MAP 2
D2

✓ ✓ ✓ **SKIBO CASTLE, DORNOCH:** 01862 894600. A vast estate once home to the formidable Carnegies (those halls in NYC, Dunfermline, etc.). They declared it to be 'heaven on earth' which may be your sentiment too. Now like an Edwardian 'gentleman's' club you can sample the atmos once, but to return you join the club. Some club! The sumptuous castle retains its original furnishings (silk wallpaper, panelling, etc.) and the service from your discreet 'hosts' is exemplary. Lodges in the grds offer more privacy, with the obligatory golf course, spa, gym and beach, all oases of relaxing indulgence – vintage Rolls Royces take you around. It is world class, but you may need to win the lottery before you can experience this kind of fairy land. Phone for details.   LOTS AND LOTS

1138
MAP 2
D1

✓ ✓ **ACKERGILL TOWER, nr WICK:** 01955 603556. One of the most genuine Highland-castle-hoolly thingies we've come across. Usually the sole domain of corporate hospitality shindigs and big events (weddings etc). The minimum number they'll take is 16 (but they won't turn away a dozen at a quiet time of year). Set in sumptuous acres: miles of sandy beach, woods to whirl in, and the 15th-century castle perched next to the sea. The whole household greets you on arrival and makes you feel part of it all. The Wick Band pipe their way down the drive as you arrive for your ceilidh, Catriona indulges you with her afternoon teas and Craig proudly cooks up a storm using ingredients from the grd; you eat inside or out – wherever the season takes you. All food, drink, activities and surprises incl in the tariff. Spontaneity no extra charge.   LOTS AND LOTS

1139
MAP 2
B2

✓ **LOCH TORRIDON, GLEN TORRIDON, nr KINLOCHEWE:** 01445 791242. Impressive former hunting lodge on lochside, surrounded by majestic mts. The atmos o/side can be affected by the weather, and within by the mood of your hosts. Dressing for dinner is expected; if not entirely necessary in this comfortable but cosy baronial house. Numerous walks poss for all abilities, fishing and Diabeg nearby (1422/COASTAL VILLAGES).

                                        20RMS JAN-DEC T/T XPETS CC XKIDS LOTS

1140
MAP 6
B2

✓ **MONACHYLE MHOR, nr BALQUHIDDER:** 01877 384622. Not so very remote, but seems so once you've negotiated the thread of rd alongside Loch Voil from Balquhidder (only 11km from the A84 Callander-Crianlarich rd) and Rob Roy's now famous grave (1707/GRAVEYARDS). Farmhouse o/looking L Voil from the magnificent Balquhidder Braes. Friendly, cosy and inexp; a place to relax in summer or winter. Rms in courtyard annex are best (4), but all have character. Fishing. Food fairly fab, well-sourced ingredients, 2 AA rosettes. Informal though you might venture J&T for dinner.

                                        10RMS JAN-DEC SOME T/T PETS CC KIDS INX

1141
MAP 9
A3

✓ **CORSEWALL LIGHTHOUSE HOTEL nr STRANRAER:** 01776 853220. Only 15mins from Stranraer (via A718 to Kirkcolm) and follow signs, but way up on the peninsula and as it suggests a hotel made out of a working lighthouse. Not much to do here perhaps except walk on the rocks and stare into your lover's eyes, but the food is v good and there are attractions nearby (Portpatrick 30 mins). At w/ends they like you to stay at least 2 nights. Suites best.   6RMS JAN-DEC T/T PETS CC KIDS EXP

1142
MAP 2
B3

THE PIER HOUSE, INVERIE, KNOYDART: 01687 462347. Currently the only restau on this far-away peninsula, though good grub at the pub nearby (1181/BLOODY GOOD PUBS). Accessible on foot (sic) from Kinlochourn (25km) or Bruce Watt's boat from Mallaig (Mon, Wed, Fri). Friendly couple offer warm hospitality in their home and surprisingly good cooking for somewhere so remote; rovers often return. Some say the better and certainly remoter option is the **DOUNE STONE LODGE** 01687 462667; 5km up the single rd. We couldn't stay, but it comes much recommended.

                                        3RMS MAR-OCT X/X XPETS XCC KIDS TOS CHP

1143
MAP 4
C2

✓ **CLOVA HOTEL, GLEN CLOVA, nr KIRRIEMUIR:** 01575 550222. Well, not that nr Kirriemuir; 25km N to head of glen on B955 and once you're there there's nowhere else to go except up. Proprietor Graham Davie arranges all kinds of activities, however, from parachuting to falconry, so there's never a dull moment and there is superb walking hereabouts (e.g. L Brandy and the classic path to L Muick). An inexp get-away-from-it all.

7RMS JAN-DEC T/T PETS CC KIDS INX

1144 **APPLECROSS HOTEL, APPLECROSS:** 01520 744262. At the end of the rd (the
MAP 2 Pass of the Cattle which is often snowed up in winter, so you can really disap-
B2 pear) N of Kyle of Lochalsh and W of Strathcarron. Cheerful, chp extremely
basic accom in a good place.

5RMS JAN-DEC X/X PETS CC KIDS INX

1145 **TOMICH HOTEL nr CANNICH:** 01456 415399. 8km from Cannich which is
MAP 2 20km from Drumnadrochit. Fabulous Plodda Falls are nearby (1456/WATER-
D3 FALLS). Cosy country inn in conservation village with added bonus of use of
swimming pool in nearby steading. Good base for outdoorsy w/end. Glen
Affric across the way.

8RMS JAN-DEC T/T PETS CC KIDS INX

1146 **INVERVAR LODGE, GLEN LYON:** 01887 877206. A retreat in Glen Lyon where
MAP 4 I haven't stayed but it comes highly rec by our Angus. Run by a Swiss/German
A3 couple they seem to be doing everything right. Delicious food free-
range/organic wherever poss, open fire, good vibes. BYOB. Glen Lyon, of
course, is amazing (1445/GREAT GLENS).

4RMS JAN-DEC X/X PETS CC KIDS INX

1147 **MULLARDOCH HOUSE, nr CANNICH, nr DRUMNADROCHIT:** 01456 415460.
MAP 2 Leaving L Ness at Drumnadrochit up Glen Urquhart to Cannich (20km), then
C3 follow R Cannich to head of glen (12km) where it's blocked by the mighty
Mullardoch Dam. Almost tangible pressure as this cosy Edwardian shooting
lodge lies below it, but only herds of red deer wander here and with 11
Munros within 20mins, it's a good place to wander, too. Good for
hunters/shooters/fishers. Their tick is reportedly long overdue, but I didn't
make it up the glen this time, so can't award one. Reports please! Fixed dinner
at 8pm.

7RMS JAN-DEC T/T PETS CC KIDS MED.EX

1148 **ARDEONAIG, LOCH TAY:** 01567 820400. On narrow S Loch Tay rd midway
MAP 4 betw Kenmore and Killin, not so remote, but feels like a long way from the city.
A3 Once you arrive you forget all that. An airy roadside inn by the water opp Ben
Lawers. Friendly staff and many dogs. Upstairs library, good food, gr scenery –
you won't miss the telly.

14RMS MAR-NOV T/X PETS CC KIDS MED.EX

1149 **CAPE WRATH HOTEL, nr DURNESS:** 01971 511212. 3km S Durness just off A838;
MAP 2 on rd to Cape Wrath Ferry (1828/COASTAL WALKS) which takes you to Britain's far-
C1 thest-flung corner and the Cliffs of Clo Mor. O/looking the loch, the sparsely furnished hotel is popular with fisherman; passing tourists also shoal up for lunch.
Fishing on 3 rivers including the celebrated Dionard and lochs. Durness Golf nearby (1870/GOLF) and there's some of Britain's most spectacular and undisturbed
coastline to wander. Excl views from some rms down Kyle of Durness; like a setting for something morose by Ibsen. 18RMS APR-OCT X/X PETS CC KIDS MED.INX

1150 **SPRINGBANK COTTAGE, ST ABBS:** 018907 71477. Centre of the village next
MAP 8 to St Abbs harbour, 5km from the A1. Not a hotel, certainly a B&B but defi-
D1 nitely a gr place to get away. Small and friendly cottage (no smk) with an outdoors tea grd open all year, popular with divers – bring a wetsuit when raining. Walk in St Abbs Head nature reserve (1581/WILDLIFE RESERVES). Few rms so
often full in summer.

3RMS FEB-DEC X/T PETS CC KIDS CHP

1151 **THE MILL HOUSE, TEMPLE:** 01875 830253. Temple is on the B6372, 5km off
MAP 7 the A7 S of Edin (our researcher's idea of a get-away from-it-all w/end). Turn rt
B2 after the village sign then down a driveway by the kirk. Gorgeous wee cottage
in riverside gdens. Cordon bleu cooking. The only place in the Lothians we
would call 'idyllic'. 3RMS APR-SEP T/T XPETS XCC XKIDS TOS MED.EX

1152 **TUSHIELAW INN, ETTRICK VALLEY:** 01750 62205. Further down the valley
MAP 8 (15 miles Selkirk) a cosy retreat. Only 3 rms, but good value. Both this hotel
B3 and the place above are close to Edin. 3RMS JAN-DEC X/T PETS CC KIDS CHP

MAP 9 **KNOCKINAAM LODGE, nr PORTPATRICK:** 01776 810471. Report: 812/SW
A3 BEST HOTELS

THREE CHIMNEYS, SKYE: 01470 511258. Report: 1117/ROADSIDE INNS,
2138/ISLAND RESTAU.

SOME HIGHLAND AND ISLAND PLACES TO CAMP

In Scotland the Best! we don't do caravan life style. In fact, because we spend a lot of time behind them on Highland roads, WE HATE CARAVANS, but wild camping is a different matter. Although it's probably irresponsible to encourage it greatly, it's a good and inexp way to experience Scotland, provided you are sensitive to the environment and respect the rights of farmers and other landowners.

1153 **KINTRA, ISLAY:** Bowmore-Port Ellen rd, take Oa turn-off then follow signs
MAP 1 7km. Restau and bar at end of rd with long beach one way, wild coastal walk
A3 the other. Camping (room also for a few caravans) on grassy strand looking out to sea; not a formal site but facs available. Also bunkhouse.

1154 **LOCHAILORT:** A 12km stretch S from Lochailort on the A861, along the
MAP 2 southern shore of the sea loch itself. A flat, rocky and grassy foreshore with a
B3 splendid seascape and backed by brooding mtns. Nearby is L nan Uamh where Bonnie Prince Charlie landed (1732/MARY, CHARLIE AND BOB). Once past the salmon farm laboratories, you're in calendar scenery; the Glenuig Inn at the southern end is a fine pub to repair to. No facs except the sea.

1155 **MULL:** Calgary Beach 10km from Dervaig, where there are toilets; also S of
MAP 1 Kilchronan on the gentle shore of L Na Keal where there is nothing but the sky
A1 and the sea. Ben More is in the background (1783/MUNROS).

1156 **GLEN ETIVE, nr BALLACHULISH and GLENCOE:** One of Scotland's gr unoffi-
MAP 2 cial camping grounds. Along the rd/river side in a classic glen (1447/GLENS)
C4 guarded where it joins the pass into Glencoe by the awesome Buachaille Etive Mor. Innumerable grassy terraces and small meadows on which climbers and walkers have camped for generations, and pools to bathe in (1516/SWIMMING HOLES). The famous Kingshouse Pub is 2km from the foot of the glen for sustenance, malt whisky and comparing midge bites.

1157 **OLDSHOREMORE, nr KINLOCHBERVIE and ACHMELVICH, nr LOCHINVER:**
MAP 2 2 superb beaches with grassy links and nr villages for supplies, the pub etc.
C1 Achmelvich has official campsite, Oldshoremore (and neighbouring coves) has only you.

THE BEST VERY SCOTTISH HOTELS

1158 ✓ ✓ **THE CEILIDH PLACE, ULLAPOOL:** 01854 612103. Off main st near pt
MAP 2 for the Hebrides, this place more than any other in the Highlands
C2 encapsulates Scottish trad culture and hospitality and interprets it in a contemporary manner. Caters for all sorts: there's an excellent hotel above (with a truly comfortable lounge – you help yourself to drinks) and a stylish restau below. A bar with occasional live music and gr bar meals. A bunkhouse across the way with cheap and cheerful (though thin-walled) accom and a bookshop where you can browse through the best new Scottish literature. Scottish-ness is all here and nothing embarrassing in sight. 23RMS JAN-DEC T/X PETS CC KIDS EXP/CHP

1159 ✓ ✓ **THE ALBANNACH, LOCHINVER:** 01571 844407. 2km up rd to
MAP 2 Baddidarach as you come from S into Lochinver on A837, at the br.
C1 Lovely 18th-century house in one of Scotland's most scenic areas, Assynt, where the mtns can take your breath away even without going up them (1756/1757/FAVOURITE HILLS). Arty atmos for creative professionals needing to unwind; which you will do in these tasteful, informal surroundings. The food is the best for miles. No smk. 5RMS MAR-DEC X/X XPETS CC XKIDS MED.INX

1160 ✓ **KILDRUMMY CASTLE HOTEL, nr ALFORD, ABERDEENSHIRE:** 01975
MAP 3 571288. 60km W of Aberdeen via A944, through some fine bucolic
B3 scenery and the green Don valley to this spectacular location with the real aura of the Highlands. Well placed if you're on the 'Castle Trail', this comfortable chunk of Scottish Baronial has the redolent ruins of Kildrummy Castle on the opposite bluff and a gorgeful of gardens betw. Some rms small, but all v Scottish. Romantic in autumn when the grds are good. J/tie for dinner.
16RMS FEB-DEC T/T PETS CC KIDS TOS EXP

1161
MAP 2
B3

✓ **ARISAIG HOUSE, ARISAIG:** 01687 450622. Another hotel in Bonnie Prince Charlie country on the 'Road to the Isles'; here there's a cave at the foot of their fields (and wonderful gdns) where he once hid – it's very near where he landed (1732/MARY, CHARLIE AND BOB). Of course it's not just any other hotel, but an elegant country house which succeeds in the apparently rare combination of refinement and r&r. Good manners, but very Scots. *Relais and Châteaux*. Chef, Duncan Gibson gets 3 AA rosettes for cooking, the Smithers family and excl staff do the rest.

14RMS APR-OCT T/T XPETS CC XKIDS TOS EXP

1162
MAP 2
B3

✓ **EILEAN IARMAIN, SKYE:** 01471 833332. Situated in Sleat area on S of island, this snug Gaelic inn nestles in the bay and is the classic island hostelry. A dram in your rm awaits you; from the adj whisky company. Bedrms in cottage across from hotel ensure you'll not be bothered by the crack from the pub. Food real good. New suites in adj steading. Mystic shore walks. Gallery and shop nearby. Always good but no longer such good value.

12RMS JAN-DEC T/T PETS CC KIDS EXP/LOTS

1163
MAP 2
B3

✓ **GLENFINNAN HOUSE, GLENFINNAN:** 01397 722235. Off the Road to the Isles (A830 Ft William to Mallaig). The MacFarlanes recently celebrated a quarter century of running their hotel in this historic house (1734/MARY, CHARLIE AND BOB). Some refurb without losing its charm, the huge rms remain intimate and cosy with open fires. Legendary sessions and ceilidhs wherever there's a gathering in the house and you get piped into dinner. Solitude still achievable in the huge grounds, or fishing or dreaming on L Shiel (boat and cruises available). Day trips to Skye and small islands, nearby.

20RMS APR-OCT X/X PETS CC KIDS MED.INX

1164
MAP 2
C4

✓ **BALLACHULISH HOUSE, BALLACHULISH:** 01855 811266. On rd A828 betw Oban and (just S of) Ft William a family house steeped in history and the folklore of the Highlands. Said to be the most haunted house in Scotland, your close encounters are more likely to be with your hospitable hosts bringing vegetables and flowers in from the gdn for dinner. More of a guesthouse than a hotel (966/INEXP HIGHLAND HOTELS).

6RMS JAN-DEC T/X PETS CC KIDS MED.EX

1165
MAP 1
C3

✓ **SAVOY PARK, AYR:** 01292 266112. 16 Racecourse Rd. In a street and area of many indifferent hotels this one, owned and run by the Henderson family for over 30 yrs, is a real Scottish gem. Many weddings here but that's the only drawback. Period features, garden, not too much tartan, but a warm cosy lived-in atmos. Round one of the fireplaces, 'blessed be God for his giftis', the Henderson's (and I) would agree.   15RMS JAN-DEC T/T PETS KIDS MED.INX

CRIEFF HYDRO, CRIEFF: 01764 655555. The quintessential Scottish family hotel. (1091/HOTELS FOR KIDS).

STONEFIELD CASTLE, TARBERT: 01880 820836 (792/ARGYLL HOTELS).

REAL RETREATS

1166
MAP 9
D2

✓ ✓ ✓ **SAMYE LING, ESKDALEMUIR, nr LOCKERBIE/DUMFRIES:** 01387 373232. Bus or train to Lockerbie/Carlisle then bus (Mon-Sat) to Boreland (0345 090510) or taxi (01576 470480). 2km from village, community consists of an extraordinary and inspiring temple, main house (with some accom), dorm and guesthouse blocks many single rms, a café (open 7 days 9am-5pm) and shop. On the hill and out of bounds the area where people really retreat; available for short retreats (up to a yr) and conferences. Much of Samye Ling, a world centre for Tibetan Buddhism, is still under construction, but they offer daily and longer stays (£15-25) and many courses in all aspects of Buddhism, meditation, tai chi, Alexander Technique, etc. Daily timetable, from prayers at 6am and work period. Breakfast/lunch and soup, etc. for supper at 6pm; all vegn. Busy, thriving community atmos; some space cases and holier-than-thous, but rewarding and unique and thriving. Probably Britain's most must-do retreat – lots of famous names. Their recent acquisition, **HOLY ISLAND**, off Arran, requires much work to turn it into a place for longer retreats. Boats leave from the pier at Lamlash, accom limited. Phone Samye Ling for details.

1167 ✓ ✓ **PLUSCARDEN, between FORRES and ELGIN:** 01343 890257.
MAP 3   Signed from main A96 (11km from Elgin) in a sheltered glen S-fac-
A2 ing with a background of wooded hillside, this is the only medieval
monastery in the UK still inhabited by monks. It's a deeply calming place. The
(Benedictine) community keep walled gdns and bees. 7 services a day in the
glorious chapel (1712/ABBEYS) which visitors can attend. Retreat for men (15
places) and women (separate, self-catering) with no time limit and no obliga-
tory charge. Write to the Guest Master Brother Gabriel, Pluscarden Abbey, by
Elgin W30 8VA; no telephone bookings. Men eat with monks (mainly vegn).
Restoration/building work always in progress (of the abbey and of the spirit).

1168 ✓ ✓ **FINDHORN COMMUNITY, FINDHORN, nr FORRES:** 01309 690311.
MAP 3   The world-famous spiritual community (now a foundation) begun
A1 by Peter Caddy and Dorothy Maclean in 1962, a village of mainly caravans and
cabins on the way into Findhorn on the B9011. Open as an ordinary caravan
park and visitors can join the community as 'short-term guests' eating and
working on-site but probably staying at recommended B&Bs. Also full programme of courses and residential workshops in spiritual growth/dance/
healing, etc. Accom mainly at Cluny Hill College in Forres. Many other aspects
and facs available in this cosmopolitan and well-organised new-age township. Excellent shop (1340/DELIS).

1169 **COLLEGE OF THE HOLY SPIRIT, MILLPORT, ISLAND OF CUMBRAE:** 01475
MAP 1 530353. Continuous ferry service from Largs (hourly in winter), then 6km bus
C3 journey to Millport. Off main st through gate in the wall, into grounds of the
Cathedral of the Isles (1685/CHURCHES) and another more peaceful world. A
retreat for the Episcopal Church since 1884, there are 19 simple but comfortable rms in the college next to the church with B&B or full board (£17-32). No
set schedule but morning and evening prayer each day, Eucharist on Sun and
occasional concerts in summer. Warden available for direction and spiritual
counselling. Fine library. Bike hire. Phone 'the Provost'. Try the island's gr café
(1277/CAFÉS).

1170 **CARBERRY TOWERS, MUSSELBURGH, nr EDINBURGH:** 0131 665 3135.
MAP 7 Sitting in extensive, well-kept grounds 3km S of Musselburgh, parts of this
B1 fine old house date back to the 15th century. Now a Christian residential and
conference centre, most accom is in new block 50m away; student-hall standard. Courses for church workers/group weekends which visitors may sometimes join. Not a quiet retreat but inexp for a break; high on 'renewal', low on
rock 'n' roll.

1171 **NUNRAW ABBEY, GARVALD, nr HADDINGTON:** 01620 830228. Cistercian
MAP 7 community earning its daily bread with a working farm in the land surround-
B1 ing the abbey – but visitors can come and stay for a while and get their heads
together in the Sancta Maria Guesthouse (a house for visitors is part of their
doctrine). Payment by donation. V Catholic monastic ambience throughout.
Guesthouse is 1km from the monastery, a modern complex built to a trad
Cistercian pattern. Services open to visitors.

1172 **SALISBURY CENTRE, EDINBURGH:** 0131 667 5438. 2 Salisbury Rd.
MAP A 'Community and creative resource' in Georgian house on capital's Southside,
xE4 est 1973 by Dr Winifred Rushforth, psychotherapist and dream specialist. Not
a retreat in the isolated sense, although 'w/end retreats' are possible. Classes
during week and w/end workshops in meditation, healing, aromatherapy,
massage, yoga, shiatzu, tai chi and pottery. Organic garden, therapy rm, some
basic accom.

1173 **CAMAS ADVENTURE CENTRE, MULL:** 01681 700404. Part of Iona
MAP 1 Community (2 others on Iona; this one is aimed at youngsters) near to
A1 Fionnphort in S of island (good bus service). No electricity, cars, TV or noise
except the waves and the gulls. Outdoor activities (e.g. canoeing, hillwalking).
2 dorms; share chores. Week-long stays. You'll probably have to relate.

GET-AWAY WEEKENDS

1174 LOCHAWESIDE

MAP 1

WHERE TO STAY
TAYCHREGGAN (791/ARGYLL HOTELS); **ARDANAISEIG** (1086/COUNTRY-HOUSE HOTELS)

WHERE TO EAT AND DRINK
LOCK 16, CRINAN HOTEL (1241/SEAFOOD); **KILCHREGGAN INN, FORD HOTEL**.

WHERE TO VISIT
THE WOODS (1811/WOODLAND WALKS); **TEMPLE WOOD** (1646/PREHISTORIC SITES).
KILMARTIN MUSEUM (2010/MUSEUMS)

1175 TARBERT, ARGYLL

MAP 1

WHERE TO STAY
STONEFIELD (792/ARGYLL HOTELS; 1098/KIDS); **THE COLUMBA** (795/ARGYLL
HOTELS); **WEST LOCH** (794/ARGYLL HOTELS).

WHERE TO EAT AND DRINK
THE ANCHORAGE (1248/SEAFOOD RESTAUS); **WEST LOCH** (*as above*); **KILBERRY
INN** (1205/BEST FOOD); **AN TAIRBERT CENTRE** W on A83 (*see below*).

WHERE TO VISIT
The **VILLAGE** itself; **ISLAY/JURA** (by ferry from Kennacraig, 7km S, *see p.281*);
GIGHA (by ferry from Tayinloan 14km SW); **ARRAN** (by ferry from Claonaig 9km
SE) **TARBERT CASTLE** (1621/RUINS) **& SKIPNESS CASTLE**; **AN TAIRBERT CENTRE**
for kids.

1176 SPEYSIDE

MAP 3

WHERE TO STAY
CRAIGELLACHIE, DELNASHAUGH, MANSION HOUSE
(*pp. 116–7*).

WHERE TO EAT AND DRINK
MANSEFIELD HOUSE HOTEL, ELGIN: 920/NE HOTELS.

ARCHIESTOWN HOTEL BISTRO: 01340 810218. Well-known spot locally for good
(2 AA rosettes) informal dining. LO 8.30pm.

AUCHENDEAN LODGE: a bit further S (nr Grantown) but imaginative cuisine
(962/INEXP HIGHLAND HOTELS).

WHERE TO VISIT
DISTILLERIES: *p. 167*; **SPEYSIDE WAY:** 1791/LONG WALKS; **BALLENDALLOCH CAS-
TLE:** on A95 midway betw Grantown and Craigellachie. Family big house with
pleasant Speyside grds. Apr-Sept 10am-5pm.; **ELGIN CATHEDRAL:** 1614/RUINS;
JOHNSONS: 1958/WOOLIES; **CHRISTIES OF FOCHABERS:** 1982/GARDEN CENTRES;
JUST ART: 2039/ART

1177 EAST NEUK OF FIFE

MAP 5

WHERE TO STAY
See p. 112-3 FIFE HOTELS/RESTAUS. Note also; **THE BELVEDERE:** way back at **WEST
WEMYSS** (*see* KIRKCALDY, *p. 294*); **ANSTRUTHER, THE HERMITAGE:** 01333 310909;
THE SPINDRIFT: 01333 310573; **THE SMUGGLERS:** 01333 310506; **ELIE, THE
SHIP INN:** 01333 330246; **ELIE, GOLF HOTEL:** 01333 330209 (877/FIFE HOTELS).

WHERE TO EAT AND DRINK
THE CELLAR, ANSTRUTHER (1242/SEAFOOD RESTAUS); **THE ANSTRUTHER FISH
BAR or RESTAU** (1269/FISH AND CHIPS); **THE PEAT INN:** (882/FIFE BEST RESTAUS);
OSTLER'S CLOSE, CUPAR (884/FIFE BEST RESTAUS); **THE BOUQUET GARNI, ELIE**
(885/FIFE BEST RESTAUS); **THE SHIP, ELIE** (1215/PUB FOOD); **OLD RECTORY, DYSART**
(886/FIFE BEST RESTAUS); **SEAFOOD CABIN, ST MONANS** (1253/SEAFOOD).

WHERE TO VISIT
THE SECRET BUNKER (2003/MUSEUMS); **CHAIN WALK, ELIE** (1835/COASTAL WALKS);
CRAIL POTTERY (1927/CRAFTS); **ST ANDREWS ATTRACTIONS** (*p. 308*); **GOLF, ST
ANDREWS** (*see p. 237*); **FISHERIES MUSEUM, ANSTRUTHER** (2018/MUSEUMS);
ISLE OF MAY (1565/BIRDS).

BLOODY GOOD PUBS

Pubs in EDIN, GLAS, ABER and DUNDEE are listed in their own sections.

1178 ✔ ✔ **DROVER'S INN, INVERARNAN:** A famously Scottish drinking
MAP 6 den/hotel on the edge of the Highlands just N of Ardlui at the head
A2 of L Lomond and 12km S of Crianlarich on the A82. Smoky, low-ceilinged
rooms, open ranges, whisky in the jar, stuffed animals in the hall and kilted
barmen; this is nevertheless the antithesis of the contrived Scottish tourist
pub.

1179 ✔ ✔ **CLUANIE INN:** 01320 340257. On A87 at head of L Cluanie 15km
MAP 2 before Shiel Br on the long rd to Kyle of Lochalsh. A trad wayside inn
C3 with good pub food, a restau and MED.INX refurb-ed accom. Perfect base for
climbing/ walking (esp the Five Sisters of Kintail, 1796/SERIOUS WALKS). A cosy
refuge.

1180 ✔ **BORESTONE BAR, BANNOCKBURN nr STIRLING:** Bloody fine pub on
MAP 6 r/about 2km from centre of Stirling. Lounge bar, but mainly notable for
C3 the public bar where you will find no wine and usually no women – and the
best whisky collection in Scotland.

1181 ✔ **OLD FORGE, INVERIE, KNOYDART:** A warm haven for visitors to this
MAP 2 remote peninsula. Suddenly you're part of the community, real ales and
B3 real characters, real pub grub. Stay along the rd. (1142/GET-AWAY-FROM-IT-ALL)

1182 ✔ **TIGH-AN-TRUISH, CLACHAN, ISLE OF SEIL:** 01852 300242. Beside the
MAP 1 much- photographed 'Bridge over the Atlantic' which links the 'Isle' of Seil
B2 with the 'mainland'. On B884, 8km from B816 and 22km S of Oban. Country
pub with rms/apartments above (with views of br). A place where no one
cares how daft your hair looks after a hard day's messing about on boats.
Food LO 8.30pm. (Mar-Oct)

1183 ✔ **CLACHAIG INN, GLENCOE:** Deep in the glen itself down the rd signed off
MAP 2 the A82, 5km from Glencoe village. Both the pub with its wood-burning
C4 stove and the lounge are woody and welcoming. Real ale and real climbers
and walkers. Handy for hostel 2km down rd. Decent food (in bar/lounge or
dining rm) and good, inexp accom. Beerfest Feb/Mar.

1184 ✔ **THE MISHNISH, TOBERMORY:** The Mish has had its refit, but it's still the
MAP 1 real Tobermory. Till 1am every night. 7 days till late. Usually live music
B1 from Scot trad to DJs and indie.

1185 **POLLACHAR INN, SOUTH UIST:** Southern tip; on the shore looking over to
MAP 2 Barra. It's a long way from Brighton. The Saturday night discos are a long way
A3 from Glasgow. Just a thought. Amazing sunsets! Some rms.

1186 **CASTLEBAY BAR, BARRA:** Adj Castlebay Hotel. Brilliant bar. All human life is
MAP 2 here. More Irish than all the Irish makeovers on the mainland. Occasional live
C3 music, conversations with strangers.

1187 **PHOENIX, INVERNESS:** 108 Academy St. Trad horseshoe bar. Always lively.
MAP 2 The lounge is the place to relax with robust food (macaroni cheese & chips)
C2 and a pint of Deuchars IPA.

1188 **TIBBIE SHIELS INN:** Off A708 Moffat-Selkirk rd. Occupies its own particular
MAP 9 place in Scottish culture, esp literature (1744/LITERARY PLACES) and in the
D2 Border hills SW of Selkirk where it nestles between 2 romantic lochs. On
Southern Upland Way (1463b/WATERFALLS) a good place to stop and refuel.

1189 **THE MURRAY ARMS and THE MASONIC, GATEHOUSE OF FLEET:** 2 adj,
MAP 9 unrelated pubs that just fit perfectly into the life of this gr wee town. Murray
B3 has accom and home-style food but it's the Masonic that has the best atmos
and pub grub.

1190 **LOCK INN, FORT AUGUSTUS:** Busy canalside (Caledonian Canal which joins
MAP 2 L Ness in the distance) pub for locals and visitors. Good grub (you should
C3 book for the upstairs restau) The Gilliegorm, reasonable malts. Food LO 9pm.
Some live music.

GREAT PUBS FOR REAL ALE

1191 ✓ **FISHERMAN'S TAVERN, DUNDEE:** In Broughty Ferry, but not too far to
MAP 4   go for gr atmos and the best collection of ales in the area. In Fort St near
C3   the seafront. Belhaven/Maclays/Theakston and guests. Low-ceilinged and
friendly (1072/DUNDEE PUBS).

1192 ✓ **THE PHEASANT, HADDINGTON:** On corner where main st divides. Old-
MAP 7   style, real-ale howf claiming to have the best selection in E Lothian. No
B2   arguments from us. Rare guests on tap, and local Belhaven brewed along the
road in Dunbar. Busy market-town atmos; pool and frequent live music. Mind
the parrot.

1193 ✓ **MOULIN INN/HOTEL, PITLOCHRY:** 2km uphill from main st on rd to Br
MAP 4   of Cally, an inn at a picturesque crossrds since 1695. Some rms and restau,
B2   but notable mainly for cosy bar and brewery out back from which comes
'Moulin Light' and the 'Ale of Atholl'. Live music some Sun. Food LO 9.30pm.

1194 ✓ **ROYAL HOTEL, COMRIE:** Main sq; public bar is behind hotel. By same
MAP 4   people who have the Bow Bar and Cloisters in Edin, a rare combination
B3   of stylish and right-on ambience, sort of city meets the country. Guests and
regulars, which incl Earthquake Ale (made by Caledonian), exclusive to pub.
Live music. Beer garden.

1195 ✓ **ROYAL HOTEL, KINGUSSIE:** Main St. Busy local with all sorts of folk, juke
MAP 2   box, snooker; gr lively atmos. Amazing range of malts packed along the
D3   shelves and a microbrewery attached, so unique ales. At their annual beerfest,
any pint for a quid.

1196 ✓ **THE FOUR MARYS, LINLITHGOW:** Main st nr rd up to palace so handy for
MAP 7   a pint after schlepping around the historical attractions. Mentioned in
A1   most beer guides. Half a dozen ales on tap incl various guests. Notable malt
whisky collection and popular locally for lunches (daily) and evening meals
(Thurs-Sat, LO 8.45pm). Open 7 days.

1197 **THE TAPPIT HEN, DUNBLANE:** By the cathedral and with a small inexp hotel
MAP 6   up-stairs (The Chimes, 4 rms, 01786 825226). Good ales (incl the Wallace),
C2   atmos and live music.

1198 **MARINE HOTEL, STONEHAVEN:** Popular local on great harbour front with
MAP 3   seats o/side; pool tables, juke box and bar meals inside. Youngish crowd. Has
C4   won awards for its cask ales – various on tap. Lounge/restau upstairs. Open all
day.

1199 **THE WOOLPACK, TILLICOULTRY:** Via Upper Mill St from main st on your way
MAP 6   to the Ochils. They come far and wide to this ancient pub. Bar food and a
D3   changing selection of ales which they know how to keep. So no change here
chaps.

1200 **CLACHNAHARRY INN, INVERNESS:** On A862 Inverness-Beauly rd just out-
MAP 2   side Inverness o/looking firth with beer grd. Long list of regulars posted, 5/6
C2   on tap when we visited, also Clachnaharry Village Ale, and three Tomintouls
'from the wood'. Heaven!

1201 **THE SHORE INN, PORTSOY:** Down at the harbour, pub was taken over in '97
MAP 3   by the Hills who know their ales (they owned a wee brewery before they
C1   came here). Food all day in summer, weekends only in winter. The place to
drink when you come for the Trad Boats fest (2202/EVENTS)

1202 **THE OLD INN, GAIRLOCH:** Southern app on A832 nr golf course, an 'old inn'
MAP 2   across an old br; a goodly selection of malts. 12 real ales in the cellar – usual
B2   suspects like McEwans 80/- but also obscurities such as Aviemore IPA.

1203 **BETTY NICOL'S, KIRKCALDY:** 299 High St at the E end. Innkeepers who know
MAP 5   and love their ales. Gr selection with usually 8 posted. Food till early even, but
B3   plenty of t/aways nearby for later. Live music. Open 7 days.

1204 **DEESIDE HOTEL, BALLATER:** 013397 55420. Stand-out hotel in Ballater for
MAP 3   proprietors enthusiasm for real ales sometimes from Tomintoul up the road.
B3   Big local following and INX rms.

SECTION 5

Good Food and Drink

Pubs in EDIN, GLAS, ABER and DUNDEE are listed in their own sections.

1205
MAP 1
B3
✓ ✓ **KILBERRY INN, KILBERRY, nr TARBERT:** 01880 770223. On B8024 from W Loch Tarbert, the coast rd of Knapdale, 22km Tarbert/32km Lochgilphead – and you might whizz past. Down to earth good honest Yorkshire home cooking! Huge blackboard menu with a plethora of pies and Kath Leadbetter's pastry that really does melt in the mouth. Eat in the parlour of a roadside inn; you'll wish you lived nearer (though there are 2 inexp rms). Come to stay, put on weight! Home-made jams and chutneys. Lunch and 6.30-9pm. Book w/ends. Cl Sun.

1206
MAP 3
C4
✓ ✓ **LAIRHILLOCK, nr NETHERLEY, STONEHAVEN:** 01569 730001. Here forever for gr pubfood, but restau renowned as one of the best places to eat in the NE: open evenings – LO 9.30pm – and Sun lunch (1009/ABER RESTAUS). Inn more informal and downright friendly. Pub and conservatory. Fine for kids. Superb cheese selection, notable malts and ales. Can app from S Deeside Rd, but simplest direction for strangers is: 15km S of Aber by main A92 towards Stonehaven, then signed Durris, go 5km to country crossrds.

1207
MAP 5
A3
✓ ✓ **UNICORN INN, KINCARDINE:** 01259 730704. More a restau in a former pub than a pub with food, and unquestionably the best place to eat hereabouts. Worth coming from Stirling for, these light, Mediterranean-style dishes in bistro atmos. Best to book at w/ends. Report: 838/CENTRAL HOTELS. Cl Sun/Mon LO 9.15pm.

1208
MAP 8
D2
✓ **THE WHEATSHEAF, SWINTON, betw KELSO and BERWICK:** 01890 860257. A hotel pub in an undistinguished village about halfway betw the 2 towns (18km) on the B6461. In deepest, flattest Berwickshire, Alan and Julie Reid serve up the best pub grub you've had since England. Open noon-2pm and 6-9pm. Cl Mon.

1209
MAP 6
D3
✓ **THE WHINSMUIR COUNTRY INN, POWMILL, nr DOLLAR:** 01577 840595. A hotel/roadhouse and pub with v reasonable accom and, a v decent place for an informal and civilised meal; good wine list etc. On A977 Kinross (12km – M90, jnct 6) – Kincardine Br. 7 days. LO 9pm.

1210
MAP 6
C3
✓ **THE CROSS KEYS, KIPPEN:** 01786 870293. Here forever in this quiet backwater town off the A811 15km W of Stirling. Bar meals by coal fire, à la carte and family restaus. A real pub food haven, and about the only thing Egon Ronay has got right in this region. LO 9.30pm.

1211
MAP 1
C3
✓ **WHEATSHEAF INN, SYMINGTON, nr AYR:** 01563 830307. 2km A77. Pleasant village off the unpleasant A77 with this busy coaching inn opposite church. Folk come from miles around to eat (book at w/ends) honest-to-goodness pub fare in various rms (roast beef every Sunday). Menu on boards. Beer garden. LO 10pm.

1213
MAP 2
C1
✓ **KYLESKU HOTEL, KYLESKU:** 01971 502231. Off A894 betw Scourie and Lochinver in Sutherland. A hotel and pub with a gr quayside location on L Glencoul where boats leave for trips to see the 'highest waterfall in Europe' (1461/WATERFALLS, 996/INEXP HIGHLAND RESTAUS). A friendly atmos with local fish, seafood (esp with legs) and yummy desserts. Noon-9.30pm.

1214
MAP 6
D3
✓ **STRATHALLAN HOTEL, DOLLAR:** Chapel Pl. All round gr pub (with 4 inexp rms above) in back st of couthie and tidy town. Ales, malts, a games selection and beer grd. Food, after going through a lean patch, is back to being probably the best in town. Definitely worth a visit after doing the glen (1800/GLEN AND RIVER WALKS).

1215
MAP 5
C3
✓ **SHIP INN, ELIE:** Pub on the bay at Elie, the perfect toon in the picturesque East Neuk of Fife (1419/COASTAL VILLAGES). Bar and rm through back, but food mainly in refurbished boathouse next door and bistro above (good view, book w/ends). Same menu throughout and blackboard specials. Real popular place esp in summer when terrace o/looking the beach goes like Bondi. LO 9.00pm. Also has 6 chp rms adj (01333 330246).

1216 **MYRTLE INN, CALLANDER:** On way in/out of town A84 S, the Doune and
MAP 6 Stirling rd. Possibly an unlikely good place to eat on the way in or out of a
C2 town lined with many indifferent restaus, but this has always done a better
than av pub meal. Good Vegn menu. LO 9pm.

1217 **HUNTING LODGE HOTEL, FALKLAND :** 01337 857226. Main st of much visit-
MAP 5 ed town in central Fife, opp the fabulous Palace (1594/CASTLES). All day menu
B3 of mainly stalwarts like 80/- ale steak pie and macaroni cheese. Beer grd a bit
removed. Open 7 days. LO 8pm.

1218 **GOBLIN HA' HOTEL, GIFFORD:** 01620 810244. Twee village in the boondocks;
MAP 7 one of 2 hotels (864/LOTHIANS HOTELS). This, the one with the gr name, serves a
B1 decent pub lunch and supper (6-9pm; 9.30pm on Fri and Sat) in lounge and
more basic version in the pub. Conservatory and grd; kids' play area.

1219 **DROVER'S INN, E LINTON:** 01620 860298. A village off A1, 35km from Edin. A
MAP 7 notable E Lothian eatery within reach of city. Restau upstairs, bistro with
B1 blackboard specials down. Can eat alfresco in summer with trains whooshing
by (1219/BEST FOOD).

1220 **TORMAUKIN INN, GLENDEVON:** 01259 781252. On A823 through wooded
MAP 4 Glen to Auchterarder, 36km E of Stirling, 16km W of M90 at jnct 6/7. Rdside inn
B4 with very pleasant accom (10 rms/MED.INX), restau and fine pub meals. À la
carte and specials; vegn dishes. W/ends busy. Lunch and 5.30-9.30pm.

1221 **THE BYRE, BRIG O' TURK:** 01877 376292. Off A821 at Callander end of the vil-
MAP 6 lage adj Dundarroch Hotel. Country inn (with new friendlier owners) in deep
C2 Trossachs. Blackboard table d'hôte in bar or (no smk) restau. Lunch and 6-9pm.

1222 **OLD BRIDGE INN, AVIEMORE:** Off Coylumbridge rd at S end of Aviemore as
MAP 2 you come in from A9 or Kincraig. 100m main st but sits in hollow. An old inn
D3 like it says with basic à la carte and more interesting blackboard specials.
Three cask ales on tap. Kids' menu, ski-bums welcome. Lunch and 6-9pm.
Bunkhouse should get up and running for spring 2000.

1223 **CAFE MAMBO, AVIEMORE:** 01479 811670. It's a city-style cafe bar in the ski zone
MAP 2 that does food (Indian, Tex-Mex, snacks) until 9pm, coffee and drinks all day and
D3 then Thurs-Sat late on, it goes all clubby. All things to all people, until 1am daily.

1224 **THE CROWN, PORTPATRICK:** 01776 810261. Hugely popular pub on harbour
MAP 9 with tables o/side in summer. Light, airy conservatory at back serving freshly
A3 caught fish. 12rms above. Locals and Irish who sail over for lunch (sic). Excl
chips LO 10pm.

1225 **OLD SMUGGLERS, AUCHENCAIRN:** 01556 640331. An alternative place to
MAP 9 stay to the Balcary Bay in this old smuggling stretch of the Solway coast
C3 (though only 3 rms). Good pub grub and village crack. LO 10pm.

1226 **THE ANCHOR, KIPPFORD:** The place to eat on the 'Scottish Riviera', esp if
MAP 9 you've walked over from Rockcliffe (2km). In summer, tables o/side look (over
C3 the rd) to the silted Solway. Elbow to elbow inside with all ages enjoying grub,
good family pub with games rm and kids menu.

1227 **THE SHIP INN, BROUGHTY FERRY:** Excellent seafront (Tay estuary) snug pub
MAP 4 with food upstairs and down (best tables at window upstairs). Famous for
C3 clootie dumpling (but not in summer). 7 days, lunch and 5-10pm
(1060/DUNDEE EAT AND DRINK).

1228 **HORSESHOE INN, EDDLESTON, nr PEEBLES:** 5km N on A703 to Edin, this
MAP 8 rdside inn is more a restau than just a pub, serving food from 7.30am right
A2 through to 3pm, and then dinner in the evenings. A hostelry worth a stop-
over (8 bedrms).

1229 **THE AULD CROSS KEYS INN, DENHOLM, nr HAWICK:** 01450 870305. Not a
MAP 8 lot of eating places to recommend in Hawick (in fact, none), so Peter and
C3 Heather Ferguson's old faithful is worth the 8km journey on the A698
Jedburgh rd. On the Green, with pub and dining lounges through the back.
Blackboard menu, heaps of choice and food. Big on Sun high tea (4-6.30pm).
No food Mon.

FOX AND HOUNDS, HOUSTON: 01505 612448.

OLD CLUBHOUSE, GULLANE: 01620 842008. Report: 870/LOTHIANS HOTELS

THE BEST VEGETARIAN RESTAURANTS

Not surprisingly, perhaps, there are precious few completely vegetarian restaus in Scotland. But there are lots in EDIN *(see p.30) and some in* GLAS *(see p. 79).*

1230
MAP 2
B3
✓ **SEAGREEN, KYLE OF LOCHALSH:** 01599 534388. On edge of town, rd to Plockton. Café/bookshop/wholefood during the day (open AYR); in another rm is a seafood restau at night (May-Sept). Not your run-of-the-mill tofu; Fiona Begg's varied and artistic menu demonstrates just how innovative vegn cookery can be. Vegan selection. No whiff of bacon sarnies here among the books. No smk. Organics ales and wine. 7 days.   MED

1231
MAP 2
B2
✓ **AN TUIREANN, PORTREE, SKYE:** Off Uig (then Struan) rd (at the Co-op). Excl gallery cafe and restau with contemp menu; salads, hot meals, snacks. Prob best coffee on Skye. Mon/Tues 10am-5pm, W-Sat 10am-9pm, Sun 12-5pm. Changing exhibs.   CHP

1232
MAP 3
A1
✓ **HELIO'S at FINDHORN COMMUNITY, FINDHORN:** You will go a long way in the N to find real vegn food, so it may be worth the detour from the main A96 Inverness–Elgin rd, to Findhorn and the famous commune (1168/RETREATS) where there is a gr deli (1340/DELIS) and a pleasant caff by the 'Hall'.   CHP

1233
MAP 2
B2
THE MOUNTAIN RESTAURANT, GAIRLOCH: 01445 712316. Restau with con- servatory and tables outside with mt view. Bookshop and adj Nature Shop with every kind of spiritual whatsits you may want. We've had complaints about the price of tea and scones – and the candlelit dinners in the eve are 'ample'. Just the job after a day on the hill, but far from dainty. V American, and a v retro debate over sexist posters in the loo being conducted by graffiti when last we visited. You won't leave without an opinion. Easter-Oct.   INX

THE BEST VEGETARIAN-FRIENDLY PLACES

EDINBIRGH *and* GLASGOW *cafés and restaus are mentioned in their own sections, see p. 30 and p. 79.*

1234 ORKNEY/SHETLAND

WOODWICK HOUSE, EVIE, ORKNEY: 01856 751330. B&B, seals, music and woodland. (2161/ORKNEY)

BURRASTOW HOUSE, WALLS, SHETLAND: 01595 809307. Good value lunches and set dinners (2162/SHETLAND).

BAYANNE HOUSE, SELLAFIRTH, YELL, SHETLAND: 01957 744219. A croft by the sea. Accom.

1235 HIGHLANDS
MAP 2

THE CEILIDH PLACE, ULLAPOOL: 01854 612103 (960/INEXP HIGHLAND HOTELS).

CAFÉ NUMBER ONE, INVERNESS: 01463 226200 (2168/INVERNESS).

BOOKSHOP CAFE, INVERNESS: 01463 239947 (2168/INVERNESS).

DUNNET HEAD TEAROOM, nr THURSO: 01847 851774 (995/INEXP HIGHLAND RESTAUS).

THREE CHIMNEYS, SKYE: 01470 511258 (2138/ISLAND RESTAUS).

BEN TIANAVAIG, PORTREE, SKYE: 01478 612152. 5 Bosville Terr, rd to Station and N.

OLD SCHOOL, DUNVEGAN, SKYE: 01470 521421 (2158/SKYE)

THE SEAFOOD RESTAURANT, KYLE OF LOCHALSH (985/INEXP HIGHLAND RESTAUS).

RIVERSIDE BISTRO, LOCHINVER: 01571 844356 (991/INEXP HIGHLAND RESTAUS).

CAFÉ BEAG, FORT WILLIAM: 01397 703601 (2166/FT WILLIAM).

OLD STATION, SPEAN BRIDGE: 01397 712535 (983/INEXP HIGHLAND RESTAUS)

1236 NORTH EAST
MAP 3

LEMON TREE, ABERDEEN: 01224 642230 (1032/ABER RESTAUS).

OWLIES, ABERDEEN: 01224 649267 (1030/ABER RESTAUS).

MILTON RESTAURANT, BANCHORY: 01330 844566 (934/NE HOTELS)

GREEN INN, BALLATER: 01339 755701 (931/NE HOTELS).

GORDON ARMS HOTEL, KINCARDINE O'NEIL, DEESIDE: 01339 884236. Halfway betw Ballater and Aberdeen. Hotel with ok-ish pub food. Organic wine list.

1237 ARGYLL
MAP 2

THE CLIFTON COFFEE SHOP, TYNDRUM: 01838 400271 (1287/TEAROOMS).

THE BOXTREE, OBAN: 01631 563542 (2169/OBAN).

ARISAIG HOUSE HOTEL, ARISAIG: 01687 450622 (1087/COUNTRY-HOUSE HOTELS).

AN TAIRBEART HERITAGE CENTRE, TARBERT: 01880 820190. On A83 S. Family fare.

1238 FIFE AND LOTHIANS
MAPS 5, 7

OSTLER'S CLOSE, CUPAR: 01334 655574 (884/FIFE RESTAUS).

THE VINE LEAF, ST ANDREWS: 01334 477497 (2176/ST ANDREWS).

BRAMBLES and THE MERCHANT HOUSE, ST ANDREWS (1304/TEAROOMS).

WATERSIDE BISTRO, HADDINGTON: 01620 825674 (865/LOTHIANS RESTAUS).

DROVER'S INN, EAST LINTON: 01620 860298 (1219/BEST FOOD).

1239 CENTRAL:
MAP 4

FARLEYER HOUSE nr ABERFELDY: 01887 820332 (890/PERTHSHIRE RESTAUS).

LET'S EAT, PERTH: 01738 643377 (905/PERTHSHIRE RESTAUS).

UNICORN INN, KINCARDINE: 01259 730704 (838/CENTRAL RESTAUS).

MYRTLE INN, CALLANDER: 01877 330919 (1216/BEST PUB FOOD).

MONACHYLE MHOR nr BALQUHIDDER: 01877 384622 (1140/GET-AWAY-FROM-IT-ALL).

KILLIECRANKIE HOTEL BAR, KILLIECRANKIE: 01796 473220 (898/PERTHSHIRE HOTELS).

1240 SOUTH AND SOUTH WEST:
MAP 8

MARMIONS, MELROSE: 01896 822245 (852/BORDERS HOTELS).

THE BEST SEAFOOD RESTAURANTS

For seafood restaus in EDINBURGH, *see p. 29; for* GLASGOW, *see p. 79.*

1241
MAP 1
B2
✓ ✓ **LOCK 16, CRINAN HOTEL, CRINAN:** 01546 830261. 8km off A816. On coast, 60km S of Oban (Lochgilphead 12km) at head of the Crinan Canal which joins L Fyne with the sea. This is the third-floor rm where you drink in the sunset over the Sound of Jura (from where your dinner has come) as well as a glass or two of perfectly complementary white wine. O/side on the quay is the boat which has landed those massive prawns, sweet clams and other creatures with legs or valves, which are cooked v simply and brought on heaped tureens to your table. Ground-floor restau has cranked up the pace recently – proprietor Nick Ryan says the only thing that's keeping him from retirement is the sense of wonder at having found a chef as good as Craig Wood (ex Atrium, Balmoral in Edin). EXP

1242
MAP 5
D3
✓ ✓ **THE CELLAR, ANSTRUTHER:** 01333 310378. The best in SE Scotland. Behind Fisheries Museum in busy East Neuk of Fife town. Fish and shellfish from beyond the harbour wall, some meat options. Cosy French bistro atmos. Full Report: 883/FIFE RESTAUS. MED

1243
MAP 3
D3
✓ ✓ **SILVER DARLINGS, ABERDEEN:** 01224 576229. Down by harbour. For many yrs one of the best restaus in the city and the NE. Exquisite chargrilled seafood. report: 1010/ABER RESTAUS. MED

1244
MAP 1
C3
✓ ✓ **MACCALLUMS, TROON:** 01292 319339. At end of long rd to the Harbour, follow the Seacat signs, this spacious quayside bistro is literally at the Seacat (ferry) terminus. Lovely fish, gr atmos. Unpretentious. Worth going down from Glasgow. 7 days, lunch and LO 9.30pm. CL Mon and Sun lunch. MED

1245
MAP 2
B2
✓ **LOCHBAY SEAFOOD, SKYE:** 01470 592235. 12km N Dunvegan; A850 to Portree, B886 Waternish peninsula coastal route. Another scenic Skye drive leads you to the door of this small cottage at end of the village row. O/looks water where your shellfish, skate or even shark have come from. Main dishes served unfussily with chips or baked potatoes. Comforting puds and Irish coffee. Simply v good – you'll need to book. Apr-Oct; lunch & LO 8.30ish. On our last visit, weirdly cl on Sat and Sun. MED

1246
MAP 1
C2
✓ **LOCH FYNE SEAFOOD AND SMOKERY:** 01499 600264. On A83 the L Lomond to Inveraray rd, 20km Inveraray/11km Rest and Be Thankful. Rdside smokery which is not merely a net across the end of the loch to catch tourists. In summer you may well have to book or wait; people come from afar for the oysters and the smokery fare, esp the kippers. Spacious, though the booths can seem cramped. House white (other whites and whisky) well chosen. Same menu all day, no 'meal times'. Shop sells every conceivable packaging of salmon, etc., 9am-9pm. Though some readers complain of indifferent service, it is busy so on balance this is a notable spot. It's always been fyne by me, something to look forward to on the long road home. INX

1247
MAP 2
B2
✓ **KISHORN SEAFOOD AND SNACK BAR, KISHORN:** 01520 733240. On A896 at Kishorn on rd betw Lochcarron (Inverness) and Sheildaig nr the rd over the hill to Applecross (1484/ROUTES). Fresh local seafood in a roadside diner. Light, bright and a real find in the middle of beautiful nowhere. 7 days 10-8pm, Sun 12-4pm. Summer only. MED

1248
MAP 1
B2
✓ **THE ANCHORAGE, TARBERT:** 01880 820881. Mediterranean refurb is in perfect sync with light touch displayed at the stoves. Complementary wines, desserts and coffee – an all round experience. Authentic location on busy quay of quintessential Highland port. 7 days Apr-Oct, tues-sat in wint. Dinner only. MED

1249
MAP 3
C4
✓ **THE TOLBOOTH, STONEHAVEN:** 01569 762287. On corner of harbour, one of the best restaus in the area in a great setting – oldest building in town. Upstairs bistro with interesting seafood menu served with flair and integrity; good wine list, some real bargains. Daily 6-9.30pm. Cl lunch. MED

1250
MAP 1
C3

✓ **FINS, FAIRLIE, nr LARGS:** 01475 568989. On main A78 8km S of Largs a seafood bistro, smokery, shop and craft/cookshop. Roadside fish farm bistro, best place to eat for miles in any direction. Chef Gillian Dick uses exemplary restraint and the wine list is similarly to the point. Lunch and dinner. Cl Mon. INX

1251
MAP 1
C3

✓ **CREELERS, BRODICK, ARRAN:** 01770 302810. Just outside Brodick on rd N to castle in a modern tourist plaza-plex. Even with their other Creelers doing so well in Edin (1251/SEAFOOD RESTAUS) Tim and Fran James still manage to keep this excl island bistro tip-top (and get the boat out). Lunch LO 10pm. Cl Mon. MED

1252
MAP 2
C2

✓ **MOREFIELD HOTEL, ULLAPOOL:** 01854 612161. Neptune's seafood platter, great fish and vegn all on offer in this quirky popular restau (Mariners) on a kind of housing estate. Bar meals are great and selection of seafood amazing; close your eyes and enjoy. People drive 100 miles for this meal – nuff said. INX.MED

1253
MAP 5
C3

THE CABIN SEAFOOD RESTAURANT, ST MONANS, FIFE: 01333 730327. West end of East Neuk Village accurately described by title and no fuss in the menu either. Terrace o/looks sea, waves lap, gulls mew etc. Bar menu lunch and dinner LO 11pm Cl Mon. MED

1254
MAP 9
A3

CAMPBELLS, PORTPATRICK: 01776 810314. Friendly, harbourside restau of recent origin ('99). Some meat dishes, but mainly seafood. Sardines were nice. 7 days lunch and LO 10pm. Cl Jan-Mar and Mons. MED

1255
MAP 2
C3

CRANNOG, FORT WILLIAM: 01397 705589. Some doubt as to the future, but at time of going to press, this remains a good bet in Ft William. Finlay Finlayson's converted boathouse is where the Cal Mac boats used to dock. Usual fresh fish and seafood from surrounding islands esp good langoustines. 7 days lunch and dinner. MED

1256
MAP 2
C1

SEAFOOD CAFÉ, TARBET, nr SCOURIE: 01971 502251. Charming conservatory restau on cove where boats leave for Handa Island bird reserve (1562/BIRDS). Julian catches your seafood from his boat (he'll also take you on a cruise) and Jackie cooks it; some take photos of the results. Cheesecake for dessert. It's so peaceful here you'll want to stay and can do so in adj self-catering barn. Located at end of unclassified rd off the A894 between Laxford Br and Scourie; best phone to check openings. Apr-Sept: Mon-Sat 12-8pm. Some Sun in summer. INX

1257
MAP 1
B1

THE PIERHOUSE, PORT APPIN: 01631 730302. At the end of the minor rd and 3km from the A828 Oban–Ft William rd in Pt Appin village rt by the tiny 'pier' where the passenger ferry leaves for Lismore. Locally caught seafood (Lismore oysters, Mallaig flatfish, hand-dived shellfish) is handed over fresh to the door by boat. Lively atmos, wine and wonderful view but mmm … we have had some complaints! (1119/INNS). INX

THE BEST FISH AND CHIP SHOPS

1258
MAP 5
B3

✓ ✓ **VALENTE'S, KIRKCALDY:** 01592 651991. 73 Overton Rd (not downtown version). Ask directions to this superb chippy in E of town; worth the detour and worth the queue when you get there. Phone if you're lost. Till 11pm. Cl Wed.

1259
MAP B
xD5

✓ ✓ **THE UNIQUE, GLASGOW:** 223 Allison St. Not exactly central, but if you're on the S-side you'll find the best fish 'n' chips in town here. Through the curtain in the café, they serve lunches, fish teas and spam fritters. Veg oil used. Old-fashioned hours, viz 8.15am-1.15pm, 3.45-9pm. That's right, 9pm – closed.

1260
MAP 3
D3

✓ ✓ **THE ASHVALE, ABERDEEN, ELGIN, INVERURIE and BRECHIN:** Original restau (1985) at 46 Gt Western Rd nr Union St, and 2 other city branches. Restau and takeaway complex à la Harry Ramsden (and they steadfastly stick to dripping). Various sizes of haddock, sole, plaice. Homemade stovies, etc., all served fresh and fast although discerning Brechiners still drive to Inverbervie (1268/see over). Open 7 days, noon-1am; restau noon-11pm Sun-Thu; till midnight Fri/Sat.

1261
MAP 3
D3

✓ ✓ **THE NEW DOLPHIN, ABERDEEN:** Chapel St. Despite the pre-eminence of the Ashvale in Aberdeen, many would rather swear by this small, always busy place just off Union St. Few tables, superb takeaway. Till 1am and 3am w/ends.

1262
MAP A
C1

✓ **L'ALBA D'ORO, EDINBURGH:** Henderson Row, nr corner with Dundas St. Large selection of deep-fried goodies, incl many vegn savouries. Inexpensive proper pasta, real pizzas and even the wine's ok. A lot more than your usual fry-up – as several plaques on the wall attest (incl *Scotland the Best!*). Open until midnight.

1263
MAP A
D2

✓ **THE RAPIDO, EDINBURGH:** 77 Broughton St. Legendary chippie. Popular with late-nighters stumbling back down the hill to the New Town, and the flotsam of the 'Pink Triangle.' 1.30am (3.30am Fri/Sat).

1264
MAP A
D2

✓ **THE DEEP SEA, EDINBURGH:** Leith Walk, opp Playhouse. Open late and often has queues but these are quickly dispatched. The haddock has to be 'of a certain size'. Trad menu. Still one of the best fish suppers you'll ever feed a hangover with. 2am-ish (3am Fri/Sat).

1265
MAP 4
C3

✓ **DEEP SEA, DUNDEE:** 81 Nethergate at bottom end of Perth Rd; v central. The Sterpaio family have been serving the Dundonians excellent fish 'n' chips since 1939; gr range – lemon sole, scampi, haddock, cod etc in veg oil. Café with aproned waitress service is a classic. V trad, so … oo tasty. Mon-Sat, 11.30am-6.40pm.

1266
MAP 4
C3

✓ **HOLDGATES, PERTH:** 146 South St. For all of this century (est 1901), this brilliant caff shop has been frying up the F&C the way we like it. Sitting-room thro' the back is a model of minimalism and functionalism. This place will be here long after the chromey makeovers have come and gone. Go sample the simple. 7 days 12-8.30pm, Sun 4pm-8.30pm

1267
MAP 4
D3

✓ **PEPPO'S, ARBROATH:** 51 Ladybridge St next to the harbour where those fish come in. Fresh as that and chips in dripping. Peppo has been here since 1951; John and Frank Orsi are carrying on the gr family trad and feeding the hordes. Mon-Fri 4-10pm, Sat-Sun 4-8pm. Then step outside and smell the smokies.

1268
MAP 3
C4

✓ **THE BERVIE CHIPPER, INVERBERVIE and STONEHAVEN:** Main st Inverbervie. Sit-in area up and downstairs and take-away. Gets through enormous amounts of haddock and cod. Lard used. New opening in Stoney on David St has queues out the door on Sat nights. Both open daily, noon-10.30pm (Inverbervie from 3pm in winter) 7 days.

1269
MAP 5
D3

✓ **THE ANSTRUTHER FISH BAR:** On the front in Fife seaside town (1419/COASTAL VILLAGES); just look for the queue. Get a gr fish supper and walk round the harbour. Lard used. Eating in is cramped (cardboard trays etc) so out is best. 7 days 11.30-10.30pm

1270
MAP 1
C3

✓ **WEST END, ROTHESAY:** 1 Gallowgate. Winner of awards (so many, we lose track) and unmissable if you're on Bute despite the ticket system. Only haddock, but wide range of other fries and fresh pizza. Uses expensive groundnut oil. Summer: 12-12am (Sun 4-11pm); winter 12-12am, Cl 2-4pm. Café in summer till 8pm. Cl Mon.

1271
MAP 9
C3

BALMORAL, DUMFRIES: Balmoral Rd. Seems as old and essential as the Bard himself. Now using groundnut oil, hence the best chip in the south. 7 days.

1272
MAP 1
B1

ONORIO'S, OBAN: George St. Legendary but this is where the wifie patiently told me, 'Anyone who says you can fry good chips in vegetable oil is having you on, son.' This is bollocks, missus (*see above*). But their lardy chips are good and you're near the seafront to eat and walk off the grease. Lunch/4-11.30pm. (Cl Sun winter.)

1273
MAP 3
C4

SANDY'S STONEHAVEN: Market Sq. The established Stoney Chipper, dealing well with the recent competition. Daily, LO 9pm. Big haddock.

1274
MAP 6
D3

CORVI'S, BO'NESS: Just squeezing in, included for its fine fish supper, and gr home-made ice cream (1334/ICE CREAM).

GREAT CAFÉS

For cafés in EDINBURGH, *see p. 40,* GLASGOW, *p. 81.*

1275
MAP 1
C3

✓ ✓ ✓ **NARDINI'S, LARGS:** 01475 674555. The Esplanade, Glas side. An institution. The epitome of the seaside cafeteria and all the nostalgia of Doon the Watter days. This airy brasserie with cake, ice cream and chocolate counters and in the back a trad tratt with full Italian à la carte and OK wines has a timeless formula which works as well today as it ever did. The light fittings like almost everything else are true originals. Summer evenings with the long light and a bowl of ice cream and the place busy with all kinds of folk is life-affirming stuff. Get you down there. High tea (4-6pm) is always a good idea. Summer till 10.30pm/winter 8pm. (1331/ICE CREAM.). No sign of Daniella now.

1276
MAP 6
C3

✓ **ALLAN WATER CAFÉ, BRIDGE OF ALLAN:** Henderson St (main st) beside the eponymous br. Real whiff of nostalgia along with the fish'n'chips and the ice cream, which are the best around. Worth coming over from Stirling (8km) for a takeaway or a seat in the comforting woody caff – and a reminisce of the life before the mall and the burgering of your high st. 7 days, 8am-9pm.

1277
MAP 1
C3

✓ **THE RITZ CAFÉ, MILLPORT:** See Millport, see the Ritz. Since 1906 and now in its fourth generation, the classic café on the Clyde. Somewhat overshadowed by Nardini's (*see above*) and a short ferry journey away (from Largs, continuous; then 6km), but it should be an essential part of any visit to this part of the coast, and Millport is not without charm. Food 'n' chips, frothy cappuccino, famous home-made ice cream (esp with melted marshmallow), Millport rock and, of course, the hot peas. 7 days, 10am-10pm forever.

1278
MAP 1
C3

✓ **TOGS, TROON:** Templehill nr main crossrds. There are 2 seaside caffs in downtown Troon (the other, the pleasingly named Venice Café, is also good), but this is the one that did it for me – it even smells like a café should. Snacks and stuff and brilliant rock. 7 days 9am-6 or 8pm (from 10am on Sun).

1279
MAP 1
D3

THE MARKET BAR AND RESTAURANT, LANARK MARKET: Hyndford Rd. Betw the auction rings and only on auction days of which there are many esp Mon/Tues/Thurs, a café from a bygone era. Farmers' sons of farmers' sons still cram the tables for canteen cooking that's always hit the spot. Jam roly-poly, jelly, apples and custard after your mince and chips. Not as funky as it was, but the walls still creak, the waitresses josh with the regulars. Go buy some ducks!

1280
MAP 2
C2

THE CASTLE RESTAURANT, INVERNESS: On rd that winds up to the castle from the main st, nr the TO and the hostels. No pandering to tourists here, but this great caff has been serving chips with everything for 40 years. Recent redecoration, but not poshed up. Pork chops, prawn cocktail, perfect fried eggs. They work damned hard. 8am-8.30pm. Cl Sun.

1281
MAP 6
B2

THE CAFÉ IN BRIG O'TURK IN THE TROSSACHS: 01877 376267. Hanging baskets of flowers o/side this shack are what you notice from the rd (the A821 12km W of Callander) in the heart of the afternoon tea belt of the Trossachs. But more substantial high teas are served: Highland stew, Cullen skink, whisky spice cake. Book for evening. Always busy, they hate name checks like this.

1282
MAP 6
C2

BEN LEDI CAFE, CALLANDER: Main st nr sq. Fish teas, and a sq meal. Unprepossessing frontage, but here is the genuine, ungentrified article – who needs an internet cafe? Take away or sit in. The best ice cream for miles around. It *is* always worth a stop in this Callander. Cl Thu.

THE BEST TEAROOMS AND COFFEE SHOPS

For EDINBURGH, *see p.38; for* GLASGOW, *p. 80.*

1283
MAP 1
C3
✓ ✓ **TUDOR RESTAURANT, AYR:** 8 Beresford Terr, nr Odeon and Burns Monument Sq. Recently changed hands after 25yrs in the same family but still a classic tea rm. Roomy, well-used, full of life. Bakery counter at front (fab cream donuts and 'fly cemeteries' as they're supposed to be) and disdainful nippy waitresses in the body of the kirk. 9am-8pm Mon-Sat, 9pm July and Aug. Open Sun in season. Trad without being tacky.

1284
MAP 8
B2
✓ ✓ **KAILZIE GARDENS TEAROOMS, PEEBLES:** On the way out of town towards Traquair (1387/GARDENS) this v civilised courtyard coffee shop is nr the Garden entrance. Superior sort of home-baking – the apple cake should be famous and it's hard to choose from the rest. Open 7 days, till 4pm Mon-Fri and 5pm at w/ends (5.30pm in summer). Apr-Oct. Fri/Sat – an excl atmos dinner.

1285
MAP 4
B3
✓ ✓ **THE GRANARY, COMRIE:** Main st parlour with gr home-bakes arranged on an old-fashioned counter. TLC coconut biscuits, tiffin, brill bics, major cakes – come with appetite. Jams/chutneys/ice cream. No smk. Mar-Oct 10am-5pm. Cl Mon. Also **TULLY BANNOCHER FARM RESTAURANT**, 2km W on A85 to Lochearnhead. Recommended roadside coffee shop/self-service diner with hot dishes, salads, etc. Open till 8.30pm. Apr-Oct.

1286
MAP 4
B7
✓ ✓ **THE POWMILL MILKBAR, nr KINROSS:** On the A977 Kinross (on the M90, jnct 6) to Kincardine Br rd, a real milkbar and a real slice of Scottish cack and cake. Apple pie and moist fly cemeteries – an essential stop on the Sunday run whatever day of the week you're passing. The paper plates do little justice to the confections they bear, but they are part of the deal, so loosen up! Hot meals and salads. Good place to take kids. 7 days, 9am-5pm (6pm w/ends, earlier in winter). (1800/GLEN AND RIVER WALKS)

1287
MAP 6
A1
✓ ✓ **THE CLIFTON COFFEE SHOP, TYNDRUM:** On A82, a strategically placed pit-stop on the drive to Oban or Ft William (just before the rd divides), with a Scottish produce shop and the 'Green Welly Shop' selling outdoor gear. Fast (Scottish) food to an unusually good standard and emporium packed with Scottish produce, from whisky to videos. Here you get the picture and the flavour of the land – this is Scotland, ken? 7 days, 8.30am-5.30pm.

1288
MAP 3
C3
✓ **THE BLACK-FACED SHEEP, ABOYNE:** 01339 887311. Nr main Royal Deeside rd through Aboyne (A93) and TO, this excellent coffee shop/gift shop is well-loved by locals but is thankfully missed by the bus parties hurtling towards Balmoral. Home-made breads and cakes, snacks; good coffee. 10am-5pm, Sun from 11am.

1289
MAP 1
B3
✓ **NORTH BEACHMORE FARM RESTAURANT, nr MUASDALE:** on A83 Tarbert–Campbeltown rd. Signposted up a steep track, 2km off the rd and into the hills. Matt and Eileen McInnes' home-cooking is v popular locally; you see why. Stunning views of the Sound of Gigha, (and on a clear day Ireland). Food excl too. Open AYR 10am-11pm. Cl weekays in Nov.

1290
MAP 1
B1
✓ **THE GLASS BARN, TOBERMORY, MULL:** Up the hill at the edge of town 500m off Dervaig rd, 2km centre. Run by (and part of) the Reade's dairy farm the people who make the excellent Mull cheddar (which you can 'win' with this book, *see p.12*), but that's not the reason I'm recommending it. Rather, it's just gr what they've done with it – go see! A glass barn full of plants, hearty soup, farm bakes. Walk from the village – it will do you good. May-Sep; Mon-Fri (Cl Sun) 10am-4pm.

1291
MAP 6
C3
✓ **PUDDLEDUCKS, BLAIRLOGIE, nr STIRLING:** On main A91 in tiny village. Hot dishes at lunch but mainly delicious cakes, and I do mean delicious. 3 ladies make 'em. Stock up on the way to the Ochils. 7 days 10.30-4.30pm.

1292
MAP 9
B3
✓ **KITTY'S TEAROOM, NEW GALLOWAY:** Main St of town in the forest. We used to rec another place here, but it changed hands for the worse. Fortunately Kitty's is an excl replacement. Some hot food and snacks, but esp renowned for Sylvia Brown's wicked cakes. Irresistible. Many teas and Costa coffee. 10am-5pm (Fri/Sat till 8.30pm) Cl Mon.

1293   **THE RIVERSIDE, ABBEY ST BATHANS:** 01361 840312. By the trout farm, nr R
MAP 8   Whiteadder in the middle of this rustic hamlet on the Southern Upland Way.
C1   A welcome place for a café (though it's more of a restau really) with friendly
service, hearty grub, incl pheasant pie, various savoury flans and puddings
which will need a bit of walking off. Tue-Sun 11am-5pm and bank hols.

1294   **THE OLD BANK, DUMFRIES:** 95 Irish St, off High St. Coffee shop in converted
MAP 9   bank (revolving doors and cornices remain) on st where Burns lived. Delicate
C3   snacks, good puds and cakes. Mon-Sat 10am-5pm.

1295   **PEEL FARM COFFEE & CRAFT SHOP nr ALYTH:** B954 to Lintrathen, 3km N. of
MAP 4   Reekie Linn (1465/WATERFALLS). Farmhouse fare and handcrafted knits, pot-
C3   tery, jewellery. Traditional, cosy, mumsie. 9am-5pm Easter-mid Oct daily.

1296   **AN CARRAIG TEAROOM, STRATHYRE:** Main st on A84 as you leave towards
MAP 6   Crianlarich (and after Munro Hotel). Look out for it, because it's quite discreet.
B2   Some hot dishes but becoming renowned for cakes, like a good tearoom
should. Excellent lentil soup. Jams and provisions. Daytime only. Cl Wed/Thur

1297   **THE TEAROOM at CLATT, nr ALFORD and INVERURIE:** In the village hall in
MAP 3   the hamlet of Clatt where local ladies display gr home-made Scottish baking.
C3, C4   I haven't been, but lots of people wrote to tell me about it, so it must be quite
special. Take A96 N of Inverurie, then B9002 follow sign for Auchleven, then
Clatt. Gr countryside. Prob only w/ends in summer.

1298   **THE HARBOUR CAFE, ROTHESAY:** 01700 505166, East Princes St. Internet
MAP 1   and espresso come to Bute. Surf the web, have a sandwich, or dinner. Urban
C3   outpost, opened Apr '99. Easter-Oct 10am-6pm daily, also 7-10pm Fri/Sat.
Reduced opening hrs in winter.

1299   **GARDEN ROOM TEASHOP, ROCKCLIFFE:** On main rd in/out of this seaside
MAP 9   cul de sac. Best on sunny days when you can sit in the garden. Snacks and
C3   cakes (though not all home-made). 10.30-5pm. Cl Tues.

1300   **COFFEE HOUSE, GRANTOWN-ON-SPEY:** 35 High St. Surprisingly authentic
MAP 2   Italian café with genuine Italian cakes, ice cream and espresso. They serve
D3   stew as well as pretty good pasta. Nice people run this place. Till 5pm.

1301   **THE COFFEE SHOPPE, FRASERBURGH:** 30 Cross St. Small front-room-of-
MAP 3   somebody's-hoose-type place. Scottish and imported cakes (e.g. carrot cake,
D1   pavlova) all home made. Mum's soup, scones and rowies. Mon-Sat, 9am-
4.30pm. Cl Wed.

1302   **BINNIE'S TEAROOM, CROMARTY:** In great wee village in Black Isle 30km NE
MAP 2   of Inverness (1414/COASTAL VILLAGES) on corner of Church St. Home-baking
D2   and some snacks. Country Kitchen opp has, in my opinion, better scones and
better jam, but my Cromarty connection says … it has to be Binnie's. Only till
4pm. Cl Wed and Sat.

1303   **KIND KYTTOCK'S KITCHEN, FALKLAND:** Folk come to Falkland (1594/CAS-
MAP 5   TLES; 1775/HILL WALKS) for many reasons, not least for afternoon tea. Several
B3   choices, this the longest established and highly regarded. Omelettes, toasties,
baked potatoes, baking. Good service. 10.30am-5.30pm. Cl Mon.

1304   **MERCHANT'S HOUSE, ST ANDREWS:** S St in the middle. Self-serve restau-
MAP 5   cum-coffee shop with urbane, relaxed, yet busy atmos. Conservatory through
C2   back though not all the plants are real! Next, but by no means least, another
place: **BRAMBLES:** 5 College St. Has similar ambience. Both have good home
bakes, hot dishes and good vegn choices. St Andrews is lucky to have these
wholesome options, but then it is that kind of a town. Both 7 days till
5/5.30pm.

1305   **DUN WHINNY'S, CALLANDER:** Off main st at Glas rd, a welcoming wee (but
MAP 6   not twee) tearoom; not run by wifies. Banoffee pie kind of thing and clootie
C2   dumpling. There's a few new caffs in Callander. This one still ok in my book.

    DUNNET HEAD TEAROOM nr THURSO: 15km N (995/INEXP HIGHLAND
RESTAUS).

THE BEST SCOTCH BAKERS

1306
MAP 5
C2
MAP 4
C3
✓ ✓ **FISHER & DONALDSON, DUNDEE/ST ANDREWS/CUPAR:** Main or original branch in Cupar and 3 in Dundee. Superior contemporary bakers along trad lines – surprising (and a pity) that they haven't gone further, although they do supply a few selected outlets (e.g. Jenners in Edin with pastries and the most excellent Dr Floyd's bread which is as good as anything you could make yourself). Main sq, Cupar; Church St, St Andrews; Whitehall St, 300 Perth Rd and Lochee, Dundee, which is v well served with decent bakers, for example:

1307
MAP 4
C3
MAP 5
C2
✓ **GOODFELLOW AND STEVEN and WALLACE'S, DUNDEE:** G&S have several branches in Dundee, Perth and Fife. Wallaces are famous for their pies and massive bridies, and have branches in Crichton St and Faraday St.

1308
MAP B
D3
✓ **BRADFORD'S:** 245 Sauchiehall St, Glas, and suburban branches in selected areas, i.e. they have not over-expanded; for a bakery chain, some lines seem almost home-made. Certainly better than all the industrial 'home'-bakers around. Individual fruit pies, for example, are uniquely yummy, and the all-important Scotch pie pastry is exemplary. (593/TEAROOMS.)

1309
MAP 1
D3
✓ **WATERSIDE BAKERY, STRATHAVEN, nr LANARK:** 01357 521260. Specialising in huge array of savoury breads: sunflower, Bavarian, sourdough, black bun and, at Christmas, stollen. They also make all their flavoured shortbreads and oatcakes. Good wholesome stuff! Mon-Sat 8am-5.30pm (Sat from 7am!)

1310
MAP 6
C2
✓ **SCOTCH OVEN, CALLANDER:** Opp Royal Hotel in busy touristy main st and one of the best things about it. Good bread, rolls, cakes, the biggest, possibly the best, tattie scones and sublime doughnuts. Also featuring what may be the perfect Scotch pie pastry. This is where to stock up for your walk on the Braes, the other great thing about Callander. Open 7 days.

1311
MAP 4
C3
✓ **McINTYRE'S, PERTH:** 81 South St. This is not the same McIntyres who once made the best morning rolls in Scotland, but all is not lost - the recipe was sold to another bakers (Tower) and this McIntyre's now sell them. Now you know!

1312
MAP 1
C2
✓ **BLACK'S OF DUNOON:** aka Cowal Cottage Bakery at 144 Argyll St, the main st of Dunoon. Popular for aeons and still influenced by the American base that used to be nearby; loads of doughnuts and muffins. The old favourites shortbread, potato scones and the like still draw the queues.

1313
MAP 8
C3
HOUSTON'S OF HAWICK: Nothing too mould-breaking about old Houston's just honest Border baking. They're at 16 Bourtree Pl as you come into Hawick from the Jedburgh rd just as they've always been. It's where I came in, too, to go to school, and I have incl the place where I found an alternative to school dinners, mainly for nostalgic reasons. They do make the best Selkirk bannocks.

1314
MAP 4
B3
BREADALBANE BAKERY, ABERFELDY: 37 Dunkeld St. On rd out of town to Grantully opp petrol stn. Home of Aberfeldy Whisky Cake (a rich fruit job with single malt flavour) and Holyrood Tarts (no, not Hollywood) and brill home-made biscuits, etc.

1315
MAP 2
D2
THE DORNOCH BAKERY, DORNOCH: Behind cathedral, a busy town bakery with a couple of tables in front of the ovens. Great selection of pies (esp fruit pies) and bread (esp milk bread). Often has queues.

1316
MAP 2
D2
ASHER'S, NAIRN: 2 branches at either end of Main St and also in Inverness (Church St), Grantown-on-Spey, Elgin and Forres. Baking on the Moray Firth for 100 years and has esp good bread and rolls. Coffee shops attached.

1317
MAP 5
B3
PILLANS AND SONS, KIRKCALDY: Nr Harbour and end of High St. Here for 100yrs or so turning out their Scottish rolls and cakes and unconventional Scotch pies (let's hope the scions of the family can put up with the early rising) – closed when last we passed so hope they're ok. Nostalgia and good Scots baking.

1318 **ADAMSON'S IN FIFE: PITTENWEEM, ELIE, CRAIL, ANSTRUTHER and**
MAP 5 **CUPAR:** Baking in the kingdom since 1887, Adamson's is one of the few places
C3 that keeps trad bakery going, not succumbing to the creaming, or industrial
D2 yeasting of everything. Where else can you find puggy buns, Hedderwick
D3 buns or raggy biscuits? Mainly small neighbourhood shops – the one in Elie
is out of Dr Finlay's Casebook. Original bake-house in Pittenweem. Go see!

1319 **AITKENS, ABERDEEN:** Glenbervie Rd and Menzies Rd, Torry (a district of Aber
MAP 3 over the br) and 202 Holburn St in city centre. They do fancy cakes, pies and
D3 all the usual, but are mainly notable as the place to get your rowies, the but-
tery rolls which are the Aberdonian contribution to breakfast considered by
many to give the croissant a run for its money. Aitkens rowies send
Aberdonians into raptures all over the world.

1320 **McLARENS, FORFAR:** Town centre next to Queens Hotel. The best in town to
MAP 4 sample the famous Forfar bridie, a meaty shortcrust pastie that'll maybe keep
D3 you going all the way to Aber. **SADDLER'S** make excl cakes esp meringues.

THE BEST ICE CREAM

1321 ✓ ✓ **LUCA'S, MUSSELBURGH, nr EDINBURGH (and EDINBURGH):** 32
MAP 7 High St. Queues out the door in the middle of a Sun afternoon in
B1 February are testament to the enduring popularity of this almost-legendary
ice cream boutique. 3 classic flavours (vanilla, choc and strawberry) and pure
ingredients attract folk from Edin (14km) though there is now a branch in
Edin at 16 Morningside Rd, a more designery Italian version (223/CAFÉS). In
cafe thro the back, basic snacks, and you might have to wait, in Edin cafe
upstairs more pizza/pasta and smart sandwiches. Mon-Sat 9am-10pm, Sun
10.30am-10pm. Edin hrs: 7 days 9am-11pm (10pm wint).

1322 ✓ ✓ **MANCINI'S, THE ROYAL CAFÉ, AYR:** 11 New Rd, the rd to Prestwick.
MAP 1 Ice cream that's taken seriously, entered for competitions and usual-
C3 ly wins. Family biz for aeons. 300 flavours at their disposal, always new ones.
Try apple crumble or their famous honeypot. Their sorbets taste better than
the fruit they're made from. They were first with the ice-cream toastie. These
Mancinis are champions of ice cream. 9.30am-11.00pm; cl Thu in winter.

1323 ✓ **THE CHOCOLATE BOX, BIGGAR:** The Taylors had been making ice cream
MAP 8 here before the Italians thought of it: the original 'family blocks' are in the
A2 café across the square, but the real vanilla scoop is here in their confectionery
shop (where the additional variety of home-made tablet, fudge and chocolates is waist-expanding). 7 days, 9-5pm (opens at 1pm Sun).

1324 ✓ **JANETTA'S, ST ANDREWS:** 31 South St. Family firm since 1908. There are
MAP 5 two Janetta's, but the one to adore is opp the Byre Theatre. Once only
C2 vanilla, Americans up for the Open asked for other flavours. Now there are 52,
incl the famous irn-bru sorbet. Also frozen yogs. Janetta's is another good reason for being a student at St Andrews. 7 days 9am-6pm.

1325 ✓ **CALDWELL'S, INNERLEITHEN:** On the High St in this ribbon of a town
MAP 8 between Peebles and Gala they've been making ice cream since 1911.
B2 Purists will approve of the fact that they still make only vanilla – chocolate
powder on top if you want. The shop sells everything from Blue Nun to bicycles. Mon-Fri till 8.30pm, Sat/Sun 7.30pm.

1326 **VISOCCHI'S, BROUGHTY FERRY/KIRRIEMUIR:** Orig from St Andrews; ice-
MAP 4 cream makers for 30 years and still with the café they opened in Kirriemuir in
C3 1953. On the main drag of the Angus town (1449/GLENS), it's a hang-out for
everybody. Broughty Ferry (Dundee's seaside suburb) more middle-class, with
a contemporary menu; home-made pasta as well as the peach melba. But
whatever comes and goes, the ice cream will go on forever. 7 days
(1068/DUNDEE EAT AND DRINK).

1327 **CASA MARCHINI, ABERDEEN:** Gt Western Rd. New premises since last edi-
MAP 3 tion, past the Amatola hotel, then beside the shops. Superior ice cream in
D3 multi flavours and ice-cream cakes to superior trad Italian recipes. This place
should be more widely recognised; it licks all the others in Aber. – Sun-Wed
until 5.30pm, Thurs-Sat until 8.30pm.

1328 **THE ALLAN WATER CAFÉ, BRIDGE OF ALLAN:** An old-fashioned café in an
MAP 6 old-fashioned town, near the eponymous br in the main st since 1902.
C3 Fabulously good fish 'n' chips and ice cream. The former now dispensed from
a modernised shop next door. Ice cream (only vanilla) in the old woody café
that smells like a real caff should. 7 days, 8am-9pm.

1329 **COLPI'S, MILNGAVIE, GLASGOW:** Opp Black Bull in Milngavie centre (pron
MAP B Mullguy) and there since 1928. Many consider this to be Glas's finest. Only
xC1 vanilla at the cone counter but strawb/choc flake/amaretto/honeycomb to
take home. There's another branch in Clydebank. Till 9pm, 7 days.

1330 **TORTOLANO'S, UDDINGSTON:** 29 Main St. 15km E of city via M74,
MAP 1 Uddingston t/off, at the lights where you turn for Bothwell Castle
D3 (1618/RUINS). Tiny confectioners/ice-cream shop with proper biscuit cones as
an option and 5 flavours (try the 'double cream') all home made by
Montecassino's Mr Tortolano. Their loss, definitely our weight gain.

1331 **NARDINI'S, LARGS:** On the Esplanade. The debate about best ice cream con-
MAP 1 tinues and this, from the celebrated Nardini empire in particular (1275/CAFÉS),
C3 but summer 1997 I had a pistachio and vanilla doublescoop on the esplanade
one balmy evening as the boat came in from Cumbrae; all was well with the
world. This ice cream was part of the magic. In summer 1999 well … it was
exactly the same.

3132 **DRUMMUIR FARM, COLLIN, nr DUMFRIES:** 5km off A75 (Carlisle/Annan) rd
MAP 9 E of Dumfries on B724 (nr Clarencefield). A real farm producing real ice cream
C3 – 'the original' still the most popular (it's creamier than vanilla), but also but-
terscotch and honeycomb. Apr-Sept noon-5.30pm. Cl Mon except July/Aug.
W/ends only in winter.

1333 **CREAM O' GALLOWAY, RAINTON, nr GATEHOUSE OF FLEET:** 01557 814040.
MAP 9 A75 take Sandgreen exit 2km, then left at sign for Carrick. Originally a dairy
B3 farm producing cheese, now you can watch them making the creamy con-
coctions which you find all over in 'good shops'. Nature trail and playground.
Apr-Oct 11am-6pm.

1334 **CORVI'S, BO'NESS:** Seaview Pl, opp car park with tourist info. Downhome fish
MAP 6 'n' chip shop that serves home-made vanilla or strawberry ice cream in
D3 premises that look like an extended version of someone's parlour. Eat in or
take away – the fish supper is the local choice. Mon-Tues 11am-6.30pm, Thurs-
Sat 11am-7.30pm.

1335 **CAPALDI'S, BRORA:** Louis has retired but his legacy lives on! Drift away on a
MAP 2 blue cloud (aniseed flavour) and take away an ice cream cake. Or just try some
D2 rhubarb delight. 7 days; 10am-9pm (Sun from 8am!).

BEN LEDI CAFÉ, CALLANDER: Main St (1282/CAFÉS).

1336 ✓ ✓ ✓ **VALVONA AND CROLLA, EDINBURGH:** 19 Elm Row, nr top of
MAP A Leith Walk. Since 1934, an Edin institution, the shop you show
E1 visitors. Full of smells, genial, knowledgeable staff and a floor-to-ceiling range
of cheese (Ital/Scot, etc.), meats, oils, wines and more. Fresh veg trucked in
from Milan markets, on-premises bakery, great caffe/bar (109/ITALIAN RESTAUS).
Also demos, tastings, Fringe venue. Second to none.

1337 ✓ **GLASS & THOMPSON, EDINBURGH:** 2 Dundas St. Exemplary and con-
MAP A temporary New Town provisioner. Selective choice of Mediterranean –
C2 style goodies to eat or take away and bread/pâtisserie; also those all-
important New Town dinner party essentials. Report: 213/TEAROOMS.

1338 ✓ **GOURMET PASTA, EDINBURGH:** 52 Morningside Rd. As the name sug-
MAP A gests, this pasta kitchen/shop in the dense dinner-party zone of
xC4 Bruntsfield sells mainly freshly-made pasta and various sauces, as good as (or
better than) you can make yourself. Also tortes, roulades, etc. Cl Sun.

1339 ✓ **SARTI'S, GLASGOW:** 113 Wellington St. Definitive corner of little Italy – a
MAP B deli/tratt here and another eating place/wine shop in Bath St (523/ITAL-
D3 IAN RESTAUS). Feels like Italy.

1340 ✓ **FINDHORN COMMUNITY SHOP, FINDHORN:** Serving the new age
MAP 3 township of the Findhorn Community and therefore pursuing a consci-
A1 entious app, this has become an exemplary and v high quality deli, worth the
detour from the A96 Inverness-Elgin rd even if you have apprehensions about
their 'thing'. Packed and carefully selected shelves; as much for pleasurable
eating as for healthy. Till 6pm. (W/ends 5pm.) Cl Tue am.

1341 **LUPE PINTO'S, EDINBURGH:** 24 Leven St nr Kings Theatre. Unusual Latin deli
MAP A (ie Mexican, Central American, Spanish). Where to go for chorizo, manchego
C4 and 20 kinds of tequila. T/away incl home-made burritos and the usual Tex-
Mex. 10am-6pm. Cl Suns.

1342 **PECKHAM'S, CENTRAL STATION, GLASGOW:** Best of several branches, most
MAP B remarkable for its location in Glas's main station. From early train times to
D4 11pm (midnight Fri/Sat, 10pm Sun), they've got everything you need from
staples to fine wines and cheeses and a good range of up-market nibbles and
quick meals. Their branch at Edinburgh Waverley is somehow not on the
same … track. The better Edin branch is at 155 Bruntsfield Pl.

1343 **GRASSROOTS, GLASGOW:** 48 Woodlands Rd, nr Charing Cross. First-class
MAP B vegn food and provisions store, everything chemically unaltered and envi-
B2 ronmentally-friendly. Gr breads and sandwiches for lunch and the best organ-
ic fruit/veg range in town. Now with vegn restau round the corner (580/GLAS
VEGN). 7days till 6pm (7pm Thur, 3pm Sun).

1344 **NESBITS, DOLLAR:** Main st of cosy town which nestles round its Academy
MAP 6 and its glorious glen (1800/GLEN AND RIVER WALKS). Sort of town you'd expect a
D3 half-decent deli and this is it. Usual stuff mainly, but hot bread and cheese
selection. Academy kids pig out on too much pocket money. Till 8pm.

1345 **BUTLER & CO, ST ANDREWS:** 10 Church St. Excl deli by the people who have
MAP 5 the seafood restau in St Monans (1253/SEAFOOD RESTAUS). Good range of
C2 Scottish and other cheeses. Cl Suns.

1346 **GORDON AND MACPHAIL, ELGIN:** South St. Purveyors of fine wines, cheeses,
MAP 3 meats, Mediterranean goodies, unusual breads and other epicurean delights
B2 to the good burghers of Elgin for nigh on a century. Traditional shopkeeping,
in the style of the 'family grocer'. G & M are widely known as bottlers of lesser-
known high-quality malts ('Connoisseurs' range') – on sale here. Some rare real
ales by the bottle too. Mon-Sat 9am-5.15pm.

1347 **THE FOOD HAMPER, HADDINGTON:** Town centre, nr clock tower. Country
MAP 7 town provisions – but for locals and visitors, shopping here is still preferable
B1 to driving to Edin. Cl Sun.

1348 **THE OLIVE TREE, PEEBLES:** 7 High St. Small emporium packed with wide
MAP 8 selection of European groceries plus local delicacies: beer, honey, cheese ad
B2 infinitum – specialises in farmhouse and unpasteurised cheeses.

1349 **MULL or TOBERMORY CHEDDAR:** From Sgriob-Ruadh Farm (pron 'Skibrua'). Comes in big 50lb cheeses and 1lb truckles. Good, strong cheddar, one of the v best in the UK. The Ingle Smokehouse in Perth make a fine oak-smoked cheddar. Loch Arthur from Beeswing in Dumfries is a tangy organic cheddar.

1350 **DUNSYRE BLUE/LANARK BLUE:** Made by Humphrey Errington at Carnwath. Next to Stilton, Dunsyre (made from the unpasteurised milk of Ayrshire cows) is the best blue in the UK. It is soft, rather like Dolcelatte. Lanark, the original, is Scotland's Roquefort and made from ewes' milk. Both can vary but are excellent. Go on, live dangerously – unpasteurise your life.

1351 **STICHILL/KELSAE:** Hand-made hard cheeses from Brenda Leddie near Kelso. Rich, hard and crumbly cheeses, found only on the more informed cheese-boards. My own favourites of the new Scottish cheeses.

1352 **CABOC/CROWDIE/GRUTH DHU:** Widely available and established soft cheeses from Highland Fine Cheeses in Tain (*see below*). Crowdie is tradition-al cottage or crofters cheese, v basic; others made from double cream rolled in oatmeal/pepper. Rich and delicious; usually avail in wee 'logs'.

1353 **CAIRNMORE:** A hard, tangy, cheddary cheese from Sorbie in Wigtownshire surprisingly made from ewes' milk, smoked or unsmoked.

AND WHERE TO FIND THEM

All the delis mentioned will have good selections (esp Valvona's). Also:

1354
MAP A
D3,xC4
MAP B
xB1
✓ ✓ **IAIN MELLIS, EDINBURGH & GLASGOW:** 30a Victoria St & 205 Bruntsfield Pl (Edin) and 492 Gr Western Rd (Glas). A real cheese-monger. Smell and taste before you buy. Cheeses from all over the UK in prime condition. Daily and seasonal specials. Cl Sun.

1355
MAP 3
D3
✓ ✓ **THE BIG CHEESE, ABERDEEN:** 22 Belmont St. Linda Davidson's rather fab deli and cheese shop where v big cheeses from Scotland and the UK are piled up around you. Snack bar opened '98 with (no surprise) fab cheeseboard and ploughman's lunch. 9.30am-5.30pm. Cl Sun.

1356
MAP A
B1
✓ **HERBIE, EDINBURGH:** 66 Raeburn Pl. Excellent selection. Clarissa Dickson-Wright is a big fan. As usual she's right. As with Scottish cheeses, it's practically impossible here to find a Brie or a blue in less than perfect con-dition. All too moreish.

1357
MAP 4
C3
✓ **MACDONALDS CHEESE SHOP, RATTRAY nr BLAIRGOWRIE:** 2km Blairgowrie on rd to Glenshee and Braemar. Discreet 'shack' you could eas-ily miss, but don't! Extraordinary selection of cheese esp Scottish and Swiss – only shop selling complete wheels of gruyere in Scotland. 7 days till 6pm.

1358
MAP 1
C3
ISLAND CHEESES, ARRAN: 5km Brodick, rd to castle and Corrie. Excellent selection of their own (the well-known cheddars but many others esp crowdie with garlic and hand-rolled cream cheeses) and others. See them being made. 7 days.

1359
MAP 2
B3
WEST HIGHLAND DAIRY, ACHMORE, nr PLOCKTON: 01599 577203. Excellent farm dairy shop selling variety of their own cheeses from ewes'/goats'/cows' milk; yogurt, ice cream and cheesecakes. Open AYR 'dawn to dusk'. Signed from village.

1360
MAP A
C2
JENNERS DEPARTMENT STORE, EDINBURGH: Princes St, top-floor.

1361
MAP 4
B2
HOUSE OF BRUAR nr BLAIR ATHOLL: Roadside emporium (1941/CRAFTS).

1362
MAP 2
C3
PETER MACLENNAN, FORT WILLIAM: 28 High St.

1363
MAP 2
C4
SCOTTISH SPECIALITY FOOD, NORTH BALLACHULISH: By Leven Hotel.

THE BEST DISTILLERY TOURS

The process is basically the same in every distillery, but some are more atmospheric and some have more interesting tours, like these:

1364
MAP 1
A3

THE ISLAY MALTS: In one day you can visit several of Scotland's most impressive distilleries and sample their gr malts. The distilleries here look like distilleries ought to. **LAGAVULIN** (01496 302400) and **LAPHROAIG** (01496 302418) are both nr Pt Ellen. They offer fascinating tours, by appointment, where your guide will lay on the anecdotes as well as the process and you get a feel for the life and history as well as the product of these world-famous places. At Laphroaig you can join their 'Friend' scheme (free) and own a piece of their hallowed ground. **BUNNAHABHAIN** and **CAOL ILA** nr Pt Askaig, **BRUICHLADDICH** on rd to Pt Charlotte, has been closed since '97 but we live in hope. **BOWMORE** has professional, more commercial, 1hr tours regularly (incl video show and the usual dram). **ARDBEG** (nr Port Ellen) how the newest visitor centre – and it opens on Sunday. All these distilleries are in settings that entirely justify the romantic hyperbole of their advertising. Worth seeing from the o/side as well as the floor.

1365
MAP 3
B2

STRATHISLA, KEITH: 01542 783044. The oldest working distillery in the Highlands, literally on the strath of the Isla river and methinks the most evocative atmos of all the Speyside distilleries. Recent refurb makes this an even classier halt. Used as the 'heart' of Chivas Regal, the malt not commonly available is still a fine dram. March-Nov, Mon-Sat 9.30am- 4pm; Sunday 12.30-4pm.

1366
MAP 2
B3

TALISKER, CARBOST, ISLE OF SKYE: From Sligachan-Dunvegan rd (A863) take B8009 for Carbost and Glen Brittle along the S side of L Harport for 5km. Skye's only distillery; since 1830 they've been making this classic after-dinner malt from barley and the burn that runs off the Hawkhill behind. A dram before the informative 40min tour. Good visitor centre. Apr-Oct 9am-4.30pm (winter 2-4.30pm). Cl w/ends except Sats July-Sept. Gr gifts nearby (1931/CRAFT SHOPS).

1367
MAP 7
B1

GLENKINCHIE, PENCAITLAND, nr EDINBURGH: 01875 342004. Only 25km from city centre (via A68 and A6093 before Pathhead), so popular. Founded in 1837 in a peaceful, pastoral place (it's 3km from the village) with its own bowling green; a country trip as well as a whisky tour. They have a 'silent season', so check (tho they still do a tour). State-of-the-art visitor centre. May-Sep tours daily until 4pm, Oct-Mar Mon-Fri until 4pm.

1368
MAP 4
B2

EDRADOUR, nr PITLOCHRY: Claims to be the smallest distillery in Scotland, producing single malts for blends since 1825 and limited quantities of the Edradour (since 1986) as well as the House of Lords' own brand. Guided tour of charming cottage complex every 20min. 4km from Pitlochry off Kirkmichael rd, A924; signed after Moulin village. Mar-Oct daily until 5pm. Nov-Dec Mon-Sat until 4pm cl Jan-Feb.

1369
MAP 4
B3

GLENTURRET, nr CRIEFF: 2km from town off A85 to Comrie. A village has almost been built around this quaint distillery, the oldest in Scotland (1775) with award-winning visitor centre. Continuous tours, restau and shop with superior range of branded products and exemplary marketing. Self-service and waitress restau. The whisky itself has a smoky, roasted aroma; it's superb in its older bottlings, e.g. 1967-72. Open AYR Mon-Sat 9.30am-4.30pm (last tour), and Sun from noon. Jan, Mon-Fri 11.30am-2.30pm.

1370

HIGHLAND PARK, KIRKWALL, ORKNEY: 2km from town on main A961 rd S to S Ronaldsay. The whisky is great and the tour one of the best. The most northerly whisky in a class and a bottle of its own. You walk through the floor maltings and you can touch the warm barley and fair smell the peat. Good combination of the industrial and trad Mar-Dec w/days (2-3.30pm only in winter).

THE BEST OF THE SPEYSIDE WHISKY TRAIL: *Well signposted but bewildering number of tours, though by no means at every distillery. Many are in rather featureless industrial complexes and settings. These are the best along with Strathisla (see above):*

1371 **THE GLENLIVET, MINMORE:** 01542 783220. Starting as an illicit dram cele-
MAP 3 brated as far S as Edin, George Smith licensed the brand in 1824 and founded
B2 this distillery in 1858, registering the already mighty name so that anyone else
had to use a prefix. After various successions and mergers, independence was
lost in 1978 when Seagrams took over. The famous Josie's Well, from which the
water springs, is underground and not shown, but small parties and a walk-
through which is not on a gantry make the tour as satisfying and as popular,
esp with Americans, as the product. Excellent reception centre with
bar/restau and shop. Apr-Oct, 10am-4pm; till 6pm July/Aug. Sundays 12.30-
4pm.

1372 **GLENFIDDICH, DUFFTOWN:** O/side town on the A941 to Craigellachie by the
MAP 3 ruins of Balvenie Castle. Well-oiled tourist operation and the only distillery
B2 where you can see the whisky bottled on the premises; indeed, the whole
process from barley to bar. Also the only major distillery that's free (incl dram).
AYR 9.30am-4.30pm not w/ends in winter. On the same rd there's a chance to
see a whisky-related industry/craft that hasn't changed in decades. The **SPEY-
SIDE COOPERAGE** is 1km from Craigellachie. You watch those poor guys from
the gantry (no chance to slack). Ayr Mon-Fri 9.30am-4.30pm (also Sats in
summer 9.30am-4pm)

1373 **GLEN GRANT, ROTHES:** In Rothes on the A941 Elgin to Perth rd. A distillery
MAP 3 tour with an added attraction viz the grds and orchard reconstructed around
B2 the shallow bowl of the glen of the burn that runs through the distillery. Tour
vouchers can be used there to take a dram in the delightful Dram Pavilion.
Mar-Oct 10-4pm (till 5pm June-Sept), from 11.30pm on Sun.

1374 **CARDHU, CARRON:** Off B9102 from Craigellachie to Grantown through
MAP 3 deepest Speyside, a small if charming distillery with its own community, a
B2 millpond, picnic tables, etc. Owned by United Distillers, Cardhu is the 'heart of
Johnny Walker' (which, amazingly, has another 30 malts in it). 9.30am-4.30pm,
Dec-Feb restricted hrs, check local TO. Mar-Nov, Mon-Fri.

1375 **DALLAS DHU, nr FORRES:** Not really nr the Spey (3km S of Forres on B9010)
MAP 3 and no longer a working distillery (ceased 1983), but instant history provided
A2 by HS and you don't have to go round on a tour. The wax workers are a bit
spooky; the product itself is more life-like. Cl Thu afternoons/Fri in winter. HS

WHERE TO FIND THE BEST SELECTION OF MALTS
GLASGOW

THE CASK AND STILL: 154 Hope St.

THE BON ACCORD: 153 North St.

EDINBURGH

BENNETS: 8 Leven St by Kings Theatre.

KAYS BAR: 39 Jamaica St.

THE BOW BAR: 80 West Bow.

CADENHEADS: 172 Canongate. The shop with the lot.

CANNY MAN'S: 237 Morningside Rd.

SCOTCH MALT WHISKY SOCIETY: The Vaults, 87 Giles St, Leith. Your search
will end here. More a club (with membership) but visitors must be signed in.

REST OF SCOTLAND

THE BORESTONE BAR, STIRLING: St Ninians, Bannockburn rd 2km from centre. Staggering range of malts in truly authentic bar on a r/bout o/side Stirling.
Even if few folk seem to drink them here, this v typical Scottish pub should be
a must on any whisky trail.

LOCHSIDE HOTEL, BOWMORE, ISLAY: More Islay malts than you ever imagined in friendly local near the distillery. Malt whisky w/ends.

ARISAIG HOTEL, ARISAIG, nr MALLAIG: On the seafront. Small, civilised
lounge and busy local. 100 malts move betw the bars.

KNOCKINAAM LODGE, PORTPATRICK: Comfortable country-house hotel; esp good lowland selection incl the (extinct) local Bladnoch (812/SW HOTELS).

CROMLIX HOUSE HOTEL, DUNBLANE: Excl and not overly expensive whisky list after dinner in civilised setting (829/CENTRAL HOTELS).

KINLOCH HOUSE HOTEL nr BLAIRGOWRIE (894/PERTHSHIRE BEST HOTELS).

SETTLE INN, STIRLING: Carefully selected shelf of malts that almost exactly matches the list I have recommended. Several Balvenies for example.

OBAN INN, OBAN: Good mix of customers, whisky and ale.

FISHERMAN'S TAVERN, BROUGHTY FERRY: (1060/DUNDEE EAT AND DRINK).

LOCK INN, FORT AUGUSTUS: Canalside setting, good food and plenty whisky.

CLACHAIG INN, GLENCOE: Over 100 malts to go with the range of ales and the range of folk that come here to drink after the hills (1183/BLOODY GOOD PUBS).

THE DROVER'S INN, INVERARNAN: Same as above, with over 100 to choose from and the rt atmos to drink them in (1178/BLOODY GOOD PUBS).

DUNAIN PARK HOTEL, INVERNESS: After dinner in one of the best places to eat hereabouts, there's a serious malts list to mull over (944/HIGHLAND HOTELS).

THE BAR AT THE CRAIGELLACHIE HOTEL: Whiskies arranged around the cosy bar of this essential Speyside hotel and the river below (915/NE HOTELS).

ROYAL HOTEL, KINGUSSIE: Main st of small town S of Aviemore. Gr local (1195/REAL ALE) and astonishing range of whiskies.

PETER MACLENNAN, FORT WILLIAM: Main st, long-established emporium with big whisky section.

HOTEL EILEAN IARMAIN, SKYE: Also known as the Isleornsay Hotel (2122/ISLAND HOTELS); not the biggest range but one of the best places to drink (it).

LOCH FYNE WHISKIES, INVERARAY: Beyond the church on the A83 a shop with 400 malts to choose from in various sizes and disguises; and whisky ware.

SLIGACHAN HOTEL, SKYE: 01478 650204. On A87 (A850) 11km S of Portree. 81 malts in Seamus' huge cabin bar. Good real-ale selection; mid-Apr, Sept festivals. Adj bunkhouse, shop, laundry, mt exhibition due for 1998.

GORDON & MACPHAIL, ELGIN: The whisky provisioner and bottlers of the Connoisseurs brand you see in other shops and bars all over. From these humble beginnings over 100yrs ago, they now supply their exclusive and rarity range to the world. 9am-5.15pm. Cl Sun.

THE WHISKY SHOP, DUFFTOWN: The whisky shop in the main st (by the clock-tower) at the heart of whisky country. Within a few miles of numerous distilleries and their sales operations, this place stocks all the product (incl many halfs). Apr-Oct 10am-9pm, Sun afternoons.

CAIRNGORM WHISKY CENTRE, INVERDRUIE, nr AVIEMORE: On main rd from Aviemore, nr Coylumbridge and adj Rothiemurcus Vistor Centre. Whisky emporium with over 500 for sale. Tasting rm (most afternoons). Open 7 days.

THE BEST MALTS AND WHEN TO DRINK THEM

Obviously, opinions vary. The following list is compiled from the consensus of several whisky buffs and 'authorities', and God knows there are plenty of them. Vintages make a discernible difference to the connoisseur; the whiskies here are fine in any of their readily available forms.

BEFORE DINNER

Bruichladdich	ISLAY	(pron 'Brew ich laddie')
Caol Ila	ISLAY	(pron 'Coal eela')
Glenmorangie	SPEYSIDE	
Tomintoul-Glenlivet	SPEYSIDE	

AFTER DINNER

Aberlour	SPEYSIDE	
Ardbeg	ISLAY	
Bowmore	ISLAY	
Bunnahabhain	ISLAY	(pron 'Bun a havan')
Glenfarclas	SPEYSIDE	
Highland Park	ORKNEY	
Lagavulin	ISLAY	(pron 'Laga voolin')
Laphroaig	ISLAY	(pron 'La froig')
Talisker	SKYE	
Tamdhu	SPEYSIDE	(pron 'Tam do')

ANYTIME

Balvenie	SPEYSIDE
Cragganmore	SPEYSIDE
Glenfiddich	SPEYSIDE
Glenkinchie	LOWLAND
Glenlivet	SPEYSIDE
Linkwood	SPEYSIDE
Macallan	SPEYSIDE
Springbank	CAMPBELTOWN

SECTION 6

Outdoor Places

THE BEST GARDENS

1376
MAP 1
C2
✔ ✔ **THE YOUNGER BOTANIC GARDEN, BENMORE:** 12km Dunoon on the A815 to Strachur. An 'outstation' of the Royal Botanic in Edin, gifted to the nation by Harry Younger in 1928, but the first plantations dating from 1820. Walks clearly marked through formal grds, woody grounds and the 'pinetum' where the air is often so sweet and spicy it can seem like the v elixir of life. Redwood avenue, terraced hill sides, views; a grd of different moods and fine proportions. Good walk nearby (1812/WOODLAND WALKS). Café. Apr-Oct 10-6pm. ADMN

1377
MAP 1
C2
✔ ✔ **CRARAE, INVERARAY:** 16km SE on A83 to Lochgilphead. The famous grds (pron 'cray') on the wooded banks of L Fyne were landscaped long ago around the gushing glen, and now seem as vast and lush as Borneo. 3 routes are marked (easiest takes 45mins). Riotous rhodies in May, gigantic hogweed in August and arbour after arbour in every season. Open AYR. Summer 9am-6pm, winter daylight hrs. ADMN

1378
MAP 2
B2
✔ ✔ **INVEREWE, POOLEWE:** on A832, 80km S of Ullapool. The world-famous grds on a promontory of L Ewe. First started in 1862, Osgood Mackenzie made it his life's work in 1883 and it continues with large crowds coming to admire his efforts. Helped by the ameliorating effect of the Gulf Stream, the 'wild' grd became the model for many others. The guided tours (1.30pm Mon-Fri Apr-Sept) are probably the best way to get the most out of this extensive gdn. No 'keep off the grass' signs but you feel you should anyway. Open AYR. ADMN

1379
MAP 3
C3
✔ ✔ **CRATHES, nr BANCHORY, ROYAL DEESIDE:** 25km W of Aber and just off A93. One of the most interesting tower houses (1663/COUNTRY HOUSES) surrounded by exceptional topiary and walled grds of inspired design and tranquil atmos. Keen gardeners will be in their scented heaven. The Golden Garden (after Gertrude Jekyll) works particularly well and there's a wild grd beyond the old wall that many people miss. All in all, a v *House and Garden* experience. Grounds open AYR 9.30am-sunset. NTS ADMN

1380
MAP 4
B4
✔ ✔ **DRUMMOND CASTLE GARDENS, MUTHILL, nr CRIEFF:** Signed from A822, 2km from Muthill and then up a long avenue, the most exquisite formal grds viewed first from the terrace by the house. A boxwood parterre of a vast St Andrew's Cross in yellow and red (esp antirrhinums and roses), the Drummond colours, with extraordinary sundial centrepiece; 5 gardeners keep every leaf in place. 7 days May-Oct 2-5pm (last adm). House not open to the public. ADMN

1381
MAP 9
A3
✔ ✔ **LOGAN BOTANICAL GARDENS, nr SANDHEAD, S of STRANRAER:** 16km S of Stranraer by A77/A716 and 2km on from Sandhead. Remarkable outstation of the Edin Botanics amongst sheltering woodland in the mild SW. Compact and full of pleasant surprises. Less crowded than other 'exotic' grds. Their 'soundwands' giving commentary on demand make it all v interesting. Salad bar not bad. The Gunnera Bog is quite extraterrestrial. Mar-Oct; 7 days, 9.30am-6pm. ADMN

1382
MAP 8
A2
✔ **DAWYCK, STOBO, nr PEEBLES:** On B712 Moffat rd off the A72 Biggar rd from Peebles, 2km from Stobo. Another outstation of the Edin Botanics; a 'recent' acquisition, though tree planting here goes back 300 yrs. Sloping grounds around the gurgling Scrape burn which trickles into the Tweed. Landscaped woody pathways for meditative walks. Famous for shrubs and blue Himalayan poppies. The chapel is closed. Gr walk on Drovers rd, 2km on Stobo Rd before entrance. Tiny basic tearoom. Mar-Oct 10am-6pm. ADMN

1383
MAP 1
C1
✔ **ANGUS' GARDEN, TAYNUILT:** 7km from village (which is 12km from Oban on the A85) along the Glen Lonan rd. Take first rt after Barguillen Grd Centre. A grd laid out by the family who own the centre in memory of their son Angus, a soldier, who was killed in Cyprus. On the slopes around a small loch brimful of lilies and ducks. An informal mix of the tended and the uncultivated, a more poignant remembrance is hard to imagine as you while an hr away in this peaceful place. Open AYR. HONESTY BOX

1384   ✓ **ARDUAINE GARDEN, nr KIMELFORD:** 28km S of Oban on A816, one of
MAP 1   Argyll's undiscovered arcadias gifted to the NTS and brought to wider
B2   attention. Creation of the microclimate in which the rich, diverse vegetation
has flourished, influenced by Osgood Mackenzie of Inverewe and its restoration a testimony to 20yrs hard labour by the Wright brothers. Let's hope that
the ongoing wrangle betw the surviving Wright brother and the NTS might
be resolved. Enter/park by L Melfort hotel, gate 100m. Until dusk.

1385   ✓ **ACHAMORE GARDENS, ISLE OF GIGHA:** 1km from ferry. Walk or cycle
MAP 1   from ferry (bike hire at post office at top of ferry rd); an easy day trip. The
B3   'big house' on the island set in 65 acres. Lush tropical plants mingle with
rhodies that flourish early (Feb-March): all due to the mild climate and head
gardener Malcolm McNeill's devotion. 2 marked walks (40mins/2hrs) start
from the walled gdn (green route takes in the sea view of Islay and Jura). The
sheer density and variety of shrubs, pond plants and trees is revealed as you
meander around this enchanting spot. Leaflet guides in jam jar at entrance.
Open AYR. (2112/MAGICAL ISLANDS.)   ADMN

1386   **PRIORWOOD, MELROSE:** Next to Melrose Abbey, a tranquil secret grd
MAP 8   behind high walls which specialises in growing flowers and plants for drying.
C2   Picking, drying and arranging is continuously in progress. Samples for sale.
Run by enthusiasts on behalf of the NTS, they're always willing to talk stamens
with you. Also includes an historical apple orchard with trees through the
ages. Heavenly jelly on sale. Mon-Sat 10am-5.30pm; Sun 1.30-5.30pm. Cl 4pm
wint.   NTS ADMN

1387   **KAILZIE GARDENS, PEEBLES:** On B7062 Traquair rd. Informal woodland grds
MAP 8   just out of town; not extensive but eminently strollable. Old-fashioned roses
B2   and wilder bits. Some poor birds in cages and the odd peacock. Excellent
courtyard teashop (1284/TEAROOMS). Kids' corner. Apr-Oct.   ADMN

1388   **PITMEDDEN GARDEN, nr ELLON:** 35km N of Aber and 10km W of the main
MAP 3   A92. Formal French grds recreated in 1950s on site of Sir Alex Seaton's 17th-
D3   century ones. The 4 gr parterres, 3 based on designs for grds at Holyrood
Palace, are best viewed from the terrace. Charming farmhouse 'museum' has
also been somewhat transplanted. For lovers of symmetry and an orderly uni-
verse only. May-Sept 10am-5.30pm.   NTS ADMN

1389   **CANDACRAIG GARDENS, STRATHDON:** On A944 from Kildrummy to Alford
MAP 3   which follows the Don through deep Aberdeenshire. A private walled cottage
B3   grd and secret world in the wild country. Gallery has changing exhibits on a
horticultural theme. A nice place to while away an afternoon (and 2 cottages
for accom if you want to stay longer). May-Sept 10am-5pm, Sun 2-6pm.

1390   **PITTODRIE HOUSE nr INVERURIE:** An exceptional walled grd in the grounds
MAP 3   of Pittodrie House Hotel at Chapel of Garioch in Aberdeenshire (912/NE
C3   HOTELS). 500m from house and largely unvisited by most of the guests, this
secret and sheltered haven is both a kitchen grd and a place for meditations
and reflections (and possibly wedding photos).

1391   **ARDKINGLAS WOODLAND, CAIRNDOW:** Off the A83 L Lomond to Inveraray
MAP 1   rd. Through village to signed car park and these mature woodlands in the
C2   grounds of Ardkinglas House on the southern bank nr the head of L Fyne. Fine
pines include the 'tallest tree in Britain'. Magical at dawn or dusk.
     HONESTY BOX

1392   **THE HYDROPONICUM, ACHILTIBUIE:** The 'Garden of the Future'; a weird
MAP 2   indoor waterworld. Geraniums cluster round the pond by the café and other
C2   plants thrive in the microclimates. Apr-Sep. Tours: hourly. Growing kits to buy;
so you can have strawberries at Christmas.   ADMN

1393   **ARD-DARAICH HILL GARDEN, ARDGOUR:** 3 km S Ardgour at Corran Ferry
MAP 2   (2185/JOURNEYS) on A861 to Strontian. Private, labour of love 'hill' and wild gar-
B4   den which you are at liberty to wander in. Specialising in rhodies, shrubs,
trees. Nursery/small gdn centre. 01855 841248.

ROYAL BOTANIC GARDEN, EDINBURGH: 352/OTHER ATTRACTIONS.

BOTANIC GARDEN and KIBBLE PALACE, GLASGOW: 702/OTHER ATTRAC-
TIONS.

THE BEST COUNTRY PARKS

1394   ✓ **DRUMLANRIG CASTLE, THORNHILL, nr DUMFRIES:** 01848 330248. On
MAP 9   A76, 7km N of Thornhill in the W Borders in whose romance and history
C2   it's steeped, much more than merely a country park; spend a good day, both
inside the castle and in the grounds. Apart from the art collection
(Rembrandts, Leonardos, Holbeins) and the Craft Courtyard (1950/CRAFT
SHOPS), the outdoor delights include: woodland and riverside walks, an adventure
playground, the 'Working Forge' and bike hire for further afield explorations
along the Nith etc. Open May-Aug; Mon-Sun 11am-4.15pm.

1395   ✓ **MUIRSHEIL, nr LOCHWINNOCH:** Via Largs (A760) or Glas (M8, jnct 29
MAP 1   A737 then A760 5km S of Johnstone). N from village on Kilmacolm rd for
C3   3km then signed. Muirshiel is name given to wider area, but park proper
begins 6km on rd along the Calder valley. Despite proximity of conurbation
(Pt Glas is over the hill), this is a wild and enchanting place for walking/picnics
etc. Trails marked to waterfall and summit views. Extensive 'events' programme:
enquiries@muirsheil.sol.co.uk Escape! (483/CAMPING.)

1396   **MUGDOCK COUNTRY PARK, nr MILNGAVIE:** Another marvellous park v
MAP 1   close to Glas reached by train to Milngavie then bus, or by car to either of 3
D2   car parks around the vast site. Highly recommended. *For more info and directions,
see* 713/CITY WALKS.

1397   **JOHN MUIR COUNTRY PARK, nr DUNBAR, EAST LOTHIAN:** Named after the
MAP 7   19th-century conservationist who founded America's National Parks (and the
B1   Sierra Club) and who was born in Dunbar. This swathe of coastline to the W of
the town (known locally as Tyninghame) is an important estuarine nature
reserve but is good for family walks and beachcombing. Can enter via B6370
off A198 to N Berwick or by 'cliff-top' trail from Dunbar (1583/WILDLIFE).

1398   **STRATHCLYDE PARK, between HAMILTON and MOTHERWELL:** 15km SE of
MAP 1   Glas. Take M8/A725 interchange or M74/jnct 5 or 6. Scotland's most popular
D3   country park, esp for water sports. Everything from canoeing to parascending;
you can hire all the gear (1906/WATER SPORTS). Also; excavated Roman bath
house, playgrounds, sports pitches and now that the trees are beginning to
mature, some pleasant walks too. Nearby Baron's Haugh (1573/BIRDS) and
Dalzell Country Park more notable for their nature trails and grds. (482/CAMPING;
1668/MONUMENTS.)

1399   **FINLAYSTONE ESTATE, LANGBANK nr GREENOCK:** A8 to Greenock, past
MAP 1   Langbank, then signed. Grand mansion home to Chief of Clan Macmillan set
C2   in formal grds in wooded estate. Leafy walks, walled grd. Rare magic.

1400   **ALMONDELL, nr EAST CALDER:** 12km from Edin city bypass. Well-managed
MAP 7   park in the valley of the R Almond set amidst an area of redundant industrial
A1   sprawl. If you've just spent light yrs trying to exit from Livingston's notorious
rd system, you'll need this green oasis with its walks through woods, meadows
and along cinder tracks. Picnic sites, visitor centre with refreshments, kids'
areas and river meadows. A71 from bypass (Kilmarnock), then B7015 (Camp)
for 7km. Park on rt just into E Calder village. Walk ahead into woods, not to rt.

1401   **MUIRAVONSIDE COUNTRY PARK:** 5km W of Linlithgow on B825. Also sign-
MAP 7   posted from J4 of the M9 Edin/Stirling. Former farm estate now run by the
A1   local authority providing 170 acres of woodland walks, parkland, picnic sites
and a visitor centre for school parties or anyone else with an interest in birds,
bees and badgers. Ranger service does guided walks Apr-Sep. Gr place to
walk off that lunch at the not-too-distant Champany Inn (184/BURGERS).

1402   **EGLINTON nr IRVINE:** Beside main A78 Largs to Ayr rd signed from
MAP 1   Irvine/Kilwinning intersection. Spacious lungful of Ayrshire nr new town
C3   nexus and traffic tribulations. Visitor centre with interpretation of absolutely
everything; network of walks. Not much left of the house. A factory makes
'ambient foods'. All a bit of a construct, but some parts are peaceful.

TENTSMUIR, nr TAYPORT: Estuarine; John Muir, on Tay (1583/WILDLIFE).

ADEN, MINTLAW, nr PETERHEAD: 1550/KIDS.

HADDO HOUSE, ABERDEENSHIRE: Beautiful grounds (1652/CO HOUSES).

KELBURNE COUNTRY CENTRE, LARGS: 1540/KIDS.

1403
MAP A
C3
✔ ✔ **PRINCES ST GARDENS, EDINBURGH:** S side of Princes St. The greenery that launched a thousand postcards – millions probably – it's Edin. This former loch – drained around the time the New Town was built – is divided by the Mound. The eastern half has pitch and putt, Winter Wonderland and the Scott Monument (382/BEST VIEWS), the western has its much-photographed fountain, open-air café and space for locals and tourists to sprawl on the grass when sunny. You'll also find the the Ross Bandstand here – heart of Edinburgh's Hogmanay (2210/ANNUAL EVENTS) and the International Festival's gobsmacking fireworks concert (2204/ANNUAL EVENTS). Louts with lager, senior citz on benches, Italian teens with daft wee rucksacks – all our lives are here. Till dusk.

1404
MAP 3
D3
✔ ✔ **HAZELHEAD PARK, ABERDEEN:** Via Queens Rd, 3km centre. Extraordinary park where the mysterious gardening skills of the Aberdonians are magnificently in evidence. Many facs incl a maze, mini-zoo, wonderful tacky tearoom and there are lawns, memorials and botanical splendours aplenty esp azalea garden in spring and roses in summer. Gr sculpture (a leaflet describes).

1405
MAP 3
D3
✔ **DUTHIE PARK, ABERDEEN:** Riverside Dr along R Dee from the br carrying main A92 rd from/to Stonehaven. The other large well-kept park with duck pond, bandstand, hugely impressive rose grds in summer, carved sculptures and the famous, though now somewhat shabby Winter Grd of subtropical palms/ferns etc (10am-almost dusk).

1406
MAP 5
A3
✔ **PITTENCRIEFF PARK, DUNFERMLINE:** The extensive park alongside the Abbey and Palace ruins gifted to the town in 1903 by Carnegie. Open areas, glasshouses, pavilion (more a function rm) but most notably a deep verdant glen criss-crossed with pathways. Lush, full of birds, good after rain.

1407
MAP 5
B3
BEVERIDGE PARK, KIRKCALDY: Also in Fife, another big municipal park with a duck and boat pond, wide-open spaces and many amusements (e.g. bowling, tennis, putting, paddling). Ravenscraig a coastal park on the main rd E to Dysart is an excellent place to walk. Gr prospect of town and Firth, coves and skerries.

1408
MAP 8
C3
WILTON LODGE PARK, HAWICK: Hawick is perhaps not overfull of visitor attractions, but it does have a pretty nice park with facs and diversions enough for everyone e.g. the civic gallery, rugby pitches (they quite like rugby in Hawick), a large kids' playground, a café and lots of riverside walks by the Teviot. Lots of my school friends lost their virginity in this park (yes Mr Angry who wrote, I can say that). All-round open-air recreation centre. S end of town by A7.

1409
MAP B
xC5
ROUKEN GLEN AND LINN PARK, GLASGOW: Both on S side of river. Rouken Glen via Pollokshaws/Kilmarnock rd to Eastwood Toll then rt. Good place to park is second left, Davieland Rd beside pond. Across park from here (or beside main Rouken Glen rd) is main visitor area with grd centre, a Chinese restau and 'Butterfly Kingdom'. Linn Park via Aikenhead and Carmunnock rd. After Kings Park on left, take rt to Simshill Rd and park at golf course beyond houses. A long route there, but worth it; this is one of the undiscovered Elysiums of a city which boasts 60 parks. Ranger Centre.

1410
MAP 4
C3
CAMPERDOWN PARK, DUNDEE: Calling itself a country park, Camperdown is the main recreational breathing space for the city and hosts a plethora of distractions (a golf course, a wildlife complex, mansion house etc). Situated beyond Kingsway, the ring-route; go via Coupar Angus rd t/off. Best walks across the A923 in the Templeton Woods.

1411
MAP 3
A2
GRANT PARK, FORRES: Forres is a frequent winner of the Bonny Bloom competitions. Grant Park, with its balance of ornamental grds, open parkland and woody hill side, is the carefully tended rose in its crown. Good municipal facs like pitch and putt, playground. Cricket in summer and topping topiary. Through woods at top of Cluny Hill, a tower affords gr views of the Moray and Cromarty Firths and surrounding forest from which the town takes its name.

THE MOST INTERESTING COASTAL VILLAGES

1412
MAP 2
B3
✓ **PLOCKTON, nr KYLE OF LOCHALSH:** A Highland gem of a place 8km over the hill from Kyle, clustered around inlets of a wooded bay on L Carron. Cottage grds down to the bay and palm trees! Some gr walks over headlands. Plockton Inn prob best bet for reasonable stay and eats (968/LESS EXP HIGHLAND HOTELS). Haven Hotel (01599 544223) also good place to eat. Plockton Hotel (CHP, pub grub). It's not hard to feel connected with the village. (1946/CRAFT SHOPS.) Hamish MacBeth made here.

1413
✓ **STROMNESS, ORKNEY MAINLAND:** 24km from Kirkwall and a different kettle of fish. Hugging the shore and with narrow streets and wynds, it has a unique atmos, both maritime and European. Some of the most singular shops you'll see anywhere and the Orkney folk going about their business. Park nr harbour and walk down the cobbled main st if you don't want to scrape your paintwork (2161/ORKNEY; 2030/GALLERIES).

1414
MAP 2
D2
✓ **CROMARTY, nr INVERNESS:** At end of rd across Black Isle from Inverness (45km NE), but worth the trip. Village with dreamy times-gone-by atmos, without being twee. Lots of kids running about and a pink strand of beach. Delights to discover include: the kirk, plain and aesthetic with countryside through the windows behind the altar; Hugh (the geologist) Miller's house/Courthouse museum; Binnie's (1302/TEAROOMS); the shore and cliff walk (1834/COASTAL WALKS) and of course the dolphins (1579/DOLPHINS). Royal Hotel is inexp and good (975/INEXP HIGHLAND HOTELS).

1415
MAP 5
A3
CULROSS, nr DUNFERMLINE: By A994 from Dunfermline or jnct 1 of M90 just over Forth Rd Br (15km). Old centre conserved and being restored by NTS. Mainly residential and not awash with craft and coffee shops. More historical than merely quaint; a community of careful custodians lives in the white, red-pantiled houses. Footsteps echo in the cobbled wynds. Palace and Town House open Easter-Sept, 11-5pm. Interesting back gardens and lovely church at top of hill (1690/CHURCHES). Pamphlet by Rights of Way Society available locally, is useful.

1416
MAP 1
B2
TOBERMORY, MULL: Not so much a village, rather the main town of Mull, set around a hill on superb Tobermory Bay. Ferry pt for Ardnamurchan, but main Oban ferry is 35km away at Craignure. Usually a bustling harbour front with quieter streets behind; a quintessential island atmos. Some good inexp hotels (and quayside hostel) well situated to explore the whole island. (2160/MULL; 2125/ISLAND HOTELS; 1111/BEST HOSTELS.)

1417
MAP 1
A3
PORT CHARLOTTE, ISLAY: A township on the 'Rinns of Islay', the western peninsula. By A846 from the pts, Askaig and Ellen via Bridgend. Rows of white-washed, well-kept cottages along and back from shoreline. On rd in, there's a creamery, an island museum and a coffee/bookshop. Also a 'town' beach and one between PC and Bruichladdich (and esp the one with the war memorial nearby). Quiet and charming, not quaint. On Sat night, join the locals for a drink at the Loch Indaal Hotel and see if the 'moonie' comes out. (2157/ISLAY; 2121/ISLAND HOTELS)

1418
MAP 9
C3
ROCKCLIFFE, nr DUMFRIES: 25km S on Solway Coast rd, A710. On the 'Scottish Riviera', the rocky part of the coast around to Kippford (1830/COASTAL WALKS). A good rock-scrambling foreshore and a village with few houses and Baron's Craig hotel; set back with gr views. Excl pub at Kippford (1226/BEST FOOD) and tearoom at Rockcliffe (1299/TEAROOMS).

1419
MAP 5
C3, D3
EAST NEUK VILLAGES: The quintessential quaint wee fishing villages along the bit of Fife that forms the mouth of the Firth of Forth, **CRAIL, ANSTRUTHER, PITTENWEEM, ST MONANS** and **ELIE** all have different characters and attractions esp Crail's harbour, Anstruther as main centre and home of Fisheries Museum (see also 1269/FISH AND CHIPS; FIFE HOTELS p.112; 1565/BIRDS) and perfect Elie (1921/WINDSURFING; 877/878/FIFE HOTELS; 1215/BEST FOOD; 1850/GREAT GOLF). Or see St Andrews p. 308. Cycling good, traffic in summer not.

1420
MAP 5
B4

ABERDOUR: Betw Dunfermline and Kirkcaldy and nr Forth Rd Br (10km E from jnct 1 of M90) or, better still, go by train from Edin (frequent service: Dundee or Kirkcaldy); before Railtrack it used to win the 'best-kept station' award. Walks round harbour and to headland, Silver Sands beach 1km, castle ruins. (1689/CHURCHES; 880/881/FIFE HOTELS.)

1421
MAP 3
C1, D1

MORAY COAST FISHING VILLAGES: From Speybay (where the Spey slips into the sea) along to Fraserburgh, some of Scotland's best coastal scenery and many interesting villages in cliff/cove and beach settings. Esp notable are **PORTSOY** with 17th-century harbour (1894/SWIMMING POOLS) – and see 2202/EVENTS; **SANDEND** with its own popular beach and a fabulous one nearby (1428/BEACHES); **PENNAN** made famous by the film *Local Hero* (the hotel/pub is cosy and cheap: 01346 561201); **GARDENSTOWN** with a walk along the water's edge to **CROVIE** (pron 'Crivee') the epitome of a coast-clinging community; and **CULLEN**, which is more of a town and has a gr beach. (925/NE HOTELS.)

1422
MAP 2
B2

DIABEG, WESTER ROSS: On N shore of L Torridon at the end of the unclassified rd from Torridon on one of Scotland's most inaccessible peninsulas. Diabeg (pron 'Jee-a-beg') is simply beautiful. Fantastic rd there and then walk!

1423
MAP 1
C3

DUNURE, AYR: 15km S of Ayr on A719, the coast rd past the Heads of Ayr (cliff walks) 10km from Culzean (1593/CASTLES). Only a few cottages, a pub, an old harbour and the dramatic ruins of Dunure Castle, once the scene of horrific tortures, now a kids' playground.

1424
MAP 9
B4

ISLE OF WHITHORN: Strange faraway village at end of the rd, 35km S Newton Stewart, 6km Whithorn (1644/PREHISTORIC SITES). Mystical harbour where low tide does mean low, saintly shoreline, a sea angler's pub (Steam Packet) v good pub grub and McWilliams' amazing leaning stores. Ninian's chapel less uplifting, but you can see why he landed.

1425
MAP 1
C3

CORRIE, ARRAN: Last but not least, the bonniest bit of Arran, best reached by bike from Brodick (2156/ARRAN). I'd like a memorial bench on that shoreline.

FANTASTIC BEACHES AND BAYS

1426
MAP 1
A2

✓ ✓ **KILORAN BEACH, COLONSAY:** 9km from quay and hotel, past Colonsay House: parking and access on hill side. Described as the finest beach in the Hebrides, it does not disappoint, even in the rain. Craggy cliffs on one side, negotiable rocks on the other and, in betw, tiers of grassy dunes. The island of Colonsay was once bought as a picnic spot. This beach was probably the reason why.

1427
MAP 1
B3

✓ ✓ **MACHRIHANISH:** At the bottom of the Kintyre peninsula 10km from Campbeltown. Walk N from Machrihanish village, or from the car park on the main A83 to Tayinloan and Tarbert at pt where it hits/leaves the coast. A joyously long strand (8km) of unspoiled orange-pink sand backed by dunes and facing the 'steepe Atlantic Stream' all the way to Newfoundland (1856/GOLF IN GREAT PLACES).

1428
MAP 2
C1

✓ ✓ **SANDWOOD BAY, KINLOCHBERVIE:** This mile-long sandy strand with its old 'Stack', is legendary, but therein lies the problem since now too many people know about it and you may have to share in its glorious isolation. Inaccessibility is its saving grace, a 7km walk from the sign off the rd at Balchrick (nr the cattle grid), 6km from Kinlochbervie; allow 3hrs return plus time there. More venturesome is the walk from the N and Cape Wrath (1828/COASTAL WALKS).

1429
MAP 2
C1

✓ **OLDSHOREMORE:** The beach you pass on the rd to Balchrick, only 3km from Kinlochbervie. It's easy to reach and a beautiful spot: the water is clear and perfect for swimming, and there are rocky walks and quiet places. **POLIN**, 500m N, is a cove you might have to yourself.

1430
MAP 1
A3

✓ **ISLAY: SALIGO, MACHIR BAY and THE BIG STRAND:** The first two are bays on NW of island via A847 rd to Pt Charlotte, then B8018 past L Gorm. Wide beaches; remains of war fortifications in deep dunes, Saligo perhaps the nicer. They say 'no swimming' so paddle with extreme prejudice. The Big Strand on Laggan Bay: along Bowmore-Pt Ellen rd take Oa t/off, follow Kintra signs. There's a restau/bar, accom, camping and gr walks in either direction, 8km of glorious sand and dunes (contains the Machrie Golf Course). An airy amble under a wide sky. (1855/GOLF IN GREAT PLACES; 1826/COASTAL WALKS.)

1431
MAP 1
B2
✓ **OSTAL BEACH/KILBRIDE BAY, MILLHOUSE, nr TIGHNABRUAICH:** Down rd from 'Millhouse corner' on B8000, a track to rt at a white house (there's a church on the left) marked 'Private Road, No Cars' (often with a chain across to restrict access). Park and walk 1km, turning rt after lochan. You arrive on a perfect white sandy crescent known locally as Ostal and, apart from stranded jellyfish and the odd swatch of sewage, in certain conditions, a mystical secret place to swim and picnic. The N coast of Arran is like a Greek island in the bay.

1432
MAP 2
A2
✓ **SOUTH UIST:** Deserted but for birds, an almost unbroken strand of beach running for miles down the W coast; the machair at its best early summer. Take any rd off the spinal A865; usually less than 2km. Good spot to try is t/off at Tobha Mor; real black houses and a chapel on the way to the sea.

1433
MAP 2
A2
✓ **SCARISTA BEACH, SOUTH HARRIS:** On main rd S of Tarbert (15km) to Rodel. The beach is so beautiful that people have been married there. Hotel over the rd is worth staying just for this, but is also a gr retreat (2124/ISLAND HOTELS). Golf course on links (1861/GOLF IN GREAT PLACES). Fab in early evening. The sun also rises.

1434
MAP 4
D3
✓ **LUNAN BAY, nr MONTROSE:** 5km from main A92 rd to Aber and 5km of deep red crescent beach under a wide northern sky. But'n'Ben at Auchmithie, is an excellent place to start or finish (907/PERTHSHIRE EATS) and good app (from S), although relative newcomer, Gordon's restau at Inverkeilor is closer (908/PERTHSHIRE EATS). Best viewpoint from Boddin Farm 3km S Montrose and 3km from A92 signed 'Usan'. Often deserted.

1435
MAP 1
B2
JURA, LOWLANDMAN'S BAY: Not strictly a beach (there is a sandy strand before the headland) but a rocky foreshore with ethereal atmos; gr light and space. Only seals break the spell. Go rt at 3-arch br to first group of houses (Knockdrome), through yard on left and rt around cottages to track to Ardmenish. After deer fences, bay is visible on your rt, 1km walk away.

1436
MAP 2
A3
VATERSAY, OUTER HEBRIDES: The tiny island joined by a causeway to Barra. Twin crescent beaches on either side of the isthmus, one shallow and sheltered visible from Castlebay, the other an ocean beach with rollers. Dunes/machair; safe swimming. There's a helluva hill betw Barra and Vatersay if you're cycling.

1437
MAP 2
A3
BARRA, SEAL BAY: 5km Castlebay on W coast, 2km after Isle of Barra Hotel through gate across machair where rd rt is signed Taobh a Deas Allathasdal. A flat, rocky Hebridean shore and skerries where seals flop into the water and eye you with intense curiosity. The better-beach beach is next to the hotel.

1438
MAP 5
C2
WEST SANDS, ST ANDREWS: As a town beach, this is hard to beat; it dominates the view to W. Wide swathe not too unclean and sea swimmable. Golf courses behind. In 1997 consistently gets 'the blue flag', but beach buffs may prefer Kinshaldy (1586/WILDLIFE), Kingsbarns (10km S), or Elie (28km S).

1439
MAP 3
C1, D1
MORAY COAST: Many gr beaches along coast from Spey Bay to Fraserburgh, notably **CULLEN** and **LOSSIEMOUTH** (town beaches) and **NEW ABERDOUR** (1km from New Aberdour village on B9031, 15km W of Fraserburgh) and **ROSE-HEARTY** (8km W of Fraserburgh) both quieter places for walks and picnics. One of the best-kept secrets is the beach at **SUNNYSIDE** where you walk past the incredible ruins of Findlater Castle on the cliff top (how did they build it? And what a place, on its grassed-over roof, for a picnic) and down to a cove which on my sunny day was quite simply perfect. Take a left going into Sandend 16km W of Banff and follow rd for 2km, turning rt and park in the farmyard. Walk from here past dovecote, 1km to cliff. See also 1833/COASTAL WALKS.

1440
MAP 2
B1, C1
NORTH COAST: To the W of Thurso, along the N coast, are some of Britain's most unspoiled and unsung beaches. No beach bums, no Beach Boys. There are so many gr little coves, you can have one to yourself even on a hot day, but those to mention are: **STRATHY** and **ARMADALE** (35km W Thurso), **FARR** and **TORRISDALE** (48km) and **COLDBACKIE** (65km). My favourite (which may be called Ceannabeinne after the hill above it, but **PETE'S BEACH** is easier to

remember) is further along where L Eriboll comes out to the sea and the rd hits the coast again 7km E of Durness. It's a small 100m cove flanked by walls of oyster-pink rock and shallow turquoise sea; perfect.

1441 **SANDS OF MORAR, nr MALLAIG:** 70km W of Ft William and 6km from
MAP 2 Mallaig, these easily accessible beaches may seem overpopulated on summer
B3 days and the S stretch nearest to Arisaig may have one too many caravan parks, but they go on for miles and there's enough space for everybody. The sand's supposed to be silver but in fact it's a v pleasing pink. Lots of rocky bits for exploration. One of the best beachy bits is (coming from Mallaig) the next bay after the estuary; park on the rd. And the bit nr the youth hostel, Camusdarroch (where *Local Hero* was filmed), further from rd, is quieter and a v good swathe of sand. Traigh, the golf course makes good use of the dunes (1873/GOOD GOLF).

1442 **THE BAY AT THE BACK OF THE OCEAN, IONA:** Easy 2km walk from frequent
MAP 1 ferry from Fionnphort, S of Mull (2109/MAGICAL ISLANDS) or hire a bike from the
A1 store on your left as you walk into the village. Paved rd most of way. John Smith, who is buried beside the abbey, once told me that this was one of his favourite places. Me too.

1443 **DORNOCH and EMBO BEACHES:** The wide and extensive sandy beach of
MAP 2 this pleasant town at the mouth of the Dornoch Firth famous also for its golf
D2 links. 4km N, Embo Sands starts with caravan city, but walk N towards Golspie. Embo is twinned with Kaunakakai, Hawaii!

THE GREAT GLENS

1444
MAP 2
C3
✓ ✓ ✓ **GLEN AFFRIC:** Beyond Cannich at end of Glen Urquhart A831, 20km from Drumnadrochit on L Ness. A dramatic gorge that strikes westwards into the wild heart of Scotland. Superb for rambles (1799/GLEN AND RIVER WALKS), expeditions, Munro-bagging (further in, beyond L Affric) and even just tootling through in the car. Shaped by the Hydro Board, L Benevean nevertheless adds to the drama. Cycling good (bike hire in Cannich) as is the detour to Tomich and Plodda Falls (1456/WATERFALLS). Stop at Dog Falls (1523/PICNICS).

1445
MAP 4
A3
✓ ✓ ✓ **GLEN LYON, nr ABERFELDY:** One of Scotland's crucial places both historically and geographically, much favoured by fishers/walkers/Munro-baggers. Wordsworth and Tennyson, Gladstone and Baden Powell all sang its praises. The Lyon is a classic Highland river tumbling through corries, gorges and riverine meadows. Several Munros are within its watershed and rise gloriously on either side. Rd all the way to the loch side (30km). Eagles soar over the remoter tops at the head of the glen stay at Invervar Lodge (1146/GET-AWAY-FROM-IT-ALL). Fishing permits from Fortingall Hotel on the way there (1123/INNS, 01887 830367). The 'oldest tree' in Europe, a rather scraggy yew, is by the church next to the hotel.

1446
MAP 2
C3
✓ ✓ **GLEN NEVIS, FORT WILLIAM:** Used by many a film director; easy to see why. Ben Nevis is only part of magnificent scenery. Many walks and convenient facs (1463/WATERFALLS; 1797/SERIOUS WALKS). Not sure about the Braveheart car park or the 'legend' of Samuel's Stone; other-wise, it's a national treasure. Check Ft William p.296 for eats.

1447
MAP 2
C4
✓ ✓ **GLEN ETIVE:** Off from more exalted Glencoe (and the A82) at Kingshouse, as anyone you meet in those parts will tell you, this truly is a glen of glens. And, as my friends who camp and climb here implore, it needs no more advertisement.

1448
MAP 2
B2
STRATHCARRON, nr BONAR BRIDGE: You drive up the N bank of this Highland river from the br o/side Ardgay (pron 'Ordguy') which is 3km over the br from Bonar Br. Rd goes 15km to Croick and its remarkable church (1694/CHURCHES). The river gurgles and gushes along its rocky course to the Dornoch Firth and there are innumerable places to picnic, swim and stroll further up. Quite heavenly on a warm day.

1449
MAP 4
C2
THE ANGUS GLENS: Glen Clova/Glen Prosen/Glen Isla. All via Kirriemuir. Isla to W is a woody, approachable glen with a deep gorge, on B954 nr Alyth (1465/WATERFALLS) and the lovely Glenisla Hotel (1126/INNS). Others via B955, to Dykehead then rd bifurcates. Both glens stab into the heart of the Grampians. 'Minister's Walk' goes betw them from behind the kirk at Prosen village over the hill to B955 before Clova village (7km). Glen Clova is a walkers' paradise esp from Glendoll 24km from Dykehead; limit of rd. Viewpoint. 'Jock's Rd' to Braemar and the Capel Mounth to Ballater (both 24km). Campsite and SYH. Also gr hotel at Clova (900/PERTHSHIRE HOTELS) and famous 'Loops of Brandy' walk (2hrs, 2-B-2); stark and beautiful.

1450
MAP 1
C2
GLENDARUEL: The Cowal Peninsula on the A886 betw Colintraive and Strachur. Humble but perfectly formed glen of R Ruel, from Clachan in S (a kirk and an inn) through deciduous meadowland to more rugged grandeur 10km N. Easy walking and cycling. W rd best. Views L Fyne and Argyll from W ridge.
2-B-2

1451
MAP 1
B1
GLEN LONAN, nr TAYNUILT: Betw Taynuilt on A85 and A816 S of Oban. Another quiet wee glen, but all the rt elements for walking, picnics, cycling and fishing or just a run in the car. Varying scenery, a bubbling burn (the R Lonan), some standing stones and not many folk. Angus' Garden at the Taynuilt end should not be missed (1383/GARDENS). No marked walks; now get lost!
2-B-2

1452
MAP 9
B3
GLEN TROOL, nr NEWTON STEWART: 26km N by A714 via Bargrennan which is on the S Upland Way (1790/LONG WALKS). A gentle wooded glen of a place around L Trool. One of the most charming, accessible parts of the Galloway Forest Park. (1735/MARY, CHARLIE, BOB.) Start of the Merrick climb (1766/HILLS).

1453 **THE SMA' GLEN, nr CRIEFF:** Off the A85 to Perth, the A822 to Amulree and
MAP 4   Aberfeldy. Sma' meaning small, this is the valley of the R Almond where the
B3   Mealls (lumpish, shapeless hills) fall steeply down to the rd. Where the rd turns
away from the river, the long distance path to L Tay begins (28km). Sma' Glen,
8km, has good picnic spots, but they get busy and midgy in summer.

1454 **STRATHFARRAR, nr BEAULY or DRUMNADROCHIT:** Rare unspoiled glen
MAP 2   accessed from A831 leaving Drumnadrochit on L Ness via Cannich (30km) or
C2   S from Beauly (15km). Signed at Struy. Arrive at gatekeeper's house. Access
restricted to 25 cars per day (Cl Tue and Sun till 1.30pm) For access Oct-Mar
01463 761260; you must be out by 6pm. 22km to head of glen past lochs.
Good climbing, walking, fishing. Peace be with you.

THE MOST SPECTACULAR WATERFALLS

*One aspect of Scotland that really is improved by rain. All the walks to these falls
are graded 1-A-1 unless otherwise stated (see p. 10 for walk codes).*

1455 ✓✓ **FALLS OF GLOMACH:** 25km Kyle of Lochalsh off A87 nr Shiel Br, past
MAP 2   Kintail Centre at Morvich then 2km further up Glen Croe to br. Walk
C3   starts other side; there are other ways, (e.g. from the SY Hostel in Glen Affric),
but this is most straightforward. Allow 5/7 hrs for the pilgrimage to one of
Britain's highest falls. Path is steep but well trod. Glomach means gloomy and
you might feel so, peering into the ravine; from precipice to pool, it's 200m.
But to pay tribute, go down carefully to ledge. Vertigo factor and sense of
achievement both fairly high. (1113/HOSTELS.)   2-C-3

1456 ✓✓ **PLODDA FALLS, nr TOMICH, nr DRUMNADROCHIT:** A831 from L
MAP 2   Ness to Cannich (20km), then 7km to Tomich, a further 5km up
C3   mainly woodland track to car park. 200m walk down through woods of Scots
Pine and ancient Douglas Fir to one of the most enchanting woodland sites
in Britain and the Victorian iron br over the brink of the 150m fall into the
churning river below. The dawn chorus here must be amazing (though I'll
never hear it). Freezes into winter wonderland (ice climbers from Inverness
take advantage). Good hotel in village (949/HIGHLANDS HOTELS).

1457 ✓ **FALLS OF BRUAR, nr BLAIR ATHOLL:** Close to the main A9 Perth-
MAP 4   Inverness rd, 12km N of B Atholl nr House of Bruar shopping experience.
B2   (1941/CRAFT SHOPS). Consequently, the short walk to lower falls is now v con-
sumer-led but less crowded than you might expect. The lichen-covered walls
of the gorge below the upper falls (1km) are less ogled and more dramatic.
Circular path is well marked but steep and rocky in places. Tempting
(1526/SWIMMING HOLES).

1458 ✓ **GLENASHDALE FALLS, ARRAN:** 5km walk from br on main rd at Whiting
MAP 1   Bay. Signed up the burn side, but uphill and further on than you think, so
C3   allow 2hrs (return). Short series of falls in a rocky gorge in the woods with
paths so you get rt down to the brim and the pools. Swim here, swim in heav-
en!   1-B-1

1459 **EAS FORS, MULL:** On the Dervaig to Fionnphort rd 3km from Ulva Ferry; a
MAP 1   series of cataracts tumbling down on either side of the rd. Easily accessible.
B1   There's a path down the side to the brink where the river plunges into the sea.
On a warm day swimming in the sea below the fall is a rare exhilaration.

1460 **EAS MOR, SKYE:** Glen Brittle nr end of rd. 24km from Sligachan. A mt water-
MAP 2   fall with the wild Cuillins behind and views to the sea. App as part of a serious
B3   scramble or merely a 30-min Cuillin sampler. Start at the Memorial Hut, cross
the rd, bear rt, cross burn and then follow path uphill.   2-C-2
Another impressive torrent of wild mt water is the **LEALT FALLS** about 20km
N of Portree on the A855 (before Kilt Rock). Beside rd; park walk and peer (you
can get down to the beach).

1461 **EAS A' CHUAL ALUINN, KYLESKU:** 'Britain's highest waterfall' nr the head of
MAP 2   Glencoul, is not easy to reach. Kylesku is betw Scourie and Lochinver off the
C1   main A894, 20km S of Scourie. There are 2hr cruises at 11am/2pm May-Sept
(and 4pm July/Aug) outside hotel (996/INEXP HIGHLAND RESTAUS). Falls are a
rather distant prospect, but you may be able to alight and get next boat. The

captain's rap will keep you going. There's also a track to the top of the falls from 5km N of the Skiag Br on the main rd (4hrs return), but you will need to take directions locally. The water freefalls for 200m, which is 4 times further than Niagara (take pinch of salt here). There is a spectacular pulpit view down the cliff, 100m to rt.
2-C-3

1462 **STEALL FALLS, GLEN NEVIS, FORT WILLIAM:** Take Glen Nevis rd at r/bout
MAP 2 o/side town centre and drive 'to end' (16km) through glen. Start from the sec-
C3 ond car park you come to, following path marked Corrour, uphill through the woody gorge with R Ness thrashing below. Glen eventually and dramatically opens out and there are gr views of the long veils of the Falls. Precarious 3-wire br for which you will also need nerves of steel. One day in Jan, of 10 of us, 2 couldn't do it. I am one (sad person). I blamed a hangover.
3-A-3

1463a **CORRIESHALLOCH GORGE/FALLS OF MEASACH:** Jnct of A832 and A835,
MAP 2 20km S of Ullapool; possible to walk down into the gorge from both rds. Most
C2 dramatic app is from the car park on the A832 Gairloch rd. Staircase to swing br from whence to consider how such a wee burn could make such a deep gash. V impressive.

1463b **THE GREY MARE'S TAIL:** On the wildly scenic rd betw Moffat and Selkirk, the
MAP 9 A708. About halfway, a car park and signs for waterfall. The lower track takes
D2 10/15mins to a viewing place still 500m from falls; the higher, on the other side of the Tail burn, threads betw the austere hills and up to L Skene from which the falls overflow (45/60mins). Mountain goats cast a wary eye.

1464 **THE FALLS OF CLYDE, NEW LANARK, nr LANARK:** Dramatic falls in a long
MAP 1 gorge of the Clyde. New Lanark, the conservation village of Robert Owen the
D3 social reformer, is signed from Lanark. It's hard to avoid the 'award-winning' tourist bazaar, but the riverbank has … a more natural appeal. The path to the Power Station is about 3km, but the route doesn't get interesting till after it, a 1km climb to the first fall (Cora Linn) and another 1km to the next (Bonnington Linn). Swimming above or below them is not advised (but it's gr). Certainly don't swim on an 'open day', when they close the station and divert all the water back down the river in a mighty surge (about once a month in summer on Sundays; details from TO: 01555 661661). There is a gr Italian restau in Lanark and one of the mills is now a hotel (474/HOTELS O/SIDE GLASGOW). New Lanark is better when the other tourists have gone home.

1465 **REEKIE LINN, ALYTH:** 8km N of town on back rds to Kirriemuir on B951 betw
MAP 4 Br of Craigisla and Br of Lintrathen. A picnic site and car park on bend of rd
C3 leads by 200m to the wooded gorge of Glen Isla with precipitous viewpoints of defile where Isla is squeezed and falls in tiers for 100ft. Can walk further along the glen. Excellent loch side restau nearby (906/PERTHSHIRE EATS) and tearoom (1295/TEAROOMS).

1466 **FALLS OF ACHARN nr KENMORE, LOCH TAY:** 5km along S side of loch on
MAP 4 unclass rd. Walk from opp engineering plant in township of Acharn; falls are
B3 signed. Steepish start then 1km up side of gorge; waterfalls on other side.

1467 **FALLS OF ROGIE, nr STRATHPEFFER:** Car park on A835 Inverness-Ullapool
MAP 2 rd, 5km Contin/10km Strathpeffer. Accessibility makes short walk (250m)
C2 quite popular to these hurtling falls on the Blackwater R. Br (built by T Army) and salmon ladder (they leap in summer). Woodland trails marked, include a circular route to Contin (1823/WOODLAND WALKS).

1468 **FOYERS, LOCH NESS:** On southern route from Ft Augustus to Inverness, the
MAP 2 B862 (1492/SCENIC ROUTES) at the village of Foyers (35km from Inverness). Park
C3 next to shops and cross rd, go through fence and down steep track to view-ing places (slither-proof shoes advised). R Foyers falls 150m into foaming gorge below and then into L Ness throwing clouds of spray into the trees (you may get drenched). Occasionally the Hydro 'turn the water off' and it just stops.

1469 **FALLS OF SHIN, nr LAIRG, SUTHERLAND:** 6km E of town on signed rd, car
MAP 2 park and falls nearby are easily accessible. Not quite up to the splendours of
C3 others on this page, but an excellent place to see salmon battling upstream (best June-Aug). Visitor centre with extensive shop; the café/restau was surprisingly good last time we tried.

1470
MAP 2
B2

LOCH MAREE: A832 betw Kinlochewe and Gairloch. Dotted with islands covered in Scots pine hiding some of the best examples of Viking graves and apparently a money tree in their midst. Easily viewed from the rd which follows its length for 15km. Bienn Eighe rises behind you and the omniscient presence of Slioch is opposite. Aultroy Vistor Centre (5km Kinlochewe), fine walks from car park further on, good accom and fishing at L Maree Hotel (969/INEXP HIGHLAND HOTELS).

1471
MAP 2
D3

LOCH AN EILEAN: An enchanted loch in the heart of the Rothiemurchus Forest (1813/WOODLAND WALKS *for directions*). There's a good visitor centre. You can walk rt round the loch (5km, allow 1.5hrs). This is classic Highland scenery, a landscape of magnificent Scots pine. It was one of Wainwright's favourites.

1472
MAP 2
C3

LOCH ARKAIG: 25km Ft William. An enigmatic loch long renowned for its fishing. From the A82 beyond Spean Br (at the Commando Monument) cross the Caledonian Canal, then on by single track rd through the Clune Forest and the 'Dark Mile' past the 'Witches Pool' (a cauldron of dark water below cataracts), to the loch. Bonnie Prince Charlie came this way before and after Culloden; one of his refuge caves is marked on a trail.

1473
MAP 6
B2

LOCH LUBHAIR, nr CRIANLARICH: The loch you pass (on the rt) on the A85 to Crianlarich (4km), in Glen Dochart, the upper reaches of the Tay water system. Small, perfect, with bare hills surrounding and fringed with pines and woody islets. Beautiful scenery that most people just go past in the car heading for Oban or Ft William. Enquire locally for kayak hire.

1474
MAP 6
B3

LOCH ACHRAY, nr BRIG O' TURK: The small loch at the centre of the Trossachs betw **LOCH KATRINE** (on which the *SS Sir Walter Scott* makes thrice-daily cruises: 01877 376316) and **LOCH VENACHAR**. The A821 from Callander skirts both Venachar and Achray (picnic sites). Ben Venue and Ben An rise above: gr walks (1760/HILLS) and views. A one-way forest rd goes round the other side of L Achray thro Achray Forest (enter and leave from the Duke's Pass rd betw Aberfoyle and Brig O'Turk). Details of trails from forest vistor centre 3km N Aberfoyle. Bike hire at L Katrine/Callander/Aberfoyle – it's the best way to see these lochs.

1475
MAP 3
B3

LOCH MUICK, nr BALLATER: At head of rd off B976, the S Dee rd at Ballater. 14km up Glen Muick (pron 'Mick') to car park, visitor centre and 100m to loch side. Lochnagar rises above (1785/MUNROS) and walk also begins here for Capel Mounth and Glen Clova (1449/GLENS). 3hr walk around loch and any number of ambles. The lodge where Vic met John is at the furthest pt (well it would be). Open aspect with grazing deer and not too much forestry.

1476
MAP 2
C1

LOCH ERIBOLL, NORTH COAST: 90km W of Thurso. The long sea loch that indents into the N coast for 15km and which you drive rt round on the main A838. Deepest natural anchorage in the UK, exhibiting every aspect of loch side scenery including, alas, fish cages. Ben Hope stands nr the head of the loch and there is a perfect beach (my beach) on the coast (1440/BEACHES). Walks from Hope.

1477
MAP 9
B3

LOCH TROOL, nr NEWTON STEWART: The small, celebrated loch in a bowl of the Galloway Hills reached via Bargrennan 14km N via A714 and 8km to end of rd. Woodland visitor centre/café on way. Good walks but best viewed from Bruce's Stone (1735/MARY, CHARLIE AND BOB) and the slopes of Merrick (1766/HILLS). An idyllic place.

1478
MAP 2
B3

LOCH MORAR, nr MALLAIG: 70km W of Ft William by the A850 (a wildly scenic route). Morar village is 6km from Mallaig and a single track rd leads away from the coast to the loch (only 500m but out of sight) then along it for 5km to Bracora. It's the prettiest part with wooded islets, small beaches, loch side meadows and bobbing boats. The rd stops at a turning place but a track continues to Tarbet and it's poss to connect with a post boat and sail back to Mallaig on L Nevis. L Morar, joined to the coast by the shortest river in Britain, also has the deepest water. There is a spookiness about it and just possibly a monster called Morag.

1479 **LOCH TUMMEL, nr PITLOCHRY:** W from Pitlochry on B8019 to Rannoch (and
MAP 4 the end of the rd), L Tummel comes into view, as it did for Queen Victoria, scin-
B2 tillating beneath you, and on a clear day with Schiehallion beyond
(1509/VIEWS). This N side has good walks (1820/WOODLAND WALKS), but the S rd
from Faskally just o/side Pitlochry is the one to take to get down to the
lochside to picnic etc. Great caravan park on B8019 at Ardquallich and a hotel,
the Queens View, 01796 473291, with great views (10 rms, cl Feb, MED.INX).

1480 **LOCH LUNDAVRA, nr FORT WILLIAM:** Here's a secret loch in the hills, but not
MAP 2 far from the well-trodden tracks through the glens and the sunny streets of Ft
C3 William. Go up Lundavra Rd from r/bout at W end of main st, out of town, over
cattle grid and on (to end of rd) 8km. You should have it to yourself; good picnic spots and gr view of Ben Nevis.

LOCH LOMOND: The biggest, maybe not the bonniest (2178/BIG ATTRAC-
TIONS).

LOCH NESS: The longest; you haven't heard the last of it (2181/BIG ATTRAC-
TIONS).

THE SCENIC ROUTES

1481
MAP 1
C2
✓ ✓ ✓ **ROTHESAY–TIGHNABRUAICH:** A886/A8003. The most celebrated part of this route is the latter, the A8003 down the side of L Riddon to Tighnabruaich along the hill sides which give the breathtaking views of Bute and the Kyles, but the whole way, with its diverse aspects of loch side, riverine and rocky scenery, is supernatural. Includes short crossing betw Rhubodach and Colintraive.

1482
MAP 2
C4
✓ ✓ ✓ **GLENCOE:** The A82 from Crianlarich to Ballachulish is a fine drive, but from the extraterrestrial L Ba onwards, there can be few rds anywhere that have direct contact with such imposing scenery. After Kinghouse and Buachaille Etive Mor on the left, the mts and ridges rising on either side of Glencoe proper are truly awesome. The visitor centre, well signposted 8km from Glencoe village, sets the topographical and historical scene. (1183/BLOODY GOOD PUBS; 1794/SERIOUS WALKS; 1722/BATTLEGROUNDS; 1747/SPOOKY PLACES; 1112/HOSTELS.)

1483
MAP 2
B3
✓ ✓ **SHIEL BRIDGE–GLENELG:** The switchback rd that climbs from the A87 (Ft William 96km) at Shiel Br over the 'hill' and down to the coast opp the Sleat Peninsula in Skye (short ferry to Kylerhea). As you climb you're almost as high as the surrounding summits and there's the classic view across L Duich to the 5 Sisters of Kintail. Coming back you think you're going straight into the loch! It's really worth driving to Glenelg (1121/INNS) and beyond to Arnisdale and ethereal L Hourn (16km).

1484
MAP 2
B2
✓ **APPLECROSS:** 120km Inverness. From Tornapress nr Lochcarron for 18km. Leaving the A896 seems like leaving civilisation; the winding ribbon heads into monstrous mts and the high plateau at the top is another planet. It's not for the faint-hearted and Applecross is a relief to see with its campsite/coffee shop and a faraway inn. The Applecross Hotel (tacky, but friendly). 1144/GET-AWAY-FROM-IT-ALL.

1485
MAP 2
A2
✓ **THE GOLDEN ROAD, SOUTH HARRIS:** The main rd in Harris follows the W coast, notable for bays and sandy beaches (1433/BEACHES). This is the other one, winding round a series of coves and inlets with offshore skerries and a treeless rocky hinterland – the classic Hebridean landscape, esp Finsbay. Tweed is woven in this area; you can visit the crofts but it would be impolite to leave without buying some gloves or something (1962/TWEED).

1486
MAP 2
B3
SLEAT PENINSULA, SKYE: The unclassified rd off the A851 (main Sleat rd) esp coming from S, i.e. take rd at Ostaig nr Gaelic College; it meets coast after 9km. Affords rare views of the Cuillins from a craggy coast. Returning to 'main' rd S of Isleornsay, pop into the gr hotel pub there (2122/ISLAND HOTELS).

1487
MAP 2
C1
LOCHINVER–ACHILTIBUIE: Achiltibuie is 40km from Ullapool; this is the route from the N; 28km of winding rd/unwinding Highland scenery; through glens, mts and silver sea. Known locally as the 'wee mad rd' (it is maddening if you're in a hurry). Passes Achin's Bookshop (1936/CRAFT SHOPS), the path to Kincraig Falls and the mighty Suilven.

1488
MAP 2
C1
LOCHINVER–DRUMBEG: The coast rd N from Lochinver (20km) is also marvellous; essential Assynt. Actually best travelled N-S so that you leave the splendid vista of Eddrachilles Bay and pass through lochan, moor and even woodland, touching the coast again by sandy beaches (at Stoer a rd leads 7km to the lighthouse and the walk to the Old Man of Stoer, 1829/COASTAL WALKS) and app Lochinver with one of the classic long views of Suilven.

1489
MAP 8
C2
LEADERFOOT–CLINTMAINS, nr ST BOSWELLS: The B6356 betw the A68 and the B6404 Kelso-St Boswells rd. This small rd, busy in summer, links Scott's View and Dryburgh Abbey (1715/ABBEYS; best found by following Abbey signs) and Smailholm Tower, and passes through classic Border/Tweedside scenery. Don't miss Irvine's View if you want to see the Borders (1507/VIEWS). Nice GH (847/BORDER HOTELS).

1490
MAP 3
B3
BRAEMAR–LINN OF DEE: 12km of renowned Highland river scenery along the upper valley of the (Royal) Dee. The Linn (rapids) is at the end of the rd, but there are river walks and the start of the gr Glen Tilt walk to Blair Atholl (1797/SERIOUS WALKS). Deer abound.

1491 **BALLATER-TOMINTOUL:** This is the ski road to the Lecht (1878/SKIING), the
MAP 3 A939 which leaves the Royal Deeside rd (A93) W of Ballater before it gets real-
B3 ly royal. A ribbon of road in the bare Grampians, past the sentinel ruin Corgarff
(open to view, 250m walk) and the valley of the trickling Don. Rd proceeds
seriously uphill and main viewpoints are S of the Lecht. There is just nobody
for miles. Walks in Glenlivet estates S of Tomintoul. Good hotel here.

1492 **FORT AUGUSTUS–DORES, nr INVERNESS:** The B862 often single-track rd
MAP 2 that follows and, for much of its latter length, skirts L Ness. Much quieter and
C3 more interesting than the main W bank A82. Starts off in rugged country and
follows the extraordinary straight rd built by Wade to tame the Highlands.
Reaches the loch side at Foyers (1468/WATERFALLS) and goes all the way to
Dores (15km from Inverness). There are paths to the shore of the loch.
Fabulous untrodden woodlands nr Errogie (marked) and the spooky grave-
yard adj Boleskin House where Aleister Crowley did his dark magic and Jimmy
Page of Led Zeppelin may have done his. 35km total; worth taking slowly.

1493 **THE DUKE'S PASS, ABERFOYLE–BRIG O'TURK:** Of the many rds through the
MAP 6 Trossachs, this one is spectacular though gets busy; numerous possibilities for
B2 stopping, exploration and gr views. Good viewpoint 4km from L Achray Hotel,
above rd and lay-by. One-way forest rd goes round L Achray. Good hill walking starts (1760/1761/1762/FAVOURITE HILLS) and L Katrine Ferry (2km) 3 times
a day Apr-Oct (01877 376316). Bike hire at L Katrine, Aberfoyle and Callander.

1494 **GLENFINNAN–MALLAIG:** The A830, Road to the Isles. Through some of the
MAP 2 most impressive and romantic landscapes in the Highlands, splendid in any
B3 weather (it does rain rather a lot) to the coast at the Sands of Morar
(1441/BEACHES). This is deepest Bonnie Prince Charlie country (1734/MARY,
CHARLIE AND BOB) and demonstrates what a misty eye he had for magnificent
settings. The rd is shadowed for much of the way by the West Highland
Railway, which is an even better way to enjoy the scenery (2187/FAVOURITE
JOURNEYS).

1495 **LOCHAILORT–ACHARACLE:** Off from the A830 above at Lochailort and turn-
MAP 2 ing S on the A861, the coastal section of this gr scenery is superb esp in the
B3 setting sun. This is the rd to Castle Tiorem, which should not be missed
(1613/RUINS); Michael McGregor's new wildlife centre nearby shouldn't be
either (1561/KIDS).

1496 **AMULREE–KENMORE:** The unclassified single track and often v narrow rd
MAP 4 that leads from the hill-country hamlet of Amulree to cosy Kenmore. Past L
B3 Freuchie, a steep climb takes you to a plateau ringed by magnificent (distant)
mts and, by the time you descend to L Tay, you may be completely intoxicat-
ed with the scenery. But don't forget to close the gates.

1497 **PURE PERTHSHIRE, MUTHILL–COMRIE:** A route you won't find in any other
MAP 4 guidebook. It takes you through some of the best scenery in central Scotland
B4 and ends up (best this way round) in Comrie with its teashops and other pleasures (1285/TEAROOMS; 1524/PICNICS). Leave Muthill by Crieff rd turning left
(2km) into Drummond Castle grounds up a glorious avenue of beech trees
(gate open 2-5pm). Visit grd (1380/GARDENS) then continue through estate. At
gate, go rt, following signs for Strowan. V quiet rd; we have it to ourselves. First
jnct, go left following signs (4km). At T-jnct, go left to Comrie (7km).

For views of and around EDINBURGH *and* GLASGOW *see p. 57 and p. 95. No views from hill or mt tops are included here.*

1498
MAP 2
B2

✔ ✔ ✔ **THE QUIRANG, SKYE:** Best app is from Uig direction taking the rt-hand unclassified rd off the hairpin of the A855 above and 2km from town (more usual app from Staffin side is less of a revelation). View (and walk) from car park, the massive rock formations of a towering, contorted ridge. Solidified lava heaved and eroded into fantastic pinnacles. Fine views also across Staffin Bay to Wester Ross. (2153/ISLAND WALKS.)

1499
MAP 2
C2

✔ ✔ ✔ The views of **AN TEALLACH** and **LIATHACH:** An Teallach, that gr favourite of Scottish hill walkers (40km S of Ullapool by the A835/A832), is best viewed from the side of little L Broom or the A832 just before you get to Dundonald.

The classic view of the other great Torridon mts (Beinn Eighe and Liathach together, 100km S by rd from Ullapool), for those who can't imagine how (or why) you would attempt to go up them, is from the track around L Clair which is reached from the entrance to the Coulin estate off the A896, Glen Torridon rd (be aware of stalking). These mts have to be seen to be believed.

1500
MAP 2
B2

✔ ✔ From **RAASAY:** There are a number of fabulous views looking over to Skye from Raasay, the small island reached by ferry from Sconser (2107/MAGICAL ISLANDS). The panorama from Dun Caan, the hill in the centre of the island (444m) is of Munro proportions, producing an elation quite incommensurate with the small effort required to get there. Start from the rd to the 'N End'.
2-B-2

1501
MAP 1
C2

✔ ✔ **THE REST AND BE THANKFUL:** On A83 L Lomond-Inveraray rd where it's met by the B828 from Lochgoilhead. In summer the rest may be from driving stress and you may not be thankful for the camera-toting masses, but this was always one of the most accessible, rewarding viewpoints in the land. Surprisingly, none of the encompassing hills are Munros but they are nonetheless dramatic. There are mercifully few carpets of conifer to smother the grandeur of the crags as you look down the valley.

1502
MAP 2
B3

✔ **ELGOL, SKYE:** End of the rd, the B8083, 22km from Broadford. The classic view of the Cuillins from across L Scavaig and of Soay and Rum. Cruises (Apr-Oct) in the *Bella Jane* (0800 731 3089) or the *Kaylea Jayne* (01687 462447) to the famous corrie of L Coruisk, painted by Turner, romanticised by Walter Scott; with 90mins ashore. A journey you'll remember.

1503
MAP 2
C2

✔ **THE SUMMER ISLES, ACHILTIBUIE:** The Summer Isles are a scattering of islands seen from the coast of Achiltibuie (and the lounge of the Summer Isles Hotel 945/HIGHLANDS HOTELS) and visited by boat from Ullapool. But the best place to see them, and the stunning perspective of this western shore is on the road to Altandhu, possibly to the pub there. On way to Achiltibuie, turn rt thro Polbain, on about 2.5km. There's a bench. Sit on it, drink in the sunset.

1504
MAP 2
B3

CAMAS NAN GEALL, ARDNAMURCHAN: 12km Salen on B8007. 4km from Ardnamurchan's Natural History Centre (1561/KIDS) 65km Ft William. Coming esp from the Kilchoan direction, a magnificent bay appears below you, where the rd first meets the sea. Almost symmetrical with high cliffs and a perfect field (still cultivated) in the bowl fringed by a shingle beach. Car park viewpoint and there is a path down. Deer graze around here.

1505
MAP 2
C3

GLENGARRY: 3km after Tomdoun t/off on A87, Invergarry-Kyle of Lochalsh rd. Lay-by with viewfinder. An uncluttered vista up and down loch and glen with not a house in sight (pity about the salmon cages). Distant peaks of Knoydart are identified, but not L Quoich nestling spookily and full of fish in the wilderness at the head of the glen. Bonnie Prince Charlie passed this way.

1506
MAP 8
C2

SCOTT'S VIEW, ST BOSWELLS: Off A68 at Leaderfoot Br nr St Boswells, signed Gattonside. 'The View', old Walter's favourite (the horses still stopped there long after he'd gone), is 4km along the rd (Dryburgh Abbey 3km further; 1715/ABBEYS). Magnificent sweep of his beloved Border country, but only in one direction. If you cross the rd, climb through the gate and head up the hill towards the jagged standing stone that comes into view, you reach …

1507 **IRVINE'S VIEW:** The full panorama from the Cheviots to the Lammermuirs.
MAP 8 This, the finest view in southern Scotland, is only a furlong further. This is
C3 where I'd like my bench – you know the kind of thing: a wee plaque saying 'He
loved the Borders' etc.

1508 **THE LAW, DUNDEE:** Few cities have such a single good viewpoint. To N of the
MAP 4 centre, it reveals the panoramic perspective of the city on the estuary of the
C3 silvery Tay. Best to walk from town; the one-way system is a nightmare. Get
chips at Luigi's (ask a local) on the way up: Dundee in a poke.

1509 **QUEEN'S VIEW, LOCH TUMMEL, nr PITLOCHRY:** 8km on B8019 to Kinloch
MAP 4 Rannoch. Car park and 100m walk to rocky knoll where pioneers of tourism,
B2 Queen Victoria and Prince Albert, were 'transported into ecstasies' by the view
of L Tummel and Schiehallion (1479/LOCHS; 1820/WOODLAND WALKS). Their
view was flooded by a hydro scheme after WW2, but you get the idea.

1510 **CALIFER, nr FORRES:** 7km from Forres on A96 to Elgin, turn rt for 'Pluscarden',
MAP 3 follow narrow rd for 5km. Viewpoint is on rd and looks down across Findhorn
A2 Bay and the wide vista of the Moray Firth to the Black Isle and Ben Wyvis.
Fantastic light.

1511 **THE MALCOLM MEMORIAL, LANGHOLM:** 3km from Langholm and signed
MAP 9 from main A7, a single-track rd leads to a path to this obelisk raised to cele-
D2 brate the military and masonic achievements of one John Malcolm. The eulo-
gy is fulsome esp compared with that for Hugh MacDiarmid on the cairn by
the stunning sculpture at the start of the path (1676/MEMORIALS). Views from
the obelisk, however, are among the finest in the S, encompassing a vista from
the Lakeland Fells and the Solway Firth to the wild Border hills. Path 1km.

1512 **DUNCRYNE HILL, GARTOCHARN, nr BALLOCH:** Gartocharn is betw Balloch
MAP 1 and Drymen on the A811, and this view, was recommended by writer and out-
C2 doorsman Tom Weir as 'the finest viewpoint of any small hill in Scotland'. Turn
up the rd at the E end of village and park 1km on left by a small wood (a sign
reads 'Woods reserved for Teddy bears'). The hill is only 470ft high and 'easy',
but the view of L Lomond and the Kilpatrick Hills is superb.

1513 **BLACKHILL, LESMAHAGOW, nr GLASGOW:** 28km S of city. Another marvel-
MAP 1 lous outlook, but in the opp direction from above. Take jnct 10/11 on M74,
D3 then off the B7078 signed Lanark, take the B7018. 4km along past Clarkston
Farm, head uphill for 1km and park by Water Board mound. Walk uphill
through fields to rt for about 1km. Unprepossessing hill which unexpectedly
reveals a vast vista of most of E central Scotland.   1-A-2

1514 **TONGUE:** From the causeway across the kyle, or following the minor rd to
MAP 2 Talmine on the W side, look S to the ben, or north to the small islands off the
C1 coast. Ask Elaine at the Ben Loyal Hotel. (970/INEXP HIGHLAND HOTELS).

SUMMER PICNICS AND GREAT SWIMMING HOLES

Care should be taken when swimming in rivers; don't take them for granted. Kids should be watched. Most of these places are trad local swimming and picnic spots where people have swum for yrs, but rivers continuously change their course and their nature. Wearing sandals or old sports shoes is a good idea.

1515
MAP 2
B3
✔ ✔ **THE FAIRY POOLS, GLEN BRITTLE, SKYE:** On a hot day, this is one of the best places on Skye to head for; swimming in deep pools with the massif of the Cuillins around you. One pool has a stone br you can swim under. Head off A863 Dunvegan rd from Sligachan Hotel (*see* p.169) then B8009 and Glenbrittle rd. 7km down just as rd begins to parallel the glen itself, you'll see a river coming off the hills. Park in lay-by on rt. 1km walk, follow this up. Lady Clair Macdonald recs also, the pools at Torrin nr Elgol.

1516
MAP 2
C4
✔ ✔ **THE POOLS IN GLEN ETIVE:** Glen Etive is a wild, enchanted place where people have been camping for yrs to walk and climb in the Glencoe area. There are many grassy landings at the river side as well as these perfect pools for bathing. The first is about 6km from the main Glencoe rd, the A82 at Kingshouse, but just follow the river and find your own. Take midge cream for evening wear.

1517
MAP 2
D3
✔ ✔ **FESHIEBRIDGE:** At the br itself on the B970 betw Kingussie and Inverdruie nr Aviemore. 4km from Kincraig. Gr walks here into Glen Feshie and in nearby woodland, but under br a perfect spot for Highland swimming. Go down to left from S. Rocky ledges, clear water. One of the best but cold even in high summer.

1518
MAP 6
A2
✔ ✔ **ROB ROY FALLS, nr INVERARNAN:** A82 N of Ardlui and 3 km past The Drover's Inn (1178/BLOODY GOOD PUBS). Sign on the rt (Picnic Area), height restriction so watch your Landcruiser. Park, then follow the path to the main waterfall where you'll be able to glimpse a secluded upper pool, through the trees. There's an overhanging rock face on one side and smooth slabs at the edge of the falls. Natural suntrap in summer, but the water is 'Baltic' at all times.

1519
MAP 8
A2
✔ **NEIDPATH, PEEBLES:** 2km from town on A72, Biggar rd; sign for castle. Park on rd in lay-by 100m further on, or down track by castle (gates shut at 5pm and they get shirty if you're still parked). Idyllic setting of a broad meander of the Tweed, with medieval Neidpath Castle, a sentinel above (open to public Apr-Sept). Two 'pools' (3m deep in av summer) linked by shallow rapids which the adventurous chute down on their backs. Usually a rope-swing at upper pool. TAKE CARE. Also see (1805/GLEN AND RIVER WALKS).

1520
MAP 8
C1
✔ **THE WHITEADDER, nr ABBEY ST BATHANS:** Can walk in from village or from Toot corner (1778/HILL WALKS); past Edenshall brochs then follow river 2km further. Easier via A6112 to Duns (6km from A1 at Granthouse), rd to rt marked Abbey St Bathans, go 500m to first corner, then rough track signed for brochs for 1km to river side at swing br. 3 superb rocky pools with the br above. Midges can be menacing, so take the lotion; river shoes useful. River pron 'Whit-adir'.

1521
MAP 3
A2
✔ **RANDOLPH'S LEAP nr FORRES:** Spectacular gorge on the mythical Findhorn which carves out some craggy scenery on its way to a gentle coast. This secret glade and fabulous swimming hole are behind a wall and it's difficult to describe how to find them succinctly (*see* 1810/WOODLAND WALKS *for directions*), but it's S of Forres and Nairn and nr Logie Steading, a courtyard of good things. One Randolph of course once leapt here; we just bathe and lie under the trees dreaming of gods (and maybe satyrs).

1522
MAP 2
C3
STRATHMASHIE, nr NEWTONMORE: On A86 Newtonmore/Dalwhinnie (on A9) to Ft William rd 7km from Laggan, watch for Forest sign, small off rd car park and lay-by. River follows rd. Last visit: a coachload of German teenagers. Ah well … and I used to have it to myself.

1523 **DOG FALLS, GLEN AFFRIC:** Half-way along Glen Affric rd from Cannich
MAP 2 before you come to the loch, a well-marked picnic spot and gr place to swim
C3 in the peaty waters surrounded by the Caledonian Forest (with trails). Birds
well sussed to picnic potential – your car covered in tits – Hitchcock or what?
(1799/GLEN AND RIVER WALKS).

1524 **Nr COMRIE:** 2 great pools of different character nr the neat little town in
MAP 4 deepest Perthshire. **THE LINN**, the town pool: go over humpback br from
B3 main A85 W to Lochearnhead, signed The Ross. After 2km there's a parking
place on left. River's relatively wide, v pleasant spot. For more adventurous,
GLENARTNEY is 5km on rd to Cultybraggan training camp (follow signs),
continue past camp and then MoD range on left until a ruined cottage on rt.
Park and walk down to river in glen. What with the twin perils of the Army and
the Comrie Angling Club, you might feel you have no right to be here, but you
do and this stretch of river is quite marvellous; you should have it to yourself.

1525 **NORTH SANNOX BURN, ARRAN:** Park at the North Sannox Bridge on the
MAP 1 A841 (rd from Lochranza to Sannox Bay) and follow the track W to the deer
C3 fence and treeline (1km). Just past there you will find a gt pool with small
waterfall, dragonflies and perhaps even an eagle or two above.

1526 **FALLS OF BRUAR, nr BLAIR ATHOLL:** Just off A9, 12km N of Blair Atholl. 250m
MAP 4 walk from **HOUSE OF BRUAR** car park and shopping experience
B2 (1941/CRAFTS) to lower fall (1457/WATERFALLS) where there is an accessible
large deep pool by the br. Cold, fresh mt water in a woody gorge. The proximity of the 'retail experience' can make it all the more daring.

1527 **THE OTTER'S POOL, NEW GALLOWAY FOREST:** A clearing in the forest
MAP 9 reached by a track, 'The Raider's Rd', running from 8km N of Laurieston on the
B3 A762, for 16km to Clatteringshaws Loch. The track is only open Apr-
Oct, has a toll of £2 and gets busy. It follows the Water of Dee and halfway
down the rd – the Otter's Pool. A bronze otter used to mark the spot (it got
nicked) and it's a place mainly for kids and paddling; but when the dam runs
off it can be deep enough to swim. Rd closes dusk. (1821/WOODLAND WALKS.)

1528 **ANCRUM:** A secret place on the quiet Ale Water (out of village towards
MAP 8 Lilliesleaf, 3km out 500m from farm sign to Hopton – a recessed gate on the
C3 rt and a rough track). A meadow, a Border burn, a surprising deep pool to
swim. Arcadia!

1529 **THE COBBY, KELSO:** A stretch of the Tweed with wide grassy banks, a tradi-
MAP 8 tional picnic/swimming spot with Floors Castle in the background. Rd to Floors
C2 and left to river. Fairly deep and wide at this point; good swimmers only.

1530 **PARADISE, SHERIFFMUIR, nr DUNBLANE:** A pool at the foot of an unex-
MAP 6 pected leafy gorge on the moor betw the Ochils and Strathallan. Here the
C2 Wharry Burn is known locally as 'Paradise', and for good reason. Take rd from
'behind' Dunblane or Br of Allan to the Sheriffmuir Inn; head downhill (back)
towards Br of Allan and park on the hump back br. Walk downsteam for 1km.
It can be midgy and it can be perfect. The inn (01786 823285), built in the
same yr as the battle (1715), has ales, food (6-8.45pm) and a warm welcome.

1531 **POTARCH BRIDGE & CAMBUS O'MAY on the DEE:** 2 places on the 'Royal'
MAP 3 Dee, the first by the reconstructed Victorian br (and nr the hotel) 3km E of
B3 Kincardine O'Neill. Cambus another stretch of river E of Ballater (6km). Locals
swim, picnic on rocks, etc, and there are forest walks on the other side of rd.
The brave jump off the bridge at Cambus – best to watch the locals and learn.
Be sensible!

1532 **INVERMORISTON:** On main L Ness rd A82 betw Inverness and Ft Augustus,
MAP 2 this is the best bit. R Moriston tumbles under an ancient br. Perfectly
C3 Highland. Ledges for picnics, invigorating pools, ozone-friendly. Nice beech
woods. Tavern/bistro nearby (1136/INNS).

1533 **DULSIE BRIDGE, nr NAIRN:** 16km S of Nairn on the A939 to Grantown, this
MAP 2 locally revered beauty spot is fabulous for summer swimming. The ancient
D2 arched br spans the rocky gorge of the Findhorn (again) and there are ledges
and even sandy beaches for picnics and from which to launch yourself or paddle in the peaty waters.

STRATHCARRON, nr BONAR BRIDGE: Pick your spot (1448/GLENS).

CENTRAL:

1534
MAP A
xA3
✓ ✓ **EDINBURGH ZOO:** 0131 334 9171. Corstorphine Rd. 4km W of Princes St. A large and long-established zoo, where the natural world from the poles to the plains of Africa is ranged around Corstorphine Hill. Enough huge/exotic/ghastly creatures and friendly, amusing ones to fill an overstimulated day. The penguins and the seals do their stuff at set times. More familiar creatures hang out at the 'farm'. Café and shop stocked with environmentally ok toys and souvenirs. Open 7 days, 9am-6pm (till dusk in winter).

1535
MAP A
E3
✓ ✓ **DYNAMIC EARTH, EDINBURGH:** 0131 558 7800. Holyrood Rd. Edinburgh's newest big attraction. A must for curious kids. See 346/ATTRACTIONS.

1536
MAP A
D3
✓ ✓ **MUSEUM OF CHILDHOOD, EDINBURGH:** 0131 5294142. 42 High St. An Aladdin's cave of toys through and for all ages. Much more fascinating than computer games – allegedly (356/OTHER ATTRACTIONS).

1537
MAP 7
B1
✓ **BUTTERFLY FARM, nr DALKEITH and EDINBURGH:** 0131 663 4932. On A7, signed Eskbank/Galashiels from ring rd (1km). Part of a big complex which includes a grd centre and the rather swish **BIRDS OF PREY CENTRE** (flying displays; kids get to handle some of the birds, phone for details 0131 654 1720). As for the bugs, the butterflies are delightful but 'orrible children will be far more impressed with the scorpions, locusts and other assorted uglies on show. Red-kneed tarantula not for the faint-hearted. 7 days, 10am-5pm.

1538
MAP A
CHILDREN'S FESTIVAL, EDINBURGH: 0131 554 6297 for info. Annual event held sometime in May. A week of shows from around the world.

1539
MAP 4
B3
AUCHINGARRICH WILDLIFE CENTRE, nr COMRIE: 4km from main st turning off at br then signed. Sympathetic coralling in picturesque Perthshire Hills that's especially good fun for kids mainly because of its easy-going atmos. Lots of baby fluffy things, some of which you can hold. Don't ask what happens to them when they grow up! Good place to start sex education. Emus and meerkats especially weird. Open AYR 10am-dusk. Coffee shop till 5pm.

1540
MAP 1
C3
KELBURN COUNTRY CENTRE, LARGS: 2km S of Largs on A78. Riding school, grds, woodland walks up the Kel Burn and a central visitor/consumer section with shops/exhibits/cafés. Wooden stockade for clambering kids; commando assault course for exhibitionist adults and less doddering dads. Falconry displays (and long-suffering owl). Kelburn continues to develop its range of attractions: a Secret Forest has appeared in the woods. Combine with Vikingar (1885/LEISURE CENTRES) for an exhausting day. Stock up with chips and Nardini's ice cream (1331/ICE CREAM). 7 days 10am-6pm. Apr-Oct. Grounds only in wint 11-5pm.

FIFE AND DUNDEE:

1541
MAP 5
B4
✓ **DEEP SEA WORLD, N QUEENSFERRY:** 01383 411411. The massively successful aquarium in a quarry which must make life hell in N Queensferry at the w/end (park'n'ride system and buses from Edin, or better still by *Maid of the Forth* from S Queensferry) (2186/FAVOURITE JOURNEYS). Habitats are viewed from a conveyor belt where you can stare at the fish and diverse divers teeming around and above you. Amazonian fish in a 'rainforest habitat'. Maximum hard sell to this all-weather attraction, but kids like it even when they've been queueing for aeons. In my view the best thing is the view from the canteen but for an 'award-winning' attraction, the cafe is appalling. Open AYR 7 days: summer 10am-6.30pm; winter 11am-5pm, w/ends 10am-6pm.

1542
MAP 5
C2
✓ **CRAIGTON PARK, ST ANDREWS:** 01334 473666. 6km SW of St Andrews on the Pitscottie rd. An oasis of fun: bouncy castles, trampolines, putting, crazy golf, boating lake, a train thro the grounds, adventure playgrounds and glasshouses. A perfect day's amusement esp for nippers. Easter-Sept; 10.30am-6.30pm, 7 days.

1543
MAP 4
C3

CAMPERDOWN PARK, DUNDEE: The large park just off the ring-road system (the Kingsway and via A923 to Coupar Angus) with a wildlife centre and a nearby play complex. Animal-handling at w/ends, but watch out: that gorilla does eat babies. 'Over 80 species'. Open AYR, but centre 10am-4.30pm, earlier in winter (1410/TOWN PARKS).

SOUTH AND SOUTH WEST:

1544
MAP 1
C3

✓ **KIDZ PLAY, PRESTWICK:** 01292 475215. Off main st at Station rd, past stn to beach and to rt. Big shed that's a soft play area for kids. Everything that the little blighters will like in the throwing-themselves-around department. Shriek city and a non-parent nightmare zone. They never had anything like this in my day, only trees (he said, Day-Glo green with envy). 7 days 9.30am-7pm.

1545
MAP 1
C3

LOUDON CASTLE, nr GALSTON: Theme park for the S of Glas hinterland. Just off A71 Kilmarnock-Edin rd (go from Glas via A77 Kilmarnock rd). Behind the ruins of the said Loudon Castle (burned out in 1941), a fair-ground which includes the 'largest carousel in Europe' and massive 'chairy plane', has been transplanted in the old walled grd. Nice setting; well kids may not notice the setting, but they won't forget the chairy plane. Open AYR 10am-dusk.

1546
MAP 1
D2

PALACERIGG COUNTRY PARK, CUMBERNAULD: 01236 720047. 6km E of Cumbernauld. 740 acres of parkland; ranger service, nature trails, picnic area and kids farm. 18-hole golf course and putting green. Exhib area with changing exhibits about forestry, conservation etc. Open AYR: 7 days; daylight hrs. Visitor centre and tearoom till 6.30pm in summer, 4.30pm winter.

1547
MAP 9
D2

THE TWEEDHOPE SHEEPDOG CENTRE, MOFFAT: 01683 221471. Viv Billingham Parkes has competed in numerous sheep trials and now shepherds the public in to watch her skilful demos. Easter-Oct; 11am/3pm or by appointment. W/ends and winter by appointment only. Check her answerphone message!

1548
MAP 8
C2

TEDDY MELROSE, TEDDY BEAR MUSEUM, MELROSE: 01896 822464. The Wynd. Charming teddy cornucopia: small rm displaying Pooh, Rupert and friends, with origin and history details alongside. Downstairs you can watch teddies being made, then ponder over which teddy keepsake to buy in the shop. Yummy cream teas in the courtyard. Open AYR: 10am-5pm. Wint Fri/Sat/Sun 11am-4pm. Small theatre behind for grown-ups in the evening (2092/THEATRES).

DRUMLANRIG CASTLE, nr DUMFRIES: 1394/COUNTRY PARKS.

NORTH-EAST

1549
MAP 3
C2

✓ **MACDUFF AQUARIUM:** On seafront E of the harbour, a family attraction for this under-rated Moray Firth port. Under-rated perhaps because neighbouring Banff gets more attention from tourists, but Duff House (2029/GALLERIES) gets much fewer visitors than this user and child-friendly sea life centre. All the fish seem curiously happy with their lot and content to educate and entertain. Open AYR 10-5pm.

1550
MAP 3
D2

✓ **ADEN, MINTLAW, nr PETERHEAD:** (pron 'Ah-den'). Country park just beyond Mintlaw on A950 16km from Peterhead. Former grounds of mansion with walks and many organised activities and events. Farm buildings converted into Heritage Centre (kids free), café etc. Adventure playground, 'working farm'. Open AYR.

1551
MAP 3
D3

✓ **STORYBOOK GLEN, nr ABERDEEN:** Fibreglass fantasy land in verdant glen 16km S of Aber via B9077, the S Deeside rd, a nice drive. Characters from every fairy tale and nursery story dotted around 20-acre park. Their fixed manic stares give them a spooky resemblance to people you may know, but kids presumably don't find them so real. Older kids may find it tame – no guns, no big technology. Indoor play area. Mar-Oct 10-6pm. Nov-Feb w/ends only 11-4pm.

HIGHLANDS

1552 ✓ **THE CAIRNGORM REINDEER HERD nr AVIEMORE:** At Glenmore Forest
MAP 2 Park on rd from Coylumbridge 12km from Aviemore. Real reindeer aplen-
D3 ty in reasonably authentic free-ranging habitat (when they come down off
the cloudy hillside in winter with snow all around). The most fun you can have
wearing GoreTex. They've come a long way from Sweden in 1952. Transport to
slope and meal for handfeeding. 1hr 30min trip. They are so …small. 11am
AYR plus 2.30pm in summer.

1553 ✓ **LEAULT FARM nr KINCRAIG:** Actually on fast bit of the main A9, but eas-
MAP 2 ier to find by looking for sign 1km S of Kincraig on the B9152. Working
D3 farm with daily sheepdog trials where Neal Ross demonstrates his extraordinary facility with dogs and sheep (and ducks). By all accounts this is gr spec-
tacle and is totally authentic in this setting. Usually noon and 4pm (May-Oct,
also 10 and 2pm July/Aug). Cl Sat.

1554 **THE HIGHLAND WILDLIFE PARK, KINCRAIG:** On B9152 betw Aviemore and
MAP 2 Kingussie. Large drive-through 'reserve' run by Royal Zoological Society with
D3 wandering herds of deer, bison etc and pens of other animals. 'Habitats', but
mostly cages. Must be time to bring back some of these bears and wolves –
sort out the deer and liven up the caravan parks. Open 10-5pm.

1555 **HIGHLAND AND RARE BREEDS FARM, ELPHIN, nr ULLAPOOL:** 01854
MAP 2 666204. Bridie and Russell Pursey's charming croft with over 30 'breeds' from
C1 the Soay sheep of St Kilda to Tamworth pigs; many feathered friends. A genuine working farm set on either side of the rd (A835 26km N of Ullapool) that's
v hooves and hands-on. There's always a baby something to pet. Farmwork
demos and tours. The sun seems to shine here all day. May-Sept, 10am-5pm; 7
days.

1556 **LANDMARK CENTRE, CARRBRIDGE:** 01479 841614. A purpose-built tourist
MAP 2 centre with audiovisual displays and a gr deal of shopping. Gr for kids mess-
D3 ing about in the woods on slides, in a 'maze' etc, in a large adventure playground. The Tower may be too· much for Granny but there are fine forest
views. Open AYR 7 days.

1557 **ISLAY WILDLIFE INFO & FIELD CENTRE, PORT CHARLOTTE:** 01496 850288.
MAP 1 Fascinating wildlife centre for all ages. Activity rm and organised day trips.
A3 (1588/WILDLIFE; 2157/ISLAY).

1558 **SEALIFE CENTRE, OBAN:** 16km N on the A828. On the shore of L Creran this
MAP 1 one of the oldest of a number of UK waterworlds still the best (another in **ST**
B1 **ANDREWS**). Environmentally conscientious they 'rescue' seals and house
numerous aquatic life. The new 'World of the Jellyfish' is the ultimate lava lamp
of baby moon-jellys floating around their glass cylinder. Café/shop/adventure
playground. Open summer, 10am- 6pm. (call for winter hrs 01631 720386)

1559 **RARE BREEDS FARM, OBAN:** 4km from town via Argyll Sq, then S (A816),
MAP 1 bearing left at church and on past golf course. A weird and wonderful collec-
B1 tion of animals in hill side pens and runs, who seem all the more peculiar
because they're versions of familiar ones – but are they sheep or dogs or
goats or what? Leaving the caging questions aside, it's a funny farm for kids
and the creatures seem keen enough for the attention and the far too many
crumbs from the tearoom table. Open 7 days in season.

1560 **ARGYLL WILDLIFE PARK, INVERARAY:** 4km W of town on A83. Another zoo-
MAP 1 type place, but with many native animals in more or less their natural habitat.
C2 Lots of them just wander and waddle about. Set amongst pinewoods on the
braes of L Fyne, there are probably even a few animals (e.g. mink and foxes),
trying to get in. Of the many badgers, wildcats, deer and multifarious wild-
fowl, only one old boar has so far escaped. Apr-Oct, 10-5pm, 7days.

1561 **NATURAL HISTORY CENTRE, ARDNAMURCHAN:** 01972 500209. A861
MAP 2 Strontian, B8007 Glenmore 14km. Photographer Michael McGregor's award
B3 winning interactive exhib; a bit of a surprise out here. Kids will enjoy, adults
may be impressed. Tearoom. Mon-Sat; 10.30am-5.30pm. Sun; 12-5.30pm.

THE BEST PLACES TO SEE BIRDS

See p. 197 for WILDLIFE RESERVES, *all of which are bird reserves, too.*

1562
MAP 2
C1
✓ ✓ **HANDA ISLAND, nr SCOURIE, SUTHERLAND:** Take the boat from Tarbet Beach 6km off A894 5km N of Scourie and land on a beautiful island run by the Scottish Wildlife Trust as a sea bird reserve. Boats (Apr-mid Sept though fewer birds after Aug) are continuous depending on demand (01971 502077/340). Crossing 15mins. Small reception hut and 2.5km walk over island to cliffs which rise 350m and are layered in colonies from fulmars to shags. Allow 3 to 4hrs. Perhaps you can persuade the boatman to go to see the cliffs and the formidable stack from below. Though you must take care not to disturb the birds, you'll be eye to eye with seals and bill to bill with razorbills. No boats on Sun. Eat at the seafood café on the cove when you return (1256/SEAFOOD RESTAUS).

1563
MAP 9
C3
✓ ✓ **CAERLAVEROCK, nr DUMFRIES:** 17km S on B725 nr Bankend, signed from rd. Park at 'The Wildlife and Wetlands Centre'. Admn to observation towers and walkways betw embankments into which hides have been built at intervals allowing fine views of surrounding wetlands. Large assemblies of numerous species; sightings posted. Gr success story for Barnacle Geese now wintering from Spitzbergen in many thousands. A well-managed site where it is poss to get so close to the birds that it's hard to imagine that they don't know you're there. Barn owl watch and special toads. Oct-April 10am-5pm. ADMN

1564
MAP 1
A1
✓ ✓ **LUNGA and THE TRESHNISH ISLANDS:** Off Mull. Sail from Iona or Fionnphort or Ulva ferry on Mull to these uninhabited islands on a 5/6hr excursion which probably takes in Staffa and Fingal's Cave. Best months are May-July when birds are breeding. Some trips allow 3hrs on Lunga. Razorbills, guillemots and a carpet of puffins oblivious to your presence. This will be a memorable day. Boat trips (01688 400242) or check Tobermory TO (01688 302182) who will advise of other boatmen. All trips dependent on sea conditions.

1565
MAP 5
D3
✓ ✓ **ISLE OF MAY, FIRTH OF FORTH:** Island at mouth of Forth off Crail/ Anstruther reached by daily boat trip from Anstruther Harbour (01333 310103), May-Oct 9am-2.30pm depending on tides. Boats hold 40-50; trip 45mins; allows 3hrs ashore. Island (including isthmus to Rona) 1.5km x 0.5km. Info centre and resident wardens. See guillemots, razorbills and kittiwakes on cliffs and shags, terns and thousands of puffins. Most populations increasing. This place is strange as well as beautiful. The puffins in early summer are, as always, engaging.

1566
MAP 7
B1
✓ **THE LAGOON, MUSSELBURGH:** On E edge of town behind the racecourse (follow rd round), at the estuarine mouth of the R Esk. Waders, sea birds, ducks aplenty and often interesting migrants on the mudflats and wide littoral. The 'lagoon' itself is a man-made pond behind and attracts big populations (both birds and binocs). This is the nearest diverse-species area to Edin (15km) and in recent yrs has become one of the most significant migrant stopovers in the UK.

1567
MAP 3
C4
✓ **FOWLSHEUGH, nr STONEHAVEN:** 8km S of Stonehaven and signed from A92 with path from Crawton. Sea bird city on spectacular cliffs where you can lie on your front and look over. The cliffs are 75m high; take gr care. 80,000 pairs of 6 species esp guillemots, kittiwakes, razorbills and also fulmar, shag, puffins. Poss to view the birds without disturbing them and see the 'layers' they occupy on the cliff face. Or go by boat twice weekly in summer from Stonehaven Harbour (check TO for details 01569 762806). Best seen May-July.

1568
MAP 4
B3
✓ **LOCH OF THE LOWES, DUNKELD:** 4km NE Dunkeld on A923 to Blairgowrie. Properly managed (Scottish Wildlife Trust) site with double-floored hide and permanent binocs. Main attractions are the captivating ospreys (from early Apr-Aug/Sept). Nest 100m over loch and clearly visible. Their revival is well documented, including diary of movements, breeding history etc. Hide 10am-5/6pm.

1569
MAP 2
D3

✓ **LOCH GARTEN, BOAT OF GARTEN:** 3km village off B970 into Abernethy Forest. Famous for the ospreys and so popular that access may be restricted until after the eggs have hatched. 2 car parks: the first has nature trails through Scots pine woods and around loch; other has the main hide 300m away. Extraordinary palaver considering there's only one pair and there are no fish in the loch so they don't feed there (anyhow fishfarms are easier). Och, but they are magnificent.

1570
MAP 1
A3

✓ **ISLAY, LOCH GRUINART, LOCH INDAAL:** RSPB reserve. Take A847 at Bridgend then B8017 turning N and rt for Gruinart. The mudflats and fields at the head of the loch provide winter grazing for huge flocks of Barnacle and Greenland geese. They arrive, as do flocks of fellow bird-watchers, in late Oct. Hides and good vantage points near rd. The Rhinns and the Oa in the S sustain a huge variety of bird life.

1571

✓ **MARWICK HEAD, ORKNEY MAINLAND:** 40km NW of Kirkwall, via Finstown and Dounby; take left at Birsay after L of Isbister cross the B9056 and park at Cumlaquoy. Spectacular sea bird breeding colony on 100m cliffs and nearby at the Loons Reserve, wet meadowland, 8 species of duck and many waders. Orkney sites include the Noup cliffs on Westray, North Hill on Papa Westray and Copinsay, 3km E of the mainland. The remoter, the merrier

1572 **ORKNEY PUFFINS:** 'Wildabout' tour's dusk puffin patrol (01856 851011). Or go solo at Costa Head, Brough of Birsay and Westray; check Kirkwall TO for latest.

1573
MAP 1
D3

BARON'S HAUGH, MOTHERWELL: nr Strathclyde Park. From Motherwell Civic Centre, take rd for Hamilton then left (1km) up Leven St, bearing rt to end (there are signs). RSPB reserve of woodland, marsh and scrub by R Clyde; a sanctuary in a heavily built-up area. Furthest of 4 hides is 1.5km walk. The wide variety of habitats offers a surprising range of species esp in winter. Dalzell Country Park adj, has trails.

1574
MAP 7
B1

THE BASS ROCK, off NORTH BERWICK: 01620 892838. 'Temple of gannets'. A gr-guano encrusted spaceship take-off ramp sticking out of the Forth and where Davie Balfour was imprisoned in RLS's *Catriona* (aka *Kidnapped II*). Weather-dependent boat trips available May-Sep courtesy of Mr Marr, from N Berwick harbour (also to nearby Fidra). Phone for details.

SCOTTISH SEABIRDS CENTRE, N BERWICK: Opening spring 2000 nr N Berwick Harbour o/looking Bass Rock and Fidra. Video and other state of the art technology bringing the birds closer to you.

1575
MAP 4
D2

MONTROSE BASIN WILDLIFE CENTRE: 1.5km south of Montrose on the A92 to Arbroath. V accessible centre, opened in '95, overlooks the basin that hosts various residents and migrants. Good for twitchers and kids. And autumn geese. Apr-oct daily 10.30am-5pm. Nov-Mar daily 10.30pm-4pm

1576
MAP 2
D1

FORSINARD NATURE RESERVE: By road, 44km from Helmsdale on the A897, or the train stops on route to Wick/Thurso. RSPB reserve, acquired in '95 following public appeal. 17, 500 acres of flow country and the birds that go with it: divers, plovers, merlins and hen harriers. Reserve open AYR; visitor centre Apr-Oct daily 9am-6pm.

1577
MAP 4
C2

LOCH OF KINNORDY, KIRRIEMUIR: 4km W of town on B951, an easily accessible site with 2 hides o/look loch and wetland area managed by RSPB. Geese in winter, gulls aplenty; always tickworthy.

1578
MAP 3
D1

STRATHBEG, nr FRASERBURGH: 12km S off main Fraserburgh-Peterhead rd, the A952 and signed 'Nature Reserve' at Crimond. Wide, shallow loch v close to coastline, a 'magnet for migrating wildfowl' and from the (unmanned) reception centre at loch side it's poss to get a v good view of them. Marsh/fen, dune and meadow habitats. In winter 30,000 geese/widgeon/mallard/swans and occasional rarities like cranes and egrets. Binocs in centre and 2 other hides; marked route around.

WHERE TO SEE DOLPHINS, WHALES AND PORPOISES

1579
MAP 2

✔ ✔ *The coast around the N of Scotland offers some of the best places in Europe from which to see whales and dolphins and, more ubiquitously, seals. You don't have to go on boat trips, though of course you get closer, the boatman will know where to find them and the trip itself can be exhilarating. A list of operators is given below. Dolphins are most active on a rising tide esp May-Sept.*

MORAY and CROMARTY FIRTHS, nr INVERNESS and CROMARTY:

The best area in Scotland. The population of bottlenose dolphins in this area well exceeds 100 and they can be seen AYR.

THE DOLPHIN WATCH and MARINE RESEARCH STATION: Just N of the Kessock Br on the A9 and adj the Tourist Information Centre. Underwater microphones pick up the chatterings of dolphins and porpoises and there's always somebody there to explain. Apr-Nov, 7 days 10am-7.30pm.

CROMARTY: Any vantage around the town is good esp S Sutor for coastal walk and an old lighthouse cottage has been converted into a research base here. Other sites in this area with helpful marker boards at **FOULIS FERRY**, W end of car park; **BALINTORE**, opp Seaboard Memorial Hall; **TARBERT NESS** beyond **PORTMAHOMACK**, end of path through reserve; and esp **CHANONRY POINT**, E end of pt beyond lighthouse. Sightings further out along the Moray Firth poss at **BURGHEAD, LOSSIEMOUTH** and **BUCKIE, SPEY BAY** and **PORTKNOCKIE**.

NORTH WEST

On the W coast, esp nr Gairloch the following places may offer sightings of orcs, dolphins and minke whales mainly in summer.

RUBHA REIDH nr GAIRLOCH: 20km N by unclassified rd beyond Melvaig. Nr the Carn Dearg Youth Hostel W of Lonemore where rd turns inland is good spot.

GREENSTONE POINT N of LAIDE on the A832 nr Inverewe Gardens and Gruinard Bay. Harbour porpoises here Apr-Dec and minke whales May-Oct.

RED POINT of GAIRLOCH: by unclassified rd via Badachro. High ground looking over N Minch and S to L Torridon. Harbour porpoises often along this coast.

OTHER PLACES

MOUSA SOUND, SHETLAND: 20km S of Lerwick (1634/PREHISTORIC SITES).

ARDNAMURCHAN, THE POINT: The most westerly point (and lighthouse) on this wildly beautiful peninsula. Go to end of rd or park nr Sanna Beach and walk round. Sanna Beach is worth going to just to walk the strand. New visitor centre with tearoom and toilets.

STORNOWAY, ISLE OF LEWIS: Heading out of town for Eye Peninsula, at Holm nr Sandwick S of A866 or from Bayble Bay (all within walking distance).

BOAT TRIPS TO SEA LIFE

FROM CROMARTY: DOLPHIN ECOSSE (01381 600323); **SEABOARD MARINE** (01862 851324) or 01862 871255 (the ferry).

FROM INVERNESS: DOLPHIN CRUISES (01463 717900); **MACAULAY CHARTERS** (01463 717337).

ON THE ISLANDS: SEA-LIFE CRUISES, MULL (01688 400223); **WILDABOUT, ORKNEY:** (01856 851011) puffin patrols at dusk.

MINCH CHARTERS, MALLAIG: 01687 462304. Every kind of mammal in all kinds of scenery: L Coruisk, Corryvreckan, St Kilda (2214/SEVEN THINGS).

LAXFORD CHARTERS: 01971 502251. Unusual islands and skerries of L Laxford (nr Handa Island); seals, birds and gr seafood back on land (1256/SEAFOOD RESTAUS).

SUMMER ISLES CRUISES: 01854 622200. The islets and seal colony. Angling if you like.

WILDLIFE CRUISES: 01955 611353. From John o' Groats; puffins, seabirds, seals. June-Aug.

... And OTTERS

1580
MAP 2
B3

Otters can be seen all over the NW Highlands in sheltered inlets, esp early morning and late evening and on an ebb tide. Skye is one of best places in Europe to see them. **OTTER SURVIVAL FUND AND VISITOR CENTRE, BROADFORD** (01471 822487) organise guided walks for all wildlife and might pt you in the rt direction.

GREAT WILDLIFE RESERVES

These wildlife reserves are not merely bird-watching places. Most of them are easy to get to from major centres; none requires permits.

1581
MAP 8
D1

✓✓ **ST ABBS HEAD, nr BERWICK:** 22km N Berwick, 9km N Eyemouth and only 10km E of main A1. Spectacular cliff scenery (1831/COASTAL WALKS), a huge sea bird colony, rich marine life and a varied flora make this a place of fascination and diverse interest. Good view from top of stacks, geos and cliff face full of serried ranks of guillemot, kittiwake, razorbill etc. Hanging grds of grasses and campion. Behind cliffs, grassland rolls down to the Mire L and its varied habitat of bird, insect and butterfly life and vegetation. Superb.

1582
MAP 3
D3

✓✓ **SANDS OF FORVIE and THE YTHAN ESTUARY, NEWBURGH:** 25km N of Aber. Cross br o/side Newburgh on A975 to Cruden Bay and park. Path follows Ythan estuary and, bearing N, enters the largest dune system in the UK undisturbed by man. Dunes in every aspect of formation. Collieston, a 17/18th-century fishing village arranged in terraces on the cliffs, is 5km away. The various coastal habitats support the largest population of eiders in UK (esp June) and huge numbers of terns. Plenty to see even from main rd lay-bys; also hides.

1583
MAP 7
B1

JOHN MUIR COUNTRY PARK, DUNBAR: The vast park betw Dunbar and N Berwick named after the naturalist/explorer who was born in Dunbar and who, in founding Yellowstone National Park in the US, is regarded as the father of the Conservation movement. Includes estuary of the Tyne (park also known as Tyninghame), cliffs, sand spits and woodland, it covers a wide range of habitats. Many bird species (e.g. 30 waders), crabs, lichens, sea and marsh plants. Enter at E extremity of Dunbar at Belhaven, off the B6370 from A1; or off A198 to N Berwick 3km from A1. Or better, walk from Dunbar by 'cliff top trail' (2km).

1584
MAP 1
C3

LOCHWINNOCH: 30km SW of Glas via M8 jnct 29 then A737 and A760 past Johnstone. Also from Largs 20km via A760. Reserve is just o/side village on loch side and comprises wetland and woodland habitats. A serious 'nature centre' incorporating an observation tower. Hides and marked trails; and a birds-spotted board. Shop and coffee shop. Good for kids. Centre 10am-5pm.
RSPB

1585
MAP 2
D3

INSH MARSHES, KINGUSSIE: 4km from town along B970 (after Ruthven Barracks, 1626/RUINS), a reserve run by RSPB but with much more than just birds to see. Trail (3km) marked out through meadow and wetland and a note of species to look out for (including 6 types of orchid). Also 2 hides (250m and 450m) high above marshes, vantage points to see waterfowl, birds of prey, otters and deer.

1586
MAP 5
C2

TENTSMUIR, betw NEWPORT and LEUCHARS: The northern tip of Fife at the mouth of the Firth of Tay, reached from Tayport or Leuchars via the B945. Follow signs for Kinshaldy Beach taking rd that winds for 4km over flat and then forested land. Park amongst Corsican pine plantation (car park closes 9pm in summer) and cross dunes to broad strand which many consider to be a better beach than the W Sands, St Andrews. Walks in both direction: W back to Tayport, E towards Eden Bird Sanctuary. Also 4km circular walk of beach and forest. Hide 2km away at Ice House Pond. Seals often watch from waves and bask in summer. Lots of butterflies. Waders aplenty and, to E, one of UK's most significant populations of eider. Most wildfowl offshore on Abertay Sands.

1587
MAP 5
B3
VANE FARM: RSPB reserve on S shore of L Leven, beside and bisected by B9097 off jnct 5 of M90. Easily reached and v busy visitor centre with observation lounge and education/orientation facs. Hide nearer loch side reached by tunnel under rd. Nature Trail on hill behind through heath and birchwood (2km circ). Good place to introduce kids to nature watching. Recent upgrading.

1588
MAP 1
A3
ISLAY WILDLIFE INFO & FIELD CENTRE, PORT CHARLOTTE: Jam-packed info centre that's v 'hands-on' and interactive. Up-to-date displays of geology, natural history (rocks, skeletons, sealife tanks). Recent sightings of wildlife, flora and fauna lists, video rm, reference library. Kids area and activity days when staff take you on a tour around the surrounding area.

1589
MAP 2
A2
BALRANALD, NORTH UIST, WESTERN ISLES: W coast of N Uist reached by the rd from Lochmaddy, then the Bayhead t/off at Clachan Stores (10km N). We have listened for the corncrake, this being one of its last strongholds but so far not a cheep. However here and there are… Many species; many different habitats.

SECTION 7

Historical Places

THE BEST CASTLES

NTS: *Under the care of the National Trust for Scotland. Hrs vary.* HS: *Under the care of Historic Scotland. Standard hrs are: Apr-end Sept Mon-Sat 9.30am-6.30pm; Sun 2-6.30pm. Oct-Mar Mon-Sat 9.30am-4.30pm; Sun 2-4.30pm.*

1590
MAP 6
C3
✓✓✓ **STIRLING CASTLE:** Some would say that Stirling is 'better' than Edin: perched on its rock above the town, it is instantly comparable. And like Edin, it's a timeless attraction that can withstand waves of tourism as it survived the centuries of warfare for which it was built. Despite this primary function, it does seem a v civilised billet, with peaceful grds and rampart walks from which the views are excellent (esp the aerial view of the Royal Grds, 'the cup and saucer' as they're known locally). The renovation of the Gr Hall will recreate the jewel in Stirling's crown demonstrating how magnificent the banquets must have been in the court of James. In summer there's v 20th C rock 'n' roll – REM played here 1999. Nice café.   HS

1591
MAP A
C3
✓✓✓ **EDINBURGH CASTLE:** Edin city centre. Impressive from any angle and all the more so from inside. Despite the tides of tourists and time, it still enthralls. Superb perspectives of the city and of Scottish history. Stone of Destiny now up there with the Crown Jewels as Big Attraction. Café and restau (superb views) with efficient, but uninspiring catering operation; open only castle hrs and to castle visitors (341/MAIN ATTRACTIONS).   HS

1592
MAP 3
A2
✓✓ **BRODIE CASTLE, nr NAIRN:** 6-7km W of Forres off main A96. More a (Z plan) tower house than a castle, dating from 1567 and still lived in by the Brodie of Brodie. With a minimum of historical hocum, this 16/17th-century, but mainly Victorian, country house is furnished from rugs to moulded ceilings in the most excellent taste. Every picture (v few gloomies) bears examination. The nursery and nannie's rm, the guest rms, indeed all the rms, are eminently habitable. I could live in the library. There are regular musical evenings and other events (01309 641371 for event programme). Tearoom and informal walks in grounds. An avenue leads to a lake; in spring the daffodils are famous. Apr-Sept 11am-5.30pm; Sun 1.30-5.30pm. W/ends in Oct. Grounds open AYR till sunset.   NTS

1593
MAP 1
C3
✓✓ **CULZEAN CASTLE, MAYBOLE:** 24km S of Ayr on A719. Impossible to convey here the scale and the scope of the house and the country park. Allow some hrs esp for the grounds. Castle is more like a country house and you examine from the other side of a rope. From the 12th century, but rebuilt by Robert Adam in 1775, a time of soaring ambition, its grandeur is almost out of place in this exposed cliff-top position. It was designed for entertaining, and the oval staircase is magnificent. Wartime associations (esp with President Eisenhower) plus the enduring fascination of the aristocracy. 560 acres of grounds including cliff top walk, formal grds, walled grd, Swan Pond (a must) and Happy Valley. Harmonious home farm is visitor centre with café, exhibits and shop etc. Open Apr-Oct 10.30am-5.30pm. Many special 'events'. Culzean is pron 'Cullane'.   NTS

1594
MAP 5
C3
✓✓ **FALKLAND PALACE, FALKLAND:** Middle of farming Fife, 15km from M90 at jnct 8. Not a castle at all, but the hunting palace of the Stewart dynasty. Despite its recreational rather than political role, it's one of the landmark buildings in Scottish history and in the 16th century was the finest Renaissance building in Britain. They all came here for archery, falconry and hunting boar and deer on the Lomonds; and for Royal Tennis which is displayed and explained. Still occupied by the Crichton-Stewarts, the house is dark and rich and redolent of those days of 'dancin and deray at Falkland on the Grene'. Apr-Oct 11-5.30pm, Sun 1.30-5.30pm. Gr walks from village (1775/HILL WALKS). (1802/GLEN WALKS).   NTS

1595
MAP 2
D2
✓ **CAWDOR CASTLE, CAWDOR, nr NAIRN and INVERNESS:** The mighty Cawdor of Macbeth fame. The family clear off for the summer and leave their romantic yet habitable castle, sylvan grounds and gurgling Cawdor Burn to you. Pictures from Claude to John Piper and Conroy, a modern kitchen as fascinating as the enormous one of yore. Even the 'tartan passage' is nicely done. The burn is the colour of tea. An easy drive (25km) to Brodie (1592/CASTLES) means you can see two of Scotland's most appealing castles in one day. Grds are gorgeous. May-early Oct, 7 days, 10am-5.30pm, 9-hole golf.

1596
MAP 4
B2
✓ **BLAIR CASTLE, BLAIR ATHOLL:** Impressive from the A9, the castle and the landscape of the Dukes of Atholl; 10km N of Pitlochry. Hugely popular; almost a holiday camp atmos. Numbered rms chock-full of 'collections': costumes, toys, plates, weapons, stag skulls, walking sticks – so many things! Upstairs, the more usual stuffed apartments including the Jacobite bits. Walk in the policies (which is more than the current Duke does v often – he lives abroad). Apr-Oct 10am-6pm.

1597
MAP 4
C3
✓ **GLAMIS, FORFAR:** 8km from Forfar via A94 or off main A929, Dundee-Aber rd (t/off 10km N of Dundee, a picturesque app). Fairy-tale castle in majestic setting. Seat of the Strathmore family (Queen Mum spent her childhood here) for 300 yrs; every rm an example of the interior of a certain period. Guided tours (continuous/50mins duration). Restau/gallery shop haven for tourists. Mid Apr-mid Oct, 10.00am. Last admn 4.45pm.

1598
MAP 1
C3
✓ **BRODICK CASTLE, ARRAN:** 4km from town (bike hire 01770 302868/302009). Impressive, well-maintained castle, exotic formal grds and extensive grounds. Goat Fell in the background and the sea through the trees many of which were flattened in the Dec '98 storm that also affected the castle. Dating from 13th century and until recently the home of the Dukes of Hamilton. An over-antlered hall leads to liveable rms with portraits and heirlooms, an atmos of long-ago afternoons. Tangible sense of relief in the kitchens now all the entertaining is over. Robert the Bruce's cell is not so convincing. Easter-Oct daily until 4.30pm (until 5pm July/Aug). Marvellous grounds open AYR.
NTS

1599
MAP 1
B1
✓ **DUART CASTLE, MULL:** 13th-century ancestral seat of the Clan Maclean who take up residence for the summer and clan gatherings. Quite a few modifications over the centuries as methods of defence grew in sophistication but with walls as thick as a truck and the sheer isolation of the place it must have made any prospect of attack seem doomed from the outset. Of course the only attacking that gets done these days is on scones in the tearoom but some scent of the old bloodthirst still remains. May-Oct 10.30am-6pm.

1600
MAP 1
B1
TOROSAY CASTLE, MULL: 3km from Craignure and the ferry. A Victorian *arriviste* in this strategic corner where Duart Castle has ruled for centuries. Not many apartments open but who could blame them – this is a family home, endearing and eccentric esp their more recent history (like Dad's Loch Ness Monster fixation). The heirlooms are valuable because they have been cherished and there's a human proportion to the house and its contents which is rare in such places. The grds, attributed to Lorimer, are fabulous, esp the Italianate Statue Walk, and are open AYR. The Mull Light Railway from Craignure is one way to go. Tearoom. Apr-Oct 10.30am-5.30pm.

1601
MAP 2
B2
DUNVEGAN CASTLE, SKYE: 3km Dunvegan village. Romantic history and setting, though more baronial than castellate, the result of mid-19th-century restoration that incorporated the disparate parts. Necessary crowd management leads you through a series of rms where the Fairy Flag, displayed above a table of exquisite marquetry, has pride of place. Grds down to the loch, where boats leave the jetty 'to see the seals'. Busy café and gift shop at gate side car park.

1602
MAP 2
B3
EILEAN DONAN, DORNIE: On A87, 13km before Kyle of Lochalsh. A calendar favourite, often depicted illuminated; and with the balloon hovering above, an abiding image from the BBC promo of '99. Inside it's a v decent slice of history for the price. The Banqueting Hall with its Pipers' Gallery must make for splendid dinner parties for the Macraes. Much military regalia amongst the bric-à-brac, but also the impressive Raasay Punchbowl partaken of by Johnson and Boswell. Mystical views from ramparts.

1603
MAP 4
B3
CASTLE MENZIES, WEEM, nr ABERFELDY: In Tay valley with spectacular ridge behind (there are walks here in the Weem Forest, part of the Tummel Valley Forest Park; separate car park). On B846, 7km W of Aberfeldy, through Weem. The 16th-century stronghold of the Menzies (pron 'Ming-iss'), one of Scotland's oldest clans. Sparsely furnished with odd clan memorabilia, the house nevertheless conveys more of a sense of Jacobite times than many more brimful of bric-à-brac. Bonnie Prince Charlie stopped here on the way to Culloden. Open farmland situation, so manured rather than manicured grounds. Apr-Oct 10.30am-5pm, Sun 2-5pm. Tearoom.

1604 **SCONE PALACE, nr PERTH:** On A93 rd to Blairgowrie and Braemar. A 'great
MAP 4   house' and home to the Earl of Mansfield and the major attraction here-
C3   abouts. Famous for the 'Stone of Scone' on which the Kings of Scotland were
crowned, now as delightful to roam in the grounds as to roam thro their his-
tory. Many contented animals greet you and a plethora of peacocks.
Easter–oct 7days 9.30am-4.45pm (last adm.)

1605 **KELLIE CASTLE, nr PITTENWEEM, FIFE:** Major castle in Fife. Dating from 14th
MAP 5   century restored by Robert Lorimer, his influence evidenced by magnificent
C3   plaster ceilings and furniture. The grds, nursery and kitchen recall all the old
Victorian virtues. The old-fashioned roses still bloom for us. Easter and May-
Sept 1.30-5.30pm, w/ends only Oct. Grounds open AYR.   ADMN

1606 **CRAGIEVAR, nr BANCHORY:** 15km N of main A93 Aber-Braemar rd betw
MAP 3   Banchory and Aboyne. A classic tower house, perfect like a porcelain minia-
C3   ture. Random windows, turrets, balustrades. Set amongst sloping lawns and
tall trees. Limited access to halt deterioration (only 8 people at a time) means
you are spared the shuffling hordes, but don't go unless you are respecter of
the NTS conservation policy. Check local TOs for latest opening hrs, but probably May-Sept 1.30pm. Last Entry 4.45pm.   NTS

1607 **DRUM CASTLE (the IRVINE ANCESTRAL HOME), nr BANCHORY:** 1km off
MAP 3   main A93 Aber-Braemar rd betw Banchory and Peterculter and 20km from
C3   Aber centre. For 24 generations this has been the seat of the Irvines. Our lot!
Gifted to one William De Irwin by Robert the Bruce for services rendered at
Bannockburn, it combines the original keep, a Jacobean mansion and
Victorian expansionism. I have twice signed the book in the Irvine Rm and
wandered through the accumulated history hopeful of identifying with
something. Hugh Irvine, the family 'artist' whose extravagant self-portrait as
the Angel Gabriel raised eyebrows in 1810, seems more interesting than most
of my soldiering forebears. Give me a window seat in the library! Grounds
have a peaceful walled rose grd (Apr-Oct 10-6pm). House: Easter-Sept 1.30-
5.30, Oct w/ends only.   NTS

1608 **BALMORAL, nr BALLATER:** On main A93 betw Ballater and Braemar. Limited
MAP 3   access to the house (i.e. only the ballrm – public functions are held here when
B3   they're in residence) so grounds (open Apr-July) with Albert's wonderful trees
are more rewarding. For royalty rooters only, and if you like
Landseers …Crathie Church along the main rd has a good rose window, an
altar of Iona marble. John Brown is somewhere in the old graveyard down
track from visitor centre (but I couldn't find him), the memorial on the hill is
worth a climb for a poignant moment and the view of the policies. The Crathie
services haven't been quite the same Sunday attraction since Di and Fergie on
a prince's arm.

1609 **DUNROBIN CASTLE, GOLSPIE:** The largest house in the Highlands, the home
MAP 2   of the Dukes of Sutherland who once owned more land than anyone else in
D2   the British Empire. It's the first Duke who occupies an accursed place in Scots
history for his inhumane replacement, in these vast tracts, of people with
sheep. His statue stands on Ben Bhraggie above the town (1672/MONUMENTS).
Living the life of English grandees, the Sutherlands transformed the castle
into a *château* and filled it with their obscene wealth. Once there were 100
servants for a house party of 20 and it had 30 gardeners. Now it's all just history. The grds are still fabulous. The castle and separate museum are open
May-mid Oct. Check 01408 633177 for times. One of the few castles you might
want to raze on first sight; the motto above the windows says 'sans peur'. Gets
the pulse racing.   ADMN

CRATHES, nr BANCHORY: 1379/GARDENS; 1663/COUNTRY HOUSES.

FYVIE, ABERDEENSHIRE: 1662/COUNTRY HOUSES.

FASQUE, nr STONEHAVEN: 1654/COUNTRY HOUSES.

FLOORS CASTLE, KELSO: 1658/COUNTRY HOUSES.

TRAQUAIR, INNERLEITHEN: 1656/COUNTRY HOUSES.

THIRLESTANE, LAUDER: 1661/COUNTRY HOUSES.

THE MOST INTERESTING RUINS

HS: *Under the care of Historic Scotland. Standard hrs are: Apr-end Sept Mon-Sat 9.30am-6.30pm; Sun 2-6.30pm. Oct-Mar Mon-Sat 9.30am-4.30pm, Sun 2-4.30pm. 'Friends of Historic Scotland' membership: 0131 668 8600 or any of the manned sites (annual charge but then free admn).*

1610
MAP 7
A1

✓ ✓ ✓ **LINLITHGOW PALACE:** Impressive from the M9 and the S app to this the most agreeable of W Lothian towns, but don't confuse the magnificent Renaissance edifice with St Michael's Church next door, topped with its controversial crown and spear spire. From the richly carved fountain in the courtyard, to the Gr Hall with its adj huge kitchens, you get a real impression of the lavish lifestyle of the court. Apparently 'underperforms' as an attraction for Historic Scotland, so some titivation may be underway.

HS

1611
MAP 9
C3

✓ ✓ **CAERLAVEROCK, nr DUMFRIES:** 17km S by B725. Follow signs for Wetlands Reserve (1563/BIRDS), but go past rd end. Fairy-tale fortress within double moat and manicured lawns, the daunting frontage being the apex of an uncommon triangular shape. Since 1270, the bastion of the Maxwells, the Wardens of the W Marches. Destroyed by Bruce, besieged in 1640; now only waiting to be turned into a movie.

HS

1612
MAP 3
C4

✓ **DUNNOTTAR CASTLE, nr STONEHAVEN:** 3km S of Stonehaven on the coast rd just off the A92. Like Slains further N, the ruins are impressively and precariously perched on a cliff top. Historical links with Wallace, Mary Queen of Scots (the odd night) and even Oliver Cromwell, whose Roundheads besieged it in 1650. Mel Gibson's *Hamlet* was filmed here (bet you don't remember that). 400m walk from car park. Can walk along cliff top from Stonehaven (2km). Mar-Oct 9am-6pm, Sun 2-5pm. Nov-Mar Weekdays only 9-dusk.

1613
MAP 2
B3

✓ **CASTLE TIORAM, nr ACHARACLE:** Romantic ruin where you don't need the saga to sense the place, and maybe the mystery is better than the history. 5km from A861 just N of Acharacle. A sign on the foreshore says 'Don't get stranded'; the walk across a short causeway adds to the experience. Recently and controversially, bought up and its future as well as its past is under review. Pron 'Cheerum'. Musical beach at nearby Kentra Bay (1832/COASTAL WALKS).

1614
MAP 3
B1

✓ **ELGIN CATHEDRAL, ELGIN:** Follow signs in town centre. Set in a meadow by the river, a tranquil corner of this busy market town, the scattered ruins and surrounding graveyard of what was once Scotland's finest cathedral. The nasty Wolf of Badenoch burned it down in 1390, but there are some 13th-century and medieval renewals. The octagonal chapterhouse is especially revered, but this is an impressive and evocative slice of history. Guided tours are v good. Around the corner, there's now a biblical garden planted with species mentioned in the Bible. (May-Sept, daily).

HS ADMN

1615
MAP 3
C3

✓ **KILDRUMMY CASTLE, nr ALFORD:** 15km SW of Alford on A97 nr the hotel (1160/SCOTTISH HOTELS) and across the gorge from its famous grds. Most complete 13th-century castle in Scotland, an HQ for the Jacobite uprising of 1715 and an evocative and v Highland site. Here the invitation in HS advertising to 'bring your imagination' is truly valid. Apr-Sep 9.30am-6.30pm.

HS

1616
MAP 2
A3

✓ **KISIMULL CASTLE, ISLE OF BARRA:** The medieval fortress, home of the MacNeils that sits on a rocky outcrop in the bay 200m offshore. Originally built in the 11th century, it was burnt in the 18th and restored by the 45th chief, an American architect, but was unfinished when he died in 1970. An essential pilgrimage for all MacNeils, it is fascinating and atmospheric for the rest of us, a grim exterior belying an unusual internal layout – a courtyard that seems unchanged and rms betwixt renovation and decay. The boatman John Allan will show you round on Mon/Wed/Sat afts. Go to the quay or phone 01871 810449. See it before HS removes the weeds and the true ravages of time.

1617 **EDZELL CASTLE, EDZELL:** 2km village off main st, signed. Pleasing red sand-
MAP 4 stone ruin in bucolic setting – birds twitter, rabbits run. Notable walled
D2 parterre grd created by Sir David Lindsay way back in 1604. The wall niches
are nice. Mary Queen of Scots was here (of course). HS

1618 **BOTHWELL CASTLE, UDDINGSTON, GLASGOW:** 15km E of city via M74,
MAP 1 Uddingston t/off into main st and follow signs. Hugely impressive 13th-cen-
D3 tury ruin, the home of the Black Douglases, o/look Clyde (with fine walks).
Remarkable considering proximity to city that there is hardly any 20th-centu-
ry intrusion except yourself. 1km from car park. Pay to go inside. HS

1619 **FORT GEORGE, nr INVERNESS:** On promontory of Moray Firth 18km NE via
MAP 2 A96 by village of Ardersier. A vast site and 'one of the most outstanding
D2 artillery fortifications in Europe'. Planned after Culloden as a base for George
II's army and completed 1769, it has remained unaltered ever since and allows
a v complete picture. May provoke palpitations in the Nationalist heart, but
it's heaven for militarists and altogether impressive. It's hardly a ruin of course,
and is still occupied by the army. HS

1620 **DUNOLLIE CASTLE, OBAN:** Just o/side town via Corran Esplanade towards
MAP 1 Ganavan. Best to walk to or park on Esplanade and then walk 1km. (No safe
B1 parking on main rd below castle.) Bit of a scramble up and a slither down, but
the views are superb. More atmospheric than Dunstaffnage and not com-
mercialised. You can climb one flight up, but the ruin is only a remnant of the
gr stronghold of the Lorn Kings that it was. The Macdougals, who took it over
in the 12th century, still live in the house below.

1621 **TARBERT CASTLE:** Tarbert, Argyll. Strategically and dramatically o/look the
MAP 1 sheltered harbour of this epitome of a West Highland pt. Unsafe to clamber
B2 over, it's for the timeless view rather than an evocation of tangible history that
it's worth finding the way up. Steps on Harbour Rd next to dental surgery.

1622 **KILCHURN CASTLE, LOCH AWE:** The romantic ruin at the head of L Awe, vis-
MAP 1 ited either by a short walk (1km) from car park off the main A85 5km E of
C1 Lochawe village (betw the Stronmilchan t/off and the Inveraray rd) or by a
fetching wee steamboat from Loch Awe Pierhead (by the station) – call 01838
200440 for details Pleasant spot for loch reflections. If you go by boat, take tea
in the railway carriage cafe while you're waiting.

1623 **ST ANDREWS CATHEDRAL:** The ruins of the largest church in Scotland
MAP 5 before the Reformation, a place of gr influence and pilgrimage. St Rule's Tower
C2 and the jagged fragment of the huge W Front in their striking position at the
convergence of the main streets and o/look the sea, are remnants of its gr
glory.

1624 **CRICHTON CASTLE, nr PATHHEAD:** 6km W of A68 at Pathhead (28km S Edin)
MAP 7 or via A7 turning E, 3km S of Gorebridge. Massive Border keep dominating the
B1 Tyne valley on knoll with church ruin nearby. Spectacular 'range' built late
16th century. 500m walk from Crichton village. Good picnic spots below by
the river. ADMN HS

1625 **TANTALLON CASTLE, NORTH BERWICK:** 5km E of town by coast rd; 500m to
MAP 7 dramatic cliff top setting with views to Bass Rock. Dates from 1350 with mas-
B1 sive 'curtain wall' to see it through stormy weather and stormy history. The
Red Douglases and their friends kept the world at bay. Wonderful beach
nearby (377/BEACHES). ADMN HS

1626 **RUTHVEN BARRACKS, KINGUSSIE:** 2km along B970 and visible from A9 esp
MAP 2 at night when it's illuminated, these former barracks built by the English
D3 Redcoats as part of the campaign to tame the Highlands after the first
Jacobite rising in 1715, were actually destroyed by the Jacobites in 1746 after
Culloden. It was here that Bonnie Prince Charlie sent his final order, 'Let every
man seek his own safety', signalling the absolute end of the doomed cause.
Life for the soldiers is well described and visualised. Open AYR. HS

1627 **URQUHART CASTLE, DRUMNADROCHIT, LOCH NESS:** 28km S of Inverness
MAP 2 on A82. The classic Highland fortress on a promontory o/look L Ness visited
C3 every yr by bus loads and boat loads of tourists. Photo opportunities galore
amongst the well-kept lawns and extensive ruins of the once formidable
stronghold of the Picts and their scions, finally abandoned in the 18th
century. ADMN HS

1628 **DOUNE CASTLE, DOUNE:** Follow signs from centre of village which is just off
MAP 6 A84 Callander-Dunblane rd. O/look the R Teith, the well-preserved ruin of a
C2 late 14th-century courtyard castle with a Gr Hall and another draughty rm
where Mary Queen of Scots once slept. Walk in the meadow.

ADMN HS

1629 **SLAINS CASTLE, betw NEWBURGH and CRUDEN BAY:** 32km N of Aber off
MAP 3 the A975 perched on the cliffs. Obviously because of its location, but also
D2 because there's no reception centre/postcard shop or guided tour, this is a
ruin that talks. Your imagination, like Bram Stoker's (who was inspired after
staying here, to write Dracula), can be cast to the winds. The seat of the Earls
of Errol, it has been gradually disintegrating since the roof was removed in
1925. Once, it had the finest dining-rm in Scotland. The waves crash below, as
always. Be careful!

THE BEST PREHISTORIC SITES

1630 ✓ ✓ ✓ **SKARA BRAE, ORKNEY MAINLAND:** 32km Kirkwall by
A965/966 via Finstown and Dounby. Can be a windy walk to
this remarkable shoreline site, the subterranean remains of a compact village
5,000 yrs old. It was engulfed by a sandstorm 600yrs later and lay perfectly
preserved until uncovered by another storm in 1850. Now it permits one of
the most evocative glimpses of truly ancient times in the UK. ADMN HS

1631 ✓ ✓ **THE STANDING STONES OF STENNESS, ORKNEY MAINLAND:**
Together with the Ring of Brodgar and the great chambered tomb
of Maes Howe, all within walking distance of the A965, 18km from Kirkwall, this
is as impressive a ceremonial site as you'll find anywhere. From same period as
Skara Brae. The individual stones and the scale of the Ring are v imposing and
deeply mysterious. The burial cairn is the finest megalithic tomb in the UK.
Seen together, they will stimulate even the most jaded sense of wonder. HS

1632 ✓ ✓ **THE CALLANISH STONES, ISLE OF LEWIS:** 24km from Stornoway.
MAP 2 Take Tarbert rd and go rt at Leurbost. The best preserved and most
A1 unusual combination of standing stones in a ring around a tomb, with radiat-
ing arms in cross shape. Predating stonehenge, they were unearthed from the
peat in the mid-19th century and have become the major historical attraction
of the Hebrides. Other configurations nearby. At dawn there's nobody else
there (except camping New-Agers). Visitor centre out of sight is a good one
with a nice caff. Free. HS

1633 ✓ **THE CLAVA CAIRNS nr CULLODEN nr INVERNESS:** Here long before the
MAP 2 most famous battle in Scottish and other histories; well worth finding.
D2 Not so well marked but continue along the B9006 towards Cawdor Castle,
that other gr historical landmark (1595/CASTLES), taking a rt at the Culloden
Moor Inn and follow signs for Clava Lodge (holiday homes), picking up HS
sign to rt. Chambered cairns in grove of trees. Really just piles of stones, but
the death rattle echo from 5,000 yrs ago is perceptible to all esp when no one
else is there. Remoteness inhibits new age attentions and allows more private
meditations in this extraterrestrial spot. HS

1634 ✓ **THE MOUSA BROCH, SHETLAND:** On small island of Mousa, off Shetland
mainland 20km S of Lerwick, visible from main A970; but to see it properly, take boat (01950 431367). Isolated in its island fastness, this is the best
preserved broch in Scotland. Walls are 13m high (originally 15m) and galleries
run up the middle, in one case to the top. Solid as a rock, this example of a
uniquely Scottish phenomenon would have been a v des res at the turn of the
last millennium.

JARLSHOF in the far S next to Sumburgh airport has remnants and ruins from
Neolithic to Viking times – 18th century, with esp impressive 'wheelhouses'.

ADMN

1635 **TOMB OF THE EAGLES, ORKNEY MAINLAND:** 33km S of Kirkwall at the foot
of S Ronaldsay; signed from Burwick. A 'recent' discovery, the excavation of
this cliff cave is on private land. You should call in at the house first and they'll
tell you the whole story. Then there's a 2km walk. Allow time; this is ethereal
stuff.

ADMN

1636 **CAIRNPAPPLE HILL, nr LINLITHGOW, WEST LOTHIAN:** App from the
MAP 7 'Beecraigs' rd off W end of Linlithgow main st. Go past the Beecraigs t/off and
A1 continue for 3km. Cairnpapple is signed. Cairn and remnants of various rings
of stones evince the long sequence of ceremonial activities that took place on
this high, windy hill betw 2800 and 500 BC. Atmos even more strange by the
very 20th-century communications mast next door. Go into the tomb.

ADMN HS

1637 **CAIRNHOLY, between NEWTON STEWART/GATEHOUSE:** 1km off main A75.
MAP 9 Signed from rd, a pleasant walk up the glen side. A mini Callanish of standing
B3 stones around a burial cairn on v human scale and in a serene setting with
views of Wigtown Bay, the S Uplands behind.

1638 **THE BROWN-AND-WHITE CATERTHUNS, KIRKTON OF MENMUIR, nr
MAP 4 BRECHIN:** 5km uphill from war memorial at Menmuir, then signed 1km. Lay-
D2 by with obvious path to both on either side of the rd. White easiest (500m
uphill). These iron-age hill top settlements give tremendous sense of scale
and space and afford an impressive panorama of the Highland line. Colours
refer to the heather-covered turf and stone of one and the massive collapsed
ramparts of the White. The Picts, on the other hand, were blue (you know, like
Mel Gibson).

IN ABERDEENSHIRE

1639 **EAST AQUHORTHIES STONE CIRCLE, nr INVERURIE, nr ABERDEEN:** Signed
MAP 3 from B993 from Inverurie to Monymusk. A circle of pinkish stones with 2 grey
C3 sentinels flanking a huge recumbent stone set in the rolling countryside of
the Don Valley. Look at Bennachie then wonder what they got up
to …(1772/HILLS).

1640 **LOANHEAD OF DAVIOT STONE CIRCLE, nr INVERURIE/ABERDEEN:** Head
MAP 3 for the village of Daviot on B9001 from Inverurie; or Loanhead, signed off
C3 A920 rd betw Old Meldrum and Insch. The site is 500m from top of village.
Impressive and spooky circle of 11 stones and one recumbent from
4000/5000 BC. Unusual second circle adj encloses a cremation cemetery from
1500 BC. Remains of 32 people were found here. Obviously, an important place
for God-knows-what rituals.

1641 **ARCHAEOLINK nr INSCH, ABERDEENSHIRE:** Geographically betw the 2 sites
MAP 3 above and within an area of many prehistoric remnants, a recent state of the
C3 art interpretative centre. Impressively modern app to history both from exterior and within, where interactive and audiovisual displays bring the food
hunter-gatherer past into the culture hunter-gatherer present. The Romans
are a bit 'Life of Brian' though. Apr-Oct 10am-5pm.

ADMN

1642 **THE GREY CAIRNS OF CANSTER, nr WICK:** 20km S of Wick, a v straight rd
MAP 2 (signed for Cairns) heads W from the A9 for 8km. The cairns are instantly iden-
D1 tifiable nr the rd and impressively complete. The 'horned cairn' is the best in
the UK. In 2500 BC these stone-piled structures were used for the disposal of
the dead. You can crawl inside them if you're agile (or at night, brave). Nearby,
also signed from A9 is:

1643 **HILL O' MANY STANES, nr WICK:** Aptly named place with extraordinary
MAP 2 number of small standing stones; 200 in 22 rows. If fan shape was complete,
D1 there would be 600. Their v purposeful layout is enigmatic and strangely
stirring.

1644 **THE WHITHORN DIG, WHITHORN:** Late 20th cent excavations are still ongo-
MAP 9 ing at the medieval priory, the shrine of St Ninian and home of the earliest
B3 church in Scotland. Not much to see but a serene spot behind main st of a forgotten town. Go further on your pilgrimage for the life affirming stuff.
(1424/COASTAL VILLAGES).

1645 **THE MOTTE OF UR, nr DALBEATTIE:** Off B794 N of Dalbeattie and 6km from
MAP 9 main A75 Castle Douglas to Dumfries rd. Most extensive bailey earthwork cas-
C3 tle in Scotland dating from 12th century. No walls or excavation visible but a
gr sense of scale and place. Go through village of Haugh (good pub with food)
and on for 2km. Looking down to rt at farm buildings the minor rd crosses a
ford; park here, cross footbridge and head to rt – the hillock is above the ford.

1646 **TEMPLE WOOD, nr KILMARTIN, nr LOCHGILPHEAD:** 2km S of Kilmartin and
MAP 1 1km (signed) from A816, 2 distinct stone circles from a long period of history
B2 betw 3000-1200 BC. Story and speculations described on boards. Pastoral
countryside and wide skies. There are other sites in the vicinity, and a good
new museum (MUSEUMS/2010).   HS

1647 **CRANNOG CENTRE, ABERFELDY:** Adj Croft-Na-Caber Water Sports Centre
MAP 4 on L Tay (1907/WATER SPORTS). Reconstruction of iron-age dwelling (there are
B3 several under the loch). Credible and worthwhile archeological project. Open
Apr-Oct.

1648 **BAR HILL, nr KIRKINTILLOCH:** A fine example of the low ruins of a Roman
MAP 1 fort on the Antonine Wall which ran across Scotland for 200 yrs early ad. Gr
D2 place for an out-of-town walk (723/VIEWS).

1649 **THE BROCHS, GLENELG:** 110km from Ft William. Glenelg is 14km from the
MAP 2 A87 at Shiel Br (1483/SCENIC ROUTES). 5km from Glenelg village in beautiful
B3 Glen Beag. The 2 brochs, Dun Trodden and Dun Telve, are the best preserved
examples on the mainland of these mysterious 1st-century homesteads. Easy
here to distinguish the twin stone walls that kept out the cold and the more
disagreeable neighbours. Free.   HS

1650 **BARPA LANYASS, NORTH UIST:** 8km S Lochmaddy, visible from main A867
MAP 2 rd, like a hat on the hill (200m away). A 'squashed' beehive burial cairn dating
A2 from 1000 BC, the tomb of a chieftain. It's largely intact and you can explore
inside, crawling through the short entrance tunnel and down through the yrs.

1651 **SUENO'S STONE, FORRES:** Signposted from Grant PK (TOWN PARKS/1411).
MAP 3 More late Dark Age than prehistoric, a 9th or 10th C carved stone, 6m high in
A2 its own glass case. Pictish, magnificent; arguments still rage over what it
shows.

GREAT COUNTRY HOUSES

1652 ✓ ✓ **HADDO HOUSE:** Tarves, by Ellon. 01651 851440. Designed by
MAP 3 William Adam for the Earl of Aberdeen, the Palladian-style mansion
D3 well known for its musical evenings. Not so much a house, more a leisure land
in the best poss taste, with country park to wander, a pleasant café, estate
shop and gentle education. Austere inside perhaps, but the basements are
the place to ponder. The window by Burne-Jones in the chapel is glorious. Excl
programme of events, both NTS and Haddo House Trust. Enjoy some good
life!

1653 ✓ ✓ **MOUNT STUART, BUTE:** 01700 503877. Unique Victorian Gothic
MAP 1 house; echoes 3rd Marquis of Bute's passion for mythology, astron-
C3 omy, astrology and religion. Amazing splendour and scale, but atmos intimate
and romantic. Beautiful Italian antiques, notable paintings and fascinating
attention to detail with surprising humourous touches. Equally grand grds,
with walks and sea views. After a day here you still won't have taken it in. May-
Oct 11am-4.30pm. Cl Tue/Thu.

1654 ✓ ✓ **FASQUE, betw STONEHAVEN and MONTROSE:** W of A92 at
MAP 3 Laurencekirk and through Victorian Fettercairn to Fasque, one of
C4 the most fascinating old houses you'll ever be permitted to wander through
on your own (or accompanied by the enthusiastic custodian). Home of
Gladstone (4 times Prime Minister) whose descendants still live in the W wing.
Shut down in 1939 till the 1970s, the world before and betw the wars was preserved and is still there for faded-grandeur connoisseurs to savour and all of
us to sense. Best is below stairs. May-Sept 7 days 11am-5.30pm. Take no
souvenirs.

1655
MAP 8
D2

✓ **MANDERSTON, DUNS:** Off A6105, 2km down Duns-Berwick rd. Described as the swan-song of the Gr Classical House, one of the finest examples of Edwardian opulence in UK. All the more fascinating because the family still live there. Below stairs as fascinating as up; sublime grds (don't miss the woodland grd on other side of the lake, or the marble dairy). Open May-end Sept, Thu/Sun 2-5.30pm.

1656
MAP 8
B2

✓ **TRAQUAIR, INNERLEITHEN:** 01896 830323. 2km from A72 Peebles-Gala rd. Archetypal romantic Border retreat steeped in Jacobite history (ask about the Bear gates). Human proportions, liveability and lots of atmos (those peacocks calling are spooky at dusk). An enchanting house and a maze in the grd. Traquair ale still brewed. 1745 cottage tearoom, pottery and candlemaking. Apr-Sept 12.30-5.30pm (opens 10.30am June-Aug) and afternoons in Oct, Fri-Sun.

1657
MAP 7
B1

GOSFORD HOUSE nr ABERLADY, EAST LOTHIAN: On A198 betw Longniddry and Aberlady, the Gosford estate is behind a high wall and strangely stunted vegetation. Imposing house with centre block by Robert Adam and the wing you visit by William Young who did Glas City Chambers. The Marble Hall houses the remarkable collections of the unbroken line of the Earls of Wemyss. Priceless (well, maybe £25m) Botticellis, Rubens and Canalettos and important portraits in delightfully informal display (hand-written cards). No tearoom or paraphernalia here, but the grounds with ornamental ponds and their Hansel and Gretel curling and ice houses are superb picnic spots. Only open Wed/Sat/Sun 2-5pm, June and July.

1658
MAP 8
C2

FLOORS CASTLE, KELSO: 01573 223333. More vast mansion than old castle, the ancestral home of the Duke of Roxburghe, o/look with imposing grandeur the town and the Tweed. 18th-century with later additions. You're led round lofty public rms past family collections of fine furniture, tapestries and porcelain. Priceless; spectacularly impractical. Good grd centre (1979/GARDEN CENTRES).

1659
MAP 8
C2

MELLERSTAIN, nr GORDON/KELSO: 01573 410225. Home of the Earl of Haddington, signed from B6089 (Kelso-Gordon) or A6105 (Earlston-Greenlaw). One of Scotland's gr Georgian houses, begun by Wm Adam in 1725, completed by Robert. Outstanding decorative interiors esp the library. May-Sept 12.30-5pm. (not Sat)

1660
MAP 8
D2

PAXTON, nr BERWICK: 01289 386291. Off B6461 rd to Swinton and Kelso about 6km from A1. Adam mansion with Chippendales, Trotters and a picture gallery which is an outstation of the National Gallery. They've made a very good job of the wallpapering. Restored Victorian boathouse and salmon fishing museum on the R Tweed. Tours (lasting 1hr) every 45mins, Apr-Oct 11am-5pm. Garden 10am-sunset

1661
MAP 8
C2

THIRLESTANE, LAUDER: 01578 722430. 2km off A68. A castellate/baronial seat of the Earls and Duke of Lauderdale and family home of the Maitlands; it must take some upkeeping. Extraordinary staterooms, esp plaster work; the ceilings must be seen to be believed. In contrast, the nurseries (with toy collection), kitchens and laundry are more approachable. May, June, Sept open Sun, Mon, Wed, Thur 2-5pm. July, Aug 2-5pm every day except Sat.

1662
MAP 3
C2

FYVIE, ABERDEENSHIRE: 40km NW Aber, an important stop on the 'Castle Trail' which links the gr houses of Aberdeenshire. Before opulence fatigue sets in, see this pleasant baronial pile first. It was lived-in until the 1980s so feels less remote than most. Fantastic roofscape and ceilings. The *best* tearoom. Tree-lined acres; loch side walks. July-Aug daily 11am-5.30pm Apr-June, Sept, Oct we 1.30-5.30pm. Grounds open AYR, 9.30am-sunset.   NTS

1663
MAP 3
C3

CRATHES, nr BANCHORY: 25km W of Aber on A93. Amidst superb grds (1379/GARDENS) a 'fairy-tale castle', a tower house which is actually interesting to visit. Up and down spiral staircases and into small but liveable rms. The notable painted ceilings and the Long Gallery at the top are all worth lingering over. 350yrs of the Burnett family are ingrained in this oak. Apr-Oct 11am-5.30pm. Grounds open AYR 9.30am-dusk.

ABBOTSFORD, nr MELROSE: Home of Walter Scott (1745/LITERARY PLACES).

GREAT MONUMENTS, MEMORIALS AND FOLLIES

These sites are open at all times and free unless otherwise stated.

1664
MAP 1
A3

✔ ✔ **THE AMERICAN MONUMENT, ISLAY:** On the SW peninsula of the island, known as the Oa (pron 'Oh'), 13km from Pt Ellen. A monument to commemorate the shipwrecks in nearby waters, of 2 American ships, the *Tuscania* and the *Ontranto*, both of which sank in 1918 at the end of the war. The obelisk o/look this sea – which is often beset by storms – from a spectacular headland, the sort of disquieting place where you could imagine looking round and finding the person you're with has disappeared. Take rd from Pt Ellen past Maltings marked Mull of Oa 9km, through gate and left at broken sign. Park and walk 1.5km steadily uphill to monument. Bird life good in Oa area.

1-A-2

1665
MAP 6
C3

✔ **WALLACE MONUMENT, STIRLING:** Visible for miles and with gr views, though not as dramatic as Stirling Castle. App from A91 or Br of Allan rd. 150m walk from car park and 246 steps up. Victorian gothic spire marking the place where Scotland's gr patriot swooped down upon the English at the Battle of Stirling Br. Mel Gibson has increased visitors though his face on the new Wallace statue is a sad joke. In the 'Hall of Heroes' the new heroines section requires a feminist leap of the imagination. The famous sword is v big. Cliff top walk through Abbey Craig woods is worth detour. Monument open daily 10am-5pm (or later in summer 01786 472140), w/ends in winter till 4pm.

ADM

1666
MAP 2
B2

THE GRAVE OF FLORA MACDONALD, SKYE: Kilmuir on A855, Uig-Staffin rd, 40km N of Portree. A 10ft-high Celtic cross supported against the wind, high on the ridge o/look the Uists from whence she came. Long after the legendary journey, her funeral in 1790 attracted the biggest crowd since Culloden. The present memorial replaced the original, which was chipped away by souvenir hunters. Dubious though the whole business may have been, she still helped to shape the folklore of the Highlands.

1667
MAP 1
D3

CARFIN GROTTO, MOTHERWELL: A723 just outside Motherwell 4km from M8, on left after 2nd garage. A homage to Lourdes, built largely by striking miners in 1921. (God's) acre of grds and pathways with reliquaries, shrines, a glass pavilion and chapel; the ghost of Ravenscraig is always in the background. Spiritual sustenance, despite the throngs, for the true believers; something of a curiosity for the rest of us. Pilgrimage centre and tearoom. Open at all times.

1668
MAP 1
D3

HAMILTON MAUSOLEUM, STRATHCLYDE PARK: Off (and visible from) M74 at jnct 5/6, 15km from Glas (1398/COUNTRY PARKS). Huge, over-the-top/over-the-tomb (though removed 1921) stone memorial to the 10th Duke of Hamilton. Guided tours daily (Easter-Sept at Wed/Sat/Sun 3pm and, even better, evenings on request; winter Sat/Sun at 2pm). Eerie and chilling and with remarkable acoustics – the 'longest echo in Europe'. Give it a shout or take your violin. Info: 01698 426213.

1669
MAP 8
C3

PENIEL HEUGH, nr ANCRUM/JEDBURGH: (pron 'Pinal-hue'.) An obelisk visible for miles and on a rise which offers some of the most exhilarating views of the Borders. Also known as the Waterloo Monument, it was built on the Marquis of Lothian's estate to commemorate the battle. It's said that the woodland on the surrounding slopes represents the positions of Wellington's troops. From A68 opposite Ancrum t/off, on B6400, go 1km past 'Woodland Centre' up steep, unmarked rd to left for 150m. Park, walk up through woods.

1670
MAP 7
B1

THE HOPETOUN MONUMENT, ATHELSTANEFORD nr HADDINGTON: The needle atop a rare rise in E Lothian and a gr vantage point from which to view the county from the Forth to the Lammermuirs and Edinburgh over there. Off A6737 Haddington to Aberlady rd on B1343 to Athelstaneford. Car park and short climb. Tower usually open and viewfinder boards at top. Good gentle 'ridge' walk E from here.

1671 **THE PINEAPPLE, AIRTH:** From Airth N of Grangemouth, take A905 to Stirling
MAP 6 and after 1km the B9124 for Cowie. It sits on the edge of a walled grd at the
C3 end of the drive. 45ft high, it was built in 1761 as a grd retreat by an unknown
architect and remained 'undiscovered' until 1963. How exotic the fruit must
have seemed in the 18th century, never mind this extraordinary folly. Open
AYR; oddly enough, you can stay there (2 twin rms, 01628 825925).

1672 **THE MONUMENT ON BEN BHRAGGIE, GOLSPIE:** Atop the hill (pron
MAP 2 'Brachee') that dominates the town, the domineering statue and plinth (over
D2 35m) of the dreaded first Duke of Sutherland; there's a campaign group that
would like to see it demolished, but it survives yet. Climb from town fountain
on marked path. The hill race go up in 10mins but allow 2hrs return. His private view along the NE coast is superb (1609/CASTLES; 2007/MUSEUMS).

1673 **McCAIG'S TOWER or FOLLY, OBAN:** Oban's gr landmark built in 1897 by
MAP 1 McCaig, a local banker, to give 'work to the unemployed' and as a memorial to
B1 his family. It's like a temple or coliseum and time has mellowed whatever
incongruous effect it may have had originally. The views of the town and the
bay are magnificent and it's easy to get up from several points in town centre.
(*See* OBAN, p. 300.)

1674 **THE VICTORIA MEMORIAL TO ALBERT, BALMORAL:** Atop the fir-covered
MAP 3 hill behind the house, she raised a monument whose distinctive pyramid
B3 shape can be seen peeping over the crest from all over the estate. Desolated
by his death, the 'broken-hearted' widow had this memorial built in 1862 and
spent so much time here, she became a recluse and the Empire trembled.
Path begins at shop on way to Lochnagar distillery, 45mins up. Forget
Balmoral (1608/CASTLES), all the longing and love for Scotland can be felt here,
the gr estate laid out below.

1675 **THE PROP OF YTHSIE, nr ABERDEEN:** 35km NW city nr Ellon to W of A92, or
MAP 3 pass on the 'Castle Trail' since this monument commemorates one George
D3 Gordon of Haddo House nearby, who was prime minister 1852-55 (the good-
looking guy in the first portrait you come to in the house). Tower visible from
all of rolling Aberdeenshire around and there are reciprocal views should you
take the easy but unclear route up. On B999 Aber-Tarves rd and 2km from
entrance to house. Take rd for the Ythsie (pron 'icy') farms, 100m. Stone circle
nearby.

1676 **THE MONUMENT TO HUGH MacDIARMID, LANGHOLM:** Brilliant piece of
MAP 9 modern sculpture by Jake Harvey on the hill above Langholm 3km from A7 at
D2 beginning of path to the Malcolm obelisk from where there are gr views
(1511/VIEWS). MacDiarmid, our national poet, was born in Langholm in 1872
and, though they never liked him much after he left, the monument was commissioned and a cairn beside it raised in 1992. The bare hills surround you. The
motifs of the sculpture were used by Scotland's favourite Celtic rock band,
Runrig, on the cover of their 1993 album, *Amazing Things*.

1677 **MURRAY MONUMENT, nr NEW GALLOWAY:** Above A712 rd to Newton
MAP 9 Stewart about halfway betw. A fairly austere needle of granite to commemo-
B3 rate a 'shepherd boy', one Alexander Murray, who rose to become a professor
of Oriental Languages at Edinburgh Univ in early 19th century. 10min walk up
for fine views of Galloway Hills; pleasant waterfall nearby. Just as he,
barefoot …

1678 **SMAILHOLM TOWER, nr KELSO and ST BOSWELLS:** The classic Border
MAP 8 tower; plenty of history and romance and a v nice place to stop, picnic what-
C2 ever. Good views. Nr main rd B6404 or off smaller B6937 – well signposted.
Open Apr-Sept 9.30am-6.30pm (Sun from 2pm). But fine to visit at any time
(1489/SCENIC ROUTES).

1679 **AIKWOOD TOWER nr SELKIRK:** 8km SE via B7009 to Eltnckbridge. Fine 16th
MAP 8 cent tower the home of Lord David and Judy Steel. Exhib of life and times of
B3 James Hogg (1744/LITERARY PLACES) and 'medieval garden'. Apr-Sept
Tues/Thur/Sun 2pm-5pm.

SCOTT MONUMENT, EDINBURGH: 382/VIEWS.

THE MOST INTERESTING CHURCHES

All 'generally open' unless otherwise stated; those marked (*) have public services.

1680
MAP 1
C1

✓ ✓ ***ST CONAN'S KIRK, LOCH AWE:** A85 33km E of Oban. Perched amongst trees on the side of L Awe, this small but spacious church seems to incorporate every ecclesiastical architectural style. Its building was a labour of love for one Walter Campbell who was perhaps striving for beauty rather than consistency. Though modern (begun by him in 1881 and finished by his sister and a board of trustees in 1930), the result is a place of ethereal light and atmos, enhanced by and befitting the inherent spirituality of the setting. There's a spooky carved effigy of Robert the Bruce, a cosy cloister and the most amazing flying buttresses. A place to wander and reflect.

1681
MAP 7
A1

✓ ✓ ***ROSSLYN CHAPEL, ROSLIN:** 12km S of Edin city centre. Take A702, then A703 from ring-route rd, marked Penicuik. Roslin village 1km from main rd and chapel 500m from village crossroads above Roslin Glen (366/WALKS OUTSIDE THE CITY). Freemason central and New Age fuel station: stories abound of the Holy Grail hidden in the walls and for the next few yrs there's a metal hood to protect the roof. For such a wee chapel, visitors can spend hrs wandering around working the place out with help from copious guidance notes. Founded by a 15th-century Sinclair, Prince of Orkney, who reinterred his illustrious 13th-century ancestor here (the latter just happened to be a Grand Prior of the Knights Templar). All holy meaningful stuff in a *Foucault's Pendulum* sense. But a special place. Episcopalian. Mon-Sat 10-5pm, 12-4.45pm Sun Coffee shop.

1682

✓ ✓ **THE ITALIAN CHAPEL, ORKNEY MAINLAND:** 8km S of Kirkwall at Lamb Holm and the first causeway on the way to St Margaret's Hope. In 1943, Italian PoWs brought to work on the Churchill Barriers transformed a Nissen hut, using the most meagre materials, into this remarkable ornate chapel. The meticulous *trompe l'œil* and wrought-iron work are a touching affirmation of faith. At the other end of the architectural scale, **ST MAGNUS CATHEDRAL** in Kirkwall is a gr edifice, but also filled with spirituality.

1683
MAP B
xC1

✓ ✓ **QUEEN'S CROSS CHURCH, GLASGOW:** 870 Garscube Rd where it becomes Maryhill Rd at Springbank St. C R Mackintosh's only church. Fascinating and unpredictable in every part of its design. Some elements reminiscent of The Art School (built in the same year 1897) and others, like the tower, evoke medieval architecture. Bold and innovative, now restored and functioning as the headquarters of The Mackintosh Society. Mon-Fri 10.00am-5pm, Sat 10am-2pm, Sun 2pm-5pm. No services. (747/MACKINTOSH.)

1684
MAP 9
C2

✓ ***DURISDEER PARISH CHURCH, nr ABINGTON AND THORNHILL:** Off A702 Abington-Thornhill rd and nr Drumlanrig (1394/COUNTRY PARKS). If I lived in this village in the hills, I'd go to church more often. It's exquisite and the history of Scotland is writ on the stones. The Queensberry marbles (1709) are displayed in the N transept and there's a cradle roll and a list of ministers from the 14th century. The plaque to the two brothers who died at Gallipoli is especially touching.

1685
MAP 1
C3

*CATHEDRAL OF THE ISLES, MILLPORT ON THE ISLAND OF CUMBRAE: Frequent ferry service from Largs is met by bus for 6km journey to Millport. Lane from main st by Newton pub, 250m then through gate. The smallest 'cathedral' in Europe, one of Butterfield's gr works (other is Keble Coll, Oxford). Here, small is outstandingly beautiful. (1169/RETREATS; 1277/CAFÉS.)

1686
MAP 2
A2

ST CLEMENTS, RODEL, SOUTH HARRIS: Tarbert 40km. Classic island kirk in Hebridean landscape (as long as the Super Quarry is never built). Simple cruciform structure with tower, which the adventurous can climb. Probably influenced by Iona. Now an empty but atmospheric shell, with blackened effigies and important monumental sculpture. Goats in the churchyard graze amongst the headstones of all the young Harris lads lost at sea in the Gr War. There are other fallen angels on the outside of the tower.

1687
MAP 2
A3

*ST MICHAEL'S CHAPEL, ERISKAY, nr SOUTH UIST/BARRA: That rare example of an ordinary modern church without history or grand architecture, which has charm and serenity and imbues the sense of well-being that a religious centre should. The focal pt of a relatively devout Catholic community who obviously care about it. Alabaster angels abound. O/look Sound of Barra. A real delight whatever your religion.

1688
MAP 5
C2
*ST ATHERNASE, LEUCHARS: The parish church on a corner of what is essentially an Air Force base spans centuries of warfare and architecture. The Norman bell tower is remarkable.

1689
MAP 5
B4
*ST FILLAN'S CHURCH, ABERDOUR: Behind ruined castle in this pleasant seaside village (1420/COASTAL VILLAGES), a more agreeable old kirk would be hard to find. Restored from a 12th-century ruin in 1926, the warm stonework and stained glass create a v soothing atmos (church may be closed, but nice graveyard).

1690
MAP 5
A3
*CULROSS ABBEY CHURCH: Top of Forth-side village full of interesting buildings and windy streets (1415/COASTAL VILLS). Worth hike up hill (signed 'Abbey', ruins are adj) for views and this well loved and looked after church. Gr stained glass (see Sandy's window), often full of flowers.

1691
MAP 6
C2
*DUNBLANE CATHEDRAL: A huge nave of a church built around a Norman tower (from David I) on the Allan Water and restored 1892. The wondrously bright stained glass is mostly 20th-century. The poisoned sisters buried under the altar helped change the course of Scottish history. This cathedral made more recently famous and seen on TV all over the world during the Dunblane tragedy.   HS

1692
MAP 3
D3
*ST MACHAR'S CATHEDRAL, ABERDEEN: The Chanonry in 'Old Aberdeen' off St Machar's Dr about 2km from centre. Best seen as part of a walk round the old 'village within the city' occupied mainly by the university's old and modern buildings. Cathedral's fine granite nave and twin-spired W Front date from 15th century, on site of 6th-century Celtic church. Noted for heraldic ceiling and 19/20th-century stained glass. Seaton Park adj has pleasant Don-side walks and …unexpected pleasures. Church open daily 9am-5pm.

1693
MAP 7
B1
*THE EAST LOTHIAN CHURCHES at ABERLADY, WHITEKIRK, ATHELSTANE-FORD: 3 charming churches in bucolic settings; quiet corners to explore and reflect. Easy to find. All have interesting local histories and in the case of Athelstaneford, a national resonance – a 'vision' in the sky nr here became the flag of Scotland, the saltire. An innovative audiovisual display explains. Aberlady my favourite.

1694
MAP 2
C2
CROICK CHURCH, nr BONAR BRIDGE: 16km W of Ardgay, which is just over the river from Bonar Br and through the splendid glen of Strathcarron (1448/GLENS). This humble and charming church is chiefly remembered for its place in the history of the Highland clearances. In May 1845, 90 folk took shelter in the graveyard around the church after they had been cleared from their homes in nearby Glencalvie. Not allowed even in the kirk, their plight did not go unnoticed and was reported in *The Times*. The harrowing account is there to read, and the messages they scratched on the windows. Sheep graze all around.

1695
MAP 1
C3
*THOMAS COATES MEMORIAL CHURCH, PAISLEY: Built by Coates (of thread fame), an imposing edifice, one of the grandest Baptist churches in Europe. A monument to God, prosperity and the Industrial Revolution. Open Apr-Sept Mon/Wed/Fri 2-4pm, service on Sun at 11am.

1696
MAP 7
B1
*THE LAMP OF THE LOTHIANS, ST MARY'S COLLEGIATE, HADDINGTON: Follow signs from E main st. At the risk of sounding profane or at least trite, this is a church that's really got its act together, both now and throughout ecclesiastical history. It's beautiful and in a fine setting on the R Tyne, with good stained glass and interesting crypts and corners. But it's obviously v much at the centre of the community, a lamp as it were, in the Lothians. Guided tours, brass rubbings (Sat), summer recitals (Sun afternoon). Coffee shop and gift shop. Don't miss Lady Kitty's grd nearby, including the secret medicinal grd, a quiet spot to contemplate (if not sort out) your condition. Mon-Sat 10am-4pm. Sun 1pm-4pm.

1697
MAP 4
B3
*DUNKELD CATHEDRAL: In town centre by lane to the banks of the Tay at its most silvery. Medieval splendour amongst lofty trees. Notable for 13th-century choir and 15th-century nave and tower. Parish church open for edifying services and purposes.

1698 **RUTHWELL CHURCH, RUTHWELL:** 10 miles SE Dumfries, B724 nr
MAP 9 Clarencefield. Collect keys from Mrs Coulthard, Kirkyett House in village; she's
D3 the fount of all knowledge concerning this important building. Unique 18ft
Runic Cross within Church, dating from 7th century. Carvings depict Biblical
scenes with monk's inscription of 'The Holy Rood' poem. Fascinating history of
its creation, preservation during the religious troubles of 1640, and subse-
quent restoration in 1823 by the community.

1699 **KEILLS CHAPEL, S of CRINAN:** The chapel at the end of nowhere. From
MAP 1 Lochgilphead, drive towards Crinan, but before you get there, turn S down the
B2 B8025 and follow it for nearly 20km to the end. Park at the farm then walk the
last 200m. You are 7km across the Sound from Jura, at the edge of Knapdale.
Early 13thC chapel (simple) but houses some remarkable cross slabs and a
7thC cross. Wave to the ghosts. HS

ST GILES CATHEDRAL, EDINBURGH: 357/OTHER ATTRACTIONS.

GLASGOW CATHEDRAL/UNIVERSITY CHAPEL: 697/700/MAIN ATTRACTIONS.

THE MOST INTERESTING GRAVEYARDS

1700 ✓✓ **GLASGOW NECROPOLIS:** The vast burial ground at the crest of the
MAP B ridge, running down to the river, that was the focus of the original
xE3 settlement of Glas. Everything began at the foot of this hill and, ultimately,
ended at the top where many of the city's most famous (and infamous) sons
and daughters are interred within the reach of the long shadow of John
Knox's obelisk. Generally open (official times), but best if you can get the full
spooky experience to yourself. Check with the TO 0141 204 4400. (697/MAIN
ATTRACTIONS.)

1701 **EDINBURGH: CANONGATE:** On left of Royal Mile going down to Palace.
MAP A Adam Smith and the tragic poet Robert Fergusson revered by Robbie Burns
E2 (who raised the memorial stone in 1787 over his pauper's grave) are buried
here in the heart of Auld Reekie. Tourists can easily miss this one. **GREYFRI-
ARS:** A place of ancient mystery, famous for the wee dog who guarded his
master's grave for 14yrs, for the plundering of graves in the early 18th century for the Anatomy School and for the graves of Allan Ramsay (prominent
poet and burgher), James Hutton (the father of geology), William McGonagall
(the 'world's worst poet') and sundry serious Highlanders. Annals of a gr city
are written on these stones. **WARRISTON:** Warriston Rd by B&Q or end of cul-
de-sac at Warriston Cres (Canonmills), up bank and along railway line.
Overgrown, peaceful, steeped in atmos. Gothic horrorland (some of those
cruising guys may like that sort of thing).

1702 **ISLE OF JURA:** Killchianaig graveyard in the N. Follow rd as far as it goes to
MAP 1 Inverlussa, graveyard is on rt, just before hamlet. Mairi Ribeach apparently
B2 lived until she was 128. In the south at Keils (2km from rd N out of Craighouse,
bearing left past Keils houses and through the deer fence), her father is buried
and he was 180! Both sites are beautiful, isolated and redolent of island history, with much to reflect on, not least the mysterious longevity of the inhabitants.

1703 **CAMPBELTOWN CEMETERY:** Campbeltown. Odd, but one of the nicest
MAP 1 things about this end-of-the-line town is the cemetery. It's at the end of a row
B3 of fascinating posh houses, the original merchant and mariner owners of
which will be interred in the leafy plots next door. Still v much in use after centuries of commerce and seafaring disasters, it has crept up the terraces of a
steep and lush overhanging bank. The white cross and row of WW2 headstones are partic affecting.

1704 **KIRKOSWALD KIRKYARD nr MAYBOLE and GIRVAN:** On main rd through
MAP 1 village betw Ayr and Girvan. The graveyard around the ruined Kirk famous as
C4 the burial place of the characters in Burns' most famous poem and a must for
Burns fans and thrill seekers. Tam O'Shanter, Souter Johnie and Kirkton Jean
all lie here.

1705 **HUMBIE CHURCHYARD:** Humbie, E Lothian 25km SE of Edin via A68 (t/off at
MAP 7   Fala). This is as reassuring a place to be buried as you could wish for; if you're
B1   set on cremation, come here and think of earth. Deep in the woods with the
burn besides; after-hrs the sprites and the spirits must have a hell of a time.

1706 **ANCRUM GRAVEYARD, nr JEDBURGH:** The quintessential country church-
MAP 8   yard; away from the village (2km along B6400), by a lazy river (the Ale Water)
C3   crossed to a farm by a humpback br and a chapel in ruins. Elegiac and deeply
peaceful (1528/PICNICS).

1707 **BALQUHIDDER CHURCHYARD:** Chiefly notable as the last resting place of
MAP 6   one Rob Roy Macgregor who was buried in 1734 after causing a heap of trou-
B2   ble hereabouts and raised to immortality by Sir Walter Scott and Michael
Caton-Jones. Despite well-trodden path, setting is poignant. For best reflec-
tions head along L Voil to Inverlochlarig. Beautiful Sunday evening concerts in
kirk July/Aug. (check with local TOs).

1708 **LOGIE OLD KIRK, nr STIRLING:** A crumbling chapel and an ancient graveyard
MAP 6   at the foot of the Ochils. The wall is round to keep out the demons, a burn gur-
C3   gles beside and there are some fine and v old stones going back to the 16th
century. Take rd for Wallace Monument off A91, 2km from Stirling, then first rt.
The old kirk is beyond the new.

1709 **CHISHOLM GRAVEYARD, nr BEAULY:** Last resting place of the Chisholms
MAP 2   and 3 of the largest Celtic crosses you'll see anywhere, in a secret and atmos-
C2   pheric woodland setting. 10km S Beauly on A831 to Struy, 1km before Cnoc
Hotel opp Erchless Estate and through a white iron gate on rt. Walk 250m.

1710 **TUTNAGUAIL, DUNBEATH:** An enchanting cemetery 5km from Dunbeath,
MAP 2   Neil Gunn's birthplace, and found by walking up the 'Strath' he describes in his
D1   book *Highland River* (1743/LITERARY PLACES). With a white wall around it, this
graveyard, which before the clearances once served a valley community of
400 souls, can be seen for miles. Despite isolation, it's still used.

THE GREAT ABBEYS

1711 ✓ ✓ **IONA ABBEY:** This hugely significant place of pilgrimage for new
MAP 1   age and old age pilgrims and tourists alike is reached from
A1   Fionnphort, SW Mull, by frequent Calmac Ferry (5min crossing). Walk 1km.
Here in 563 BC St Columba began his mission for a Celtic Church that changed
the face of Europe. Cloisters, graveyard of Scottish kings and, marked by a
modest stone, the inscription already faded by the weather, the grave of John
Smith father of our Blair New World. Regular services. Good shop (1938/CRAFT
SHOPS). Residential courses and retreats (MacLeod Centre adj, 01681 700404)
include a 'Christmas house party' (2109/MAGICAL ISLANDS).

1712 ✓ ✓ **PLUSCARDEN ABBEY, betw FORRES and ELGIN:** A fully working
MAP 3   monastic community (1167/RETREATS) in one of the most spiritual of
A2   places. Founded by Alexander II in 1250 and being restored since 1948.
Benedictine services (starting with Matins at 5am through Prime-Terce-Sext-
None-Vespers at 6pm and Compline at 8.05pm) open to public. The ancient
honey-coloured walls, the brilliant stained glass, the monks' Gregorian chant:
the whole effect is a truly uplifting experience. The bell rings down the valley.
Open at all times.

1713 ✓ ✓ **PAISLEY ABBEY:** Town centre. An abbey founded in 1163, razed (by
MAP 1   the English) in 1307 and with successive deteriorations and renova-
C3   tions ever since. Major restoration in the 1920s brought it to present-day
cathedral-like magnificence. Exceptional stained glass (the recent window
complementing the formidable Strachan E Window), an impressive choir and
an edifying sense of space. Sunday Services (11am/6.30pm) are superb, esp
full-dress communion and there are open days (1st Sat July, 2nd Sat Sept)
with coffee in the cloisters, organ music and the tower open for climbing.
Otherwise Abbey open AYR 10am-3.30pm. Café/shop.

1714 ✓ ✓ **JEDBURGH ABBEY:** The classic abbey ruin; conveys the most com-
MAP 8   plete impression of the Border abbeys built under the patronage of
C3   David I in the 12th century. Its tower and remarkable Catherine window are

still intact. Excavations have unearthed first example of a 12th-century comb (worth half a million quid!). It's now displayed in the excellent visitor centre which brilliantly illustrates the full story of the abbey's amazing history. Best view from across the Jed in the 'Glebe'. Apr-Sep 9.30am-6.30pm, Oct-Mar until 4.30pm.   HS

1715 ✓ **DRYBURGH ABBEY, nr ST BOSWELLS:** One of the most evocative of
MAP 8   ruins, an aesthetic attraction since the late 18th century. Sustained innu-
C2   merable attacks from the English since its inauguration by Premonstratensian
Canons in 1150. Celebrated by Sir Walter Scott, buried here in 1832 (with his biographer Lockhart at his feet), its setting, amongst huge cedar trees on the banks of the Tweed is one of pure historical romance. 4km A68. (1506/VIEWS.)
                                                                                                                  HS

1716 **CROSSRAGUEL ABBEY, MAYBOLE:** 24km S of Ayr on A77. Built 1244, one of
MAP 1   first Cluniac settlements in Scotland, an influential and rich order, stripped in
C4   the Reformation. Now an extensive ruin of architectural distinction, the ground plan v well preserved and obvious. Open daily.   HS

1717 **SWEETHEART, NEW ABBEY nr DUMFRIES:** 12km S by A710. The endearing
MAP 9   and enduring warm red sandstone abbey in the shadow of Criffel, so named
C3   because Devorguilla de Balliol, devoted to her husband (he of the Oxford College), founded the abbey for Cistercian monks and kept his heart in a casket which is buried with her here. No roof, but the tower is intact. (821/SW HOTELS.)   HS

1718 **MELROSE ABBEY:** Another romantic setting, the abbey seems to give an
MAP 8   atmos to the whole town. Built by David I (what a guy!) for Cistercian monks
C2   from Rievaulx from 1136, there wasn't much left, spiritually or architecturally, by the Reformation. Once, however, it sustained a huge community, as evinced by the widespread excavations. There's a museum of abbey, church and Roman relics; soon to include Robert the Bruce's heart, recently excavated in the grds. Same hrs as Jed.   HS

1719 **ARBROATH ABBEY:** 25km N of Dundee. Founded in 1178 and endowed on an
MAP 4   unparalleled scale, this is an important place in Scots history. It's where the
D3   Declaration was signed in 1320 to appeal to the Pope to release the Scots from the yoke of the English (you can buy facsimiles of the yellow parchment; the original is in the Scottish Records Office in Edin). It was to Arbroath that the Stone of Destiny (on which Scottish kings were traditionally crowned) was returned after being 'stolen' from Westminster Abbey in the 1950s and is now at Edinburgh Castle.   HS

THE GREAT BATTLEGROUNDS

Chosen for accessibility and sense of history as well as historical significance.

1720 **CULLODEN, INVERNESS:** Signed from A9 and A96 into Inverness and about
MAP 2　8km from town. Extensive battlefield on either side of the rd before you even
C2　get to the (v full-on) visitor centre. Positions of the clans and the troops
marked out across the moor; flags enable you to get a real sense of scale. If
you go in spring you see how wet and miserable the Moor can be (the battle
took place on 16 April 1746). No matter how many other folk are there wandering down the lines, a visit to this most infamous of battlefields can still
leave a pain in the heart. Centre 9am-6pm (winter 10am-4pm) Cl Jan. Ground
open at all times for more personal Cullodens.　　　　　　　　　　　　NTS

1721 **BATTLE OF THE BRAES, SKYE:** 10km Portree. Take main A850 rd S for 3km
MAP 2　then left, marked 'Braes' for 7km. Monument is on a rise on rt. The last battle
B2　fought on British soil and a significant place in Scots history. When the clearances, uninterrupted by any organised opposition, were virtually complete
and vast tracts of Scotland had been depopulated for sheep, the Skye crofters
finally stood up in 1882 to the Government troops and said enough is
enough. A cairn has been erected nr the spot where they fought on behalf of
'all the crofters of Gaeldom', a battle which led eventually to the Crofters Act
which has guaranteed their rights ever since. At the end of this rd at
Peinchorran, there are fine views of Raasay (which was devastated by clearances) and Glamaig, the conical Cuillin, across L Sligachan.

1722 **GLENCOE:** Not much of a battle, of course, but one of the most infamous mas-
MAP 2　sacres in British history. Much has been written (John Prebble's *Glencoe* and
C4　others) and the visitor centre provides audiovisual scenario. There's the
Macdonald monument nr Glencoe village and the walk to the more evocative
Signal Rock where the bonfire was lit, now a happy woodland trail in this
doom-laden landscape. About 4km return from centre. (1747/SPOOKY PLACES.)

1723 **SCAPA FLOW, ORKNEY MAINLAND and HOY:** Scapa Flow, surrounded by
various of the southern Orkney islands, is one of the most sheltered anchor-
ages in Europe. Hence the huge presence in Orkney of ships and personnel
during both wars. The Germans scuttled 54 of their warships here in 1919 and
many still lie in the bay. The *Royal Oak* was torpedoed in 1939 with the loss of
833 men. Much still remains of the war yrs (especially if you're a diver,
1919/DIVING): the rusting hulks, the shore fortifications, the Churchill Barriers
and the ghosts of a long-gone army at Scapa and Lyness on Hoy. Excl 'tour' on
MV Guide with remote controlled camera exploring 3 wrecks. 01856 811360.

1724 **LILLIARD'S EDGE, nr ST BOSWELLS:** On main A68, look for Lilliard's Edge
MAP 8　Caravan Park 5km S of St Boswells; park and walk back towards St Boswells to
C2　the brim of the hill (about 500m), then cross rough ground on rt along ridge,
following whin hedge. Marvellous view attests to strategic location. 200m
along, a cairn marks the grave of Lilliard who, in 1545, joined the Battle of
Ancrum Moor against the English 'loons' under the Earl of Angus. 'And when
her legs were cuttit off, she fought upon her stumps'. An ancient poem etched
on the stone records her legendary … feet.

1725 **KILLIECRANKIE, nr PITLOCHRY:** The first battle of the Jacobite Risings where,
MAP 4　in July 1689, the Highlanders lost their leader Viscount (aka Bonnie) Dundee,
B2　but won the battle, using the narrow Pass of Killiecrankie. One escaping soldier
made a famous leap. Well-depicted scenario in visitor centre; short walk to 'The
Leap'. Battle viewpoint and cairn is further along rd to Blair Atholl, turning rt
and doubling back at Little Chef and on, almost to A9 underpass (3km from visitor centre). You get the lie of the land from here. Many good walks.

1726 **BANNOCKBURN, nr STIRLING:** 4km town centre via Glas rd (it's well sign-
MAP 6　posted) or jnct 9 of M9 (3km), behind a rather sad hotel. Some visitors might
C3　be perplexed as to why 24 June 1314 was such a big deal for the Scots and,
apart from the 50m walk to the flag-pole and the huge statue, there's not a lot
doing. But the visitor centre does bring the scale of it to life, the horror and the
glory. The battlefield itself is thought to lie around the orange building of the
High School some distance away, and the best place to see the famous wee
burn is from below the magnificent Telford Br. Ask at centre (5km by road).

MARY QUEEN OF SCOTS 1542–87

LINLITHGOW PALACE: Where she was born (1610/RUINS).

HOLYROOD PALACE, EDINBURGH: And lived (342/MAIN ATTRACTIONS).

1727
MAP 6
B3
INCHMAHOME PRIORY, PORT OF MENTEITH: The ruins of the Priory on the island in Scotland's only lake, where the infant Queen spent her early years in the safe keeping of the Augustinian monks. Short journey by boat from quay nr lake hotel. Signal the ferryman by turning the board to the island, much as she did. 7 days, 9.30am-6pm (Sun from 2pm). Delights of the Trossachs surround you.   HS

1728
MAP 8
C3
MARY QUEEN OF SCOTS' HOUSE, JEDBURGH: In grds via Smiths Wynd off main st. Historians quibble but this long-standing museum claims to be 'the' house where she became ill in 1566, but somehow made it over to visit the injured Bothwell at Hermitage Castle 50km away. Tower house in good condition; displays and well-told saga. Easter-Nov 10am-4.45pm, Sun 4.30pm. wint hrs vary slightly.

1729
MAP 4
C4
LOCH LEVEN CASTLE, nr KINROSS: The ultimate in romantic penitentiaries; on the island in the middle of the loch and clearly visible from the M90. Not much left of the ruin to fill out the fantasy, but this is where Mary spent 10 months in 1568 before her famous escape and her final attempt to get back the throne. Sailings Apr-Sept, 9am-6pm in small launch from Kirkgate Park. 7min trip, return as you like.

1730
MAP 9
C3
DUNDRENNAN ABBEY, nr AUCHENCAIRN and KIRKCUDBRIGHT: Mary Queen of Scots got around and there are innumerable places, castles and abbeys where she spent the night. This, however, was where she spent her last one on Scottish soil. She left next day from Pt Mary (nothing much to see there except a beach – it's 2km along the rd that skirts the sinister MoD range – the pier's long gone and … well, there's no plaque). The Cistercian abbey of Whitemonks (established 1142), which harboured her on her last night, is now a tranquil ruin.   HS

'In my end is my beginning,' she said, facing her execution which came 19 yrs later.

1731
MAP 7
B1
Her 'death mask' is displayed at **LENNOXLOVE HOUSE**, nr **HADDINGTON**; it does seem on the small side for someone who was supposedly 6 feet tall!

BONNIE PRINCE CHARLIE 1720–88

1732
MAP 2
A3
PRINCE CHARLIE'S BAY, ERISKAY: The uncelebrated, unmarked and beautiful beach where Charlie first landed in Scotland to begin the Jacobite Rebellion. Nothing much has changed and this crescent of sand with soft machair and a turquoise sea is still a secret place. 1km from township heading S. (2114/MAGICAL ISLANDS.)

1733
MAP 2
B3
LOCH NAN UAMH, nr ARISAIG, THE PRINCE'S CAIRN: 7km from Lochailort on A830, 48km Ft William. Signed from the rd, a path leads down to the left. This is the 'traditional' spot (pron 'Loch Na Nuan') where Charlie embarked for France in Sept 1746, having lost the battle and the cause. The rocky headland also o/look the bay and skerries where he'd landed in July the year before to begin the campaign. This place was the beginning and the end and it has all the romance necessary to be utterly convincing. Is that a French ship out there in the mist?

1734
MAP 2
B3
GLENFINNAN: The place where he 'raised his standard' to rally the clans to the Jacobite cause. For a while on that August day in 1745 it had looked as if only a handful were coming. Then they heard the pipes and 600 Camerons came marching from the valley (where the viaduct now spans). That must have been one helluva moment. Though it's thought that he actually stood on the higher ground, there is a powerful sense of place and history here. The visitor centre has an excellent map of Charlie's path/flight through Scotland – somehow he touched all the most alluring places! Tower can be climbed. NTS

CULLODEN, nr INVERNESS: 1720/BATTLEGROUNDS.

ROBERT THE BRUCE 1274–1329

1735
MAP 9
B3

BRUCE'S STONE, GLEN TROOL, nr NEWTON STEWART: 26km N by A714 via Bargrennan (8km to head of glen) which is on the S Upland Way (1790/LONG WALKS). The fair Glen Trool is a celebrated spot in the Galloway Forest Park (1452/GLENS). The stone is signed and marks the area where Bruce's guerrilla band rained boulders down on the pursuing English in 1307 after they had routed the main army at Solway Moss. Good walking, incl Merrick (1766/HILLS).

1736
MAP 6
C3

BANNOCKBURN, nr STIRLING: The climactic battle in June 1314, when Bruce decisively whipped the English and got himself the kingdom (though Scotland was not recognised as independent until 1328, just before his death). The scale of the skirmish can be visualised at the visitor centre, but not so readily 'in the field' (1726/BATTLEGROUNDS).

1737
MAP 4
D3

ARBROATH ABBEY: Not much of the Bruce trail here, but this is where the famous Declaration was signed that was the attempt of the Scots nobility united behind him to gain international recognition of the independence they had won on the battlefield. What it says is stirring stuff; the original is in Edin (1719/ABBEYS).   HS

1738
MAP 5
A3

DUNFERMLINE ABBEY CHURCH: Here, at last, some tangible evidence, his tomb. Buried in 1329, his remains were discovered wrapped in gold cloth, when the site was being cleared for the new church in 1818. Many of the other gr kings, the Alexanders I and III, were not so readily identifiable (Bruce's ribcage had been cut to remove his heart). With gr national emotion he was reinterred underneath the pulpit. The church (as opposed to the ruins and Norman nave adj) is open Apr-Sept 9.30am-5pm. Gr café in Abbot House thro graveyard (2004/MUSEUMS).

1739
MAP 8
C2

MELROSE ABBEY: On his deathbed Bruce asked that his heart be buried here after it was taken to the Crusades to aid the Army in their battles. The lead casket containing it has recently been excavated from the chapter house and, after inspections in Edin by HS, it'll be displayed here.   HS

1740 **ROBERT BURNS (1759–96), ALLOWAY, AYR AND DUMFRIES:** A well-marked
MAP 9 heritage trail through his life and haunts in Ayrshire and Dumfriesshire. His
C3 howff at Dumfries is v atmospheric. Best is at **ALLOWAY:** The Auld Brig o'
Doon and the Auld Kirk where Tam o' Shanter saw the witches dance are more
evocative than the Monument and surrounding grds or, 1km up the rd, the
cottage (his birthplace; little atmos) and the state-of-the-art Tam o' Shanter
Experience where you are 'transported back to 18th-century Ayrshire by 20th-
century technology' (I don't think he'd have been overimpressed – the shop
here is a temple of tat).

1741 **AYR:** The Auld Kirk off main st by river; graveyard with diagram of where his
MAP 1 friends are buried; open at all times. **DUMFRIES:** House where he spent his
C3 last yrs and mausoleum 250m away at back of a kirkyard stuffed with extrav-
MAP 9 agant masonry. 10km N of Dumfries on A76 at **ELLISLAND FARM** is the most
C3 interesting of all the sites. The farmhouse with genuine memorabilia e.g. his
mirror, fishing-rod, a poem scratched on glass, original manuscripts. There's his
favourite walk by the river where he composed 'Tam o' Shanter' and a strong
atmos about the place. Farmer/curator Les Byers will let you in to see when
he's at home. **BROW WELL, nr RUTHWELL** on the B725 20km S Dumfries and
nr Caerlaverock (1563/BIRDS), is a quiet place, a well with curative properties
where he went in the latter stages of his illness. Not many folk go to this one.

1742 **LEWIS GRASSIC GIBBON (1901–34), ARBUTHNOT, nr STONEHAVEN:**
MAP 3 Although James Leslie Mitchell left the area in 1917, this is where he was born
C4 and spent his formative years. Visitor centre (01561 361668; Apr-Oct 7 days
10am-4.30pm) at the end of the village (via B967, 16km S of Stonehaven off
main A92) has details of his life and can point you in the direction of the
places he writes about in his trilogy, *The Scots Quair*. The first part, *Sunset Song*,
is generally considered to be one of the gr Scots novels and this area, the
HOWE OF THE MEARNS, is the place he so effectively evokes. Arbuthnot is
reminiscent of 'Kinraddie' and the churchyard 1km away on the other side of
rd still has the atmos of that time of innocence before the war which pervades
the book. His ashes are here in a grave in a corner. From 1928 to when he died
6yrs later at the age of only 33, he wrote an incredible 17 books.

1743 **NEIL GUNN (1891–1973), DUNBEATH, nr WICK:** Scotland's foremost writer
MAP 2 on Highland life, only now receiving the recognition he deserves, was brought
D1 up in this NE fishing village and based 3 of his greatest yarns here, particularly *Highland River*, which must stand in any literature as a brilliant evocation of
place. The **STRATH** in which it is set is below the house (a nondescript terraced house next to the Stores) and makes for a gr walk (1804/GLEN AND RIVER
WALKS). There's a commemorative statue by the harbour, not quite the harbour
you imagine from the books. Gunn also lived for many yrs nr **DINGWALL** and
there is a memorial on the back rd to Strathpeffer and a wonderful view in a
place he often walked (on A834, 4km from Dingwall).

1744 **JAMES HOGG (1770–1835), ST MARY'S LOCH, ETTRICK:** 'The Ettrick
MAP 8 Shepherd' who wrote one of the great works of Scottish literature, The
B3 *Confessions of a Justified Sinner*, was born, lived and died in the valleys of the
YARROW and the **ETTRICK**, some of the most starkly beautiful landscapes in
Scotland. **ST MARY'S LOCH** on the A708, 28km W of Selkirk: there's a com-
memorative statue looking over the loch and the adj and supernatural seeming L of the Lowes. On the strip of land betw is **TIBBIE SHIELS** pub (and hotel),
once a gathering place for the writer and his friends (e.g. Sir Walter Scott) and
still a notable hostelry. Across the valley divide (11km on foot, part of the S
Upland Way (1790/LONG WALKS), or 25km by rd past the Gordon Arms Hotel is
the remote village of **ETTRICK**, another monument and his grave (and Tibbie
Shiels') in the churchyard. He was born, lived, died and was buried within this
one acre. James Hogg exhib at Aikwood (1679/MONUMENTS).

1745 **SIR WALTER SCOTT (1771–1832), ABBOTSFORD, MELROSE:** No other place
MAP 8 in Scotland (and few anywhere) contains so much of a writer's life and work.
C2 This was the house he rebuilt from the farmhouse he moved to in 1812 in the
countryside which he did so much to popularise. The house is still lived in by
his descendants and the library and study are pretty much as he left them,

including 9,000 rare books, antiquarian even in his day. There are pleasant grounds and topiary and a walk by the Tweed which the house o/look. His grave is at **DRYBURGH ABBEY** (1715/ABBEYS). House open Apr-Oct 10am-5pm; Sun 2-5pm. (in summer 10am)

1746
MAP 7
MAP A

ROBERT LOUIS STEVENSON (1850–94), EDINBURGH: Though Stevenson travelled widely – lived in France, emigrated to America and died and was buried in Samoa – he spent the first 30 yrs of his short life in Edin. He was born and brought up in the New Town, living at **17 HERIOT ROW** from 1857-80 in a fashionable town house which is still lived in (not open to the public). Most of his youth was spent in this newly built and expanding part of the city in an area bounded then by parkland and farms. Both the **BOTANICS** (352/OTHER ATTRACTIONS) and **WARRISTON CEMETERY** (1701/GRAVEYARDS) are part of the landscape of his childhood. However, his fondest recollections were of the **PENTLAND HILLS** and, virtually unchanged as they are, it's here that one is following most poignantly in his footsteps. The 'cottage' at **SWANSTON** (a delightful village with some remarkable thatched cottages reached via the city bypass/Colinton t/off or from Oxgangs Rd and a br over the bypass; the village nestles in a grove of trees below the hills and is a good place to walk from), the ruins of **GLENCORSE CHURCH** (ruins even then and where he later asked that a prayer be said for him) and **COLINTON MANSE** can all be seen, but not visited. The fact is, Edinburgh has no Stevenson Museum (though his lifetime was relatively recent and his acclaim international). You can always stay at the **HAWES INN** in South Queensferry and dream of *Kidnapped*.

IRVINE WELSH (c1958 –): Literary immortality awaits confirmation. Tours (*that* toilet etc) likely any day. **ROBBIES BAR:** might suffice (274/'UNSPOILT' PUBS).

THE REALLY SPOOKY PLACES

1747 **HIDDEN VALLEY, GLENCOE:** The secret glen where the ill-fated Macdonalds
MAP 2 hid the cattle they'd stolen from the Lowlands and which became (with poli-
C4 tics and power struggles) their undoing. A narrow wooded cleft takes you
betw the imposing and gnarled '3 Sisters' Hills and over the threshold (God
knows how the cattle got there) and into the huge bowl of Coire Gabhail. The
place envelops you in its tragic history, more redolent perhaps than any of the
massacre sites. Park on the A82 5km from the visitor centre 300m W of 2 white
buildings (one as steading) on either side of the rd (Alt-na-reigh). Cross rd and
follow clear path down to and across the R Coe. Ascend keeping burn to left;
1.5km further up, it's best to ford it. Allow 3hrs. (1722/BATTLEGROUNDS.)   2-B-2

1748 **UNDER EDINBURGH OLD TOWN:** Two mentions here – Mary King's Close, a
MAP A medieval st under the Royal Mile closed in 1753; and the Vaults under North
D3 Br – built in the 18th century and sealed up around the time of the
Napoleonic Wars. History underfoot for unsuspecting tourists and locals alike.
Mercat Tours (0131 661 4541) will take you both places. Glimpses of a rather
smelly subterranean life way back then. It's dark during the day, but at
night …

1749 **THE YESNABY STACKS, ORKNEY MAINLAND:** A cliff top viewpoint that's so
wild, so dramatic and, if you walk near the edge, so precarious that its super-
naturalism verges on the uneasy. Shells of lookout posts from the war echo
the melancholy spirit of the place. ('The bloody town's a bloody cuss/No
bloody trains, no bloody bus/And no one cares for bloody us/In bloody
Orkney' – first lines of a poem written then, a soldier's lament.) Nr Skara Brae,
it's about 30km from Kirkwall and way out west.

1750 **THE FAIRY GLEN, SKYE:** A place so strange, it's hard to believe that it's mere-
MAP 2 ly a geological phenomenon. Entering Uig on the A855 (becomes A87) from
B2 Portree, there's a turret on the left (Macrae's Folly). Take rd on rt marked
Balnaknock for 2km and you enter an area of extraordinary conical hills
which, in certain conditions of light and weather, seems to entirely justify its
legendary provenance. Your mood may determine whether you believe they
were good or bad fairies, but there's supposed to be an incredible 365 of
these grassy hillocks, some 35m high – how else could they be there?

1751 **CLAVA CAIRNS, nr CULLODEN, INVERNESS:** Nr Culloden (1720/BATTLE-
MAP 2 GROUNDS) these curious chambered cairns in a grove of trees nr a river in the
C1 middle of 20th-century nowhere can be seriously X-Files (1633/PREHISTORIC
SITES for details).

1752 **THE CLOOTIE WELL on the road betw TORE on the A9 and AVOCH:** Spooky
MAP 2 spooky place on the rd towards Avoch and Cromarty 4km from the r/bout at
C2 Tore N of Inverness. Easily missed, but it's on the rt side of the rd going E. What
you see is hundreds of rags (actually pieces of clothing) hanging on the
branches of trees around the spout of an ancient well. They go way back up
the hill behind and have probably been here for decades. Don't wish you were
here. This has what you'd call strong (but strange) vibrations.

1753 **BURN O' VAT, nr BALLATER:** This impressive and rather spooky glacial curi-
MAP 3 ousity on Royal Deeside is a popular spot and well worth the short walk. 8km
B3 from Ballater towards Aberd on main A93, take A97 for Huntly for 2km to a
recently refurbed car park at the Muir of Dinnet nature reserve. Some scrambling to reach the huge cavern from which the burn flows to L Kinord. Forest
walks, busy on fine weekends, but v odd when you catch it quiet. July '99,
Keith saw a vision here (she was wearing a Scotland's Natural Heritage t-shirt).

1754 **CRICHOPE LINN, nr THORNHILL:** A supernatural sliver of glen inhabited by
MAP 9 water spirits of various temperaments. Take rd for Cample on A76 Dumfries to
C2 Kilmarnock rd just S of Thornhill; at village (2km) take left for 2km. Discreet
sign and gate in bank on rt is easy to miss, but quarry for parking 100m further on, on left, is more obvious. Follow path upsteam on trickling Cample
water for 1km until you're at the gorge. Hope you come back. (and take care
on the path! One reader lost his dog here – really!)

1755 **SALLOCHY WOOD, LOCH LOMOND:** B837, N of Balmaha, look for Sallochy

MAP 6 Wood car park on the left. Cross back over the rd, away from L Lomond, and

B3 follow the trail signs, up the hill. After the large Cedar tree, the path takes you into the woods. Slippery going (on the exposed tree roots) then an unexpected clearing in middle of dense undergrowth. This is the ruined hamlet of Wester Sallochy. Surrounded by gloomy conifers, the roofless buildings still stand, awaiting the return of their long-dead tenants. Not a place to visit at night, but some do, and they leave their mark …

THE NECROPOLIS, GLASGOW: 1700/GRAVEYARDS.

HAMILTON MAUSOLEUM, STRATHCLYDE PARK: 1668/MONUMENTS.

LOANHEAD OF DAVIOT, nr OLDMELDRUM, ABERDEENSHIRE: 1640/PREHISTORIC SITES.

SECTION 8

Strolls, Walks and Hikes

Popular and notable hills in the various regions of Scotland but not including Munros or difficult climbs. Always best to remember that the weather can change v quickly. Take an OS map on higher tops. See p. 10 for walk codes.

1756
MAP 2
C1

SUILVEN, LOCHINVER: From close or far away, this is one of Scotland's most awe-inspiring mountains. The 'sugar loaf' can seem almost insurmountable, but in good weather it's not so difficult. Route from Inverkirkaig 5km S of Lochinver on rd to Achiltibuie, turns up track by Achin's Bookshop (1936/CRAFT SHOPS) on the path for the Kirkaig Falls; once at the loch, you head for the Bealach, the central waistline through an unexpected dyke and follow track to the top. The slightly quicker route from the N (Glencanisp) following a stalkers' track that eventually leads to Elphin, also heads for the central breach in the mt's defences. Either way it's a long walk in; 8km before the climb. Allow 8hrs return. At the top, the most enjoyable 100m in the land and below – amazing Assynt. 731m. Take OS map.   2-C-3

1757
MAP 2
C2

STAC POLLAIDH/POLLY, nr ULLAPOOL: This hill described variously as 'perfect', 'preposterous' and 'gr fun', certainly has character and, rising out of the Sutherland moors on the rd to Achiltibuie off the A835 N from Ullapool, demands to be climbed. Route everyone takes is from the car park by L Lurgainn 8km from main rd. Head for the central ridge which for many folk is enough; the path to the pinnacles is exposed and can be off-putting. Best half day hill climb in the N. 613m. Allow 3-4hrs return.   2-B-3

1758
MAP 1
C3

GOAT FELL, ARRAN: Starting from the car park at Cladach before Brodick Castle grounds 3km from town, or from Corrie further up the coast (12km). Worn path, a steady climb, rarely much of a scramble but a rewarding afternoon's exertion. Some scree and some view! 874m. Allow 5hrs.   2-B-2

1759
MAP 1
C2

THE COBBLER (BEN ARTHUR), ARROCHAR: Perennial favourite of the Glas hill walker and, for sheer exhilaration, the most popular of 'the Arrochar Alps'. A motorway path ascends from the A83 on the other side of L Long from Arrochar (park in lay-bys nr Succoth rd end; there are always loads of cars) and takes 2.5-3hrs to traverse the up'n'down route to the top. Just short of a Munro at 881m, it has 3 tops of which the N peak is the simplest scramble (central and S peaks for climbers). Way not marked; consult.   2-B-3

SIX MAGNIFICENT HILLS IN THE TROSSACHS

1760
MAP 6
B3

BEN VENUE and BEN AN: 2 celebrated tops in the Highland microcosm of the Trossachs around L Achray, 15km W of Callander; strenuous but not difficult and with superb views. Ben Venue (727m) is the more serious; allow 4-5 hrs return. Start from Kinlochard side at Ledard or more usually from behind L Achray Hotel: 100m along 'Forest Path' go left and then it's way-marked. Ben An (415m) starts with a steep climb from the main A821 along from the old Trossachs Hotel. Scramble at top. Allow 2 to 3hrs.   2-B-3

1761
MAP 6
B2

BEINN ANT-SIDHIEN, STRATHYRE: (pron 'Ben Sheann'). Another Trossachs favourite and not taxing. From village main rd (the A74 to Lochearnhead), cross bridge opp Monro Hotel, turn left after 200m then 500m to steep start through woods. O/look village and views to Crianlarich and Ben Vorlich (*see below*). 600m. 1.5hrs.   2-B-3

1762
MAP 6
B3

DOON HILL, THE FAERIE KNOWE, ABERFOYLE: Legendary hillock in Aberfoyle, only 1hr up and back, so a gentle elevation into faerie land. The tree at the top is the home of the 'People of Quietness' and there was once a local minister who had the temerity to tell their secrets (in 1692). Go round it 7 times and your wish will be granted, go round it backwards at your peril (well, you wouldn't would you?). Go from end of main st and opp jnct of Trossachs/Callander rd take small rd past hotel for 2km, veering left. Better still, ask!   1-B-1

1763
MAP 6
B2

THE GOLDEN HILL, BEN OUR, LOCH EARN: A relatively easy climb which feels like a real mountain walk and with dramatic vews of the big hills around it, Ben Vorlich and the Ben Lawyers group and the Balquhidder Braes. Starts S of Lochearnhead on the S Lochearn rd 1.5km from its jnct with the A84. Park after white castle and church before crossing the R Ample. Follow river track for 1.5km to a footbridge then another past Glenample Farm. Curve round to the back of Ben Our, the path peters out nr the top. 3hrs return.　　　　2-B-3

1764 **BEN VORLICH:** The big hill itself is also approached from the S Lochearn rd; MAP 6　from Ardvorlich House 5km from A84. Enter 'East Gate' and follow signs for B2　open hillside of Glen Vorlich. Track splits after 1.5km, take right then SE side of come to N ridge of mountain. Allow 5hrs ret.　　　　2-B-3

1765 **CRIFFEL, NEW ABBEY, nr DUMFRIES:** 12km S by A710 to New Abbey, which MAP 9　Criffel dominates. It's only 569m, but seems higher. Exceptional views from C3　top as far as English lakes and across to Borders. Granite lump with brilliant outcrops of quartzite. The annual race gets up and back to the Abbey Arms in under an hr; you can take it easier. Start 3km S of village, t/off A710 by one of the curious painted bus shelters signed for Ardwell Mains Farm. Park before the farm buildings and get on up.　　　　2-A-2

1766 **MERRICK, nr NEWTON STEWART:** Go from bonnie Glen Trool via Bargrennan MAP 9　14km N on the A714. Bruce's Stone is there at the start (1735/MARY, CHARLIE B2　AND BOB). The highest peak in S Scotland (843m), it's a strenuous though straight-forward climb in glorious scenery. 4hrs.　　　　2-B-3

1767 **NORTH BERWICK LAW:** The conical volcanic hill, a beacon in the E Lothian MAP 7　land-scape. **TRAPRAIN LAW** nearby, is higher, tends to be frequented by rock B1　climbers, but has major prehistoric significance as a hillfort citadel of the Goddodin and a definite aura. NBL is easy and rewarding – leave town by Law Rd, path marked beyond houses. Views 'to the Cairngorms' (!) and along the Forth.　　　　BOTH 1-A-1

1768 **RUBERSLAW, DENHOLM, nr HAWICK:** The smooth hummock that sits above MAP 8　the Teviot valley and affords views of 7 counties, incl Northumberland. At C3　424m, it's a gentle climb taking about 1hr from the usual start at Denholm Hill Farm (private land, be aware of livestock). Leave Denholm at corner of Green by shop and go past post office. Take left after 3km to farm.　　　　2-A-2

1769 **TINTO HILL, nr BIGGAR and LANARK:** A favourite climb in S/Central MAP 1　Scotland with easy access to start from A73 nr Symington, 10km S of Lanark. D3　Park 100m behind Tinto Hills farm shop, after stocking up with rolls and juice. Good track, though it has its ups and downs before you get there. Braw views. 707m. Allow 3hrs.　　　　2-A-2

1770 **CONIC HILL, BALMAHA, LOCH LOMOND:** An easier climb than the Ben up MAP 6　the rd and a good place to view it from, Conic, on the Highland fault line, is B3　one of the first Highland hills you reach from Glas. Stunning views also of L Lomond from its 358m peak. Ascend thro woodland from the corner of Balmaha car park. Watch for buzzards and your footing on the final crumbly bits. May be closed for lambing season Apr-May. 1.5hrs up.　　　　2-A-2

1771 **KINNOULL HILL, PERTH:** Various starts from town (the path from beyond MAP 4　Branklyn Grds on the Dundee Rd is less frequented) to the wooded ridge C3　above the Tay with its tower and incredible views to S from the precipitous cliffs. Surprisingly extensive area of hill side common and it's not difficult to get lost. The leaflet/map from Perth TO helps. Local lurv spot after dark.　1-A-1

1772 **BENNACHIE, nr ABERDEEN:** The pilgrimage hill, an easy 528m often busy at MAP 3　w/ends but never a let-down. Various trails take in 'the Taps'. Trad route from C3　Rowan Tree nr Chapel of Garioch (pron 'Geery') signed Pittodrie off A96 nr Pitcaple. Also from Essons car park on rd from Chapel-Monymusk, which is steeper. Or from other side the Lord's Throat rd, a longer, more forested app from banks of the Don. All car parks have trail-finders. From the fortified top you see what Aberdeenshire is about. 2hrs. Bennachie's soulmate, **TAP O' NOTH**, is 20km W. Easy app via Rhynie on A97 (then 3km).　　　　2-B-2

1773 **DUNADD, KILMARTIN, N of LOCHGILPHEAD:** Less of a hill, more of a lump, MAP 1　but it's where they crowned the kings of Dalriada for half a millennium. Stand B2　on top when the Atlantic rain is sheeting in and … you get wet like the kings did. For more info, try **KILMARTIN HOUSE MUSEUM** nearby (MUSEUMS/2010)
　　　　2-C-3

HILL WALKS

The following ranges of hills offer walks in various directions and more than one summit. They are all accessible and fairly easy. See p. 10 for walk codes.

1774
MAP 2

WALKS ON SKYE: Obviously many serious walks in and around the Cuillins (1786/MUNROS, 1793/SERIOUS WALKS), but almost infinite variety of others. Can do no better than read a gr book, *50 Best Routes on Skye and Raasay* by Ralph Storer (avail locally), which describes and grades many of the must-dos.

1775
MAP 5
B3

LOMOND HILLS, FIFE, nr FALKLAND: The conservation village lies below a prominent ridge easily reached from the main st esp via Back Wynd (off which there's a car park). More usual app to both E and W Lomond, the main tops, is from Craigmead car park 3km from village towards Leslie trail-finder board. The celebrated Lomonds (aka the Paps of Fife), aren't that high (West is 522m), but they can see and be seen for miles. Also start from radio masts up rd from A912 E of Falkland.   3-10KM CIRC XBIKES 2-A-2

An easy rewarding single climb is **BISHOP'S HILL** Start opp the church in Scotlandwell. A steep path veers left and then there are several ways up. Allow 2hrs. Gr view of L Leven, Fife and a good swathe of Central Scotland. Gliders glide over.

1776
MAP 8
C3

THE EILDONS, MELROSE: The 3 much-loved hills or paps visible from most of the Central Borders and easily climbed from the town of Melrose which nestles at their foot. Leave main sq by rd to stn (the Dingleton rd), after 100m a path begins betw 2 pebble-dash houses on the left. You climb the smaller first, then the highest central one (422m). You can make a circular route of it by returning to the golf course. Allow 1.5hrs.   3KM CIRC XBIKES I-A-2

1777
MAP 6
D3

THE OCHILS: Usual app from the 'hillfoot towns' at the foot of the glens that cut into their S-facing slopes, along the A91 Stirling-St Andrews rd. Alva, Tillicoultry and Dollar all have impressive glen walks easily found from the main streets where tracks are marked (1800/GLEN AND RIVER WALKS). Good start nr Stirling from the Sheriffmuir rd uphill from Br of Allan or, from the old graveyard (1708/GRAVEYARDS), take the steep rd up. From last houses about 3km, there's a lay-by on the rt and a reservoir just visible on the left. There are usually other cars here. A stile leads to the hills which stretch away to the E for 40km and afford gr views for little effort. Highest point is Ben Cleugh, 721m. Swimming place nearby is Paradise (1530/PICNICS).   2-40KM SOME CIRC XBIKES 1/2-B-2

1778
MAP 7
B2

THE LAMMERMUIRS: The hills SE of Edin that divide the rich farmlands of E Lothian and the valley of the Tweed in the Borders. Mostly a high wide moor land but there's wooded gentle hill country in the watersheds of the southern rivers and spectacular coastal scenery betw Cockburnspath and St Abbs Head. (1581/WILDLIFE; 1831/COASTAL WALKS.) The eastern part of the S Upland Way follows the Lammermuirs to the coast (1790/LONG WALKS). Many moorland walks begin at the car park at the head of Whiteadder Reservoir (A1 to Haddington, B6369 towards Humbie, then E on B6355 through Gifford), a mysterious loch in the bowl of the hills. Excellent walks also centre on Abbey St Bathans to the S – head off A1 at Cockburnspath. Through village (1293/TEAROOMS) to Toot Corner (signed 1km) and off to left, follow path above valley of Whiteadder to Edinshall Broch (2km). Further on, along river (1km), is a swing bridge and a fine place to swim (1520/PICNICS). Circular walks possible; ask in village.   5-15KM SOME CIRC MTBIKES 1/2-B-2

1779
MAP 8
D3

THE CHEVIOTS: Not strictly in Scotland, but they straddle the border and Border history. There are many fine walks starting from Kirk Yetholm (incl the Pennine Way which stretches 400km S to the Peak district) incl an 8km circular route of typical Cheviot foothill terrain that follows the actual border for half its route (leaflet available in the pub). Most forays start at Wooler 20km from Coldstream and the border. Cheviot itself (2,676ft) has wide boggy plateau, Hedgehope via the Harthope Burn usually more fun.

THE CAMPSIE FELLS, nr GLASGOW: 714/WALKS OUTSIDE THE CITY.

THE PENTLAND HILLS, nr EDINBURGH: 364/WALKS OUTSIDE THE CITy.

SOME GREAT MUNROS

There are almost 300 hills in Scotland over 3,000ft as tabled by Sir Hugh Munro in 1891. Munro-bagging has become v popular and there are numerous books which give route details. The Munros selected here have been chosen for their relative ease of access both to the bottom and thence to the top. They all offer rewarding climbs, but none should be attempted without proper clothing (esp boots) and sustenance for the journey. You may also need an OS map. Always remember that the weather can change quickly in the Scottish mts.

1780 **BEN LOMOND, ROWARDENNAN, LOCH LOMOND:** Many folk's first Munro,
MAP 6 given proximity to Glas (soul and city). It's not too taxing a climb and has
B3 rewarding views (in good weather). 2 main ascents: 'tourist route' is easier, from toilet block at Rowardennan car park (end of rd from Drymen), well-trodden all the way; or 500m up past Youth Hostel, a path follows burn – the 'Ptarmigan Route'. Circular walk poss. 974m. 3hrs up.

1781 **AN TEALLACH, TORRIDON:** Sea-level start from Dundonnell on the A832 S of
MAP 2 Ullapool, so easy to find. This, one of the most awesome peaks in Scotland is
C2 not the ordeal it looks. Path well trod and once up there are gr scrambling opportunities for the nimble. Peering over the pinnacle of Lord Berkeley's Seat down to L na Sheaallag is a jaw-drop. Take a day (a good day). 1,062m.

1782 **BEINN ALLIGIN, TORRIDON:** The other gr Torridon trek – you may as well go
MAP 2 for it! Car park by br on rd to Inveralligin and Diabeg, walk thro woods over
B2 moor by tumbling river. Left at fork then a steepish pull up onto the Horns of Alligin. You can cover 2 Munros in a circular route that takes you across the top of the world, up there with mighty Liathach and Beinn Eighe. 985m.

1783 **BEN MORE, MULL:** The 'cool, high ben' sits in isolated splendour, the only
MAP 1 Munro, bar the Cuillins, not on the mainland. Has a sea-level start from a lay-
B1 by on the coast rd B8073 that skirts the southern coast of L Na Keal, then a fairly clear path through the bleak landscape. Can be slightly tricky nr the top (don't think about it without good boots), but there are fabulous views across the islands, even as far as Ireland. 966m.

1784 **BEN WYVIS, nr GARVE:** Standing apart from its northern neighbours, you can
MAP 2 feel the presence of this mt from a long way off. Just to N of main A835 rd from
C2 Inverness-Ullapool and v accessible from it, park 6km N of Garve (48km from Inverness) and follow marked path by stream and through the forest. Vast plantations all around but you leave them behind and the app to the summit is by a soft and mossy ridge. Magnificent 1,046m.

1785 **LOCHNAGAR, nr BALLATER:** Described as a fine, complex mt, its nobility and
MAP 3 mystique apparent from afar, not least Balmoral Castle. App via Glen Muick
B3 (pron 'Mick') rd from Ballater to car park at L Muick (1475/LOCHS). Path to mt well signed and well trodden. 18km return, allow 6-8hrs. Steep at top. Apparently on a clear day you can see the Forth Br. 1,155m.

1786 **BLA BHEINN, SKYE:** The magnificent massif, isolated from the other Cuillins,
MAP 2 has a sea-level start and seems much higher than it is. The *Munro Guide*
B3 describes it as 'exceptionally accessible'. It has an eerie jagged beauty and – though some scrambling is involved and it helps to have a head for exposed situations – there are no serious dangers. Take A881 from Broadford to Elgol through Torrin and park 1km S of the head of L Slapin, walking W at Allt na Dunaiche along N bank of stream. Bla Bheinn (pron 'Blahven') is an enormously rewarding climb and permits rapid descent for scree runners to shorten the usual time of 8hrs. 928m.

1787 **BEN LAWERS, between KILLIN and ABERFELDY, PERTHSHIRE:** The massif
MAP 4 of 7 summits includes 6 Munros that dominate the N side of L Tay. They are
A3 linked by a twisting ridge 12km long that only once falls below 800m and, if you're v fit, it's poss to do the lot in a single day starting from the N or Glen Lyon side. The Munro beginner or non-bagger should start and plan route at the visitor centre 5km off the A827 nr Lawers.

1788 **MEALL NAN PTARMIGAN:** The part of the ridge to the W of Lawers (above),
MAP 4 which takes in a Munro and several tops, is not arduous and is immensely
A3 impressive. In 3hrs you can get up, along some of it and back, and feel gr for

the rest of the week. Start 1km further on from visitor centre down 100m track and through gate. Head up to saddle, paths indistinct, but just climb. At the top the path becomes clear, as does your reason for being here.

LONG WALKS

Once again, these walks require preparation, route maps, v good boots etc. But don't carry too much. Sections are always poss. See p. 10 for walk codes.

1789 **THE WEST HIGHLAND WAY:** The 150km walk which starts at Milngavie 12km
MAPS o/side Glas and goes via some of Scotland's most celebrated scenery to
1, 2 emerge in Glen Nevis before the Ben. The route goes: Mugdock Moor-Drymen-L Lomond-Rowardennan-Inversnaid-Inverarnan-Crianlarich-Tyndrum-Br of Orchy-Rannoch Moor-Kingshouse Hotel-Glencoe-The Devil's Staircase-Kinlochleven. The latter part from Br of Orchy is the most dramatic. The Br of Orchy Hotel (01838 4000208) (1118/ROADSIDE INNS) and Kingshouse (01855 851259), both historic staging posts, are recommended, as is the Drover's Inn, Inverarnan (836/CENTRAL HOTELS). It's a good idea to book accom (allowing time for muscle fatigue) and don't take too much stuff. Info leaflet/pack from shops or Scottish Natural Heritage (01397 704716).

MAP 1 **START:** Officially at Milngavie (pron 'Mull-guy') Railway Stn (reg service from
D2 Glas Central, also buses from Buchanan St Bus Stn), but actually from Milngavie shopping precinct (Douglas St) 500m away; an inauspicious ramp down to Allander River by the side of Victoria Wine and then behind Presto supermarket. However, the countryside is close. Start from other end 1km down Glen Nevis rd from r/bout on A82 N from Ft William. Way is well marked, but you must have a route map.
                                                                                    2-B-3

1790 **SOUTHERN UPLAND WAY:** 350km walk from Portpatrick S of Stranraer
MAP 9 across the Rhinns of Galloway, much moorland, the Galloway Forest Park, the
A3 wild heart-land of Southern Scotland, then through James Hogg country (1744/LITERARY PLACES) to the gentler E Borders and the sea at Pease Bay (official end, Cockburnspath). Route is Stranraer-N Luce-Dalry-Sanquhar-Wanlockhead-Beattock-St Mary's L-Melrose-Lauder-Abbey St Bathans. The first and latter sections are the most obviously picturesque but highlights include L Trool, the Lowther Hills, St Mary's L, R Tweed. Usually walked W to E, the SU Way is a formidable undertaking ... (Info SNH as above). St Cuthberts Way in the Borders is a doddle by comparison (check local TOs).

START: Portpatrick by the harbour and up along the cliffs past the lighthouse. or Cockburnspath. Map is on side of shop at Cross.
                                                                                    2-B-3

1791 **SPEYSIDE WAY:** The walk that follows R Spey from the coast at Speybay betw
MAP 3 Buckie and Lossiemouth to Ballindalloch (there have been plans to extend much further S to Boat of Garten) with side spurs to Dufftown from Craigellachie up Glenfiddich (5km) and to Tomintoul follow the R Avon (pron 'A'rn') regarded currently as the end of the walk (24km). Main section from coast to Ballindalloch through Fochabers and Craigellachie is about 50km and closely follows the river. Much less strenuous than SU or WH Ways. Tomintoul spur has more hill walking character and a gr viewpoint at 600m. Throughout walk you are in whisky country with opportunities to visit Cardhu, Glenlivet and other distilleries nearby (1371/1374/WHISKY). Trail criss-crosses river.

START: Usual start is from coast end. Speybay is 8km N of Fochabers; the first marker is by the banks of shingle at the river mouth.
                                                                                    1-A-3

1792 **GLEN AFFRIC:** In enchanting Glen Affric and L Affric beyond (1799/GLEN AND
MAP 2 RIVER WALKS; 1444/GLENS; 1523/PICNICS), some serious walking begins on the
C3 32km Kintail trail. Done either W-E starting at the Morvich Outdoor Centre 2km from A87 nr Shiel Br, or E-W starting at the Affric Lodge 15km W of Cannich. Route can include one of the approaches to the Falls of Glomach (1455/WATERFALLS). In mid-June, this strenuous walk is the first part of an Iron Man-type race called the Highland Cross where 600 self-confessed crazies complete the trail W-E with a 50km cycle dash to Beauly in 3.5hrs. Poss stopover at one of Scotland's remotest (and, amongst walkers, most celebrated) hostels, the refurb 'Allt Beithe'. Otherwise allow 10hrs.
                                                                                    2-C-3

SERIOUS WALKS

None of these should be attempted without OS maps, proper equipment and preparation. Hill or ridge walking experience may be essential.

1793
MAP 2
B3
THE CUILLINS, SKYE: Much scrambling and, if you want it, serious climbing over these famously unforgiving peaks. The Red ones are easier and many walks start at the Sligachan Hotel on the main Portree-Broadford rd. Every July there's a hill race up Glamaig; the conical one which o/look the hotel. Most of the Black Cuillins incl the highest, Sgurr Alasdair (993m), and Sgurr Dearg, 'the inaccessible pinnacle' (978m), can be attacked from the campsite or the youth hostel in Glen Brittle. Good guides are *Introductory Scrambles from Glen Brittle* by Charles Rhodes, or '50 Best Routes in Skye and Raasay' by Ralph Storer both available locally, but you will need something. Take extreme care! (2179/BIG ATTRACTIONS; 1114/1115/HOSTELS; 1460/WATERFALLS; 1786/MUNROS; 1515/PICNICS.) 3-C-3

1794
MAP 2
C4
AONACH EAGACH, GLENCOE: One of several poss major expeditions in the Glencoe area and one of the world's classic ridge walks. Not for the faint-hearted or the ill-prepared. It's the ridge on your rt for almost the whole length of the glen from Altnafeadh to the visitor centre (where you might consult over the route). Start from the main rd and once you're up and have hopped across, do resist the descent from the last summit (Sgorr nam Fiannaidh) to the welcoming bar of the Clachaig Hotel. On your way, you'll have come close to heaven, seen Lochaber in its immense glory and recon-noitred some fairly exposed edges and pinnacles. As I've said before, go with somebody good. (1482/SCENIC ROUTES; 1183/BLOODY GOOD PUBS; 1112/ HOS-TELS; 1722/BATTLEGROUNDS.) 3-C-3

1795
MAP 2
C3
BEN NEVIS: Start on Glen Nevis rd, 5km Ft William town centre by br opp youth hostel or from visitor centre (4km town) over br and past Achintee Farm (gentler start). These paths lead to the same main route which continues to the top (many consider the tourist route to be v dull, but it is the safest). Allow the best part of a day (and I do mean the best – the weather can turn quickly here). Many people are killed every yr, even experienced climbers. It is the biggest, though not the best; you can see 100 Munros on a clear day (i.e. about once a yr.) You climb it because … well, because you have to. Go pre-pared (but you can hire boots etc on Glen rd). 2-B-3

1796
MAP 2
C3
THE FIVE SISTERS OF KINTAIL and THE CLUANIE RIDGE: Both generally started from A87 along from Cluanie Inn (1179/BLOODY GOOD PUBS) and they will keep you rt; usually walked E to W. Sisters is an uncomplicated but inspir-ing ridge walk, taking in 2 Munros and 2 tops. Not as strenuous as it looks, though it's a hard pull up and you descend to a point 8km further up the rd (so arrange transport). Many side spurs to vantage-points and wild views. The Cluanie or S ridge is a classic which covers 7 Munros. Starts at inn; 2 ways off back onto A876. Both can be walked in a single day (Cluanie allow 9hrs). (1113/HOSTELS.) 3-C-3

From the Kintail Centre at Morvich off A87 nr Shiel Br another long distance walk starts to Glen Affric (1792/LONG WALKS).

1797
MAP 2
D3
GLEN MORE FOREST PARK: from Coylumbridge and L Morlich; 32km. (2) joins (3) beyond L Morlich and both go through the Rothiemurchus Forest (1813/WOODLAND WALKS) and the famous **LAIRIG GHRU**, the ancient Rt of Way through the Cairngorms which passes betw Ben Macdui and Braeriach. Ascent is over 700m and going can be rough. This is one of the gr Scottish trails. At end of June, the Lairig Ghru Race completes this course E-W in 3.5hrs, but generally this is a full-day trip. The famous shelter, Corrour Bothy betw 'Devil's Point' and Carn A Mhaim, can be a halfway house. Nr Linn of Dee, routes (1) and (2/3) converge and pass through the ancient Caledonian Forest of Mar. Going E-W is less gruelling and there's Aviemore to look forward to!

GLEN AFFRIC: Or rather beyond Glen Affric and L Affric (1799/GLEN WALKS; 1444/GLENS), the serious walking begins (1792/LONG WALKS).

GLEN AND RIVER WALKS

See also GREAT GLENS, p. 180. Walk codes are on p. 10.

1798 GLEN TILT, BLAIR ATHOLL: A walk of variable length in this classic Highland
MAP 4 glen, easily accessible from the caravan park off the main A9 in Blair Atholl.
B2 Trail leaflet from park office and local TOs. Fine walking and unspoiled scenery
begins only a short distance into the deeply wooded gorge of the R Tilt, but
to cover the circular route it's necessary to walk to 'Gilbert's Br' (9km return) or
the longer trail to Gow's Br (17km return). Begin here also the gr route into the
Cairngorms leading to the Linn of Dee and Braemar, joining the track from
Speyside which starts at Feshiebridge or Glenmore Forest (1797/SERIOUS
WALKS).   UP TO 17KM CIRC XBIKE 1-B-2

1799 GLEN AFFRIC, CANNICH, nr DRUMNADROCHIT: Easy short walks are
MAP 2 marked and hugely rewarding in this magnificent glen well known as the first
C3 stretch in the gr E-W route to Kintail (1796/SERIOUS WALKS) and the Falls of
Glomach (1455/WATERFALLS). Starting pt of this track into the wilds is at the
end of the rd at L Affric; there are many short and circular trails indicated here.
Car park is beyond metal rd 2km along forest track towards Affric Lodge (cars
not allowed to lodge itself). Track cl in stalking season. Easier walks in famous
Affric forest from car park at Dog Falls. 7km from Cannich (1523/PICNICS).
Waterfalls and spooky tame birds. Good idea to hire bikes at Drumnadrochit
or Cannich (Caravan Park). Don't miss Glen Affric (1444/GLENS).

5/8KM CIRC BIKE 1-B-2

1800 DOLLAR GLEN, DOLLAR, nr STIRLING: The classic fairy glen in Central
MAP 6 Scotland, positively hoaching with water spirits, reeking of ozone and euphor-
D3 ic after rain. 20km from Stirling by A91, or 18km from M90 at Kinross jnct 6.
Start from top of tree-lined ave on either side of burn or from further up rd
signed Castle Campbell where there's a car park and a path down into glen.
The Castle at head of glen is open 7 days till 6pm (Oct-Mar till 4pm), and has
boggling views. There's a circular walk back or take off for the Ochil Tops, the
hills that surround the glen. There are also first-class walks (less frequented)
up the glens of the other hillfoot towns, Alva and Tillicoultry; they also lead to
the hills (1777/HILL WALKS).   3KM + TOPS CIRC XBIKE 1-A-2

1801 RUMBLING BRIDGE, nr DOLLAR: Formed by another burn running off the
MAP 6 same hills, an easier short walk in an Ochil Glen with something of the chas-
D3 mic experience and the added delight of the unique double br (built 1713).
There's a pt here at the end of one of the walkways under the br where you
are looking into a Scottish jungle landscape as the Romantics imagined. Nr
Powmill on A977 from Kinross (jnct 6, M90) then 2km. Nearby is **BRIDGE
BYGONES**, an antique/coffee shop (w/ends till 5pm) and esp **THE POWMILL
MILKBAR** serving excellent home-made food for 35 yrs. It's 5km W on the
A977. Open 7 days till 5pm (6pm weekends) (1286/TEAROOMS). Go after your
walk! **GARTWHINZEAN HOTEL**, 1km further on, is a roadhouse with decent
bar food all day.   3KM CIRC XBIKE 1-A-1

1802 FALKLAND, FIFE: If you're in Falkland for the Palace (1594/CASTLES) or the tea-
MAP 5 room (1303/TEAROOMS), this short amble up an enchanting glen should be
B3 added to your afternoon. Head thro vill for Falkland School (an activity centre
for visiting groups) – you can take a car into the estate – and look for gardens
behind it. The glen and the path are obvious. Gushing burn, waterfalls – you
can even walk behind one.   3KM CIRC XBIKE 1-A-2

1803 THE BIG BURN WALK, GOLSPIE: A non-taxing, perfect little glen walk
MAP 2 through lush diverse woodland. Variations poss, but start just beyond
D2 Sutherland Arms (973/HIGHLAND INEXP HOTELS) in the garage yard which is just
off the A9 before Dunrobin Castle. Go past derelict mill and under aqueduct
following river. A real supernature trail unfolds with ancient tangled trees,
meadows, waterfalls, cliffs and much wildlife. 3km to falls, return via route to
castle woods for best all-round intoxication.   6KM CIRC XBIKE 1-B-1

1804 THE STRATH at DUNBEATH: The glen or strath so eloquently evoked in Neil
MAP 2 Gunn's Highland River (1743/LITERARY PLACES), a book which is as much about
D1 the geography as the history of his childhood. A path follows the river for
many miles. A leaflet from the Dunbeath Heritage Centre points out places on

the way. It's a spate river and in summer becomes a trickle; hard to imagine Gunn's salmon odyssey. It's only 500m to the broch, but it's worth going into the hinterland where it becomes quite mystical (1710/GRAVEYARDS).　　1-A-1

1805 **TWEEDSIDE, PEEBLES:** The river side trail that follows the R Tweed from town
MAP 8 (Hay Lodge Park) past Neidpath Castle (1519/PICNICS) and on through classic
A2 Border wooded countryside crossing river either 2.5km out (5km round trip) at Manor Br 6km out (Lyne Footbr, 12km). Local pamphlet, The Bridges of Peebles, worth finding at TO.　　5/12KM CIRC XBIKE 1-A-1

Other good Tweedside walk between Dryburgh Abbey and Bemersyde House grounds. Start at either end.

1806 **GLEN LEDNOCK, nr COMRIE:** Can walk from Comrie or take car further up to
MAP 4 monument or drive further into glen to reservoir (9km) for more open walks.
B3 From town take rt off main A85 (to Lochearnhead) at Deil's Cauldron restau. Walk and Deil's Cauldron (waterfall and gorge) are signed after 250m. Walk takes less than 1hr and emerges on rd nr Lord Melville's monument (climb for gr views back towards Crieff, about 25 mins). River below in woody gorge.　　3/5KM CIRC XBIKE 1-A-1

1807 **BRIDGE OF ALVAH, BANFF:** Details: 1822/WOODLAND WALKS, mentioned here
MAP 3 because the best bit is by the river and the br itself. The single span crossing
C1 was built in 1772 and stands high above the river in a sheer-sided gorge. The river below is deep and slow. In the rt light it's almost Amazonian.

1808 **THE GANNOCHY BRIDGE AND THE ROCKS OF SOLITUDE, nr EDZELL:** 2km
MAP 4 N of village on B966 to Fettercairn. There's a lay-by after br and a wooden door
D2 in wall. Through it is another green world and a path above the rocky gorge of the R North Esk (1km). Huge sandstone ledges over dark peaty pools. You don't have to be alone (well maybe you do).　　2KM XCIRC XBIKE 1-A-1

1809 **Nr TAYNUILT:** A walk (recommended by readers) which takes in education
MAP 1 with recreation. It goes via Bonawe Ironworks (2017/MUSEUMS) and L Etive
C1 along the river side to a swing br and thence to Inverawe Smokehouse (open to the public; café). Walk back less interesting but all v nice. Ask in Taynuilt for start.　　10 KM CIRC BIKE 1-A-1

WOODLAND WALKS

1810 **RANDOLPH'S LEAP nr FORRES:** Tricky to explain how to find this spectacu-
MAP 3 lar gorge of the plucky little Findhorn lined with beautiful beechwoods and a
A2 gr place to swim or picnic (1521/PICNICS), so listen up. Go either: 10km S of Forres on the A940 for Grantown, then the B9007 for Ferness and Carrbridge. 1km from the sign for Logie Steading (2045/BUY ART) and 500m from the nar-row stone br, there's a pull-over place on the bend. The woods are on the other side of the rd. Or: take the A939 S from Nairn or N from Grantown and at Ferness take the B9007 for Forres. Approaching from this direction, it's about 6km along the rd; the pull-over is on your rt. If you come to Logie Steading you've missed it; don't – you will miss one of the sylvan secrets of the N.

1811 **LOCHAWESIDE:** Unclassified rd on N side of loch betw Kilchrenan and Ford,
MAP 1 centred on Dalavich. Illustrated brochure available from local hotels around
B2, C2 Kilchrenan and Dalavich post office, describes 6 walks in the mixed, mature forest all starting from car parking places on the rd. 3 starting from the Barnaline car park are trail-marked and could be followed without brochure. Avich Falls route crosses R Avich after 2km with falls on return route. Inverinan Glen is always nice and the track from the car park N of Kilchrenan on the B845 back to Taynuilt isn't on the brochure, may be less travelled and also fine.　　2-8KM CIRC XBIKE 2-A-2

1812 **PUCK's GLEN nr DUNOON:** Close to the gates of the Younger Botanic Garden
MAP 1 at Benmore (1376/GARDENS) on the other side of the A815 to Stracher 12km N
C2 of Dunoon. A short, exhilarating woodland walk from a convenient car park. Ascend thro' trees then down into a faery glen, foll the burn back to the rd. Some swimming pools.　　3KM CIRC XBIKE 1-A-1

1813 **ROTHIEMURCHUS FOREST, nr AVIEMORE:** The place to experience the
MAP 2   magic and the majesty of the gr Caledonian Forest and the beauty of Scots
D3   pine. App from B970, the rd that parallels the A9 from Coylumbridge to
Kincraig/Kingussie. 2km from Inverdruie nr Coylumbridge follow sign for L an
Eilean; one of the most perfect lochans in these or any woods. Loch circuit
5km (1471/LOCHS).

1814 **ARIUNDLE OAKWOODS:** Strontian. 35km Ft William via Corran Ferry. Walk
MAP 2   guide brochure at Strontian TO. Many walks around L Sunart and Ariundle:
B3   rare oak and other native species (esp on the wetter ground). You see how v
different was the landscape of Scotland before the Industrial Revolution used
up the wood. Start over town br, turning rt for Polloch. Go on past Cosy Knits,
with good home-baking café and park. 2 walks; well marked.

5KM CIRC MTBIKE 1-A-2

1815 **BALMACARRA:** 5km S Kyle of Lochalsh on A87. A woodland walk around the
MAP 2   shore of L Alsh, centred on Lochalsh House. Mixed woodland in fairly formal
B3   grd setting where you are confined to paths. Views over to Skye. A fragrant
and verdant amble.

3KM CIRC XBIKE 1-A-1

1816 **THE BIRKS O' ABERFELDY:** Circular walk through oak, beech and the birch (or
MAP 4   birk) woods of the title, easily reached and signed from town main st (1km).
B3   Steep-sided wooded glen of the Moness Burn with attractive falls esp the
higher one spanned by br where the 2 marked walks converge. This is where
Burns 'spread the lightsome days' in his eponymous poem.

3KM CIRC XBIKE 1-A-2

1817 **THE HERMITAGE, DUNKELD:** On A9 2km N of Dunkeld. Popular, easy, accessi-
MAP 4   ble walks along the glen and gorge of R Braan with pavilion o/look the Falls
B3   and, further on, 'Ossian's Cave'. Several woody walks around Dunkeld/Birnam
– good leaflet from TO.

2KM CIRC XBIKE 1-A-1

1818 **GLENMORE FOREST PARK, nr AVIEMORE:** Along from Coylumbridge (and
MAP 2   adj Rothiemurchus) on rd to ski resort, the forest trail area centred on L
D3   Morlich (sandy beaches, good swimming, water sports). Visitor centre has
maps of walk and bike trails and an activity programme.

1819 **ABOVE THE PASS OF LENY, CALLANDER:** A walk through mixed forest
MAP 6   (beech, oak, birch, pine) with gr Trossachs views. Start from MAIN car park on
C2   A84 4km N of Callander (the Falls of Leny are on opp side of rd, 100m away)
on path at back, to the left – path parallels rd at first (don't head straight up).
Way-marked and boarded where marshy, the path divides after 1km to head
further up to crest (4km return) or back down (2km).

2 OR 4KM CIRC XBIKE 1-A-2

1820 **LOCH TUMMEL WALKS, nr PITLOCHRY:** The mixed woodland N of L Tummel
MAP 4   reached by the B8019 from Pitlochry to Rannoch. Visitor centre at Queens
B2   View (1509/VIEWS) and walks in the Allean Forest which take in some historical sites (a restored farmstead, standing stones) start nearby (2-4km). There
are many other walks in area and the Forest Enterprise brochure is worth following (available from visitor centre and local TOs). (1479/LOCHS.)

1821 **THE NEW GALLOWAY FOREST:** Huge area of forest and hill country with
MAP 9   every type and length of trail incl section of S Upland Way from Bargrennan
B3   to Dalry (1790/LONG WALKS). Visitor centres at Kirroughtree (5km Newton
Stewart) and Clatteringshaws L on the 'Queen's Way' (9km New Galloway)
with easy routes around them. Glen and L Trool are v fine (1452/GLENS); the
'Retreat Oakwood' nr Laurieston has 5km trails. The Smithy in New Galloway
has walk books and walk food (1292/TEAROOMS). There's a river pool on the
Raiders' Rd (1527/PICNICS). One could ramble on …

1822 **DUFF HOUSE, BANFF:** Duff House itself is the major attraction around here
MAP 3   (2029/PUBLIC GALLERIES), but if you've time it would be a pity to miss the wood-
C1   ed policies and the meadows and riverscape of the Deveron. An illustrated
map on the back of the free brochure for the house (available from local TOs)
shows the route. To the Br of Alvah where you should be bound is about 7km
return. See also 1807/GLEN AND RIVER WALKS.

1823 **TORRACHILTY FOREST and ROGIE FALLS nr CONTIN and STRATHPEFFER:**
MAP 2   Enter by old br just o/side Contin on main A835 W to Ullapool or further along
C2   (4km) at Rogie Falls car park. Shame to miss the falls (1467/WATERFALLS), but

the woods and gorge are pleasant enough if it's merely a stroll you need. Ben Wyvis further up the rd is the big challenge (1784/MUNROS).

1824 **ABERNETHY FOREST nr BOAT OF GARTEN:** 3km from village off B970, but
MAP 2 hard to miss because the famous ospreys are signposted from all over
D3 (1569/BIRDS). Nevertheless this woodland reserve is a tranquil place among native pinewoods around the loch with dells and trails. Many other birdies twittering around your picnic. They don't dispose of the midges.

1825 **FOCHABERS** on main A98 about 3km E of town are some excellent woody
MAP 3 and winding walks around the glen and Whiteash Hill (2-5km). Further W on
B2 the **MORAY COAST: CULBIN FOREST** – head for Cloddymoss or Kentessack off A96 at Brodie Castle 12km E of Nairn. Acres of Sitka in sandy coastal forest.

WHERE TO FIND SCOTS PINE

Scots pine, along with oak and birch etc, formed the gr Caledonian Forest which once covered most of Scotland. Native Scots pine is v different from the regimented rows of pine trees that we associate with forestry plantations and which now drape much of the countryside. It is more like a deciduous tree with reddish bark and irregular foliage; no two ever look the same. The remnants of the gr stands of pine that are left are beautiful to see, mystical and majestic, a joy to walk among and no less worthy of conservation perhaps than a castle or a bird of prey. Here are some places you will find them:

ROTHIEMURCHUS FOREST: 1813/WOODLAND WALKS.

GLENTANAR, ROYAL DEESIDE: Nr Ballater, 10-15km SW of Aboyne.

Around Braemar and **GRANTOWN-ON-SPEY**.

STRATHYRE, nr CALLANDER: S of village on rt of main rd after L Lubnaig.

ACHRAY FOREST, nr ABERFOYLE: Some pine nr the Duke's Pass rd, the A821 to L Katrine, and amongst the mixed woodland in the 'forest drive' to L Achray.

BLACKWOOD OF RANNOCH: S of L Rannoch, 30km W of Pitlochry via Kinloch Rannoch. Start from Carie, fair walk in. 250-year-old pines; an important site.

ROWARDENNAN, L LOMOND: End of the rd along E side of loch nr Ben Lomond. Easily accessible pines nr the loch side, picnic sites etc.

Shores of **LOCH MAREE** and around **LOCH CLAIR, GLEN TORRIDON:** Both nr the Beinn Eighe National Park. Woodland centre on A832 N of Kinlochewe.

GLEN AFFRIC, nr DRUMNADROCHIT: 1444/GLENS. Biggest remnant of the Caledonian Forest in classic glen. Many strolls and hikes poss. Try Dog Falls (on main rd) for Affric introduction.

Native pinewoods aren't found S of Perthshire, but there are fine plantation examples in southern Scotland at:

GLENTRESS, nr PEEBLES: 7km on A72 to Innerleithen. Mature forest up the burn side, though surrounded by commercial forest.

SHAMBELLIE ESTATE, nr DUMFRIES: 1km from New Abbey beside A710 at the Shambellie House, 100yds sign. Ancient stands of pine over the wall amongst other glorious trees; this is like virgin woodland. Planted 1775–1780. Magnificent.

COASTAL WALKS

1826
MAP 1
A3
✓ ✓ **KINTRA, ISLAY:** On Bowmore-Pt Ellen rd take Oa t/off: then Kintra signed 7km. Good restau/bar with B&B in season, a place to camp (1153/HIGHLAND CAMPING), a fabulous beach (1430/BEACHES) which runs in opp direction and a notable golf course behind it (1855/GOLF IN GREAT PLACES). This walk leads along N coast of the Mull of Oa, an area of diverse beauty, sometimes pastoral, sometimes wild, with a wonderful shoreline. In café a detailed route map has been annotated with pictures. ANY KM XCIRC XBIKE 2-B-2

1827
MAP 3
D2
✓ ✓ **THE BULLERS OF BUCHAN, nr PETERHEAD:** 8km S of Peterhead on A975 rd to/from Cruden Bay. Park and walk 100m to cottages. To rt is precarious and spectacular cliff top walk to Cruden Bay (3km), to left the walk to Longhaven Nature Reserve, a continuation of the dramatic cliffs and more sea bird city. The Bullers is at start of walk, a sheer-sided 'hole' 75m deep with an outlet to the sea thro a natural arch. Walk round the edge of it, looking down on layers of birds (who might try to dive-bomb you away from their nests); it's a wonder of nature on an awesome coast. Take gr care.

1828
MAP 2
C1
✓ ✓ **CAPE WRATH and the CLIFFS OF CLO MOR:** Britain's most NW point reached by ferry from 1km off the A838 4km S of Durness by Cape Wrath Hotel; a 10min crossing then 40min minibus ride to Cape. Ferry holds 14 and runs May-Sept, 9.30am-4.30pm (01971 511376). At 280m Clo Mor are the highest cliffs in UK; 4km round trip from Cape. MoD range – access may be restricted. In other direction, the 28km to Kinlochbervie is one of Britain's most wild and wonderful coastal walks. Beaches incl Sandwood (1428/BEACHES). While in this NW area: **SMOO CAVE** 2km E of Durness.

1829
MAP 2
C1
OLD MAN OF STORR, nr LOCHINVER: The easy, exhilarating walk to the dramatic sea stack, 3km from lighthouse off unclassified rd 14km N Lochinver. Park and follow sheep tracks; cliffs are high and steep. 1-B-2

1830
MAP 9
C3
ROCKCLIFFE TO KIPPFORD: An easy stroll along the 'Scottish Riviera' through woodland nr the shore (2km) past the 'Mote of Mark' a Dark Age hill ft with views to Rough Island. The better cliff top walk is in the other direction to Castlepoint, but Kippford has The Anchor to look forward to (1226/BEST FOOD; 1418/COASTAL VILLAGES) (1299/TEAROOMS).

1831
MAP 8
D1
ST ABBS HEAD: The most dramatic coastal scenery in S Scotland, scary in a wind, rhapsodic on a blue summer's day. Extensive wildlife reserve and trails through coastal hills and vales to cliffs. Cars can go as far as lighthouse, but best to park at visitor centre nr farm on St Abbs village rd 3km from A1107 to Eyemouth and follow route (1581/WILDLIFE). 5-10KM CIRC XBIKE 1-B-2

1832
MAP 2
B3
SINGING SANDS, ARDNAMURCHAN: Park at Arivegaig 3km Acharacle and cross wooden br, following track round side of Kentra Bay. Follow signs for Gorteneorn, and walk through forest track and woodland to beach. As you pound the sands they should 'sing' to you whilst you bathe in the the beautiful views of Rum, Eigg, Muck and Skye (and just possibly the sea). Check at TO for directions and other walks booklet. 6KM XCIRC BIKE 1-B-1

1833
MAP 3
B1
EAST FROM CULLEN on the MORAY COAST: This is the same walk mentioned with reference to Sunnyside (1439/BEACHES) a golden beach with a fabulous ruined castle (Findlater) that might be your destination, there's a track E along from Harbour. 2hrs return. Superb coastline. 8KM XCIRC XBIKE 1-A-1

1834
MAP 2
D2
CROMARTY, THE SOUTH SOUTARS: The walk from Cromarty village (1414/COASTAL VILLAGES; 1302/TEAROOMS) round the tip of the S promontory at the narrow entrance to the Cromarty Firth. E of vill; coastal path hugs shoreline then ascends thro' woodland to headland. Good bench! Go further to top car park and viewpt panel. Return by rd. There may be dolphins out there! 5KM CIRC XBIKE 1-A-1

1835
MAP 5
C3
THE CHAIN WALK, ELIE: Unique and adventurous headland scramble at the W end of Elie (and Earlferry), by golf course. Hand- and footholds carved into rock with chains to haul yourself up. Watch tide; don't go alone. 2-B-2

SECTION 9

Sports

SCOTLAND'S GREAT GOLF COURSES

Those listed open to non-members and available to visitors (incl women) at most times, unless otherwise stated. Handicap certificates may be required.

AYRSHIRE (MAP 1)

1836　**GLASGOW GAILES/WESTERN GAILES:** 01294 311347/311649. Superb links
C3　courses next to one another, 5km S of Irvine off A78.

1837　**ROYAL OLD COURSE, TROON:** V difficult to get on. No wimmen. Staying at
C3　Marine Highland Hotel (01292 314444) helps. Easier is **THE PORTLAND COURSE:** Across rd from Royal. Both 01292 311555. And 805/AYRSHIRE HOTELS for the adj Piersland House Hotel.

1838　**OLD PRESTWICK:** 01292 477404. Original home of the Open and 'every chal-
C3　lenge you'd wish to meet'. Hotels opp (eg the Golf View 01292 671234) cost less than a round. Unlikely to get on w/ends.

1839　**TURNBERRY:** 01655 331000. Ailsa (championship) and Arran. Sometimes
C4　poss by application. Otherwise you must stay at hotel. (800/AYRSHIRE HOTELS.) Superb.

1840　**BELLEISLE, AYR:** 01292 441258. Good parkland course. Easy to get on.
C3

EAST LOTHIAN (MAP 7)

Note: There is a gr booklet available at the local TO, entitled 'Golf in East Lothian'.

1841　**GULLANE NO.1:** 01620 842255. One of 3 varied courses surrounding charm-
B1　ing village on links and within driving distance (35km) of Edin. Muirfield is nearby, but you need intro. Gullane is okay most days except Sat/Sun. (Handicap required for no.1 only – under 24 men, 30 ladies.) No.3 best for beginners. Visitor centre acts as clubhouse for non-members on nos. 2/3. Clubhouse for members/no.1 players only.

1842　**NORTH BERWICK EAST AND WEST:** E (officially the Glen Golf Club) has stun-
B1　ning views. A superb cliff-top course and is not too long, 01620 892726. W more taxing (esp the classic 'Redan') used for Open qualifying; a v fine links. Also has 9-hole kids' course, 01620 892135.

1843　**MUSSELBURGH:** The original home of golf (really: golf recorded here in
B1　1672), but this local authority-run 9-hole links is not exactly top turf and is enclosed by Musselburgh Racecourse. Nostalgia still appeals though. **ROYAL MUSSELBURGH** nearby compensates. It dates to 1774, fifth-oldest in Scotland. Busy early mornings and Fri afternoons, 01875 810139.

NORTH-EAST (MAPS 2, 3 and 4)

1844　**CARNOUSTIE:** 01241 853789. 3 good links courses; even poss (with handicap
MAP 3　cert) to get on the championship course (though w/ends difficult). Every hole
D3　has character. Buddon Links is cheaper and often quiet. Combination tickets available. A well-managed and accessible course, increasingly a golfing must.

1845　**MURCAR, ABERDEEN:** 01224 704354. Getting on Royal Aber Course is diffi-
MAP 3　cult for most people, but Murcar is a testing alternative, a seaside course 6km
D3　N of centre off Peterhead rd signed at r/bout after Exhibition Centre. Handicap cert needed. Municipal course at Hazlehead (good course, ish condition).

1846　**CRUDEN BAY, nr PETERHEAD:** 01779 812285. On A975 40km N of Aber.
MAP 3　Designed by Tom Simpson and ranked in UK top 50, a spectacular links course
D2　with the intangible aura of bygone days. Quirky holes epitomise old-fashioned style. W/ends difficult to get on.

1847　**NAIRN:** 01667 452787. Traditional seaside links course and one of the easiest
MAP 2　championship courses to get on. Good clubhouse, friendly folk. Nairn Dunbar
D2　on other side of town also has good links.

1848 **ROYAL DORNOCH:** 01862 810219. Sutherland championship course laid out
MAP 2 by Tom Morris in 1877. Amongst top 10 courses in UK, but not busy or inces-
D2 santly pounded. No poor holes. Stimulating sequences. Probably the most
northerly gr golf course in the world – and not impossible to play.

FIFE (MAP 5)

1849 **ST ANDREWS:** 01334 475757. The home and Mecca of golf, v much part of the
C2 town (2176/HOLIDAY CENTRES) and probably the largest golf complex in
Europe. Old Course most central, celebrated. Application by ballot the day
before (handicap cert needed). For Jubilee (1897, upgraded 1989) and Eden
(1914, laid out by Harry S. Holt paying homage to the Old with large, sloping
greens), apply the day before. New Course (1895, some rate the best) easiest
access. Less demanding are the new Strathtyrum and Balgove (upgraded 9-
hole for beginners) courses. All 6 courses contiguous and 'in town'; the
newish. Dukes Course (part of Old Course Hotel) is 3km away. Phone for reservations (and ballot). A whole lot of golf to be had – get your money out!

1850 **ELIE:** Book 01333 330301. Splendid open links maintained in top condition;
C3 can be windswept. The starter has his famous periscope and may be watching you. Adj 9-hole course, often busy with kids, is fun.

1851 **CRAIL:** 01333 450278. Originally designed by the legendary Tom Morris, links
D2 and park; all holes in sight of sea. Not exp; easy to get on.

1852 **LUNDIN LINKS:** 01333 320202/ladies 320832. Challenging seaside course
C3 used as Open qualifier. Some devious contourings. There is a separate course
for women.

1853 **LADYBANK:** 01337 830814. Best inland course in Fife; Tom Morris-designed
B2 again. V well kept and organised. Good facs. Tree-lined and picturesque.

GOOD GOLF COURSES IN GREAT PLACES

All open to women, non-members and inexpert players (except Luss).

1854 ✓ **LOCH LOMOND GOLF CLUB, LUSS:** On A82 1km from conservation vil-
MAP 1 lage of Luss. Exclusive American-owned club; membership only 5000
C2 bucks! We can buy a cheaper season ticket to see the annual World
Invitational tournament (early July; tickets 0990 661661); but no access to
plebs to clubhouse. 18 holes of scenic golf by the Loch, with Jack Nicklaus due
to design additional course soon. This is golfing for gold.

1855 ✓ **MACHRIE:** 01496 302310. Isle of Islay. 7km Pt Ellen. Worth going to Islay
MAP 1 (BA's airstrip adj course or Calmac ferry from Kennacraig nr Tarbert) just
A3 for the golf. The Machrie (Golf) Hotel does deals. Old-fashioned course to be
played by feel and instinct. Splendid, sometimes windy isolation with a warm
bar and restau at the end of it. The notorious 17th, 'Iffrin' (it means Hell), vor-
tex shaped from the dune system of marram and close-cropped grass, is one
of many gr holes. 18.

1856 ✓ **MACHRIHANISH:** 01586 810213. By Campbeltown (10km). Amongst the
MAP 1 dunes and links of the glorious 8km stretch of the Machrihanish Beach
B3 (1427/BEACHES). The Atlantic provides thunderous applause for your triumphs
over a challenging course. 9/18.

1857 ✓ **SOUTHERNESS, SOLWAY FIRTH:** 01387 880677. 25km S of Dumfries by
MAP 9 A710. A championship course on links on the silt flats of the Firth. Despite
C3 its prestige, visitors do get on. 10-12pm and 2-4pm. Under the wide Solway
sky, it's pure – southerness. 18.

1858 ✓ **ROSEMOUNT, BLAIRGOWRIE:** 01250 872622. Off A93, S of Blairgowrie.
MAP 4 An excellent, pampered and well-managed course in the middle of green
C3 Perthshire, an alternative perhaps to Gleneagles, being much easier to get on
(most days) and rather cheaper (though not at w/ends). 18.

1859 **GLENCRUITTEN, OBAN:** 01631 562868. Picturesque course on the edge of
MAP 1 town. Head S (A816) from Argyll Sq, bearing left at church. Course is signed.
B1 Quite tricky with many blind holes. Can get busy, so phone first. 18.

1860 **GAIRLOCH:** 01445 712407. Just as you come into town from the S on A832, it looks over the bay and down to a perfect, pink, sandy beach. Small clubhouse with honesty box. Not the world's most agonising course; in fact, on a clear day with views to Skye, you can forget agonising over anything. 9/18.

MAP 2
B2

1861 **HARRIS GOLF CLUB, SCARISTA, ISLE OF HARRIS:** 01859 511218 (the captain, but no need to phone). Just turn up on the rd betw Tarbert and Rodel and leave £7 in the box. First tee commands one of the gr views in golf and throughout this basic, but testing course, you are looking out to sea over Scarista beach (1433/BEACHES) and bay. The sunset may put you off your swing.

MAP 2
A2

1862 **NEW GALLOWAY:** Local course on S edge of this fine wee toon. Almost all on a slope but affording gr views of L Ken and the Galloway Forest behind. No bunkers and only 9 short holes, but exhilarating play. Easy on, except Sun. Just turn up. Clubs can be hired at The Smithy coffee shop in the village.

MAP 9
B3

1863 **MINTO, DENHOLM:** 01450 870220. 9km E Hawick. Spacious parkland in Teviot valley.

MAP 8
C3

1864 **VERTISH HILL, HAWICK:** 01450 372293. A more challenging hill course. Both among the best in Borders. 18.

MAP 8
C3

1865 **ROXBURGH HOTEL GOLF COURSE nr KELSO:** 01573 450331. Only championship course in the Borders. Designed by Dave Thomas along banks of R Teviot. Open non-res. Details (844/BORDER HOTS).

MAP 8
C2

1866 **TAYMOUTH CASTLE, KENMORE:** 01887 830228. Spacious green acres around the enigmatic empty hulk of the castle. Well-tended and organised course betw A827 to Aberfeldy and the river. Inexp, and guests at the Kenmore Hotel (899/PERTHSHIRE HOTELS) get special rate. 18.

MAP 4
B3

1867 **GIFFORD:** 01620 810591. Dinky inland course on the edge of a dinky village, bypassed by the queue for the big E Lothian courses and a guarded secret among the regulars. Generally ok, but phone starter (above) for avail. 9.

MAP 7
B1

1868 **STRATHPEFFER:** 01997 421219. V hilly (and we do mean hilly) course full of character and with exhilarating Highland views. Small-town friendliness. You are playing up there with the gods and some other old codgers. 18.

MAP 2
C2

1869 **ELGIN:** 01343 542884. 1km from town on A941 Perth rd. Many memorable holes on moorland/parkland course in an area where links may lure you to the coast (Nairn, Lossiemouth). 18.

MAP 3
B1

1870 **DURNESS:** 01971 511364. The most N golf course on mainland UK, on the wild headland by Balnakeil Bay, looking over to Faraid Head. The last hole is 'over the sea'. Only open since 1988, it's already got cult status. 2km W Durness village. 9.

MAP 2
C1

1871 **BOAT OF GARTEN:** 01479 831282. Challenging, picturesque course in town where ospreys have been known to wheel overhead. Has been called the 'Gleneagles of the North'; certainly the best round around, though not for novices. 18.

MAP 2
D3

1872 **ROTHESAY:** 01700 503554. Sloping course with breathtaking views of Clyde. Visitors welcome. What could be finer than taking the train from Glas to Wemyss Bay for the ferry over (2182/FAVOURITE JOURNEYS) and 18 holes. Finish up with fish 'n' chips at The W End (1270/FISH AND CHIPS) on the way home.

MAP 1
C3

1873 **TRAIGH, ARISAIG:** 01687 450337. A830 Ft William-Mallaig rd, 2km N Arisaig. Pronounced 'try'- and you may want to. The islands are set out like stones in the sea around you and there are 9 hilly holes of fun.

MAP 2
B3

BEST OF THE SKIING

*In a good yr the Scottish ski season can extend from Dec (or even Nov) till the 'lambing snow' of late April. And on a good day it can be as exhilarating as anywhere in Europe. Here's a summary (**distances in kilometres**):*

	GLENSHEE	CAIRNGORM	AONACH MOR	GLENCOE	THE LECHT
DIST/EDIN	130	215	215	165	200
DIST/GLASGOW	170	235	200	150	160
NR CENTRE	Perth 65	Inverness 45	Ft Will 10	FT Will 40	Aberdeen 95
NR TOWN	Braemar 20	Aviemore 15	Ft Will 10	Ballachulish 20	Tomintoul 11
NO OF RUNS	38	28	35	15	17
BEGINNERS	10	11	8	3	6
INTERMED	26	15	12	11	10
GOOD	2	2	1	15	1
NO OF TOWS	26	17	12	7	12
CAFÉS	3	4	3 + units	1	1
GOOD FOR	*Size*	*Size*	*Uplift*	*Fewer crowds*	*Fewer crowds*
	Access from rd	*Non-skiing*	*Access*	*Nr road*	*Nr road*
	Views Glas Maol	*Views*	*Views/Sunsets*	*Views*	*Families*
	2 distinct areas	*Beginners*	*Ski School*	*Most alpine*	*Near NE*
	Snowboarding	*Snowboarding*	*Café*		

1874 GLENSHEE

MAP 4
B3

BASE STATION: 013397 41320. **SCHOOL:** 01250 885255 or 01250 885 216.

WHERE TO STAY

DALMUNZIE HOUSE: 01250 885 226. 9km S. Country house. Golf. Family-run. MED.EX

BRIDGE OF CALLY HOTEL: 01250 886231. 36km S. **GLENISLA, KIRKTON OF GLENISLA:** 01575 582223. 32km SE (1131/INNS). INX

SPITTAL OF GLENSHEE: 01250 885204. 8km S. Cheap'n'cheerful. MED.INX

WHERE TO EAT

CARGILLS BISTRO, BLAIRGOWRIE: 01250 876735 (909/PERTHSHIRE EATS).

DALMUNZIE/BRIDGE OF CALLY HOTEL/GLENISLA: *as above.*

APRÉS-SKI

BLACKWATER INN: 17km S on main rd. A good all-round pub. Occasional live music.

SKI HIRE

BRIDGE OF CALLY SKI HIRE: Opp hotel (phone as above). On the way. **BLACKWATER SKI HIRE:** Also on main rd to slopes, but nearer.

1875 CAIRNGORM

MAP 2
D3

BASE STATION: 01479 861261. SCHOOL: 01479 810296/810655.

WHERE TO STAY

CORROUR HOUSE: 01479 810220. 11km W (1090/COUNTRY-HOUSE HOTELS). INX

COYLUMBRIDGE: 01479 810661. 10km W. Nearest and best of modern Aviemore hotels. 2 pools/sauna. Ski hire. Okay restau. Comfort when you need it. MED.EX

CAIRNGORM, AVIEMORE: 01479 810630. Main st of main town. Busy bar. Rms not unreasonably priced and lots of them. INX

THE OSPREY, KINGUSSIE: 01540 661510. 32km S. Good value tho kitsch. MED.INX

WHERE TO EAT

THE CROSS, KINGUSSIE: 01540 661166 (956/HIGHLANDS HOTELS).

THE BOATHOUSE, KINCRAIG: 01540 651394 (988/INEXP HIGHLANDS RESTAUS).

THE OLD BRIDGE, AVIEMORE: Welcoming, good atmos (1222/BEST FOOD).

APRÉS-SKI

THE WINKING OWL, AVIEMORE: At end of main st. Owl's Nest.

ROYAL HOTEL, KINGUSSIE: Real ales (8) and malts (1195/REAL ALE).

SKI HIRE

COYLUMBRIDGE HOTEL: 01479 810661. Behind hotel, run by Caird Sport (major operators) and nearest to slopes. Open mornings and 4–6.30pm.

1876 AONACH MOR/THE NEVIS RANGE

MAP 2
C3

BASE STATION: 01397 705825. **SCHOOL:** 01397 705825.

WHERE TO EAT and STAY

See **FORT WILLIAM**, *p. 296.*

APRÉS-SKI

No pub in immediate vicinity. Nearest all-in ski centre is **NEVIS SPORT, FORT WILLIAM**: 01397 704921. Bar (side entrance) till 11pm. Self-serve café all day till 5pm. Bookshop and extensive ski/outdoor shop on ground floor. Also ski hire.

SKI HIRE

As above (01397 704921), also Ellis Brigham (01397 706220), and base stn.

1877 GLENCOE

MAP 2
C4

BASE STATION: 01855 851226. **SCHOOL:** 01855 851226.

WHERE TO EAT and STAY

See **FORT WILLIAM**, *p. 261,* and also:

ISLES OF GLENCOE HOTEL, BALLACHULISH: 01855 811602. Modern development leisure centre incl pool. Good touring base (1099/KIDS).

CLACHAIG INN, GLENCOE: 01855 811 252. Famous 'outdoor inn' for walkers, climbers etc with pub (1183/BLOODY GOOD PUBS), pub food and inexp accom.

KINGSHOUSE HOTEL: 01855 851259. The classic travellers' inn 1km from A82 through Glen and nr slopes (8km). Pub with food/whisky. Inexp rms.

APRÉS-SKI

As above, especially Clachaig Inn and Kingshouse.

SKI HIRE

At base stn.

1878 THE LECHT

MAP 3
B3

BASE STATION: 019756 51440. **SCHOOL:** 019756 51412.

WHERE TO STAY

Nearest town (28km S) with big choice of hotels is Ballater.

RICHMOND ARMS, TOMINTOUL: 01807 580777. Also on sq. Trad hotel, log fires. A v good prospect. 24 rms. MED.INX

DARROCH LEARG, BALLATER: 013397 55443 (913/NE HOTELS). LOTS

GLENAVON HOTEL, TOMINTOUL: 01807 580218. On sq in nearest town. CHP

WHERE TO EAT

GREEN INN, BALLATER: 013397 55701 (931/NE HOTELS). MED

THE WHITE COTTAGE, nr ABOYNE: 01339 886265 (2177/HOLIDAY CENTRES).
MED

TOMINTOUL HOTELS above. INX

APRÉS-SKI

GLENAVON HOTEL, TOMINTOUL: 01807 580218. Good large bar for skiers, walkers (S end of Speyside Way is here) and locals.

ALLARGUE HOTEL, COCKBRIDGE: 019756 51410. On rd S to Ballater 5km from slopes and o/look Corgarff Castle and the trickle of the R Don. Rms also.

SKI HIRE

From ski centre, 019756 51440.

WEATHER AND ROAD REPORTS

Dial 0891 654 then:

655 **CAIRNGORM**; 656 **GLENSHEE**; 658 **GLENCOE**; 660 **NEVIS RANGE**; 657 **THE LECHT**

OTHER SKI HOTLINES (ALL AREAS) ARE: 0891 654654 or 0891 500440.

THE BEST SLEDGING PLACES

Locals will know where the best slopes are. Here's my suggestions for EDIN/GLAS:

EDINBURGH

1879
MAP A
xC4
xA3
E3

THE BRAID HILLS: The connoisseur's choice, you sledge down friendly and not-too-challenging slopes in a crowded L S Lowry landscape that you will remember long after the thaw. Off Braid Hills Drive at the golf course. Can walk in via Blackford Glen Rd. **CORSTORPHINE HILL:** Gentle broad slope with woodland at top and trails (363/CITY WALKS) and a busy rd at the bottom. App via Clermiston Rd off Queensferry Rd. **QUEEN'S PARK:** The lesser slopes that skirt Arthur's Seat, and further in around Hunter's Bog for the more adventurous or less sociable sledger.

GLASGOW

1880
MAP B
xB1
xC1
xC5

KELVINGROVE PARK: At Park Terr side. No long runs but a winter wonderland when the rime's in the trees. **GARTNAVEL HOSPITAL GROUNDS:** In W end (Hyndland) off Gr Western Rd. You can play safe sledging into the playing field, or more adventurously through the woodlands. **QUEEN'S VIEW:** On A809 N of Bearsden 20km from centre. A v popular walk (721/BEST VIEWS) is also a gr place to sledge. Variable slopes off the main path. The Highlands can be seen on a clear day. **RUCHILL PARK:** In N of city (722/BEST VIEWS) and **QUEEN'S PARK** in S.

THE BEST LEISURE CENTRES

1881
MAP 4
C3
✓ **PERTH LEISURE POOL:** 01738 635454. A perfect example of the mega successful water-based leisure-land; makes you wonder where everyone went before they existed. Large, shaped pool with o/side section (open also in winter, when it's even more of a novelty); 2 flumes, 'wild water channel', whirlpools etc. 25m 'training' pool for lengths (sessions). Outdoor kids' area. Excellent facility. I go often (because it's open late). Daily 10am-10pm.

1882
MAP 2
C2
✓ **AQUADOME, INVERNESS:** 01463 667500. Inverness's all-weather attraction. Leisure waters; incl 3 flumes, wave machine and toddler area. Huge competition pool for serious swimming and luxurious health suites; massages, hydrotherapy and (ladies) that essential bikini line wax. All in all, a bigger splash. Phone for opening hrs.

1883
MAP 7
B1
✓ **DUNBAR POOL:** 01368 865456. Model of its kind, o/look old harbour (where folks used to swim on a summer's day) and castle ruins. Cool, modern design amidst the warm red sandstone. Flumes and wave machine that mimics the sea o/side; lengths just possible in betw (though it's often v crowded). 7 days till 8pm (6pm at w/kends).

1884
MAP 1
C3
MAGNUM CENTRE, IRVINE: 01294 278381. From Irvine's throughway system, follow signs for Harbourside, then Magnum. Same report as last time – sorry couldn't go back. In an unalluring 'big shed', this phenomenally successful pleasuredrome provides every conceivable diversion from the monotony of my namesake o/side. From soothing bowls to frenetic skating, pools, cinema, cafés, courses, you name it. Secrete endorphins and other hormones.

1885
MAP 1
C3
VIKINGAR!, LARGS: 01475 689777. Suddenly fulfilled all the needs and gaps in this busy visitor area of the Clyde coast – a pool and sports centre, a theatre, an indoor attraction and a dab of heritage. Got the award. But hey … it works. It won't exercise your intellect, but the other bits will tone up. Times for various facilities vary.

1886
MAP 1
D2
THE TIME CAPSULE, MONKLANDS: 01236 449572. They say Monklands, but where you are going is downtown Coatbridge about 15km from Glas via M8. Known rather meanly as the 'Tim Capture' (local joke – you don't want to know!). A leisure (rather than swimming) pool and ice-rink lavishly fitted out on prehistoric monster theme. Even if you haven't been swimming for yrs, this is the sort of place you force the flab into the swimsuit. Cafés and view areas. Facs of the clean-up-your-act variety (e.g. squash, sauna). 10am-10pm.

1887
MAP 1
D3
DOLLAN AQUA CENTRE, TOWN CENTRE PARK, EAST KILBRIDE: 01355 260000. An excl family leisure centre. 50m pool, fitness facs, soft play area and Scotland's first inter-active flume, (aquatic pin ball machine with you as the ball!) – there had to be a twist. Mon-Wed 7.30am-10pm, Thurs/Fri 8am-10pm, Sat/Sun 8am-6pm.

1888
MAP B
xA3
SCOTSTOUN LEISURE CENTRE: 0141 9594000. Clydeside expressway then A814, rt at Victoria Park lights, first left after r/about. Danes Drive. If 'modernity is suburban' this is state of the art. 10 lane pool, sports halls, health suite, dance studio and gym. Outdoor footie and tennis – it's enormous. Call for times, but open till 10pm. Tues is women only from 6pm.

1889
MAP 5
C2
EAST SANDS LEISURE CENTRE, ST ANDREWS: 01334 476506. From S St take rd for Crail then follow signs. About 2km from centre. Bright and colourful centre o/look the E Sands, the less celebrated beach of St Andrews. Mainly a fairly conventional pool with 25m lane area as well as 50m water slide, toddlers' pool etc. Also 2 squash courts, gym with Pulsestar machines, 'remedial suite', bar and café. 7 days 7.30/8.30pm; Sat/Sun till 5pm. Times may vary.

1890
MAP 5
B3
BEACON LEISURE CENTRE, BURNTISLAND: 01592 872211. On the front of this quietly-getting-on-with-it Fife town nr Kirkcaldy. Family fun pool centre with 'landmark' beacon thing and external flume tubes. It does work. Loadsa kids and 'waves' do come, but latest swimming in area (check times). 7 days.

1891
MAP 2
D3
BEACH LEISURE CENTRE, ABERDEEN: 01224 655401. Beach Esplanade across rd from beach itself. Multisports facility with bars and cafés. 'Leisure' Pool isn't much use for swimming (Aber has many others, 1899/SWIMMING POOLS) but it's fun for kids with flumes etc. Linx Ice Arena is adj for skating, curling, ice hockey. O/side is the long long beach and the N Sea.

THE BEST SWIMMING POOLS AND SPORTS CENTRES

For EDINBURGH, *see p.57; for* GLASGOW, *see p.96. And see* LEISURE CENTRES *p 242.*

1892
MAP 3
C4
✓ **STONEHAVEN OUTDOOR POOL, STONEHAVEN:** The 'Friends of Stonehaven Outdoor Pool' won the day (eat your hearts out N Berwick) and they've saved a gr pool that goes from length to strength. Fabulous 1930s Olympic-sized heated salt-water pool. There are midnight swims in midsummer most Wednesdays (is that cool, or what?). June-Aug only: 11am-7.30pm (10-6pm w/ends).

1893
MAP 1
C2
✓ **GOUROCK BATHING POOL:** 01475 631561. The only other open-air (proper) pool in Scotland that's still open! On coast rd S of town centre 45km from central Glas. 1950s-style leisure. Heated, so it doesn't need to be a scorcher (brilliant, but choc-a-block when it is). Open 'in season' 10am-8pm, Sun till 6pm.

1894
MAP 3
C1
✓ **PORTSOY OPEN-AIR POOL:** One of the most engaging of the villages on this N Aberdeenshire coast 7km W of Banff with a pool flushed by the sea in an idyllic setting. Run by local swimming club with changing facs and great wee tearoom, it's only open Jun-Aug but take advantage of it on any sunny day. 50th anniversary in 1996. Long may it chill us out. Head W from centre or main A98.

1895
MAP 5
A3
✓ **CARNEGIE CENTRE, DUNFERMLINE:** 01383 723211. Pilmuir St. Excellent all-round sports centre with many courses and classes. 2 pools (ozone-treated), 25m, and kids' pool. Lane swimming lunch time and evenings. Authentic Turkish and Aeretone Suite with men's, women's and mixed sessions. Large gym with Powersport stations etc. Badminton, squash, aerobic classes. Usually open till 9pm (including pool), but check. Keeping Dunfermline fitter then most of us.

1896
MAP B
xE2
✓ **BISHOPBRIGGS SPORTS CENTRE, GLASGOW:** 0141 772 6391. 147 Balmuildy Rd. At the N edge of Glas, best reached by car or 1km walk from stn; adj Forth and Clyde Canal walkway (711/CITY WALKS). Large, modern, efficient with 33.3m pool, gym, sauna, bar, café etc. Open 9am-10pm (pool hours vary).

1897
MAP 7
A1
✓ **LINLITHGOW POOL:** 01506 846358. On edge of pleasant town off rd to Lanark. Modern light and airy sports centre with sauna and steam room at the pool side and W Lothian outside the windows. Excellent community facility, well designed and laid out. All towns should enjoy this quality of life. I go here often for a swim and a slice of it.

1898
MAP 8
B2
GALASHIELS POOL: 01896 752154. An award winning pool in the Central Borders on the edge of parkland with picture windows bringing the outside in. No leisurama nonsense, just a good deck-level pool (25m). Pool in Hawick also good. Phone for opening hrs.

1899
MAP 3
D3
ABERDEEN BATHS: 01224 587920. City well served with swimming pools. 3 in suburbs are not esp easy to find, though Hazlehead (01224 310062) is signed from inner ring road to W of centre. Bon Accord Baths are a fine example of a municipal pool; recently refurbished, they're centrally situated behind the W end of Union St. Annie Lennox learned to swim here. The newer Beach Leisure Centre has just about thought of everything (1891/LEISURE CENTRES).

1900
MAP 2
D2
GOLSPIE SWIMMING POOL: 01408 633437. A neat little pool (20m) next to the High School. Nothing too high tech, but a friendly atmos and a friendly mural at one end. Hrs vary.

1901
MAP 1
A3
MACTAGGART CENTRE, BOWMORE, ISLAY: 01496 810767. Eco-friendly pool (heated by adj distillery) o/look bay. Interesting whisky cask shaped ceiling and good fitness suite. Laundry facs. Cl Mon.

THE BEST WATER SPORTS CENTRES

1902
MAP 5
C3
✓ **ELIE WATERSPORTS, ELIE:** 01333 330962 (day) 330942 (night). Gr beach location in totally charming wee town where there's enough going on to occupy non-watersporters. Easy lagoon for first timers and open season for non-experienced users. Wind-surfers, kayaks, water-ski. Also mt bikes. (885/FIFE EATS, 875/878/FIFE HOTELS, 1215/PUB FOOD, 1850/GOLF).

1903
MAP 1
B1
✓ **LINNHE MARINE:** 01631 730227. Lettershuna, Port Appin. 32km N of Oban on A828 nr Portnacroish. Established, personally run business in a fine sheltered spot for learning and ploutering. They almost guarantee to get you windsurfing over to the island in 2hrs. Individual or group instruction. Wayfarers, Luggers and fishing-boats. New laser clay pigeon shooting. Moorings. Castle Stalker and Lismore are just round the corner; the joy of sailing. May-Oct.

1904
MAP 1
C3
✓ **SCOTTISH NATIONAL WATERSPORTS CENTRE, LARGS AND CUMBRAE:** 01475 674666. Centre for all kinds of water sports in a doon-the-watter situation, mainly at Millport on Cumbrae, but with general sports centre on mainland. Improved facs '99. Ferry betw.

1905
MAP 7
A1
✓ **PORT EDGAR, SOUTH QUEENSFERRY:** 0131 331 3330. At end of village, under and beyond the Forth Road Br. Major marina and water sports centre. Berth your boat, hire anything from a Wayfarer to a canoe or just use the jetty to kick off some windsurfing or jet-skiing. Big tuition programme for kids. Easter-Oct.

1906
MAP 1
D3
✓ **STRATHCLYDE PARK:** 01698 266155. Major water sports centre 15km SE of Glas and easily reached from most of Central Scotland via M8 or M74 (jnct 5 or 6). 200-acre loch and centre with instruction on sailing, canoeing, windsurfing, rowing, water-skiing and hire facs for canoes, Mirrors, Wayfarers, windsurfers and trimarans. Sessions: summer 9.30am-10pm; winter 9.30am-5pm.

1907
MAP 4
B3
CROFT-NA-CABER, nr KENMORE, LOCH TAY: 01887 830588. S side of loch, 2km from village. Purpose-built water sports centre with instruction and hire of windsurfers, canoes, kayaks, dinghies, motor boats as well as waterskiing, river rafting (down the Tay from Aberfeldy to white water at Grandtully: pure exhilaration), archery and clay shooting. A v good all-round activities centre in a gr setting but some say not what it was and that chalet accom should be avoided.

1908
MAP 2
C3
GREAT GLEN WATER PARK: 01809 501381. 3km S Invergarry on A82. On shores of tiny L Oich and L Lochy in the Gr Glen. Wonderful spot, with many other lochs nearby. Day visitors welcome with windsurfers, Wayfarers, kayaks, canoes and also mountain bikes and fishing rods for hire. Mainly, however, a chalet park with all the usual condo/timeshare facs (you can rent by the week).

1909
MAP 1
C3
CASTLE SEMPLE COUNTRY PARK, LOCHWINNOCH: 01505 842882. 30km SW Glas M8 jnct 29, A737 then A760 past Johnstone. Also 25km from Largs via A760. Loch (nr village) is 3km x 1km and at the Rangers Centre you can hire windsurfers, dinghies, canoes etc. Bird Reserve on opp bank (1584/WILDLIFE). Peaceful place to learn.

1910
MAP 1
C2
KIP MARINA, INVERKIP: 01475 521485. Major sailing centre on Clyde coast 50km W of Glas via M8, A8 and A78 from Pt Glas heading S for Largs. A yacht heaven as well as haven of Grand Prix status. Sails, charters, pub/restau, chandlers and myriad boats. Diving equipment jet skis and dinghies for hire.

1911
MAP 5
B3
LOCHORE, nr LOCHGELLY: 01592 414300. From Dunfermline-Kirkcaldy motorway take Lochgelly t/off into town and follow signs for Lochore Country Park. Small, safe loch for learning and perfecting. Canoes, dinghies and esp windsurfing. Instruction and hire. Park contains a good adventure playground.

1912
MAP 2
D3
LOCHINSH WATERSPORTS, KINCRAIG: 01540 651272. On B970, 2km from Kincraig towards Kingussie and the A9. Marvellous loch side site launching from gently sloping dinky beach into forgiving waters of L Inch. Hire of canoes, dinghies (Mirrors, Toppers, Lasers, Wayfarers) and windsurfers as well

as rowing boats; river trips. An idyllic place to learn. Watch the others and the sunset from the balcony restau above (988/INEXP HIGHLAND RESTAUS). Sports 9am-5pm, Apr-Oct.

1913   **LOCH MORLICH WATERSPORTS nr AVIEMORE:** 01479 861221. By Glenmore
MAP 2   Forest Park, part of the plethora of outdoor activities hereabouts (skiing, walk-
D3   ing etc). This is the loch you see from Cairngorm and just as picturesque from the woody shore. Canoes/kayaks/rowing boats and dinghies (Wayfarers, Toppers, Optimists) with instruction in everything. Evening hire poss.

1914   **LOCHEARNHEAD WATERSPORTS:** 01567 830330. On A85 nr jnct with A84 is
MAP 6   a water sports centre where they suggest you'll never be out of your depth.
B2   Certainly the loch is wide open and (usually) gently lapping. Kayaks, Canadian canoes and dinghies. Water-skiing, jet-biking and mountain bike hire. Café.

1915   **RAASAY OUTDOOR CENTRE, nr SKYE:** 01478 660266. Excl activity place! Day
MAP 2   visits or holidays.
B2

1916   **WIGBAY SAILING CENTRE, STRANRAER:** 01776 703535. Tuition and power-
MAP 9   boating.
A3

THE BEST DIVING SITES

Scotland's seas are primal soup, full of life and world-class sites as hard core divers already know. The E coast can be tricky if the wind is blowing from the N or E, therefore the W coast is preferable (the further N the better). Thanks to the Gulf Stream it's not cold, even without a dry suit, and once you're down it's like flying thro the Botanics (says my friend Tim Maguire). So when you see all those crazies walking into the sea, remember, they may know something that you don't know. Some day I will go down! This page due to Tim.

1917   ## WEST COAST
MAP 2

THE OUTER HEBRIDES: excellent with fantastic visibility esp off the W coast of **HARRIS** where you can plop in virtually anywhere.

ST KILDA: offers the best diving in the UK, but it's the hardest to get to. On the edge of the Continental Shelf and the whale migration route, it has huge drop-offs and upwellings of life. Book boat and board well in advance – excursions on MV Kuma best: 01851 672381.

THE SUMMER ISLES: from Ullapool harbour. Wrecks, lee shores and unpolluted waters.

MAP 1   **OBAN:** Scuba central with lots of sites in the neighbourhood and easy access
B1   to the isles. Charter a boat and search for scallops in **THE GARVELLACH** or dive the wrecks in the **SOUND OF MULL**. Somewhere off **TOBERMORY** there is reputedly, one of Scotland's most enigmatic wrecks, a Spanish galleon. Easier to find are dolphins off the coasts of **ISLAY & TIREE** and see 1579/DOLPHINS for other likely spots.

1918   ## EAST COAST

MAP 8   **ST ABBS HEAD:** Accessible from the shore (1831/COASTAL WALKS) or by boat
D1   from **EYEMOUTH**, a marine reserve, so leave the lobsters alone. The spectacular Cathedral Rock is encrusted with green and yellow dead men's fingers and in August /Sept is a sanctuary for breeding fish (this cathedral is as beautiful as St Giles and is distinctly non-denominational). Nearby shore-based diving at **DUNBAR** is shallow, safe and simple.

MAP 5   **THE ISLE OF MAY:** across the Forth is more advanced. Take a boat from
D3   Anstruther (1565/BIRDS). Main site is Piccadilly Circus, a central atrium fed by gullies, full of friendly seals.

ORKNEY

SCAPA FLOW: The world-famous underwater burial site where the Germans scuttled their fleet in 1918. Think Gaudalcanal, but colder. Although the scrappies have been in, there are still dozens and cruisers down there. Most lie in 35-40m deep, so plan carefully. Majorly eerie!

DIVE OPERATORS (Don't leave home without one).

NATIONAL

Dive Scotland. 0131 441 2001. Andrew Adams and James Hogg. Friendly, knowledgeable and resourceful. Will organise trips and training anywhere and to suit all levels of experience.

LOCAL

EDINBURGH: Edinburgh Dive Centre 0131 229 4838.

OBAN: Oban. Nervous Wrecks 01631 566000. Oban Divers 01631 566618. Alchemy 01631 720337.

ULLAPOOL: Ullapool. Atlantic Diving Services (Achiltibuie) 01854 622261.

ORKNEY: Diving Cellar 01856 850055. Dolphin Scuba 01856 731269. Scapa Flow Scuba 01856 851218.

THE BEST WINDSURFING

FOR BEGINNERS AND INSTRUCTION (*see also* WATER SPORTS).

STRATHCLYDE PARK, nr MOTHERWELL and GLASGOW:01698 266155.

CROFT-NA-CABER, KENMORE, LOCH TAY:01887 830588.

LINNHE MARINE, nr OBAN:01631 730227.

LOCHWINNOCH, between PAISLEY and LARGS:01505 842882.

LOCHORE MEADOWS, LOCHGELLY, FIFE:01592 860264.

TIGHNABRUAICH SAILING SCHOOL, TIGHNABRUAICH:01700 811396.

SCOTTISH NATIONAL WATERSPORTS CENTRE, CUMBRAE AND LARGS: 01475 674666.

STRATHCLYDE PARK, nr MOTHERWELL and GLASGOW: 1398/COUNTRY PARKS. Lots to do in this recreational zone of the conurbation. Water may not be so turquoise.

ELIE, EAST NEUK OF FIFE: 01333 330962. Small, friendly windsurfing and water sports operation on the beach (beyond the Ship Inn).

WINDSURFING SPOTS

1920 WEST COAST

MAP 1 **MACHRIHANISH:**Wave-sailing, fabulous long beach (1427/BEACHES). Mainly
B3   at Air Force base end.

C3   **PRESTWICK/TROON:**Town beaches.

C3   **ISLAND OF CUMBRAE:**Millport beach.

C3   **MILARROCHY BAY, LOCH LOMOND:** 8km from Drymen (45km N of Glas).
W/end centre run by 7th Wave. Second beach up from Balmaha. Picturesque.

1921 EAST COAST

MAP 3 **FRASERBURGH:**Town beach.

MAP 4 **LUNAN BAY:**12km N of Arbroath. Also surfing.

MAP 5 **CARNOUSTIE:**Town beach.

MAP 7 **ST ANDREWS:**W Sands.

LONGNIDDRY/GULLANE:25/35km E of Edin via A1 and A198.

PEASE BAY:14km S of Dunbar, 60km S of Edin via A1 (1926/SURFING).

1922 NORTH COAST

MAP 2 **THURSO:**Many beaches nr town and further W to choose from (1440/BEACH-ES).

FOR ENTHUSIASTS

1923 **ISLAND OF TIREE:** The windsurfing capital of Scotland. 40km W of Mull.
MAP 1 Countless clean, gently sloping beaches all round island (and small inland
A1   loch) allowing surfing in all wind directions. Accom basic: Tiree Lodge Hotel
(01879 220368), Kirkapol Guest House (01879 220 729) or self-catering (Oban
TO 01631 563122). Loganair fly every day except Sunday (0141 889 1311) and
Calmac run ferries from Oban 3 or 4 times a week (01475 650100).

INFORMATION/BOARD HIRE:

BOARDWISE, GLASGOW:3146 Argyle St. 0141 334 5559.

BOARDWISE, EDIN: Lady Lawson St. 0131 229 5887.

THE BEST SURFING BEACHES

A surprise for the sceptical: Scotland has some of the best surfing beaches in Europe. Forget the bronzed beachboys and lemon bleached hair, surfing in Scotland is titanium-lined, rubber and balaclavas, and you get an ice cream head even encased in the latest technology. The main season is Sept-Dec. Surfees probably don't divulge their favourite beach, but the following are good bets. Don't surf alone. This page is based on information from Neil Butler.

1924 WEST COAST

MAP 2
A1, B1

ISLE OF LEWIS: Probably the best of the lot. Go N of Stornoway, N of Barvas, N of just about anywhere. Leave the A857 and your day job behind. Not the most scenic of sites, but the waves have come a long way, further than you have. Derek at Stornoway Surf and Sports (01851 705862) will tell you when and where to go.

MAP 1
B3

MACHRIHANISH: Nr Campbelltown at the foot of the Mull of Kintyre. Long strand to choose from (1427/BEACHES). Jamie at Clan Skates in Glasgow (0141 339 6523) usually has an up-to-date satellite map and a idea of both the W and (nearest to central belt) Pease Bay (*see below*).

1925 NORTH COAST

MAP 2
C1, D1

STRATHY BAY: Nr Bettyhill on the N coast hafway betw Tongue and Thurso on the A836. Go past the village, park at the graveyard. Once in the foam, paddle to the rt. From here to Cape Wrath the power and quality of the waves detonating on the shore justify comparisons with Hawaii.

MAP 2
D1

THURSO: Surf City, well not quite, but it's a good base to find your own waves. Esp to the E of town at Dunnet Bay – a 5km long beach with excellent reefs at the N end.

MAP 2
D1

WICK: On the Thurso rd at Ackergill to the S of Sinclair's Bay (1138/GET-AWAY-FROM-IT-ALL). Find the ruined castle and taking care, clamber down the gully to the beach. A monumental reef break, you are working against the backdrop of the decaying ruin drenched in history, spume and romance.

1926 EAST COAST

MAP 3
D3

NIGG BAY: Just S of Aberdeen (not to be confused with Nigg across from Cromarty) and off the vast beach at Lunan Bay (1434/BEACHES) betw Arbroath and Montrose.

MAP 7
xB1

PEASE BAY: S of Dunbar nr Cockburnspath on the A1. The nearest surfie heaven to the capital. The caravan site has parking and toilets. V consistent surf here.

SECTION 10

Shopping

See also WHERE TO BUY ART, p. 264.

1927
MAP 5
D2

✓ **CRAIL POTTERY, CRAIL, FIFE:** At the foot of Rose Wynd, signposted from main st (best to walk). In a tree-shaded Mediterranean courtyard and upstairs attic is a cornucopia of brilliant, useful, irresistible things. Open 10am-5pm (Sun 2-5pm). Don't miss the harbour nearby, one of the most romantic neuks in the Neuk. Pity there's nowhere decent in Crail for tea.

1928
MAP 2
D2

✓ **ANTA FACTORY SHOP, FEARN, nr TAIN:** Off B9175 from Tain to the Nigg ferry, 8km through Hill of Fearn, on corner of disused airfield. Shop with adj pottery. Much tartan curtain fabric; many rugs, throws and pots. You can commission furniture to be covered in their material. Free to wander round the pottery; no organised tours. Shop. AYR daily 10am-5pm, pottery Mon-Fri only.

1929
MAP 2
C1

✓ **HIGHLAND STONEWARE, LOCHINVER and ULLAPOOL:** On rd to Baddidarach as you enter Lochinver on A837; and in Mill St, Ullapool, on way N beyond centre. A modern large-scale pottery business incl a shop/warehouse and studios that you can walk round (Lochinver is more *engagé*). Similar to the 'ceramica' places you find in the Med, but not too terracotta – rather, painted and patterned stoneware in set styles. Gr selection, pricey – but you may have luck rummaging in the Lochinver discount section. Mail-order service. Open AYR.

1930
MAP 2
B2

EDINBANE POTTERY, EDINBANE, SKYE: 500m off A850 Portree (22km) – Dunvegan rd. Long-established and reputable working pottery where all the various processes are often in progress. Earthy pots of every shape and size; unusual 'lantern' plant holders. Open AYR 9am-6pm. 7 days in summer.

1931
MAP 2
B2

SKYE SILVER, COLBOST, SKYE: 10km Dunvegan on B884 to Glendale. Long established and reputable jewellery made and sold in an old schoolhouse by the rd in distant corner of Skye, but 3 chimneys restau nearby (2138/ISLANDS RESTAUS). Well-made, Celtic designs, good gifts. AYR 7 days, 10am-6pm.

1932
MAP 2
C3

KILN ROOM POTTERY AND COFFEE SHOP, LAGGAN: On main A86 rd, E-W route to Ft William and Skye from Newtonmore. Simple, usable pottery made by the long wood-fired kiln method, with distinctive warm colouring. Selected knitwear and useful things. Home-made cakes and scones; the stuff of life. 9am-6pm, 7 days. Now with bunk rms out back v inx incl comfy lounge with gr vista (01528 544231).

1933
MAP 2
B3

GLENELG CANDLES, GLENELG: Signed from glen rd which comes over the hill from Shiel Bridge (1483/SCENIC ROUTES) and hard to miss. Wooden cabin/coffee shop with multifarious candles and local art. Home-made food. AYR 9.30pm-6pm (Sat/Sun 10am-5pm).

1934
MAP 2
C1

BALNAKEIL, DURNESS, SUTHERLAND: From Durness and the main A836 rd, take Balnakeil and Faraid Head rd for 2km W. Founded in the 1960s in what one imagines was a haze of hash, this craft village is still home to those seeking to 'downshift'. Varied paintings, pottery, fruit wine (01971 511354) and weaving in the different prefab huts where the community members live and work (the site used to be an early warning station). Lotte Glob *is* (01971 511354) v good. Village open Apr-Oct 10am-6pm. Café, and plans for (another) restau when last we passed.

1935
MAP 2
B2, B3

SKYEBATIKS, ARMADALE and PORTREE, SKYE: 400m from Mallaig ferry and in centre. V original Sri Lanka 'batiks'- cotton fabrics of ancient Celtic designs in every shape and size. Mainly hand-made, majorly colourful; a unique souvenir of Skye. Same people have nice outdoor shop adj in Portree.

1936
MAP 2
C1

ACHIN'S BOOKSHOP, LOCHINVER: At Inverkirkaig 5km from Lochinver on the 'wee mad rd' to Achiltibuie (1487/SCENIC ROUTES). Unexpected selection of books in the back of beyond providing something to read when you've climbed everything. Outdoor wear too and gr hats. The path to Kirkaig Falls and Suilven begins at the gate. Easter-Oct 7 days; 9.30am-6pm. Adj café 10am-5pm. Winter, Mon-Sat 10am-5pm (unless he has to pop out on Guinness).

1937 KNOCKAN STUDIO, ULLAPOOL: Argyll St. Ian and Linda Combe's excellent
MAP 2 shop with some well-crafted jewellry, some with real Scottish gold. Bonny
C2 stones. Mon-Sat 9am-5pm AYR. They also have a gallery at Elphin. 28km N on
the A835 – summer only. Big refurb in '99, reopening spring 2000.

1938 IONA ABBEY SHOP: Iona via Calmac ferry from Fionnphort on Mull. Crafts
MAP 1 and souvenirs in a room off the Abbey cloisters, the proceeds from which sup-
A1 port a worthy, committed organisation. Christian literature, tapes etc, but
mostly artefacts from nearby and around Scotland. Celtic crosses much in evidence, but then this is where they came from! Mar-Oct 9.30am-5pm.

1939 CARBOST CRAFT POTTERY, CARBOST and PORTREE: Judith Nicholl's fami-
MAP 2 ly business nr the Talisker distillery (1366/WHISKY) produces an array of trad
B2 pottery, incl the notable 'torn pots'. Her shop in Bayfield Rd, Portree (nr TO)
sells these and other innovative glassware, soft furnishings, pictures etc. Some
inspired designs and ideas. Open AYR Mon-Sat; 9am-lateish. Pottery; Apr-Sept
9am-5pm.

1940 BRODIE COUNTRY FARE: By main A96 betw Nairn and Forres, nr Brodie
MAP 3 Castle (1592/CASTLES). Not a souvenir shoppie in the trad sense, more a drive-
A2 in one-stop shopping experience. Quality deli food (organic chutneys), a fairly up-market boutique designer womanswear and every crafty tartanalia of
note. The self-serve restau gets as busy as a motorway café. 7 days till
5.30/7pm Thurs.

1941 HOUSE OF BRUAR, PITLOCHRY: Another roadside emporium and shopa-
MAP 4 holic honey pot this time on the A9 N of Blair Atholl esp for those who just
B2 missed Pitlochry. General Harrods in the N feel (I'd still recommend
McNaughtons; 1963/OUTDOOR SHOPS), though the food side is sound (good
range of Scottish cheeses, Mackays ice cream etc). Falls nearby for more spiri-
tual sustenance (1457/WATERFALLS). 7 days, till 8pm (6pm in winter).

1942 OCTOPUS CRAFTS, nr FAIRLIE, nr LARGS: On main A78 Largs to Ayr rd.
MAP 1 Smaller set up than above, but, crafts, wines and cookshop an excellent restau
C3 (1250/SEAFOOD RESTAUS) and a seafood deli. An all-round road side experience.
Everything here is hand-made and/or hand-picked. Even the wines are well
chosen. Good pots. Glass and wood. They also run courses. Cl Mon.

1943 BALBIRNIE CRAFT CENTRE, MARKINCH: Follow signs for Balbirnie Park from
MAP 5 Glenrothes road system, but off the A92. Farmyard courtyard of craft work-
B3 shops and retail in country park nr Balbirnie House Hotel (873/FIFE HOTELS).
Jewellery, glasswork, ceramics, leather and embroidery – bit of everything
really. Nice that something's made in Glenrothes that isn't made in millions. 7
days (Sun afternoons only).

1944 ALDIE WATER MILL, TAIN: 01862 893786. Off the A9 nr S Tain. Restored pic-
MAP 2 turesque mill with local history in the beams. Adj craft shop houses individual,
D2 attractive home furnishings all locally made. The tapestry scenes, made from
hand dyed/spun wools and jute, framed with driftwood are done real good.
Pippa Lee's sturdy willow basketry is the real McCoy and her jewellery unique.
Ware from the nearby pottery, which you can also visit (there's also a guest-
house up the track). 7 days; 10am-5pm in season – phone at other times.

1945 BORGH POTTERY, BORVE, ISLE OF LEWIS: On NW coast of island a wee way
MAP 2 from Stornoway, but not much of a detour from the rd to Callanish where you
A1 are probably going. Alex and Sue Blair's pleasant gallery of handthrown pots
with strong glazes; domestic and grd wear. Some knits. Open AYR 9-6pm. Cl Sun.

1946 THE STUDIO CRAFT SHOP, PLOCKTON: 8km over hill from Kyle at the corner
MAP 2 of the two 'main' streets in this picturesque and much-loved village
B3 (1412/COASTAL VILLAGES). Well-chosen knick-knacks, jewellery and good selec-
tion of local artist's work. 10am-1pm, 2-6pm. Cl Sun.

1947 JUST SCOTTISH, STONEHAVEN: Small selective arts/crafts shop in main st
MAP 3 adj the sq. Anta and other brand leaders, but other interesting stuff like,
C4 Jonathan Eadie's candelabras. 10am-5.30pm. Cl Sun.

1948 GALLOWAY LODGE PRESERVES, GATEHOUSE OF FLEET: On main st of com-
MAP 9 pact town. Packed with local jams, marmalades, chutneys and pickles. Scottish
B3 pottery by Anta, Highland, Stoneware and Dunoon. Good presents and jam
for yourself. 9.30am-5pm Mon-Sat, and Sun afternoons in summer.

1949 **CRAFTS AND THINGS, nr GLENCOE VILLAGE:** On A82 betw Glencoe village
MAP 2 and Ballachulish. Eclectic mix of so many baubles that some are literally hang-
C4 ing from the rafters. Mind, body & spirit books (like this one) and reasonably
priced knit/outerwear. Good coffee shop, with local artist's work on walls. All-
round nice place. Feb-Dec 9am-5.30pm (maybe later in summer).

1950 **DRUMLANRIG CASTLE, nr THORNHILL, nr DUMFRIES:** A whole day out of
MAP 9 things to do (1394/COUNTRY PARKS) including the craft centre in the old sta-
C2 ble/courtyard to the side of the house. Studio-type shops with leather work,
jewellery, dried flowers and T-shirts. Hire a bike and ride while you decide.

WHERE TO BUY GOOD WOOLLIES

1951 ✓ **JUDITH GLUE, KIRKWALL, ORKNEY:** Opp the cathedral. Distinctive
hand-made jumpers, the runic designs are a real winner. Also the widespread but individual Highland and Joker stoneware (jewellery and animal
clocks v popular), condiments and preserves. The landscape prints of Orkney
are by twin sister, Jane. Open AYR 7 days 9am-6pm.

1952 ✓ **NUMBER TWO, EDINBURGH:** St Stephen Pl. They were here on the cor-
MAP A ner of St Stephen Pl in the first 1960s flush of alternative culture, long
C1 before their trail-blazing range of Scottish machine and hand-made knitwear
could be called 'designer'. Still innovative, still filling the shop with the cardies
that Liz Taylor once admired.

1953 ✓ **LYNDA USHER, BEAULY:** 01463 783017. Knits and the 100% natural
MAP 2 yarns, plus textiles and nice linen shirts for men. V selective and based on
C2 the owner's personal choice; Lynda is a big name in Scottish knitting circles.
Open AYR; Mon-Sat 10am-6pm (and some Suns in summer) (til 5pm in win-
ter).

1954 ✓ **BELINDA ROBERTSON:** 0131 225 1057. 22 Palmerston Pl, Edin. Queen of
MAP A the commissioned cashmere creations; you can only choose from the
B3 *prêt-à-porter* collection in her showroom here (or in London). Her team of 7
girls design and process the stock which is made up in Hawick. **HILARY
ROHDE'S** the other cashmere designer par excellence. She's too big time
even to give out a phone-number (and I promised I wouldn't).

1955 ✓ **HUNTER'S OF BRORA, BRORA, SUTHERLAND:** Main rd N (the A9)
MAP 2 towards Helmsdale. Certainly among the best of the larger scale mill-
D2 type emporia. Bales of their own stylish tweeds or choose from the made up
clothing selection. Trad but unstuffy stalwarts, and some gr hats – the bow
brim is a must. Open AYR Mon-Sat, 10am-5.30pm, Sun 10am-4pm.

1956 **RAGAMUFFIN, SKYE:** On Armadale Pier, so one of the first or last things you
MAP 2 can do on Skye is rummage through the Ragamuffin store and get a nice knit.
B3 Every kind of jumper and some crafts in this Aladdin's cave; incl tweedy things
and hats. Talk of rebuilding the shack soon. They're also in Edin in the Royal
Mile. **OVER THE RAINBOW:** Quay St, Portree (rd down to harbour) can be
expensive but is individual and generally excellent.

1957 **CORNER GALLERY, KIRKCUDBRIGHT:** Corner of the Main St just as you arrive
MAP 9 from the A755 otherwise – in the middle! Designer knitwear incl Iva Knight
C3 and Quernstone. Pretty nice stuff. Mon-Sat 10-5pm, cl 1-2pm and Thur aft in
wint.

1958 **JOHNSTONS CASHMERE CENTRE, ELGIN:** Large Mill Shop kind of operation
MAP 3 and full-blown visitor attraction nr the Cathedral (1614/RUINS). 'The only
B1 British mill to transform fibre to garment' (yarns spun at their factory in Elgin
and made into garments in the Borders) and though this is more British High
St than Bloomingdales, New York, these jumpers will keep you just as warm.
Flood in summer '97 saw a major refurb – new exhib area, AV, and coffee shop.
Actually impressive. Mon-Sat 9am-5.30pm, summer 9am-6pm and Suns
July/Aug.

1959 **ST ANDREWS WOOLLEN MILL, ST ANDREWS:** At the bottom end of N St nr
MAP 5 the Old Course, a vast emporium/indoor market of every conceivable woolly
C2 from heavy knits to mitts. Some of the big names (you know, Nick Faldo),
hand-mades, cashmere and also tweeds, kilts etc. Mon-Sat 9am-5pm and Sun

in season. **AUCHTERLONIES** next door has, since 1895, had everything anyone would ever need on a golf course; more or less a must for the golf-crazed tourist. Same hrs.

1960
MAP 8
B2
LOCHCARRON VISITOR CENTRE, GALASHIELS: If you're in Galashiels (or Hawick), which grew up around woollen mills, you might expect to find a good selection of woollens you can't get everywhere else; and bargains. Well, tough! There's no stand-out place, but L Carron (formerly 'Peter Anderson') is a big tourist attraction with mill tours (Open AYR 4 times a day), exhibits and an okay mill shop. Hawick did invent the Y-front.

1961
MAP 8
C3
CHAS N. WHILLANS, HAWICK (PEEBLES and elsewhere): Their main shop is in Hawick (Teviotdale Mills, over the bridge at S end of main st; instead of continuing on A7, turn rt and they're on the rt). They stock all the local big names incl a good range of Pringle, Lyle & Scott and Braemar. Best to stick to the classic cuts; the 'fashion' versions are not too warm and not too cool.

HARRIS TWEED

1962
MAP 2
A2
THE REAL HARRIS TWEED, ISLE OF HARRIS: To be awarded the Harris Tweed Orb Mark, this distictive wool cloth has to be hand woven from yarn which has been dyed and spun in the Outer Hebrides. Much is processed industrially and finds its way into jackets etc in department stores all over the world. The real McCoy however is still woven and worked in Harris, mainly in the S in places on or off the Golden Road (1485/SCENIC ROUTES). The places to recommend are:

CLO MOR, LICEASTO: 10km S of Tarbert. The true trad passed on from the doyenne of Harris Tweed making, Marion Campbell to Anne Campbell who here dyes her own wool over an open fire using lichens, heather flowers, indigo, ragwort etc, the wool spun by hand on a trad spinning wheel. The tweeds are hand-waulked, treaded in soapy water, pounded on a wooden board and washed in the stream. Authentic this is! Ann receives visitors Mon-Fri 9am-5pm (or phone 01859 530364).

LUSKENTYRE HARRIS TWEED: NO 6, LUSKENTYRE: 2km off W coast on main rd S to Scarista and Rodel. Donald and Maureen Mackay's place is notable for their bright tartan tweed. 9.30am-6pm Cl Sun.

JOAN McCLENNAN: NO 1, DRINISHADDER: Further down the Golden Rd. I don't know, but I've been told, this is where you find the real golden fleece. Go look for it.

THE BEST OUTDOOR SHOPS

Includes outfitters (gentlemen's outfitters) and some mention of kilts.

1963
MAP 4
B2
✓ ✓ **MACNAUGHTON'S, PITLOCHRY:** Station Rd on corner of main st and opp Hunter's (same firm) who sell the outdoor/non-Scottish end of their incredible range. A vast old-fashioned outfitter with acres of tartan attire – incl obligatory tartan pyjamas and dressing gowns! Make their own cloth, and 9m kilts prepared in 10 wks. This really is the real McCoy. 7 days till 5.30pm (4pm Sun).

1964
MAP A
C2
✓ ✓ **GRAHAM TISO, EDINBURGH:** 0131 225 9486 Rose St; just one of the many outlets of this legendary outdoor suppliers (warehouse outlet in Commercial St, Leith) also at outposts in – **INVERNESS, ABERDEEN, DUNDEE, GLASGOW, STIRLING, AYR, EAST KILBRIDE** too! Whether you're off to climb a Munro or just planning a Sunday stroll they can kit you out and equip you. Probably the biggest range of boots in Scotland.

1965
MAP A
xE1
✓ ✓ **KINLOCH ANDERSON, EDINBURGH:** Commercial St, Leith. A bit of a trek from uptown, but firmly on the tourist trail and rightly so. Experts in Highland dress and all things tartan; they've supplied *everybody*. They design their own tartans, have a good range of men's tweed jackets; even rugs. Mon-Sat 9am-5.30pm (5pm winter).

1966 **STEWART, CHRISTIE & CO, EDINBURGH:** 63 Queen St. Est 1792 and still sell-
MAP A ing breeches! (On request.) Highland outfitter, tailor and saddlery – tartan
C2 waistcoats, Harris Tweed jackets, sporrans etc. 9am-5.30pm. Sat till 5pm. Cl
Sun.

1967 **NOTE:** Rather than buy an expensive new kilt or have one made, there are a
MAP A few places in Edin where you can buy second-hand. **ARMSTRONGS:** 83
C3 Grassmarket and 313 Cowgate, Mon-Sat; **ST STEPHENS ST:** second-hand
C1 shops with jackets, kilts, tweeds etc when available Mon-Sat. Also believe it or
E1 not: **THE ARMY AND NAVY STORES:** Brunswick Pl, Leith Walk.

1968 **GREEN WELLY SHOP, TYNDRUM:** On main A82 rd W to Oban/Ft William. Adj
MAP 6 Clifton coffee shop (1287/TEAROOMS). Outdoorwear emporium in strategic
A1 position, with racks of Goretex and other membranes. Berghaus, Barbour and
the all-important midge helmet (now, there's a souvenir!). 7 days, till 5.30pm.

1969 **MORTIMERS & RITCHIES, GRANTOWN ON SPEY:** 3 & 41-45 High St (the
MAP 2 main st) respectively of this respectable Speyside holiday town where fishing
D3 gear is somewhat in demand (though odd to find 2 similar high quality shops
adj). Mortimers more exclusively angling for your custom, but both have a big
range of flies. Outdoor clothing with all the big names betw them and every
shade of olive. Ritchies also have guns if you want to kill something. Both cl
Sun.

1970 **NANCY BLACK, OBAN:** 3 shops around Argyll Sq in centre of Oban, a 'chan-
MAP 1 dlery', an outdoor shop (all the big names in breathable linings) on the corner
B1 and a fashion-for-fogeys shop in the middle. From Scottish knits to Swiss army
knives. Cl Sun.

1971 **NEVIS SPORT, FORT WILLIAM:** 01397 704921; the pyramid shaped building
MAP 2 nr the High St. Extensive ski/outdoor shop; specialising in hill walking and
C3 climbing gear. Snowboards and skis for hire. Self-serve café, bar and craft
shop. Total out-door experience and since it might be raining in Ft William,
this shop is a good place to while away some time … indoors.

1972
MAP 1
B1
✓ **KINLOCHLAICH HOUSE, APPIN:** On main A28 Oban-Ft William rd just N of Pt Appin t/off, the West Highlands' largest nursery/grd centre. Set in a large walled grd filled with plants and veg soaking up the climes of the warm Gulf stream. Donald Hutchison and daughter nurture these acres enabling you to reap what they sow; with a huge array of plants on offer it's like visiting a friend's grd and being able to take home your fave bits. Charming cottages for let 01631 730342. 7 days: 9am-5.30pm (10.30am Sun). Cl Sun in winter.

1973
MAP 7
A1
✓ **DOUGAL PHILIP'S WALLED GARDEN CENTRE, nr S QUEENSFERRY:** 0131 319 1122. 18km from Edin. Perhaps the only plant shop in the world where the drive in makes you feel like a character from Jane Austen – you're driving towards the hugely stately Hopetoun House, a major visitor attraction in itself which o/looks the Forth, open Easter-Oct 10am-5.30pm). DP's is in its old walled grd. This is where Edinburgh's discerning gardeners come for their greens. Vendor of Captain Scarlet roses. Dougal does know his onions. Open AYR 10am-5.30pm.

1974
MAP 2
D3
✓ **INSHRIACH, nr KINCRAIG, nr AVIEMORE:** On B970 betw Kincraig and Inverdruie (which is on the Coylumbridge ski rd out of Aviemore), a grd centre, nay a nursery, that puts most others in the shade. Specialising in alpines and bog plants, but with neat beds of all sorts in the grounds of the house by the Spey and frames full of perfect specimens, this is a potterer's paradise. Mon-Fri 9am-5pm, Sat 9am-4pm. Cl Sun.

1975
MAP B
xB1
✓ **FINDLAY CLARK, MILNGAVIE, GLASGOW:** In Campsie countryside N of city, 20km from centre via A81 or A807 (Milngavie or Kirkintilloch rds) or heading for Milngavie (pron 'Mullguy'), turn rt on Boclair Rd. Vast grd complex and all-round visitor experience; an institution. 'Famous' coffee shop (the famous waitresses are local babes and what they turn into), saddlery with everything except horses; labels from Crabtree & Evelyn to Fisons, plus books, clothes and piles of plants; and live pets. 9am-9pm (till 7pm in winter).

1976
MAP 6
B2
BEN LOMOND NURSERY, BALMAHA, LOCH LOMOND: Nearer Conic Hill than Ben Lomond, on the B837 just before Balmaha. Family-run, supplying the trade and gardeners in the know, as well as passing motorists, particularly with bedding plants grown in their greenhouses on the side of the loch. 9.00am-6pm, Coffee shops. 7 days.

1977
MAP 2
C2
DOCHFOUR, LOCH NESS: On A82 Inverness-Ft William rd 12km S of Inverness. 20 acres of terraced Victorian grd in the grounds of Dochfour House. Yew hedges with not a leaf out of place enclose formal grds for ambling about in. Largish shrubs are esp cheap. Pick your plants by example. Open 7 days 10am-5pm (Sat/Sun 2-5pm).

1978
MAP 2
C2
BRIN SCHOOL FIELDS, FLICHITY, nr INVERNESS: Off A9 S of Daviot, 12km S of Inverness, then 10km W along rd to Farr. An old school and playground dedicated to herbs, plants and all the potions and lotions that come from them. Tearoom in the school room. Mar-Oct 9am-6pm, Sun 2-5pm.

1979
MAP 8
C2
FLOORS CASTLE, KELSO: 3km outside town off B6397 St Boswells rd (grd centre has separate entrance to main visitors' gate in town). Set amongst lovely old greenhouses within walled grds some distance from house, it has a showpiece herbaceous border all round. Nice coffee shop and patio. Centre is open AYR. 10am-5pm. (1658/COUNTRY HOUSES.)

1980
MAP 4
C3
CHRISTIE'S NURSERY, KIRRIEMUIR: 01575 572977. On long straight stretch of A926 to Blairgowrie in the village of Westmuir, 3km from Kirriemuir. Looking towards the Sidlaw Hills, this is a family-run nursery specialising in hardy plants (orchids, alpines etc) with unique stocks of rare plants. This is where those in the know go for gentians, (they are world specialists), primulas and advice about the rock grd. Mar-Oct 10am-6pm; outwith these times, phone first.

1981
MAP 4
C3
GLENDOICK, GLENCARSE, nr PERTH: On A85, 10km from Perth, in the fertile Carse of the Tay. A large grd centre notable esp for rhododendrons and azaleas, a riot of which can be viewed in the nursery behind (May only). V popular coffee shop. 7 days till 6pm.

1982 **CHRISTIE'S, FOCHABERS:** On A98 going into town from Buckie side. Huge
MAP 3 grd centre and forest nursery, the centre of a family empire which has florists,
B2 the Spey Bay Hotel and a golf course. Good for shrubs, indoor plants etc and
a gr place for keen and not-so-keen gardeners to browse around. Famous floral clock strutting peacock, and aviary – an all- round shopping/recreational
experience. 9am-5pm, 7 days (from 10am Sun).

1983 **KESKE NURSERIES, CLACHAN, NORTH UIST:** In the remote heart of wild and
MAP 2 watery N Uist on main rd to Benbecula S of Lochmaddy and just after Clachan
A2 Stores and the t/off for Bayhead a cottage nusery and a … bus full of plants
(tomatoes when we visited). Idiosyncratic app, but certainly the Hebridean
choice for trees, shrubs, veg and bedding plants. Go on, make a statement –
plant a tree in this treeless tract. Open AYR 1pm-late. Cl Sun.

1984 **SMEATON GARDENS, EAST LINTON:** 2km from village on N Berwick rd
MAP 7 (signed Smeaton). Up a drive in an old estate is this walled grd going back to
B1 early 19th century. Wide range; good for fruit (and other) trees, herbaceous
etc. Nice to wander round, an additional pleasure is the 'Lake Walk' halfway
down drive through small gate in woods. 1km stroll round a secret finger lake
in magnificent mature woodland. You're only supposed to go during grd hrs
(10am-4.30, Sun from 11.30; cl w/ends Jan/Feb).

1985 **THE CLYDE VALLEY:** The lush valley of the mighty Clyde is grd centre central.
MAP 1 Best reached say from Glas by M74, jnct 7, then A72 for Lanark. Betw Larkhall
D3 and Lanark there's a profusion to choose from and many have sprouted cof-
fee/craft shops. Pick your own fruit in summer and your own picnic spot to eat
it.

1986 **DOBBIES, MONIFIETH:** 01382 530333. Recent addition to Dobbies Scottish
MAP 4 chain (Mar '99) – but the biggest garden centre in the country. A bit corporate,
D3 but huge. Daily 9am-6pm (until 8pm Wed & Thurs).

THE BEST MARKETS

1987
MAP B
E4

✓ ✓ **THE BARROWS, GLASGOW:** A market spread out around the streets and alleys in the E End, app via the Tron at the end of Argyle St and then the Gallowgate. Acres of cheap stuff, old and new, in shops, doorways, stalls, sheds and round the back. As with all gr markets, it's full of character and characters and it's still possible to find bargains and collectibles. Wander and rummage all over, but look esp for the Square Yard and the Cartwheel opp in Stevenson St West (parallel to Gallowgate) and also for the Upstairs Market in Gibson St at the side of Barrowlands (770/GLASGOW NIGHTLIFE) where you'll find the Barras as it always was, plus everything from clairvoyants to the latest scam (e.g. computer games, bootleg tapes). Sat and Sun only, 10am-5pm.

1988
MAP 4
C3

DENS ROAD, DUNDEE: A kind of mini-Barrowland on the hill N of town centre area of Dundee. By car you have to negotiate the bewildering and irritating one-way system. The market, which sells all kinds of junk, cheap essentials and nonsense, is all undercover in sheds and has a particular atmos. Open Tue, Fri, w/ends.

1989
MAP 1
D3

LANARK MARKET: Principally a cattle auction but also all the other animals incl pets. The sweat and dust of the ring, and of interest to those of us who ain't farmers or butchers, for the atmos and the café (1279/CAFÉS). There's nothing quite like it in Scotland. Every Mon, but many other days 01555 662281.

1990
MAP 7
A1

INGLISTON, outside Edin on A8 nr Airport; **EAST FORTUNE**, off A1 E of Haddington; **KINROSS** jnct 5/6 of the M90. All tacky markets on unattractive sites nr Edin. Possibly declining popularity due to bootsales and just as well. They're all on Sundays. I mention them just in case you wonder what the traffic's all about, but best to avoid.

1991
MAP A
C3
xE1

EDINBURGH MARKETS: The remarkable thing about Edin and all its aspirations to be seen as a major European city is that, unlike all the others, it doesn't have a st market. All attempts to actuate one are met with huge popular support e.g. the Grassmarket Fair (w/ends during the Festival), the Market on the Shore, Leith in early June. The Meadows Festival. But, for various reasons, there's nothing more permanent yet. Till then, trains to Glas leave regularly.

AUCTIONS AND JUNKYARDS

1992
MAP 1
C3

✓ **BURNTHILLS DEMOLITION, QUARRELTON, JOHNSTON, nr GLASGOW:** 01505 329644. M8 to Paisley, town centre then follow signs for Johnstone. Left at 'Iceland' at the top of the rise, left again at the police stn, rt into S William St and it's on your left around the bend. A yard, full of Victorian sinks and a warehouse that's an Aladdin's cave of fascinating and useful junk; old bikes, stuffed polar bears, stained glass and lots of stuff whose original purpose has long been forgotten. Quite spooky upstairs; watch out for The Mummy! Mon-Sat 9am-5pm Sun noon-5pm. About 12km from airport.

1993
MAP 2
D2

✓ **AULDEARN ANTIQUES, AULDEARN, nr NAIRN:** Doris Milton's cornucopia of junk, quality antiques and architectural salvage in an old manse 2km from main st (via Lethen Rd) which is 3km from main A96 Nairn-Forres rd. Serene spot for browsing through courtyard of shops and a churchful of furniture. Kids welcome. 7 days until 5.30pm.

1994
MAP 7
B1

SAM BURNS' YARD, PRESTONPANS, nr EDINBURGH: 01875 810600. On the coast rd out of Musselburgh; if you get to Prestonpans you've missed it. By a gate in the wall you'll see cars on the kerb of a long straight stretch. The yard has piles of old bikes, assorted 'stuff' and is full of domestic and office furniture stored both outdoors and in sheds. Popular with Sunday browsers although you wonder who might want a rusted filing cabinet or a second-hand toilet. 7 days until 5pm, Sun from 12.30pm.

1995
MAP A
xD1

EASY (EDINBURGH ARCHITECTURAL SALVAGE YARD): 554 7077. Couper St off Coburg St (at N end of Gr Jnct St nr mini roundabout). Warehouseful of original house fittings and the place to go for baths, sinks, radiators, fireplaces, doors (there are rows of them) and all the other bits of Old Edin that used to be thrown out but which are now worth lots. Similar set ups at Angus Architectural Antiques, Hill St, Montrose, in harbour area (01674 674291) and **TAYMOUTH ARCHITECTURAL**, Perth Rd, Dundee (01382 666833).

1996
MAP B
A3

R McTEAR and J.A. CATHCART, GLASGOW: McTear's at the Clydeway Business Centre Elliot Pl. overlooking the SECC has sales every Fri (view Thu) and Cathcart's at 20 Anchor Lane off St. Vincent Pl near George Sq. on Wed. Mornings. See the *Herald* on Mon for details.

1997
MAP A
xE1
D1

FINDLAY'S AUCTIONEERS: 554 4422. Edinburgh has lost not only its famously funky Lyon & Turnbull Lane Sales, but also Philips (house and specialist sales). This leaves Findlays to fill the breach from their sale rms in Jane St, Leith. Sat sales (viewing Fri 8am-8pm and Sat 8am onwards). **LYON & TURN-BULL:** Broughton Pl at the end. Having said the above, the legendary name is scheduled to be back at the time of going to press with an auction room in a converted church (the ill-fated Palladium, closed by noise-resistant neighbours). Presumably, they will advertise times, viewings, etc in *The Scotsman*.

1998
MAP 5
B2

LADYBANK AUCTION: Kinloch St along from railway stn in flat village in middle of farming Fife. Weekly sale of all kinds of household stuff from Victoriana through nifty 1950s to 1970s collectibles. Eminently worth a gander. Fri 6pm. Viewing Thu till 9pm, Fri from 10am.

1999
MAP 6
C2

ROBERTSON'S AUCTION, KINBUCK: 01786 822603. 6km N of Dunblane on B8033. Second Sat every month and alternate Fri at 10am. Viewing: Thur and Fri 9am-4pm, (and Thur 7.30-9pm). Antiques/domestic furniture-stripping.

COMRIE AUCTION: 01764 670613. In old church on main st. Occasional Tues at 10.30am. Viewing: Sat 10am-1pm, Mon 9am-6pm. **CRIEFF AUCTION:** 01764 653276. Galvelmore St off rd in from S. Times vary so check. These 3 salerooms in Perthshire are like 'country sales'; general goods and antiques. Gr for furniture and bric-à-brac. Much of it finds its way into antique shops. These sales can be addictive.

2000
MAP 4
D2

TAYLOR'S AUCTIONS, MONTROSE: 01674 672775. Panmure Row. Auction Rooms for regular sales of household furniture and effects every second Sat and some Fridays, when they do specialised items like wine. Some antique and quality stuff but all kinds incl bric-à-brac, jewellery, grd furniture (viewing: Fri 2-5pm and 6-9pm; Sat 9am onwards). Often fascinating just to wander round; you're bound to see something you want.

2001
MAP 7
B1

LESLIE and LESLIE, HADDINGTON: 01620 822241. Market St. An outside of Edinburgh auction rm where wheelers and dealers have oft come for supplies. You can cut out the middleman here. Phone for times.

SECTION 11

Museums, Galleries, Theatres and Music

THE MOST INTERESTING MUSEUMS

For EDINBURGH *galleries, see pp. 51-2;* GLASGOW, *see pp.91-2.*

2002
MAP 7
B1
✓ ✓ **MUSEUM OF FLIGHT, nr HADDINGTON, E LOTHIAN:** 01620 880308. 3km from A1 S of town. In the old complex of hangars and nissen huts at the side of E Fortune, an airfield dating to World War I (there's a tacky open-air market on Sundays), a large collection of planes from gliders to jets and esp wartime memorabilia has been respectfully restored and preserved. Inspired and inspiring displays; not just boys' stuff. Marvel at the bravery back then and sense the unremitting passage of time. From E Fortune the airship R34 made its historic Atlantic crossings. AYR 7 days; 10.30am-5pm (till 6pm Jul-Aug).

2003
MAP 5
D3
✓ ✓ **THE SECRET BUNKER, nr CRAIL/ANSTRUTHER:** 01333 310301. The nuclear bunker and regional seat of government in the event of nuclear war – a twilight labyrinth beneath a hill in rural Fife so vast, well documented and complete, it's utterly fascinating and quite chilling. Few 'museums' are as authentic or as resonant as this, even down to the 1950s records in the jukebox in the claustrophobic canteen. Makes you wonder what 300 people would have felt like incarcerated down there, what the Cold War was all about and what secrets They are cooking up these days. Apr-Oct 10am-5pm.

2004
MAP 5
A3
✓ **THE ABBOT HOUSE, DUNFERMLINE:** Maygate in town centre 'historic area'. V fine conversion of ancient house demonstrating the importance of this town as a religious and trading centre from the beginning of this millennium to medieval times. Encapsulates history from Margaret and Bruce to the Beatles. One of the few tourist attractions where 'award-winning' is a reliable indicator of worth. Café and tranquil grd; gate to the graveyard and Abbey. 7 days 10am-5pm.

2005
MAP 1
B2
✓ **EASDALE ISLAND FOLK MUSEUM:** On Easdale, an island/township reached by a 5min (continuous) boat service from Seil 'island' at the end of the B844 (off the A816, 18km S of Oban). Something special about this grassy hamlet of white-washed houses on a rocky outcrop which has a pub, a tearoom and a craft shop, and this museum across the green. The history of the place (a thriving slate industry erased one stormy night in 1881, when the sea drowned the quarry) is brought to life in displays from local contributions. Easter-Sept 11am-5pm.

2006
MAP 2
B1
✓ **THE BLACK HOUSE AT ARNOL, LEWIS:** 01851 710501. The A857 Barvas rd from Stornoway, left at jnct for 7km, then rt through township for 2km. The trad thatched dwelling of the Hebrides, with earth floor, bed boxes and central peat fire (no chimney hole), occupied both by the family and their animals. Remarkably, this house was lived in until the 1960s. Smokists may reflect on that peaty fug. Open AYR: Cl Fri in wint. Cl Sun and Fri in wint and maybe lunchtimes. HS

2007
MAP 2
D1
✓ **STRATHNAVER MUSEUM, BETTYHILL:** 01641 521418. On N coast 60km W of Thurso in a converted church which is v much part of the whole appalling saga: a graphic account of the Highland clearances told through the history of this fishing village and the Strath that lies behind it from whence its dispossessed population came; 2,500 folk were driven from their homes – it's worth going up the valley (from 2km W along the main A836) to see (esp at Achenlochy) the beautiful land they had to leave in 1812 to make way for sheep. For opening outside advertised times, call 01641 521335. Apr-Oct Mon-Sat 10am-5pm (cl at lunchtime).

2008
MAP 3
D1
✓ **SCOTLAND'S LIGHTHOUSE MUSEUM, FRASERBURGH:** At Kinnaird Head nr Harbour. A top attraction, so signed from all over. Purpose-built and v well done. Something which may appear to be of marginal interest made vital. In praise of the prism and the engineering innovation and skill that allowed Britain once to rule the seas (and the world). A gr ambition (to light the coastline) spectacularly realised. *At Scotland's Edge* by Allardyce and Hood (or its follow-up) is well worth taking home. The tour guide is like James Robertson Justice with better patter. Apr-Oct 10am-6pm (Sun afternoons); winter closes at 4pm.

2009 **WEST HIGHLAND MUSEUM, FORT WILLIAM:** Cameron Sq off main st, listed
MAP 2 building next to TO. Good refurb yet retains mood; the setting doesn't over-
C3 shadow the contents. 7 rms of Jacobite memorabilia, archeology, wildlife,
clans, tartans, arms etc all effectively evoke the local history. Gr oil paintings
line the walls, incl drawn battle plan of Culloden. The anamorphic painting of
Charlie isn't so bonny, but a fascinating snapshot all the same. Cl Sun except
July/Aug (2-5pm).

2010 **KILMARTIN HOUSE:** N of Lochgilphead on the A816. 01546 510278. Centre
MAP 1 for landscape and archeology interpretation, opened summer '97 so first
B2 appearance in this book. Want to know why Kilmartin Glen is littered with historic sites? Then come here. Intelligent, interesting, run by a small independent trust. Excellent organic cafe – deserves to be supported. AYR 10am-
5.30pm daily.

2011 **PICTAVIA, BRECHIN:** 01356 626241. S of Brechin on the Forfar rd at Brechin
MAP 4 Castle Garden Centre opened summer '99 to give a multimedia interpretation
D2 of our Dark Age ancestors. Sparse on detail, high on interactivity. Listen to
some music, pluck a harp and argue about the Battle of Dunnichen – was it
that important? AYR Mon-Sat 9-6pm, Sun 10am-6pm (5pm winter).

2012 **SUMMERLEE, COATBRIDGE:** 01236 431261 West Canal St. Follow signs. Here
MAP 1 in the Iron Town is this tribute to the industry, ingenuity and graft that pow-
D2 ered the Industrial Revolution and made Glas gr. Anyone with a mechanical
bent or an interest in the social history of the working class will like it here;
totty kids and bored teens may not. Tearoom. 10am-5pm. Winter (12-5pm
w/ends).

2013 **SKYE MUSEUM OF ISLAND LIFE:** Kilmuir on Uig-Staffin rd, the A855, 32km N
MAP 2 of Portree. The most authentic (or at least official) of several converted cot-
B2 tages on Skye where the poor crofter's life is recreated for the enrichment of
ours. The small thatched township includes agricultural implements as well as
domestic artefacts, many of which illustrate an improbable fascination with
the royal family. Flora Macdonald's grave is nearby (1666/MONUMENTS).

2014 **AUCHENDRAIN, INVERARAY:** 8km W of town on A83. A whole township
MAP 1 reconstructed to give a v fair impression of both the historical and spatial
C2 relationship betw the cottages and their various occupants. Longhouses and
byre dwellings; their furniture and their ghosts. 7 days. Apr-Sept 9.30am-5pm
(not Sat in Apr-Sept) (10am in winter).

2015 **INVERARAY JAIL:** 'The story of Scottish crime and punishment' (sic) told in
MAP 1 'award-winning' reconstruction of courtroom with cells below, where the
C2 waxwork miscreants and their taped voices bring local history to life. Makes
you think that guided tours of Peterhead can't be far off. Open AYR, 10am-
6pm (opens 9.30am in summer).

2016 **ARCTIC PENGUIN aka MARITIME HERITAGE CENTRE, INVERARAY:** 'One of
MAP 1 the world's last iron sailing ships' moored so you can't miss it at the loch side
C2 in Inveraray. More to it than would seem from the outside; displays on the history of Clydeside (the *Queens M* and *E* memorabilia etc), Highland Clearances,
the Vital Spark. Lots for kids to get a handle (or hands) on. 7 days 10am till
6pm; 5pm winter.

2017 **BONAWE IRONWORKS MUSEUM, TAYNUILT:** At its zenith, (late 17th – early
MAP 1 18th century), this ironworks was a brutal, fire-breathing monster, as 'black as
C1 the Earl of Hell's waiscoat'. But now, all is calm as the gently sloping grassy
banks carry you around from warehouse to foundry and down onto the
banks of L Etive to the pier, where the finished product was loaded on to ships
to be taken away for the purpose of empire-building (with cannonballs). Apr-
Sept daily until 6.30pm; Oct-Nov daily until 4.30pm; cl Dec-Mar.

2018 **SCOTTISH FISHERIES MUSEUM, ANSTRUTHER:** 01333 310628. In and
MAP 5 around a cobbled courtyard o/look the old fishing harbour in this busy East
D3 Neuk town. Excellent evocation of trad industry still alive (if not kicking).
Impressive collection of models and actual vessels incl those moored at adj
quay. Crail harbour 9km up the coast, for the full picture (and fresh crab/lob-
ster). Open AYR 10am-5.30pm, Sun 11am-5pm (cl 4.30pm in winter).

2019 **ROBERT SMAIL'S PRINTING WORKS, INNERLEITHEN:** Main st. A trad print-
MAP 8 ing works till 1986 and still in use. Fascinating vignettes/instant history. Have
B2 a go at hand setting, then have a go at Caldwell's cone holding (1325/ICE
CREAM). May-Oct, Mon-Sat 10am-5pm, Sun 2-5pm. W/ends in Oct. (Cl 1-2pm).

2020 **SHAMBELLIE HOUSE MUSEUM OF COSTUME, NEW ABBEY, nr DUMFRIES:**
MAP 9 Another obsession that became a museum. On 2 floors of this country house
C3 set among spectacular woodlands. Fab frocks etc from every 'period'. Apr-Oct
11am-5pm.

2021 **ABERFELDY WATER MILL, ABERFELDY:** Mill St off main st. Excellent renova-
MAP 4 tion made all the more authentic because it was restored in 1983 by a 7th-
B3 generation miller, Tom Rodger, and once again is producing good healthy
(organic) oatmeal that you can buy for your porridge. The weight of the water
in the buckets turns the wheel; life goes round. The tearoom serves, amongst
other things, a v fine fly cemetery. Apr-Oct 10am-5pm (Sun cl. 5.30pm).

2022 **WICK HERITAGE CENTRE, BANK ROW:** 01955 605313. Amazing civic muse-
MAP 2 um run by volunteers. Jam-packed with items about the sea, town and land.
D1 Donald Dewar should ensure these people get OBEs or something.

2024 **ABERDEEN MARITIME MUSEUM:** 01224 337700. Shiprow. Aberdeen faces
MAP 3 the sea – and this place tells you the stories. Films, exhibits, photos and paint-
D3 ings, from sail to oil. Decent cafe. Mon-Sat 10am-5pm, Sun 12-3pm.   ADM

THE MOST INTERESTING PUBLIC GALLERIES

For EDINBURGH, see p. 51-2; GLASGOW, p. 91-2.

2025
MAP 3
D3
✓ **ABERDEEN ART GALLERY:** Schoolhill. Major gallery with temp exhibits and eclectic permanent collection from Impressionists to Bellany. Large bequest from local granite merchant Alex Macdonald in 1900 contributes fascinating collection of his contemporaries: Bloomsburys, Scottish, Pre-Raphaelites. Excellent watercolour rm. An easy and rewarding gallery to visit. 10am-5pm (Sun 2-5pm).

2026
MAP 4
C3
✓ **THE FERGUSSON GALLERY, PERTH:** Marshall Pl on corner of Tay St in distinctive round tower (former waterworks). The assembled works on two floors of J D Fergusson 1874-1961. Though he spent much of his life in France, he had an influence on Scottish art and was pre-eminent amongst those now called the Colourists. It's a long way from Perth to Antibes 1913 but these pictures are a draught of the warm S. Mon-Sat 10-5pm.

2027
MAP 5
B3
✓ **KIRKCALDY MUSEUM AND ART GALLERY:** Nr railway stn, but uptown Kirkcaldy isn't easy to find your way around, so ask. One of the best galleries in central Scotland. Splendid introduction to the History of 19th/20th-century Scottish art. Lots of Colourists/McTaggart/Glasgow Boys. And Sickert to Redpath. Museum ain't bad also. Kirkcaldy doesn't get a lot of good press, but this and the parks (1407/PARKS) are worth the journey (plus Valente's – 1258/FISH AND CHIPS). 7 days till 5pm.

2028
MAP 9
C3
✓ **HORNEL GALLERY, KIRKCUDBRIGHT:** Broughton House where he lived, now a fabulous evocation with collection of his work and atelier as was. 'Even the Queen was amazed'. The beautiful garden stretching to the river is a real eye opener. April-Oct. 7 Days 1-5.30pm.   NTS

2029
MAP 3
C1
✓ **DUFF HOUSE, BANFF:** Nice walk and easy to find from town centre. Important outstation of the National Gallery in meticulously restored Adam house with interesting history and spacious grounds. Ramsays, Raeburn, portraiture of mixed appeal and an El Greco. Maybe OTT for some, but major attraction in the area (go futher up the Deveron, 1822/WOODLAND WALKS).

2030
THE PIER ART GALLERY, STROMNESS, ORKNEY MAINLAND: On main st (1413/COASTAL VILLAGES), a gallery on a small quay which could have come lock, stock and canvases from Cornwall. Permanent St Ives-style collection of Barbara Hepworth, Ben Nicholson, Paolozzi and others shown in a *simpatico* environment with the sea o/side. Temporary exhibs downstairs. A breath of art. Cl Mon.

2031
MAP 1
C3
PAISLEY ART GALLERY AND MUSEUM: High St. Permanent collection of the world famous Paisley shawls and history of weaving techniques. Other exhibs usually have a local connection and an interactive element. Notable Greek Ionic-style building. Mon-Sat 10am-5pm.

2032
MAP 1
C3
MACLAURIN GALLERY, AYR: In Rozelle Park and the only art in these parts. Temporary exhibs change every month (incl local artists' work). 5 galleries, and additional 5 rms of art in Rozelle Hse; craft shop. Apr-Oct: Mon-Sat 10am-5pm, Sun 2-5pm.

2033
MAP 9
C3
✓ **SCULPTURE AT GLENKILN RESERVOIR, nr DUMFRIES:** Take A75 to Castle Douglas and rt to Shawshead; into village, rt at T-jnct, left to Dunscore, immediate left, signed for reservoir. Follow rd along loch side and park. Not a gallery at all but sculpture scattered amongst the hills, woods and meadows around this reservoir in the Galloway Hills 16km SE of Dumfries. One or two are obvious, the others you just have to find. Epsteins and Moores. I found 3 (there are thought to be 6 in all), but not the King and Queen who had their heads removed – now, that's vandalism. This is an enchanting place; art plays its part.

2034 McEWAN GALLERY nr BALLATER, DEESIDE: A surprising place but for many
MAP 3 years this cottage gallery has been dealing in 19th/20th century, mainly
B3 Scottish art. Delightful house. They wrote the book! Summer exhibs, but open
AYR 10am-6pm (Sun 2-6pm). 300m up A939 Tomintoul rd.

2035 THE LOST GALLERY, MIDDLE OF NOWHERE, ABERDEENSHIRE: Best
MAP 3 reached off the A944 Strathdon rd at Bellabeg, though don't follow the sign
B3 for 'Lost', the one you see in postcards. Fabulous small gallery of work by con-
temporary Scottish artists incl the owners. AYR 11am-5pm. Cl Tues.

2036 STRATHEARN GALLERY, CRIEFF: 32 W St (western extension of Main St).
MAP 4 Highly regarded (by Scottish Crafts Council and others) gallery with pottery
B3 downstairs. Fine and applied arts. Open AYR: Thu-Sat in winter and cl Sun.

2037 ART-TM, INVERNESS: 20 Bank St. 01463 712240. Excellent Scottish Arts
MAP 2 Council-backed gallery with regular arts and crafts shows. Even the staff are
C2 surprised to find something like this here. Tues-Sat 11am-6pm.

2038 TOLQUHON GALLERY, nr ABERDEEN: 01651 842343. Betw Ellon and
MAP 3 Oldmeldrum and nr Haddo House (1652/COUNTRY HOUSES) and Pitmedden
D3 (1388/GARDENS) – follow signs for castle, an interesting ruin for kids to clam-
ber. Real art at realistic prices. (Pron 'T'hon'.) 11am-5pm, Sun 2-5pm. Cl Thu.

2039 JUST ART, FOCHABERS: Main st, the A96 through Fochabers E of Elgin.
MAP 3 Changing exhibs of serious and selected mainly Scottish artists. Good ceram-
B2 ics. A must stop on this rd along the coast. See 1982/GARDEN CENTRES.

2040 ST ANDREWS FINE ART: Crowded walls of Scottish art from 1800-present.
MAP 5 Includes some good work from kent contemporaries. Peploe-Redpath and
C2 their chums.

2041 KRANENBURG & FOWLER FINE ARTS, OBAN: Star Brae, 01631 562323. Geoff
MAP 1 and Jan source work from artists that ranges from the polite to the interest-
B1 ing. Small group of regular exhibitors and others. Mon-Sat 9.30am-6pm.

2042 MORVERN GALLERY, BARVAS, ISLE OF LEWIS: Coast rd just N of Barabhas
MAP 2 5km from Callanish and those stones. Farm steading kind of gallery (now
B1 expanded) with well-selected work, mainly local. Painting, tapestry, ceramics
and fab original knits. Baking. AYR 10am-5pm. Cl Sun.

2043 GALLERY HEINZEL, ABERDEEN: 21 Spa St. Major commercial gallery in city
MAP 3 with credibility. A showcase for NE arts with changing exhibs. Frequent atten-
D3 dees of the Glasgow Art Fair Tues-Sat 10am-5.30pm. Next dr is an artists stu-
dio workshop, Studio 25, Sat only.

2044 SCOTTISH SCULPTURE WORKSHOPS, LUMSDEN nr ALFORD and HUNTLY:
MAP 2 Affordable sculpture for your house, garden or square. Exhib area. Interesting
C3 art in a wee place N of nowhere. Mon-Fri, 9am-5pm.

2045 LOGIE STEADING nr FORRES: Estate courtyard in beautiful countryside
MAP 2 10km S of Forres though not so obvious to find. Nr pleasant woodland walk
A2 and picnic spot. For directions, see 1810/WOODLAND WALKS. Well chosen art
and ceramics from Highland artists and workshops. Tearoom. Certainly one of
the best small galleries in N Scotland and well worth detour from the coast or
the A9. May-Oct Tues-Sun 10.30am-5pm.

The following are excl gallery/studios to see work by contemp artists.

2046
MAP B **GLASGOW PRINT STUDIOS:** 22 King St, Merchant City/Tron area.
E4
2047 EDINBURGH PRINTMAKERS WORKSHOP: 23 Union St off Leith Walk
MAP A
D1 **PEACOCK PRINT and PHOTOGRAPHIC STUDIOS, ABERDEEN:** 21 Castle St.
2048
MAP B **THE DEGREE SHOWS, EDINBURGH/GLASGOW ART SCHOOLS:** Work from
E4 final-year students. Discover the Bellanys/Howsons of the future. 2-week exhi-
bition after manic first night (mid June).

2049 THE GLASGOW ART FAIR: The Scottish market place for contemporary art
MAP B with mainly home-grown and London galleries with Scottish connections.
D3 Held in mid April in pavilions in George Square. 0141 552 6027 for details.

EDINBURGH

Edin's gay scene continues to develop as the 'pink triangle' around the Playhouse and Broughton St.

BARS AND CLUBS

2050
MAP A
D2

NEW TOWN BAR: 538 7775. 26 Dublin St. Basement and v sub-basement bar in residential New Town. Mixed crowd. Island bar good for eyes across the rm. Downstairs – called **INTENSE**, open Thu-Sun – is fairly intense; cruisy and gets full-on. That carpet has seen the lot. 7 days till 1.30am; w/ends 2.30am.

2051
MAP A
D2

PLANET OUT: 524 0061. Few doors down from the Playhouse by taxi rank (for the dash home) and opp the Deep Sea (for the fish supper if you haven't pulled). Retro poppy look and amiable, mixed crowd. 7 days till 1am. Then you go up the street to …

2052
MAP A
D2

CC BLOOMS: 556 9331. Next to Playhouse. Bar up, disco down. Main event of the evening for most and last port of call for many, so can get *desperate*. Often queues to get in and nr 3am, to get off. After this there's only the 'Gardens of Fun' – more risky than frisky, so get it on here. 7 days till 3am. (340/LATE BARS)

2053
MAP A
C2

FRENCH CONNECTION: 225 7651. Rose St Lane N nr Castle St. Intimate bar out on a limb in the drinking zone. But that has its attractions. You will not come and go unnoticed. Oldies and youngies; the twain do meet. 7 days till 1am.

2054
MAP A
E2

STAG AND TURRET: 478 7231. 1 Montrose Terr, Abbeyhill nr well-known cruising area. Friendly local more laid back than the above. 7 days till 1am.

OTHER PLACES

2055
MAP A
D2

BLUE MOON CAFÉ: 556 2788. 36 Broughton St. Friendly and always busy neighbourhood café at the heart of quarter with all-day menu and committed agenda. Non-gay friendly. 2/3 rms with food, drink and conversation. If you are arriving in Edin and don't know anybody, come here first. Food 7 days till 11.15pm, 12.15am w/ends. (221/CAFÉS)

2056
MAP A
E1

NO. 18: 553 3222. 18 Albert Pl. Sauna for gentlemen. 12-10pm. Sun 2-10pm.

2057
MAP A
D1

TOWNHOUSE HEALTH CLUB: 556 6116. 51 E Claremont St, just down from Broughton St. New sauna, open til 11pm.

HOTELS

2058
MAP A
D2

MANSFIELD HOUSE: 556 7980. 57 Dublin St. Small New Town guest house and OK gay stay. Candelabra in the hall, various other camperie. Breakfast on a tray. No public rms – you'll have to leave your door open. New Town Bar (*see above*) up the st.　　5RMS　JAN-DEC　X/X　XPETS　XCC　XKIDS　MED.INX

2059
MAP A
B3

ST VALERY GH: 337 1893. 36 Coates Gardens, W End. Gay-friendly rather than gay GH by the people who used to have the Linden Hotel.
20RMS　JAN-DEC　T/T　XPETS　CC　KIDS　INX

2060
MAP A
xE1

GARLANDS: 554 4205. 48 Pilrig St. Quiet st of many other guesthouses about 2km from scene (but nr sauna). 6RMS　JAN-DEC　X/T　PETS　XCC　KIDS　CHP

2061
MAP A
xE4

SOUTHSIDE GH: 668 4422. 8 Newington Rd nr Commonwealth Pool. Not too far away and well-appointed GH, mainly gay. No smk.
7RMS　JAN-DEC　X/T　XPETS　CC　KIDS　INX

GLASGOW

BARS AND CLUBS

2062
MAP B
D4

DELMONICA'S: 552 4803. 68 Virginia St. Newly refurbed stylish pub with long bar and open plan in quiet lane in Merchant City. Food till 7pm. Pally, pre-club crowd later on. Some event nights. 7 days till 12midnight.

2063
MAP B
D4

POLO LOUNGE: 553 1221. 84 Wilson St. Classiest Glas gay bar yet by same people who own Delmonica's (*see above*) and Caffe Latte (*see below*). Comfortable and clubbable by day, cruisier by night. Downstairs disco (Fri-Sun) with 3am licence; otherwise till 1am (one of the few pubs in town serving after midnight). (680/PRE-CLUB BARS)

2064
MAP B
C4

WATERLOO BAR: 221 7539. 306 Argyle St. Old-established bar and clientele. Not really for trendy young things. You might not fancy anybody but they're a friendly down-to-earth old bunch. 7 days till 12midnight.

2065
MAP B
E4

COURT BAR: 552 2463. 69 Hutcheson St, centre of Merchant City area. Long-going small bar that's fairly straight till mid-evening. 7 days till midnight.

2066
MAP B
D3

SADIE FROSTS: 332 8005. 8 W George St, in front of Queen St Stn and underneath Burger King. Downtown cruisy bar, well placed for the brief encounter. Gets jumpy nr closing time. Incorporates **SAPPHO**, a bar for pool-playing girls. 7 days till midnight.

2067
MAP B
D4

BENNETS: 552 5761. 80 Glassford St. For 20yrs the real disco. Everybody goes in the beginning – and in the end. Late '90s face-lift, so she's looking good again. Wed-Sun 11pm-3am, Tue is 'traditionally' straight night.

OTHER PLACES

2068
MAP B
D4

CAFFE LATTE: 553 2553. Corner of Virginia St and Wilson St. Café-bistro at heart of gay st; not at all cloney. Laid-back atmos; snacks and food all day till 12midnight.

2069
MAP B
D4

CENTURION SAUNA: 248 4485. 19 Dixon St, above Aer Lingus and St Enoch's. Till 10pm or later (some Sat all-nighters).

2070
MAP B
C4

THE LANE: 221 1802. 60 Robertson St, nr Waterloo (*see above*) opp side of Argyle St, lane on rt. You 'look for the green light'. Sauna and private club. You wouldn't call it upmarket. 7 days, afternoons till 10pm.

HOTEL

2071
MAP B
C1

ALBION HOTEL: 339 8620. 405 N Woodside Rd, off Gr Western Rd. Currently Glasgow's only prospect is gay-friendly (i.e. they advertise in *Gay Times*) rather than gay. It's a start.   16RMS   JAN-DEC   T/T   XPETS   CC   KIDS   INX

ABERDEEN

Gay scene in Aberdeen in disarray at time of going to press. Only one bar/club:

2072
MAP 3
D3

CLUB 2000: 01224 596999. 62 Shiprow, off Market St. Gay club open late night only. 7 days 9pm-2am. Adm Fri/Sat, free other times.

DUNDEE

2073
MAP 4
C3

CHARLIE'S BAR: 01382 226840. 75 Seagate nr Cannon Cinema. Okay and recently improved pub, small-city scene, but if you're in Dundee for the night, you might. 7 days till 11pm/midnight.

2074
MAP 4
C3

LIBERTY NIGHTCLUB: 01382 200660. 124 Seagate. Along from the above so follows on. Bar and dancefloor. Everybody knows everybody else, but not you. This may have its advantages. Wed-Sun till 2.30am. Also …

2075
MAP 4
C3

BAR XS: 01382 200660. St Andrews Lane. Behind and above Liberty's. Small bar, a pre-club bar on disco nights (reduced tickets avail at bar). 7 days till midnight (11pm Sun).

HOTELS ELSEWHERE

Not many, but Auchendean more than just 'gay-friendly'.

2076
MAP 2
D3

AUCHENDEAN LODGE, DULNAIN BRIDGE: 01479 851347. A Highland retreat in an area with lots of outdoorsy things to do. Innovative cooking. (Eric and Ian well on the case 962/INEXP HIGHLAND HOTELS). Essential reading: Linklater's *The Prince in the Heather*, or try and find your own.
7RMS   JAN-DEC   X/T   PETS   CC   KIDS   TOS   MED.EX

THE MOST HAPPENING NIGHTCLUBS

Many of the best clubs come and go and there's little point in mentioning them here. Some are only on once a week with no permanent venue. Consult The List *magazine (Edin and Glas) for up-to-date info, and look for flyers.*

2077 GLASGOW
MAP B

Glas is a club city, but the dreaded curfew remains. Stampede when the pubs shut etc – check venues for current 'rules'.

D4   Clubs at **THE ARCHES: RELIEF, COLOURS, LOVE BOUTIQUE and others:** 221 9736. At the Arches Theatre, Midland St (754/BEST CLUBS), w/ends only. Glasgow's finest. DJs by rotation. Vaulted archways, serious sound system and v up-for-it crowd. Big Millennium renovations 2000.

D4   **ARCHAOS:** 204 3189. 25 Queen St. Huge dance emporium on 3 floors incl Betty's Mayonnaise. Central dance floor has state-of-the-art lighting. Balconies upstairs for action-checking and chilling. Atmos more rarified the higher you go.

D4   **THE TUNNEL:** 204 1000. 84 Mitchell St. Once defined club culture in Glas. Still high glam quotient and designer ambience with vogue-ish crowd. W/ends (Ark and Triumph, summer 1997) and student nights. On same circuit as Liverpool's Cream, so big name DJs every month.

C3   **ALASKA:** 248 1777. 142 Bath Lane. Behind the Spy Bar in Bath St with which it has relations. Cool spot for w/ends only (though students thing on Tues at time of going to press).

D4   **THE APARTMENT:** 221 6381. 23 Royal Exchange Sq. Colin and Kelly Barr's stylish drinking club kind of disco for older more discerning types. Exclusivity is part of the deal, but they have been known to let in any old footballer and hairdresser. However, sometimes getting in here is just too much hassle for groovers of a certain age. Thu-Mon from 11pm.

D4   **BABAZA:** 204 0101. Royal Exhange Sq. Downstairs (from above), a basement groovebox around a bar. Not young crowd, not old – y'know in the middle. Adm after 11pm Wed-Sun, but open 7 days.

D4   **THE SUB CLUB:** 248 4600. 22 Jamaica St. Long-running, but revamped and still v much a scene. Eclectic music policy. Fri/Sat Psy phi/Sub Culture at time of going to press. (some Thurs and Suns).

D4   **YANG:** 248 8484. 33 Queen St. Underneath Archaos (above) and same totally mainstream up-for-it Glasgow crowd, maybe younger, maybe fresher. Bar open 7 days. Club thing varies.

C3   **THE GARAGE:** 332 1120. 490 Sauchiehall Street. The big night out for cheap drinks, chart sounds and copping off. Totally unpretentious. Live bands as advertised.

2078 EDINBURGH
MAP A

Edin club culture still getting better. Most clubs are still weekly or occasional events, but they tend to use the same venues. These are the ones to check:

D2   **EDEN:** 478 7434. 14 Picardy Pl. V new at time of going to press, but likely to become major Edin club venue. Same people have The Outhouse (315/these ARE HIP) and good location nr Playhouse and gay zone. 2 floors in former casino. Likely Fri-Sun.

D2   **THE VENUE:** 557 3073. Calton Rd behind Waverley Stn. Long-established (in club terms) venue for clubs on w/end nights (mainly live bands during the week). Top nights – **PURE** (considered a major club night in Scotland) **TRIBAL FUNKTION, DISCO INFERNO.**

D2   **THE BONGO CLUB** 556 5204. 14 New St. A small door in a big wall above a huge underground parking lot (formerly the bus garage). Big windows onto small rooms where a committed crowd have created a club which is truly underground. No isms here incl ageism. W/ends, but sadly closing 2000.

D3   **LA BELLE ANGELE:** 225 2774. Hastie's Close off Cowgate at Gilded Balloon. W/ends. Occupants vary, we couldn't say.

C4 **CAVENDISH:** 228 3252. West Tollcross, upstairs it has the long-running **THE MAMBO CLUB** Fri and Sat (on 2 floors) African/reggae/generally good vibes music for v mixed crowd – good for oldies who like to dance.

D3 **MERCADO:** 226 4224. 36-39 Market St behind Waverley Stn. Probably Edinburgh's longest-running club venue. Recent revamp and infusion of good club organisers means that it's a go-area again – try **TIME TUNNEL** (with Trendy Wendy) on Fri or **COLOURS OF LOVE**.

D1 Two clubs that we hope hang around (but who knows): soul jazz grooves at **LIZZARD LOUNGE** in **CAFE GRAFFITI** on Sat (Mansfield Pl Church) and **CLUB LATINO** which moves around, so look for flyers.

C2 **THE DOME:** 624 8633. George St. Home to **WHY NOT?** a kind of disco-mating venue for over-25s.

REST OF SCOTLAND

CLUBS IN ABERDEEN, see p. 130.

2079
MAP 7
A1
BATHGATE, ROOM AT THE TOP: 01506 635123. Menzies Rd, Bathgate. You can spend half an hr driving round the centre of Bathgate before you twig that the huge thing next to Safeway is a purpose-built nightclub – UK's biggest. (Cream and Ministry of Sound? Well … who knows?) Proprietor does-n't like the word superclub, hyperbole wouldn't do it justice (capacity of 2600) but more dance floors, bars, nooks and (snogging) crannies than you can use.

2080
MAP 4
C3
DUNDEE, MARDI GRAS: 01382 205551. S Ward St. Capacity crowd of 1,250 most w/ends. Late '90s fave with Dundonians who like commercial sounds and good lights. Jazz bar, vodka bar, with large seating areas from where you check out who's in and what they're wearing. Mainly High St. Security relatively low-key. They have umbrellas if it's raining when you queue. Tues-Sun 10.30pm-2.30am.

2081
MAP 2
C2
INVERNESS, BLUE: 01463 222712. Rose St. Find Safeways: this relatively recent purpose-built club is opp the supermarket and behind its pub, the Forty-Five (good unpretentious, contemporary bar). Designed by the same team who did the Glasgow's Tunnel this is a v good groove to find so far N of Manchester. Bars up and down. Good floor and a v young crowd. Thur-Sun.

2082
MAP 6
C3
STIRLING, FUBAR: 01786 472619. Maxwell Place. Now long-established bar and club in downtown Stirling. Most of its moments probably passed, but mixed crowd with oldies and kids on separate floors. W/ends.

2083
MAP 5
B3
KIRKCALDY, JACKIE O'S: 01592 264496. On the Esplanade. Unpretentious, non-stressful *palais de danse*. Wed-Sat 9pm-2am. Still going after all these yrs (unlike Jackie). And behind it: **CAESAR'S:** 01592 201389. Second danceria on same esplanade and not much to choose, but similarly packed w/ends. Everyone seems to be wearing River Island (including me) and people sing along to the hits of the moment. Bouncers bounce. Thur-Sun till 2am. Also in Fife, nearby in **DUNFERMLINE** the nitespots are: **LIBERTY** 25 Kirkgate – 2 storey dance halls, music from every damned decade. 7 days; phone for hrs 01383 621515. **LORENZO MARKS**, St Margarets St; an old fave still packs them in.

2084
MAP 1
C3
SALTCOATS, METROPOLIS: 01294 602213. Hamilton St in centre of small town N of Ayr, 45km from Glas. Unlikely toon for a nightspot, but clubbers have been converging here for a wee while now. Mainly kids stuff, but check for oldie sessions if you're in the area for the night (ok I know that's unlikely). Thur-Sat.

2085
MAP 1
C3
AYR, CLUB DE MAR: 01292 611136. 1 Arthur St. The older of the two main and mainly w/end clubs in Ayr ain't at all bad. The other **X-ESS:** 01292 885717 off the main (pedestrianised) st behind Burger King; ain't bad either. Both are close geographically and spiritually to the High St. And musically – expect Radio One night-time stuff. Both are friendly and safe as House. Oldies will survive; but many find themselves more negotiable at **CLUB 30** in Main St. Ayr is (officially) an E free zone.

THE MOST INTERESTING THEATRES AND CINEMAS

For EDINBURGH, *see pp. 60-1; and* GLASGOW, *see p. 100.*

2086 **MULL LITTLE THEATRE, DERVAIG, MULL:** 01688 400377. 'The smallest the-
MAP 1 atre in Britain' is still there after more than 25 years. On edge of dinky Dervaig,
A1 10km from Tobermory. Bar and acceptable restau adj at the Druimard
Country-House Hotel. Tiny auditorium, so you're almost on top of the actors.
Never predictable. Its incongruity is part of its appeal. Easter-Oct. Curtain up
8.30pm. Cosy seats; cosy intervals.

2087 **CUMBERNAULD THEATRE:** 01236 732887. Nr old part of this new town on a
MAP 1 rise o/look the ubiquitous dual carriageway (to Stirling). Follow signs for
D2 Cumbernauld House. Bar/café-restau and 300-seat theatre (in the round) with
a mixed programme of one-nighters and short runs of mainly Scottish touring companies. Also concerts, drama workshops and kids' programmes. A
community-based and vital theatre, one of the better reasons to 'relocate in
Cumbernauld'.

2088 **BOWHILL LITTLE THEATRE, BOWHILL HOUSE, nr SELKIRK:** 01750 20732.
MAP 8 Tiny theatre off the courtyard below Bowhill House with intermittent mixed
B3 programme (must phone), but always delightful, esp with supper afterwards
(also phone to book).

2089 **PITLOCHRY THEATRE:** 01796 472680. Modern rep theatre across river from
MAP 4 main st performing usually 6 plays on different nights of the week. With a
B2 well-chosen programme of classics and popular works, the 500-seat theatre is
often full. V mixed Sunday concerts and foyer fringe events. Coffee bar open
at all times. Best places to eat before or after show: Portnacraig adj, by river
(01796 472777), or excellent East Haugh House on rd S, 2km town centre
(01796 473121).

2090 **EDEN COURT THEATRE, INVERNESS:** 01463 234234. An important theatre
MAP 2 complex making a vital contribution to the cultural life of the Highlands.
C2 Diverse programme of theatre, dance, variety, all kinds of music, opera, trad –
the occasional coup. Easy to book by credit card; lots do sell out. Theatre bar
and the Ness down there. Cinema programme of selected art-house/first-run
movies. What would Inverness watch without it? Good luck, Colin!

2091 **BYRE THEATRE, ST ANDREWS:** 01334 476288. Abbey St or South St. Serious
MAP 5 theatre in receipt of big lottery funding, so total rebuild still going on at time
C2 of going to press. Watch their space … then theirs.

2092 **THE WYND, MELROSE:** 01896 823854. Hidden behind the Teddy Melrose
MAP 8 shop (1548/KIDS) this 80 seater regularly entertains locals and even Edin folk.
C2 Ibsen, musicals, folk and jazz film. Intimate atmos in an intimate town.

2093 **CAMPBELTOWN PICTURE HOUSE:** 01586 553657. Campbeltown, Argyll.
MAP 1 Cinema Paradiso on the Kintyre peninsula. Lovingly preserved art deco gem;
B3 a shrine to the movies. Opened 1913, closed 1983, but such was the tide of
nostalgic affection that it was refurbished and reopened resplendent in 1989.
Shows mainly first-run films. To see a film here and emerge onto the
esplanade of Campbeltown L is to experience the lost magic of a night at the
pictures.

2094 **THE NEW PICTURE HOUSE, ST ANDREWS:** 01334 473509. On North St. 'New'
MAP 5 means 1931 and, apart from adding another screen (the small Cinema 2), it
C2 hasn't changed much, as generations of students will remember with fond-
ness. Mainly first-run flicks and Oct-May, there's a programme of late-night
cult/art movies. You can still smoke in the rear balcony. So quaint! So refreshingly non-smokist.

2095 **THE ROXY, KELSO:** 01573 224609. Horsemarket. A cinema from my youth, still
MAP 8 remarkably here and unchanged; still the smell of hot celluloid. Few better
C2 places to watch a first-run movie or an art flick and enjoy 'real Scottish pop-
corn'. Sun, Tues, Wed, Sat (early) and bingo on Mon, Thur & Fri/Sat. Don't you
ever close.

2096
MAP A
EDINBURGH (see also 428-431/NIGHTLIFE and festivals see below).

Good bars to frequent, some with regular and some with occasional live music, include:

SANDY BELL'S aka THE FORREST HILL BAR: Famous and forever. Sometimes you could look in and wonder why; other times you know you're in exactly the rt place. Music every night except Tues and Sun. **FIDDLER'S ARMS:** Grassmarket. And fiddle they do on Monday nights. Good crack and blether at all times. **WEST END HOTEL BAR:** 225 3656. Palmerston Pl. A good place to stay or just to hang out with the Highlanders. Some trad folk live at w/ends and whenever (26/INDIVIDUAL HOTELS). Finally **ROYAL OAK** Infirmary St. Late-night singaround (338/LATE BARS).

2097
MAP B
GLASGOW (see also 763-769/NIGHTLIFE).

THE CLUTHA VAULTS: 167 Stockwell St. E end nr Clyde. Gr atmos for the drink and the music. Mixed programme: readings Tues, bluegrass Sat afternoons. **HALT BAR** Woodlands Rd. Amongst a mixed music programme, always some folk for the kind of folk who inhabit the bar (634/GREAT 'GLASGOW' PUBS). Wednesdays. **RIVERSIDE:** 0141 248 3144. Fox St off Clyde St. Fri and Sat have ceilidh dances with a proper band and the full works. Doors open 8pm, band on 9pm and often full by 10pm. Just as you imagined it. **SCOTIA BAR:** 112 Stockwell St. The folk club and writers' retreat and all things non-high cultural. Club meets Wed night and Sat afternoon. Always the 'right folk' here (638/GREAT 'GLASGOW' PUBS). **VICTORIA BAR:** Bridgegate. Near the Scotia and a similar set-up. Fri and Sat night sessions of Irish/Scottish trad music.

2098
REST OF SCOTLAND

CEILIDH PLACE, ULLAPOOL: (960/INEXP HIGHLAND HOTELS).

DEAN TAVERN, NEWTONGRANGE: Home of the estimable Nitten folk club on Thursdays.

VICTORIA INN, HADDINGTON: Haddington Folk Club on Wednesdays.

THE ROAD HOUSE, DUNFERMLINE: Dunfermline Folk Club on Wednesday.

MISHNISH HOTEL, TOBERMORY, MULL: (1184/BLOODY GOOD PUBS).

PICK OF THE FOLK FESTS

GLASGOW CONCERT HALL, CELTIC CONNECTIONS: 0141 332 6633. Major jamboree every Jan. 3 weeks of concerts, ceilidhs and gatherings. Broad appeal.

EDINBURGH: 0131 557 1050. 10 days before Easter. The biggest festival.

INVERNESS: 01738 623274. Easter w/end. 01349 830388. Highland Festival 3 days, end June. 01463 715757. Summer Festival July/Aug, Balnain House.

SHETLAND: 01595 694757. Mid-April long (and they mean long) w/end.

GIRVAN: 01465 712128. Early May long w/end.

ORKNEY: 01856 851331. End of May 3 days.

ISLAY: Local TO for details. End of May over 2 weeks, till June.

ARRAN: 07990 593535. Early June 6 days.

KILLIN, nr STIRLING: Local TO for details. End of June. A gr newcomer 3 days.

STONEHAVEN: Local To for details. Mid-July 3 days.

SKYE: 01470 532436 but in soLocal TO for details

ISLE OF BUTE: Local TO for details. End July long weekend, trad.

AUCHTERMUCHTY: Local TO for details. Mid-August w/end.

TARBERT: Local TO for details. End Sept long w/end.

THE BEST OF ROCK AND POP MUSIC

2099
MAP A

EDINBURGH (dial 0131)

INGLISTON EXHIB CENTRE and **MURRAYFIELD STADIUM:** Rarely used, biggies only (U2, The Stones, the Pope). **PLAYHOUSE THEATRE:** 557 2590. Major theatre in Scotland, most regular programme, holds 3,000. More infrequent as concert venue while they get thro the musicals (surely not many to go). **USHER HALL:** 228 1155. Gr auditorium, but mainly classical. **THE VENUE:** 0131 557 3073 and **LA BELLE ANGELE:** 225 2774. Main small club venues for emerging and local bands. Check *The List* (whats on magazine) for programmes. **QUEEN'S HALL:** 668 2019. Most diverse (choral, jazz, art pop). Good atmos. Used every night; your best bet if you just want to go somewhere for decent music.

2100
MAP B

GLASGOW (dial 0141)

SCOTTISH EXHIBITION AND CONFERENCE CENTRE: 248 3000. Scotland's major venue for arena rock'n'roll – smaller **CLYDE AUDITORIUM** (aka the Armadillo) is adj. Used occasionally. **ROYAL CONCERT HALL:** 332 6633. Full programme of mainly classical music, but also a civilised theatre for more thoughtful pop. **BARROWLANDS:** Doesn't have its own box office. Ticket info 287 7777. The world-famous ballroom; pure rock'n'roll. Must be sampled (770/NIGHTLIFE). **PAVILION THEATRE:** 332 1846. Intimate, tiered music hall with v mixed programme incl hypnotism and hip and hyped pop. **KING TUT'S WAH WAH HUT:** 221 5279. St Vincent St. City's main club venue for live bands; well established on national circuit. **THE CATHOUSE** 248 6606. 15 Union St. Club venue for contemporary rock. **THE GARAGE:** 332 1120. 490 Sauchiehall St. Largish club for emerging bands. **13th NOTE:** 553 1638. Cafe in King St, also Clyde St. Bright, eclectic, indie.

For all of the above check *The List*, fortnightly what's on guide (avail all central belt newsagents) for details.

2101
MAP 3
D3

ABERDEEN (dial 01224)

ABERDEEN EXHIBITION HALL: 824824. Similar to SECC above, but only a few major acts go this distance (tho Oasis did).

MUSIC HALL: 632080. Medium-range civic (sit/stand).

CEILIDHS IN THE CITY

One element of Scottish culture enjoying a revival is the ceilidh (though fashion-ability waning). This is not just an excuse to down large amounts of alcohol, but is a friendly get-together easy to join in. Trad dances like the Gay Gordons and eightsome reels are usually 'called' and most of them are easy to pick up. Ceilidhs in towns and villages likely to be more impromptu affairs, but see p. 284 for Ceilidhs in Skye. Mull also a good bet.

2102
MAP B
C4
THE RENFREW FERRY, GLASGOW: Enter by Clyde Pl via Jamaica St Br from N of river or Bridge St. A real ferry moored on the Clyde – brilliant ambience for ceilidhs and gigs of all kinds. Fri 9pm-2am. Tickets at quay or in adv from Ticket Centre, Candleriggs (0141 227 5511), usually sold out by 10pm. Visitors and locals. Gr bands.

2103
MAP B
D4
THE RIVERSIDE, GLASGOW: 0141 248 3144. Fox St off Clyde St. The place that started the ceilidh revival in Glas. Upstairs in quiet st, the joint is jumping. Fri/Sat from 8pm, fills up quickly. Good band. Good, mixed crowd.

2104
MAP A
C2
THE ASSEMBLY ROOMS, EDINBURGH: 0131 220 4349. George St. Municipal halls but grand, the venue for all kinds of culture (esp during the Festival), and though a long way from the draughty village hall kind of jig, they've been positively reeling to the sounds of the Robert Fish Band. Ceilidhs generally last Fri of the month. Watch local press, e.g. *The List* magazine for details and pay at door.

2105
MAP A
B3
WEST END HOTEL, EDINBURGH: 0131 225 3656. 35 Palmerston Pl. Edinburgh's Heilan' hame hotel has occasional sessions of music/singing and story-telling (more like a trad ceilidh) but no dancing. This is where to come (or phone) to find out where the others are (occasional ceilidhs held in the church hall nearby).

2106
MAP A
xA4
CALEDONIAN BREWERY, EDINBURGH: Contact: 337 1286. Slateford Rd. At time of going to press, regular ceilidhs in the Festival Hall of the brewery from 8pm-11.45pm. Bands vary but the couple of hundred heuchin' teuchin' pun-ters have a good time regardless.

SECTION 12

The Islands

THE MAGICAL ISLANDS

2107
MAP 2
B2

✓ ✓ **RAASAY:** A small car ferry (car useful, but bikes best) from Sconser betw Portree and Broadford on Skye takes you to this, the best of places. The distinctive flat top of Dun Caan presides over an island whose history and natural history is Highland Scotland in microcosm. The village with MED. INX hotel and bar (and rows of mining-type cottages) is 3km from jetty. The Outdoor Centre (01478 660226) in the big hoose (once the home of the notorious Dr No who, like others before him, allowed Raasay to go to rack and ruin) has courses galore. They'll put you up if they've got rm (mostly bunkrooms). The views from the lawn, or the viewpoint above the house, or better still from Dun Caan with the Cuillins on one side and Torridon on the other, are quite brilliant (2148/ISLAND WALKS). There's a ruined castle, a secret rhododendron-lined loch for swimming, seals, otters and eagles. Much to explore. Go quietly here. *Regular Calmac ferry from Sconser, but not Sun.*

2108
MAP 1
B2

✓ ✓ **JURA:** Small regular car ferry from Pt Askaig on Islay takes you into a different world. Jura is remote, scarcely populated and has an ineffable grandeur indifferent to the demands of tourism. Ideal for wild camping, alternatively the serviceable hotel and pub (2133/ISLAND HOTELS) in the only village (Craighouse) 15km from ferry at Feolin. Walking guides available at hotel and essential esp for the Paps, the hills that maintain such a powerful hold over the island. Easiest climb is from Three Arch Br; allow 6hrs. In May they run up all of them and back to the distillery in 3hrs. Jura House's walled grd is a hidden jewel set above the S coastline; myriad wildflowers and Australasian trees with scenic walks to the shore. The Corryvreckan whirlpool (2155/ISLAND WALKS) is another lure, but you may need a lift in a 4 wheel drive to get close enough to walk, and its impressiveness depends upon tides. Orwell's house (Barnhill; where he wrote 1984) is not open, but there are many fascinating side tracks: the wild west coast; around L Tarbert; and the long littoral betw Craighouse and Lagg. (Also 1435/BEACHES; 1702/GRAVEYARDS.) With one rd, no st lamps and over 2,000 deer the sound of silence is everything. *Western Ferries (01496 840681) regular 7 days, 5min service from Pt Askaig.*

2109
MAP 1
A1

✓ ✓ **IONA:** Needs little commendation from mortal me; and many people think there are too many visitors already. Packed with daytrippers – not so much a pilgrimage, more an invasion – but Iona still enchants, esp if you can get away to the Bay at the Back of the Ocean (1442/BEACHES) or watch the cavalcade from the hill above the Abbey. Or stay: Argyll Hotel best (01681 700334) or B&B. Abbey shop isn't bad (1938/CRAFT SHOPS). Everything about Iona is benign; even the sun shines here when it's raining on Mull. *Reg 5min Calmac service from Fionnphort till 6 or 7pm (earlier in winter).*

2110
MAP 2
B3

✓ ✓ **EIGG:** After changing hands, much to-do and cause célèbre, the islanders seized the time and Eigg is finally theirs; and of course, ours. A wildlife haven for birds and sealife; otters, eagles and seal colonies. Scot Wildlife Trust warden does weekly walks around the island. July is the 'Month of Music' with lots of ceilidhs. Refurb tearoom at pier. Licenced and evening meals. Bicycle hire 01687 482417. 2 croft houses at Cleadale near Laig bay and the Singing Sands beach; contact Sue Kirk 01687 482405 (knows loads about all aspects of island). She also offers full board accom and caters for vegn and other diets. 2,000 sheep on island. *CalMac (from Mallaig) 01687 462403 or (better, from Arisaig) Arisaig Marine 01687 450224 every day in summer. No car ferry; but motorbikes poss. Day trips to Rum and Muck.*

2111
MAP 2
B3

✓ ✓ **RUM:** The large island in the group S of Skye, off the coast at Mallaig. The Calmac ferry plies betw Canna, Eigg, Muck and Rum but not too conveniently and it's not easy to island-hop and make a decent visit (but *see below*). Rum the most wild and dramatic has an extraordinary time-warp mansion in Kinloch Castle which lets out 4 of its incredible rms to guests, but is mainly a museum (guided tours tie in with boat trips). Below stairs a hostel contrasts to the antique opulence above. Also a bistro, but it must be pre-booked (no lunch). Details: 2134/ISLAND HOTELS. Rum is run by Scottish Natural Heritage and there are fine trails, climbs, bird-watching spots. Coffee-shop at the Community Hall (open for day-trippers). 2 simple walks are marked for the 3hr visitors, but the island reveals its mysteries more slowly. The Doric temple mausoleum to George Bullough, the industrialist whose Highland fantasy the castle was, is a 12km (6hr) walk across the island to Harris Bay. Sighting the sea eagles may be one of the best things that ever happens to you. *Calmac ferry from Mallaig via Eigg (3.5hrs) or Canna at an ungodly hr. Better from Arisaig (Murdo Grant 01687 450224) Tues/Thur in summer (3hrs ashore).*

2112
MAP 1
B3

✓ **GIGHA:** Romantic small island off Kintyre coast; with classic views of its island neighbours. Easy access to mainland (20min ferry trip) contributes to an island atmos that lacks any feeling of isolation. The island remains a whole estate; with grds open at the main house (1385/GARDENS) and the hotel run by the family (2131/ISLAND HOTELS) providing comfortable surroundings, Gigha cheeses and seafood. The locals are relaxed (now) and friendly; with bike hire, B&B (CHP) and good home-cooking available courtesy of the estimable McSporran family at the post office on the ferry rd (01583 505251). Best Walk: Left after golf course (9 hole), through gate and follow track (signed Ardailly) past Mill L to Mill and shore; gr views to Jura (1-B-2). See: Double Beach, where the Queen once swam off the Royal Yacht; two crescents of sand on either side of the N end of the isthmus of Eilean Garbh (seen from rd but path poorly marked). *Calmac ferry from Tayinloan on A83, 27km S of Tarbert (Glas 165km). One an hour in summer, fewer in winter. Cars exp and unnecessary.*

2113
MAP 1
A1

✓ **ULVA:** Off W coast of Mull. A boat leaves Ulva Ferry on the B8073 26km S of Dervaig. Idyllic wee island with 5 well-marked walks incl to the curious basalt columns similar to Staffa, or by causeway to the smaller island of Gometra; plan routes at boathouse 'interpretive centre' and tearoom (with Ulva oysters). No accom. A charming Telford church has services 4 times a yr. Ulva is a perfect day away from the rat race of downtown Mull. *Continuous 5min service during day in summer. Ferryman: 01688 500226.*

2114
MAP 2
A3

✓ **ERISKAY:** Made famous by the sinking nearby of the SS *Politician* in 1941 and the salvaging of its cargo of whisky, immortalised by Compton Mackenzie in *Whisky Galore*, this Hebridean gem has all the 'idyllic island' ingredients: perfect beaches (1732/MARY, CHARLIE AND BOB), a hill to climb, a pub (called the Politician and telling the story round its walls; it sells decent pub food all day in summer), and a small, frequent ferry. There's only limited B & B and no hotel, tho plans for accom at the Politician are afoot. but camping is ok if you're discreet. Eriskay and Barra together – the pure island experience. (Also 1687/CHURCHES *and see* THE WESTERN ISLES *p.284*). *Car ferry (01878 720261) from Ludaig, S Uist (10km S Lochboisdale) 5 per day AYR. Passenger boat (01878 720238) 3/4 per day, acc to tides, also serves Barra.*

2115
MAP 2
A3

✓ **MINGULAY:** Deserted mystical island nr the southern tip of the Outer Hebrides, the subject of one of the definitive island books, *The Road to Mingulay*. Now easily reached in summer by daily trip from Castlebay, Barra with 2hr journey and 3hrs ashore (enquire at TO or Castlebay Hotel, the boat operators 01871 810223). Last inhabitants left 1912. Ruined village has the poignant air of St Kilda; similar spectacular cliffs on W side with fantastic rock formations, stacks and a huge natural arch – best viewed from boat. Mingulay was up for sale in '99, but at time of going press only birds and sheep live here.

2116
MAP 1
A2

✓ **COLONSAY:** Accessible to daytrippers in summer (with the ferry round trip); this island haven of wildlife, flowers and beaches (1426/BEACHES) deserves more than a few hrs exploration. V congenial hotel and pub (2130/ISLAND HOTELS); self-catering units nearby. Some holiday cottages, but camping discouraged. Interesting coffee/craft/shop adj to hotel. A wild 18-hole golf course. Semi-botanical grds adj to Colonsay House and fine walks, esp to Oronsay (2151/ISLAND WALKS). Lucy McNeill's home cooking and painting (incl t-shirts) activities available. at 'The Barn'. *Calmac from Oban (or Islay) Mon, Wed, Fri. Crossing takes just over 2hrs.*

2117
MAP 1
B1

LISMORE: Sail from Oban (car ferry) or better from Pt Appin 5km off main A828 the Oban-Ft William rd, 32km N Oban and where there's a seafood bar/restau/hotel (1257/SEAFOOD RESTAUS), to sit and wait. A rd goes down the centre of the island, but there are many hill and coastal walks and even the nr end round Pt Ramsay feels away from it all. History, natural history and air. Bike hire on island from Mary McDougal 01631 760213 who will deliver to ferry. Tearoom (not always open) 3km S of ferry, a pleasant stroll. *Calmac service from Oban, 4 or 5 times a day (not Sun). From Pt Appin (32km N of Oban) several per day. 5mins. Last back 8.15pm 9.30 high season, but check (6.15pm winter).*

CALMAC: 0990 650000

THE BEST ISLAND HOTELS

2118
MAP 2
A2
✓✓ **THE HOUSE OVER-BY at THE THREE CHIMNEYS, SKYE:** 01470 511258. At Colbost 7km W of Dunvegan by the B884 to Glendale. Recent new build (that looks like it's been there forever) of 6 quietly luxurious and tastefully decorated rms, adj or just over-by from the Spiers' notable, almost legendary restau (2138/ISLAND RESTAUS). Separate dining rm for healthy buffet b/fast. Outside the sheep, the sea and the sky. This is where to come for the pamper yourself w/end. 6RMS JAN-DEC T/T PETS CC KIDS TOS INX

2119
MAP 2
A3
✓ **CASTLEBAY HOTEL, BARRA:** 01871 810223. Prominent position o/look bay and ferry dock. You see where you're staying long before you arrive. Exceptionally good value hotel at the centre of Barra life with nice owners who are always there. They run the boats to Eriskay and Mingulay, so they can sort out your days out. Good restau and bar meals (2159/WESTERN ISLES). Adj bar one of the best bars for crack and car culture in Scotland and with more than a dash of the Irish (1186/BLOODY GOOD PUBS).

12RMS JAN-DEC T/T PETS CC KIDS INX

2120
MAP 2
B3
✓ **KINLOCH LODGE, SKYE:** 01471 833333. S of Broadford in Sleat Peninsula, 18km Ryliakin, 55km Portree. The ancestral, but not overly imposing home of Lord and Lady Macdonald now with newly built house adj – adding 5 v well appointed rms and spacious, country drawing rm. Lady Clair is Clair Macdonald of cookery fame, so her many books for sale, cookery courses in Nov and Mar and her hand in all the wonderful things you eat (all meals in the Lodge itself). Some Lodge rms small and less exp. See 2137/RESTAUS.

10+5RMS JAN-DEC X/T XPETS KIDS TOS LOTS

2121
MAP 1
A3
✓ **PORT CHARLOTTE HOTEL, ISLAY:** 01496 850360. The Leavey family had a choice: stay in LA or refurb a hotel in Islay. The rest is (recent) history. Modern, discreet approach in this fine whitewashed village (COASTAL VILLAGES/1417), good whisky choice, and good food for a kitchen so far-flung. Tourists in summer, hardcore twitchers in winter … and us anytime.

10RMS JAN-DEC T/T PETS CC MED.EX

2122
MAP 2
B3
✓ **EILEAN IARMAIN, SKYE:** 01471 833332. Isleornsay, Sleat. 60km S of Portree. Tucked into the bay this Gaelic inn with its gr pub and quite good food provides famously comfortable base in S of the island. Dear as well as dear, but a Skye must.

12RMS + NEW SUITES JAN-DEC T/T PETS CC KIDS TOS EXP

2123
MAP 2
A2
✓ **ARDVOURLIE CASTLE, HARRIS:** 01859 502307. Just off main rd 45mins S Stornaway (16km N Tarbert). Not so much a castle, but a charming Victorian lodge meticulously restored by Derek Martin, a former professor at Imperial College and his sister Pamela. Huge bathrooms. Dinner by gaslight. Derek is an excellent chef. Everything home-made. Gradually developing grds down to loch. They've planted 7,000 trees. Reporting people and places like this gives the task of this book both a purpose and a pleasure.

4RMS APR-OCT X/X XPETS XCC KIDS TOS EXP

2124
MAP 2
A2
✓ **SCARISTA HOUSE, SOUTH HARRIS:** 01859 550238. 21km Tarbert, 78km Stornaway. On the W coast famous for its beaches and o/look one of the best (1433/BEACHES). Self-catering in separate block, but fixed menu meals in dining room o/look sea are excellent. No TVs, phones, but many books. The golf course over the rd is exquisite. Hotel for sale at time of going to press. Phone first. 5RMS MAY-SEPT X/X PETS CC KIDS TOS EXP

2125
MAP 1
B1
✓ **WESTERN ISLES HOTEL, TOBERMORY, MULL:** 01688 302012. Victorian edifice more reminiscent of a stn hotel in town – till you see the view from your bedrm. Great atmos, individual rms (rates vary) and lounges. Refurb conservatory also looks over the harbour and bay. This hotel is the epitome of grand island hospitality. 26RMS JAN-DEC T/T PETS CC KIDS TOS MED.EXP

2126
MAP 1
C3
✓ **KILMICHAEL, BRODICK, ARRAN:** 01770 302219. On main rd to castle/Corrie, take left at bend by golf course and you're in the country. 3km down track is this delightful small country-house hotel with v individual rms and many ornaments. Good bookcase, nice Japanese items, best hotel on the island. And the most trad-classic cuisine.

6RMS JAN-DEC T/T PETS CC KIDS TOS EXP

2127 **KILLIECHRONAN HOUSE, MULL:** 01680 300403. 6km from Salen on B8035
MAP 1 off main A849 Craigmore – Tobermory Rd. About 22km Tobermory (the
B1 nightlife). Comfortable, relaxing Victorian lodge in large estate in the middle
of Mull. Prob the best dinner on the island. Friendly service.

6RMS APR-OCT T/X PETS CC KIDS TOS EXP

2128 **CALGARY FARMHOUSE, MULL:** 01688 400256. 7kms S of Dervany (30 mins
MAP 1 Tobermory) nr beautiful Calgary Beach. Roadside bistro/restau (2143/ISLAND
A1 RESTAUS) with rms and gallery/coffee shop. All basic and v sympatico. Matthew
makes furniture. Family-friendly. 2 new lofts above gallery.

9RMS APR-OCT X/X PETS CC KIDS TOS MED.INX

2129 **BAILE-NA-CILLE, TIMSGARRY, UIG, LEWIS:** 01851 672242. 58km W of
MAP 2 Stornoway via Garynahine and Leurbost. A far-away and much-loved refuge
A1 which takes you in and restores the battered spirit. O/look sea. Easy-going;
you're one of the family and they welcome yours (1095/KIDS). Couldn't visit
this time round, but things don't change much. No smk.

9RMS MAR-OCT X/X PETS CC KIDS MED.INX

2130 **ISLE OF COLONSAY HOTEL:** 01951 200316. 400m from ferry (and they will
MAP 1 collect you) a convivial, comfortable island spot. If you sit in the bar for long
A2 enough you'll meet all the islanders. Adj 'Poirots' coffee/craft shop sells and
publishes books! Picnic boat trips to seal colony or wildflower places are
among many activities arranged. See 2116/MAGICAL ISLANDS.

11RMS JAN-DEC X/T PETS CC KIDS MED.EX

2131 **THE GIGHA HOTEL, ISLE OF GIGHA:** 01583 505254. A short walk from the
MAP 1 ferry (or they will collect you) on an island perfectly proportioned for a short
B3 visit; easy walking and cycling. Resident's lounge peaceful with dreamy views
to Kintyre. Good menu with local produce in bar or dining-rm. Island life without the remoteness. Some special break rates.

13RMS APR-OCT T/T PETS CC KIDS TOS MED.EX

2132 **VIEWFIELD HOUSE, PORTREE, SKYE:** 01478 612217. One of the first hotels
MAP 2 you come to in Portree on the rd from S (driveway opp gas stn); you need look
B2 no further. Individual, grand but comfortable, full of antiques and memorabilia, though not at all stuffy; this is also one of the best-value hotels on the
island. Log fires, communal dinner (they like you to eat in); you have the run
of a remarkable country house.   11RMS APR-OCT X/X PETS CC KIDS MED.EX

2133 **JURA HOTEL:** 01496 820243. Craighouse, 15km from Islay ferry at Feolin.
MAP 1 Serviceable, basic hotel o/look Small Isles Bay; will oblige with all
B3 walking/exploring requirements. Pub is social hub of island. Rms at front may
be small, but have the views.   18RMS JAN-DEC X/X PETS CC KIDS INX

2134 **KINLOCH CASTLE, RUM:** 01687 462037. The fantastic OTT edifice of a
MAP 2 Victorian entrepreneur George Bullough now mainly a museum, but 4 opu-
B3 lent rms are available. The bathrooms are from another world. Servant quar-
ters have hostel accom. Bistro dining by arrangement. Island has superb
wildlife. Run by Scottish Natural Heritage.

4RMS + HOSTEL JAN-DEC X/X X/PETS XCC KIDS EXP/CHP

2135 **ISLE OF BARRA HOTEL, BARRA:** 01871 810383. The other hotel in Barra once
MAP 2 owned by George Macleod who has the Castlebay. Euroblock exterior, but
A3 comfortable inside with gr setting and rms o/look fab Tangasdale Beach. Nr
Seal Bay (1437/BEACHES) and other quiet places. Bar the locals like. 3km from
town (and bike hire, 2159/WESTERN ISLES).

30RMS APR-SEPT X/T PETS CC KIDS MED.INX

2136 **FLODIGARRY, SKYE:** 01470 552203. Staffin, 32km N of Portree. A romantic
MAP 2 country house o/look the sea, with Flora Mac's cottage in the grounds. Good
B2 food, gr crack in the bar; you'll be reeling. Report: 1089/COUNTRY-HOUSE HOTELS.

20RMS JAN-DEC X/X PETS CC KIDS TOS EXP

THE BEST RESTAURANTS IN THE ISLANDS

2137
MAP 2
B3
✓ ✓ **KINLOCH LODGE, SKYE:** 01471 833333. In S on Sleat Peninsula, 55km S of Portree signed off the 'main' Sleat rd, along a long characterful track. Lord and Lady MacDonald's family home/hotel offers a taste of the high life without hauteur; a setting and setup especially appreciated by Americans and other visitors. Lady Claire's stints at the stoves are renowned, as are the cookery books that result. Dinner almost a theatrical event, (the dining-rm: lined with oils, furnished with antiques, glinting with silver). Fixed menu. Perfect cheeses but you simply must leave rm for the puds. **EXP**

2138
MAP 2
B2
✓ ✓ **THE THREE CHIMNEYS, SKYE:** 01470 511258. Colbost. 7km W Dunvegan on B884 to Glendale. Shirley and Eddie Spear's friendly and authentic island restau in a converted cottage on the edge of the best kind of nowhere. Best ingredients and local, natch! Jan-Dec. Lunch, afternoon tea, dinner LO 9pm. Cl Sun in winter. The perfect choice! **EXP**

2139
MAP 1
C3
✓ **KILMICHAEL HOTEL, ARRAN:** 01770 302219. 3km from seafront rd in Brodick, this is the place to go for dinner. Report: 2126/HOTELS. **MED**

2140
MAP 2
A1
✓ **BONAVENTURE, LEWIS:** 01851 672474. Aird Wig S of Timsgarry on B8011, about 30kms W of Stornaway via A858. This is about as far-flung as you can get and many will be the most wee westerly restau in the UK. I haven't been, but by all and many accounts it's quite brilliant. Often fully booked for dinner. Chef/prop Richard Leparoux late of the estimable La Bagatelle in Edin prepares French. Scottish food from mainly local ingreds (obviously). Nautical theme in unusual ex RAF base. Get on your yacht and if you're in Lewis, go manger. Lunch and dinner LO 9pm. Tues-Sat. Cl Nov-Mar. **MED**

2141
MAP 2
B2
HARLOSH HOUSE, SKYE: 01470 521367. Nr Dunvegan (6km S signed off A863). O/look the wide sweep of L Bracadale and distant Cuillins. Peter Elford's big rep restau with 3 AA rosettes tho' I've never quite taken to it myself. I can't feel the vibe, but others have a damned good (set) dinner (no lunch); emphasis on local seafood. **6RMS MED**

2142
MAP 2
A3
CASTLEBAY HOTEL, CASTLEBAY: 01871 810223. V decent plain cooking in informal dining-rm or bar o/look castle and bay. Scores mainly when fresh from the bay (lobster) or off the beach (cockles in garlic butter), but their sticky toffee pudding is exactly as it ought to be. Inexpensive wines. **MED**

2143
MAP 1
A1
CALGARY FARMHOUSE AND DOVECOTE RESTAU, MULL: 01688 400256. 7km from Dervaig on B8073 nr Mull's famous beach. Roadside farm setting with inexp light, piney bedrms and a bistro/wine bar restau using local produce. Relaxed, cosmo atmos. Patron also makes grd furniture! Gallery/coffee shop in summer. A quiet spot over the hill from busy wee Tobermory. **INX**

2144
MAP 2
B2
AN TUIREANN, SKYE: 01478 613306. On Struan Rd, edge of Portree (direction Uig from main rd into Portree from Sligachan). Not so much a restau, more a café-bar in an arts centre. This is where to go in Skye for interesting local and national touring exhibs and for Kate Terley's contemp mainly vegn snacks and meals. Best coffee. 10am-9pm (till 6pm Mon/Tues). Sun noon-5pm (wint hrs may vary). **INX**

2145 **LOCHBAY SEAFOOD, SKYE:** 12km N Dunvegan (2158/KYE). **INX**

2146 **CREELERS, ARRAN:** 01770 302810. Edge of Brodick (2156/ARRAN). **MED**

2147 **BUSTA HOUSE, SHETLAND:** 01806 522506. 35km N of Lerwick (2162/SHETLAND). **MED**

FANTASTIC WALKS IN THE ISLANDS

For walk codes, see p. 10.

2148 DUN CAAN, RAASAY: Still one of my favourite island walks – to the flat top of
MAP 2   a magic hill (1500/VIEWS). Take ferry (2107/MAGICAL ISLANDS), ask for route from
B2   Inverarish. Go via old iron mine; looks steep when you get over the ridge, but
it's a dawdle. And amazing.   10KM XCIRC XBIKE 2-B-2

2149 THE LOST GLEN, HARRIS: Take B887 W from Tarbert almost to the end
MAP 2   (where at Hushinish there's a good beach, maybe a sunset), but go rt before
A2   the Big House (signed Chliostair Power Stn). Park here or further in and walk
up to dam (3km from rd). Take rt track round reservoir and the left around the
upper loch. Over the brim you arrive in a wide, wild glen; an overhang 2km
ahead is said to have the steepest angle in Europe. Go quietly; if you don't see
deer and eagles here, you're making too much noise on the gneiss.
12KM RET XCIRC XBIKE 2-B-2

2150 CARSAIG, MULL: In S of island, 7km from A849 Fionnphort-Craignure rd nr
MAP 1   Pennyghael. 2 walks start at pier: going left towards Lochbuie for a spectacu-
B1   lar coastal/woodland walk past Adnunan Stack (7km); or rt towards the
imposing headland where, under the cliffs, the Nuns' Cave was a shelter for
nuns evicted from Iona during the Reformation. Nearby is a quarry whose
stone was used to build Iona Abbey and much further on (9km Carsaig), at
Malcolm's Pt, the extraordinary Carsaig Arches carved by wind and sea.
15/20KM XCIRC XBIKE 2-B-2

2151 COLONSAY: (2116/MAGICAL ISLANDS). From hotel or the quay, walk to Colonsay
MAP 1   House and its lush, overgrown intermingling of native plants and exotics
A2   (8km round trip); or to the priory on Oronsay, the smaller island. 6km to 'the
Strand' (you might get a lift with the postman) then cross at low tide, with
enough time (at least 2hrs) to walk to the ruins. Allow longer if you want to
climb the easy peak of Ben Oronsay. Tide tables at shop or hotel.
12+6KM XCIRC BIKE 1-A-2

2152 THE OLD MAN OF STORR, SKYE: The enigmatic basalt finger visible from the
MAP 2   Portree-Staffin rd (A855). Start from car park on left, 12km from Portree.
B2   There's a well-defined path through or around the clump of woodland
towards the cliffs and a steep climb up the grassy slope to the pinnacle which
towers 165ft tall. Gr views over Raasay to the mainland. Lots of space and rabbits and birds who make the most of it.   5KM XCIRC XBIKE 2-B-2

2153 THE QUIRANG, SKYE: See 1498/VIEWS for directions to start pt. The strange
MAP 2   formations have names (e.g. the Table, the Needle, the Prison) and it's possible
B2   to walk round all of them. Start of the path from the car park is easy. At the first
saddle, take the second scree slope to the Table, rather than the first. When
you get to the Needle, the path to the rt betw two giant pinnacles is the easiest of the 3 options. From the top you can see the Hebrides. This place is
supernatural; whole parties of school girls could disappear here. So be careful.   6KM XCIRC XBIKE 2-B-2

2154 HOY, ORKNEY: There are innumerable walks on the scattered Orkney Islands
MAP 2   and on Hoy itself; on a good day you can get round the north part of the
island and see some of the most dramatic coastal scenery anywhere. A passenger ferry leaves Stromness 2 or 3 times a day and takes 30mins. Make
tracks N or S from jnct nr pier and use free Hoy brochure from TO so as not to
miss the landmarks, the bird sanctuaries and the Old Man himself.
20/25KM CIRC MTBIKE 2-B-2

2155 CORRYVRECKAN, JURA: The whirlpool in the Gulf of Corryvreckan is notori-
MAP 1   ous and classified by the Royal Navy as unnavigable. Betw Jura and Scarba; to
B2   see it go to far N of Jura. From end of the rd at Ardlussa (25km Craighouse, the
village), there's a rough track to Lealt then a walk (a local may drive you) of
12km to Kinuachdrach, then a further walk of 3km. Phenomenon best seen at
certain states of tide. Consult hotel (2133/ISLAND HOTELS) and get the walk
guide. (2108/MAGICAL ISLANDS). Alternative trip by boat; Craobh Haven boats
(01852 500664).   6/24KM XCIRC XBIKE 2-C-2

THE BEST OF ARRAN

FERRY: Ardrossan-Brodick, 55mins. 6 per day Mon-Sat, 4 on Sun. Ardrossan-Glas, train or rd via A77/A71 1.5hr. Claonaig-Lochranza, 30mins. 10 per day (summer only). *The best way to see Arran is on a bike. See foot of page.*

WHERE TO STAY

KILMICHAEL HOUSE, BRODICK: 01770 302219. 3km from the main rd through town down a lane in real country. Attention to detail and guests. Refined atmos, some nice antique touches. All rms v individual. *The* place to eat on Arran, but book (2126/ISLAND HOTELS).

6RMS JAN-DEC T/T XPETS CC KIDS TOS MED.EX

AUCHRANNIE HOUSE, BRODICK: 01770 302234. Old house enlarged but not altogether enhanced by mod cons. Some rms do look into 'the country'. Good pool, gym. Arran's other up-market hotel; conservatory restau (two AA rosettes) and busy with bar meals. Time-share city in grounds.

28RMS JAN-DEC T/T XPETS CC KIDS TOS MED.EX

GRANGE HOUSE, WHITING BAY: 01770 700263. Shore rd, the esplanade. Among many other hots, this one stands out. Well and tastefully appointed. No restau, but a relaxing stay. No smk. In Michelin.

7RMS APR-OCT X/T XPETS CC KIDS MED.INX

CORRIE HOTEL: 01770 810273. Cheap, cheerful sea- and roadside hotel in cosy Corrie. Good crack in bar. Seaview best.

18RMS APR-OCT X/X CC PETS KIDS INX

S.Y. HOSTELS: at Lochranza (01770 830631) and Whiting Bay (01770 700339). Both busy Grade 2s in picturesque areas (Mar-Oct), 25 and 15km from Brodick.

CAMPING AND CARAVAN PARKS: at Glen Rosa (01770 302380) 4km Brodick; Lamlash (01770 600251), Lochranza (01770 830273). And Glen Rosa has idyllic river side camping.

WHERE TO EAT

CREELERS, BRODICK: 01770 302810. Widely commended seafood restau 2km from Brodick on castle/Corrie rd. Cheerful, consistently good. They catch and smoke their own. They're thinking of selling up (autumn '99) so might be there in 2000, might not … (131/SEAFOOD RESTAUS.) MED

CARRAIG MHOR, LAMLASH: 01770 600453. On front, a proper restau amongst the usual seaside fodder, and a real chef (Peter Albrich). Book. Seafood esp. Dinner only, 7-9pm. MED

BURLINGTON HOTEL, WHITING BAY: 01770 700255. Kitchen under the direction of Robin Gray who also runs an organic produce business. The sous-chefs work abroad in the winter and the food is top-notch. Björk sings in the background. Easter-Oct, dinner daily. INX

HAROLD'S: 01770 830264. At the Distillery Visitor Centre, Lochranza. Good light menu in light even clinical rm with running water accompaniment. Phone for times. INX

BRODICK BAR: Best pub food in Brodick? Yes. Bar snacks, then turns into more of a bistro in the eve. Food until 10pm. Cl Sun. CHP

WINEPORT, CLADCACH: 01770 302977. Simple new bistro (summer '99) in developing 'centre' at start of Goat Fell walk. No frills, but you'll want that pasta and beer once you've finished. By the time you're reading this, there will be a microbrewery at Cladach too.

WHAT TO SEE

BRODICK CASTLE: 5km walk or cycle from Brodick. Impressive museum and grds. Tearoom. Flagship NTS property. (1598/CASTLES.) NT

GOAT FELL: 6km/5hr gr hill walk starting from the car park at Cladach nr Castle and Brodick or sea start at Corrie. Free route leaflet at TO. (1758/HILLS.)

2-A-2

GLENASHDALE FALLS: 4km, but 2hr forest walk from Glenashdale Br at Whiting Bay. Steady, easy climb, silvan setting. (1458/WATERFALLS.)   1-B-1

CORRIE: The best village 9km N Brodick. Go by bike. Good pub. (1425/COASTAL VILLAGES.)

MACHRIE MOOR STANDING STONES: Off main coast rd 7km N of Blackwater Foot. Various assemblies of Stones, all part of an ancient landscape. We lay down there.

GLEN ROSA, GLEN SANNOX: Fine glens – Rosa nr Brodick, Sannox 11km N.

1-B-2

WHAT TO DO

GOLF: Lots of it. Brodick (01770 302513); Lochranza (01770 830273); Lamlash (01770 600296); Whiting Bay (01770 700487). Corrie and Machrie (9 holes). **TENNIS/ SWIM:** Enquiries TO. **CYCLE HIRE:** Brodick 3 places along front, but esp Brodick Cycles (302460); also Whiting Bay (700382). 3-speed or mountain bikes.

TOURIST INFO: 01770 302140. **CALMAC:** 0990 650000.

THE BEST OF ISLAY AND JURA

2157
MAP 1
B3

FERRY: Kennacraig-Pt Askaig: 2hrs, Kennacraig-Pt Ellen: over 2hrs. Pt Askaig-Feolin, Jura: 5mins, frequent daily (01496 840681).

BY AIR: from Glas to Pt Ellen Airport in S of island. BA 0345 222111.

WHERE TO STAY

PORT CHARLOTTE HOTEL, PORT CHARLOTTE: 01496 850360. Restored Victorian inn and gdns on seafront of conservation village. Restful place, restful views. Good bistro style menu, the best around.

10RMS JAN-DEC T/T PETS CC KIDS MED.EX

HARBOUR INN, BOWMORE: 01496 810330. Accom may be expanding in 2000. Lovely conservatory with bay views and gr food by proprietor chef Scott Chance. Lunch and 7-9pm; must book.

4RMS JAN-DEC T/T PETS CC KIDS MED.INX

KILMENY FARM, nr BALLYGRANT: 01496 840668. De luxe home from home; antique furniture, hill views. House party atmos: scones and pancakes on arrival, sherry before dinner (shared table).

3RMS JAN-DEC X/X XPETS XCC KIDS TOS MED.INX

THE MACHRIE, PORT ELLEN: 01496 302310. 7km N on A846. Ongoing refurb not reached the chalets yet. Restau and bar meals in clubhouse atmos. Gr beach and golf. Restau in old byre; ask Elspeth about the aphrodisiac qualities of local cheddar; some self-cat chalets.

16RMS JAN-DEC T/T PETS CC KIDS MED.INX

BRIDGEND HOTEL, BRIDGEND: 01496 810212. On roadside betw Bowmore and Pt Charlotte. Some rms small. Good lounge bar.

10RMS JAN-DEC T/T PETS CC KIDS MED.EX

LOCHSIDE HOTEL, BOWMORE: 01496 810244. Probably best selection of Islay malts in the world; Alistair Birse delights in them and his 'whisky weekends'.

MED.INX

JURA HOTEL, CRAIGHOUSE: 01496 820243. The hotel for the island. Situated in front of the distillery by the bay. Front rms best.

18RMS JAN-DEC X/X PETS CC KIDS INX

CAMPING, CARAVAN SITE, HOSTEL at Kintra Farm. 01496 302051. Off main rd to Pt Ellen; take Oa rd, follow Kintra signs 7km. July-August B&B in farm-house. Grassy strand, coastal walks. **ISLAY YOUTH HOSTEL** Pt Charlotte 01496 850385.

WHERE TO EAT

HARBOUR INN, BOWMORE and **PORT CHARLOTTE HOTEL:** *see above.*

CROFT KITCHEN: Pt Charlotte. 01496 850230. Joy and Douglas Law have combined this coffee (latte, macchiato) and gift shop by day, with restau by night. March-October 10am-8.30pm. Book in season.   INX

THE OLD GRANARY: Kintra Farm (as Camping, above). Good basic menu in 'barn' setting. Walk on beach after. May-Aug 5.30-11pm daily.   CHP

BALLYGRANT INN: 01496 840277. S of Pt Askaig. Pub grub, curry a speciality. Hit the right night and you might get some live music with your pakora.

3RMS INX

WHAT TO SEE

ISLAY: THE DISTILLERIES esp Laphroaig and Lagavulin (classic settings) by Pt Ellen; tours by appointment. Bowmore has regular glossy tour; Ardbeg, open daily, good cafe (1364/WHISKY); **MUSEUM OF ISLAY, THE CREAMERY** (aka The Islay Cheese Co), **WILDLIFE INFO AND FIELD CENTRE** (1588/WILDLIFE): all at Pt Charlotte; **AMERICAN MONUMENT** (1664/MONUMENTS); **OA and LOCH GRUINART** (1570/BIRDS); **PORT CHARLOTTE** (1417/COASTAL VILLAGES); **KINTRA** (1826/COASTAL WALKS); **FINLAGGAN:** The romantic, sparse ruin on 'island' in L Finlaggan: last home of the Lords of the Isles. Off A846 5km S of Pt Askaig. Cross the fen by br or boat.

JURA: (2108/MAGICAL ISLANDS); **THE PAPS OF JURA; CORRYVRECKAN, BARN-HILL** (2155/ISLAND WALKS); **KILLCHIANAIG, KEILS** (1702/GRAVEYARDS); **LOW-LANDMAN'S BAY** (1435/BEACHES); **JURA HOUSE WALLED GARDEN.**

WHAT TO DO

GOLF at Machrie (1855/GOLF IN GREAT PLACES); **PONY-TREKKING** at Rockside Farm (01496 850231), Ballyvicar (01496 302251); **SWIMMING** at Bowmore (01496 810767); **BIKE HIRE:** Polly Taylor (01496 850488), **MARINE CHARTERS:** 01496 850436.

TOURIST INFO: 01496 810254. **CALMAC:** 0990 650000.

THE BEST OF SKYE

2158
MAP 2

THE BRIDGE: the hump (which is all it has given to a lot of the locals); unro-mantic but convenient; from Kyle. **THE FERRIES:** Mallaig-Armadale, 30mins. Tarbert (Harris)-Uig, 1hr 45mins (Calmac, as Mallaig). **THE BEST WAY TO SKYE** is Glenelg-Kylerhea, 10mins. Continuous Apr-Oct (not Suns in April) 01599 511302.

WHERE TO STAY

(See also ISLAND HOTELS, *esp The House-Over-By, p. 246).*

EILEAN IARMAIN: 01471 833332. 15km S of Broadford on A851. V Gaelic inn on bay with dreamy views, good food and gr pub no longer cheap (2122/ISLAND HOTELS).   12RMS JAN-DEC T/X PETS CC KIDS EXP

FLODIGARRY: 01470 552203. 30km N Portree on A855. Far-flung N of the island; the views exceptional. Relaxed country-house ambience; local liveli-ness in the bar. (1089/COUNTRY-HOUSE HOTELS.)
20RMS JAN-DEC X/X PETS CC KIDS TOS EXP

VIEWFIELD HOUSE, PORTREE: 01478 612217. One of the oldest island hous-es; it's been in the MacDonald family over 200yrs. Unique and antique atmos. (2132/ISLAND HOTELS.)   11RMS APR-OCT X/X PETS CC KIDS MED.EX

ROSEDALE, PORTREE: 01478 613131. Snug harbour location; some rms small but well appointed refurb and central.

18RMS JAN-DEC T/T PETS CC KIDS MED.EX

CUILLIN HILLS HOTEL, PORTREE: 01478 612003. On the edge of Portree (off rd N to Staffin) nr waters edge. Secluded mansion house hotel with nice conservatory. Decor slightly iffy (you may like leather-studded furniture and draped 4-posters) but gr views from most rms.

25RMS JAN-DEC T/T PETS CC KIDS MED.EX

SKEABOST: 01470 532202. 11km W of Portree on A850. Tranquil country house in lovely grds with 9-hole golf and salmon fishing on R Snizort. Chef Angus McNab of the McNabs. 26RMS MAR-DEC T/T PETS CC KIDS TOS MED.EX

UIG HOTEL, UIG: 01470 542205. N of island nr ferry to Hebrides; on hill side with gr views, friendly welcome tho basic.

17RMS APR-OCT T/T PETS CC KIDS MED.EX

DUNTULM CASTLE HOTEL, TROTTERNISH: 01470 552213. Adj Flodigarry (*see above*) and same owners. O/look Tulm island and Outer Hebrides. An idyllic place at a real good price; no frills or thrills.

29RMS APR-OCT X/T PETS CC KIDS CHP

TALISKER HOUSE, TALISKER: 01478 640245. Not really a hotel, but too good to leave out. Situated nr beautiful Talisker bay, this lovely family home is a retreat from Skye tours. Good hill walking and fishing in nearby lochs.

3RMS MAR-NOV X/X XPETS XCC KIDS MED.INX

S.Y. HOSTELS: At Kyleakin (biggest, nearest mainland), Armadale (interesting area in S), Broadford, Glen Brittle (v Cuillin), Uig (for N Skye, ferry to Hebrides). **INDEPENDENT HOSTELS** at Kyleakin and Staffin (1115/1114/HOSTELS) and just about everywhere else.

CAMP/CARAVAN PARKS: Glen Brittle (01470 521206). L Greshernish at Edinbane; 18km Portree (01470 582230) – gr site and facs. Uig and Staffin – ask at TO.

WHERE TO EAT

THREE CHIMNEYS: 01470 511258. 7km W of Dunvegan on B884. Superb home cooking gets even better! (2138/ISLAND RESTAUS). MED

KINLOCH LODGE: 01471 833333. 13km S Broadford off A851. Classy food in almost theatrical atmos at Lady Claire's table(s) (2137/ISLAND RESTAUS). EXP

HARLOSH HOTEL: 01470 521367. Nr Dunvegan, off A863 (5km). Peter Elford's unpretentious but highly regarded (fixed) menu. 3 AA whatsits. Apr-Oct. (2141/ISLAND RESTAUS.) MED

LOCHBAY SEAFOOD: 01470 592235. 12km N Dunvegan off A850. Small; simple fresh seafood in loch side setting, but closed Sat/Sun (1245/SEAFOOD RESTAUS). INX

AN TUIREANN CAFE: 01478 613306. Nr Portree. Coffee shop/gallery. Good food and chat in a cultural caff. (2144/ISLAND RESTAU; 1231/VEGN RESTAUS). Also **BEN TIANAVAIG** (1235/VEGN-FRIENDLY RESTAUS).

HARBOUR VIEW, PORTREE: 01478 612069. Bosville Terr on rd to Staffin and N Skye with harbour view at least from the door. Local seafood in intimate bistro dining rm (some game). Non pretentious, well-judged cooking. 7 days lunch and dinner (not Sun lunch). LO 10pm

CREELERS, BROADFORD: 01471 822281. Signed from A87 rd from Kyleakin and bridge to Portree just as you come into Broadford. Small cabin seafood restau in a housing scheme, but good local rep. 7 days in season 12-10pm.

THE OLD SCHOOL, DUNVEGAN: 01470 521421. On main rd/st in Dunvegan. Long established, serviceable bistro. Good vegn. 7 days, lunch and dinner in season. LO 9pm.

PASTA SHED, ARMADALE: no number. On the quayside at Armadale where the Mallaig ferry comes in. Simple pasta/pizza but best to get Alistair MacPhail to knock you up some super-fresh seafood. Exotic drinks like ginseng teas. 7 days in season 9am-7.30pm.

THE HAYLOFT, TORRIN nr BROADFORD: 01471 866366. 18km Broadford (rd to Elgol) by single-track rd, so it's a schlepp, but locals say always worthwhile. Chef Les Macleod presides in former steading; mainly seafood. 7 days in season. Lunch and 6-9pm, but it's a long way – phone first.

ARDVASAR HOTEL: 01471 844223. Sleat in far S near Mallaig ferry. Local choice for pub grub.   MED

THE LOWER DECK, PORTREE: 01478 613611. On harbour where Dan and Joan Corrigall buy the fish they sell locally and serve here. Taste the sea. Takeaway next door has seafood sandwiches. Apr-Oct 7 days 11am-9.30pm.
                                                                                   INX

SLIGACHAN HOTEL: Surprisingly good seafood in hotel (not pub). See also 1366/WHISKY.

WHAT TO SEE

THE CUILLINS (2179/BIG ATTRACTIONS); **RAASAY** (2107/MAGICAL ISLANDS); (2148/ISLAND WALKS); **THE QUIRANG** (1498/VIEWS); (2153/ISLAND WALKS); **OLD MAN OF STORR** (2152/ISLAND WALKS); **DUNVEGAN** (1601/CASTLES); **EAS MOR** (1460/WATERFALLS); **ELGOL** (1502/VIEWS); **SKYEBATIKS** (1935/CRAFT SHOPS); **SKYE MUSEUM OF ISLAND LIFE** (2013/MUSEUMS); **FLORA MACDONALD'S GRAVE** (1666/MONUMENTS); **SKYE SILVER, EDINBANE POTTERY** and **CARBOST CRAFT** (1931/1930/1939/CRAFT SHOPS); **FAIRY POOLS** (1515/PICNICS); **SLIGACHAN HOTEL:** (1366/WHISKY).

WHAT TO DO

GOLF at Skeabost (*previous page*) and Sconser (01478 650351); **FISHING:** ask at hotels; Skeabost, Eilean Iarmain (*previous page*) and Greshhornish House (01470 582266); **SWIMMING** at Portree Pool (01478 612655); **BIKE HIRE:** Island Cycles (01478 613121); Fair Winds Bicycle Hire (01471 822270); **RIDING:** (01470 532233).

CEILIDHS: In this most Highland of islands 3 hoolies are worth mentioning, all welcoming to visitors; **SKYE SCENE CEILIDH, TIGH NA SCIRE, PORTREE** (enquire TO). Mon and Wed in season and Tues (July-Sept). Touristy, but charming. **CEOL IS CNAC** at the **AROS CENTRE** S of Portree. Most Thur/Fri in season (01478 613750) Touristy but authentic. **FLODIGARRY COUNTRY-HOUSE HOTEL:** 32km N Portree. V north, v Staffin and the stuff of a damned good shindig. Every Sat, plus other nights. Backpackers from adj hostel (1114/HOSTELS), locals and hotel guests happily get down. Till 11.30pm-ish.

TOURIST INFO: 01478 612137. **CALMAC:** 0990 650000.

THE BEST OF THE WESTERN ISLES

2159
MAP 2

FERRIES: Ullapool-Stornoway, 2hrs 30mins, (not Sun). Oban/Mallaig-Lochboisdale, S Uist and Castlebay, Barra; 5hrs. Uig on Skye-Tarbert, Harris (not Sun) or Lochmaddy, N Uist 1hr 45mins. Also Leverburgh, Harris-Otternish, S Uist Check Calmac. Local ferry: Ludag, S Uist-Eoligarry, Barra. check local TOs.

BY AIR: BA 3 times daily (2 Sat; not Sun). Inverness/Glas. Local 01851 702340. BA Otter to Barra/Benbecula from Glas (1 a day). Linkline 0345 222111.

WHERE TO STAY

ARDVOURLIE CASTLE, N HARRIS: 01859 502307. 14km N of Tarbert on shore of L Seaforth in hills of N Harris. Victorian hunting lodge. Fab (2123/ISLAND HOTELS).

SCARISTA HOUSE, S HARRIS: 01859 550238. 20km S of Tarbert. Nr famous but often deserted beach; celebrated retreat. Also Self-catering accom (2124/ISLAND HOTELS).

BAILE-NA-CILLE: 01859 672242. Nr Uig 50km W of Stornoway off A858. Welcoming old manse in far W. Report: 2129/ISLAND HOTELS.

CASTLEBAY HOTEL, CASTLEBAY, BARRA: 01871 810223. O/looks ferry terminal in main town. Excellent value. Good food. Brilliant bar (2119/ISLAND HOTELS; 1186/BLOODY GOOD PUBS).

ISLE OF BARRA HOTEL, BARRA: 01871 810383. Modern purpose-built hotel on gr beach 3km W of Castlebay. Seaviews are see views (2135/ISLAND HOTELS).

ROYAL HOTEL, STORNOWAY, LEWIS: 01851 702109. The best value and most central of the 3 main hotels in town. All usual comforts. Barnacle bistro and Boatshed (probably 'best' hotel dining).

26RMS JAN-DEC T/T PETS CC KIDS MED.INX

PARK GUEST HOUSE, STORNOWAY: 01851 702485. James St. Refurbished town house with surprisingly good menu and comfy rms. Superior guesthouse and a place to eat even if not staying.

9RMS JAN-DEC X/T XPETS XCC XKIDS TOS CHP

LEACHIN HOUSE, TARBERT, N HARRIS: 01859 502157. 2km N on A859. Small, Victorian family house. Personal touch in furnishings, food and your excursions. Shared dinner. A Wolesly Lodge.

2RMS JAN-DEC X/T XPETS XCC KIDS INX

LOCHBOISDALE HOTEL, LOCHBOISDALE, S UIST: 01471 822270. In last town nr tip of Uists at ferry terminal o/look bay. Mainly fishing hotel with all rods catered for. Gr local bar. Rms vary.

18RMS JAN-DEC X/T PETS CC KIDS MED.EX

POLLACHAR INN, S UIST: 01878 700215. S of Lochboisdale nr small ferry for Eriskay/Barra (2114/ISLANDS) an inn at the end of the known world. Excl value, good crack and the view/sunset across the sea to Barra. Occasional wild discos.

10RMS JAN-DEC X/X PETS CC KIDS MED.INX

HOSTELS: Simple hostels within hiking distance. 2 in Lewis, 2 in Harris, 1 each in N and S Uist (Barra pending). Excellent hostelling holiday prospect (1110/HOSTELS).

WHERE TO EAT

BONAVENTURE, AIRD UIG: 01851 672474. 30km W of Stornaway to the end of the rd (A858 then B8011). A corner of France far from home. Report 2140/ISLAND RESTAUS.

PARK GUEST HOUSE and **THE BOATSHED**, the **ROYAL HOTEL, STORNOWAY:** (*see above*). The top two in town. Park is a restau so don't be put off by guesthouse tag. V TOS (Tues-Sat). Latter a bit up-market with seafood emphasis. High teas then LO 9pm.

TIGH MEALROS, GARYNAHINE, LEWIS: 01851 621333. On A858 22km SW Stornoway. 2km S of Callanish. Unpretentious surf 'n' turf. Scallops (dived) a special. BYOB (but watch the narrow entrance when you leave). Open AYR. LO 9pm.

COPPER KETTLE, DALBEG, LEWIS: 01851 710592. 6km N of Carloway W of Stornoway. Signed off main rd down track to lily-filled lochan. Tables on terrace in summer for tea and tiny restau with excellent plain cooking. Must book dinner.

COFFEE SHOPS at **AN LANNTAIR GALLERY, STORNOWAY**, and **CALLANISH VISITOR CENTRE, LEWIS**. The latter esp good. Daytime hrs (1632/PREHISTORIC SITES).

ARDVOURLIE and **SCARISTA HOUSE, HARRIS:** (*see above*). Dinner possible for non-residents. Both a drive from Stornoway. Fixed menus. Book well in advance.

FIRST FRUITS TEAROOM, TARBERT, HARRIS: Nr TO and ferry to Uig. Home-cooking that hits the spot if a bit stodgy (you may have walked or come far for this). Good atmos. 10.30am-early evening (8pm July/Aug). Lunch only, in winter.

TOURIST INFO: (Stornoway) 01851 701818. **CALMAC:** 0990 650000.

THE BEST OF MULL

FERRY: Oban-Craignure, 40mins. Main route; 5-8 a day. Lochaline-Fishnish, 15mins. 9-15 a day. Kilchoan-Tobermory, 35mins. 7 a day (not Sun in winter).

WHERE TO STAY

WESTERN ISLES, TOBERMORY: 01688 302012. High above town, classic views over bay; real individuality, fire in foyer, gr conservatory. Good suites and restau. Report: 2125/HOTELS   26RMS JAN-DEC T/T PETS CC KIDS TOS MED.EX

TIRORAN HOUSE: 01681 705232: In S of Mull, a treat and a retreat run by the people who used to have the L Melfort Hotel and No. 20, the gr deli in Oban, so they know about hospitality and they know about food. Nr Iona.
6RMS + COTT MAR-NOV X/X XPETS CC KIDS MED.EXP

ARGYLL HOTEL, IONA: 01681 700334. 2 rms from ferry on seashore o/looking Mull on rd to abbey. Laid-back, cosy accom, cottage rms, home cooking, good vegn. (2109/ISLANDS)   17RMS APR-OCT X/X PETS CC KIDS INX

KILLIECHRONAN HOUSE: 01680 300403. Set in its own 5,000 acre estate in the wooded bay in the W of the narrowest part of the island. Intimate old lodge house; comfort in mind (2127/ISLAND HOTELS).
6RMS MAR-OCT T/X PETS CC XKIDS TOS EXP

CALGARY FARMHOUSE, CALGARY: 01688 400256. Nr Dervaig on B8073 nr Mull's famous beach. Gallery/coffee shop and good bistro/restau. Report: 2128/HOTELS   9RMS APR-OCT X/T PETS CC KIDS MED.INX

TOBERMORY HOTEL: 01688 302091. On waterfront, cheapish/cheerful. Gr location.   17RMS JAN-DEC X/X PETS CC KIDS MED.INX

DRUIMARD COUNTRY HOUSE, DERVAIG: 01688 400345. Small, country place beside Mull Little Theatre and heart of Mull village; conservatory bar, books. Bistro style dining; see the show first.
5RMS JAN-DEC T/T PETS CC KIDS MED.EX

S.Y. HOSTEL: In Tobermory main st on bay (1111/HOSTELS).

CARAVAN PARKS: At Fishnish (all facs, nr Ferry) Craignure and Fionnphort.

CAMPING: Calgary Beach, Fishnish and at Loch Na Keal shore.

WHERE TO EAT

KILLIECHRONAN HOUSE: 01680 300403. As above. 25mins Tobermory, but prob the most intimate/elegant dinner on the island. Book.   EXP

WESTERN ISLES: 01688 302012. (*See above.*) Good dining-rm, *cuisine marché*; bar meals in refurbished conservatory undoubtedly the nicest rm in town; (2125/ISLAND HOTELS.)   MED

CALGARY FARMHOUSE: 01688 400256. Dovecote Restaurant. Local produce in v atmospheric wine-bar setting, run by mellow people (2143/ISLAND RESTAUS).   INX

THE GLASS BARN: 2km Tobermory centre. Highly recommended (1290/TEA-ROOMS).

BACK BRAE, TOBERMORY: 01688 302422. Just off the front, up the Back Brae. Bar on first floor and bistro/restau up top. Prob Tobermory's best non-hotel bet for dinner. Imaginative menu esp specials. 7 days (Fri/Sat in winter) LO 9.30pm.   MED

ISLAND BAKERY, TOBERMORY: 01688 302225, Main St. Bakery-deli with excl take-away pizza by Joe Reade the son of the cheese people (**GLASS BARN** above). Bottle of wine – box of pizza – sit by the sea. 7 days LO 9pm (w/end only in wint).   CHP

THE ANCHORAGE, TOBERMORY: 01688 302313. Main St. Haven't been able to try, but good local reports. Family-owned by fishing folk, so mainly seafood. 7 days, lunch and LO 9.30pm. Winter hrs will vary.   INX

WHAT TO SEE

TOROSAY CASTLE: Walk or train (!) from Craignure. Fabulous grds and fascinating insight into an endearing family's life. Teashop. (1600/CASTLES.) **DUART CASTLE:** 5km Craignure. Seat of Clan Maclean. Impressive from a distance, good view of clan history and from battlements. Teashop. (1599/CASTLES.) **EAS FORS:** Waterfall on Dervaig to Fionnphort rd. V accessible series of cataracts tumbling into the sea (1459/WATERFALLS). **THE MISHNISH:** No mission to Mull complete without a night at the Mish (1184/BLOODY GOOD PUBS), though MacGochann's over the bay gives it a run for its money.

WHAT TO DO

Excursions to **IONA** (from Fionnphort) and **ULVA** (from Ulva Ferry) (2109/2113/MAGICAL ISLANDS); **STAFFA** (from Fionnphort or Iona) and **THE TRESH-NISH ISLES** (Ulva Ferry or Fionnphort). Marvellous trips in summer (1564/BIRDS); walks from **CARSAIG PIER** (2150/ISLAND WALKS); or up **BEN MORE** (1783/MUNROS); **CROIG** and **QUINISH** in N, nr Dervaig and **LOCHBUIE** off the A849 at Strathcoil 9km S of Craignure: these are all serene shorelines to explore. **AROS PARK** forest walk, from Tobermory, about 7km round trip. **GOLF:** Tobermory (01688 302020). Craignure (01688 302372). Both 9 holes. **FISHING:** Info: 'Tackle and Books' (01688 302336).

TOURIST INFO: 01688 302182. **CALMAC:** 0990 650000.

THE BEST OF ORKNEY

2161   **FERRY:** P&O (01224 572615) Stromness: from Aber – Tue and Sat, takes 8hrs; from Scrabster – 2/3 per day and 2 on Sun (winter: 2 daily, n/o Sun) takes 2hrs. From John O'Groats to Burwick (01955 611353), 40mins, up to 5 a day in summer.

BY AIR: BA (0345 222111) to Kirkwall: from Aber – 3 daily; from Edin – 2 daily; from Glas – 3 daily. No flights on Sun.

WHERE TO STAY

FOVERAN HOTEL, ST OLA: 01856 872389. A964 Orphir rd; 4km from Kirkwall. Scandinavian style hotel is a friendly informal place serves trad food using best local ingredients; separate vegn menu. offering gr value. Comfortable light rms; grdn o/look Scapa Flow. Good restau.

8RMS   FEB-DEC   T/T   PETS   CC   KIDS   TOS   MED.INX

AYRE HOTEL, KIRKWALL: 01856 873001. Roy and Moira Dennison have spent several years refurb their family hotel in line with TO standards; which has resulted in them having the highest grading on the island. Situated on the harbour front, the whole place is well tidy and well established. It's where to stay in Kirkwall.

33RMS   JAN-DEC   T/T   PETS   CC   KIDS   MED.EX

BARONY, BIRSAY: 01856 721327. 40km from Kirkwall. Basic accom in wild corner by loch. Brown trout fishing, walks, sea air. Cabin style 'HMS Hampshire' bar.

10RMS   APR-OCT   T/T   PETS   CC   KIDS   MED.INX

MERKISTER, HARRAY: 01856 771366. A fave with fishers and twitchers; handy for archaeological sites and just poss the Orkney hotel of choice. À la carte or table d'hôte in the conservatory o/look the loch.

13RMS   JAN-DEC   T/T   PETS   CC   KIDS   MED.EX

STROMNESS HOTEL: 01856 850298. Orkney's biggest hotel, recent refurb. Central and picturesque. We haven't stayed.

42RMS   MAR-NOV   T/T   PETS   CC   KIDS   MED.INX

OAKLEIGH HOTEL, STROMNESS: 01856 850447. Basic accom (kids free if sharing) in family hotel on cobbled st in old town. Cellar restau; good vegn dishes. Harbour out back.

6RMS   JAN-DEC   X/T   PETS   XCC   KIDS   CHP

WOODWICK HOUSE, EVIE: 01856 751330. Comfy country house and gdn, nr shore with views of islets. Managed by the Dandelion Trust charity, it's a gr retreat. Home cooking, local produce. Good value.

5RMS   APR-OCT   X/T   XCC   KIDS   MED.INX

S.Y. HOSTELS: 01856 850589. At Stromness (excellent location, Grade 2), Kirkwall (the largest), Hoy, Rackwick, Eday and the wonderful Papa Westray. **PEEDIE HOSTEL, KIRKWALL:** 01856 874500. Ayre Rd; by the sea. Private bedrm, own keys.

CAMPING/CARAVAN: At Kirkwall and Stromness (both 01856 873535).

WHERE TO EAT

THE CREEL, ST MARGARET'S HOPE: 01856 831311. On S Ronaldsay, 20km S of Kirkwall. In the wild area where seals vie with the fishermen. Excl table (2 AA rosette) though fairly exp. Many sauces over meat or fish. Clootie for pud or Orkney cheeses. Popular with the islanders. Dinner only. Seal Rescue Centre nearby. Also well-appointed 3 rms, a good choice B+B.

3RMS A GOOD CHOICE B+B   MED

FOVERAN HOTEL, ST OLA: 01856 872389. 4km Kirkwall. *As above.*   MED

HAMNAVOE, STROMNESS: 01856 850606. Leslie's Close off main st. Seafood is their speciality, but they do haggis, neeps and tatties. Apr-Sept/Oct; Tue-Sat 7pm-late.   INX

THE STRYND, KIRKWALL: 01856 871552. Up lane beside TO. New, bright sun-flower tearoom; snacks, home made cakes. Mon-Sat 10am-5pm, Sun in season.   CHP

THE COFFEE SHOP, STROMNESS: Nr the harbour office. Good toasties, black-board specials. Gets busy – fill yourself up before the ferry journey! Apr-Oct; Mon-Sat 9am-6.30pm, Sun 9am-5pm.   CHP

WHAT TO SEE

SKARA BRAE: 25km W Kirkwall. Amazingly well-preserved underground labyrinth, a 5,000-year-old village (1630/PREHISTORIC SITES).

THE OLD MAN OF HOY: on Hoy; 30min ferry 2 or 3 times a day from Stromness. 3hr walk along spectacular coast (2154/ISLAND WALKS).

STANDING STONES OF STENNESS, THE RING OF BRODGAR, MAES HOWE: Around 18km W of Kirkwall on A965. Strong vibrations (1631/PREHISTORIC SITES).

YESNABY SEA STACKS: 24km W of Kirkwall. A precarious cliff top at the end of the world (1749/SPOOKY – or spiritual – PLACES).

ITALIAN CHAPEL: 8km S of Kirkwall at first causeway. A special act of faith. (1682/CHURCHES).

SKAILL HOUSE: at Skara Brae. 17th century 'mansion' built on Pictish ceme-tery. Set up as it was in the 1950s; with Captain Cook's crockery in the dining-rm looking remarkably unused. Apr-Sep; 7 days 9.30am-6.30pm (11.30am on Sundays) or by appointment – 01856 841501. Tearoom and visitor centre and HS link with Skara.

ST MAGNUS CATHEDRAL (1682/CHURCHES); **STROMNESS** itself (1413/COASTAL VILLAGES); **PIER ART GALLERY** (2030/INTERESTING GALLERIES); **TOMB OF THE EAGLES** (1635/PREHISTORIC SITES); **MARWICK HEAD** and many of the smaller islands (1571/BIRDS); **SCAPA FLOW** (1723/BATTLEGROUNDS; 1919/DIVING); **HIGHLAND PARK** (1370/WHISKY); **PUFFINS:** (1572/BIRDS)

WHAT TO DO

GOLF: Golf courses open to public at Kirkwall and Stromness. **SWIMMING:** Pools at Kirkwall, Stromness and Hoy. **FISHING:** Permits not required, though permission needed to fish at L of Skile. **SCUBA DIVE:** PADI training, trips, guesthouse, shop at Burray (01856 731269). **BIKE HIRE:** Rousay Pier (01856 821293).

TOURIST INFO: 01856 872856 or 01856 850716.

2162 **FERRY:** P&O (01224 572615) Aber-Lerwick 14hrs (leaves 6pm arrives 8am) Mon-Fri (not Tues Jun-Aug). Also via Orkney (leaves Aber on Sat at noon and Stromness at noon on Sun; arrives 8pm; also Tue Jun-Aug).

BY AIR: BA (linkline 0345 222111, Shetland 01950 460345) from Aber (4 a day, 2 Sat, 2 Sun). From Inverness (1 a day, not w/ends). From Glas (2 a day, 1 Sat & Sun). From Edin (1 a day, not Sun). From Wick (1 a day, not Sun).

WHERE TO STAY

BURRASTOW HOUSE: 01595 809307. 40 mins from Lerwick. Most guides and locals agree this is the place to stay on Shetland. Peaceful Georgian house with views to Island of Vaila. Wonderful home-made/produced food. Full of character with food, service and rooms the best on the island.

5RMS MAR-DEC X/X PETS CC KIDS MED.EX

BUSTA HOUSE: 01806 522506. Historic country house at Brae just over 30 mins from Lerwick. This is the other place to go. High standards, gr malt selection. Service unpredictable.

20RMS JAN-DEC T/T PETS CC KIDS MED.EX

SUMBURGH HOTEL, SUMBURGH: 01950 460201. Refurbished manor house in v S of mainland 42 km from Lerwick. Next to airport and Jarlshof excavations. Sea views as far as Fair Isle (50km S). Beaches and birds! Wide and relatively cheap menu.   32RMS JAN-DEC T/T PETS CC KIDS MED.INX

KVELDRO HOTEL, LERWICK: 01595 692195. Pron 'Kel-ro'. Probably best proposition in Lerwick; o/look harbour. Reasonable standard at a price. Locals do eat here.   16RMS JAN-DEC T/T CC KIDS LOTS

SCALLOWAY HOTEL, SCALLOWAY: 01595 880444. Main St. Good accommodation but our spies say don't eat here.

24RMS JAN-DEC T/T PETS CC KIDS MED.INX

WESTINGS HOTEL, WHITENESS: 01595 840242. 12 km from Lerwick. Breathtaking views down Whiteness Voe. Excellent base for exploring. Large selection of real ales and three different menus. Campsite alongside.

6RMS JAN-DEC T/T CC KIDS MED.INX

S.Y. HOSTEL in Lerwick, Isleburgh House: 01595 692114. Beautifully refurbished and v central.

CAMPING BODS (fisherman's barns). Cheap sleep in wonderful sea-shore settings. **THE SAIL LOFT** at Voe; **GRIEVE HOUSE** at Whalsay; **WIND HOUSE LODGE** at Mid Yell; **VOE HOUSE** at Walls; **BETTY MOUAT's COTTAGE** at Dunrossness; **JOHNNIE NOTIONS** at Eashaness. Remember to take sleeping mats. Check TO for details.

CAMPING/CARAVAN: CLICKIMIN, LERWICK 01595 741000. **LEVENWICK** 01950 422207.

WHERE TO EAT

BURRASTOW HOUSE, WALLS & BUSTA HOUSE, BRAE: (see above). The best meal in the islands.

MONTY'S BISTRO and **DELI, LERWICK:** 01595 696555. Mounthooley St nr TO. Deli with takeaway and upstairs bistro. Renovated building in light Med décor. Best bet in town. Good service and quality menu. Bistro: Cl Sun/Mon. Lunch and LO 9pm.   MED

LERWICK HOTEL: 01595 692166 and the **KVELDRO HOTEL:** 01595 692195 Have pub food and fairly reliable dining-rms (the Kveldro is 'up-market' and exp).

Pub food also recommended at the following:

THE WESTINGS, WHITENESS: 01595 840745. Max's Restaurant has varied menu of Turkish and Greek dishes together with usual pub fare and plenty of vegn options. Also do takeaway. LO 9.30pm. **THE MID BRAE INN, BRAE:**32km N of Lerwick, 01806 522634. Lunch and supper till 9pm, 7 days. **HERRISLEA HOUSE, TINGWALL:**01595 840208. 7km NW of Lerwick. Lunch and supper till 9pm, 7 days. Basic, good home cooking. Also have nice acccomodation.

DA HAAF RESTAURANT, SCALLOWAY: 01595 880328. Part of the North Atlantic Fisheries College, Port Arthur. Basically a canteen but fresh Shetland seafood overlooking the harbour at reasonable prices more than makes up for the plastic trays and fluorescent lights.

SCALLOWAY FISH AND CHIP SHOP: New Rd, by the castle. Quite the freshest and best fish and chips in Shetland, (if not Scotland, some say) can also sit in.

OSLA's CAFE, LERWICK:01595 696005. Mounthooly St, just up from Monty's. Best cafe, also supper on Thurs-Sat, LO 9pm. Incredibly good value. Cosy & very child friendly. Art exhibitions on walls.

WHAT TO SEE

MOUSA BROCH and **JARLSHOF** (1634/PREHISTORIC SITES), also **CLICKIMIN** broch. During July and August, recently discovered Iron Age excavations can be viewed at Old Scatness, 5 mins from airport.

ST NINIAN'S ISLE, BIGTON:8km N of Sumburgh on W Coast. An island linked by exquisite shell-sand. Hoard of Pictish silver found in 1958 (now in Edin). Beautiful, serene spot.

SCALLOWAY: 7km W of Lerwick, a township once the ancient capital of Shetland, dominated by the atmospheric ruins of Scalloway Castle.

SHETLAND WOOLLEN COMPANY is worth a rummage.

NOUP OF NOSS, ISLE OF NOSS, off BRESSAY:8km W of Lerwick by frequent ferry and then boat (also direct from Lerwick 01595 692577), May-Aug only. Excellent.

UP HELLY AA: Festival Lerwick on the last Tuseday in Jan. Ritual with hundreds of torchbearers and much fire and firewater. Norse, northern and pagan. A wild time. Permanent exhibition at St Sunniva Street. Lerwick.

SEA RACES: The Boat Race every summer from Norway. Part of the largest North Sea international annual yacht race.

BONHOGA GALLERY & WEISDALE MILL CAFE:01595 830400.

GO -KARTING:01950 477509, and **GOLF RANGE:** at Moor Park, Gulberwick 01595 694959.

TOURIST INFO:01595 693434.

SECTION 13

Local Centres
Where to eat and stay, what to do and see

WHERE TO STAY

FAIRFIELD HOUSE: 01292 267461. Fairfield rd. 1km centre on the front. Rarely that the 'best' hotel in town is the best – this is! De luxe facs incl pool/sauna/steam, conservatory brasserie and breakfast and notable (2 AA rosettes) Fleur de Lys restau. 45RMS JAN-DEC T/T PETS CC KID EXP

NORTHPARK HOUSE: 01292 442336. 3km from centre on rd to Alloway and Burns Country Trail. Comfy Ayrshire mansion in park setting nr Belleisle (1840/GREAT GOLF). Some weddings. Good restau.

5RMS JAN-DEC T/T PETS CC KIDS MED.EX

LOCHGREEN HOUSE: 01292 313343. Monktonhall Rd, Troon 12km N on way in from Ayr. White seaside mansion nr famous golf courses of Troon (1837/GREAT GOLF). Elegant setting and décor; civilised wining and dining.

14RMS (7 IN COURTYARD) JAN-DEC T/T PETS CC KIDS EXP

SAVOY PARK: 01292 266112. 16 Racecourse Rd. Period mansion house with fab public rms. Family-run for 30yrs. See (1165/SCOTTISH HOTELS).

15RMS JAN-DEC T/T PETS CC KIDS MED.INX

PIERSLAND, TROON: 01292 314747. 12km N of Ayr (805/AYRSHIRE HOTELS).

BRIG O'DOON, ALLOWAY: 01292 442466. 5km S of Ayr Romantic, many weddings, few rms. (806/AYRSHIRE HOTELS).

KYLESTROME: 01292 262474. 11 Miller Rd. Refurb *à la mode*. Nr centre. Not a lot of character, but adequate. 12RMS JAN-DEC T/T PETS CC KIDS TOS MED.EX

OLD RACECOURSE: 01292 262873. 2 Victoria Park. On corner of Old Racecourse (arterial) Rd, 2km from centre. 'Modernised', good value. Locally rated for food incl afternoon/high teas. 8RMS JAN-DEC T/T PETS CC KIDS INX

THE RICHMOND: 01292 265153. 38 Park Circus. Best of bunch in sedate terrace nr centre. Nice folk. 6RMS JAN-DEC X/T XPETS XCC KIDS CHP

S.Y. HOSTEL: 01292 262322. Craigwiel Rd, off Racecourse Rd close to seafront, 10min walk to centre. Sleeps 86. Book ahead service (essential June, July, Aug).

CARAVAN SITES: Cragie Park nr centre. 01292 264909. 90 pitches, no tents. Good location is Heads of Ayr, 9km S on A719 rd to Dunure/Culzean 442269. Most facs at Sundrum Castle, 10km E off A70; 'holiday camp atmos', 570057.

WHERE TO EAT

Ayr is well served by the 5 places below which cover the range from seriously good food to trad Scottish caff cuisine. Look no further than:

FOUTERS: 01292 261391. 2 Academy St (807/AYRSHIRE RESTAUS). Still the best!

THE HUNNY POT: 37 Beresford Terr off centre but nr TO, Popular café/restau with exemplary home-baking and light meals. Costa coffee Mon-Sat 10am-10pm, Sun 10am-9pm.

THE STABLES: 41 Sandgate, downtown location in courtyard of shops. Coffee shop/bistro with wine bar ambience and enlightened attitude. Imaginative Scottish menu. No smk rm. Till 5pm. Cl Sun. INX

THE TUDOR RESTAURANT: 8 Beresford St (1283/TEAROOMS). Superb caff. Till 8pm.

FAIRFIELD HOUSE: 01292 267461. Fairfield rd. 1km centre on the front. Rarely that the 'best' hotel in town is the best – this is! De luxe facs incl pool/sauna/steam, conservatory brasserie and breakfast and notable (2 AA rosettes) Fleur de Lys restau.

THE REST ...

PETIT PIERRE: 01292 282087. 4 River Terr adj the Auld Brig. Rescued in the demise of the Pierre Victoire empire by 2 women on the staff and now run along the same bistro lines (with cheap lunches) Mon-Sat lunch and LO 10pm (cl Mon night). CHP

CECCHINI'S: 01292 317171. 72 Fort St (also in Troon at 72 Fort St). Excl Italian and Med restau run by the estimable Cecchini family. Mon-Sat, lunch and LO 10pm.

PIERRINO'S: 01292 269087. Alloway Pl. The other credible Italian. LO 10pm.

INX

WHAT TO SEE

CULZEAN (1593/CASTLES); **DUNURE VILLAGE** (1423/COASTAL VILLAGES) and nr (3km S on the A719) the **ELECTRIC BRAE; BURNS HERITAGE TRAIL** (1740/LITERARY PLACES); **GAILES/TROON/PRESTWICK/TURNBERRY/BELLEISLE** (see GREAT GOLF, p. 236); **MAGNUM, IRVINE** (1884/LEISURE CENTRES); **GO BANANAS** (1544/KIDS); **CLUBS** (2085/NIGHTCLUBS).

WHAT TO DO

SWIMMING: V good pool complex at S Beach Rd (01292 269793), and at Prestwick, off the road in from Ayr (01292 474015). **RIDING:** Ayrshire Equitation Centre, all standards, country setting. Book! 01292 266267. **TENNIS:** Good all-weather courts at Citadel Pl and Craigie Av near Craigie Park. Just turn up.

TOURIST OFFICE: Burn's Statue Sq. 01292 288688. Jan-Dec.

THE BEST OF DUMFRIES

2164
MAP 9

WHERE TO STAY

COMLONGON CASTLE, CLARENCEFIELD: 01387 870283. 14 km S via A75 t/off at Collin on B724. Turn rt at Clarencefield, signed for hotel and up 2 km avenue of trees to privately owned castle with hotel in adj manor house. Ownership handed-on down the family, so refreshing breeze has blown through the old place. Ghost however, still in residence. Romantic spot; popular for weddings.

12RMS MAR-DEC T/T XPETS CC KIDS EXP

CAIRNDALE: 01387 254111. Surprising spa concealed within this corporate friendly old faithful; conference centre now being added. Visiting somebodies stay here. Café is popular lunch venue for all sorts.

77RMS JAN-DEC T/T PETS CC KIDS EXP

STATION HOTEL: 01387 254316. 49 Lovers' Walk. The best all-round business/tourist hotel in town with decent upgrading of the trad stn-hotel elegance and ambience (from 1896); central and often full. 'Bistro' as well as dining-rm.

32RMS JAN-DEC T/T PETS CC KIDS MED.EX

ABBEY ARMS 01387 850489 (821/SW HOTELS). **CRIFFEL INN** 01387 850305 both in **NEW ABBEY** 12 km S of Dumfries A710. 2 gr pubs on either side of the green in this lovely wee vill where sweetheart Abbey is the main attraction (1717/ABBEYS).

4/5RMS JAN-DEC X/T PETS CC KIDS INX

EDENBANK/LAURELBANK: 2 reasonably-priced places on Laurieknowe, a main rd leading S from centre. Edenbank (01387 252759) is a small town house hotel with bar. Lauriebank (269388) more a guesthouse, privately owned, more intimate.

10/4RMS JAN-DEC/FEB-NOV T/T/X/T PETS CC/XCC KIDS INX/CHP

No SYH, Dumfries College accom: ask at TO. Caravans: **BARNSOUL:** 01387 730249. 10km W by A75. Spacious, rural site almost working farm. Gr outlook. Apr-Oct.

WHERE TO EAT

WISHARTS: 01387 259679. Mill Rd on opp riverbank from town centre and TO. Upstairs in old mill now the Robert Burns restau. Pretty much *the* restau in the SW never mind Dumfries. Waiting for food guide recognition in 2000 editions. Weird because when we went looking for it, nobody knew where it was (cross R Nith by pedestrian bridges, centre though not restau is marked).

We couldn't eat, but all reports excl. Tues-Sat lunch & dinner (lunch by appointment only in wint).   EXP

PIZZERIA IL FIUME: 01387 265154. Hidden inside Dock Park by St Michael's Br, underneath Riverside pub. Usual Italian menu but gr pizzas and cosy tratt atmos. 6-10pm 7 days.   INX

BENVENUTO: 01387 259890. 42 Eastfield Rd, off Brooms Rd – follow signs for Cresswell Maternity Hospital. Sort of surreal wooden hut setting next to owner's chippy. 5pm-late. 7 days.   INX

BRUNO'S: 01387 255757. 3 Balmoral Rd, off Annan Rd. Well-established Italian eaterie beside **BALMORAL** chippy (1271/FISH AND CHIP SHOPS). 6-10pm, Cl Tue.
                                                                                       INX

PIERRE'S: 01387 265888. 117 Queensbury St adj Tam O' Shanter Inn. Dropping Victoire from title but still safest bet for bistro food in town. 7 days. Lunch and LO 10.30pm (cl Sun even).   INX

THE OLD BANK: 01387 253499. Snacks in converted bank.

WHAT TO SEE

ROCKCLIFFE (1418/COASTAL VILLAGES); **ROCKCLIFFE TO KIPPFORD** (1830/COASTAL WALKS); **SOUTHERNESS** (1857/GOLF IN GREAT PLACES); **SWEETHEART ABBEY** (1717/ABBEYS); **CRIFFEL** (1765/HILLS); **CAERLAVEROCK** (1563/BIRDS); **CAERLAVE-ROCK CASTLE** (1611/RUINS); **ELLISLAND FARM** (1741/LITERARY PLACES). **GARDENS** (all off A75): **CASTLE KENNEDY GARDENS** 75 acres laid out around 2 acre lily pond, 2 lochs; rare species. Apr-Sep 10am-5pm. **GLENWHAN GARDENS, DUNRAGIT** enchanting 12 acre hill side, tamed and lovingly hewn into lush overflowing haven. Gr views and walks. Mar-Oct 10am-5pm. **THREAVE GARDEN, nr CASTLE DOUGLAS** for all seasons. AYR 9.30am-sunset.

WHAT TO DO

SWIMMING: Modern pool on river side nr Buccleuch St Br (01387 252908); **GOLF:** Southerness 25km S on A710 or Powfoot, 20km SW on B724 (01461 700327); **RIDING:** Barend at Sandyhills on 34km S on A710 (01387 780663).

TOURIST OFFICE: Whitesands. 01387 253862. Jan-Dec.

THE BEST OF DUNFERMLINE AND KIRKCALDY

2165 ## WHERE TO STAY

MAP 5

KEAVIL HOUSE HOTEL, CROSSFORD, DUNFERMLINE: 01383 736258. 3km W of Dunfermline on A994 towards Culross (1415/COASTAL VILLAGES) and Kincardine. Rambling mansion house in grounds within a suburban area of town, converted into modern business-type hotel with all facs incl separate leisure club (not bad pool). Best Western.

                              33RMS JAN-DEC T/T PETS CC KIDS TOS MED.EX

DAVAAR HOUSE HOTEL, DUNFERMLINE: 01383 736463. Grieve St which is a bugger to find; you'll have to ask. Georgian mansion in suburban st. Serviceable accom. Local reputation for food.

                              8RMS JAN-DEC T/T PETS CC KIDS TOS   MED.INX

STRATHEARN HOTEL, KIRKCALDY: 01592 652210. Frankly there's nowhere in Kirkcaldy you'd even recommend to your mother-in-law, the 2 'business' hotels, the Dean Park and the Parkway included. This hotel on Wishart Pl opp Ravenscraig Park on coast rd and main rd E from town, about 3km from centre may suffice. Ravenscraig is a beautiful coastal park for respite.

                              18RMS JAN-DEC T/T PETS CC KIDS INX

THE BELVEDERE, W WEMYSS, nr KIRKCALDY: 01592 654167. However, this is worth the 8km trek E of town via A955 coast rd. At beginning of neat village, a curious mixture of dereliction and conservation. Views of bay and Kirkcaldy from comfortable rms in cottages and on the seafront, all white and with red-tiled roofs. Nice pictures, decent menu.

21RMS JAN-DEC T/T PETS CC KIDS MED.INX

No hostels (SYH at Falkland is miles away, good) or campsites to recommend. Along coast from Kirkcaldy starting at Lundin Links (15km E), there are many.

WHERE TO EAT IN AND AROUND DUNFERMLINE

IL PESCATORE, LIMEKILNS: 01383 872999. 7km from town via B9156 or to Rosyth, then Charlestown. Recently refurbished favourite and the best pasta etc around. Now has 6 inexp rms above. Once we came from Edin and had my birthday do here. It's esp good for that kind of thing. 7 days, LO 11pm.   INX

BRIO: corner of Guildhall and Abbot St nr Abbot house. Noisy, trendy-ish (v ish) bar-cafe with predictable food. LO 5pm.

NOBLE CUISINE: 620555. Up-market-ish Cantonese. 7 days, LO 11pm.   INX

THE NEW VICTORIA: 724175. The 'Vic' upstairs opp City Chambers at end of the High St since 1923. 50 main courses; an institution. 7 days till 7pm (later w/ends).

WHERE TO EAT IN AND AROUND KIRKCALDY

THE OLD RECTORY, DYSART: 01592 651211. 5km E (886/FIFE RESTAUS).

LA GONDOLA: 640085. N Harbour. The best Italian with live Enzo on Suns.

FEUARS ARMS: 205025. 66 Commercial St. V good pub food west of town nr high flats. Best in town for informal meal and atmos. Lunch and dinner w/ends.

MAXIN: 01592 263406. 5 High St at the W end. The best Chinese. 7days.   INX

VALENTE'S: 01592 205774. Not sit-in, but *absolutely the best* fish, and chips of national importance (1258/FISH AND CHIPS).

WHAT TO SEE

ABBOT HOUSE, DUNFERMLINE (2004/MUSEUMS); **PITTENCRIEFF & RAVEN-SCRAIG PARKS, DUNFERMLINE** (1406/1407/TOWN PARKS) and **BEVERIDGE PARK, KIRKCALDY** (1407/TOWN PARKS); **CARNEGIE CENTRE, DUNFERMLINE** (1895/SWIMMING POOLS); **DUNFERMLINE ABBEY** (1738/MARY, CHARLIE AND BOB); **KIRKCALDY ART GALLERY** (2027/PUBLIC GALLERIES); **PILLANS, KIRK-CALDY** (1317/BAKERS); **BETTY NICOL'S** (1203/REAL ALES); **JACKIE O'S & CAE-SAR'S, KIRKCALDY** (2083/NIGHTCLUBS).

WHAT TO DO

SWIMMING/INDOOR SPORTS: *As above.* **GOLF:** Kirkcaldy is nr some of the best (see golf, p. 236). **TENNIS:** Both towns have municipal and private courts. Check TO. **DUNFERMLINE:** Abbot House, Maygate. 01383 720999. Easter-Sept.

TOURIST OFFICES

DUNFERMLINE: Abbot House, Maygate. 01383 720999. Easter-Sept.

KIRKCALDY: 19 White's Causeway. 01592 267775. Jan-Dec.

WHERE TO STAY

INVERLOCHY CASTLE: 01397 702177. 5km out on A82 Inverness rd. One of Scotland's gr hotels. Victorian elegance recently refurb and impeccable service. (938/HIGHLANDS HOTELS).   17RMS JAN-DEC T/T XPETS CC KIDS LOTS

THE MOORINGS: 01397 772797. Banavie (follow signs), 5km out on A830 Corpach/Mallaig rd. O/look the Caledonian canal by 'Neptune's Staircase'. Refurb nautical theme, piped music, ok dining-rm (1 AA rosette). Mariner's 'Wine Bar' more fried.   21RMS JAN-DEC T/T PETS CC KIDS TOS MED.INX

HIGHLAND HOTEL: 01397 702291. Union Rd. High above town (best place to be), with gr views esp when you walk out the front door to the terraced lawns. Rms basic but foyer has character. Conveyor belt to the Highlands, but you may find untrendy tackiness charming.
112RMS MAR-NOV X/T PETS CC KIDS MED.INX

ONICH HOTEL: 01855 821214. At Onich 16km S on A82. Loch side; good value (951/HIGHLANDS HOTELS).

LODGE ON THE LOCH: 01855 821237. In Onich, quite stylish peace and quiet (950/HIGHLAND HOTELS).

GLENLOY LODGE: 01397 712700. 1920s compact groud-level house beside R Loy. Tucked away in scenic location.   9RMS DEC-OCT X/X PETS XCC KIDS INX

S.Y. HOSTEL at GLEN NEVIS: 01397 702336. 5km from town by picturesque but busy Glen Nevis rd. The Ben is above. Grade 1. Fax poss. Many other hostels in area (ask at TO for list) but esp **FW BACKPACKERS:** 01397 700711, Alma Rd.

CAMPING/CARAVAN SITE, GLEN NEVIS: 01397 702191. Nr hostel. Well-run site, mainly caravans (also for rent). Many facs incl restaus and much going on.

WHERE TO EAT

INVERLOCHY (as above): 3 AA rosettes

CRANNOG: 01397 705589. On loch front. Seafood (1255/SEAFOOD RESTAUS).

THE MOORINGS: 01397 772797. 5km by A830. (*See above.*)

No 4: 01397 704222. Cameron Sq behind the TO. At last, perhaps a restaus to write home about in Ft William town. These people know their salmon and some other things about food, presentation etc so prob the poshest plate in town. À la carte and daily specials. Lunch and LO 9.30pm. Cl Sun.   MED

AN CRANN, BANAVIE: 01397 772077. 7km centre via Mallaig rd, then signed at Banavie. A local favourite, this stone barn nestles in the countryside and offers eclectic mix. V Scottish, v friendly. Easter-Oct: 12-4pm and 6-9pm, but phone first.   INX

CAFÉ BEAG, GLEN NEVIS: 01397 703601. 5km along Glen Nevis rd; past 'Braveheart' car park (!) and visitor centre. Alpine looking cabin, cosy atmos; open fires, books, games – retreat here from the rain. Bar food all day, restau even LO 9.30pm.   INX

CAFÉ CHARDON: Coffee shop upstairs at Peter Maclennan's well-kent emporium in the main st (or access via side lane). The auld alliance continues here with pastry thingies and every kind of filled roll. Mon-Sat 9-5pm.   CHP

WHAT TO SEE

Most of the good things about Ft William are outside the town, but these incl some v big items esp the Ben and the Glens (Glens Nevis as well as Coe):

GLENCOE: 30km S (1482/SCENIC ROUTES; 1794/SERIOUS WALKS; 1722/BATTLE-GROUNDS); **GLEN NEVIS** (1446/GLENS); **BEN NEVIS:** 6km E on Glen Nevis rd (1795/SERIOUS WALKS); **WEST HIGHLAND WAY** (1789/LONG WALKS); **STEALL**

FALLS, Glen Nevis (1462/WATERFALLS); **GLENCOE SKIING** (1877/SKIING); **AONACH MOR SKIING** (1876/SKIING) **MUSEUM** (2009/MUSEUMS). **NEVIS RANGE GONDOLA:** Aonach Mor (*see below*), open AYR, is a big attraction. Go up for the incredible view and the air and the Ben over there.

WHAT TO DO

GOLF: Ft William Golf Club (01397 704464). 5km towards Inverness on A82; **SWIMMING/SPORTS:** Lochaber Centre (01397 704 359). Beyond main st and Alexandra Hotel. Squash, sauna, 2 gyms, climbing wall, swimming (with flume). **TENNIS:** One court at Lochaber Centre, free of charge. **SKIING:** Aonach Mor (01397 705825). 12km via A82. Scotland's most modern ski resort (1876/SKIING). Gondola goes up in summer for the view. **BIKE HIRE:** Off-Beat Bikes (01397 704008). Main St and ski base stn.

TOURIST OFFICE: Cameron Square. 01397 703781. Jan-Dec.

THE BEST OF THE BORDER TOWNS

2167
MAP 8

Hawick and Galashiels are the largest centres in the region, but distances betw towns aren't gr. This page includes Selkirk, Melrose and Jedburgh, all within 20km. See also the best hotels and restaus in the borders, pp. 99–100.

WHERE TO STAY

ROXBURGH HOTEL, KELSO: 01573 450331 (844/BORDERS HOTELS).   LOTS

BURTS, MELROSE: 01896 822285 (846/BORDERS HOTELS).   MED.EX

WOODLANDS, GALA: 01896 754722. Windyknowe Rd off A7 in Edin direction, A72 to Peebles. Substantial mansion above town centre with elegant hall, spacious public rms and local reputation for food and service.
9RMS JAN-DEC T/T PETS CC KID MED.EX

JEDFOREST COUNTRY HOTEL, JEDBURGH: 01835 840222 (849/BORDERS HOTELS)

EDNAM HOUSE HOTEL, KELSO: 01573 224168 (850/BORDERS HOTELS)

DRYBURGH ABBEY HOTEL nr ST BOSWELLS: 01835 822261 (847/BORDERS HOTELS)

HUNDALEE HOUSE, JEDBURGH: 01835 863011. 1km S. Jedburgh off A68. Lovely 1700 manor house in 10 acre gdn. Brilliant value, gr base, views of Cheviot hills. Nr the famously old Capon Tree.
5RMS MAR-OCT X/T XPETS XCC KIDS CHP

WHITCHESTER, HAWICK: 01450 377477. On Roberton Rd off A7, 4km S of Hawick. They call it a 'Christian guesthouse' and this may be a tad Jesus-sandal for some, but it is the best-value accom in the area and the house is tastefully done. Dinner has vegn option. Non-alcoholic wines (*sic*), but you can BYOB (thank God).
7RMS FEB-DEC X/X PETS CC KIDS TOS MED.INX

GLEN HOTEL and HEATHERLIE HOTEL, SELKIRK: 01750 20259/21200. Both family-run hotels in manor houses with views over town. Well-run, dependable. Selkirk makes a good touring centre.
8/7RMS JAN-DEC T/T X/T PETS/XPETS CC KIDS INX

CROSS KEYS, KELSO: 01573 223303. Recently refurb, alternative to Roxburgh and Ednam House; it dominates the impressive square. Front rms best.
27RMS JAN-DEC T/T PETS KIDS MED.INX

S.Y. HOSTELS: V good in this area (1107/HOSTELS).

CAMP/CARAVAN PARK: at Jedwater, Camptown, 11km S Jedburgh. 01835 840 219.

WHERE TO EAT

MARMIONS, MELROSE: 01896 822245 (852/BORDERS HOTELS).

MELROSE STATION, MELROSE: 01896 822546 (854/BORDERS HOTELS).

BURTS HOTEL, MELROSE and KINGS ARMS (PUB FOOD): Local faves (846/BORDERS HOTELS).

AULD CROSS KEYS, DENHOLM: 01450 870305 (1229/PUB FOOD)

LE PROVENCALE, NEWTOWN ST BOSWELLS: 01835 823284. Monksford Rd signed as you come off the A68 Edin Rd from N. Rene & Elizabeth Duzelier have worked in the hotel trade across Europe and offer euro know-how for local enjoyment. Authentic French food and wine. Lunch and 7-9pm. Cl Sun/Mon.   INX

GREEN'S DINER, GALASHIELS: 01896 757667. 4 Green Street. Latino eaterie proclaiming to be, 'exactly like nowhere else' which it certainly is in Gala. 3 separate menus: all day, coffee, dinner offer eclectic mix and buzzing atmos. Tues 10am-5pm, Wed-Sat 10am-10pm. Cl Sun/Mon   CHP

HERGÉS BAR BISTRO, GALASHIELS: 01896 750400. 58 Island St on rd to Peebles. Wine-bar ambience, locals rate, we haven't tried. Sat night-pub only. Lunch and 6-9pm 7days.

SHISH TANDOORI, GALASHIELS: 01896 758735. 82-86 High St. Haven't tried but comes highly recommended locally. Food cooked fresh to order.   INX

WHAT TO SEE

THIRLESTANE CASTLE, LAUDER (1661/COUNTRY HOUSES); **TWEED FISHING** (*see below*); **PENIEL HEUGH** (1669/MONUMENTS); **MARY QUEEN OF SCOTS' HOUSE** (1728/MARY, CHARLIE AND BOB); **ANCRUM** (1706/GRAVEYARDS; 1528/PICNICS); **ABBEYS** (1714/JEDBURGH; 1715/DRYBURGH; 1718/MELROSE); **PRIORWOOD** (1386/GARDENS); **ABBOTSFORD** (1745/LITERARY PLACES); **EILDON HILLS** (1776/HILL WALKS); **RUBERSLAW** (1768/HILLS); **SCOTT'S VIEW/IRVINE'S VIEW** (1506/1507/VIEWS); **LILLIARD'S EDGE** (1724/BATTLEGROUNDS); **LOCHCARRON** and **CHAS WHILLANS** (1960/1961/WOOLLIES); **TEDDY MELROSE** (1548/KIDS).

WHAT TO DO

SWIMMING: V good leisure facs both in and around Hawick and Galashiels. Galashiels Pool (01896 752154) at Livingston Pl up the hill from the one-way main st is excellent (1898/SWIMMING POOLS). Hawick's Teviotdale Leisure Centre (01450 374440) has squash courts, a gym (Universal) and a pool with fun stuff as well as length swimming. Jedburgh and Selkirk also have pools. GOLF: Good courses at Minto, nr Denholm (01450 870220) (18); Selkirk (01750 20621) (9); Melrose (01896 822855) (9); Hawick (01450 372293) (18); Jedburgh (01835 863587) (9). All picturesque, in fair condition, available to visitors. RIDING: Cowdenknowes, Earlston (01896 848020). Kailzie Stables nr Peebles. TENNIS: Galshiels, Abbotsford Terr; Hawick, Wilton Lodge Park; also Melrose. CYCLE HIRE: Galashiels, 58 High St (01896 757587); Hawick, 45 N Br St (01450 373352); Peebles, 3 High St (01721 720844). FISHING: There can be last-minute vacancies even on the famous Tweed. Tweed Foundation (01896 848271); J Leeming's independent agency (01573 470280). Tackle: Angler's Choice, Melrose (01896 823070); Tweedside Tackle, Kelso (01573 225306).

TOURIST INFORMATION:

HAWICK: Common Ground. 01450 372547. Apr-Oct.

GALASHIELS: 01896 755551. Apr-Oct.

JEDBURGH: Murray's Green. 01835 863435. Jan-Dec.

THE BEST OF INVERNESS

WHERE TO STAY – THE BEST

CULLODEN HOUSE: 01463 790461 (940/HIGHLANDS HOTELS).   LOTS

DUNAIN PARK HOTEL: 01463 230512 (944/HIGHLANDS HOTELS).   EXP

BUNCHREW HOUSE: 01463 234917 (947/HIGHLANDS HOTELS).   LOTS

KINGSMILLS HOTEL: 01463 237166. Culcabock Rd. In suburban area S of centre nr A9. Modern, v well-appointed hotel with high standards; excellent bedrms. Gets v busy in high season.   84RMS JAN-DEC T/T PETS CC KIDS EXP

WHERE TO STAY – THE BEST OF THE REST

STATION HOTEL: 01463 231926. Academy St. Works as a v central, bit old-fashioned hotel/meeting place. Midst of one-way system; train is best arrival. Good foyer; grand staircase leading to variable rms. Gloomy dining-rm. The trad Highlander hotel.   70RMS JAN-DEC T/T PETS CC KIDS EXP

COLUMBA: 01463 231391. Ness Walk nr main br, o/looks river and castle – central, convenient (though parking tricky). Reasonable facs. 'Scottish Entertainment' and bus parties.   86RMS JAN-DEC T/T PETS CC KIDS MED.EX

ARDMUIR/BRAENESS/FELSTEAD: 01463 231151/712266/231634. 3 hotels on Ness Bank, along the river opp Eden Court and v central. Felstead more a guesthouse and cheaper. All family-run, basic. Many other hotels in this st. These ones are decent value.   11/7RMS VARIES X/T PETS CC KIDS MED.INX

3 GOOD HOSTELS. S Y HOSTEL: 01463 231771. Victoria Drive; Large official hostel. More funky are the **STUDENT HOSTEL**: 236556. 8 Culduthel Rd, and 3 doors down **BAZPACKERS** 717663.

CAMPING AND CARAVAN PARKS: Most central (2km) at **BUGHT PARK**, 01463 236920. Well-equipped and large-scale municipal site on flat river meadow. Many facs. App via A82 Ft William rd. More picturesque at **SCANIPORT**, 01463 751351. 8km SW on B862, the scenic route to Ft Augustus. Rural.

WHERE TO EAT

DUNAIN PARK HOTEL: As above. 3 adj elegant dining-rms; drawing rm for avant/après. The country-house hotel on the L Ness edge of town where the good burghers come for Ann Nicholl's honest-to-goodness cookery and wish they'd left more rm for the puds. Excl wines; and malt list.   MED

CAFÉ ONE: 01463 226200. 10 Castle St nr the Castle. On site of many previous attempts incl 2 different Pierre Victoires, at last a restau that really works. Contemporary décor and cuisine in hands of good team. Reasonably priced for this standard of food and service.   MED

LA RIVIERA at the **GLEN MORISTON HOTEL:** 01463 223777. Ness Bank. On rd along river. Comfortable elegant dining-rm with effective Italian menu well known as a place to eat in this town (MED). Same owners run:

RIVA: 01463 237377. 4 Ness Walk by the main br. Central, immediately popular (opened 1997) Italian café/restau open all day, every day (Suns from 2pm) for coffee and ice cream (Capaldi's 1335/ICE CREAM) and full pasta/pizza range in Pazzo's adj.   INX

STEAKHOUSE No 10: 01463 714884. 10 Bank St on busy river side st. Much meat, but some crêpes too in small riverside howf. Mon-Sat and LO 9pm, Sun 6-9pm.   INX

BOATH HOUSE, AULDEARN: 01667 454896. Just off A96 3km E of Nairn. Sympathetically converted building about 30mins from Inverness. Chef Charlie Lockely accumulating AA rosettes. (941/HIGHLAND HOTELS)   MED

SHAPLA: 01463 241919. 2 Castle rd on town side of br from Riva above. Indian restau with the usual menu. Roadside rm and better upstairs lounge with river views. Open late (LO 11.30pm). Locals have always rated **RAJA**: 237190, behind the post office in town.   INX

THE LEMON TREE: 18 Ingle St, pedestrianised town centre st and other entrance from behind M&S. Unlikely high st location for unpretentious family-run café with home-bakes, own burgers, etc. Mon-Sat 9am-5pm. CHP

CASTLE RESTAURANT: Castle St. Excellent greasy spoon (1280/CAFÉS).

WHAT TO SEE

THE NESS ISLANDS: R Ness islands joined by iron br to both banks. A fine stroll of an evening. App via Bught Park or Ness Walk (by Eden Court) and from Dores Rd. **ART.TM**, the town's new art gallery (BUY ART/2037). **BALNAIN HOUSE:** Centre for the Study and Appreciation of Scottish Trad Music on Huntly St, the riverside. Café and shop, library and chat (Gaelic, if you want). 10am-5pm. **LEAKEY'S BOOKSHOP:** Church St, Scotland's biggest 2nd hand bookshop in the old Gaelic kirk with good cafe. Mon-Sat 10am-5.30pm. **CULLODEN** (1720/BATTLEGROUNDS); **CLAVA CAIRNS** (1633/PREHISTORIC SITES); **LOCH NESS** (2181/BIG ATTRACTIONS); **THE PHOENIX** (1187/BLOODY GOOD PUBS); **EDEN COURT THEATRE** (2090/THEATRES); **SOUTH BANK, LOCH NESS** (1492/SCENIC ROUTES); **GLEN AFFRIC** (1444/GLENS); **AQUADOME** (1882/LEISURE CENTRES).

WHAT TO DO

GOLF: Inverness Golf Club (01463 239882); Torvean (on A82) (01463 711434) Championship course at Nairn (01667 452787), 25km E (1847/GREAT GOLF). **SWIMMING:** Aquadome (01463 667500) (1882/LEISURE CENTRES). **RIDING:** Highland Riding Centre (01456 450220), Drumnadrochit along L Ness. **TENNIS:** Inverness Tennis and Squash Club. Bishop's Rd (01463 230751). Also Municipal Courts at Bellfield Park (just turn up, 7 days). **CYCLE HIRE:** Gt Glen Cycle Hire 01397 703015. Also at Bazpackers Hostel (*above*) 717663.

TOURIST OFFICE: Castle Wynd. 01463 234353. Jan-Dec.

THE BEST OF OBAN

2169
MAP 1

WHERE TO STAY

MANOR HOUSE: 01631 562087. Gallanach Rd. On S coast rd out of town towards Kerrera ferry, o/look bay. Quiet elegance in contemp style, and a restau that serves (in an intimate dining-rm) probably the best meal in town. Gets a little rushed at lunchtime, dinner better. If your timing's rt, you might catch the local lighthouse engineers taking off on a sortie in their tiny chopper from the pad o/side. 11RMS JAN-DEC T/T PETS CC KIDS TOS EXP

BARRIEMORE HOTEL: 01631 566356. Corran Esplanade. The last in a long sweep of hotels to N of centre and, though I'd have to admit that I haven't tried all of them, I'd say this was streets above the rest. Nice people in residence, gr view of the sea. B&B only (796/ARGYLL HOTELS).
11RMS MAR-NOV X/T PETS CC KIDS INX

GLENBURNIE HOTEL: 01631 562089. Corran Esplanade. And this one is also good. Run by the inimitable Strachan family, the sherry is free and the guests just keep coming back. We will too. 14 RMS MAR-OCT X/T PETS CC KIDS MED.EX

CALEDONIAN HOTEL: 01631 563133. Station Sq. There are several Victorian/municipal gothic edifices in Oban from the days when, as now, there were many visitors. Hard to know what to recommend: rms vary enormously, as does service etc. Here at least you are definitely at the centre of things – the pt. Try to get a rm at the front; and eat out. 70RMS JAN-DEC T/T PETS CC KIDS MED.EX

S.Y. HOSTEL: 01631 562025. On Esplanade (i.e. on the front). Grade 1.

CAMPING/CARAVAN SITES: Ganavan Sands, along coast rd (3km); grassy site adj to beach/leisure area (not quiet, plenty to do). 80 pitches, no tents. 016315 66479.

WHERE TO EAT

AIRDS HOTEL: 01631 730236. Pt Appin. 40km N by A828. A long way to go for dinner, but if you're in the area you just might want to eat at one of the best restaus in Scotland (789/ARGYLL HOTELS). EXP

THE KITCHEN GARDEN: 01631 566332. 14 George St. Deli-cafe that does v good candlelit dinners in the evening (MED). Now the best stand-alone restau in town. Open daily until 9.45pm in season; because it's new, they're not sure about winter opening yet.

THE WATERFRONT AT THE PIER: 01631 563110. Good seafood right by the train station. Open L and LO 9pm ish, Mar-Dec MED

THE MANOR HOUSE: (*see above*). The best hotel dining-rm in town. Creative sauces on fresh seafood and other good things. Booking essential. EXP

JULIE'S COFFEE HOUSE: 01631 565952. 33 Stafford St. Only 6 tables, so it's worth booking for dinner. Just three or four choices for each course, but what there is comes freshly prepared. INX

THE BOXTREE: 01631 563542. 108 George St. Friendly little bistro in the middle of town. Better than you'd expect on this or any other main st. All day. inx

THE STUDIO: 01631 562030. Craigard Rd off main st at Balmoral Hotel. Up the hill to find this here forever, candle-lit restau. Surprising menu. Often have to book. Apr-Oct, 5-10pm. IXP

THE BARN BAR: 01631 564618. 6km S at Lerags nr Foxholes Hotel. Popular out-of-town run for good pub food in bistro atmos. Kids welcome. Attached to chalet park but not unpleasant situation. Good 7 days, 12noon-9pm (Closed Jan). INX

WHAT TO SEE

DUNOLLIE CASTLE: On rd to Ganavan (1620/RUINS); **GLEN LONAN:** Gr wee glen starting 8km out of town (1451/GLENS); **SEALIFE CENTRE:** 16km N on A28 (1558/KIDS); **RARE BREEDS FARM:** 4km S from Argyll Sq (1559/KIDS); **KRANENBURG & FOWLER FINE ARTS; OBAN INN:** (*see* WHISKY, *p. 167*); **McCAIG'S TOWER or FOLLY:** You can't miss it, dominating the skyline. A circular granite coliseum. Superb views of the bay. Many ways up, but a good place to start is via Stevenson St, opp Cally Hotel. Free, Open AYR (1673/MONUMENTS). **KERRERA:** The island in the Sound reached by regular ferry from coast rd to Gallanach (4km town). Ferries at set times, but several per day – check TO. A fine wee island for walking, but pack your lunch. **LISMORE:** The other, larger island (2117/MAGICAL ISLANDS). Ferry from Oban (Calmac) or Pt Appin (passengers only). **DUNSTAFFNAGE CASTLE:** Signed and visible off A85 betw Oban and Connel (7km). 13th-century. V early type of castle, more of a ft, really. Unoccupied, except for the odd Clan McDougall spectre rattling around in the dungeons. Impressive setting and in good repair. Chapel in the woods **ARDCHATTAN:** 20km N via Connel. Along N shore of L Etive, a place to wander amongst ruins and grds. Tearoom. If you're along that way, go to the end of the rd at Bonawe where the famous granite that cobbled the world was (and still is) quarried. Bonawe Ironworks is open as a museum.

WHAT TO DO

GOLF: Glencruitten (01631 562868) (1859/GOLF IN GREAT PLACES); **SWIMMING:** Oban swimming pool at Dalriach Rd (01631 566800); **PONY-TREKKING:** Achnalarig Farm, Glencruitten (01631 562745); **WINDSURFING:** Linnhe Marine (01631 730227), 32km N via A828. Incl waterski and sailing (1903/WATER SPORTS); **FISHING:** Plenty on lochs and R Awe and Avich – check TO; **BIKE HIRE:** Oban Cycles (01631 566996).

TOURIST INFO: Argyll Sq. 01631 563122. Jan-Dec.

WHERE TO STAY

BALLATHIE HOUSE, KINCLAVEN: 01250 883268. 20km N of Perth via Blairgowrie rd A93/left follow signs after 16km just before the famous beech hedge; or A9 and 4km N, take B9000 through Stanley. Former baronial hunting lodge beside the R Tay. Relaxed and informal atmos in definitive country house. Kevin MacGillivray's award-winning food. Fishing by arrangement with Estate office. Separate lodge at good rate. Nice people above and below stairs.

38RMS JAN-DEC T/T PETS CC KIDS TOS LOTS

HUNTINGTOWER HOTEL: 01738 583771. Crieff rd (1km off A85, 3km W of ring route A9 signed). Elegant, modernised mansion house o/side town. Good grds with spectacular copper beech. Subdued, panelled restau with decent menu (esp lunch) and wine list. Good service.

34RMS JAN-DEC T/T PETS CC KIDS TOS MED.EX

ROYAL GEORGE: 01738 624455. Tay St by the Perth Br over the Tay to the A93 rd to Blairgowrie and relatively close to Dundee rd and motorway system. Br is illuminated at night. Georgian proportions and elegance. Queen Victoria came by in 1842 now popular with farmers.

39RMS JAN-DEC T/T PETS CC KIDS MED.EX

SUNBANK HOUSE: 01738 624882. 50 Dundee Rd. On main rd out of town over river but removed from traffic and with good views of town and Tay. Inexp 'de luxe' small hotel, feels like home. Nr Branklyn Gdns/Kinnoull Hill.

9RMS JAN-DEC T/T XPETS CC KIDS INX

S.Y. HOSTEL: 01738 623658. 107 Glasgow Rd in suburban area off main rd 1km centre. Grade 1 hostel, mostly larger dorms. No café.

CAMPING AND CARAVAN PARKS: SCONE RACECOURSE, 01738 552323. 4km NE of centre via A93 to Blairgowrie and left after Scone Palace. Grassy, flat site set amongst whispering pines. 150 pitches. Also **CLEEVE**, 01738 639521, off Glasgow Rd near ring route (2km) and 3km from centre. Narrow tree-ringed site nr rd. Sheltered, but some traffic noise. 100 pitches.

WHERE TO EAT

LET'S EAT: 01738 643377. 77 Kinnoull St. The place to eat (905/PERTHSHIRE RESTAUS) and now, **LET'S EAT AGAIN:** 633771 (905/PERTHSHIRE EATS)

KERACHERS: 01738 449777. Corner of South St and Scott St. Seafood corner restau run by notable local supplier. Downstairs lounge and upstairs bistro style dining. Excl ingredients and service. Cl Sun. Lunch and LO 9.30pm.

INX(BAR)/MED

EXCEED: 01738 621189. 65 S Methven St. Large, woody brasserie restau with varied menu, blackboard specials best. Cl Tues. Lunch and LO 10pm INX

1774: 01738 451774. 10 N Port. Fairly authentic French bistro. Intimate, discreet where you might make off with a farmer's wife. Cl Sun/Mon. Lunch and LO 9pm. MED

LOUIS': 01738 447999. 181 South St. Big airy restau best when it's bustling. Mainly Italian, but some variations. 7 days till 10pm.

KRUNGTHAI: 01738 633090. 161 South St. Another of the Thai places that have bobbed up everywhere like a prawn in a tom yum soup. Authentic fare offered by Thai owner/chef has earned good local rep. Lunch and till 11pm, 7 days (11.30pm w/ends). INX

PACO'S: 01738 622290. 16 St John's Place in 'cafe quarter'. Surprisingly cosmo feel to airy café in the centre of one of Scotland's most conservative towns. More Mex than most. CHP/MED

BIANCO'S: 01738 446698. St John's Pl by the church and as above, in the emerging cafe quarter. Outside tables in summer. Down the line Italian, but bought in puds. Mon-Sat, all day till 10pm. INX

THAT BAR: 01738 634523. 147 South St. Perthshire trendy, designery bar (with pool table & big TV) but proper food upstairs. INX

MARCELLO'S: 143 South St. Pizza pasta pitstop. Takeaway only. Noon-11pm (midnight Fri/Sat). Good looking guys knead the dough. INX

BETTY'S: 67 George St. Old-world parlour tearoom with gr home-baking, dish of the day and delicate soups. Opp art gallery. Licensed. 10am-5.30pm. Cl Sun.

LEMON TREE: Mill St. Innovative veggie restau above good gift shop. INX

ALMONDBANK INN: 01738 583242. Main St, Almondbank. Old pub looking down to R Almond in village 4km along Crieff rd W of ring route and A9. Pub lunches/suppers (6.30-8.30pm). Popular with locals. Book w/ends. INX

DELI-CIOUS: 46 Methven St. Small, cheery take-away and sit-in coffee shop. Some hot dishes. 7.30am – evening, Suns 11am-7pm. INX

HOLDGATES FISH TEAS: South St. Report: (1266/FISH 'N' CHIPS). A classic! INX

WHAT TO SEE

KINNOULL HILL (1771/HILLS); **FERGUSSON GALLERY** (2026/PUBLIC GALLERIES); **GLENDOICK** (1981/GARDEN CENTRES).

CHERRYBANK GARDENS/BRANKLYN GARDENS: Cherrybank is off Glasgow Rd, 18 acres of formal grds around the offices of United Distillers, notable esp for heathers. Open May-Oct 9am-5pm. Branklyn is signed off Dundee Rd beyond Queen's Br; park and walk 100m. A tightly packed cornucopia of typical grd flowers and shrubs. Open 7 days 9.30am-dusk.

PERTH THEATRE: 01738 621031. Established 1935 and Scotland's most successful repertory theatre (Ewan MacGregor got his first break here). Bar/coffee bar and restau. Essential all-round centre even for non-theatregoers.

WHAT TO DO

SWIMMING: Excellent large leisure centre with flumes pool and 'training' pool for lengths. Part of it is outdoors. Best app via Glasgow Rd (01738 630535) (1881/LEISURE CENTRES). **SPORTS CENTRE:** The Gannochy or 'Bells' Complex for multigym (Universal), squash (5 courts), badminton etc. Hay St off Barrack St (01738 622301). **GOLF:** Interesting course on Moncreiffe Island in the middle of the Tay (01738 625170). Good course at Murrayshall, New Scone. Excellent course at Blairgowrie (01250 872622) (1858/GOLF IN GREAT PLACES).

TOURIST INFO: 45 High St. 01738 638353. Jan-Dec.

THE BEST OF STIRLING

WHERE TO STAY

2171
MAP 6

THE GEAN HOUSE, ALLOA: 01259 219275. 12km E (831/CENTRAL HOTELS).

STIRLING HIGHLAND: 01786 475444 (832/CENTRAL HOTELS).

BLAIRLOGIE HOUSE: 01259 761441. 7km E on A91 (833/CENTRAL HOTELS).

PARK LODGE: 01786 474862. 32 Park Terrace off main Kings Park Rd, 500m from centre. Rather posh hotel in town house nr the park and golf course. Objets and lawns. Dinner taken (and recommended) at the Heritage, below. Mrs Pillinger's B&B at number 35 also looks good.

10RMS JAN-DEC T/T PETS CC KIDS MED.EX

THE HERITAGE: 01786 473660. 16 Allen Park, a quiet suburban st v close to centre, TO and main Bannockburn Rd. Owned by same folk as above; cheery French chef. Georgian town house. 4RMS JAN-DEC T/T PETS CC KIDS MED.INX

PORTCULLIS HOTEL: 01786 472290. Castle Wynd, which is no more than a cannonball's throw from the castle itself and one of the best locations in town. Pub and pub food (with noise) below; upstairs only 4 rms, but 3 have brilliant views of Castle/graveyard/town and plain.

5RMS JAN-DEC X/T PETS CC KIDS MED.INX

STIRLING MANAGEMENT CENTRE: 01786 451666. Not strictly speaking a hotel, but is as good as. Fully serviced rms on the univ campus (7km from centre in Br of Allan). Usually not full. Sports/entertainment facs nearby. Not so cheap anymore for distant location.

76RMS JAN-DEC T/T XPETS CC KIDS MED.INX

THE GOLDEN LION: 01786 475351. 8 King St. V central, large, functional with not so gr 'Great Food Stop', but handy for shops/stn/Stirling stuff.

71RMS JAN-DEC T/T PETS CC KIDS MED.EX

S.Y. HOSTEL: 01786 473442. On rd up to castle in recently renovated jail is this new-style hostel, more like a budget hotel (1105/HOSTELS).

CAMPING AND CARAVAN PARK: WITCHES CRAIG at **BLAIRLOGIE**, 01786 474947. 5km E on A91, St Andrews rd. Small park conveniently located and in meadow below the wonderful Ochils. Wallace Monument shows you the way home. Apr-Oct.

WHERE TO EAT

HERMANN'S: 01786 450632. At the 'Tolbooth' and on rd up to Castle but location likely to change at time of going to press. Hermann Aschaber's corner of Austria where schnitzels and strudels figure along with Cullen Skink and other good Scottish produce. 2 level, ambient well run rms with cheery aproned staff. MED

No 39 BROAD ST: 01786 473929. As title on rd up to Castle. Long standing restau site, this the latest version has Scottish theme to food and décor with pikestaffs upstairs, softer tartans in the bistro. INX

SCHOLARS at the **STIRLING HIGHLAND HOTEL:** 01786 473052. The up-market, up-by-the-Castle eaterie in town, the Stirling Highland a good conversion of an old school hence the name (832/CENTRAL HOTELS). Tries to live up to reputation. EXP

PACOS: 01786 446414. Nr TO in town centre. Tex-mex restau as the one in Perth. Woody ambience. LO 10.30pm. INX

OLIVIA'S: 01786 446277. Baker St. Contemp Scottish bistro that is making an effort. We haven't tried. TOS. Lunch and dinner. LO 9.30pm. Cl Sun/Mon in wint. INX

THE EAST INDIA COMPANY: 01786 471330. 7 Viewfield Pl. Still proclaim to be the best Indian in town (Michelin agrees). Good atmos in woody basement rm. Pakora bar for snacks upstairs. Open 7 days till 11pm. INX

KAM'S GARDEN: 01786 446 445. 4 Viewfield Pl nr E India (above) so best Chinese and best Indian adj. Calm; and Kam cuisine. LO 11.30pm 7 days. INX

ITALIA NOSTRA: 01786 473208. 25 Baker St. Gr name. The tratt to try (Bar Italia, Br of Allan at the Walmer Hotel also recommended). The fetching neckerchiefs have long gone, but fetching waiters remain. Busy atmos. 7 days. 11/12pm. CHP

CAFÉ ALBERT at the **ALBERT HALL:** 01786 446930. Unusual success story for a café/bistro created in a municipal hall. Hot dishes, baguettes, snacks. Newspapers and a relaxed atmos. Mon-Sat 9am-5pm. CHP

THE BARNTON BAR AND BISTRO: 01786 461698. Barnton St opp main post office. Perenially popular. Jukebox. All-day breakfast, baked potatoes, hefty sandwiches. Newspapers. 7 days. Food till 7.45pm, then bar takes over. CHP

ALLAN WATER CAFE, BRIDGE OF ALLAN: 8km up the rd in Br of Allan main st nr br itself. Great café, the best fish 'n' chips 'n' ice cream (1276/CAFÉS). CHP

WHAT TO SEE

STIRLING CASTLE (1590/CASTLES); **WALLACE MONUMENT/THE PINEAPPLE** (1665/1671/MONUMENTS); **BANNOCKBURN/SHERIFFMUIR** (1726/BATTLE-

GROUNDS); **THE OCHILS** (1777/HILL WALKS; 1800/GLEN AND RIVER WALKS); **LOGIE OLD KIRK** (1708/GRAVEYARDS); **PARADISE** (1530/PICNICS); **DUNBLANE CATHE-DRAL** (1691/CHURCHES).

STIRLING OLD TOWN JAIL: St John's St on rd up to Castle. Guided tour and put-up job, but rather well done. Live actors. Kids will be quiet or simply tortured. Open AYR (4pm winter).

THE GHOST WALK: A stroll through old part of the town nr the castle: 'a world of restless spirits and lost souls' (sound familiar?). Info: TO or 01786 447150.

RAINBOW SLIDES: Nr Railway Stn. A leisure centre with good 25m pool and gym (Pulsestar) and for kids 3 water slides of varying thrill factors. Open 7 days (Sat and Sun till 4pm). Check times: 01786 462521.

WHAT TO DO

SWIMMING/SPORTS: (*see above*). There's also a pool at the University Sports Centre and at the Stirling Highland Hotel (with squash). **GOLF:** Stirling Golf Course v central at Queens Rd. Quite testing and one of best in area (01786 464098). **BIKE HIRE:** Stewart Wilson Cycles, 49 Barnton St (01786 465292).

TOURIST INFO: Dumbarton Rd. 01786 475019. Jan-Dec.

THE BEST OF ULLAPOOL

WHERE TO STAY

ALTNAHARRIE INN: 01854 633230. 2km Ullapool other side of L Broom (by private boat). One of the v best (1080/COUNTRY-HOUSE HOTELS).
8RMS APR-OCT X/X PETS CC KIDS LOTS

THE CEILIDH PLACE: 01854 612103. 14 W Argyle St. Eclectic individualism; something to celebrate (960/INEXP HIGHLAND HOTELS). Also cheap 'bunkhouse' accom.
24RMS JAN-DEC T/X PETS CC KIDS EXP/CHP

MOREFIELD HOTEL: 01854 612161. Edge of town A835 heading N. Surreal location in midst of housing estate. Small motel cabins and gr seafood amongst big varied menu (1252/SEAFOOD RESTAUS).
10RMS JAN-DEC T/T PETS CC KIDS INX

S.Y. HOSTEL: 01854 612254. On Shore St (the front) converted from cottages. Grade 2. Can book by fax. Also at Achiltibuie (same number) 40km by rd, 22km by footpath. A good base for this scenic area; book in summer.

CAMPING/CARAVAN SITE: 01854 612054. Ardmair Pt. 6km N on A835.

WHERE TO EAT

THE CEILIDH PLACE: *as above.*

THE MOREFIELD HOTEL: *as above.*

SCOTTISH LARDER: 01854 612185. Ladysmith St. Lauri Chilton's restau serves hearty Scottish fare; pies, veggie, salads, local seafood. Daily 5.30-9pm. Adj guesthouse.
INX

WHAT TO SEE

CORRIESHALLOCH GORGE: 20km S (1463a/WATERFALLS); **AN TEALLACH** 40km S by rd (1499/VIEWS); **ACHILTIBUIE:** 40km NW (1487/SCENIC ROUTES); **STAC POLLAIDH** (pron 'Polly', 1757/HILLS); **HIGHLAND STONEWARE** and **KNOCKAN GALLERY** 1929/1937/CRAFT SHOPS); **HIGHLAND RARE BREEDS FARM** (1555/KIDS). **LOCH BROOM** pool/leisure centre 01854 612884.

TOURIST INFO: Argyle St. 01854 612135. Easter-Nov.

WHERE TO STAY

FORSS HOUSE HOTEL, nr THURSO: 01847 861201. 8km W on A836. The MacGregor's family home set in 20 woodland acres by the sea is the best quality hotel for miles. Popular restau (you should book), over 200 malts in the bar comfortable spacious rms and 5 chalets in the grounds too. Breakfast in the conservatory then birds, walks, old mill and waterfall. Fishing.

10RMS JAN-DEC T/T PETS CC KIDS TOS MED.EX

PORTLAND ARMS, LYBSTER: 01593 721208. On main A9 20km S of Wick and 45km S of Thurso by A895. A coaching inn since 1851; still hospitable. New owners and hotel enjoying a rolling refurb over 1999/2000; a popular stop. Many opportunities to eat, and you will.

22RMS JAN-DEC T/T PETS CC KIDS TOS MED.INX

BORGIE LODGE HOTEL, nr BETTYHILL: 01641 521332. A836 12km W of Tongue. Secluded trad huntin', shootin', fishin' sort of a place: 20 hill lochs and 2 rivers with salmon and trout. Shooting on the adj 12,000 acre estate and Jacqui's acclaimed cooking to come home to. Another MacGregor establishment – Peter's brother has Forss House (above).

7RMS FEB-OCT X/T PETS CC KIDS TOS MED.INX

ROYAL HOTEL, THURSO: 01847 893191. Trail St in town centre. Sprawling stone inn upgraded to comfortable commercialism. All mod cons and pool/leisure complex planned for 2000 (maybe). Some say it can be cold here in Thurso – so take your vest. A hotel for visitors.

105RMS JAN-DEC T/T XPETS CC KIDS MED.INX

NORTHERN SANDS HOTEL, DUNNET: 01847 851270. Ask a local for a good, wee hotel and they'll point you here. Just S of Dunnet village, on the bay. Even does takeaway pizza.

12RMS JAN-DEC T/T PETS CC KIDS MED.INX

MACKAYS HOTEL, WICK: Union Street. 01955 602323. Basic but welcoming. Business travellers during week, family-run (the Lamonts).

27RMS JAN-DEC T/T XPETS CC XKIDS MED.INX

BREADALBANE HOUSE HOTEL, WICK: 01955 603911. Family hotel close to harbour and town centre. Victorian house with cosy dining-rm, adj bar and large bedrms.

10RMS JAN-DEC X/T PETS CC KIDS INX

QUAYSIDE B&B, HARBOUR QUAY, WICK: Haven't stayed, but heard good reports. E-mail them on quaysidewick@compuserve.com

ACKERGILL TOWER, nr WICK: 01955 603556. A rare treat (1138/GET-AWAY-FROM-IT-ALL)

S.Y. HOSTEL: 01955 611424. At Canisbay, John O'Groats (7km). Wick 25km. Regular bus service. The furthest flung youth hostel on the mainland.

CAMPING AND CARAVAN PARK, DUNNET BAY: 01847 821319. On grassy strand nr wonderful crescent of beach; a nature reserve. 14km N of Thurso. **THURSO,** Scrabster Rd: 01955 603761. Exposed cliff top site to W of town.

WHERE TO EAT

FORSS HOUSE HOTEL, PORTLAND ARMS, BORGIE LODGE HOTEL: (*all as above*)

LA MIRAGE, HELMSDALE: 60km S. Viva Las Vegas! (987/INEXP HIGHLAND RESTAUS). INX

THE NORTHERN SANDS: (*see above*).

THE FERRY INN, SCRABSTER: 01847 892814. 3km W of Thurso in busy pt area o/look BP and ferry terminal for Orkney. 'Turf' (meat) on upper deck and 'surf' (fish) on top deck. Adj bar. Lunch and 6-9.30pm, 7 days. INX

DUNNET TEA-ROOM by DUNNET HEAD: 01847 851774. 15km N of Thurso by coast rd. Extensive menu. Apr-Oct 3-8pm (995/INEXP HIGHLAND RESTAUS). CHP

OLD SMIDDY INN, THRUMSTER: 01955 651256. 7km S of Wick on A9. Bar/restau/café full of smiddyish stuff. Snacks, meals and blackboard specials. 7 days; Sun-Thur 12-2pm, 5.30-8.30pm; Fri and Sat all day. LO 9pm.   CHP

QUEENS HOTEL Wick town centre. Haven't tried, but both popular with locals for bar food.   INX

WHAT TO SEE

DUNBEATH: 32km S of Wick (1743/LITERARY PLACES; 1804/GLEN AND RIVER WALKS); **CAIRNS OF CAMSTER:** 15km S of Wick (1642/PREHISTORIC SITES); **BET-TYHILL MUSEUM:** 50km W of Thurso (2007/MUSEUMS); **NORTH COAST BEACHES** (1440/BEACHES).

WICK HERITAGE CENTRE: 01955 605393. In town centre; June-Sept. Mon-Sat 10am-5pm. (INTERESTING MUSEUMS/2022). **CAITHNESS GLASS CENTRE, WICK:** 01955 602286. Home of popular gift ware; factory and visitor centre; by the airport.

THE TRINKIE: A walk along the rocky coast E of Wick or drive through housing schemes until cliff rd appears (ask locals). Flat rocks, an open-air pool; a good spot. 2km further for the 'Brig O'Trams'.

WHALIGOE STEPS: On A9 N of Lybster; down track nr cottages and septic tank, by Cairn O' Get sign. Infamy regained after Billy Connolly's visit; 318 (Keith counted) stone cliff steps to sea where herrings used to be landed and cured. Unsignposted so ask locally for directions if lost, and go carefully.

WILDLIFE CRUISE, JOHN O' GROATS: 01955 611353. June-Aug; 90min trips to sea stacks, birds and **JOHN O' GROATS – ORKNEY:** May-Sept day trips.

WHAT TO DO

SWIMMING: Wick (01955 603711), Thurso (01847 893260). Both central. **GOLF:** Wick (01955 602726), Thurso (01847 893807), Reay (01847 811288). **SURFING AND WINDSURFING:** Esp round Thurso. TO have leaflet about beaches. **RIDING:** Dunnet Trekking. Glorious trekking on Dunnet Beach (01847 851689). **BIKE HIRE:** From Wheels (01955 603636). **VIKING BOWL:** built using old US naval bowling lanes; cinema soon (01847 895050).

TOURIST INFO:

WICK: Whitechapel Rd. 01955 602596. Jan-Dec.

THURSO: Riverside. 01847 892371. Apr-Oct.

HOLIDAY CENTRES

2174
MAP 2

PITLOCHRY

WHERE TO STAY

KILLIECRANKIE HOTEL: 01796 473220 (898/PERTHSHIRE HOTELS).   MED.EX

PINE TREES: 01796 472121. Off Main St (897/PERTHSHIRE HOTELS).   MED.EX

DUNFALLANDY HOUSE: 01796 472648. Just out of town (2km), but away from all that. Dinner a treat. V good value country-house hotel. 9 rms. MED.INX

WHERE TO EAT

KILLIECRANKIE HOTEL: Go those miles (5) to dinner; or bar meals! (*above*).   INX

EAST HAUGH HOTEL: 01796 473121. 3km S off A9. Gr bar meals/restau. MED

PORTNACRAIG: 01796 472777. By theatre, on river. An insider choice.   INX

OLD SMITHY: 01796 472356. Main St. Coffees/restau. 7 days. LO 8.30pm.   INX

MILL POND BISTRO: Burnside, 500m up Braemar rd. A good find.   MED

PRINCE OF INDIA: 01796 472275. Off main st by McNaughtons. Unusually good Indian.   MED

MOULIN INN: 01796 472196. Notable for pub food and atmos (1193/REAL ALE). 6km uphill. LO 9.30pm.   CHP

WHAT TO SEE

THE SALMON LADDER: From Main St and across dam to see 34-pool fish ladder (salmon leaping May-Oct, if you're lucky) and Hydro Board displays (sic); **BEN VRACKIE:** Local fave with fab Trossachs views climbed from Moulin (2km from town). Rd behind Moulin Inn. Car park. 734m. Scree at top; and goats; **FASKALLY WOODS/LINN OF TUMMEL WALKS:** Well-marked woodland walks around L Faskally and Garry R. Can incl the Linn (rapids) and Pass of Killiecrankie (1725/BATTLEGROUNDS). Start: town/Garry bridge/visitor centre; **WOOLLEN SHOPS:** Many major chains and local shops in one small area/the main st. **PITLOCHRY THEATRE** (2089/THEATRES); **QUEEN'S VIEW** (1509/VIEWS); **EDRADOUR DISTILLERY** (1368/WHISKY); **MACNAUGHTON'S** (1963/OUTDOOR SHOPS); **MOULIN INN** (1193/REAL ALE).

INVERARAY

WHERE TO STAY

GEORGE HOTEL: 01499 302111. On main st and in the Clark family for centuries (no, really – 1790). A gr value hotel – ales, good pub food, real fires.   CHP

LOCH FYNE HOTEL: 01499 302148. On A83 rd out of town towards W, o/look loch. Personally run. Good bar meals.   MED.INX

WHERE TO EAT

THE GEORGE/LOCH FYNE HOTELS: Bar meals esp. (*See above.*)   CHP

LOCH FYNE OYSTER BAR: 01499 600236. 14km E on A83.   INX

CREGGANS INN: 01369 860279. 32km E and S via A83/A815. On opp bank of L Fyne, but 35mins by rd. Bar meals/restau.   MED

WHAT TO SEE

INVERARAY CASTLE: Home of the Duke of Argyll and clan seat of the Campbells. Spectacular entrance hall; chronicle of Highland shenanigans unfurls in the gilded apartments. Fine walks in grounds esp to the prominent hill and folly (45mins up). Apr-Oct. **CRARAE:** 15km S on A83; **ARDKINGLAS WOODLAND:** 17km E on A83 (1391/GARDENS). **AUCHINDRAIN:** 8km S on A83; **INVERARAY JAIL** (2015/MUSEUMS); **ARGYLL WILDLIFE PARK:** 4km S on A83 (1560/KIDS).

ST ANDREWS

WHERE TO STAY

OLD COURSE HOTEL: 01334 474371 (872/FIFE HOTELS).   LOTS

RUFFLETS: 01334 472594 (874/FIFE HOTELS).   EXP

RUSACKS: 01334 474321. A Forte hotel, rather exp (but most hotels in St Andrews are overpriced). Near all courses and overlooking the 18th of the Old. Nice sun-lounge, but dining-room is v indoors.   LOTS

ASHLEIGH HOUSE: 01334 475429. 37 St Mary's St. On Crail rd (A917) towards E Sands Leisure Centre 1km centre. Golfy, on a budget.   INX

ARGYLE HOUSE: 01334 473387. 127 North St. On corner of Murray Park with numerous guest-house alternatives. This one is central and adequate. INX

NUMBER TEN: 01334 474601. 10 Hope St. Bit of Edinburgh New Town in calm st nr centre. Georgian elegance etc. 10 rms. INX

GLENDERRON: 01334 477951. 9 Murray Park. A guest house with only 5 rms, but tasteful and good value. The one to choose on this street of a myriad. INX

MORTON OF PITMILLY and **KILCONQUHAR:** Self-catering. Excl. Check TO.

WHERE TO EAT

THE PEAT INN: 01334 840 206. 15km SW (882/FIFE HOTELS). EXP

THE VINE LEAF: 01334 477497. 131 South St. Excl new contemporary restau thro' passageway behind the baked potato place looking out to 'herb gdn'. Light, inventive menu not so meaty. Good vegn. Tues-Sat, dinner only. MED

THE DOLL'S HOUSE: 01334 477422. Church Sq. V central café/restau that caters well for kids (and teenagers). Eclectic range, smiley people and tables outside in summer. INX

GRANGE INN: 01334 472670. 4km E off Anstruther rd A917. V popular country pub with good local rep. Book w/ends.

CIAO ROMA: 01334 472090. 89 South St. Branch of Edinburgh Italian, here to good effect. Bustling atmos. Relatively exp, but good pasta and open late. MED

NEW BALAKA: 01334 474825. 'Best Curry in Scotland' winner. Certainly as good as many in the city top ten. MED

MERCHANT'S HOUSE and **BRAMBLES** (1304/TEAROOMS). Both excellent. Daytime.

WHAT TO SEE

THE TOWN ITSELF: The lanes, cloisters, gardens and the University halls and colleges; the harbour and the botanic gardens. Perfect lawns; **THE CASTLE RUINS:** Founded in 13th cent on promontory; good for clambering over. 'Escape tunnel' to explore (if not tall). Spooky by night along this shore; **BRITISH GOLF MUSEUM:** Sophisticated audio-visual exhibition illustrating history and allure of the game. Even non-players will enjoy. **THE HIMALAYAS:** the most brilliant putting green; piles of fun, near the beach. Apr-Oct till 8pm, 7 days. Many **GOLF COURSES** (1849/GREAT GOLF); **WEST SANDS/KINSHALDY BEACH** (1438/BEACHES); **LEUCHARS CHURCH:** 9km by A91 N (1688/CHURCHES); **TENTSMUIR:** 20km by A91/A919 N (1586/WILDLIFE); **NEW PICTURE HOUSE** (2084/THEATRES); **JANETTA'S** (1324/ICE CREAM); **ST ANDREWS FINE ART; CATHEDRAL** (1623/RUINS); **SEALIFE CENTRE; EAST SANDS** (1889/LEISURE CENTRES).

2177
MAP 3

ROYAL DEESIDE: BALLATER AND BANCHORY

WHERE TO STAY

DARROCH LEARG, BALLATER: 01339 755443. Town mansion above/off (at tight bend) A93 on way in from Braemar. Excellent nosh. (913/NE HOTELS.) MED

BANCHORY LODGE, BANCHORY: 01330 822625 (921/NE HOTELS). EXP

RAEMOIR, BANCHORY: 01330 824884. Large mansion in secluded grounds 3km town by Raemoir Rd off A93. Relaxed and discreet. 9-hole golf and tennis. Growing rep for food. LOTS

TOR-NA-COILLE, BANCHORY: 01330 822242. Town mansion above/just off main A93 on way in from Ballater. Nr golf. Antiques in tasteful/individual rms.

EXP

WHERE TO EAT

DARROCH LEARG, BALLATER: 01339 755443. The other Deeside hoteliers aspire to. (*see above*).

THE OAK ROOM, BALLATER: 01339 755858.

EXP

THE GREEN INN, BALLATER: 01339 755701. With 3 inexpensive rms above. Scottish fresh prod, home cooking. (931/NE HOTELS).

MED

THE BLACK-FACED SHEEP, ABOYNE: 01339 887311. Near main rd. Coffee shop/gift shop with excellent home-baking. Daytime hrs (1288/TEAROOMS).

MILTON RESTAURANT: 01330 844566 (934/NE HOTELS).

MED

THE WHITE COTTAGE, nr ABOYNE: 01339 886265. On main A93 4km towards Banchory. Cottage dining and conservatory. Good home-cooking/atmos.

MED

WHAT TO SEE

CRAIGIEVAR/DRUM (1606/1607 CASTLES); **FASQUE** (1654/COUNTRY HOUSES); **CRATHES** (1379/1663 GARDENS/COUNTRY HOUSES); **BALMORAL** (1608/CASTLES); **LOCHNAGAR** (1785/MUNROS); **ALBERT MEMORIAL** (1674/MONUMENTS); **GLEN MUICK** (1475/LOCHS); **CAMBUS O'MAY** (1531/PICNICS); **GOLF:** Well-managed/picturesque courses, open to visitors at both Ballater (013397 55567), and Banchory (01330 822447). Both 18 holes; **FISHING:** Difficult, not impossible, on Dee or on R Feugh (N bank only) – permits from Feughside Inn (01330 850225); **WALKS:** Walks down both sides of the Dee, esp Ballater to Cambus O'May, 7km; **VIEWPOINTS:** Up Craigendarroch, the Hill of the Oaks, Ballater, from Braemar Rd (45mins). Scolty Hill and Monument, Banchory. Ask for directions.

SECTION 14

The Likes of You and Me

THE BIG ATTRACTIONS

Amongst the 'top ten' (paid admn) and the 'top ten' (free admn) visitor attractions, the following are really worth seeing:

KELVINGROVE ART GALLERY; THE BURRELL COLLECTION: 695/696/MAIN ATTRACTIONS.

THE MUSEUM OF TRANSPORT; THE GLASGOW BOTANICS; THE GALLERY OF MODERN ART: 701/702/703/OTHER ATTRACTIONS.

THE PEOPLE'S PALACE, GLASGOW: 698/MAIN ATTRACTIONS.

EDINBURGH CASTLE; HOLYROOD PALACE; EDINBURGH ZOO; THE NATION-AL GALLERY; DYNAMIC EARTH: 341/342/348/347/346/ATTRACTIONS.

THE EDINBURGH BOTANICS: 352/OTHER ATTRACTIONS.

CULZEAN CASTLE; STIRLING CASTLE: 1593/1590/CASTLES.

ABERDEEN ART GALLERY: 2025/PUBLIC GALLERIES.

THE OTHER MAJOR ATTRACTIONS ARE:

2178 **LOCH LOMOND:** App via Stirling and A811 to Drymen or from Glas, the A82
MAP 6 Dumbarton rd to Balloch. Britain's largest inland waterway and a trad play-
B3 ground, especially for Glaswegians; jet-skis, show-off boats.

W bank Balloch-Tarbert is most developed: marinas, cruises, ferry to Inchmurrin Island. Luss is tweeville, like a movie set (it is used in the Scottish TV soap High Road) and a good place to buy that souvenir tea towel. Rd more picturesque beyond Tarbert to Ardlui (1106/HOSTELS); see 1178/BLOODY GOOD PUBS for the non-tourist/real Scots experience of the Drover's Inn at Inverarnan.

E bank more natural, wooded; good lochside and hill walks (1780/MUNROS). Rd winding but picturesque beyond Balmaha towards Ben Lomond (1109/HOS-TELS).

2179 **THE CUILLINS, SKYE:** This hugely impressive mt range in the S of Skye, often
MAP 2 shrouded in cloud or rain, is the romantic heartland of the Islands. The Red
B3 Cuillins are smoother and nearer the Portree-Broadford rd; the Black Cuillins gather behind and are best approached from Glen Brittle (1793/SERIOUS WALKS; 1460/WATERFALLS). This classic, untameable mt scenery has attracted walkers, climbers and artists for centuries. It still claims lives regularly. For best views apart from Glen Brittle, see 1486/SCENIC ROUTES; 1502/VIEWS. Vast range of walks and scrambles (see also 1515/PICNICS).

2180 **THE DISCOVERY, DUNDEE:** The main attraction in Dundee now closely fol-
MAP 4 lowed by the Art Centre. Central river side location at Discovery Point and
C3 state-of-the-art visitor centre. This tall-masted ship, built in Dundee for the 1901 Antarctica expedition with Scott and Shackleton, lies permanently at anchor. 10am-5pm (till 4pm Nov-Mar), opens 11am on Sun. But don't miss the frigate **UNICORN** further along in dockland, the oldest British warship afloat.
ADMN

2181 **LOCH NESS:** Most visits start from Inverness (2168/INVERNESS) at the N end via
MAP 2 the R Ness. Ft Augustus is at the other end, 56km S. L Ness is part of the still-
C3 navigable Caledonian Canal linking the E and W coast at Ft William. Many small boats line the shores of the R Ness, and one of the best ways to see the loch is on a cruise from Inverness (Jacobite Cruises 01463 233999) or Drumnadrochit (L Ness Cruises 01456 450202). Most tourist traffic uses the main A82 N bank rd converging on Drumnadrochit where the L Ness Monster industry gobbles up your money. If you must, the 'official' L Ness Monster Exhibition is the one to choose. On the A82 you can't miss Urquhart Castle (1627/RUINS); see also Dochfour (1977/GARDEN CENTRES). But the two best things about L Ness are: the S rd (B862) from Ft Augustus back to Inverness (1492/SCENIC ROUTES; 1468/WATERFALLS); and the detour from Drumnadrochit to Cannich to Glen Affric (20-30km) (1444/GLENS; 1799/GLEN AND RIVER WALKS; 1456/WATERFALLS).

MY FAVOURITE SCOTTISH JOURNEYS

A miscellany of memorable journeys by trains, boats and planes.

2182 **WEMYSS BAY–ROTHESAY FERRY:** Calmac 01475 650100. The glass-roofed
MAP 1 stn at Wemyss Bay is the railhead from Glas (60km by rd on the A78), and has
C3 the atmos and vitality of an age-old terminus. The frequent ferry (Calmac) has
all the Scottish traits and sausage rolls you can handle, and Rothesay (with its
winter grd and castle and period seaside mansions) appears out of blood-
smeared sunsets and rain-sodden mornings alike, a gentle watercolour from
summer holidays past. Go to the (Victorian) toilet when you get there.

2183 **LOCH ETIVE CRUISES:** 01866 822430, though booking not essential. From
MAP 1 Taynuilt (Oban 20km) through the long narrow waters of one of Scotland's
C3 most atmospheric lochs, a 3hr journey in a small cruiser with indoor and outdoor seating. Pier is 2km from main Taynuilt crossroads on A85. Leaves 2pm
(and 10.30am in summer not Sat/Sun). Travel into the heart of the Highlands,
the loch sides inaccessible by car; deer and golden eagles may attend your
journey.

2184 **GLENELG–KYLERHEA:** The shorter of the 2 remaining ferry journeys to Skye
MAP 2 now the br has come, and definitely the best way to get there if you're not
B3 pushed for time. The drive to Glenelg from the A87 is spectacular (1483/SCENIC
ROUTES) and so is this 5min crossing of the deep Narrows of Kylerhea. Apr-Oct
(frequent) 9am-6pm and Sun in summer (10am-6pm). 01599 511302.

2185 **CORRAN FERRY:** From Ardgour on A861-Nether Lochaber on the A82 across
MAP 2 the narrows of L Linnhe. A convenient 5min crossing which can save time to
C3 pts S of Mallaig and takes you to the wildernesses of Moidart and
Ardnamurchan and which is a charming and fondly regarded journey in its
own rt. Runs continuously until 8.50pm summer, 6.20pm winter.

2186 **THE MAID OF THE FORTH CRUISE TO INCHCOLM ISLAND:** 0131 331 4857.
MAP 7 The wee boat (though they say it holds 200 people) which leaves every day at
A1 different times (phone for details) from Hawes Pier in S Queensferry (15km
Central Edin via A90) opp the Hawes Inn, just under the famous railway br
(351/MAIN ATTRACTIONS) and also from the pier at N Queensferry. 45min trips
under the br and on to Inchcolm, an attractive island with walks and an
impressive ruined abbey. Much birdlife and also many seals. 1hr 30mins
ashore. Tickets at pier.

2187 **THE WEST HIGHLAND LINE** Info: 0345 484950. One of the most picturesque
MAP 2 railway journeys in Europe and quite the best way to get to Skye from the S.
Travel to Ft William from Glas, then relax and watch the stunning scenery, the
Bonnie Prince Charlie country (MARY, CHARLIE AND BOB, pp.217-8) and much
that is close to a railwayman's heart go past the window. Viaducts and tunnels
over loch and down dale. Also possible to make the same journey (from Ft
William to Mallaig and/or return) by steam train on certain days. Journey time
just under 2hrs. Check on 01463 239026 or 01524 732100. For anyone inter-
ested in trains, there's a museum in the restored stn at Glenfinnan. Trains for
Mallaig leave from Glas Queen St about 3 times a day and take about 5hrs.

2188 **FROM INVERNESS:** Info on 0345 484950. Two less-celebrated but mesmeris-
MAP 2 ing rail journeys start from Inverness. The journey to Kyle of Lochalsh no
longer has an observation car in the summer months, so get a window seat
and take an atlas; the last section through Glen Carron and around the coast
at Loch Carron is especially fine. There are 4 trains a day and it takes 2hrs
30mins. Inverness to Wick is a 3hr 30min journey. The section skirting the E
coast from Lairg-Helmsdale is full of drama and is then followed by the trans-
fixing monotony of the Flow Country (it's the best way to see it). There are 4
trains a day in summer.

2189 **THE PLANE TO BARRA:** Most of the island plane journeys pass over many
MAP 2 smaller islands (e.g. Glas-Tiree, Glas-Stornoway, Wick-Orkney) and are fascinating on a clear day, but BA's daily flight to Barra is doubly special because
the island doesn't have an airport and you land on Cockleshell Beach in the N
of the island (11 km from Castlebay) after a splendid app. The Otter holds only
15 passengers and leaves and lands according to the tide. 0345 222111.

THE ESSENTIAL SCOTTISH BOOKS

FICTION

Iain Banks, *The Wasp Factory*; *The Bridge*

George Douglas Brown, *The House with the Green Shutters*

George Mackay Brown, *Greenvoe*; *The Masked Fisherman*

John Buchan, *The 39 Steps/Short Stories*

Lewis Grassic Gibbon, *Sunset Song*

Neil Gunn, *Highland River*; *The Silver Darlings*

Alasdair Gray, *Lanark*

Meg Henderson, *Finding Peggy*

Archie Hind, *The Dear Green Place*

James Hogg, *Confessions of a Justified Sinner*

Robin Jenkins, *The Cone Gatherers*

A L Kennedy, *Night Geometry and the Garscadden Trains*

William McIlvanney, *Docherty*

Ian Rankin, *The Black Book*

Bess Ross, *A Bit of Crack and Car Culture*

Sir Walter Scott, *The Heart of Midlothian*; *The Two Drovers and Other Stories*; *Old Mortality*

Alan Spence, *Its Colours They Are Fine*

Robert Louis Stevenson, *Kidnapped*; *Master of Ballantrae*; *Catriona*; *Dr Jekyll and Mr Hyde*

Muriel Spark, *The Prime of Miss Jean Brodie*

Alexander Trocchi, *Cain's Book*; *Young Adam*

Alan Warner, *Morvern Callar*

Irvine Welsh, *Trainspotting*

NON-FICTION

Boswell and Johnson, *Journey to the Western Islands*

Derek Cooper, *Skye*

Jim Crumley, *A High And Lonely Place*

Tom Devine, *The Scottish Nation: 1700–2000*

Raymond Eagle, *Seton Gordon: A Highland Gentleman*

Antonia Fraser, *Mary Queen of Scots*

George MacDonald Fraser, *The Steel Bonnets*

Elizabeth Grant of Rothiemurchus, *Memoirs of a Highland Lady*

Muriel Gray, *The First Fifty: Munro-Bagging without a Beard*

Osgood Mackenzie, *100 Years in the Highlands* (out of print but still available at Inverewe Grds)

Charles Maclean, *The Story of St Kilda*

Gavin Maxwell, *Ring of Bright Water*

William Poucher, *The Magic of Skye*

John Prebble, *1000 Years of Scotland's History*; *The Lion in the North*; *The Highland Clearances*; *Culloden*; *Glencoe*

TC Smout, *A History of the Scottish People*

Nigel Tranter, *The Story of Scotland*

George Way and Romilly Squire, *The Collins Scottish Clan & Family Encyclopedia*

POETRY

Robert Burns, *Collected Songs and Poems*

Sorley Maclean, *Collected Poems*

Norman McCaig, *Collected Poems*

A FEW THINGS THE SCOTS GAVE THE WORLD

The population of Scotland has never exceeded 5 million (well let's not split hairs).

The decimal point

Logarithms

The Bank of England

The overdraft

Cannabis (the active principle)

Documentary films

Colour photographs

Encyclopaedia Britannica

Postcards

The gas mask

Theory of Combustion

The advertising film

The bus

The steam engine

The locomotive

The fax machine

The photocopier

Video

The telephone

Television

Radar

Helium

Neon

The telegraph

Street lighting

The lawnmower

Kinetic energy

Electric light

The alpha chip

The Thermos flask

The hypodermic syringe

Finger-printing

The kaleidoscope

Anaesthesia

Antiseptics

Golf clubs

The 18-hole golf course

Tennis courts

The bowling green

Writing paper

The thermometer

The gravitating compass

The threshing machine

Insulin

Penicillin

Interferon

The pneumatic tyre

The pedal bicycle

The modern road surface

Geology

Artificial ice

Morphine

Ante-natal clinics

Bovril

Marmalade

The self-acting fountain pen

The Mackintosh

Gardenias

Dolly, the cloned sheep

Not bad really!

THE BEST EVENTS

2190   **UP HELLY AA:** Info: 01595 693434. Traditionally on the 24th day after Christmas, but now always the last Tues in Jan. A mid-winter fire festival based on Viking lore where 'the Guizers' haul a galley thro the streets of Lerwick and burn it in the park; and the night goes on.   JAN

2191
MAP B
D3   **CELTIC CONNECTIONS, GLASGOW:** Tickets and info: 0141 227 5511. A huge festival of Celtic music from round the world held in the Royal Concert Hall and other city venues over 2/3 weeks. Concerts and ceilidhs.   JAN

     BURNS NIGHT: The National Bard celebrated with supper. No single major event.   JAN 25TH

2192
MAP B
D3   **GLASGOW ART FAIR, GLASGOW:** Info: 0141 552 6027 (as long as I'm still involved). Britain's most significant commercial art fair o/side London held in mid-April in tented pavilions in George Sq with selected galleries from Scotland and UK.   APRIL

2193
MAP 8
C2   **MELROSE SEVENS:** Info TO 01896 822555. Border town of Melrose completely taken over by tournament in their small is beautiful rugby ground. 7-a-side teams from all over incl international. It's just a good place to go, fanatical or not. *See p.* 297 for accom and eats.   APRIL

2194
MAP 5
C3   **FIFE POINT TO POINT, LEVEN, FIFE:** 01333 360229. Major 'society' i.e. county set, get-together at Balcormo Mains Farm. Sort of Scottish equivalent of Henley with horses organised by Fife Fox and Hounds. Range Rovers, hampers and Hermes.   APRIL

2195
MAP 1
B2   **PAPS OF JURA HILL RACE, ISLE OF JURA:** Details from the hotel 01496 820243. The amazing hill race up and down the 3 Paps or distinctive peaks (total of 7 hills altogether) on this large remote island (2108/MAGICAL ISLANDS). About 150 runners take part on the 14 mile challenge from the distillery in Craighouse, the village.   MAY

2196
MAP 1
C3/D3   **FLOWER SHOWS, STRATHCLYDE PARK & AYR:** Info 01292 612000. Many Scottish towns hold flower shows, mainly in autumn, but the newly created (1997) National Gardening Show run by the Royal Horticultural Society is now a major event in the gardening calendar. Info 01698 252565 and for Park see (1398/COUNTRY PARKS). The show in Ayr run by the local authority is the biggest flower and vegetable show.   MAY/JUNE & AUGUST

2197
MAP 8
C3   **COMMON RIDINGS, BORDER TOWNS:** Info Jedburgh TO 01835 863435. The Border town festivals. Similar formats over different weeks with 'ride-outs' (on horseback to outlying villages etc) , 'shows', dances and games, culminating on the Fri/Sat. Total local invovement. Hawick is first, then Selkirk, Peebles/Melrose, Gala, Jedburgh, Kelso and Lauder end of July.   MAY-JULY

2198
MAP A
xA3   **ROYAL HIGHLAND SHOW, INGLISTON SHOWGROUND, EDINBURGH:** 0131 333 2444. The premiere agricultural show in Scotland and for the farming world, the event of the year. Animals, machinery, food and shopping. Compulsive for some, big day out for the masses.   JUNE

2199
MAP 8
D1   **SEAFOOD FESTIVAL, EYEMOUTH:** Eyemouth TO 018907 50678 for details. A festival of seafood: from its landing and preparation through to eating. Accompanied by non-stop music, st theatre and that awful Morris dancing! Over 1 w/end days.   JUNE

2200
MAP 2
A3   **BARRA LIVE, BARRA:** Contact Hector MacInnes 01871 810270. A massive ceilidh with strong Irish flavour, the high point of the summer on this fabulous island. Everybody comes. Held in a marquee on Tangusdale Machair by the beach.   JULY

2201
MAP 4
C3   **GAME FAIR, PERTH:** Held in the rural and historical setting of Scone Palace, this is a major Perthshire day out and a gathering for the hunting, shooting, fishing and of course, shopping brigade. Details: 01738 552300.   JULY

2202
MAP 3
C1   **SCOTTISH TRADITIONAL BOAT FESTIVAL, PORTSOY:** Perfect little festival in perfect little Moray coast town nr Banff over a w/end in late June/early July. Old boats in old and new harbours, open-air ceilidhs, great atmos. 01261 843598.   JULY

2203
MAP 4
C4
T IN THE PARK, BALADO AIRFIELD nr KINROSS: Scotland's highly succesful pop festival with all that is current in Britpop and beyond. The T stands for Tennents, the sponsors who are much in evidence. Not as life style affirming as Glastonbury, but among the best fests in the UK.   JULY

2204
MAP A
EDINBURGH FESTIVAL, EDINBURGH: 0131 557 1700. The 3 week 'biggest arts festival in the world' with the Military Tattoo and major opera/music/drama. The big fireworks are on the final Saturday. Incorporates The Fringe Festival with hundreds of events every night; Fringe Sunday on the second w/end. Also the International Film Festival. A jazz Festival and (mainly for delegates on a bit of a jolly) the TV festival. Edin is full.   AUGUST

2205
MAP B
E5
THE WORLD PIPE BAND CHAMPIONSHIPS, GLASGOW: Unbelievable numbers (3-4000) of pipers competing and seriously doing their thing on Glasgow Green.   AUGUST

2206
MAP 5
C2
LEUCHARS AIR SHOW, LEUCHARS nr ST ANDREWS: Info: 01334 839000. Major air-show held over one day in RAF airfield with flying displays, exhibitions, classic cars etc.   SEPT

2207
MAP 1
B1
TOUR OF MULL RALLY, ISLE OF MULL: Info Tobermory TO 01688 302182. The highlight of the national rally calendar is this raging around Mull w/end. Though drivers enter from all over the world, the overall winner for the last few yrs has been a local man. There's usually a waiting list for accom, but camping ok and locals put you up.   OCTOBER

2208
MAP 3
D3
ABERDEEN ALTERNATIVE FESTIVAL, ABERDEEN: Arts festival with bias towards music. Also drama, comedy etc. Usually interesting programmes. Tickets 01224 641122.   OCTOBER

2209
ST ANDREWS NIGHT: Not such a big deal, but dinners etc and cultural ID.
NOV 30TH

2210
MAP A
EDINBURGH HOGMANAY, EDINBURGH: Everywhere gets booked up, but accom 557 1700; info 473 3800. One of the world's major winter events and utterly mega for the Millennium. Launched with a Torchlight Procession through the city centre and a Fire Festival on Calton Hill and with a full 4 day largely populist programme (7 days for the Millenium). Main event is the Street Party on 31st; you need a wrist-band. You have to hope that everyone will be good as well as happy. It's my party and I'll cry if I want to, but I'm usually just amazed.   DEC/JAN

SMELLING THE ROSES

Scotland the Best! comes out every two years and in the year of publication, there's a summer of intense activity, driving round Scotland, doing the research. Although it may appear to be a dream job, eating in great restaurants, always finding the best places, its not exactly relaxing and one can never stop long enough to properly enjoy the places we recommend that you do. Sometimes, friends come along for the ride. This summer, an old mate did just this, spending more time in the car than out but getting a whirlwind tour of some of Scotland's most spectacular scenery and sampling some brilliant food and hospitality. When we got back, I asked him if he'd enjoyed the trip. He had of course but with one proviso: such was our schedule that we never had a chance , as he put it, to 'stop and smell the roses'. Fortunately, this is not always the case and in alternate years, I can go at an easier pace and appreciate more. In the blur of this fast-forwarding, overloaded and short-attention-span world, we must be able to pause. I know this better than anyone. So here are some of the rare moments from during the research for this edition when we were actually able to stop and inhale.

BEN AN: An autumn day in the mid-term of this book, before the planning of the new edition had begun. With two friends I climbed Ben An in the Trossachs (1760/HILLS). From the steep start, we gradually pulled clear of the tree line and on that still and limpid afternoon, the Trossachs was revealed in all its purple glory. We had pies and donuts from The Scotch Oven in Callander (possibly the best in Scotland 1310/BAKERS), and as we neared the top we found that the slope was covered in blueberries (not the English blueberries, not brambles blueberries!). What a feast we had at the summit. A feast for the eye and the stomach. A buzzard trembled in the air and banked away across Loch Katrine. That was a moment to savour.

GARBAGE IN THE GARDENS, JEDI IN THE VENUE: *Keith writes:* Another summer, another burst of research on *Scotland the Best!* But before setting off on my travels, there was a moment's respite between one piece of work and another on 1st July. Scotland's new parliament was officially opened, Concorde flew up Princes Street, and Garbage headlined the celebratory gig in Princes Street Gardens (xxx/PARKS). Shirley Manson's obvious pride and humility was completely at odds with her normal bad girl image. I lost my friend in the crowd afterwards, watched a spectacular street theatre performance at the Mound, then went to The Venue for a late drink where a House Club was showing *Return of the Jedi* on a big screen as a backdrop. Han Solo and repetitive beats then home via The Deep Sea for chips (1264/FISH 'N' CHIPS). Scotland the Best?

THE WHITEADDER: 1999 was a very mixed summer in Scotland and there's always the problem of sunny days corresponding with days off. But one Sunday when we had planned to go for a picnic, it did actually turn out sunny and warm. We left later than planned and the idea was to find a river pot where we could swim. I suggested the Whiteadder near Abbey St Bathans. The scenic route through the Lammermuirs took ages and there were cars and picnickers everywhere. My friends were already disgruntled and impatient when we got to 'Toot Corner' (1520/SWIMMING HOLES) and it was a much longer walk than I had remembered. They wanted to stop at the nearest river-bank, but I kept pushing them on to this brilliant spot for swimming. When we got there we had it to ourselves. Impatience was dispelled in the sunshine. The water was bliss, there were no midges. We could smell the wild garlic. All was well with the world … in the end.

FLOWERS BY THE BRIDGE: *Keith writes:* The House of Bruar is a high-class roadside emporium not far from Blair Atholl on the A9 (1941/CRAFTS). But behind the car park, there's access to a fine short walk up a tumbling Highland river, with rock pools and the obligatory aged bridge. (Much preferable to geegaws.) On Monday 19th July, by the old bridge, there sat a small glass jar of flowers, fresh in the rain. I had been thinking about a pithy phrase to coin the contrast between nature and retail but the memorial just stopped me in my tracks.

THE FESTIVAL FIREWORKS: They've been going for 18 years and so have I, but occasionally, the Festival Fireworks still stuns you (and it's not even one of my events!). In 1999, late in the evening, we drove into town, there was hardly any traffic, we parked nearby (somebody just pulled out), the crowds were thinner than expected (we got through) and we found a great spot in the gardens just as the fireworks began. That evening was so mild and the city had a fantastic warm buzz. These spectacular gardens (1403/TOWN PARKS), this brilliant, dynamic city! I'd say Millennium Edinburgh is a privilege to be part of.

THE EXTREME CHAPEL: *Keith writes:* Turn south from Crinan down Knapdale, skirting the west of Loch Sween, and the road finally stops at a spit of land that feels like the end in more than a geographical sense. There stands Keills Chapel (1699/CHURCHES). The 800-year-old building is far from spectacular, but it houses some great cross slabs and the 7th century Celtic cross that used to stand outside. Walk up behind the chapel, look west and south to Jura and Islay, then think about the Kingdom of Dalriada and those people from Ireland that gave us our name.

THAT DEPOPULATION MOMENT: *Keith writes:* Carl, the owner of the Port Charlotte Hotel (2121/ISLAND HOTELS), was chatting about the business, past jobs (which included twiddling the knobs for The Undertones), and a pet interest – depopulation. 'Imagine Islay in the middle of the last century when there were four or five times as many people here. Where else has suffered that outflow?', he asked. As we thought it over, he handed me a 20-year-old Port Ellen single malt from a local distillery that had closed years ago. The bouquet of the Highlands. It was the best thing I drank on my travels. Island life: peripheral, but with its own intensities.

2211 **LOCHNAGAR ON THE LONGEST DAY:** Nr Ballater via L Muick. Leave evening
MAP 3 before and camp/keep your vigil kind of thing. 4hrs to get up. Take map, good
B4 boots, food, dram etc. From first light across the Cairngorm Plateau, the Dee
Valley, Morvern, Bennachie appear; and God, if you're lucky. Later, in Aug the
Royal Family are beneath you (1785/MUNROS).

2212 **SANDWOOD BAY, KINLOCHBERVIE:** Another place to go in the long light of
MAP 2 summer days. It's a fair trek from the N (Cape Wrath) or even (more usually)
C1 the southern app via Balchrick and Kinlochbervie (1428/BEACHES). Take a tent,
some beers and wine; a few friends. Sit in the long sunset and/or the dawn.
The summer will pass; and the winter.

A WEEKEND AWAY WITH GOOD FRIENDS OR SOMEONE YOU LOVE: As
long as it's sympatico, does it really matter where? There are plenty suggestions in preceding pages (*see esp p. XX, and pp. XXX*, GET-AWAY-FROM-IT-ALL). But
for that special pampering **KINNAIRD, CROMLIX, ISLE OF ERISKA** are among
the v best country hotels in Britain. The food, the service; the grounds are
yours (1077/COUNTRY-HOUSE HOTELS) or **THE HOUSE OVER-BY** in faraway Skye
– the treat retreat (2118/ISLAND HOTELS).

2213 **THE TRESHNISH ISLANDS:** Go especially when the puffins are there too. The
MAP 1 trip to the Treshnish (from Ulva Ferry on Mull) on a summer's day is a voyage
A1 of discovery (incl Staffa). Go in July, walk amongst these enchanting creatures
before they disappear back into the cold Atlantic. Purify the soul. (1564/BIRDS.)

2214 **ST KILDA:** The most westerly islands in the UK, 110 miles into the Atlantic.
MAP 2 Remote, symbolic, superlative in every way, ingrained deep in the spiritual
xA2 heart of the Scots. The community evacuated in 1930 represented the last in
an age of innocence and freedom now gone forever; life was hard but perfectly attuned to this dramatically beautiful place. Highest sea cliffs in UK, pre-
mier sea bird breeding stn. Village of Hirta conserved. NTS (0131 226 5922)
arrange 'working parties' (May-Aug, 14-day trips from Oban) or boat charter
from Oban 3 times a yr (0831 121156), 10-day cruises or *MV Kuma*, a former
research vessel out of Uig on Lewis: 01851 672381.

2215 **THE AONACH EAGACH or THE CLUANIE RIDGE:** Two awe-inspiring ridges; in
MAP 2 good weather among the most exhilarating walks in the world. The first is def-
C4/C3 initely not for the faint-hearted, but most of us could do them once in a lifetime. So do them before you're too doddery. And go with someone who's
done them before or knows hill-walking. Just go with somebody good
(1794/1796/SERIOUS WALKS).

2216 **THE JED and THE CARTER BAR, nr JEDBURGH:** A personal odyssey that I'm
MAP 8 saving for the New Millennium. I was born and lived all my childhood nr the
C3 the banks of the R Jed in Jedburgh. I've long had the notion to follow the river
much further than we often did as lads, into the Cheviots to find its source. It's
close to the Carter Bar, the southern border with England on the A68. But
crossing here, can be done any day – it's the high place where the Borders of
Scotland are spread out before you with hardly a house in sight. There are a
couple of hamburger vans and the occasional piper, but otherwise it's a stirring place and quite the best way to arrive in Scotland. Jedburgh is 18km
down the rd. There's Robert the Bruce's cave high up in cliff side on your left
at the first br, 2km from town. And the ancient Capon Tree, 500m further on. I
came here once again on the day I finished this edition of *Scotland the Best!*
for a final perspective. I hope this book will see you well. The Carter Bar is a
good place to come in; a good place to leave.

Until the next time – cheerio!

LIST OF MAPS

NOTE: The maps give general guidance on attractions in an area – they are not exact. For more precise details, refer to the text.

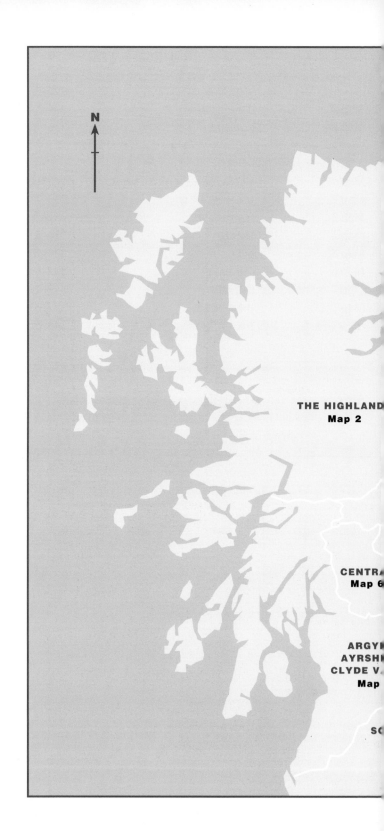

N

THE HIGHLAND
Map 2

CENTRA
Map 6

ARGYI
AYRSHI
CLYDE V.
Map

SC

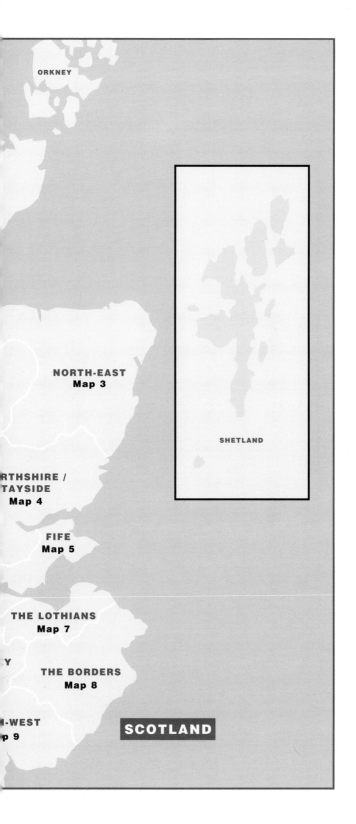

ORKNEY

NORTH-EAST
Map 3

SHETLAND

RTHSHIRE /
TAYSIDE
Map 4

FIFE
Map 5

THE LOTHIANS
Map 7

Y

THE BORDERS
Map 8

-WEST
p 9

SCOTLAND

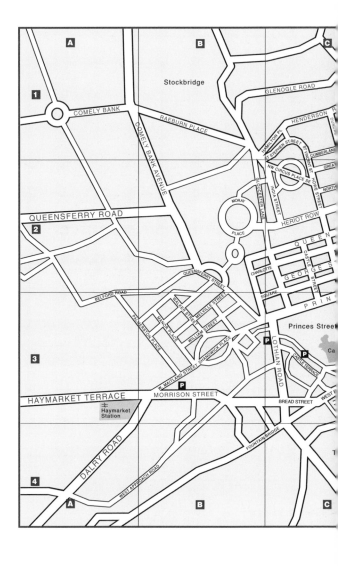

MAP A: Edinburgh City Centre

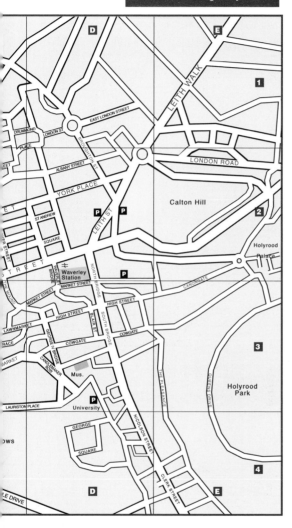

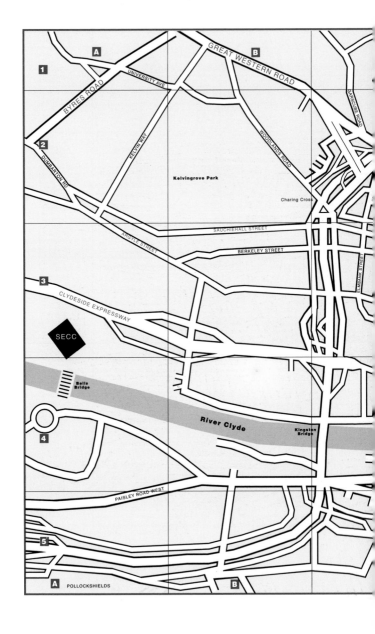

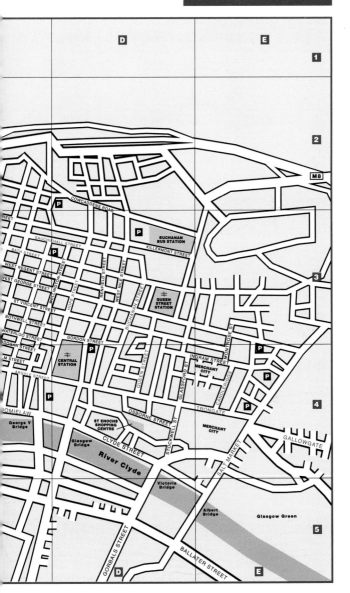

MAP B: Glasgow City Centre

D · E

1

2

M8

P · COWCADDENS ROAD

P · BUCHANAN BUS STATION

SAUCHIEHALL STREET · KILLERMONT STREET

BATH STREET

P

WEST REGENT STREET

WEST GEORGE STREET

QUEEN STREET STATION

ST VINCENT STREET

3

BOTHWELL STREET

WATERLOO STREET

GORDON STREET

ADOGAN STREET

M STREET · P · INGRAM STREET · P

CENTRAL STATION · MERCHANT CITY

ARGYLE STREET · P

P

ROMIELAW · P · OSBORNE STREET · TRONGATE · P

4

George V Bridge · ST ENOCHS SHOPPING CENTRE · MERCHANT CITY

Glasgow Bridge · CLYDE STREET · GALLOWGATE

River Clyde · STOCKWELL ST · SALT MARKET

Victoria Bridge

Albert Bridge · Glasgow Green

5

GORBALS STREET · BALLATER STREET

D · E

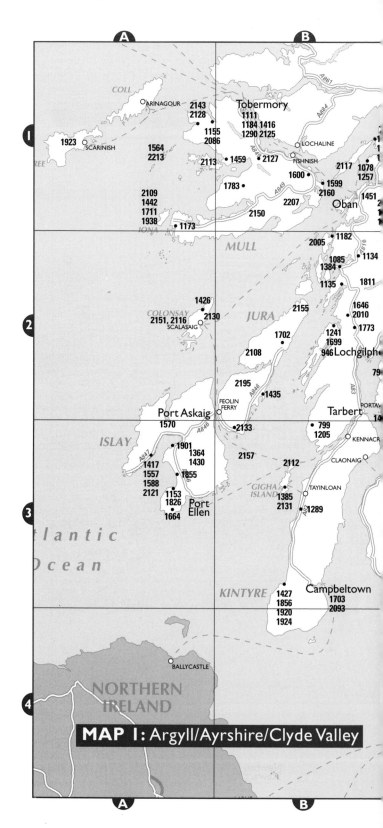

MAP 1: Argyll/Ayrshire/Clyde Valley

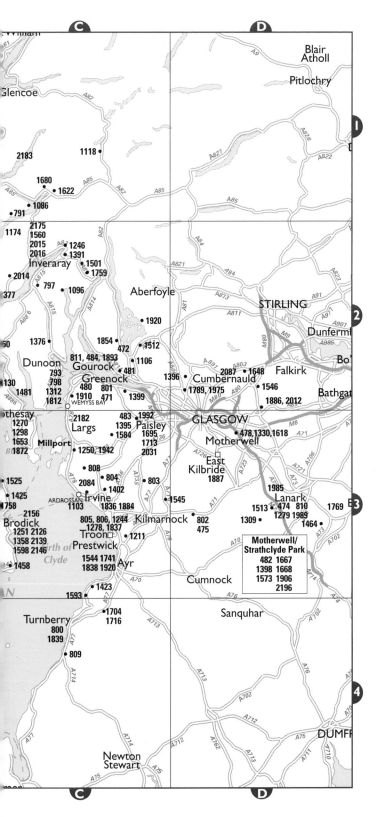

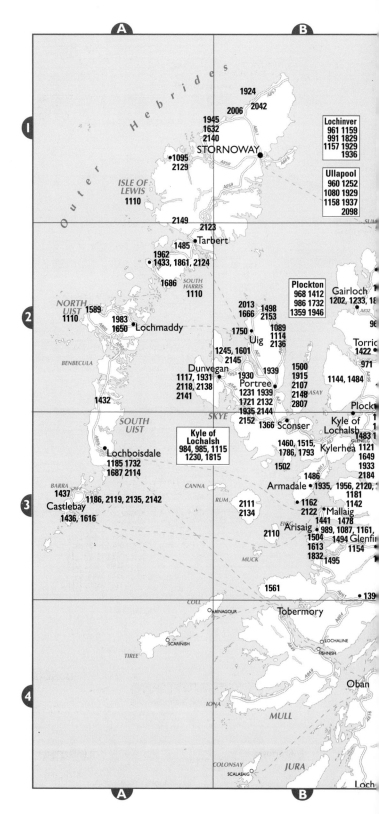

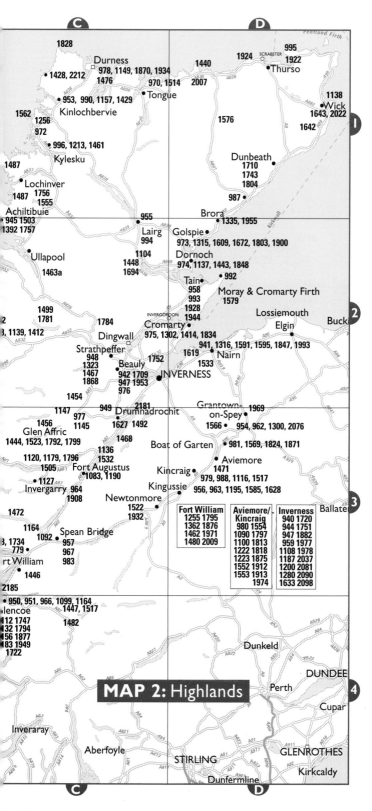

MAP 2: Highlands

Pentland Firth

C

D

1828

Durness
978, 1149, 1870, 1934
1476

• 1428, 2212

• 953, 990, 1157, 1429

Kinlochbervie

1562
1256
972

• 996, 1213, 1461

Kylesku

1487

• Lochinver
1487 1756
1555

Achiltibuie
• 945 1503
1392 1757

• Ullapool

1463a

1499
1781

2
, 1139, 1412

Dingwall

Strathpeffer
948
1323
1467
1868

Beauly
942 1709
947 1953
976

1454

1147
977 949
1456 1145
Glen Affric
1444, 1523, 1792, 1799

1120, 1179, 1796
1505 Fort Augustus
1083, 1190

• 1127
Invergarry 964
1908

1472

1164
1092 • 957
779 • 967
rt William 983

• 1446

2185

• 950, 951, 966, 1099, 1164
lencoe 1447, 1517
112 1747
32 1794
56 1877
83 1949
1722

1440
2007

970, 1514

• Tongue

1924 SCRABSTER 995
1922
• Thurso

1138
• Wick
1643, 2022

1642

1576

Dunbeath
1710
1743
1804

987 •

Brora

• 955 • 1335, 1955

Lairg
994

Golspie •
973, 1315, 1609, 1672, 1803, 1900

1104
Dornoch
1448 974• 1137, 1443, 1848
1694

Tain•
958 • 992
993
1928
1944

Moray & Cromarty Firth
1579

Lossiemouth

Elgin Buck

2

INVERGORDON

Cromarty •
975, 1302, 1414, 1834

941, 1316, 1591, 1595, 1847, 1993

1619 • Nairn
1533

1752

• INVERNESS

940 1720
944 1751
947 1882
959 1977
1108 1978
1187 2037
1200 2081
1280 2090
1633 2098

2181
Drumnadrochit

Grantown-
on-Spey • 1969

1627 1492

1566 • 954, 962, 1300, 2076

1468

Boat of Garten • 981, 1569, 1824, 1871

1136
1532

• Aviemore
Kincraig 1471

979, 988, 1116, 1517

Kingussie • 956, 963, 1195, 1585, 1628

Newtonmore
1522
1932

Fort William
1255 1795
1362 1876
1462 1971
1480 2009

Aviemore/
Kincraig
980 1554
1090 1797
1100 1813
1222 1818
1223 1875
1552 1912
1553 1913
1974

Inverness
940 1720
944 1751
947 1882
959 1977
1108 1978
1187 2037
1200 2081
1280 2090
1633 2098

Ballate

3

Spean Bridge

1482

Dunkeld

DUNDEE

Perth

Cupar

4

Inveraray

Aberfoyle STIRLING GLENROTHES

Kirkcaldy

Dunfermline

C D

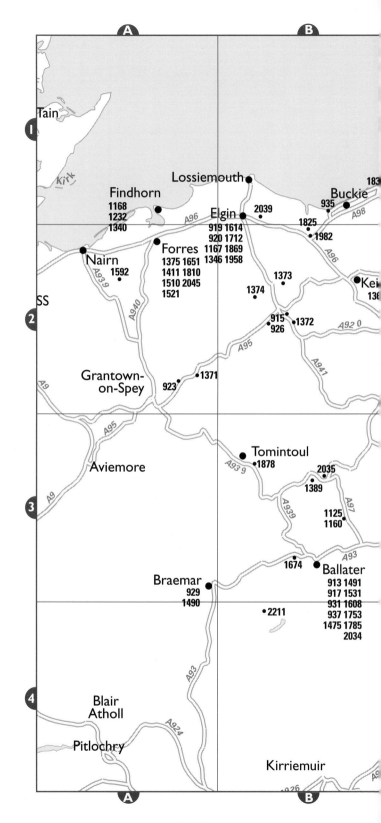

Tain

I

Kirk

SS

2

3

4

Lossiemouth

Findhorn
1168
1232
1340

Buckie
935

183

Elgin
919 1614
920 1712
1167 1869
1346 1958

2039

1825
1982

A96

A98

Forres
1375 1651
1411 1810
1510 2045
1521

Nairn
1592

A939

A940

1373

1374

Kei
136

915
926

1372

A92 0

A95

A941

Grantown-
on-Spey

923

1371

A9

A95

Tomintoul
1878

A939

2035
1389

Aviemore

A9

1125
1160

A939

A97

A93

1674

Ballater
913 1491
917 1531
931 1608
937 1753
1475 1785
2034

Braemar
929
1490

2211

A93

Blair
Atholl

A924

Pitlochry

Kirriemuir

A926

A9

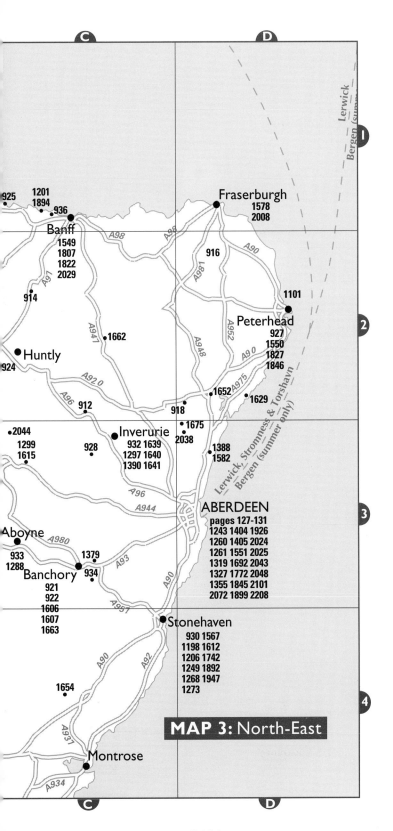

MAP 3: North-East

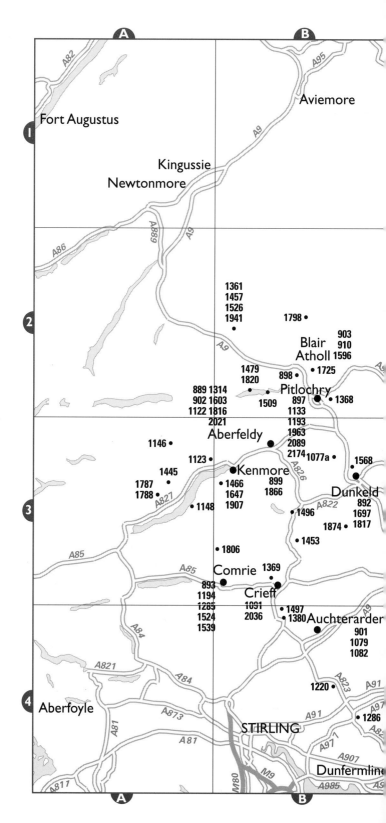

Fort Augustus

Aviemore

Kingussie
Newtonmore

1361
1457
1526
1941

1798 •

Blair
Atholl

903
910
1596

1479   898 •   • 1725
1820

889 1314   • Pitlochry   • 1368
902 1603   1509   897
1122 1816   1133
2021   1193
Aberfeldy   1963
1146 •   2089
          2174 1077a   • 1568
1123 •
1445   ● Kenmore   Dunkeld
1787   • 1466   899   892
1788   1647   1866   1697
    • 1148   1907   1817
             • 1496   1874 •
                        • 1453
        • 1806
Comrie   1369
893 ●   • Crieff
1194   1051
1285   2036   • 1497
1524   • 1380 Auchterarder
1539   901
                    1079
                    1082

Aberfoyle   1220 •
                    • 1286
        STIRLING

        Dunfermline

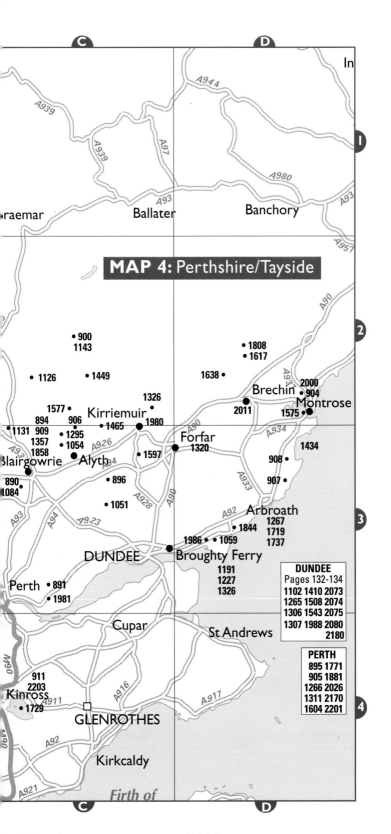

MAP 4: Perthshire/Tayside

In

Braemar Ballater Banchory

• 900
1143

• 1808
• 1617

• 1126   • 1449   1638 •   Brechin • 2000
                                        • 904
                              2011   Montrose
1326   1575 •
1577 •
894   906   Kirriemuir
• 1131 909 • 1295 • 1465 • 1980   Forfar   1434
1357 • 1054   1320
1858   908 •
Blairgowrie • Alyth • 1597   907 •
890
1084   • 896

• 1051   Arbroath
                                      1267
                                      1844   1719
DUNDEE   1986 • • 1059   1737
          Broughty Ferry
Perth • 891   1191
    • 1981   1227
                                      1326

Cupar   St Andrews

911
2203
Kinross
• 1729
GLENROTHES

Kirkcaldy

Firth of

| DUNDEE |
| Pages 132-134 |
| 1102 1410 2073 |
| 1265 1508 2074 |
| 1306 1543 2075 |
| 1307 1988 2080 |
| 2180 |

| PERTH |
| 895 1771 |
| 905 1881 |
| 1266 2026 |
| 1311 2170 |
| 1604 2201 |

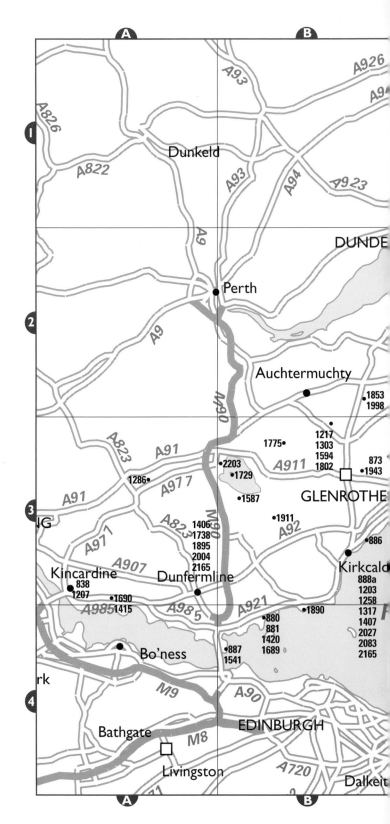

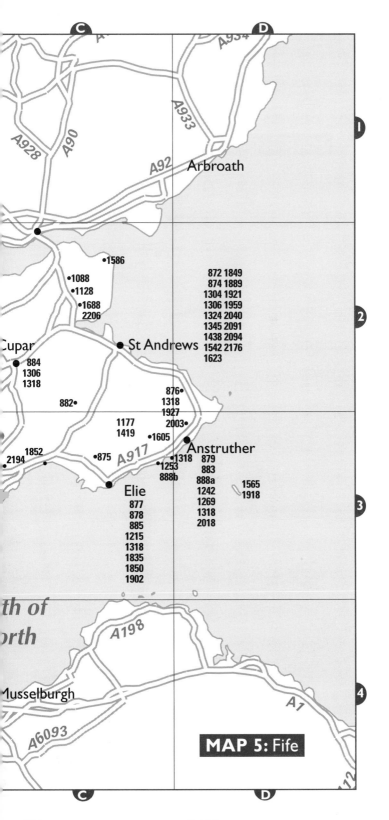

Arbroath

•1586

•1088
•1128
•1688
2206

Cupar   St Andrews

884
1306
1318

882•

876•
1318
1927
2003•

1177
1419
•1605

1852   •875   A917

2194•

•1318 Anstruther
•1253   879
888b   883
         888a   1565
Elie   1242   1918
877   1269
878   1318
885   2018
1215
1318
1835
1850
1902

872 1849
874 1889
1304 1921
1306 1959
1324 2040
1345 2091
1438 2094
1542 2176
1623

th of

A198

rth

Musselburgh

A6093

A1

MAP 5: Fife

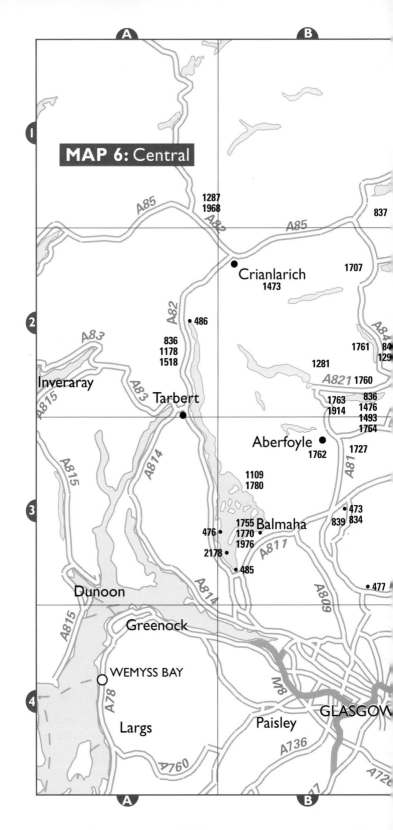

MAP 6: Central

1287
1968

837

Crianlarich
1473

1707

486

836
1178
1518

1761

84
129

1281

A821 1760

Inveraray

Tarbert

1763
1914

836
1476
1493
1764

Aberfoyle
1762

1727

1109
1780

473
839 834

476

1755
1770
1976

Balmaha

2178

485

477

Dunoon

Greenock

WEMYSS BAY

GLASGOW

Largs

Paisley

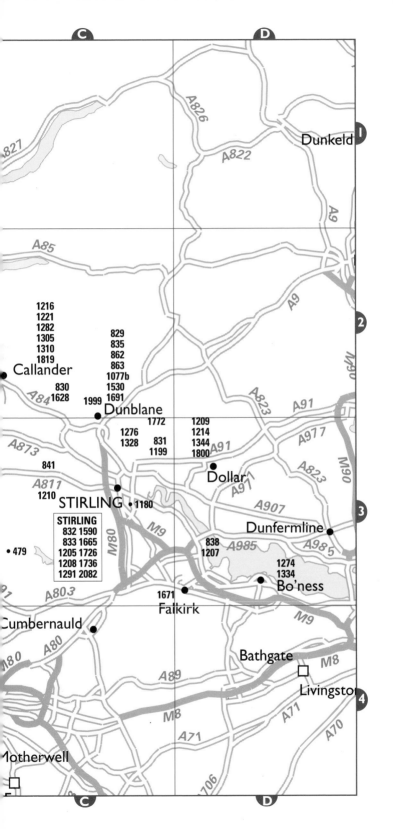

C

D

A826

A827

A822

Dunkeld **1**

A9

A85

A9

A823 A91

1216
1221
1282
1305
1310
1819

829
835
862
863
1077b
1530
1691

2

M90

Callander

830
1628

1999

A84

Dunblane

1772

1209
1214
1344
1800

A91

A977

A823

M90

1276
1328

831
1199

A873

841

A811

1210

STIRLING •1180

STIRLING
832 1590
833 1665
1205 1726
1208 1736
1291 2082

•479

M80

M9

Dollar

838
1207

A985

A907

A91

Dunfermline

A985

3

1274
1334

Bo'ness

A803

1671

Falkirk

M9

Cumbernauld •

A80

M180

A89

Bathgate

A91

Motherwell

M8

A71

A89

M8

A71

A706

Livingston **4**

A71

A70

C

D

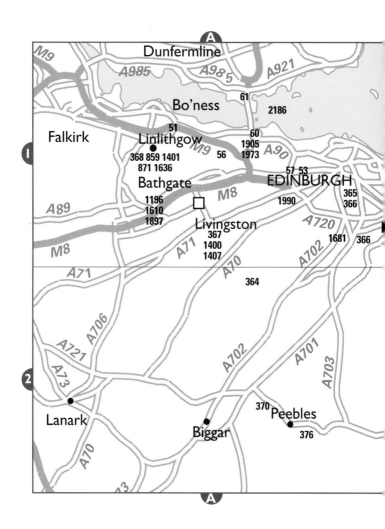

Dunfermline
A985
A98
A921
Bo'ness
61
2186
Falkirk
51
Linlithgow
M9
60
1905
1973
56
A90
368 859 1401
871 1636
57 53
EDINBURGH
Bathgate
365
366
1196
1610
1897
M8
1990
A89
A720
M8
Livingston
A702
1681
366
367
1400
1407
A70
A71
A71
364
A706
A721
A73
A702
A701
A703
Lanark
370
Peebles
A70
Biggar
376
73
M9

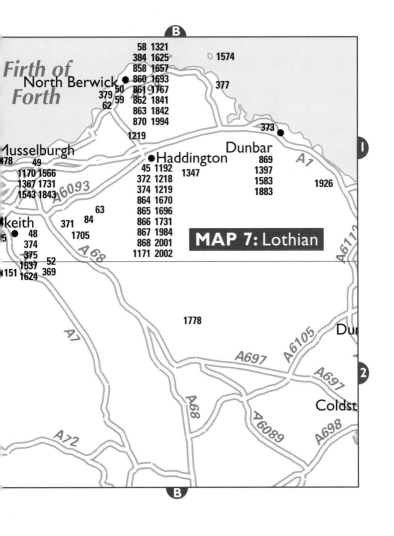

Firth of Forth

North Berwick

58 1321
384 1625
858 1657
860 1693
861 1767
862 1841
863 1842
870 1994
379 50
62 59
1219

⌂ 1574

377

373

Musselburgh

478
49
1170 1566
1367 1731
1543 1843

A6093

Haddington

45 1192
372 1218
374 1219
864 1670
865 1696
866 1731
867 1984
868 2001
1171 2002

1347

Dunbar

869
1397
1583
1883

A1

1926

MAP 7: Lothian

keith
48
374
375
1537
1624

371 84
63

1705

52
369

A68

A6112

1778

A7

A697

A6105

Du

A68

A697

Coldst

A6089

A698

A72

341   M A P S

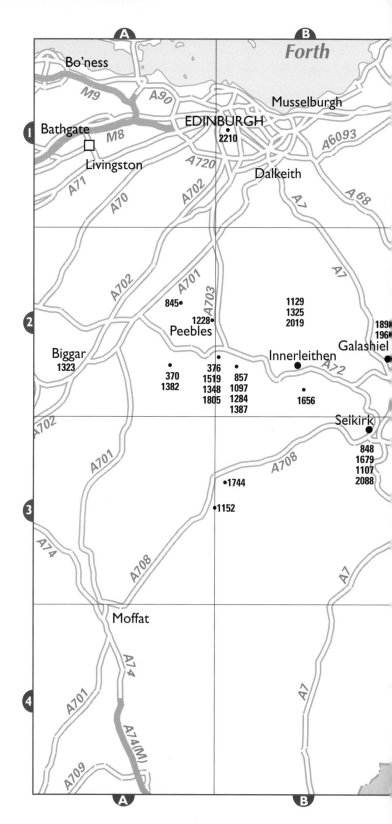

Forth

Bo'ness

M9

A90

Musselburgh

Bathgate

M8

EDINBURGH
2210

A6093

Livingston

A720

Dalkeith

A71

A70

A702

A7

A68

A702

A701

845

A703

1129
1325
2019

1898
196

Galashiel

Biggar
1323

Peebles
1228

Innerleithen

A72

376
1519
1348
1805

857
1097
1284
1387

1656

370
1382

A702

Selkirk

A701

A708

848
1679
1107
2088

•1744

•1152

A74

A708

A7

Moffat

A74

A701

A74(M)

A7

A709

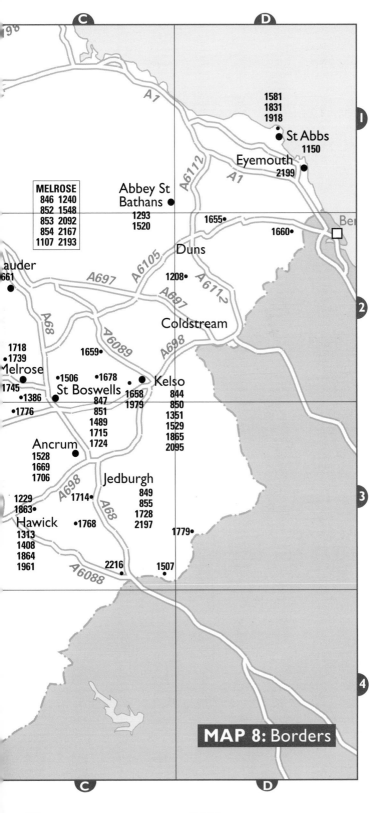

98

A1

1581
1831
1918
● St Abbs
1150

Eyemouth
2199

A6112

A1

MELROSE
846 1240
852 1548
853 2092
854 2167
1107 2193

Abbey St
Bathans ●

1293
1520

1655●

Ber

1660●

□

auder
661
●

A697

A6105

Duns

1208● A6112

A68

Coldstream

A6089

A698

A697

1718
●1739

1659●

Melrose
●

1745

●1506   ●1678

St Boswells
1658
847
851
1489
1715
1724

Kelso
844
850
1351
1529
1865
2095

●1386

●1776

1979

Ancrum
1528
1669
1706

A698

1714●

Jedburgh
849
855
1728
2197

A68

1229
1863●

Hawick
1313
1408
1864
1961

●1768

1779●

A6088

2216●

1507●

MAP 8: Borders

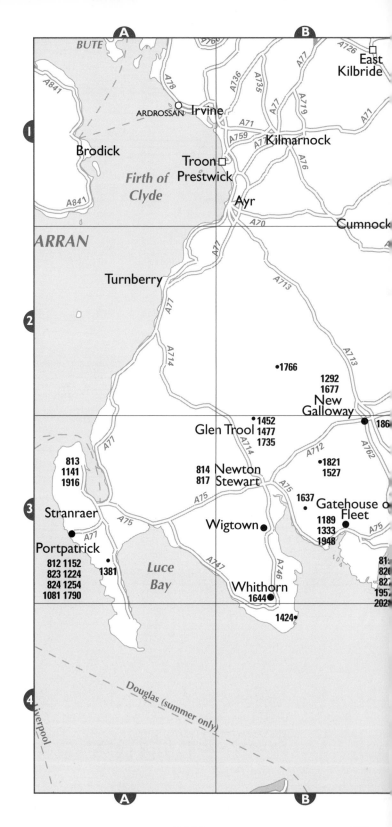

BUTE

A841

A726

East
Kilbride

A778

A736

A735

A77

A719

A71

ARDROSSAN ○ Irvine

A71

A759

A7

Brodick

*Firth of
Clyde*

Troon □
Prestwick

Kilmarnock

A76

A841

Ayr

Cumnock

A70

ARRAN

Turnberry

A713

A77

A714

•1766

1292
1677

New
Galloway

•186

Glen Trool

•1452
1477
1735

A714

A712

A762

813
1141
1916

A77

•1821
1527

814 Newton
817 Stewart

A75

1637 Gatehouse o
Fleet

A75

Stranraer

A75

Wigtown •

1189
1333
1948

Portpatrick

A77

Luce
Bay

A747

A746

81
820
82
195
202

812 1152
823 1224
824 1254
1081 1790

•1381

Whithorn
1644 ●

1424 •

Liverpool

Douglas (summer only)

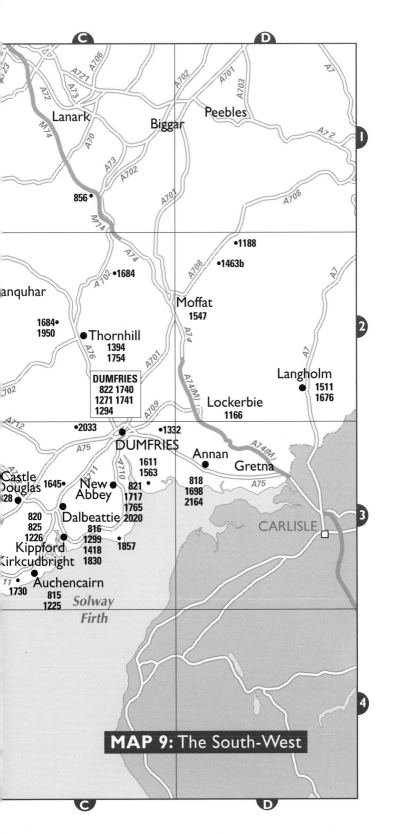

MAP 9: The South-West

Lanark
Biggar
Peebles

856 •

ǎnquhar

•1684

Moffat
1547

1684•
1950

•Thornhill
1394
1754

•1188

•1463b

Langholm
1511
1676

DUMFRIES
822 1740
1271 1741
1294

•2033

•1332

Lockerbie
1166

DUMFRIES

Annan

Gretna

1611
1563

Castle
Douglas
28 •

1645•

•New
Abbey

821
1717
1765
2020

818
1698
2164

820
825
1226

Dalbeattie

816
1299
1418
1830

•1857

CARLISLE

Kippford

ǐrkcudbright

11 •
1730

•Auchencairn

815
1225

Solway
Firth

INDEX